ALIPHATIC FLUORINE COMPOUNDS

BY

A. M. LOVELACE

•

DOUGLAS A. RAUSCH

•

WILLIAM POSTELNEK

Organic Materials Branch, Materials Laboratory

Wright Air Development Center

American Chemical Society
Monograph Series

REINHOLD PUBLISHING CORPORATION

NEW YORK

CHAPMAN & HALL, LTD. LONDON

Library of Congress Catalog Card No. *58–8250*

REINHOLD PUBLISHING CORPORATION

Publishers of Chemical Engineering Catalog, Chemical Materials Catalog, Materials in Design Engineering, Progressive Architecture, Automatic Control; Advertising Management of American Chemical Society

Printed in U.S.A. by
THE GUINN CO., INC.
New York 1, N. Y.

GENERAL INTRODUCTION

American Chemical Society's Series of Chemical Monographs

By arrangement with the Interallied Conference of Pure and Applied Chemistry, which met in London and Brussels in July, 1919, the American Chemical Society was to undertake the production and publication of Scientific and Technologic Monographs on chemical subjects. At the same time it was agreed that the National Research Council, in cooperation with the American Chemical Society and the American Physical Society, should undertake the production and publication of Critical Tables of Chemical and Physical Constants. The American Chemical Society and the National Research Council mutually agreed to care for these two fields of chemical progress. The American Chemical Society named as Trustees, to make the necessary arrangements of the publication of the Monographs, Charles L. Parsons, secretary of the Society, Washington, D. C.; the late John E. Teeple, then treasurer of the Society, New York; and the late Professor Gellert Alleman of Swarthmore College. The Trustees arranged for the publication of the ACS Series of (a) Scientific and (b) Technological Monographs by the Chemical Catalog Company, Inc. (Reinhold Publishing Corporation, successor) of New York.

The Council of the American Chemical Society, acting through its Committee on National Policy, appointed editors (the present list of whom appears at the close of this sketch) to select authors of competent authority in their respective fields and to consider critically the manuscripts submitted.

The first Monograph of the Series appeared in 1921. After twenty-three years of experience certain modifications of general policy were indicated. In the beginning there still remained from the preceding five decades a distinct though arbitrary differentiation between so-called "pure science" publications and technologic or applied science literature. By 1944 this differentiation was fast becoming nebulous. Research in private enterprise had grown apace and not a little of it was pursued on the frontiers of knowledge. Furthermore, most workers in the sciences were coming to see the artificiality of the separation. The methods of both groups of workers are the same. They employ the same instrumentalities, and frankly recognize that their objectives are common, namely, the search for new knowledge for the service of man. The officers of the Society therefore combined the two editorial Boards in a single Board of twelve representative members.

Also in the beginning of the Series, it seemed expedient to construe rather broadly the definition of a Monograph. Needs of workers had to be recognized. Consequently among the first hundred Monographs appeared works in the form of treatises covering in some instances rather broad areas. Because such necessary works do not now want for publishers, it is considered advisable to hew more strictly to the line of the Monograph character, which means more complete and critical treatment of relatively restricted areas, and, where a broader field needs coverage, to subdivide it into logical subareas. The prodigious expansion of new knowledge makes such a change desirable.

These Monographs are intended to serve two principal purposes: first, to make available to chemists a thorough treatment of a selected area in form usable by persons working in more or less unrelated fields to the end that they may correlate their own work with a larger area of physical science discipline; second, to stimulate further research in the specific field treated. To implement this purpose the authors of Monographs are expected to give extended references to the literature. Where the literature is of such volume that a complete bibliography is impracticable, the authors are expected to append a list of references critically selected on the basis of their relative importance and significance.

Preface

This book is concerned with a comprehensive treatment of the preparation and properties of all classes of aliphatic fluorine compounds. The subject is approached from the point of view of preparative organic chemistry and is arranged in a general order similar to the arrangement of treatises on classical organic chemistry. Each chapter is devoted to a specific class or classes of fluoroorganic compounds such as alkanes, alkenes, alcohols, etc. The first chapter describes various fluorination processes which may be employed for the introduction of fluorine into an organic compound. Wherever possible, the influence of fluorine on the chemical and physical properties of various classes of compounds is noted. Likewise, similarities and differences in reactivities and properties between fluorine-containing organic compounds and their hydrocarbon analogs are pointed out. Special attention is given to recent advances in the field, and where applicable, industrial or commercial importance of organic fluorine compounds is indicated.

Each chapter is complete with a bibliography and tables which describe physical properties of the compounds listed. An explanation of the tables is given on page vi. The literature has been extensively reviewed from Moissan's time up to and including the year 1955. In some cases, papers published in 1956 and early 1957 have been utilized. However, every published paper on the subject is not included in the bibliographies, nor has every organic fluorine compound prepared been included in the tables. But quite a representative number of the contributions to the subject have been incorporated in the book.

From the time of Moissan until the advent of World War II, the activity in the field of fluorocarbon chemistry has been relatively modest. However, during this period, research was stimulated by the discovery that certain fluorocarbons (Freons, Genetrons) possessed physical, chemical and physiological properties which made their application for refrigerants very desirable. During World War II the requirements for materials with the unusual properties of chemical inertness and thermal stability generated a crash program on fluorocarbon research. These properties which are characteristic of organic fluorine compounds are responsible for the continuing emphasis being placed upon research in this field. During the last decade numerous fluorocarbon products have gained wide-spread recognition for applications such as: propellants, wetting agents, textile treating agents, pharmaceutical intermediates, lubricants, elastomers, adhesives, sealants, plastics, films, protective coatings and fire extinguishing agents.

Some fluorine-containing starting materials and intermediates are commercially available to the research chemist. Representative chlorofluoro- and bromofluoromethanes and -ethanes are available under the trade names of Freons (E. I. duPont de Nemours, Inc.) and Genetrons (General Chemical Division of Allied Chemical and Dye Company). In addition, materials of this type may be available from Pennsalt Chemicals Corp. and the Chemical Division of Union Carbide Company. A few fluorine-containing olefins such as chlorotrifluoroethylene may also be available. The Minnesota Mining and Manufacturing Company markets certain perfluorocarboxylic acids. Additional fluoroorganic compounds may be obtained from certain specialty chemical companies.

The chemist undertaking a research program in organic fluorine chemistry for the first time should acquaint himself with the hazards associated with the handling of fluorocarbons as well as hydrogen fluoride. Generally such information necessary for the safe handling of these materials can be made available by the supplier.

The satisfactory analysis of fluorocarbon compounds requires, in many cases, that special techniques be employed. A comprehensive review of this subject by P. J. Elving, C. A. Horton and H. H. Willard is contained in Simons' "Fluorine Chemistry."*

The authors are extremely grateful to Professor A. L. Henne, The Ohio State University; Professor Henry Gilman, Iowa State University; Professor J. D. Park, University of Colorado; Dr. O. R. Pierce, Dow Corning Corporation; and Professors Paul Tarrant, Richard Dresdner and J. A. Young, University of Florida for reviewing portions of the manuscript and offering pertinent and timely suggestions as well as other valuable advice. The authors are also much indebted to Dr. C. H. Ruof and Dr. M. H. Wilt of Mellon Institute for critically reading the entire manuscript.

Alan M. Lovelace
Douglas A. Rausch
William Postelnek, Major, USAF
Materials Laboratory
Wright Air Development Center
United States Air Force
Air Research and Development Command
Wright-Patterson Air Force Base, Ohio

August 1957

*Simons, J. H., "Fluorine Chemistry," Vol. II, New York, Academic Press, Inc., 1954.

Table of Contents

CHAPTER		PAGE
I	Fluorination	1
II	Alkanes	31
III	Alkenes and Alkynes	100
IV	Alcohols	137
V	Ethers	155
VI	Ketones, Aldehydes and Acetals	180
VII	Carboxylic Acids	201
VIII	Acyl Halides and Anhydrides	219
IX	Esters	229
X	Nitrogen Compounds—I	259
XI	Nitrogen Compounds—II	282
XII	Organometallic and Organometalloidal Compounds	307
XIII	Sulfur Compounds	330

List of Tables

TABLE NUMBER		PAGE
1	Acyclic Alkanes	48
2	Cyclic Alkanes	80
3	Alkenes	113
4	Dienes and Trienes	122
5	Alkynes and Allenes	125
6	Cyclic Alkenes	126
7	Alcohols	145
8	Diols	151
9	Unsaturated Alcohols	152
10	Aliphatic and Alicyclic Ethers	164
11	Olefinic Ethers	169
12	Cyclic Ethers	172
13	Hydroxy Ethers	176
14	Ketones	190
15	Diketones and Hydroxy Ketones	194
16	Copper Chelates of β-Diketones	195
17	Aldehydes	196
18	Acetals and Hemiacetals	197
19	Hydrates of Ketones and Aldehydes	197
20	Monobasic Acids	210
21	Dibasic Acids	215
22	Acyl Halides	224
23	Acid Anhydrides	226
24	Monoesters	239
25	Diesters and Triesters	246
26	Unsaturated Monoesters	250
27	Unsaturated Diesters	252
28	Hydroxyesters	253
29	Ketoesters	254
30	Amides	268
31	Imides	272
32	N-Bromo Amides	273
33	Amidines	273

TABLE NUMBERS		PAGE
34	Ureas	274
35	Carbamates	275
36	Nitriles	276
37	Keto Nitriles	278
38	Isocyanates	278
39	Thiocyanates	279
40	α-Keto Thiocyanates	279
41	Amines	295
42	Imines and Azomethines	299
43	Quaternary Ammonium Salts	299
44	Triazines	300
45	Diazo Compounds	302
46	Nitroso Compounds	302
47	Nitro Compounds and Nitrites	303
48	Miscellaneous Nitrogen Compounds	304
49	Lithium Compounds	320
50	Magnesium Compounds	320
51	Zinc Compounds	320
52	Mercury Compounds	321
53	Cadmium Compounds	321
54	Boron Esters	321
55	Silicon Compounds	322
56	Phosphorus Compounds	324
57	Phosphorus Esters	325
58	Arsenic Compounds	326
59	Antimony Compounds	327
60	Selenium Compounds	327
61	Sulfur Compounds	344

Explanation of Tables

Each chapter is accompanied by tables which are separated for convenience by functional groups. In most cases, only compounds whose structure has been proven are included. The nomenclature used, is in most cases, that which is generally accepted or that which is used in the original literature. The methods refer to the appropriate subdivision of the text in which the general reaction is discussed. The methods are numbered serially for each chapter. The first number or numbers refer to the chapter, the last two numbers designate the method in that chapter.

All compounds are arranged by empirical formula in each table according to the accepted Chemical Abstract order. Where several structures apply to a given empirical formula they are arbitrarily listed under that empirical formula.

The yields reported are the actual yields from the original literature and where applicable, a range is indicated. The references are those for the paper or papers describing the preparation of the compound and refer only to the bibliography of that chapter.

The physical constants when available follow the appropriate compound. All boiling, melting and freezing points are in degrees centigrade and pressures are in millimeters of mercury. Indices of refraction (n_D^t) are for sodium light at the temperature t° C. Densities (d_4^t) are referenced to water at 4°C and recorded at temperature t°C. When the temperature (t) is the same for the refractive index and density it is listed in the right column (t°C). If the density was recorded at a different temperature this is added in parentheses following the density.

CHAPTER I

Fluorination

TABLE OF CONTENTS

		PAGE
Introduction		1
Method Number		
101	Fluorides of Group IA Elements; Potassium	3
102	Fluorides of Group IB Elements; Copper, Silver, Gold	3
103	Fluorides of Group IIA Elements; Calcium	5
104	Fluorides of Group IIB Elements; Mercury and Zinc	5
105	Fluorides of Group III Elements; Aluminum, Thallium, and Boron	6
106	Fluorides of Group IV Elements; Silicon, Tin and Lead	6
107	Fluorides of Group V Elements; Antimony, Bismuth, and Arsenic	7
108	Fluorides of the Transition Elements; Cobalt, Iron, Chromium, Manganese and Titanium	10
109	Reaction of Hydrogen Fluoride with Unsaturated Compounds: Addition and Substitution	12
110	Substitution with Hydrogen Fluoride	15
111	Electrochemical Process	17
112	Direct Fluorination	20
113	Halogen Fluorides	23
Bibliography		24

INTRODUCTION

This chapter is concerned with the methods and processes for the introduction of fluorine into organic compounds, more specifically the formation of the carbon-fluorine bond. Subsequent chapters deal mostly with the reactions of organic fluorine compounds. Three main processes have been used for the preparation of organic fluorine compounds; these are (A) the use of metallic fluorides, (B) the use of hydrogen fluoride, and (C) the use of fluorine.

The use of metallic fluorides can involve either substitution of organic halides or direct replacement of hydrogen. The reactivity of the more important metal fluorides are summarized in the following table:

Group of Periodic Table	Metallic Fluoride	Substitution of Organic Halides	Direct Replacement of Hydrogen
IA	KF	+	
IB	CuF	+	
	AgF	+	
	AgF_2	+	+
IIA	CaF_2	+	
IIB	HgF	+	
	HgF_2	+	+
III	TlF	+	
IV	SnF_4	+	
	PbF_4	+	+
V	SbF_3	+	
	SbF_3Cl_2	+	
	SbF_5	+	
Transition Elements	TiF_4	+	
	CrF_3	+	
	MnF_3	+	+
	FeF_3	+	
	CoF_3	+	+

Although nickel is not included in this table it is of importance as a material for the construction of fluorination reactors and it is probable that the nickel fluoride formed plays some part in the fluorination reaction.

Hydrogen fluoride is probably the most important present-day reagent for the preparation of organic fluorine compounds. Hydrogen fluoride is extensively used in the commercial preparation of fluorine-containing organic compounds. It is used either in conjunction with a metal salt or metal oxide to generate an active metal fluoride, for fluorinating organic halides, for addition to unsaturated compounds, and in the electrochemical fluorination process.

Fluorine is used to directly fluorinate various organic compounds or to prepare various active metal fluorides such as cobaltic fluoride or manganic fluoride.

METHOD 101 Fluorides of Group IA Elements; Potassium

The substitution reaction between potassium fluoride and organic monochlorides and monobromides yields monofluoroorganic compounds. In addition, potassium fluoride reacts with alkyl tosylates or dimethyl sulfone to yield monofluoroalkanes (cf. Method 208). Various classes of haloorganic compounds have been fluorinated by means of substitution with potassium fluoride. Mono- and dichloro- and bromoalkanes were converted into the fluorides.[37,71,72,113,114,169] Halogen-containing alcohols,[112,114,129,170] esters,[16,70,71,169,187] ethers,[70,72,170] and amides[4] have also been similarly fluorinated. Ethyl- and methylchlorocarbonate have been converted into the respective fluorocarbonates.[70,169]

Various conditions have been employed in using potassium fluoride as a fluorinating agent. Heating the organic halide and anhydrous potassium fluoride in anhydrous glycerol or ethylene glycol generally results in reasonable yields of alkyl fluorides. Reaction temperatures employed range from 50° for the fluorination of $CH_2BrCO_2CH_3$[169] to 150° to 200° for the fluorination of n-$C_{11}H_{23}Cl$.[70] However, no studies of optimum reaction conditions have been reported. High pressure autoclaves have been used as reaction vessels as well as conventional laboratory glassware.

Attempted fluorination of 4-chlorobutanol and its esters by this method led to the formation of tetrahydrofuran when the reaction was carried out at 120°. However, at lower temperatures, low yields of the fluorinated alcohol were obtained.[172]

The use of the fluorides of the other alkali metals as fluorinating agents is not readily apparent from a review of the literature.

METHOD 102 Fluorides of Group IB Elements; Copper, Silver, and Gold

Copper fluoride is very seldom used as a fluorinating agent and it is only of historical interest. Midgley and Henne[153] treated carbon tetrachloride with a mixture of cupric fluoride and antimony sulfate and obtained CF_2Cl_2. Gleave[64] fluorinated carbon disulfide with hydrogen fluoride and cupric chloride and isolated CF_3Cl, CF_2Cl_2, and CF_3Cl. Gleave also treated carbon under similar conditions and obtained $CFCl_3$, and CF_2Cl_2.

Fluorides of silver are very effective fluorinating agents and have been widely employed. Silver fluoride (AgF) was used by early investigators to prepare alkyl fluorides. Moissan[160,164] prepared methyl, ethyl, and isopropyl fluorides from the respective iodides with this reagent. Meslans[152] treated $CH_2ICH{=}CH_2$ with AgF and isolated $CH_2FCH{=}CH_2$. Chabrie[34,35] used this reagent to fluorinate CCl_4 and obtained CF_4. Swarts[216] found that treatment of n-amyl chloride with AgF yielded the fluoride but also resulted in coupling and olefin formation.

The observation was made by Henne[92] that the relative ease of replacement of halogens by inorganic fluorides is I > Br > Cl and that side reactions occur more readily with iodides and less readily with chlorides. The former part of this observation is especially true when considering polyhalogenated carbon atoms; for example, $CClBr_2CO_2C_2H_5$ was converted to $CFClBrCO_2C_2H_5$ using AgF.[207] More recently silver fluoride was used to replace iodine and chlorine on fluorocarbon haloarsines such as $(CF_3)_2AsI$, $(CF_3)_3AsCl_2$ (cf. Method 1227).

Henne[92] also points out that the disadvantages of using silver fluoride lie in the fact that it is difficult to prepare in anhydrous form and that only half the available fluorine is used due to the formation of the compound AgF · AgCl, during the fluorination reaction.

Silver fluoride, besides being used to replace halogens in alkyl halides,[34,35,151,160,164,213,216] can be used to replace halogens in esters,[26,173,187,207,214] ethers[215] and nitriles.[74]

Silver difluoride (AgF_2) is a powerful fluorinating agent, comparable to cobaltic fluoride (cf. Method 108). It should be noted that while AgF replaces halogens, AgF_2 replaces hydrogen as well. It can be prepared by the action of fluorine on silver foil[51] or on silver halides.[182] Silver difluoride is believed to be the active agent when silver plated copper packing is used in the direct fluorination process (cf. Method 112). Important knowledge of its use was gained during World War II. McBee and Bechtol[136,137,138] prepared a series of perfluorinated fused ring compounds from aromatic hydrocarbons using AgF_2; temperatures employed were in the range of 160° to 400°. The reactor consisted of a bed of the silver salt over which fluorine gas was passed. The hydrocarbon vapor was swept through the reactor with nitrogen and the products were collected in traps at the end of the system. Such hydrocarbons as indene, napthalene, acenaphthene, phenanthrene and others were converted into the completely fluorinated saturated ring systems. Ethylbenzene and *p*-cymene were likewise fluorinated.[142] Kellogg and Cady[125] reacted methanol with AgF_2 and isolated CF_3OF (cf. Chapter IV).

Liquid phase fluorination of heptanes and lubricating oil fractions with AgF_2 was also extensively studied during World War II. The reaction was carried out in a fluorinated solvent at a reflux temperature of 240° for several hours.[202] Various halogenated polynuclear hydrocarbons and ketonic materials were fluorinated using AgF_2 in the liquid phase.[202]

Silver difluoride was also used in the intermediate or final fluorination stages after a chlorocarbon was partially fluorinated by use of the Swarts reaction. In the final step in the conversion of chlorofluoroheptanes to perfluoroheptane, silver difluoride was found to be more effective than cobaltic fluoride in the vapor-phase reaction at 300° to 325°.[202]

Sharpe[194] found that $AuBrF_6$ reacted violently with either carbon tetrachloride or benzene.

METHOD 103 Fluorides of Group IIA Elements; Calcium

Of this group of fluorides only calcium fluoride has been used as a fluorinating agent, and then only in conjunction with other inorganic fluorides. The use of calcium fluoride for this purpose is considered to be relatively unimportant. A French patent[50] describes the preparation of a mixture of chlorofluoromethanes from carbon tetrachloride using a mixture of calcium fluoride and antimony pentachloride. Bockemuller[20] employed a mixture of AgF and CaF_2 and Ruff used a mixture of HgF and CaF_2 for the fluorination of haloalkanes. Midgley and Henne[153] treated carbon tetrachloride with a mixture of calcium fluoride and antimony sulfate and obtained CF_2Cl_2.

METHOD 104 Fluorides of Group IIB Elements; Mercury and Zinc

Mercurous fluoride has been prepared by the action of hydrofluoric acid on mercurous carbonate or by the reaction of sodium fluoride and mercurous nitrate. This fluorinating agent was used by Swarts to fluorinate $C_5H_{11}Cl$,[216] $C_2H_5OCH_2CHBrCH_2Br$,[215] $CH_2ICO_2CH_3$,[207] and $CH_2BrCH_2CO_2CH_3$.[214] The reaction was generally carried out at 160° for 24 hours. Swarts also found that the use of mercurous fluoride in fluorinating alkyl chlorides did not result in coupling or olefin formation as in the case of AgF. Henne and Renoll[102] studied this fluorination reaction and found that good yields of monoalkyl fluorides could be obtained from monoiodides and monobromides, but poor yields were obtained from monochlorides and polyiodides. Fluorination of polychlorides resulted in the loss of hydrogen chloride.

Mercuric fluoride is a more effective agent for halogen substitution and can be prepared by the action of fluorine on mercury salts. It is quite hygroscopic, a characteristic which limited its early application.

Henne and Midgley[98] prepared HgF_2 in a copper reaction vessel by the action of fluorine gas on mercuric chloride. Fluorination with this reagent resulted in good yields of products from polyiodides or polybromides; polychlorides were unreactive and were used as solvents for the reaction.

A great improvement in fluorination technique was introduced by Henne[91] when he demonstrated that the *in situ* preparation of HgF_2 could be accomplished by the reaction of HgO and anhydrous hydrogen fluoride. The water formed in this reaction combined with excess HF and floated on top of the layer of chloroform or methylene chloride which was used as a solvent. By this technique halogenated esters and alkanes were fluorinated in good yields at $-20°$. Further study showed that fluorination of $RCHCl_2$ could be readily accomplished by this procedure.[103] Side reactions occurred when the Swarts reaction was used on this type of compound and the difluoride was produced only with great difficulty.

Mercuric fluoride was tested as a fluorinating agent for hydrocarbons but the rapidity of the reaction of HgF_2 with air limited its use for this purpose.[48]

Huckel[118] treated both ICN and CH_3CN with mercuric fluoride at 160°. From the first reaction, cyanuryl fluoride, $(FCN)_3$ was the product obtained and in the case of acetonitrile a mixture of $CH_3CF_2NF_2$, $CH_2{=}CFNF_2$, $CH_3CF{=}NF_2$ and $CH_2{=}C{=}NF$ was obtained. Similar results were observed by Nerdel[166] in the fluorination of acetonitrile.

Zinc fluoride can be used to produce acyl fluorides from acyl chlorides.[92]

METHOD 105 Fluorides of Group III Elements; Aluminum, Thallium, and Boron

Aluminum fluoride has been investigated as a fluorinating agent in both the liquid phase and the vapor phase reactions. It is believed that the reaction involves disproportionation (cf. Method 214) rather than substitution. Miller and Calfee[156] reacted CCl_3F with AlF_3 at 105° and isolated a mixture consisting of CCl_2F_2, $CClF_3$ and CCl_4. In the vapor phase at 300° to 400° the interaction of CH_3CClF_2 and AlF_3 resulted in the formation of CH_3CF_3.[155] At 375°, both $CHClF_2$ and $CHCl_2F$ yielded CHF_3[156] and at 650° to 700°, treatment of CCl_3CClF_2 with AlF_3 resulted in the formation of a mixture of CCl_2F_2, CCl_4, CF_3Cl, $CF_2ClCFCl_2$, $CCl_2{=}CFCl$, and $CCl_2{=}CCl_2$.[33]

Thallous fluoride replaces chlorine in acyl chlorides, and alkyl chlorocarbonates at low temperatures.[67,70,174] Bromo- or iodoacetic esters are converted to the fluoro- derivative with TlF in refluxing ether or ethanol.[4,175,176,177]

Boron trifluoride has been used in conjunction with hydrogen fluoride and in this respect functions only as a catalyst (cf. Method 109).

METHOD 106 Fluorides of Group IV Elements; Silicon, Tin and Lead

References to the use of silicon and tin fluorides are few. Silver- and mercury fluorosilicate were employed by Paterno and Spallino[171] to fluorinate alkyl iodides to the corresponding fluorides. Whalley[230] treated 1,1-dichloroethane with hydrogen fluoride in the presence of 2.5 percent $SnCl_4$ and obtained a mixture of CH_3CHClF and CH_3CHF_2. Under similar conditions other chloroethanes yielded mixtures of fluorochloroethanes. This reaction was carried out at 50° to 100° and at 100 to 200 psi. The use of SnF_4 as a vapor phase fluorinating agent for hydrocarbons was found to be unsatisfactory.[56]

Henne and Waalkes[106] prepared PbF_4 *in situ* from the reaction of HF and PbO_2 in the presence of chlorofluoroolefins and observed that fluorine added across the double bond. Some of the olefins which were fluorinated and the resultant products are as follows:

$$CF_3CCl{=}CCl_2 \rightarrow CF_3CClFCFCl_2$$

$$CF_3CCl{=}CFCl \rightarrow CF_3CClFCF_2Cl$$

$$CCl_2{=}CCl_2 \rightarrow CCl_2FCCl_2F$$

$$CHCl{=}CCl_2 \rightarrow CHClFCCl_2F$$

The reaction was initiated at $-78°$ and a short time after reaching room temperature the reaction was completed. Similar results were observed when the reaction was carried out at 80° for 3 hours.[99,107,226]

The use of PbF_4 as a fluorinating agent for hydrocarbons in the vapor phase was investigated during World War II and was found unsatisfactory due to the formation of a liquid eutectic mixture of PbF_4 and PbF_2 which was corrosive to the reactor.[56] McBee[145,146] employed PbF_4 to fluorinate aromatic hydrocarbons. Benzene yielded perfluorocyclohexane at a reaction temperature of 200°.

METHOD 107 Fluorides of Group V Elements; Antimony, Bismuth, and Arsenic

The most important fluorides of the Group V metals are those of antimony. Little use has been found for the fluorides of arsenic and bismuth for the introduction of fluorine into organic molecules. Swarts first discovered that the fluorides of antimony could be used to replace other halogens with fluorine in organic molecules. Since this discovery numerous variations and refinements have been found to both accelerate and predict the course of the reaction. Today the Swarts reaction contributes, to a large degree, to the number of commercial fluorocarbons produced.

Henne has contributed in a large measure to a better understanding of the Swarts reaction. His studies of the fluorination of chlorocarbons has made available a mass of information from which the reactivities of various halogen groupings may be determined.

Many different antimony halides may be used in the Swarts reaction. Antimony trifluoride is commercially available and may be used as such. Hydrogen fluoride is less reactive toward replacement reactions as pointed out in Method 110. However, the use of a small amount of $SbCl_3$ in the presence of an excess of hydrogen fluoride is an effective fluorinating system which continually regenerates SbF_3. It has been found, however, that the presence of pentavalent antimony facilitates the Swarts reaction and this has led to numerous combinations of reagents such as: SbF_3—$SbCl_5$, SbF_2Cl_3, SbF_3Cl_2, SbF_5, SbF_3—Cl_2, SbF_3—Br_2, SbF_3Cl_2—HF, SbF_3—SbF_3Cl_2, SbF_3—Cl_2—HF, $SbCl_5$—HF. The reaction is generally carried out with no solvent other than the chlorohydrocarbon. Temperatures employed depend upon the desired fluorocompound, the reactivity of the chlorohydrocarbon, and the potency of the fluorinating agent. The Swarts reaction is generally carried out on chlorohydrocarbons; some work has been done with bromo- and iodo- compounds but they quite frequently lead to complex mixtures of products. The more highly chlorinated the starting compound is, the easier the reaction proceeds.

Henne[92] has most adequately demonstrated the reactivity of various groupings in chlorocarbons and a repetition at this point is not warranted. However, a brief summary of his observations is in order. Using antimony trifluoride with pentavalent antimony as the fluorinating reagent the following observations were made. The —CCl_3 group is the most reactive yielding —CCl_2F and —$CClF_2$ and less readily, —CF_3 groups. The —$CHCl_2$ group is converted slowly to —CHClF and to —CHF_2 with still greater difficulty. The groupings —CH_2Cl and —CHCl— are unaffected by the same treatment.

Some attention may be paid at this point to the Swarts reaction as carried out on bromohydrocarbons. Considerably less work has been done in this area. The following table indicates some of the types of materials fluorinated and the resulting products:

Starting Material	Fluorination Agent	Reaction Conditions	Products	Reference
$CHBr_3$	SbF_3, Br_2	110–120°/24 hrs.	$CHBr_2F$ $CHBrF_2$	212
$CH_2BrCHBr_2$	SbF_3, Br_2	100°	$CH_2BrCHFBr$ CH_2BrCHF_2	211
CH_2BrCBr_3	SbF_3	135°/12 hrs.	$CH_2BrCFBr_2$ CH_2BrCF_2Br	213
$CHBr_2CHBr_2$	SbF_3/Br_2		$CHBr_2CHFBr$ $CHBr_2CHF_2$	210
$CH_2BrCBr_2CH_2Br$	SbF_3/Br_2	150°	$CH_2BrCF_2CH_2Br$	139

A most interesting empirical formula has been proposed by Mantell and Herbst[149] for predicting the alternative reaction sites in the Swarts reaction. The empirical formula is proposed as follows: $A = BC\Sigma\Delta EM$; A is the number given the reactivity of the site, the larger the number the greater the reactivity; B is a constant which equals 1.00 for all sites containing less than two fluorine atoms and 0.42 for sites containing two fluorine atoms; C is equal to 1.00 for all sites where chlorine is being replaced and 1.46 for sites where bromine is being replaced; E is the electronegativity of the substituent atom minus the electronegativity of the carbon atom; M is the bond refractivity of the carbon-substituent bond. The summation sign indicates the summing of the ΔEM values for the substituents present at the site. Numerous examples are available in the literature which substantiate this empirical rule.

The Swarts reaction as carried out on chloroalkanes has been described earlier and is of considerable commercial significance. Another use of this reaction is in the fluorination of chloroalkenes. In this case, replacement of allylic chlorine atoms by fluorine proceeds much more readily to give —CF_3 groupings:

$$\mathrm{C{=}\underset{|}{C}{-}CCl_3 \longrightarrow C{=}\underset{|}{C}{-}CF_3}$$

The following table will only serve to show the relative ease with which this reaction proceeds using various types of chloroalkenes:

Starting Material	Fluorination Agent	Reaction Conditions	Products	Yields
$CCl_2{=}CClCCl_3$	SbF_3	150°	$CCl_2{=}CClCCl_2F$ $CCl_2{=}CClCClF_2$ $CCl_2{=}CClCF_3$	13[108] 28[108] 43[108]
$CCl_2{=}CClCCl{=}CCl_2$	SbF_3Cl_2		$CF_3CCl{=}CClCF_3$	95[105]
$CHCl{=}\overset{CH_3}{\overset{\vert}{C}}{-}CCl_3$	SbF_3		$CHCl{=}\overset{CH_3}{\overset{\vert}{C}}{-}CF_3$	70[104]
$CCl_2{=}CClCCl_3$	$SbCl_5+HF$	147°	$CCl_2{=}CClCF_3$	69[43]
$CCl_2{=}CClCCl_3$	$HF+Sb^{5+}$	23–47°/12 hrs.	$CCl_2{=}CClCF_3$	77[65]
$CF_2ClCF{=}CFCF_2Cl$	SbF_3	40°/30 min.	$CF_3CF{=}CFCF_3$	80[83]
$CH_2{=}CHCCl_3$	$SbF_3+SbF_3Cl_2$	−10° to −5°/2 hrs.	$CF_3CH{=}CH_2$	51[84]
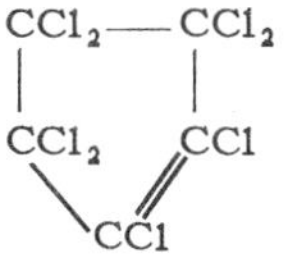	$SbF_3+SbF_3Cl_2$	1 hr/up to 100 psi	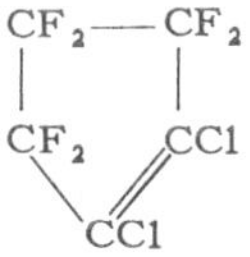	72[130]
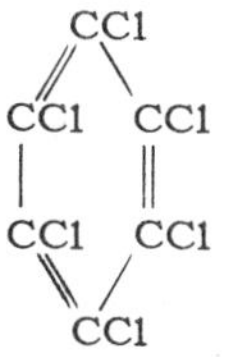	$SbCl_5+HF$	250°/1 hr.	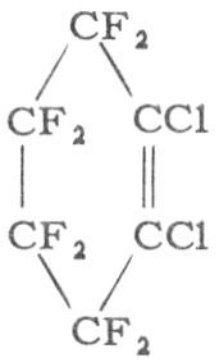	44[148]

The literature contains a multitude of examples of the use of antimony fluorides for the fluorination of chloroalkenes. It is conceivable that the ease of fluorination of certain chloroalkanes is a result of the formation of an intermediate chloroalkene.

The treatment of allylic chloroalkenes with antimony halides may result in a rearrangement, which is not too surprising. A typical rearrangement of this type is reported by Whaley and Davis[228] in the fluorination of $CCl_2{=}CClCHCl_2$:

$$CCl_2{=}CClCHCl_2 \xrightarrow{SbF_3} \begin{cases} CHCl{=}CClCF_3 & (26\%) \\ CHCl{=}CClCF_2Cl & (21\%) \\ CCl_2{=}CClCHF_2 & (24\%) \end{cases}$$

$$CCl_2{=}CClCHCl_2 \xrightarrow{SbF_3 + SbCl_5} CHCl{=}CClCF_3 \quad (92\%)$$

A small amount of pentavalent antimony hastens the fluorination reaction as well as the allylic shift.

The Swarts reaction can also be applied to the fluorination of functional organic chloro-compounds such as ethers,[21] acyl chlorides,[206,207,209] esters,[70] and sulfides.[222,225]

METHOD 108 Fluorides of the Transition Elements; Cobalt, Iron, Chromium, Manganese and Titanium

The use of cobaltic fluoride to prepare fluorocarbons directly from hydrocarbons was developed to a pilot-plant stage during World War II by investigators working for the former Manhattan Engineering District (Atomic Energy Commission) and various aspects of this work have been described in detail.[27,57,202] The reactor consisted of a copper tube surrounded by a heater into which was packed $CoCl_2$ which was converted to CoF_2 by anhydrous HF at 350° to 450°. Fluorine gas was then passed into the reactor at 200° to 300° to convert cobaltous fluoride to cobaltic fluoride. The hydrocarbon vapors, diluted with nitrogen, were passed through the reactor at a temperature of 105° to 325°. (When liquid hydrocarbons were reacted with CoF_3 violent reactions occurred.) Feed ratios, dilution ratios, length of reactor tube and temperature conditions were studied in order to obtain optimum yields. Pure *n*-perfluoroheptane was obtained in a 78 percent yield from *n*-heptane and perfluorodimethylcyclohexane was obtained in an 88 percent yield from xylene. A continuous reactor was designed and operated which also provided for the refluorination of spent CoF_3.

Various other fluorocarbons were prepared by this process. They include perfluorobutane, -pentane, -cyclopentane, -dimethylcyclopentane,

-methylcyclohexane, and -*o*-, -*m*- and -*p*-dimethylcyclohexane, among among others. Polychlorofluoroheptanes, polynuclear aromatic hydrocarbons and lubricating oil fractions were also fluorinated by this process.[202]

Haszeldine[80,86] described the complete fluorination of various alkanes, haloalkanes and alkyl aromatics by the use of CoF_3 at 350°. Stacey[203] fluorinated benzene and naphthalene by this process; Barlow and Tatlow[7] prepared perfluorobicyclohexane from biphenyl in a similar manner. Barbour, Barlow and Tatlow[6] fluorinated a series of hydrocarbons of the type $C_6H_5(CH_2)_nC_6H_5$, (where n = 1 to 6) to the completely fluorinated saturated analogs. Chlorobenzene and *o*-dichlorobenzene were likewise fluorinated with CoF_3 at 350° and perfluorocyclohexane, the mono- and dichloroperfluorocyclohexanes were obtained.[219]

Although previous work indicated that the use of CoF_3 as a fluorinating agent proceeds best in the vapor phase, Roylance, Tatlow and Worthington[180] reacted *o*-dichlorobenzene with CoF_3 and $LiAlH_4$ in ether at 0°, and obtained 1,2-dichloroperfluorocyclohexane as well as perfluorocyclohexane. Benning and Park[12] fluorinated $CCl_2{=}CCl_2$ with a mixture of Co_2O_3 and HF at 200° and isolated $CFCl_2CFCl_2$. Gochenour[66] treated $CF_3CCl{=}CClCF_3$ with CoF_3 at 165° to 216° and also obtained the addition product, namely $CF_3CClFCClFCF_3$. Bigelow[17] attempted to fluorinate acetone with CoF_3 at 60° and observed that cleavage occurred with the formation of CF_4 and CHF_3.

Nitrogen compounds were found to undergo fluorination by the use of cobaltic fluoride. Coates[40] treated CF_3CN with CoF_3 and isolated $C_2F_5NF_2$ and CF_3CF_3. Thompson and Emeleus[220] fluorinated trimethylamine in the vapor phase over CoF_3 to produce $(CF_3)_2NF$; Haszeldine[77,78,79,81] fluorinated various tertiary amines over CoF_3 at 250° and obtained the perfluorinated analogs.

Silvey and Cady[195] produced CF_3SF_5 by treating either carbon disulfide or methyl mercaptan with CoF_3 at 250° (cf. Method 1307). Emeleus[54] reacted $(CF_3)_3As$ with CoF_3 in a hot tube and observed the formation of $(CF_3)_2AsF$ (cf. Method 1227).

Manganese trifluoride was evaluated as a fluorinating agent for the conversion of a naphthenic base stock lubricating oil into a fluorolubricating oil.[56] A higher yield was obtained in the vapor phase fluorination at 147° to 218° with MnF_3 than with CoF_3. The trifluoride was prepared as follows:

$$MnCl_2 + HF \longrightarrow MnF_2 \text{ (white solid)}$$
$$MnF_2 + F_2 \longrightarrow MnF_3 \text{ (purple solid)}$$

McBee[147] fluorinated $C_3Cl_5F_3$ at 300° over MnF_3 and obtained a mixture of more highly fluorinated chloropropanes. When this mixture was passed over MnF_3 at 350°, perfluoropropane was obtained. Manganese trifluoride was employed by Fear and Thrower[55] to fluorinate benzene in the vapor phase. The reaction was carried out in a copper reactor at 200° to 350° and the fluorination product was a complex mixture of polyfluorocyclohexanes, from which were isolated octa- and heptafluorocyclohexene.

Chromic fluoride (CrF_3) was employed by Benning and Park[11,14,15] in conjunction with hydrogen fluoride in fluorination reactions. The compound to be fluorinated together with HF was passed over a bed of CrF_3 on carbon at temperatures varying from 275° to 880°, at various contact times. Such treatment of $CClF_3$ produced CF_4 in high yields; when CF_2ClCF_2Cl was similarly fluorinated, $CClF_3$ and CF_3CClF_2 were obtained. A mixture of methane, chlorine and hydrogen fluoride yielded dichlorodifluoromethane. Similar use of $FeCl_3$ on activated carbon was made to fluorinate CCl_4 with HF to CF_2Cl_2.[46]

The use of titanium tetrafluoride in fluorination has only been as a catalyst in conjunction with hydrogen fluoride (cf. Method 110). Treatment of carbon tetrachloride with HF over TiF_4 yielded CCl_2F_2.[117]

METHOD 109 Reaction of Hydrogen Fluoride with Unsaturated Compounds: Addition and Substitution

Hydrogen fluoride adds readily to hydrocarbon olefins to yield monofluoroalkanes (cf. Method 202). The reaction is generally carried out without a catalyst. The addition proceeds in accordance with Markownikoff's rule; the fluorine atom attaches itself to the carbon atom containing the least number of hydrogen atoms. Thus: $CH_3CH{=}CH_2$, and $CH_2{=}C{=}CH_2$ yield CH_3CHFCH_3 and $CH_3CF_2CH_3$, respectively. Yields up to 80 percent are obtained.[2,37,68] An apparently simple reaction is complicated, however, by the fact that the instability of monofluoroalkanes makes the reaction reversible. Monofluoroalkanes are difficult to purify since trace amounts of water or acid result in their decomposition. Hydrogen fluoride itself will initiate decomposition and isomerization. As one might expect, secondary and tertiary fluorides are particularly bad in this respect. Because of this reversibility of the reaction, the addition of hydrogen fluoride to olefins at elevated temperatures or for extended periods of time results in decomposition and/or polymerization. The addition of hydrogen fluoride to ethylene, however, is practical. If a mixture of ethylene and hydrogen fluoride is warmed to 90°, yields of the order of 80 percent of ethyl fluoride are obtained.[68] Hydrogen fluoride will open the cyclopropane ring to give *n*-propyl fluoride if the reaction is carried out at 0°.[68] Careful control of the temperature must be maintained if appreciable quantities of isopropyl fluoride are to be avoided. Harmon[76] has also carried this reaction out on perfluorocyclopropane and obtained 1-hydroperfluoropropane.

The addition of hydrogen fluoride to olefins containing a chlorine atom on a carbon atom of the double bond is an excellent procedure for the preparation of fluoro- or chlorofluoroalkanes. The products of these additions are more stable than the monofluoroalkanes. Henne and his coworkers have contributed much to the elucidation of this reaction. Considering first only monochloroolefins, the reaction may be controlled to yield the chlorofluoroalkane. If higher temperatures and an excess of hydrogen fluoride are employed the difluoroalkane may result.

The following examples represent the temperatures employed and the mono-addition products obtained.

Olefin	Product	Temperature °C.	Reference
$CH_2{=}CHCl$	CH_2CHClF	150	189
$(CH_3)_2C{=}CHCl$	$(CH_3)_2CHClF$	−23 to 0	101
$CH_3CCl{=}CHCl$	$CH_3CClFCH_2Cl$	120	101
$CH_2ClCCl{=}CH_2$	$CH_2ClCClFCH_3$	50 to 60	94, 107

When an excess of hydrogen fluoride is used the intermediate chlorofluoroalkane may eliminate hydrogen chloride and a second mole of hydrogen fluoride may add:

Olefin	Product	Temperature °C	Yield	Reference
$CH_2ClCCl{=}CH_2$	$CH_2ClCF_2CH_3$	50 to 60	4	94
$CH_3CCl{=}CHCH_3$	$CH_3CF_2CH_2CH_3$	−78 to 30	67	96
$C_2H_5CCl{=}CHCH_3$	$C_2H_5CF_2C_2H_5$	−80 to 60	67–73	93
$(CH_3)_2CHCH_2CCl{=}CH_2$	$(CH_3)_2CHCH_2CF_2CH_3$	−78 to 30	70	178
$CH_3CH_2CH_2CCl{=}CH_2$	$CH_3CH_2CH_2CF_2CH_3$	−78 to 30	64	178

The addition of hydrogen fluoride to chloroolefins containing the structure $>C{=}CCl_2$ may result in three possible products, the amount of each compound formed, depending again upon the temperature and ratio of reactants. The addition of hydrogen fluoride to vinylidene chloride or trichloroethylene will serve to illustrate this reaction:

$$CH_2{=}CCl_2 + HF \xrightarrow[50\%]{65^\circ/3\ hrs} CH_3CFCl_2$$ [101]

$$CH_2{=}CCl_2 + HF \xrightarrow[59\%]{140^\circ/14\ hrs} CH_3CF_2Cl$$ [140]

$$CH_2{=}CCl_2 + HF \xrightarrow[74\%]{180\text{–}195^\circ/35\ hrs} CH_3CF_3$$ [140]

$$CHCl{=}CCl_2 + HF \xrightarrow{200\text{–}228^\circ/8\ hrs} CH_2ClCFCl_2 + CH_2ClCF_2Cl + CH_2ClCF_3$$ [75,140,205]

$$(CH_3)_2CHCH{=}CCl_2 + HF \rightarrow (CH_3)_2CHCH_2CFCl_2\ (10\%)$$ [217]

$$(CH_3)_2CHCH_2CF_2Cl\ (60\%)$$ [217]

$$(CH_3)_2CHCH_2CF_3\ (2.3\%)$$ [217]

The addition of hydrogen fluoride to fluorine-containing olefins also occurs readily. Henne and Hinkamp[97] added hydrogen fluoride to $C_2H_5CH{=}CF_2$ by allowing the mixture to warm to room temperature and obtained yields of 96 to 99 percent of $CF_3C_3H_7$. Addition has also been reported to take place with $CF_2{=}CF_2$[76] and $(CF_3)_2C{=}CF_2$[22] to give CHF_2CF_3 and $(CF_3)_3CH$. Miller and co-workers[158] effected the addition of hydrogen fluoride to $CH_2{=}CF_2$ and $CHCl{=}CF_2$ employing AlF_3 catalyst in a nickel tube at 300°. Similar additions are claimed in a patent by Arnold[1] using boron trifluoride as a catalyst at 95°:

$$CCl_2{=}CCl_2 + HF + BF_3 \xrightarrow[13\%]{95^\circ/24\ hrs} CHCl_2CCl_2F$$

$$CF_3CH{=}CClF + HF + BF_3 \xrightarrow[70\%]{95^\circ/24\ hrs} CF_3CH_2CClF_2$$

$$CF_3CCl{=}CCl_2 + HF + BF_3 \xrightarrow[12\%]{95^\circ/24\ hrs} CF_3CHClCCl_2F$$

and by Chapman[36] using $SnCl_4$ as a catalyst.

The addition of hydrogen fluoride to alkynes proceeds very easily and under certain conditions uncontrollably (cf. Methods 202 and 304). Acetylene and hydrogen fluoride react at room temperature to yield both $CH_2{=}CHF$ and CH_3CHF_2. There are, however, numerous references to the use of various catalysts; the following table will attempt to summarize these reactions:

Catalyst	Temperature	Products	Reference
CuCN	100–240°C	$CH_2{=}CHF$	38
FSO_3H	0°C	CH_3CHF_2	31
Ni Shavings	25°C	CH_3CHF_2	69
Al_2O_3	600°F	$CH_2{=}CHF$ CH_3CHF_2	111
AlF_3	600°F	$CH_2{=}CHF$	110
Zn-Hg Chromite	146°C	$CH_2{=}CHF$	231
BF_3	22°C	CH_3CHF_2	28

Hydrogen fluoride has been added to numerous other alkynes;[69,82,100,110,168] in most cases the difluoroalkane was the sole product. The addition of hydrogen fluoride to vinylacetylene using a mercuric catalyst is claimed as a good procedure for the preparation of 2-fluoro-1,3-butadiene.[8,41,159]

Hydrogen fluoride has been employed by Knunyants[127,128] to open the epoxide ring in the following manner (cf. Method 406):

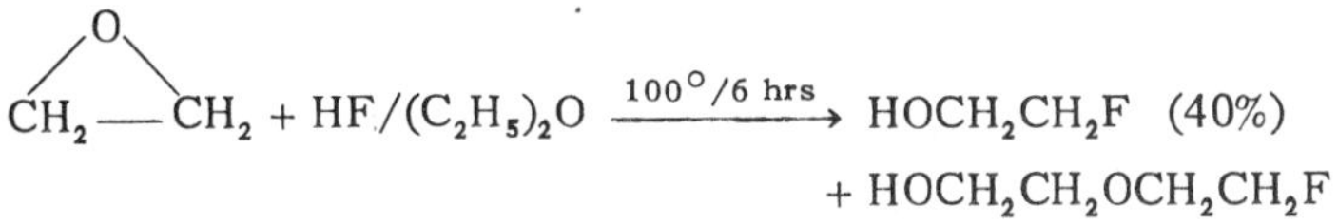

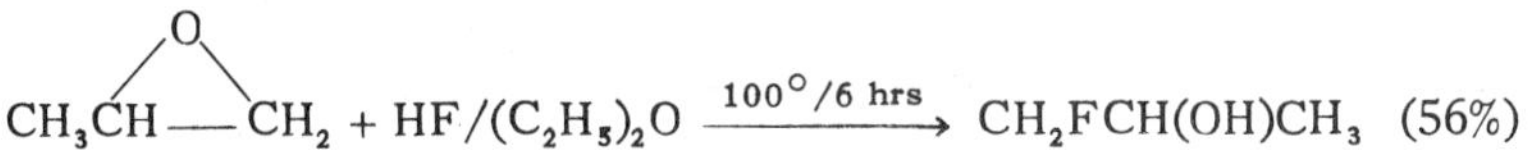

$$\overset{O}{\overset{\diagup\diagdown}{CH_2 \!-\! CH_2}} + HF/(C_2H_5)_2O \xrightarrow{100°/6 \text{ hrs}} HOCH_2CH_2F \quad (40\%)$$
$$+ HOCH_2CH_2OCH_2CH_2F$$

$$\overset{O}{\overset{\diagup\diagdown}{CH_3CH \!-\! CH_2}} + HF/(C_2H_5)_2O \xrightarrow{100°/6 \text{ hrs}} CH_2FCH(OH)CH_3 \quad (56\%)$$

Hydrogen fluoride has also been added to a number of unsaturated functional organic compounds. Addition has been accomplished with undecylenic acid, oleic acid, octadecanol, cyanic acid, and $CH_3C\!\equiv\!CCO_2H$.[109,119,135,150]

METHOD 110 Substitution with Hydrogen Fluoride

The substitution of fluorine for chlorine or bromine using only anhydrous hydrogen fluoride proceeds with difficulty. Only reactive chlorine atoms of polychloroalkanes or allylic chlorine atoms may be replaced with facility. The following table will indicate some of the products obtained from this type of fluorination:

Starting Material	Reaction Conditions	Products	% Yield	Reference
CCl_4	230–240°/1000 psi	CCl_3F	63	24
CH_3CCl_3	144°/1.75 hrs	CH_3CCl_2F	94	25
		CH_3CClF_2		
	210°/5200 psi/16.3 hrs	CH_3CF_3	80	140
CH_2ClCCl_3	225°/20 min	CH_2ClCCl_2F	80	25
$CHCl_2CCl_3$	225°/15 min	$CHCl_2CCl_2F$	77	25
$CCl_2\!=\!CClCCl_3$	155°/2 hrs	$CCl_2\!=\!CClCCl_2F$	3	25
		$CCl_2\!=\!CClCClF_2$	3	
		$CCl_2\!=\!CClCF_3$	33	

The ready replacement of allylic chlorine or bromine atoms has been previously mentioned. A particular case will serve to demonstrate the ease with which this reaction proceeds. Tarrant[217] fluorinated $(CH_3)_2CClCH_2CCl_3$ in a stainless steel autoclave using anhydrous hydrogen fluoride at a temperature of 130° for four hours. The sole product obtained was $(CH_3)_2CClCH_2CF_3$; no mono- or difluoro compounds were obtained. It was later shown that if this reaction were carried out at lower temperatures in a copper vessel, hydrogen chloride was eliminated and $(CH_3)_2C = CHCCl_3$ was formed. This latter olefin, when treated with hydrogen fluoride at $115°$ gave $(CH_3)_2CClCH_2CF_3$. Thus, it is concluded that the fluorination proceeds according to the following scheme:

$$
\underset{\underset{Cl}{|}}{\overset{\overset{CH_3}{|}}{CH_3CCH_2CCl_3}} \xrightarrow{HF} \overset{\overset{CH_3}{|}}{CH_3C}=CHCCl_3 \xrightarrow{HF}
$$

$$
\overset{\overset{CH_3}{|}}{CH_3C}=CHCF_3 \xrightarrow{HCl} \underset{\underset{Cl}{|}}{\overset{\overset{CH_3}{|}}{CH_3CCH_2CF_3}}
$$

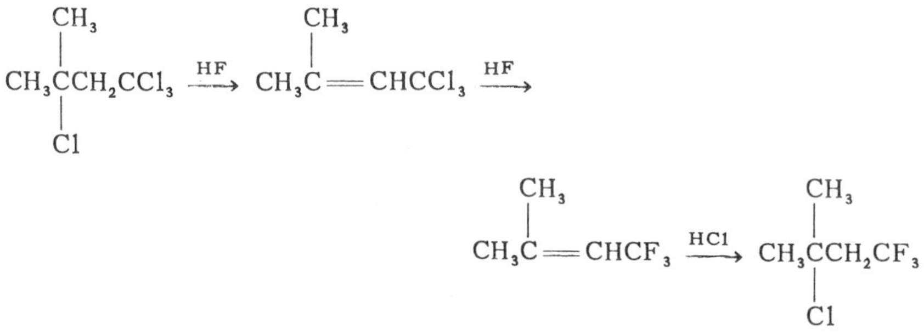

The use of anhydrous hydrogen fluoride has been extended to other bromo- and chloroalkanes. Of general interest are the following type reactions:

$$CF_2BrCH_2CHFBr + HF \xrightarrow{125°/4\ hrs} CF_3CH_2CHFBr\ [218]$$

$$CF_2BrCH_2CHBrCH_3 + HF \xrightarrow{135°/18\ hrs} CF_3CH_2CHBrCH_3\ [218]$$

$$C_2H_5CBrClCH_2Br + HF \xrightarrow{0°} C_2H_5CF_2CH_2Br\ [47]$$

$$CH_3CHClC_3H_7 + HF \xrightarrow{35-50°/80-100\ psi/18\ hrs} CH_3CF_2C_3H_7\ [178]$$

More practical use of hydrogen fluoride as a fluorinating agent may be made if it is used in conjunction with a catalyst. Many such catalysts have been reported in the patent literature and their commercial use depends to a large extent on the ease with which one can control the degree of fluorination.

An example of the type of catalysts used is chromic fluoride. Several patents are devoted to the use of a chromic fluoride on carbon as a catalyst.[11,14,15,133] Benning and Park[14] described the conversion of $CClF_3$ to CF_4 in a 88.5 percent yield by passing a mixture of hydrogen fluoride and the chlorofluorocarbon over CrF_3 on carbon with a contact time of 11 to 12 seconds at $880°$. Further work by Benning and co-workers[15] describes the preparation of $CClF_3$ and CF_3CClF_2 using a similar fluorination procedure on $CClF_2CClF_2$. Earlier work resulted in a patent on the preparation of CCl_2F_2 which was prepared by passing a mixture of methane, chlorine and hydrogen fluoride over this same catalyst.[11]

Whalley[230] employed tin tetrachloride as a catalyst with the following results:

$$CH_3CHCl_2 + HF + SnCl_4 \xrightarrow[100-200\text{ psi}]{50-100^\circ} CH_3CHClF\ (40\%) + CH_3CHF_2\ (20\%)$$

$$CH_2ClCCl_3 + HF + SnCl_4 \xrightarrow[100-200\text{ psi}]{50-100^\circ} CH_2ClCCl_2F\ (46\%) + CH_2ClCClF_2\ (5\%)$$

Other catalysts have been used and found effective and a few of these are listed to indicate the variety of materials tried: TiF_4,[117] BF_3,[9] $FeCl_3$ on activated charcoal,[46] KF-HF,[229] charcoal,[126] CuO on Al_2O_3.[232] Work has continued on this approach and has undoubtedly resulted in more effective catalysts for the utilization of hydrogen fluoride as a commercial fluorination agent.

METHOD 111 Electrochemical Process

One of the most interesting processes for the production of completely fluorinated organic compounds is the electrochemical process. This process which was discovered and developed by J. H. Simons[197] offers a commercial method of preparing completely fluorinated compounds directly from organic compounds and hydrogen fluoride.

The fluorination cell is constructed of any metal resistant to hydrogen fluoride and is a single compartment cell. The electrodes are arranged in a pack, the anodes are generally constructed of nickel while the cathodes may be of iron or nickel. The cell is charged with hydrogen fluoride, the organic reactant, and if necessary, an organic or inorganic electrolyte. The cell is run at low potentials of 5 to 6 volts and the current may vary from 5 to 2000 amperes depending on the size of the cell. The hydrogen fluoride is stripped from the effluent gases by a condenser and returned to the cell. The less volatile fluorinated products remaining in the cell, because of their high density and insolubility in hydrogen fluoride, may be withdrawn from the bottom of the cell. The exact conditions employed in any one run determine the products and their conversions. Degradation of the carbon skeleton may occur under certain conditions. A more thorough discussion of this topic may be found in Simons' book[199].

This procedure may be employed with varying degrees of effectiveness on a number of organic materials including hydrocarbons, acyl halides, ethers, *t*-amines, sulfides, etc. Some of the products obtained from this reaction using various starting materials are as follows:

Carboxylic Acids or Anhydrides

Initial Compounds (X = F, Cl)	Product
CH_3COX	CF_3COF
C_2H_5COX	C_2F_5COF
C_3H_7COX	C_3F_7COF
$C_5H_{11}COX$	$C_5F_{11}COF$
$C_7H_{15}COX$	$C_7F_{15}COF$
$C_{13}H_{27}COX$	$C_{13}F_{27}COF$
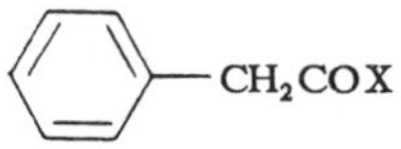	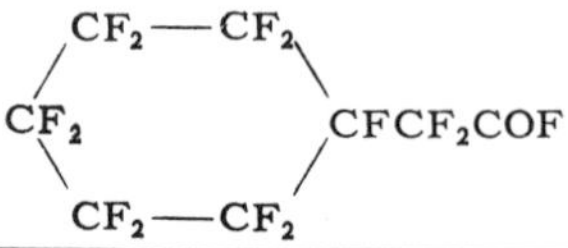

Ethers[121,123,198]

Initial Compound	Product
$C_3H_7OC_3H_7$	$C_3F_7OC_3F_7$
$C_6H_{13}OC_6H_{13}$	$C_6F_{13}OC_6F_{13}$
$CH_3OCH_2CH_2OCH_3$	$CF_3OCF_2CF_2OCF_3$
$C_2H_5OCH_2CH_2OCH_2CH_2OC_2H_5$	$C_2F_5OCF_2CF_2OCF_2CF_2OC_2F_5$
$CH_2CH_2CH_2O$ (ring)	$CF_2CF_2CF_2O$ (ring)
$CH_2CH_2CH_2CH_2O$ (ring)	$CF_2CF_2CF_2CF_2O$ (ring)

Amines[122,124]

Initial Compound	Product
$(CH_3)_3N$	$(CF_3)_3N$
$(C_2H_5)_3N$	$(C_2F_5)_3N$
$(C_4H_9)_3N$	$(C_4F_9)_3N$
$(C_2H_5)_2NCH_2CH_2N(C_2H_5)_2$	$(C_2F_5)_2NCF_2CF_2N(C_2F_5)_2$
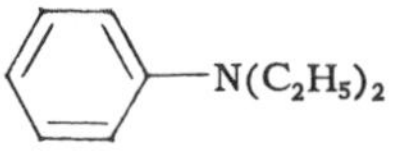	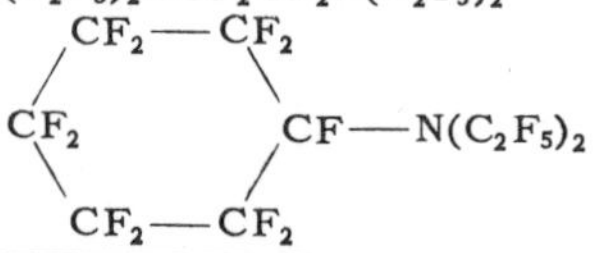

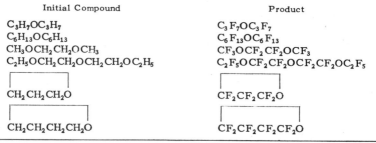

Sulfides[39,49,115,193] (cf. Methods 1307 and 1308)

Initial Compound	Product
CS_2	$CF_3SF_5 + F_5SCF_2SF_5$
CH_3SCH_3	$CF_3SF_5 + (CF_3)_2SF_4$
$C_2H_5SC_2H_5$	$C_2F_5SF_5 + (C_2F_5)_2SF_4$
$C_4H_9SC_4H_9$	$C_4F_9SF_5 + (C_4F_9)SF_4$

Fluorocarbons may be prepared by this procedure starting with either a carboxylic acid or a hydrocarbon, and an electrolyte such as water must be used in the latter case.

A second electrolytic process has been discribed by workers at the General Electric Company[62,63,233,234]. This process involves the electrolysis of mixtures of hydrogen fluoride and chlorohydrocarbons. The temperature of electrolysis affects both the distribution and yields of products as well as the efficiency of the reaction. In the electrolysis of methylene chloride the following products were obtained; $CHFCl_2$, CF_2Cl_2 and CHF_2Cl. These products accounted for 80 percent by weight of the methylene chloride charged. Some chlorination is reported to occur. The cell is constructed of iron with a central nickel anode. In the case of chlorohydrocarbons which are immiscible with the hydrogen fluoride, a rotating anode increases the yield of products and minimizes degradation. The addition of an alkali metal fluoride is necessary in certain cases to form a conducting mixture. The following table will show the effect of agitation on the electrolytic fluorination of $CHCl{=}CCl_2$:

Step	Product	Static % Yield	240 RPM % Yield	1000 RPM % Yield
1	$CHFClCFCl_2$	50	67	82
2	$CF_2ClCFCl_2$	30	22	12
3	decomposition	20	1	6

This method has been applied to other chloroalkanes and chloroacids. The latter type compounds undergo extensive decarboxylation.

A British patent[23] describes the electrolysis of a mixture of chloroform, hydrogen fluoride and lithium fluoride and reports as products, CF_4, $CClF_3$, CHF_3, $CClF_3$, $CHClF_2$, CCl_2F_2, $CHCl_2F$ and CCl_3F.

Schmidt and Schmidt[191,192] describe a study of the anode reactions in electrochemical fluorination of organic compounds using anhydrous hydrogen fluoride. Two types of cells were used; one made of polyvinylchloride with a single nickel anode and a single nickel cathode; the other cell was similar to the type employed by Simons. These workers carried out the fluorination of carboxylic acids to the monofluorination stage[191]. For example β-fluoropropionic acid was prepared from propionic acid, and the methyl esters of α-, β-, and γ-fluorobutyric acid were prepared from methyl butyrate. The investigation of the electrochemical fluorination of olefins using non-aqueous solvents was also described by these workers[192]. It was found that non-aqueous solvents were practical for electrochemical fluorination of non-polar organic compounds; anhydrous acetic acid was found to be the best solvent. Simple addition of fluorine to olefinic compounds can be carried out in this fashion:

$$CHCl{=}CCl_2 + HF/\text{acetonitrile} \xrightarrow{\bar{e}} CHClFCCl_2F$$

$$(C_6H_5)_2C{=}CH_2 + HF/\text{glacial acetic acid} \xrightarrow{\bar{e}} (C_6H_5)_2CFCH_2F.$$

METHOD 112 Direct Fluorination

The action of fluorine on a carbon compound can be likened to a combustion process where the reaction products are carbon tetrafluoride and hydrogen fluoride. Early attempts to fluorinate hydrocarbons in the vapor phase resulted in "burning" of the compound with frequent explosions taking place.

The earliest attempt to directly fluorinate methane, chloroform and carbon tetrachloride was made by Moissan.[161] Carbon tetrafluoride was obtained as the main product together with unidentified polymeric products. Ruff and Keim[184] directly fluorinated carbon tetrachloride vapor which was diluted with nitrogen by passing the vapors together with fluorine gas over a bed of cobaltic fluoride. The products obtained were tetrafluoromethane and various chlorofluoromethanes.

Calfee and Bigelow[30] found that the violence of the vapor phase fluorination reaction could be moderated by introducing fluorine through a vertical reactor tube made of brass, nickel or Monel which was packed with copper wire screen. Another moderating influence was found to be the dilution of fluorine with nitrogen. By use of this technique, ethane was fluorinated to C_2F_6 together with partially fluorinated ethanes. The carbon skeleton remained essentially intact; that is no polymers were formed, although some CF_4 was produced. Employment of this technique in further studies afforded Bigelow as well as other investigators a more practical tool for vapor phase fluorination. Chlorocarbons such as C_2H_5Cl yielded CF_3Cl and CF_3CCl_2F.[32] Fluorination of methane proved to be more complicated than ethane. Hadley and Bigelow[73] proposed a free radical polymerization mechanism to explain the production of C_2F_6 and C_3F_8 in addition to the expected CF_4 from methane.

Cady and co-workers[29] made the next refinement in vapor phase fluorination technique when they packed the reactor with silver-plated copper turnings. By use of this apparatus, *n*-heptane was fluorinated to *n*-perfluoroheptane. The use of silver with fluorine results in the formation of silver difluoride (AgF_2) which might be considered to be the important fluorinating agent in this reaction (cf. Method 103). Musgrave and Smith[165] fluorinated *n*-octene to *n*-perfluorooctane using similar conditions. These workers used copper turnings plated with various metals such as gold, silver, nickel, cobalt, etc.

The most recent advance of importance in vapor phase fluorination technique is the jet fluorination process devised by Tyczkowski and Bigelow.[224] The design of the reactor is based on the principle of a Meker burner, incorporating two concentric tubes with gas inlets. Fluorine is introduced in the outer tube and the organic compound is fed through the inner jet tube with nitrogen as a diluent. A jet pump increases internal circulation and dilutes the fluorine with inert reactor gas. When ethane is fluorinated in this reactor a 92 percent conversion to C_2F_5H and C_2F_6 can be obtained. The temperature at the top of the reactor where the fluorination products are collected is $64°$. The flow rates of fluorine and reactant, molar reaction ratios and fluorine dilution ratios are important parameters which influence the types and amounts of reaction products.

An important advantage in this system is the virtual retention of identity of the original carbon skeleton in the fluorination process and under optimum conditions no cleavage products or polymers are formed when ethane is fluorinated. Another advantage is the elimination of the necessity for metal packing in the reactor. Refinements in design of the jet reactor and a study of flow rates, dilution ratios and molar reactant ratios by Bigelow and Detoro[18] have made it possible to control the fluorination of ethane to optimum yields of either CF_3CF_3, CF_3CHF_2 or CF_3CH_2F.

In the past, direct fluorination in the vapor phase has been a cumbersome process not particularly suitable to industrial application. However, the jet reactor shows considerable promise for more widespread use especially if future refinements in the process allow for selective substitution.

Liquid phase direct fluorination has not been extensively employed. Bockemuller[20] bubbled fluorine which was diluted with carbon dioxide into a solution of cyclohexane in carbon tetrachloride and isolated monofluorocyclohexane. Bigelow and Pearson[12] introduced fluorine into a solution of hexafluorobenzene in carbon tetrachloride and isolated a low yield of $C_6F_6Cl_6$. Bockemuller[20] also fluorinated $CCl_2{=}CCl_2$ at $-80°$ and obtained $CFCl_2CFCl_2$. Miller[154,157] devised a liquid fluorinator consisting of a U-tube with vertical arms joined at the bottom by a flat section. Fluorine was introduced in one arm and the organic compound was placed in the other arm of the tube which was equipped with a stirrer. With this apparatus chlorofluoroalkenes were fluorinated with addition, substitution and disproportionation taking place.

The first successful attempt to fluorinate carbon in the form of wood charcoal was made by Lebeau and Damiens[132] who obtained CF_4, C_2F_6, C_3F_8 and other materials. An earlier attempt by these workers resulted in the isolation of only CF_4.[131] Ruff and Bretschneider[181] fluorinated graphite and Norite with a deficiency of fluorine and isolated a polymeric material with the formula $(CF)_x$ which decomposed explosively when heated. A study of the fluorination of various allotropic forms of carbon was made by Simons[196] and Simons and Block.[199A,199B] The various fluorocarbons isolated and characterized included CF_4, C_2F_6, C_3F_8, C_4F_{10}, and C_5F_{12}. More recently a novel variation was reported in a patent by Mantell, Passino and Teeters[150] who fluorinated Norite in the presence of either bromine or chlorine. The reaction was carried out from 412° to 538° and nitrogen was used as a diluent. Mixtures of chlorofluorocarbons or bromofluorocarbons containing up to four carbon atoms were obtained.

Fluorination of benzene, first reported by Fukuhara and Bigelow[19] indicated that addition as well as substitution occurred. The products isolated and identified were *cyclo*-C_6F_{12}, *cyclo*-C_6HF_{11}, *cyclo*-C_5F_{10}, C_4F_{10}, C_3F_8, CF_4 and perfluorodicyclohexane. Thompson, Tarrant and Bigelow[221] fluorinated α-methylnaphthalene over silver-plated copper wire packing and isolated a low yield of $C_{11}F_{20}$. Other aromatic hydrocarbons were subjected to vapor phase fluorination by Gilbert and Bigelow[61] who used copper shot packing in a brass tube. Fluorination of 1,3,5-tris(trifluoromethyl) benzene resulted in the formation of the completely fluorinated trimethylcyclohexane as well as intermediate hydrogen-containing compounds. Similar treatment of 1,4-bis(trifluoromethyl)-benzene, benzotrifluoride and fluorobenzene resulted in the production of completely and partially fluorinated saturated derivatives. Musgrave and Smith[165] fluorinated naphthalene in the vapor phase using gold plated copper turnings as the tube packing. Perfluorodecahydronaphthalene was isolated from the reaction. This technique was also employed by Haszeldine and Walaschewski[89] in the complete fluorination of such compounds as toluene, xylene, ethylbenzene and naphthalene.

Organic compounds containing various functional groups have also been subjected to direct fluorination. Fukuhara and Bigelow[58] treated acetone with fluorine in the vapor phase and isolated $(CF_3)_2C{=}O$, CH_2FCOCH_3, CF_4 and CF_3COF. Holub and Bigelow[116] fluorinated tetrahydrofuran and methyl ethyl ketone to the completely fluorinated products. Liquid phase fluorination of carboxylic acids was accomplished by Bockemuller;[20] *n*-butyric acid yielded a mixture of β- and γ-fluorobutyric acids. Isobutyric acid was fluorinated to α-fluoroisobutyric acid and crotonic acid was converted to the addition product, α,β-difluorobutyric acid.

Nitrogen compounds have been directly fluorinated with varying results. Ruff and Giese[183] prepared CF_3NO by fluorinating silver cyanide (cf. Chapter XI). Further study of the fluorination of silver cyanide by Ruff and Willenberg[186] resulted in the isolation and identification of hexafluoroazomethane $CF_3N{=}NCF_3$ (cf. Chapter XI). Coates, Harris and Sutcliffe[40] fluorinated potassium ferricyanide and potassium ferrocyanide in the liquid phase and obtained CF_3NF_2 (cf. Chapter XI). Attempted liquid phase fluorination of acetonitrile by Cuculo and Bigelow[44] yielded $CF_3CF_2NF_2$ as the only nitrogen-containing product together with various fluorocarbons. More recent studies on the direct fluorination of nitrogen compounds have been more encouraging. Bigelow and co-workers[60] fluorinated mono-, di- and trimethylamines, ethylenediamine and ethyleneimine in the vapor phase over copper gauze packing. The results of the fluorination reactions are summarized below:

$$CH_3NH_2 + F_2 \rightarrow CF_3NF_2,\ CF_3CF_2NF_2,\ (CF_3)_2NF,\ C_2F_6,\ CF_4$$

$$(CH_3)_2NH + F_2 \rightarrow CF_3NF_2,\ CF_3CF_2NF_2,\ (CF_3)_2NF,\ (CF_3)_3N,\ C_2F_6,\ CF_4$$

$$(CH_3)_3N + F_2 \rightarrow CF_3NF_2,\ CF_3CF_2NF_2,\ (CF_3)_2NF,\ (CF_3)_3N,\ C_2F_6,\ CF_4$$

$$H_2NCH_2CH_2NH_2 + F_2 \rightarrow (CNF_3)_2,\ CF_3NF_2,\ CF_3CF_2NF_2,\ CF_3N{=}NCF_3$$

$$CH_2CH_2NH + F_2 \rightarrow (CF_3)_2NF,\ CF_3N{=}NCF_3,\ (CF_3)_2N{-}N(CF_3)_2$$

The properties of the hexafluoroazomethane prepared by these workers compared favorably to the same compound prepared by Ruff and Willenberg.[186]

Malononitrile and dimethyl formamide were fluorinated under similar conditions:[3]

$$NCCH_2CN + F_2 \rightarrow F_2NCF_2CF_2CF_2NF_2,\ CF_3CF_2CF_2NF_2,$$
$$CF_2CF_2CF_2N{=}N,\ CF_2CF_2CF_2NFNF,\ C_3F_8.$$

$$(CH_3)_2NCH(=O) + F_2 \rightarrow (CF_3)_2NF_2,\ CHF_2NFNFCF_3,\ COF_2,\ CF_4$$

Direct fluorination of sulfur compounds has also been reported. Silvey and Cady[195] exposed CH_3SH to vapor phase fluorination and isolated CF_3SF_5 and $CSHF_7$ (cf. Method 1308). Neudorffer[167] attempted the fluorination of thiophene but obtained only perfluorocyclobutane and perfluorocyclopentane (cf. Chapter XIII). Carbon disulfide was converted to CF_3SF_5 by vapor phase fluorination[223] (cf. Method 1307).

METHOD 113 Halogen Fluorides

Chlorine trifluoride, bromine trifluoride and iodine pentafluoride have been used as fluorinating agents. They are strong oxidizing agents; ClF_3 was used as an incendiary agent during World War II by the Germans.

Chlorine trifluoride can be prepared by the process of Ruff and Krug[155] which involves direct reaction of the elements at -170°, or by Shenk's method; the reaction of the two gases at 200°.[199] Because of its great reactivity this compound has not been extensively used as a fluorinating agent. However, Huckel[118] fluorinated CF_2BrNO_2 and obtained small yields of CF_3NO_2. Collins, *et al.*[42] reacted both wood charcoal and graphite with ClF_3 at temperatures greater than 350° and isolated a mixture of chlorofluoromethanes, -ethanes, and -propanes. Ellis and Musgrave[52] fluorinated carbon tetrachloride with ClF_3 at 0°; the products isolated from this reaction were CCl_3F and CCl_2F_2.

Bromine trifluoride was first prepared by Moissan who combined the gases in the cold.[162] Banks[5] was able to effect a 94 percent conversion of CBr_4 to $CBrF_3$ with this reagent. Carbon tetrachloride yielded a mixture of CCl_2F_2 and CCl_3F. McBee and co-workers[143,144] fluorinated hexachlorobenzene and trifluoromethyl pentachlorobenzene with BrF_3 and isolated perhalogenated cyclohexanes and methylcyclohexanes containing 2 or 3 chlorine atoms. Low tempetature substitution of iodine in $C_2F_5CFICF_3$ and C_2F_5CClFI was accomplished by Haszeldine[85,88] by the use of BrF_3; the resulting products were perfluorobutane and 1-chloroperfluoropropane, respectively.

Iodine pentafluoride has been more widely employed as a fluorinating agent than the other halogen fluorides. This reagent was first prepared by Moissan[162,163] by the ignition of iodine in fluorine gas at room temperature. Ruff and Keim[184] reacted carbon tetrachloride with IF_5 at room temperature and isolated CF_4, CF_2Cl_2, CF_3Cl and CCl_3F. Fluorination of iodoform by use of this reagent was carried out by Simons, Bond and McArthur[200] at a temperature of 0° to 90° and fluoroform was obtained as the main product. When carbon tetraiodide was treated under similar conditions, the main product was perfluoroethane.

This type of fluorination reaction was studied by Banks[5] who obtained an 83% yield of CBr_2F_2 from CBr_4 when the reaction was carried out at 90°; carbon tetraiodide yielded mainly CF_3I. Emeleus and Haszeldine[53] prepared CF_3CF_2I from CF_2ICF_2I and IF_5.

Simons and Brice[201] reported the reaction of liquid IF_5 and perfluoroolefins at a temperature of 115°. In all cases reported, the elements of iodine and fluorine were observed to add across the double bond, and yielded the perfluoroalkyl iodide (cf. Method 202). Such olefins as tetrafluoroethylene, perfluoropropene, perfluorobutene-1, perfluorocyclobutene, and perfluorocyclohexene exhibited this type of addition. The reaction of IF_5 with carbon disulfide to yield sulfides of the type $CF_3(S)_xCF_3$ (cf. Method 1305) was effected by Haszeldine and Kidd[87] at 195° using an autoclave.

BIBLIOGRAPHY

1. Arnold, R. C., U. S. Patent 2,558,703(1951).
2. Austin, P. R., and Coffman, D. D., *J. Am. Chem. Soc.*, **75**, 4834(1953).

3. Avonda, F. P., Gervasi, J. A., and Bigelow, L. A., *J. Am. Chem. Soc.*, **78,** 2799(1956).
4. Bacon, J. C., Bradley, C. W., *et al.*, *J. Am. Chem. Soc.*, **70,** 2653(1948).
5. Banks, A. A., Emeleus, H. J., *et al.*, *J. Chem. Soc.*, **1948,** 2188.
6. Barbour, A. K., Barlow, G. B., and Tatlow, J. C., *J. Applied Chem.* **2,** 127(1952).
7. Barlow, G. B., and Tatlow, J. C., *J. Chem. Soc.*, **1952,** 4695.
8. Barney, A. L., U. S. Patent 2,437,148(1948).
9. Bayer, British Patent 684,117(1952).
10. Benning, A. F., and Park, J. D., U. S. Patent 2,384,499(1945).
11. Benning, A. F., and Park, J. D., U. S. Patent 2,407,129(1946).
12. Benning, A. F., and Park, J. D., U. S. Patent 2,437,993(1948).
13. Benning, A. F., and Park, J. D., U. S. Patent 2,490,764(1949).
14. Benning, A. F., Park, J. D., and Krahler, S. E., U. S. Patent 2,458,551 (1949).
15. Benning, A. F., Park, J. D., and Krahler, S. E., U. S. Patent 2,576,823 (1951).
16. Bergmann, E. D., *J. Chem. Soc.*, **1953,** 3786.
17. Bigelow, L. A., *J. Am. Chem. Soc.*, **72,** 4879(1950).
18. Bigelow, L. A., and Detoro, F. E., 130th Meeting American Chemical Society, Atlantic City, New Jersey, September 1956.
19. Bigelow, L. A., and Pearson, J. H., *J. Am. Chem. Soc.*, **56,** 2773(1934).
20. Bockemuller, W., *Ann.*, **506,** 20(1933).
21. Booth, H. S., and Burchfield, P. E., *J. Am. Chem. Soc.*, **57,** 2070(1935).
22. Brice, T. J., LaZerte, J. D., and Pearlson, W. H., *J. Am. Chem. Soc.*, **75,** 2698(1953).
23. British Thompson-Houston Company Ltd., British Patent 668,609(1952).
24. Brown, J. H., and Whalley, W. B., British Patent 576,189(1946).
25. Brown, J. H., and Whalley, W. B., *J. Soc. Chem. Ind.*, **67,** 331(1948).
26. Buckle, F. J., Pattison, F. L. M., and Saunders, B. C., *J. Chem. Soc.*, **1949,** 1471.
27. Burford, W. B., Fowler, R. D., *et al.*, *Ind. Eng. Chem.*, **39,** 319(1947).
28. Burk, R. E., Coffman, D. D., and Kalb, G. H., U. S. Patent 2,425,991(1947).
29. Cady, G. H., Grosse, A. V., *et al.*, *Ind. Eng. Chem.*, **39,** 291(1947).
30. Calfee, J. D., and Bigelow, L. A., *J. Am. Chem. Soc.*, **59,** 2072(1937).
31. Calfee, J. D., and Bratton, F. H., U. S. Patent 462,359(1949).
32. Calfee, J. D., Fukuhara, N., *et al.*, *J. Am. Chem. Soc.*, **62,** 267(1940).
33. Calfee, J. D., and Miller, C. B., U. S. Patent 2,674,630(1954).
34. Chabrie, C., *Compt. rend.*, **110,** 280(1890).
35. Chabrie, C., *Compt, rend.*, **111,** 747(1890).
36. Chapman, J., and Roberts, R., British Patent 627,773(1949).
37. Chapman, N. B., and Levy, J. L., *J. Chem. Soc.*, **1952,** 1673.
38. Clark, J. W., U. S. Patent 2,626,963(1953).
39. Clifford, A. F., El-Shamy, H. K., *et al.*, *J. Chem. Soc.*, **1953,** 2372.
40. Coates, G. E., Harris, J., and Sutcliffe, T., *J. Chem. Soc.*, **1951,** 2762.
41. Coffman, D. D., and Salisbury, L. F., U. S. Patent 2,451,612(1948).
42. Collins, J. H., Wadsworth, K. D., and Leech, H. R., British Patent 653,879 (1951).
43. Crawford, J. W. C., Wallsgrove, E. R., and Imperial Chemical Industries Ltd., British Patent 623,227(1949).

44. Cucolo, J. A., and Bigelow, L. A., *J. Am. Chem. Soc.*, **74,** 710(1952).
45. Darrall, R. A., Smith, F., *et al.*, *J. Chem. Soc.*, **1951,** 2329.
46. Daudt, H. W., and Youker, M. A., U. S. Patent 2,005,707(1935).
47. Dickey, J. B., U. S. Patent 2,624,746(1953).
48. Downing, F. B., Benning, A. F., and McHarness, R. C., U. S. Patent 2,551,573(1951).
49. Dresdner, R., *J. Am. Chem. Soc.*, **79,** 69(1957).
50. duPont, French Patent 730,874(1931).
51. Ebert, M. S., Rodowskas, E. L., and Frazer, J. C. W., *J. Am. Chem. Soc.*, **55,** 3056(1933).
52. Ellis, J. F., and Musgrave, W. K. R., *J. Chem. Soc.*, **1953,** 1063.
53. Emeleus, H. J., and Haszeldine, R. N., *J. Chem. Soc.*, **1949,** 2948.
54. Emeleus, H. J., Haszeldine, R. N., and Walaschewski, E. G., *J. Chem. Soc.*, **1952,** 1552.
55. Fear, E. J. P., and Thrower, J., *J. Appl. Chem.*, **5,** 353(1955).
56. Fowler, R. D., Anderson, H. C., *et al.*, *Ind. Eng. Chem.*, **39,** 343(1947).
57. Fowler, R. D., Burford, W. B., *et al.*, *Ind. Eng. Chem.*, **39,** 293(1947).
58. Fukuhara, N., and Bigelow, L. A., *J. Am. Chem. Soc.*, **63,** 788(1941).
59. Fukuhara, N., and Bigelow, L. A., *J. Am. Chem. Soc.*, **63,** 2793(1941).
60. Gervasi, J. A., Brown, M., and Bigelow, L. A., *J. Am. Chem. Soc.*, **78,** 1679(1956).
61. Gilbert, A. R., and Bigelow, L. A., *J. Am. Chem. Soc.*, **72,** 2411(1950).
62. Gilbert, A. R., Prober, M., and Wolfe, J. K., 124th Meeting American Chemical Society, Chicago, Illinois, September 1953.
63. Gilbert, A. R., and Wolfe, J. K., 122nd Meeting American Chemical Society, Atlantic City, New Jersey, September 1952.
64. Gleave, W. W., British Patent 463,930(1937).
65. Gochenour, C. I., U. S. Patent 2,558,703(1951).
66. Gochenour, C. I., U. S. Patent 2,555,857(1951).
67. Goswami, H. C., and Sarkar, P. B., *J. Indian Chem. Soc.*, **10,** 537(1933).
68. Grosse, A. V., and Linn, C. B., *J. Org. Chem.*, **3,** 26(1938).
69. Grosse, A. V., and Linn, C. B., *J. Am. Chem. Soc.*, **64,** 2289(1942).
70. Gryszkiewicz-Trochimowski, E., Sporzynski, A., and Wnuk, J., *Rec. trav. chim.*, **66,** 413(1947).
71. Gryszkiewicz-Trochimowski, E., Sporzynski, A., and Wnuk, J., *Rec. trav. chim.*, **66,** 427(1947).
72. Gryszkiewicz-Trochimowski, E., and Gryszkiewicz-Trochimowski, O., *Bull. soc. chim. France*, **1953,** 123.
73. Hadley, E. H., and Bigelow, L. A., *J. Am. Chem. Soc.*, **63,** 3302 (1940).
74. Halbedel, H. S., Cardon, S. Z., and Schenk, W. J., U. S. Patent 2,442,290 (1948).
75. Harmon, J., U. S. Patent 2,399,024(1946).
76. Harmon, J., U. S. Patent 2,404,374(1946).
77. Haszeldine, R. N., Research, **3,** 430(1950).
78. Haszeldine, R. N., *J. Chem. Soc.*, **1950,** 1638.
79. Haszeldine, R. N., *J. Chem. Soc.*, **1950,** 1966.
80. Haszeldine, R. N., *J. Chem. Soc.*, **1950,** 3617.
81. Haszeldine, R. N., *J. Chem. Soc.*, **1951,** 102.
82. Haszeldine, R. N., *J. Chem. Soc.*, **1952,** 3490.
83. Haszeldine, R. N., *J. Chem. Soc.*, **1952,** 4423.

84. Haszeldine, R. N., *J. Chem. Soc.*, **1953**, 3371.
85. Haszeldine, R. N., *J. Chem. Soc.*, **1953**, 3559.
86. Haszeldine, R. N., *J. Chem. Soc.*, **1953**, 3565.
87. Haszeldine, R. N., and Kidd, J. M., *J. Chem. Soc.*, **1953**, 3219.
88. Haszeldine, R. N., and Steele, B. R., *J. Chem. Soc.*, **1953**, 1592.
89. Haszeldine, R. N., and Walaschewski, E. G., *J. Chem. Soc.*, **1950**, 2689.
90. Hauptschein, M., and Braun, R. A., *J. Am. Chem. Soc.*, **77**, 4930(1955).
91. Henne, A. L., *J. Am. Chem. Soc.*, **60**, 1569(1938).
92. Henne, A. L., in "Organic Reactions," Vol. II, New York, John Wiley and Sons, Inc. (1944).
93. Henne, A. L., and DeWitt, E. G., *J. Am. Chem. Soc.*, **70**, 1548(1948).
94. Henne, A. L., and Haeckl, F. W., *J. Am. Chem. Soc.*, **63**, 2692(1941).
95. Henne, A. L., and Haeckl, F. W., *J. Am. Chem. Soc.*, **63**, 3476(1941).
96. Henne, A. L., and Hinkamp, J. B., *J. Am. Chem. Soc.*, **67**, 1194(1945).
97. Henne, A. L., and Hinkamp, J. B., *J. Am. Chem. Soc.*, **67**, 1197(1945).
98. Henne, A. L., and Midgely, T., *J. Am. Chem. Soc.*, **58**, 884(1936).
99. Henne, A. L., and Newby, T. H., *J. Am. Chem. Soc.*, **70**, 130(1948).
100. Henne, A. L., and Plueddeman, E. P., *J. Am. Chem. Soc.*, **65**, 587(1943).
101. Henne, A. L., and Plueddeman, E. P., *J. Am. Chem. Soc.*, **65**, 1271(1943).
102. Henne, A. L., and Renoll, M. W., *J. Am. Chem. Soc.*, **60**, 1060(1938).
103. Henne, A. L., Renoll, M. W., and Leicester, H. M., *J. Am. Chem. Soc.*, **61**, 938(1939).
104. Henne, A. L., Shepard, J. W., and Young, E. J., *J. Am. Chem. Soc.*, **72**, 3577(1950).
105. Henne, A. L., and Trott, P. J., *J. Am. Chem. Soc.*, **69**, 1820(1947).
106. Henne, A. L., and Waalkes, T. P., *J. Am. Chem. Soc.*, **67**, 1639(1945).
107. Henne, A. L., and Waalkes, T. P., *J. Am. Chem. Soc.*, **68**, 496(1946).
108. Henne, A. L., Whaley, A. M., and Stevenson, J. K., *J. Am. Chem. Soc.*, **63**, 3478(1941).
109. Henne, A. L., and Zimmerscheid, W. J., *J. Am. Chem. Soc.*, **69**, 281(1947).
110. Hillyea, J. C., and Wilson, J. F., U. S. Patent 2,471,525(1949).
111. Hillyea, J. C., and Wilson, J. F., U. S. Patent 2,634,300(1953).
112. Hoffmann, F. W., *J. Am. Chem. Soc.*, **70**, 2596(1948).
113. Hoffmann, F. W., *J. Org. Chem.*, **14**, 105(1949).
114. Hoffmann, F. W., *J. Org. Chem.*, **15**, 425(1950).
115. Hoffmann, F. W., and Simmons, T. C., *et al.*, 130th Meeting American Chemical Society, Atlantic City, New Jersey, September 1956.
116. Holub, F. F., and Bigelow, L. A., *J. Am. Chem. Soc.*, **72**, 4879(1950).
117. Hovey, R. S., and Carnell, P. H., U. S. Patent 2,439,299(1948).
118. Huckel, W., Nachr, Akad. Wiss Gottinger, *Math-physik Klasse*, **1946**, No. 1, 55.
119. I. G. Farbenind, French Patent, 799,432(1936).
120. Kauck, E. A., and Diesslin, A. R., *Ind. Eng. Chem.*, **43**, 2332(1951).
121. Kauck, E. A., and Simons, J. H., U. S. Patent 2,594,272(1952).
122. Kauck, E. A., and Simons, J. H., U. S. Patent 2,616,927(1952).
123. Kauck, E. A., and Simons, J. H., British Patent 672,720(1952).
124. Kauck, E. A., and Simons, J. H., British Patent 666,733(1952).
125. Kellogg, K. B., and Cady, G. H., *J. Am. Chem. Soc.*, **70**, 3986(1948).
126. Kinetic Chemicals Inc., British Patent 428,445(1935).
127. Knunyants, I. L., *Compt. rend. acad. sci, U.R.S.S.*, **55**, 223(1947).

128. Knunyants, I. L., Kil'disheva, O. V., and Petrov, I. P., *Zhur. Obshchei. Khim.*, **19**, 95(1949).
129. Knunyants, I. L., Kil'disheva, O. V., and Bykhovskaya, E., *Zhur. Obshchei. Khim.*, **19**, 101(1949).
130. Latif, A., *J. Indian Chem. Soc.*, **30**, 524(1953).
131. Lebeau, P., and Damiens, A., *Compt. rend.*, **182**, 1340(1926).
132. Lebeau, P., and Damiens, A., *Compt. rend.*, **191**, 939(1930).
133. Leicester, F. D., British Patent 468,447(1937).
134. Ligett, W. B., McBee, E. T., and Lindgren, V. V., U. S. Patent 2,480,080 (1949).
135. Linhard, M., and Betz, K., *Ber.*, **73**, 177(1940).
136. McBee, E. T., and Bechtol, L. D., *Ind. Eng. Chem.*, **39**, 380(1947).
137. McBee, E. T., and Bechtol, L. D., U. S. Patent 2,459,780(1949).
138. McBee, E. T., and Bechtol, L. D., U. S. Patent 2,459,782(1949).
139. McBee, E. T., Hass, H. B., *et al.*, *J. Am. Chem. Soc.*, **69**, 944(1947).
140. McBee, E. T., Hass, H. B., *et al.*, *Ind. Eng. Chem.*, **39**, 409(1947).
141. McBee, E. T., Pierce, O. R., and Higgins, J. F., *J. Am. Chem. Soc.*, **74**, 1736(1952).
142. McBee, E. T., and Ligett, W. B., U. S. Patent 2,606,212(1952).
143. McBee, E. T., Lindgren, V. V., and Ligett, W. B., *Ind. Eng. Chem.*, **39**, 359(1947).
144. McBee, E. T., Lindgren, V. V., and Ligett, W. B., U. S. Patent 2,489,969 (1949).
145. McBee, E. T., and Robb, R. M., U. S. Patent 2,533,132(1950).
146. McBee, E. T., and Robb, R. M., U. S. Patent 2,567,569(1951).
147. McBee, E. T., and Robb, R. M., U. S. Patent 2,578,721(1951).
148. McBee, E. T., Wiseman, P. A., and Bachman, G. B., *Ind. Eng. Chem.*, **39**, 415(1947).
149. Mantell, R. M., and Herbst, R. L. Jr., 128th Meeting American Chemical Society, Minneapolis, Minnesota, September 1955.
150. Mantell, R. M., Passino, H. J., and Teeters, W. O., U. S. Patent 2,684,987 (1954).
151. Meslans, M., *Compt. rend.*, **110**, 717(1890).
152. Meslans, M., *Compt. rend.*, **111**, 882(1890).
153. Midgley, T., and Henne, A. L., U. S. Patent 2,013,062(1935).
154. Miller, W. T., J. Am. Chem. Soc., *62*, 341(1940).
155. Miller, C. B., and Bratton, F. H., U. S. Patent 2,478,932(1949).
156. Miller, W. T., and Calfee, J. D., U. S. Patent 2,676,996(1954).
157. Miller, W. T., Ehrenfeld, R. L., *et al.*, *Ind. Eng. Chem.*, **39**, 401(1947).
158. Miller, C. B., and Smith, L. B., U. S. Patent 2,669,590(1954).
159. Mochel, W. E., Salisbury, L. F., *et al.*, *Ind. Eng. Chem.*, **40**, 2285(1948).
160. Moissan, H., *Compt. rend.*, **110**, 952(1890).
161. Moissan, H., *Ann. de chim. et phys.*, (6) **19**, 272(1891).
162. Moissan, H., "Le Fluor et ses Composes," Paris, G. Steinheil(1900).
163. Moissan, H., *Compt. rend.*, **135**, 363(1902).
164. Moissan, H., and Meslans, M., *J. Fort. Chem.*, **1888**, 931.
165. Musgrave, W. K. R., and Smith, F., *J. Chem. Soc.*, **1949**, 3021.
166. Nerdel, F., *Naturwissenschaften*, **39**, 209(1952).
167. Neudorffer, J., *Compt. rend.*, **244**, 1983(1952).

168. Newman, M. S., Renoll, M. W., and Averbach, L., *J. Am. Chem. Soc.*, **70**, 1023(1948).
169. Olah, Gy., and Pavlath, A., *Acta. Chim. Acad. Sci. Hung.*, **3**, 191(1953).
170. Olah, Gy., and Pavlath, A., *Acta. Chim. Acad. Sci. Hung.*, **3**, 425(1953).
171. Paterno, E., and Spallino, R., *Atti. Acad. Lincei*, **16**, (2) 160, 1900.
172. Pattison, F. L. M., Howell, W. C., *et al.*, *J. Org. Chem.*, **21**, 739(1956).
173. Pattison, F. L. M., and Saunders, B. C., *J. Chem. Soc.*, **1948**, 2745.
174. Ray, P. C., *Nature*, **132**, 173(1933).
175. Ray, P. C., Goswami, H. C., and Ray, A. C., *J. Indian Chem. Soc.*, **12**, 93 (1935).
176. Ray, P. C., and Ray, A. C., *J. Indian Chem. Soc.*, **13**, 427(1936).
177. Ray, P. C., Sarkar, P. B., and Ray, A. C., *Nature*, **132**, 749(1933).
178. Renoll, M. W., *J. Am. Chem. Soc.*, **64**, 115(1942).
179. Renoll, M. W., U. S. Patent 2,364,818(1944).
180. Roylance, J., Tatlow, J. C., and Worthington, R. E., *J. Chem. Soc.*, **1954**, 4426.
181. Ruff, O., and Bretschneider, O., Z. anorg. allgem. Chem., *217*, 1(1934).
182. Ruff, O., and Giese, M., *Z. anorg. allgem. Chem.*, **219**, 143(1934).
183. Ruff, O., and Giese, M., *Ber.*, **69B**, 684(1936).
184. Ruff, O., and Keim, R., *Z. anorg. allgem. Chem.*, **201**, 245(1931).
185. Ruff, O., and Krug, H., *Z. anorg. allgem. Chem.*, **190**, 270(1930).
186. Ruff, O., and Willenberg, W., *Ber.*, **73B**, 724(1940).
187. Saunders, B. C., and Stacey, G. J., *J. Chem. Soc.*, **1948**, 1773.
188. Saunders, B. C., Stacey, G. J., and Wilding, I. G. E., *J. Chem. Soc.*, **1949**, 773.
189. Scherer, O., U. S. Patent 2,146,354(1939).
190. Scherer, O., Platz, C., and Soll, J., German Patent 621,977(1936).
191. Schmidt, H., and Schmidt, H. D., *J. Prakt. Chem.*, **2**, 105(1955).
192. Schmidt, H., and Schmidt, H. D., *J. Prakt. Chem.*, **2**, 250(1955).
193. Severson, W. A., Brice, T. J., and Coon, R. I., 128th Meeting American Chemical Society, Minneapolis, Minnesota, September 1955.
194. Sharpe, A. G., *J. Chem. Soc.*, **1949**, 2901.
195. Silvey, G. A., and Cady, G. H., *J. Am. Chem. Soc.*, **72**, 3624(1950).
196. Simons, J. H., U. S. Patent 2,456,027(1948).
197. Simons, J. H., *J. Electrochem. Soc.*, **95**, 47(1949).
198. Simons, J. H., U. S. Patent 2,500,388(1950).
199. Simons, J. H., "Fluorine Chemistry", Vol. I, New York, Academic Press, Inc. (1950).
199A. Simons, J. H., and Block, L. P., *J. Am. Chem. Soc.*, **59**, 1407(1937).
199B. Simons, J. H., and Block, L. P., *J. Am. Chem. Soc.*, **61**, 2962(1939).
200. Simons, J. H., Bond, R. I., and McArthur, R. E., *J. Am. Chem. Soc.*, **62**, 3477(1940).
201. Simons, J. H., and Brice, T. J., U. S. Patent 2,614,131(1952).
202. Slesser, C., and Schram, S. R., "Preparation, Properties, and Technology of Fluorine and Organic Fluoro Compounds," New York, McGraw-Hill Book Company, Inc. (1951).
203. Stacey, M., *Royal Inst. Chem. Gt. Brit. and Ireland*, **1948**, 1.
204. Stilmar, F. B., U. S. Patent 2,553,217(1951).
205. Stover, W. A., U. S. Patent 2,622,106(1952).
206. Swarts, F., *Bull. soc. chim. France*, (3), **13**, 992(1895).

207. Swarts, F., *Bull. soc. chim. France*, (3), **15**, 1135(1896).
208. Swarts, F., *Bull. soc. chim. France*, (3), **15**, 1134(1896).
209. Swarts, F., *Bull. acad. roy. Belg.*, (3) **35**, 849(1898).
210. Swarts, F., *Rec. trav. chim.*, **17**, 231(1898).
211. Swarts, F., *Bull. acad. roy. Belg.*, **1909**, 728.
212. Swarts, F., *Bull. sci. acad. roy. Belg.*, **1910**, 113.
213. Swarts, F., *Bull. sci. acad. roy. Belg.*, **1911**, 563.
214. Swarts, F., *Rec. trav. chim.*, **33**, 252(1914).
215. Swarts, F., *Bull. soc. chim.*, **25**, 103(1919).
216. Swarts, F., *Bull. soc. chim. Belg.*, **30**, 302(1921).
217. Tarrant P., Attaway, J., and Lovelace, A. M., *J. Am. Chem. Soc.*, **76**, 2343 (1954).
218. Tarrant, P., Lovelace, A. M., and Lilyquist, M. R., *J. Am. Chem. Soc.*, **77**, 2783(1955).
219. Tatlow, J. C., and Worthington, R. E., *J. Chem. Soc.*, **1952**, 1251.
220. Thompson, J., and Emeleus, H., *J. Chem. Soc.*, **1949**, 3080.
221. Thompson, R. Y., Tarrant, P., and Bigelow, L. A., *J. Am. Chem. Soc.*, **68**, 2187(1946).
222. Truce, W. E., Birum, G. H., and McBee, E. T., *J. Am. Chem. Soc.*, **74**, 3594 (1952).
223. Tyczkowski, E. A., and Bigelow, L. A., *J. Am. Chem. Soc.*, **75**, 3523(1953).
224. Tyczkowski, E. A., and Bigelow, L. A., *J. Am. Chem. Soc.*, **77**, 3007(1955).
225. Van Vleck, R. T., U. S. Patent 2,562,994(1951).
226. Waalkes, T. P., U. S. Patent 2,466,189(1949).
227. Whaley, A. M., U. S. Patent 2,451,185(1948).
228. Whaley, A. M., and Davis, H. W., *J. Am. Chem. Soc.*, **70**, 1026(1948).
229. Whalley, W. B., British Patent 580,140(1946).
230. Whalley, W. B., U. S. Patent 2,452,975(1948).
231. Whitman, G. M., U. S. Patent 2,401,850(1946).
232. Whitman, G. M., U. S. Patent 2,578,913(1951).
233. Wolfe, J. K., and Gilbert, A. R., 122nd Meeting American Chemical Society, Atlantic City, New Jersey, September 1952.
234. Wolfe, J. K., and Gilbert, A. R., 124th Meeting American Chemical Society, Chicago, Illinois, September 1953.

CHAPTER II

Alkanes

TABLE OF CONTENTS

		PAGE
Introduction		32
Method Number		
201	Addition of Halogens to Unsaturated Compounds	33
202	Addition of Hydrogen Halides to Unsaturated Compounds	34
203	Direct Halogenation	35
204	Halogen Interchange	37
205	Addition of Alkanes to Olefins by Free Radical Catalysts	37
206	Addition of Alkanes to Olefins by Lewis Acid Catalysts	40
207	Decarboxylation of Acids, Acid Salts, Acyl Halides and Anhydrides	40
208	Decomposition of Tosylates and Other Esters	42
209	Wurtz-Type Condensation	43
210	Dimerization of Olefins	43
211	Reduction of Halides	44
212	Reduction of Unsaturated Compounds	44
213	Deamination of Amides with Hypohalites	45
214	Pyrolysis	45
215	Disproportionation	46
216	Halogenation of Alcohols and Ketones	46
217	Cleavage of Ethers	47
218	Decomposition of Diazo Compounds and Quaternary Ammonium Fluorides	47
TABLE 1	Acyclic Alkanes	48
TABLE 2	Cyclic Alkanes	80
Bibliography		92

INTRODUCTION

Fluorocarbons of the general formula C_nF_{2n+2} are extremely thermally stable and remarkably resistant to oxidation, to the effects of strong acids and bases, and to chemical attack in general. However, Wethington[332A] found that F^{18} exchanges with fluorine in such compounds as $CF_3CF{=}CF_2$, CF_4, C_4F_{10} and $(C_2F_5)_2O$. At a temperature of 250°, 15 parts per thousand of fluorine atoms were exchanged using F^{18} isotopic fluorides of the alkali metals. Fluorocarbons are characterized by their higher densities and lower refractive indices than their hydrocarbon analogs. A comparison of fluorocarbons and hydrocarbons with respect to their boiling points and melting points is shown in the following table:

COMPARISON OF *n*-FLUOROCARBONS AND *n*-HYDROCARBONS

No. of C Atoms	B.P. °C		M.P. °C	
	Fluorocarbon	Hydrocarbon	Fluorocarbon	Hydrocarbon
1	−128	−161	−184	−182
2	−79	−89	−100	−183
3	−38	−42	−183	−188
4	−2	−0.5	−85	−138
5	30	36	−97	−130
6	60	69	−74	−94
7	82	98	−80	−91

Other usual properties of the fluorocarbons are extremely low surface tension, low kinematic viscosity, and low dielectric constants as compared with hydrocarbons.

Partially fluorinated hydrocarbons can be chlorinated, brominated, and dehydrofluorinated. The early work on chlorofluorocarbons was accomplished by Swarts in Belgium, Ruff in Germany, and Midgley and Henne in the United States. The work of Midgley and Henne led to the commercial materials known as Freons (E. I. duPont Co.). These materials find widespread use as refrigerants, dispensing propellants for various household products, and industrial solvents. Bromine-containing fluorocarbons such as CBr_2F_2 and $CBrF_3$ are useful as fire-extinguishing agents.

Fluorocarbons containing other halogens or hydrogen are more chemically reactive than fluorocarbons themselves. For example compounds of the type $R_f^*CFX_2$ (where X = H, F, Cl, Br, or I) can be oxidized to the

*Throughout the text, R_f is used to denote a perfluoroalkyl group.

corresponding carboxylic acid, and CF_3CCl_3 can be hydrolyzed to trifluoroacetic acid. Dehalogenation of halofluorocarbons leads to olefin formation. Compounds of this type R_fI form Grignard reagents and react with many other metals and metalloids. These reactions are further described in other chapters of this book.

METHOD 201 Addition of Halogens to Unsaturated Compounds

Halogens add to fluorine-containing olefins in the same manner as they add to unsaturated hydrocarbons. The liquid-phase addition of chlorine to fluoroolefins in the presence of sunlight was first reported by Meslans.[224] Henne and co-workers,[146,152-4,178,179] using a small amount of water as catalyst also effected the addition of chlorine to fluoroolefins. Henne and Zimmerscheid[180] found it necessary to use an artificial ultraviolet source to successfully chlorinate $\overline{CCl{=}CCl(CF_2)_2CF_2}$. In general, liquid phase chlorination of fluorine-containing olefins occurs without substitution, but in the vapor phase some substitution of the addition product also occurs. In the vapor phase chlorination of $CH_2[CF_2C(CH_3){=}CH_2]_2$ McBee, Pierce, and Chen[218] obtained 42 percent of the substituted addition product $CH_2[CF_2CCl(CH_3)CHCl_2]_2$ as well as a 56 percent yield of the expected addition product. Upon chlorinating $CHCl{=}CClCHF_2$ in the vapor phase, Hauptschein and Bigelow[103] obtained $CCl_3CCl_2CHF_2$ as well as the addition product. It is interesting to note that the hydrogen atom on the $-CHF_2$ group was not replaced; this phenomenon is further discussed in Method 203.

Catalytic vapor-phase chlorination of fluoroolefins was reported; Henne, Sheppard, and Young[175] using $FeCl_3$ as a catalyst, added chlorine to $CF_3C(CH_3){=}CH_2$ in the dark at 0°, and Park, Lycan, and Lacher[255] using the same catalyst at 100°, added chlorine to $CHF{=}CF_2$. Using antimony trichloride as a catalyst at 140°, McBee, Truchan, and Bolt[219] added chlorine to $CF_3CH{=}CCl_2$.

Bromination of fluorine-containing olefins readily occurs without substitution either in the liquid or vapor phase and in either the presence or absence of light. Swarts[298,299,304,305] was the first to report the addition of bromine to fluoroolefins in the liquid phase. Pierce, McBee, and Judd[261] added bromine to $C_3F_7CH{=}CHCH_3$ in the absence of light at room temperature; the reaction was reported to be exothermic. Bromination of $CFCl{=}CFClCFCl_2$ at 50° in the presence of sunlight was reported[273] and using ultraviolet light, Brice, LaZerte, and Pearlson[40] added bromine to $(CF_3)_2C{=}CF_2$ in the presence of catalytic amounts of water and acetamide. The bromination of $CF_3CH{=}CH_2$ at 140° yielded $CF_3CHBrCF_2Br$[214] and the addition of bromine to $C_3F_7CH{=}CH_2$ at 114° to 143° in the presence of activated carbon yielded $C_3F_7CHBrCH_2Br$.[260]

The addition of iodine to highly fluorinated olefins has been reported and tetrafluoroethylene was iodinated at 20° to 150° under pressure of 25 psi.[265] Emeleus and Haszeldine[81] accomplished the same addition in a sealed tube at 170°, as did Coffman, *et al.*[63] in the presence of ether at 60°. The addition product obtained was unstable and lost iodine upon standing. The iodination of $CF_2{=}CFCl$ at room temperature in a sealed tube gave an addition product which was also unstable and lost iodine upon distillation.[12]

Compound halogens such as iodine monochloride and bromine monochloride have been added to fluorinated olefins in the dark. The addition of iodine monochloride to $CF_2{=}CFCl$ yielded $CF_2ClCFClI$ together with some $CF_2ClCFCl_2$. Barr[12] accomplished this reaction by bubbling $CF_2{=}CFCl$ through a $CF_2ClCFCl_2$ solution of ICl at 0°, while Hazeldine[101] accomplished the same addition using an autoclave. Some explosions have been reported using the autoclave method of addition as the reaction is very exothermic. Park, Seffel, and Lacher[257] added iodine monochloride to $CF_2{=}CFH$ and obtained $CF_2ClCFHI$. Iodine monobromide was added to $CF_2{=}CFCl$ and $CF_2{=}CH_2$ and good yields of $CF_2BrCFClI$ and CF_2BrCH_2I were obtained.[118,134] Simons and Brice[286] treated perfluorocyclohexene with IF_5 and observed that the elements of iodine and fluorine added across the double bond resulting in the formation of *cyclo*-$C_6F_{11}I$.

METHOD 202 Addition of Hydrogen Halides to Unsaturated Compounds

The addition of hydrogen fluoride to unsaturated hydrocarbons has been discussed in Method 109. Grosse and Linn[94] obtained isoporpyl fluoride upon addition of hydrogen fluoride to propylene and Scherer[280] obtained good yields of $CHClFCH_3$ upon addition of hydrogen fluoride to vinyl chloride, demonstrating the applicability of Markownikoff's rule. The addition of hydrogen fluoride to alkenes and alkynes occurs under a variety of conditions. Monofluoroalkanes are unstable in the presence of traces of water and lose HF upon heating; especially secondary or tertiary alkyl fluorides. Henne and Pleuddeman[165] added hydrogen fluoride to $CH_2{=}CCl_2$ at 65° to obtain CH_3CFCl_2 and they also showed, that at low temperatures, branched olefins such as $(CH_3)_2C{=}CHCl$ gave good yields of the addition product, $(CH_3)_2CHCHClF$. Stover[294] added hydrogen fluoride to $CHCl{=}CCl_2$ under a pressure of 2,500 psi and obtained CH_2ClCCl_2F.

The addition of hydrogen fluoride to acetylene in the preparation of vinyl fluoride is discussed in Methods 190 and 304; however, complete hydrofluorination of acetylene has been accomplished with various catalysts.[50,95] In all cases 1,1-difluoroethane was the observed product. Grosse and Linn[95] reacted alkynes with liquid hydrogen fluoride at –70° to 57°. Henne and Arnold[140] hydrofluorinated olefins in the presence of BF_3 and Chapman and Levy[60] used $SnCl_4$ as a catalyst at 0°. In Method 109 it was shown that the addition of hydrogen fluoride to olefins containing other halogens may result in some substitution by fluorine.

The addition of hydrogen chloride to fluorinated olefins usually requires catalytic means. Benning, Downing, and Plunkett[23] added hydrogen chloride to $CF_2{=}CF_2$ at 300° over activated carbon in a carbon tube. Haszeldine[124] added hydrogen chloride to $CH_3CH{=}CF_2$ at 150° over $AlCl_3$ catalyst and obtained $CH_3CH_2CF_2Cl$.

Hydrogen bromide has been added to fluoroolefins using both ionic and free radical catalysts. There are indications that the structures of the addition product are identical in either case. Park, Sharrah, and Lacher[258] passed $CF_2{=}CFCl$ and hydrogen bromide over a mixture of carbon and calcium sulfate at 90° and obtained $CF_2BrCHClF$. Haszeldine and Steele[135] obtained the same results using ultraviolet light. In another example Henne and co-workers[156,162] added hydrogen bromide to $CF_3CH{=}CH_2$ in the presence of either $AlBr_3$ or ultraviolet light and obtained the same product in either case, namely $CF_3CH_2CH_2Br$. The fact that the addition to this olefin proceeds contrary to Markownikoff's rule, can be explained if one considers that the presence of the highly electronegative $—CF_3$ group affects the polarization of the double bond so that the central carbon atom has a partially negative charge, $CF_3 \leftarrow \overset{\delta-}{CH} {=} \overset{\delta+}{CH_2}$. Haszeldine[123] added hydrogen bromide to perfluoropropene at 60° over $AlBr_3$ catalyst and obtained CF_3CHFCF_2Br. Addition of hydrogen bromide to $CF_2{=}CF_2$ and $CF_2{=}CFCl$ in the presence of ultraviolet light yielded CF_2HCF_2Br and $CF_2BrCFClH$, respectively.[135]

METHOD 203 Direct Halogenation

Since direct fluorination was discussed in Chapter I this method will refer to the substitution of hydrogen by halogens other than fluorine. Collie[64] first reported the chlorination of a fluoroalkane in 1889, and he obtained CH_2ClF from methyl fluoride and chlorine in the presence of sunlight. Henne and Renoll[171] first indicated the stepwise nature of chlorination of fluorocarbons by studying the chlorination of $CH_3CF_2CH_3$. They found that further chlorination of $CH_3CF_2CH_2Cl$ favors replacement of hydrogen on the chlorine-containing carbon atom rather than on the carbon atoms not containing chlorine. Henne and Whaley,[177] in a study of sunlight-catalyzed chlorination of $CH_3CH_2CF_3$ found that the hydrogen on the carbon atom α to the $—CF_3$ group is not as readily replaced as the hydrogen on the carbon atom β to the $—CF_3$ group, and the final chlorination product was $CCl_3CH_2CF_3$. However, they also found that chlorination of $CH_3CHClCF_3$ yielded $CH_3CCl_2CF_3$, demonstrating that the tendency to accumulate chlorine on the same carbon atom is stronger than the repressive effect of the adjacent $—CF_3$ group.

The phenomenon of the directive influence of the $—CF_2—$ and $—CF_3$ groups was further studied by Henne and Hinkamp[152,153] in the chlorination of $CH_3CF_2C_2H_5$ and $CF_3CH_2C_2H_5$. They found that chlorine readily replaces hydrogen on $—CH_2—$groups α to, and on $—CH_3$ groups β to $—CF_2—$groups. Chlorination of $CH_3CF_2C_2H_5$ in the presence of sunlight and water yielded 2 parts of $CH_3CF_2CHClCH_3$ and 3 parts of $CH_3CF_2CH_2CHCl_2$, but no $CH_2ClCF_2C_2H_5$. In the chlorination of $CF_3CH_2CH_2CH_3$ it was also observed that hydrogen atoms on carbon atoms β and γ to the $—CF_3$ group are replaced by chlorine atoms, but hydrogen atoms on the α carbon atoms are not replaced. The reaction products were $CF_3CH_2CH_2CH_2Cl$, $CF_3CH_2CHClCH_2Cl$, and other isomers, but $CF_3CHClCH_2CH_3$ was not obtained.

Chlorination of fluorinated alkanes has been accomplished in the vapor phase as well as in the liquid phase and ultraviolet light has been found to be useful in both cases. Vapor-phase chlorination has the advantage of commercial application as a continuous process. The disadvantage of liquid-phase chlorination is that it may require from several hours to as long as one week for completion. McBee, *et al.*[204,210] chlorinated CF_2ClCH_3 to CF_2ClCCl_3 at 185° in 5.3 hours; but by using light from a 200 watt incandescent lamp, the chlorination of $CF_3CH_2CH_3$ to $CF_3CH_2CHCl_2$ was effected at 365° to 390° in a continuous process with a 2.7 second contact time. Thermal chlorination of CH_2F_2 at 810° in a graphite tube is reported to give high yields of CF_2Cl_2.[53]

Bromination of fluorine-containing alkanes usually requires that it be accomplished at elevated temperatures. The replacement of terminal hydrogens of perfluoroalkyl mono- and di-hydrides with bromine can be effected at 600°.[38,287,288] Benning and Park[29] brominated perfluoroalkyl hydrides in the presence of water vapor and ultraviolet light. McBee, *et al.*,[210] brominated fluorine-containing alkanes at 500° with a contact time of 25 seconds.

Perfluorocyclopropane was converted to 1,3-dibromohexafluoropropane by aqueous bromine.[100] Haszeldine[117] iodinated CH_2BrF at 180° to 260° and obtained CHBrFI.

METHOD 204 Halogen Interchange

The replacement of a halogen by one higher in the periodic table is readily accomplished, especially in the fluorination of halocarbons as discussed in Chapter I. Chlorine can replace bromine and iodine, and bromine can replace iodine in halogenated fluoroalkanes. Hauptschein, Stokes, and Grosse[107] chlorinated $Br(CF_2)_3Br$ for 8 hours at 100° and obtained $Cl(CF_2)_3Br$. Haszeldine[115,116,126,127,132-4] chlorinated various fluorocarbon iodides in a sealed tube in the presence of ultraviolet light. The substitution of bromine for iodine was effected by treating $C_5F_{11}I$ with bromine at 80° to 90°.[105] When $CF_3CH_2CH_2I$ was brominated in a sealed tube at 380° the corresponding bromide was obtained,[115] Fluorocarbon bromides have also been obtained by reacting the corresponding iodides with bromine in the presence of ultraviolet light.[133,136] In an attempt to prepare $CF_2ClCFClCN$ by the reaction of $CF_2ClCFClI$ with BrCN, Park, Rausch, and Lacher[256] only obtained $CF_2ClCFClBr$.

The reverse type of halogen interchange, where a halogen has been replaced by one lower in the periodic table, has been accomplished only to a limited extent. Saunders, Stacey, and Wilding[279] treated CH_2FCH_2Cl with PBr_3 at 100° and obtained CH_2FCH_2Br. Swarts[300] treated CHF_2CH_2Br with anhydrous calcium iodide in the presence of alcohol at 110° and obtained CHF_2CH_2I. Miller[232] exchanged bromine in CCl_2FBr with iodine by the use of sodium iodide in anhydrous acetone. The reaction was carried out at 100° in the presence of ultraviolet light and an 18 percent yield of CCl_2FI was obtained. Since the sodium bromide which is formed is insoluble in acetone the reaction is forced toward completion.

METHOD 205 Addition of Alkanes to Olefins by Free Radical Catalysts

Addition of non-fluorinated haloalkanes to fluorine-containing olefins, addition of fluoroalkyl halides to both fluorine- and non-fluorine-containing olefins, and the addition of certain hydrocarbons to fluorinated olefins can readily be accomplished by free radical means. However, many investigators have been unable to add fluoroalkyl halides to chlorinated olefins, even vinyl chloride. The generally accepted mechanism of free radical addition to olefins is as follows:

$$RX \xrightarrow{h\nu} R\cdot + X \qquad \text{Initiation}$$

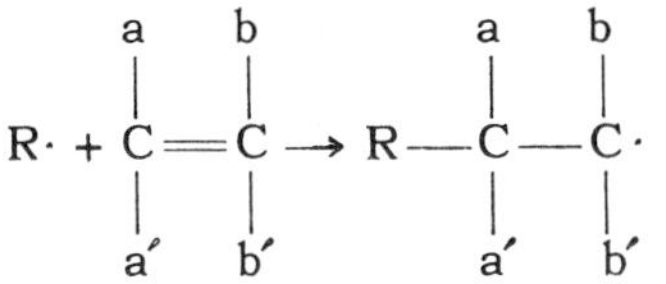

Propagation

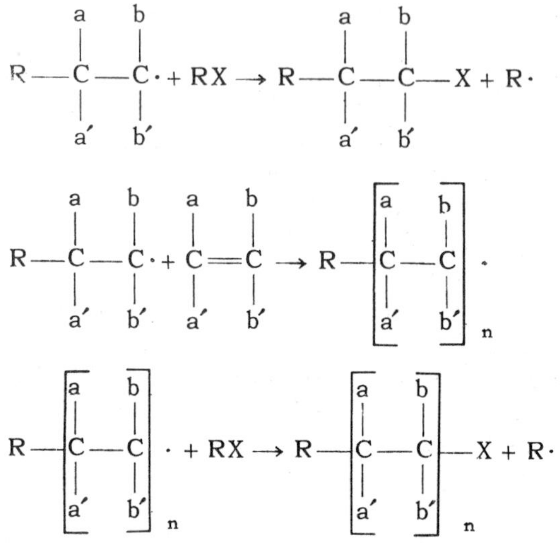

$$R-\overset{\overset{a}{|}}{\underset{\underset{a'}{|}}{C}}-\overset{\overset{b}{|}}{\underset{\underset{b'}{|}}{C}}\cdot + RX \rightarrow R-\overset{\overset{a}{|}}{\underset{\underset{a'}{|}}{C}}-\overset{\overset{b}{|}}{\underset{\underset{b'}{|}}{C}}-X + R\cdot \qquad \text{Termination}$$

$$R-\overset{\overset{a}{|}}{\underset{\underset{a'}{|}}{C}}-\overset{\overset{b}{|}}{\underset{\underset{b'}{|}}{C}}\cdot + \overset{\overset{a}{|}}{\underset{\underset{a'}{|}}{C}}=\overset{\overset{b}{|}}{\underset{\underset{b'}{|}}{C}} \rightarrow R-\left[\overset{\overset{a}{|}}{\underset{\underset{a'}{|}}{C}}-\overset{\overset{b}{|}}{\underset{\underset{b'}{|}}{C}}\right]_n\cdot \qquad \text{Telomerization}$$

$$R-\left[\overset{\overset{a}{|}}{\underset{\underset{a'}{|}}{C}}-\overset{\overset{b}{|}}{\underset{\underset{b'}{|}}{C}}\right]_n\cdot + RX \rightarrow R-\left[\overset{\overset{a}{|}}{\underset{\underset{a'}{|}}{C}}-\overset{\overset{b}{|}}{\underset{\underset{b'}{|}}{C}}\right]_n-X + R\cdot \qquad \text{Telomer Termination}$$

Either peroxide, heat, or ultraviolet light can be used for radical initiation except in the case where hydrocarbons are added to fluoro-olefins and then only peroxide catalysts have been reported to be effective. In the presence of benzoyl peroxide as well as acetyl peroxide, CCl_4,[61,77] CCl_3Br,[53,124,162] and CCl_3I[119] have been added to fluoroolefins. Certain fluoroalkyl halides fail to undergo addition to both fluorinated and non-fluorinated olefins because of the strong electronegative effect of fluorine which represses the homolytic scission of these molecules into free radicals. The free radical addition of $CFCl_3$, CF_2Cl_2 and CF_3Br to olefins has not been reported, although CF_3I,[125,162,257] CF_2Br_2,[320,322] and CF_2ClBr[321] have been found to add. The addition of hydrocarbons to $CF_2{=}CF_2$ in the presence of organic peroxides was reported by Barrick.[16,18] For example, the addition of butane yielded $C_4H_9CF_2CF_2H$, and the addition of cyclohexane yielded $cyclo$-$C_6H_{11}CF_2CF_2H$.

In the free radical addition of perhaloalkanes to fluorine-containing olefins, the structure of the addition product can be predicted on the basis of an empirical rule suggested by the authors.[261A] If RX is added to the olefin $\overset{\overset{a}{|}}{\underset{\underset{a'}{|}}{C}}=\overset{\overset{b}{|}}{\underset{\underset{b'}{|}}{C}}$, and if $\Sigma(EAR)_{aa'} < \Sigma(EAR)_{bb'}$, where E is the Pauling electronegativity and AR is the atomic refraction of a, a', b, b', then

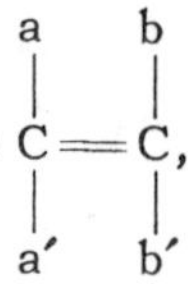

the orientation will be $R \underset{\underset{a'}{|}}{\overset{\overset{a}{|}}{C}} \underset{\underset{b'}{|}}{\overset{\overset{b}{|}}{C}} X$. The radical $R \cdot$ attacks the

olefinic carbon atom with the lowest ΣEAR of its substituents. For example:

$$CCl_3Br + CF_2 = CFCl \xrightarrow{Bz_2O_2} CCl_3CF_2CFClBr \; [158]$$
$$EAR = 9.6 \qquad 23.6$$

$$CF_2ClCFClI + CHF = CF_2 \xrightarrow{Bz_2O_2} CF_2ClCFClCHFCF_2I \; [322]$$
$$EAR = 7.1 \qquad 9.6$$

In free radical additions to propenes, butenes, and higher olefins, substituents on the β-carbon atoms are not considered in the summations because these appear to have a neglibible effect on the orientation. The orientation appears to be independent of the nature of the attacking free radical and means of radical initiation. Listed below are additional examples based on this rule as well as EAR values for some of the common elements.

Alkane	R·	X·	Olefin	Addition Product	Ref.
CF_3I	$CF_3 \cdot$	$I \cdot$	$CH_2 = CHCF_3$	$CF_3CH_2CHICF_3$	139
CCl_3Br	$CCl_3 \cdot$	$Br \cdot$	$CF_2 = CFCl$	$CCl_3CF_2CFClBr$	158
CF_2ClBr	$CF_2Cl \cdot$	$Br \cdot$	$CH_2 = CHCH_3$	$CF_2ClCH_2CHBrCH_3$	321
CF_3I	$CF_3 \cdot$	$I \cdot$	$CH_3CH = CF_2$	$CF_3CH(CH_3)CF_2I$	124

ATOM	H	F	Cl	Br	I	C
EAR	2.31	4.80	18.0	24.9	33.4	6.0

Perfluorinated neopentane $CF_3 \underset{\underset{CF_3}{|}}{\overset{\overset{CF_3}{|}}{C}} CF_3$ was prepared by Dresdner[75A] by the reaction between $(CF_3)_2SF_4$ and $CF_3CF = CF_2$ at 520° which is the decomposition temperature of $(CF_3)_2SF_4$.

In the free radical additions to olefins, telomers of the general structure, $R \left[\underset{\underset{a'}{|}}{\overset{\overset{a}{|}}{C}} \underset{\underset{b'}{|}}{\overset{\overset{b}{|}}{C}} \right]_n X$, are easily formed. Addition of CF_3I to

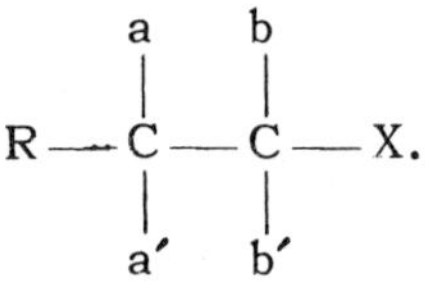

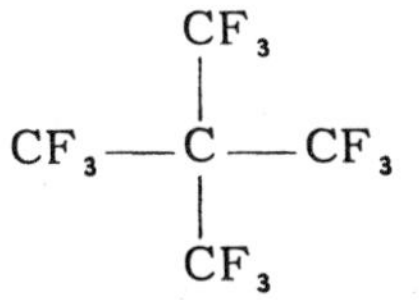

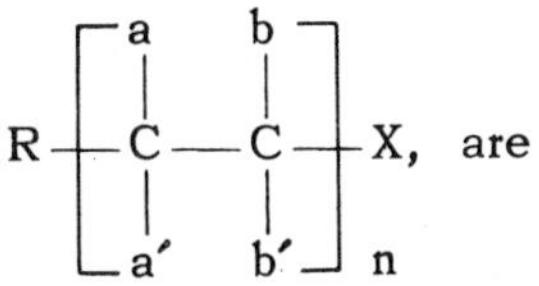

$CF_2{=}CF_2$ yields a series $CF_3(CF_2CF_2)_nI$, where n = 1 to 7.[125] Other olefins which yield telomers are $CH_2{=}CHF$,[318,322] $CH_2{=}CF_2$,[136,257,318,322] $CHF{=}CF_2$,[318,322,323] $CF_2{=}CFCl$,[127,158,166] and $CF_3CH{=}CH_2$.[116] Telomers are said to be produced upon addition of CF_3I to ethylene as well as the one-to-one addition product.[110] In general the ratio of the yield of higher molecular weight telomers to the one-to-one adduct is increased as the ratio of the olefin to the alkane is increased. This method is a convenient way to prepare long chain fluorinated compounds without resorting to fluorination reactions. Haszeldine[127] discusses several other factors favoring the telomerization reaction.

METHOD 206 Addition of Alkanes to Olefins by Lewis Acid Catalysts

The addition of CCl_4 to $CF_2{=}CFCl$ using $AlCl_3$ catalyst usually results in a mixture of products and different modes of addition have been reported. The expected addition product is $CCl_3CFClCF_2Cl$[157] which is the reverse of that obtained under free radical conditions and corrects the earlier reported orientation of $CCl_3CF_2CFCl_2$.[61] Disproportionation (cf. Method 215) resulting from the presence of $AlCl_3$ produces products of the empirical formulas $C_3Cl_5F_3$ and $C_3Cl_6F_2$[3,61] and the addition of $CHCl_3$,[3,61] $CHCl_2F$,[3] $CHClF_2$,[64] $(CH_3)_2CHCl$[12] and $(CH_3)_3CCl$[12] to $CF_2{=}CFCl$ also indicates disproportion in the presence of $AlCl_3$. The yields of the desired addition products in this type of reaction are generally low. Addition of chloromethanes to $CF_2{=}CF_2$ in the presence of $AlCl_3$ have been reported to occur without disproportionation.[16,61,190]

Zinc chloride catalyzes the addition of $(CH_3)_3CH$ to tetrafluoroethylene with the formation of telomers as well as the simple addition product.[16] The addition of $(CH_3)_3CF$ to $CH_2{=}CH_2$ has been effected with BF_3 as a catalyst.[282]

METHOD 207 Decarboxylation of Acids, Acid Salts, Acyl Halides and Anhydrides

The decarboxylation of fluorinated acids in the presence of a halogen has been reported by many investigators. Haszeldine[100] treated CF_2HCO_2H with bromine at 180° to 260° and obtained a high yield of CF_2HBr. Brice and Simons[39] obtained n-$C_6F_{13}I$ from perfluoroheptanoic acid and iodine in the presence of pyridine at elevated temperatures. LaZerte[198] prepared perfluorinated alkyl bromides from the corresponding acids and bromine at 350°. A modified Kolbe synthesis of perfluoroethane was reported by Swarts[313] by the electrolysis of trifluoroacetic acid.

The well known Hunsdiecker reaction as applied to the silver salts of highly fluorinated acids in the presence of a halogen was first reported by Henne and Finnegan,[147] and subsequently by Haszeldine,[117] Hauptschein,[109] and Brice and Simons.[39] Fluoroalkanes containing terminal —CF_2Cl, —CF_2Br, and —CF_2I groups can be prepared in this manner. The silver salts of perfluoroacids decarboxylate at a lower temperature than do those containing some hydrogen or chlorine. For example, CF_3Cl can be prepared from silver trifluoroacetate at room temperature in 90 percent yield;[113] however, decarboxylation of CH_2FCO_2Ag in the presence of bromine requires a temperature of 180° to 260°.[117] Brice and Simons[39] prepared n-$C_6F_{13}Br$ from the silver salt of perfluoroheptanoic acid in the presence of bromine and pyridine at 60° to 70°. Decarboxylation of silver salts of fluorinated acids in the presence of iodine were reported by Hauptschein and co-workers[105,109] as requiring a temperature of 100° for 6 hours; however, the silver salt of chlorofluoroacetic acid, $CHClFCO_2Ag$, in the presence of iodine required a temperature of 180° to 260° for decarboxylation.[117] In a study of this reaction Crawford and Simons[67] treated several perfluorocarboxylic acid silver salts with iodine and with bromine at room temperature in fluorocarbon solvents and obtained the corresponding perfluoroalkyl halides in high yields. The intermediate complexes of the general structure $(C_nF_{2n+1}COO)_2AgX$ were isolated. Henne and Zimmer[179A] isolated CF_3COOBr and CF_3COOI in the decarboxylation of silver trifluoroacetate in the presence of the respective halogens.

The double silver salts of fluorinated dicarboxylic acids are readily decomposed in the presence of halogen, to yield the fluoroalkyl dihalides. Hauptschein and Grosse[109] prepared $I(CF_2)_3I$ in an 18 percent yield from silver perfluoroglutarate at 120°; an additional product obtained was reported to be the lactone, $\overline{OCF_2CF_2CF_2CO}$. However Tiers[327A] proved by nuclear magnetic resonance that the compound obtained is really the isomer, perfluorosuccinyl fluoride, $(CF_2COF)_2$. Haszeldine[130] prepared $(—CFClCF_2Cl)_2$ from $(—CFClCF_2CO_2Ag)_2$ in the presence of chlorine. The dibromide was also prepared at 80° to 90°.[108]

Decarboxylation of the sodium salt of perfluoropropionic acid in the presence of bromine at 260° yielded CF_2BrCF_2Br; the intermediate product most likely being $CF_2{=}CF_2$ (cf. Method 306) which absorbed bromine.[117] LaZerte, *et al.*[196] decarboxylated the sodium salts of perfluorinated carboxylic acid in the presence of ethylene glycol at 170° to

190° and obtained the corresponding hydrides. For example, n-$C_5F_{11}CO_2Na$ yielded n-$C_5F_{11}H$. Barlow, Stacey, and Tatlow[9] decarboxylated the sodium salt of perfluoro-2-methyladipic acid in a similar manner and obtained 1,4-dihydroperfluoro-2-methylbutane.

Decarboxylation of silver salts of perfluorocarboxylic acids at high temperatures in the absence of halogens results in coupling (cf. Method 209). Haszeldine and Leedham[129] obtained perfluorobutane when they heated $C_2F_5CO_2Ag$ at 245°. Kirshenbaum, Streng, and Hauptschein[192] obtained C_2F_6 upon treating silver trifluoroacetate at 400° to 440° and also obtained n-perfluorohexane from $(C_3F_7CO)_2O$ and silver oxide at 410° in the presence of copper wire. A novel type of coupling was reported by Hauptschein and Grosse[104] when n-C_6F_{14} was obtained by heating $C_3F_7CO_2Ag$ and C_3F_7I at 275° to 335°.

LaZerte, Pearlson and Kauck[198] obtained a quantitative yield of CF_3Br by heating trifluoroacetic anhydride with bromine at 300° to 650°. The same workers pyrolyzed trifluoroacetyl bromide at 650° and obtained CF_3Br.[179] The decarboxylation of alkyl fluorocarbonates, $ROC(=O)$—F, to yield an alkyl fluoride RF was reported by Nakanski, Myers, and Jensen.[245,246] For example, $C_2H_5OC(=O)$—F heated in the presence of pyridine at 100° to 110° yielded ethyl fluoride. In the presence of BF_3-ether complex, the reaction occurred at 50°.

METHOD 208 Decomposition of Tosylates and Other Esters

This is a convenient method for the conversion of a fluorinated or non-fluorinated alcohol into a fluoroalkyl halide or an alkyl fluoride in high yields. Tiers[326] first reported this reaction and prepared R_fCH_2Cl, R_fCH_2Br, and R_fCH_2I by heating the tosyl ester of the alcohol with the corresponding sodium halide in ethylene glycol at 150° to 220°. The tosylates can be easily prepared from p-toluenesulfonyl chloride and the alcohol in the presence of pyridine. Edgell and Parts[78] converted the tosylates of methanol, ethanol and other alcohols into alkyl fluorides by heating with potassium fluoride in β,β'-dihydroxyethyl ether at 160° to 250°. These workers similarly prepared $C_2F_5CH_2F$. McBee, Campbell and Roberts[209] obtained similar results by treating tosylates in the presence of potassium halides and diethylene glycol at 240°. Grosse and Linn[94] prepared CH_3F by the action of potassium fluoride on dimethyl sulfone.

Esters of fluorinated alcohols and phosphorous- and phosphoric acids decompose in the presence of halogen to give the corresponding fluoroalkyl halides. Swarts[312] treated $CF_3CH(CH_3)OPBr_2$ with bromine and obtained $CF_3CHBrCH_3$. Krogh, Reid, and Brown[193] brominated the triphosphate esters of CF_3CH_2OH and $C_3F_7CH_2OH$ at room temperature, and obtained the corresponding bromides.

METHOD 209 Wurtz-Type Condensation

Wurtz-type condensation or coupling occurs with fluoroalkyl iodides and bromides, but not with fluoroalkyl chlorides or fluorides. Haszeldine[118] prepared $(CF_2ClCFCl—)_2$ by exposing $CF_2ClCFClI$ to ultraviolet light. Exposure of $CF_2BrCFClI$ to ultraviolet light in the presence of mercury yielded $(CF_2BrCFCl—)_2$. When CF_3CF_2CFClI was reacted with zinc and dioxane at 110° for 48 hours, $(CF_3CF_2CFCl—)_2$ was produced.[133] Henne[145] treated C_3F_7I with zinc and acetic anhydride at 40° to 45° in the presence of methylene chloride and obtained n-C_6F_{14}. Henne and Postelnek[167] prepared $(CF_2ClCFCl—)_2$ from $CF_2ClCFClI$ using the same technique.

Internal coupling or ring closure was observed by Harmon[100] to take place when $Br(CF_2)_3Br$ was treated with zinc dust; the product was perfluorocyclopropane. Tarrant, Lovelace and Lilyquist[322] reported the synthesis of $CH_2CF_2C(CH_3)_2$ (cyclic) by treating $BrCF_2CH_2CBr(CH_3)_2$ with zinc and n-propanol in the presence of zinc chloride.

METHOD 210 Dimerization of Olefins

Heating a fluoroolefin of the type $CF_2{=}CX_2$ (where X may be halogen or hydrogen) in a pressurized vessel generally results in the formation of cyclic dimers. The presence of a polymerization inhibitor generally favors dimerization rather than polymerization. Henne and Ruh[173] found that the addition normally occurs in such a way as to obtain "head-to-head" and "tail-to-tail" cyclic compounds. For example, $CF_2{=}CFCl$ dimerizes to $CF_2CF_2CFClCFCl$ (cyclic) at 200°.[45,100,101,173,280] However, Miller[231] passed the same olefin through a pyrex tube at 550° and obtained in addition to the cyclic dimer, an olefin of the structure, $CF_2{=}CFCFClCF_2Cl$. Haszeldine and Osborne[131] prepared $CFCl{=}CFCFClCFCl_2$ by passing $CFCl{=}CFCl$ through a silica tube at 230° to 300° (cf. Method 311). Tetrafluoroethylene was dimerized under pressure at 200° to perfluorocyclobutane, as well as at 1340° over a platinum filament.[100] The dimerization of $CCl_2{=\!=}CF_2$ to $CF_2CF_2CCl_2CCl_2$ was accomplished at 200° in an autoclave, but the reverse type of addition was obtained in the presence of hydrogen fluoride, yielding $CF_2CCl_2CF_2CCl_2$.

Mixed olefins can be co-dimerized into cyclic structures. For example, $CF_2{=\!=}CF_2$ and $CH_2{-\!-}CH_2$ yielded $CF_2CF_2CH_2CH_2$,[62] $CF_2{=\!=}CCl_2$ and $CF_2{=\!=}CFCl$ yielded $CF_2CF_2CClFCCl_2$,[194] and $CF_2{=\!=}CF_2$ and $CH_2{=\!=}C(CH_3)_2$ yielded $CF_2CF_2CH_2C(CH_3)_2$.[14]

METHOD 211 Reduction of Halides

Catalytic hydrogenation of fluoroalkyl chlorides, bromides and iodides replaces chlorine, bromine, and iodine atoms but not fluorine. Dichlorodifluoromethane is reduced to CH_2F_2 and $CHClF_2$ at 685° in a platinum lined tube.[30] Similarly, CF_2ClCF_2Cl can be reduced at 700° in a copper packed nickel tube to give a mixture of CF_2HCF_2Cl and CF_2HCF_2H.[35] Methane is not as effective as hydrogen in the reduction of CF_2Cl_2. At 720° to 760° only a small amount of CF_2ClH is produced by using methane and a platinum catalyst and most of the starting material is recovered.[222] The reduction of CF_3I to CF_3H is accomplished with hydrogen in the presence of mercury and ultraviolet light at 170° or in the absence of mercury and light at 250°.[116] Lithium aluminum hydride can be used to reduce cyclic fluoroalkyl chlorides.[9,47,272,324] Swarts[305] reports that the reduction of $CHBr_2F$ to CH_3F and CH_2BrF with zinc and ethanol readily occurs. This method can also be successfully applied to the reduction of iodides and chlorides.[132,133] Zinc and dioxane,[137] zinc and *n*-propanol,[322] and magnesium in ether[37] are reported as reducing agents for fluoroalkyl halides. Zinc and either dilute HCl,[132,321,322] dilute H_2SO_4,[136] or NH_4Cl[262] also effectively reduce these compounds. Haszeldine[108] reports the reduction of a series of perfluoroalkyl iodides to the corresponding hydrides with alcoholic potassium hydroxide at 100° as well as with hydrogen at 350°.

METHOD 212 Reduction of Unsaturated Compounds

Fluorine-containing olefins and dienes are reduced to the alkanes with hydrogen and a nickel catalyst in absolute ethanol at 100° and 100 atmospheres of pressure;[15,17] $CH_3CF_2CH{=\!=}CH_2$ yields $CH_3CF_2CH_2CH_3$

and $CH_2{=}CFCH{=}CH_2$ yields $CH_3CHFC_2H_5$. Raney nickel and hydrogen at 30° and 10 atmospheres of pressure has been used for the reduction of $CF_3CH{=}CH_2$.[116] Trifluoromethylacetylene can be reduced to $CF_3CH_2CH_3$ also using Raney nickel.[116] Swarts[308] reduced benzotrifluoride with a platinum black catalyst to trifluoromethylcyclohexane. However, the reduction of chlorodifluoromethylbenzene under the same conditions yielded difluoromethyltoluene, toluene and methylcyclohexane.

METHOD 213 Deamination of Amides with Hypohalites

Husted and Kohlhase[187] found that when perfluoroamides are treated with alkaline hypohalites, perfluoroalkyl halides are obtained instead of amines as in the conventional Hofmann rearrangement. For example, $C_2F_5CONH_2$ in the presence of aqueous sodium hydroxide and bromine yields C_2F_5Br. Similarly prepared were CF_3Br, C_3F_7Br, C_3F_7Cl. Deamination of perfluorobutyramide in the presence of chlorine yields $CF_3CF{=}CF_2$ and C_3F_7H in addition to C_3F_7Cl. When perfluoroamides are treated with alkaline hypoiodite, the perfluoroalkyl iodide is not obtained and the hydride is the sole product; for example, $C_3F_7CONH_2$ yields C_3F_7H.

METHOD 214 Pyrolysis

This method relates to the conversion of fluoroalkanes from other alkanes and degradation of polymers under pyrolytic conditions, either in the presence or absence of catalysts or other agents. In the commerical process for making tetrafluoroethylene by pyrolysis of CF_2HCl (cf. Method 301), many by-products are obtained, depending upon reaction conditions. The pyrolysis of CF_2HCl above 650° at 1 atmosphere in a carbon, silver or platinum tube yields a family of alkanes of the general type, $H(CF_2)_nCl$ (up to n = 12).[25,72,75,254] In addition, some perfluorocyclobutane is also obtained.[72,75] This compound is also isolated in the pyrolysis of CF_2ClCF_2Cl in the presence of hydrogen at 700° to 750° in a platinum tube.[30] When this same pyrolysis was carried out in the presence of hydrogen at 700° in a copper-packed nickel tube, CH_2F_2, CCl_2F_2 and $CHClF_2$ are formed.[35] when CF_2Cl_2 is pyrolyzed under the same conditions, CHF_2CHF_2 results.[30] If CF_2Cl_2 is passed over molten tellurium at 500°, $Cl(CF_2)_nCl$ is produced.[5] Similarly, $H(CF_2)_3H$ is prepared by the pyrolysis of CF_2HBr in a platinum-lined tube at 615°.

Simons[288] pyrolyzed C_3F_8 in a Monel tube at 785° to 855° in the presence of hydrogen and CHF_3 and CH_2F_2 were isolated; in the presence of bromine, CF_3Br and C_2F_5Br were obtained. Rogers and Cady[271] passed C_5F_{12} over a platinum filament at a temperature in excess of 900° and isolated CF_4, C_2F_6, C_3F_8, C_3F_6 and $(C_2F_4)_n$ from the reaction mixture. Ruff and Bretschneider[277] and Simons[285] subjected CF_4 to an electric arc discharge and obtained C_2F_6 and C_3F_8. By the same procedure Thornton, Burg, and Schlesinger[325] isolated $CClF_3$, CF_4 and $C_2Cl_2F_4$ from dichlorodifluoromethane.

When "Teflon" was heated in an Inconel tube at 570° to 630° perfluorocyclobutane were obtained together with a mixture of olefins[22] (cf. Method 309).

METHOD 215 Disproportionation

The rearrangement of halogens on a carbon skeleton is usually effected by the use of a Lewis acid such as aluminum chloride. Murray[243] prepared $CClF_3$ in a 96 percent yield from CCl_2F_2 or CCl_3F using $AlCl_3$ or $AlBr_3$ at 75° to 100° and at 5 to 150 psi. Trifluoromethane was similarly obtained from $CHClF_2$ or $CHCl_2F$ at -20° to 50°.[244] Pailthorp[253] produced $CClF_3$ and CCl_2F_2 by heating CCl_3F over $AlCl_3$ or Al_2O at 187°. In the disproportionation of CF_2ClCF_2Cl over $AlCl_3$ at 55° to 60° Miller[230] obtained CCl_3CF_3, together with minor amounts of other isomers. Simons[285] treated $CClF_3$ with calcium iodide and obtained tetrafluoromethane.

METHOD 216 Halogenation of Alcohols and Ketones

The halogenation of trifluoroethanol and partially fluorinated higher alcohols to the corresponding halides has been reported. However the halogenation of more highly fluorinated long chain alcohols of the general formula $C_nF_{2n+1}CH_2OH$ has not been reported at this time. Swarts[303,307,313] brominated CF_3CH_2OH, CF_2HCH_2OH and CFH_2CH_2OH with PBr_3 and obtained the corresponding bromides. Saunders[279] chlorinated monofluoroethanol with thionyl chloride and Hoffmann[184] chlorinated monofluoroethanol with phosphorus pentachloride. Gilman and Jones[90] prepared CF_3CH_2I from the corresponding alcohol using iodine and red phosphorus. Walborsky, *et al.*,[332] prepared fluoroalkyl iodides from fluoroalcohols using potassium iodide and phosphoric acid, while McBee, *et al.*[216] used red phosphorus and iodine. Swarts[310] treated trifluoromethylcyclohexanone with bromine at 108° for 17 days and obtained the corresponding dibromide. The reaction of non-fluorinated alcohols with hydrogen fluoride results in mixtures of primary and secondary alkyl fluorides. Due to the instability of these compounds, the method has not gained widespread use.

METHOD 217 Cleavage of Ethers

Haszeldine[122] treated C_3F_7OR, where R = CH_3, C_2H_5, or n-C_3F_7 with 5 percent aqueous sodium hydroxide and obtained C_3F_7H. Tiers[327] cleaved perfluoroethers with $AlCl_3$ at 175° to 230° in an autoclave and from $(n\text{-}C_6F_{13})_2O$ obtained n-$C_5F_{11}CCl_3$, and from $(n\text{-}C_4F_9)_2O$ obtained n-$C_3F_7CCl_3$ (cf. Method 506). Smorgonskii[290] heated ethyl ether with fluorobenzene in the presence of $SnCl_4$ or $SbCl_5$ and obtained C_2H_5F. Ethyl fluoride was also produced when ethyl ether was heated with chlorobenzene and boron trifluoride.[290]

METHOD 218 Decomposition of Diazo Compounds and Quaternary Ammonium Fluorides

Gilman and Jones[89] prepared CF_3CHI_2 by treating CF_3CHN_2 with iodine. These workers also treated CF_3CHN_2 with hydrogen iodide in toluene at −75° and obtained a 77 percent yield of CF_3CH_2I, while a 5 percent yield of the compound was obtained by treating trifluoroethanol with iodine and red phosphorus[90] (cf. Method 216). Krogh[193] decomposed the diazotization product of $C_3F_7CH_2NH_2$ in the presence of hydrogen iodide and obtained $C_3F_7CH_2I$. Collie[64] decomposed the quaternary ammonium salt $[N(CH_3)_4]^+F^-$ and obtained CH_3F.

TABLE 1

ACYCLIC ALKANES

Empirical Formula	Structural Formula	Method	Yield %	B.p. °C/mm.	F.p. or M.p. °C	n_D^t	d_4^t	t°C	Ref.
$CBrClF_2$	$CBrClF_2$	203		−2.5	−140		1.917	0	11
		203		−3.97	−159				274
		207	63–91	−4					117
$CBrF_3$	$CBrF_3$	203	90	−60.5 to −59.0					37,287
		207	88–98	−59					106,113,198 199,209
		214		−63 to −58					37,38,288
		213							187
		113	94						7
CBr_2ClF	CBr_2ClF	203	71	79.5–80.5					117
CBr_2F_2	CBr_2F_2	113							7
		203		20–25					11,288
		207	81	25					117
CBr_3F	CBr_3F	113		106.2 (Calc)					7
$CClF_3$	$CClF_3$	107	75–95	−81 to −85					195,334,335
		112		−82					56,285
		207	88–90						106,113,249
		214							38
		215	96						204
CCl_2FI	CCl_2FI	204	18	90.0	−107.0	1.5100	2.3134	20	232
		207	78						117
CCl_2F_2	CCl_2F_2	102							91
		105							233
		107							141,226,227, 264
		108							185
		113		−28 to −26					113
		203	82.7						53,55
		207	88	−29.5					117,313
		215							54
		216		−25					302

CCl_3F	CCl_3F	101		23–27					333
		102							91
		112							228,285
		113		23–25					80
		203							53
CF_3I	CF_3I	113		−22.5					7
		207	89–94	−22.5		1.3790	2.3608 (−32)	−42	249,113
CF_4	CF_4	102							58
		112		−128	−184				49,68,240, 285
		215							285
CHBrClF	CHBrClF	107		38	−65		1.9058	16	297
		105	25	36.11/756	−115				32
		207	73	36.5					117
CHBrFI	CHBrFI	203	19	35/70					117
$CHBrF_2$	$CHBrF_2$	107		−14.5					305
		203							274
		207	88	−15					117
$CHBr_2F$	$CHBr_2F$	107		64.9/757			2.4256	18.5	305
		207	64	64.5					117
CHClFI	CHClFI	207	35	35/150					117
$CHClF_2$	$CHClF_2$	207	91	−41					117
		211							30,222
		214	4						214
$CHCl_2F$	$CHCl_2F$	107		14.5			1.426	0	290
		207	73	9.0					117
$CHFI_2$	$CHFI_2$	102, 103		100.3	−34.5				278
		207	18	50/50					117
CHF_2I	CHF_2I	102, 103		21.6	−122.0				278
		207	93	20.5					117
CHF_3	CHF_3	102							225,241
		102, 103		−84.4	−160				278

TABLE 1 (*continued*)

Empirical Formula	Structural Formula	Method	Yield %	B.p. °C/mm.	F.p. or M.p. °C	n_D^t	d_4^t	t°C	Ref.
CHF_3		103, 107	80	−82.2					143
		105							233
		107	80–95	−84					143,334,335
		113							285
		211	81–89						116
		213		−81					73
		214							73,188,282
		215	97						244
CH_2BrF	CH_2BrF	207	62	17.5					117
		211							305
CH_2ClF	CH_2ClF	203							64
		207	52	8.5					117
				−9					143
CH_2FI	CH_2FI	102		53.4		1.491	2.366	20	330
		207	55			1.490		20	117
CH_2F_2	CH_2F_2	102		−51.6					172
		211	19						30
		214							35,188,288
CH_3F	CH_3F	214		−78.5	−114.8		0.8817	−78.5	96
		208	59.7–89.4						76,78
		211							305
		219							64
CD_3F	CD_3F	208	80.5						79
C_2BrClF_3I	$CF_2BrCFClI$	201	84	82/195		1.482		25	118
$C_2BrCl_2F_3$	CF_3CCl_2Br	203	18.8	69.2		1.3977	1.950	20	182
	$CF_2ClCFClBr$	204	80	45.1/330		1.3830	1.912	20	256
C_2BrF_5	C_2F_5Br	203		−23 to −21					37,125,287, 288
C_2BrF_5		207	97–98	−21 to −20		1.2966	1.8098(0)	29.8	106,117,198, 247
		213		−18.5 to					187

				−17.5					
$C_2Br_2ClF_3$	$CF_2BrCFClBr$	201	4	92–92.5		1.425		25	118
				93.1	−72.9	1.4278	2.2478	20	174
				92.9		1.4272	2.2318	20	203
$C_2Br_2Cl_2F_2$	CF_2BrCCl_2Br			117.1	46				203
	$CFClBrCFClBr$			139.7	32.5				203
		201		138.8–138.9	45.5				179
$C_2Br_2Cl_3F$	$CFClBrCCl_2Br$			122.5					203
$C_2Br_2F_4$	CF_2BrCF_2Br	207	43	46.4					117,249
				46.4	−112		2.149	25	203
$C_2Br_3F_3$	CF_3CBr_3	203		113.1					204,210
$C_2Br_4F_2$	$CFBr_2CFBr_2$	201		186.5/758	62.5				299
	CF_2BrCBr_3	201		185	99				306
C_2Br_5F	$CFBr_2CBr_3$				198(d)				251,253
$C_2ClF_2I_2$	$CF_2ICFClI$	201	30–35	54–5/20 d./760					12
C_2ClF_5	C_2F_5Cl	107							21
		112	8–13	−38					68,203,236
		203		−36					125
		207	83–94	−38 to −37		1.2678	1.5678	−42.2	106,117,249
$C_2Cl_2F_3I$	$CF_2ClCFClI$	201	97	99–9.5		1.449		20	118
		201		43–4/100		1.4474	2.1959 $\left(\frac{25}{20}\right)$	25	12
$C_2Cl_2F_4$	CF_3CFCl_2	112							56
				−2					203
				3.6	−56.6				174
	CF_2ClCF_2Cl	107							142
		112	17.4–19						236
		207		3.8					249
		214	61	3.6					5
$C_2Cl_3F_3$	CF_3CCl_3	107		45.9	14.2	1.3610	1.5790	20	179,203
		112		45–46	14	1.360		20	68
		203		46	13				314
		215	50–55	46.4	13.5–14.0	1.3603	1.5771	20	230,235
	$CF_2ClCFCl_2$	107		46.5–47.6	−36 to −37	1.35572	1.56354	25	34,195,203

TABLE 1 (*continued*)

Empirical Formula	Structural Formula	Method	Yield %	B.p. °C/mm.	F.p. or M.p. °C	n_D^t	d_4^t	t °C	Ref.
$C_2Cl_3F_3$		112	10.5–14.8						236
		201	16						121
		207	78	47					127
		214	6.9	47.5–48.0					45
$C_2Cl_4F_2$	CF_2ClCCl_3	201		91.5	40.6				155,203
		203	18	91	52				210,301
		206	81–90	91.8	42				51,57
		215		91–92	40.5–0.6				229,230,235
$C_2Cl_4F_2$	$CFCl_2CFCl_2$			92.8	24.65	1.41297	1.64470	25	203
		107		91.0	26.5	1.4264	1.64(30)	23	34
		108	32	92.8	26.5	1.4115		30	28
		113	1–20						228,235,236
		207	71–79	92–93					131
C_2Cl_5F	C_2Cl_5F			137.9	101.3				203
		107		136.8	100.0		1.74	25	34
		113							228
		203	12	134–6					103
$C_2F_4I_2$	CF_2ICF_2I	201	74–91	112–13		1.4895	2.6293	25	63,81,129, 265
		207	35	112–13					117,249
C_2F_5I	C_2F_5I	114	85–100	13					81,129,286
		207	85–94	12.5–13.0		1.3378	2.0718 (28)	0.5	109,117,249
C_2F_6	C_2F_6	112							49,68,200
		113							285
		207		−79 to −78	−103				192,313
		214		−79	−100.6				1,277
$C_2HBrClF_3$	$CF_2BrCHClF$	202	76–88	52.5, 46/691.5		1.3685	1.8638	25	135,255,258
$C_2HBrCl_2F_2$	$CF_2BrCHCl_2$	202		88.48/621.2		1.4349	1.9043	25	258
C_2HBrF_4	CF_2BrCF_2H	202	66	12.5, −3.5/62.5					135,258

$C_2HBr_2ClF_2$	$CF_2BrCHBrCl$			118.7		1.4611	2.2319	25	159
$C_2HBr_2Cl_2F$	$CFBrClCHBrCl$			163.5		1.5106	2.2833	23	159
$C_2HBr_2F_3$	CF_3CHBr_2	203	7	71.5–73		1.4029	2.224	24	204,210
	$CF_2BrCFHBr$	201	82	76/760		1.4191	2.274 (27.4)	24	255
$C_2HBr_3F_2$	$CF_2BrCHBr_2$	201		143.4–3.5/754		1.50215	2.60769	17.5	306
	$CFBr_2CFHBr$	107		146			2.60772	17.5	299
C_2HBr_4F	$CFBr_2CHBr_2$	107		106.4/24	d./760 mm		2.9094	17	305
	$CFHBrCBr_3$	201		204/760					298
C_2HClF_3I	$CF_2ClCFHI$	201		77/627		1.4320	2.181	20	257
C_2HClF_4	CF_2ClCF_2H	113		−13					68
		202	90	−10.2	−117				23,24
		211	19						35
		214		−10					75,254
$C_2HCl_2F_3$	$CF_2ClCFHCl$			28.0			1.496	10	159
		201	90	28.2		1.3371	1.498 (27.4)	15	255
	CF_3CHCl_2	203	15						210
$C_2HCl_3F_2$	$CF_2ClCHCl_2$			71.9		1.3889	1.55868	25	159
			5						210
	$CFCl_2CFHCl$			72.5		1.39419	1.55868	20	159
	CF_2HCCl_3			73.0		1.39787	1.56613	20	159
C_2HCl_4F	$CFCl_2CHCl_2$			116.6	−82.6	1.44873	1.62232	20	159
		110		116–18/742					41,42
		112							228
		202	12.3						2
		203							103
	$CFHClCCl_3$			117.0	−95.35	1.45253	1.62525	20	159
		203	6–50	116.5					103,301
$C_2HF_3I_2$	CF_3CHI_2	218	87	59/39			2.595	22	89
C_2HF_5	C_2F_5H	112		−42	−103				68,336
		202		−48 to −45					100
		207	98	−50/740					196
		202				1.50124		19	304

TABLE 1 (*continued*)

Empirical Formula	Structural Formula	Method	Yield %	B.p. °C/mm.	F.p. or M.p. °C	n_D^t	d_4^t	t °C	Ref.
$C_2H_2BrClF_2$	$CF_2HCHBrCl$	107		82.3–3.5/743		1.4173	1.879(20)	23	168
	CF_2BrCH_2Cl	204		71/770		1.404		20	134
	CF_2ClCH_2Br			68.4	−75.8	1.4018	1.8300	20	174
$C_2H_2BrCl_2F$	$CHBrClCHClF$	107		124.7–125.1/736		1.4776	1.932	20	168
	CCl_2FCH_2Br	102		110.8		1.4626	1.8472	25	268
$C_2H_2BrF_2I$	CF_2BrCH_2I	201	95	84/216		1.504		20	134
$C_2H_2BrF_3$	CF_3CH_2Br			26.3	−93.9	1.3331	1.7881	20	174
		107	85	26.7					328
		203	50	25.4					204,210
		208	3.5						193
		208	97.2						209
	CF_2BrCH_2F	102		24.8–5.0					305
	$CF_2HCHBrF$			40–41/735		1.36175	1.874	10	168
$C_2H_2Br_2F_2$	CF_2BrCH_2Br			93.2	−61.3	1.4456	2.2238	20	174
		107		92.8		1.44815	2.2423	17.5	306
	CF_2HCHBr_2	107		107.5		1.46223	2.31204	20	298
		110							144
$C_2H_2Br_3F$	$CFBr_2CH_2Br$	107		162.7		1.50215	2.6054	17.5	306
		201		163					304
	$CHBrFCHBr_2$	107		178		1.56383	2.67369	18	298
		211	17						35
		214	14						30
$C_2H_2ClF_3$	CF_3CH_2Cl			6.93	−105.5	1.3090	1.389	0	168,174
		109, 110	32						210
		107	90	6					20,334,335
$C_2H_2Cl_2F_2$	CF_2ClCH_2Cl	107		46.8	−101.2	1.36193	1.4163	20	155
		110	31–39	46–46.5		1.3620			99,210,295
		203		45–7					103
	CF_2HCHCl_2	107		60			1.49448	17	301
		203		58–60					103

$C_2H_2Cl_3F$	$CFCl_2CH_2Cl$	105							19
		107		88.0	−104.7	1.42484	1.42269	20	155
		109	80	88–9/753					42,44
		203	23	88.5		1.4250		20	103
	$CFHClCHCl_2$	203		101–3		1.4390		20	103
		107							301
$C_2H_2F_3I$	CF_3CH_2I	104	53	55					134
		208	28–81	54.5–5.5		1.3981	2.142	25	193,326
		216	77	54.5–5.0			1.989	23	90
$C_2H_2F_4$	CF_3CH_2F	208	35.5	−26/736					78
	CF_2HCF_2H	103							68
		104		−23					168
		214							188
C_2H_3BrClF	$CHClFCH_2Br$	104		96.6		1.45463	1.82193	20	169
$C_2H_3BrF_2$	CF_2HCH_2Br	107		57					300,304
		216		57.3	−74.5	1.39400	1.82445 (18.5)	10.5	303
$C_2H_3Br_2F$	$CHBrFCH_2Br$	107, 201		122.5/761		1.50124	2.25706 (17)	19.5	304
		109							144
$C_2H_3ClF_2$	CF_2ClCH_3	107		−9.6					169
		109	59						210
		110		−9.5					142
		203	70–84						52,154
	CF_2HCH_2Cl	107		35.1		1.3528	1.312	15	169
$C_2H_3Cl_2F$	$CFCl_2CH_3$	110	68	31.7–1.8		1.38679	1.2673	5	169,210
		202	50	32	−103.5	1.3600	1.250	10	165
	$CFClHCH_2Cl$	107		73.7–3.9		1.41132	1.3814	20	169
		202	25.5						2
$C_2H_3F_2I$	CF_2HCH_2I	204							300
$C_2H_3F_3$	CF_3CH_3	105							237
		107	87	−47.0–46.7					169,335
		109	74–80	−46.7					205,210
		212		−46.8	−107				314
	CHF_2CH_2F	104		10–11					169
C_2H_4BrF	CH_2FCH_2Br	101	25–68	70–74					98,184,250

TABLE 1 (*continued*)

Empirical Formula	Structural Formula	Method	Yield %	B.p. °C/mm.	F.p. or M.p. °C	n_D^t	d_4^t	t °C	Ref.
$C_2H_4B_rF$		104		71.5–71.8		1.42261	1.7044	25	169
		204	57	71–74					279
		208	78.9	71–72					78,266
		216		71–72.5					184,307
C_2H_4ClF	$CHClFCH_3$	107		16.1–16.2					169
		202	16						252,280
	CH_2FCH_2Cl	101	17	50–56					250
		208	60–64.4	52–3		1.3775	1.1747	20	78,266
		216	44–69.4	53.2		1.3727	1.1675	25	184,220,279
C_2H_4FI	CH_2FCH_2I	104		98–102					169
$C_2H_4F_2$	CHF_2CH_3	107		−24.7					169
		109							280
		202	65						50,95
	CH_2FCH_2F	102							59
		104		10–11					168,169
		202							181,291
		208	78.4–89.1	30.7					78
C_2H_5F	C_2H_5F			−37.1	−143.2	1.3033	0.8176	−37.1	96
		104							239
		110							223
		202	81	−37.7	−143.2	1.3057		−40	94
		207	63–86						245
		208	64–85.6						78,85
		217	10–30						290
C_3BrClF_6	$Cl(CF_2)_3Br$	204		35.7		1.3022	1.5518 (27.2)	22.2	108
$C_3BrCl_2F_5$	$CF_3CBrClCF_2Cl$	107		90.1–91.8	23.5–24.5	1.3795		26	222
$C_3BrCl_3F_4$	$CF_3CBrClCFCl_2$	107		131–3	68.9				263
$C_3BrCl_4F_3$	$CCl_3CF_2CFClBr$	208							157,158
C_3BrF_7	$CF_3(CF_2)_2Br$	108	80	12					123
		203	80	11–12					29,37,287, 125
		204		15–16					9

C_3BrF_7		207	66–97	12–13		1.3070	1.8746 (0°)	−29.8	65,106,117, 198,249, 199
		213	65–70	15–15.2/742					187
$C_3Br_2Cl_2F_4$	$CF_3CFBrCBrCl_2$	201		154	35.5–37				147
$C_3Br_2F_6$	$CF_3CFBrCF_2Br$	201	85	70.2		1.3592		20	102,261
		203		71–71.5					37,287,100
		207							117
	$Br(CF_2)_3Br$	207		74.2		1.3526	2.1162 (30.2)	27.8	108,249
C_3ClF_6I	C_2F_5CClFI	205	84	58/330		1.381		20	133
C_3ClF_7	$C_2F_5CF_2Cl$	113	75						133
		203		−3 to 0					29,108,287
		207	71–91	−1 to −2		1.2781	1.5572(0)	−29.8	106,117,133, 249
		213		8–14					187
	$(CF_3)_2CFCl$	108	14	−2					93
		112	24.7						236
$C_3Cl_2F_6$	$C_2F_5CCl_2F$	204	75	35					133
	$CF_3CFClCF_2Cl$	106							176
		107	60	34.7	−136	1.3029	1.5896	20	176
		108	13.8	34.7					93
		112		34.5		1.3013–27		20	102
		201	90						133
	$Cl(CF_2)_3Cl$	107		35.8		1.3030	1.5730	20	36
		203		34.6					73
		207		35.7					249
		214	22.4	35.5					214
$C_3Cl_3F_5$	$C_2F_5CCl_3$	203	43	70.5		1.3527		20	182
	$CF_3CFClCCl_2F$	106	41	73.4		1.3530		20	331
		107	28	73.5		1.3529	1.6643	20	176
		108	56	73.5		1.3540		20	93
	$CF_3CCl_2CF_2Cl$	107		72	−4.3	1.3519	1.6681	20	178,219
		201		72	−4.3	1.3519	1.6681		176,178
		215	70	71–2	−5	1.3490		25	230,235

TABLE 1 (*continued*)

Empirical Formula	Structural Formula	Method	Yield %	B.p. °C/mm.	F.p. or M.p. °C	n_D^t	d_4^t	t °C	Ref.
$C_3Cl_3F_5$	$CF_2ClCFClCF_2Cl$	107	70	73.7		1.3512	1.6631	20	163
		112		73.7	−72	1.3512		20	102
		206	54	72–3		1.3578	1.6429	25	61,190
$C_3Cl_4F_4$	$CF_3CFClCCl_3$	201		112.4–2.6	12.1	1.4002	1.7254	20	151,176
	$CF_3CCl_2CCl_2F$	107		112–4	41.7				176,178
	$CF_2ClCF_2CCl_3$	203		113.95	−92.78	1.3966	1.7034	20	148
		203		112–2.5		1.3961	1.6992	20	213
		205		114.5		1.3974	1.6927	25	61,190
	$CF_2ClCFClCCl_2F$	203		112.2	−58	1.39797	1.7226	20	151,171
	$CF_2ClCCl_2CF_2Cl$	107	27	112	−42.9	1.39584	1.7199	20	151,171,219
	$CFCl_2CF_2CFCl_2$	206	24	112.5–115		1.3980	1.9005	25	61
$C_3Cl_5F_3$	$CF_3C_2Cl_5$	201		153.1	109.1				178
		203							111
		215	5	151.8–2.0	108.9–9.2				230
	$CF_2ClCFClCCl_3$	203		153.3	−14.8	1.43919	1.7702	20	151,171
	$CFCl_2CF_2CCl_3$	206	3	155.5–7.0	55.6	1.4399	1.7608	25	61
				152–4		1.43887	1.7607	20	170
	$CF_2ClCCl_2CFCl_2$	107		152.3	−4.9	1.4359	1.77023	20	151,171
	$CFCl_2CFClCFCl_2$	107		154.7		1.4387	1.7624	20	163
$C_3Cl_6F_2$	$CCl_3CF_2CCl_3$	107		194.4	−12.9	1.47996	1.8105	20	160
		203		194–4.4	−15.8	1.48064	1.8136	20	6,170,172
		206	9	196.5–6.7	−5	1.4777	1.7925	25	61
	$C_2Cl_5CF_2Cl$	203			50.8				172
	$CFCl_2CFClCCl_3$	203		196	−55	1.4791	1.8080	20	148
	$CFCl_2CCl_2CFCl_2$	107		194.2	29.8	1.47418	1.79151	35	160
C_3Cl_7F	$F(CCl_2)_3Cl$	107		236.8	97				160
	$CCl_3CFClCCl_3$	203	53	105/14	7.6–8.4	1.5194	1.8515	20	150,163
$C_3F_6I_2$	$I(CF_2)_3I$	207	18.2	131		1.4516	2.5812	20	109,249
C_3F_7I	$F(CF_2)_3I$	113		39					286
		207	86.7–90	41.2		1.3272	2.0628	20	109,117,249
C_3F_8	$CF_3CF_2CF_3$	108	5	−39					123
		113		−36	−183				200,284
		214							285

C_3HBrF_6	$CF_3CHBrCF_3$	203		31.5–2.5					204
	CF_3CHFCF_2Br	202	81	35.5, 30/624		1.3031	1.8016	25	123,207,258
		207							197
$C_3HBr_2Cl_3F_2$	$CHF_2CClBrCCl_2Br$	203							103
$C_3HBr_2F_5$	$CF_3CHBrCF_2Br$	201		88		1.3780	2.1637 (23)	25	219
		202	50	87		1.379		20	136
	$CF_2BrCHFCF_2Br$	205	9	35/78.5		1.3816	2.1025	25	322
C_3HClF_6	C_2F_5CHClF	211	60–80	20					133
	$CF_3CHClCF_3$	107	16	14.5–15			1.5415	4	219
	$H(CF_2)_3Cl$	214		21		1.29	1.556	20	25,72,75,254
$C_3HCl_2F_5$	$C_2F_5CHCl_2$	203	28.5	45.5		1.3196	1.543(25)	20	209
	$CF_3CFClCHClF$	201	80	56		1.339		20	133
	$CF_3CHClCF_2Cl$	107	50	50.4		1.3208	1.5564 (22)	24	219
	CF_2ClCF_2CFClH	206	46	51–3		1.3262	1.5492	25	61,190
	$CF_2ClCFClCHF_2$	113	5	56		1.3288		20	102
$C_3HCl_3F_4$	$CF_3CHClCFCl_2$	107	56	87–7.3		1.3699	1.6174 (23)	24	219
		202	12						2
	$CF_2ClCF_2CHCl_2$	203		91.7–1.9		1.3750	1.5877	20	213
		206	83	91.2		1.3704	1.6115	25	69,190
	$CF_2ClCCl_2CHF_2$	107		92–2.5		1.3787	1.645	20	69
	$CF_2ClCClFCHClF$	107		89.8		1.3855	1.6403	20	151,171
	$CFCl_2CF_2CHClF$	206	20	90–1					61
$C_3HCl_4F_3$	$CF_3CCl_2CHCl_2$	201	52–72	125.1–6.5		1.4180	1.6757	24	111,114,219
	$CF_2HCCl_2CFCl_2$	107		134.6	65.1				69
	$CF_2ClCHClCFCl_2$	107		128.7	−42.9	1.4159	1.67471	25	151,171
	$CF_2ClCFClCHCl_2$	107		129.8		1.41967	1.69124	20	151,171
		206	10.2	125–30		1.4141		29	149
	$CFCl_2CF_2CHCl_2$	206	2	127		1.4189	1.6704	25	61
$C_3HCl_5F_2$	$CF_2ClCCl_2CHCl_2$	107		168.4		1.46241	1.73162	20	160
	$CF_2HC_2Cl_5$	201		174	139–40				103
		203		175.2	139.9				69
	$CFCl_2CHClCCl_2F$	107		167.4		1.45972	1.71720	20	160

TABLE 1 (*continued*)

Empirical Formula	Structural Formula	Method	Yield %	B.p. °C/mm.	F.p. or M.p. °C	n_D^t	d_4^t	t °C	Ref.
$C_3HCl_5F_2$	$CHCl_2CF_2CCl_3$	203		174		1.46410	1.7557	20	170
		206		171–2		1.4621	1.7241	20	61
C_3HCl_6F	$CHCl_2CFClCCl_3$	203		87/14	−33.5 to −31.6	1.5012	1.7714	20	150,176
	$CHCl_2CCl_2CCl_2F$	107		210		1.44510	1.77304	20	160
	$CFCl_2CHClCCl_3$	107		207(d)		1.5015	1.76188	20	160
	$CFHClCCl_2CCl_3$	206	38	209–11		1.5072		25	61
C_3HF_7	$F(CF_2)_3H$	110		−18.5 to −17					100
		107		−18 to −17					29
		207	97	−16					196
		211	4–88.5	−19 to −17/740					37,117,125, 137
		213	25–40						187
		217	81–88						120
	CF_3CFHCF_3	108	4	−18					123
		214							9
$C_3H_2BrClF_4$	$CF_2ClCH_2CF_2Br$	205	35	79		1.3669	1.7890	25	321
$C_3H_2BrF_5$	$C_2F_5CH_2Br$	208	81	46.5		1.3204	1.756	25	209
	$CF_3CH_2CF_2Br$	107	31	47–7.3		1.3228	1.784	20	278
		202	40	44		1.319		20	136
		204	55	44		1.320		18	136
$C_3H_2Br_2Cl_2F_2$	$CHF_2CClBrCHClBr$	203		87/24	−45	1.5078		20	103
$C_3H_2Br_2F_4$	$CHF_2CFBrCHFBr$	201		116.5		1.4190		20	102
	$CF_2BrCH_2CF_2Br$	205	28	42/85		1.3974	2.0943	25	322
$C_3H_2Br_3F_3$	$CF_3CBr_2CH_2Br$	201	98	162, 79–81/46		1.4831		25	115,161
	$CF_3CHBrCHBr_2$	201	95	167–8, 70/30		1.438		25	115
$C_3H_2ClF_5$	$C_2F_5CH_2Cl$	208	75	27.2		1.292	1.395	20	209
	$CF_3CH_2CF_2Cl$	104	5	28.4	−107	1.2875	1.4372	20	176
		202	70						2

$C_3H_2Cl_2F_3I$	$CF_3CH_2CCl_2I$	204	17	142–3					115
$C_3H_2Cl_2F_4$	$CF_2ClCF_2CH_2Cl$	107		67.9		1.3464	1.5225	20	213
		104		62.8	−75	1.3449		20	148
	$CF_2HCFClCHFCl$	112		76		1.3551		20	102
$C_3H_2Cl_3F_3$	$CF_3CH_2CCl_3$	203		153.1	109				176,178
	$CF_3CHClCHCl_2$	201		106					178
	$CF_3CCl_2CH_2Cl$	201	90	104–5		1.392		25	115
$C_3H_2Cl_3F_3$	$CFCl_2CF_2CH_2Cl$	104		109.5	−79.8		1.5814	20	148
		107		108.3		1.3954	1.5813	20	213
$C_3H_2Cl_4F_2$	$CF_2HCCl_2CHCl_2$	201		147.6	−59	1.4479	1.6582	20	69,163
	$CF_2ClCH_2CCl_3$			132		1.4290	1.576	28	211
	$CCl_3CF_2CH_2Cl$	203		151.18	−17.13	1.4440	1.6386	20	148,170
				150.8–0.9		1.4459	1.6404	20	213
$C_3H_2Cl_5F$	$CCl_3CClFCH_2Cl$	203							176
		206		72/14	−34.4	1.4871	1.6867	20	150
$C_3H_2F_5I$	$CF_3CH_2CF_2I$	205	90	72		1.3731	2.039	20	134,257
	$C_2F_5CH_2I$	208	81	70.5		1.3728	2.038(25)	20	209
$C_3H_2F_6$	$C_2F_5CH_2F$	208	13.8	1.2					78
		214		10–11					73
	$CF_3CH_2CF_3$	104	84	−0.7	−93.62				176
		107	85	0.5–1.0					322
$C_3H_3BrClF_3$	$CF_3CBrClCH_3$	203		69		1.3790	1.708	25	204,210
	$CF_3CHBrCH_2Cl$	107		94–96					122
	$CF_3CH_2CHBrCl$	203	41	91–2		1.395			115
$C_3H_3BrCl_2F_2$	$CF_2ClCHBrCH_2Cl$	107	30	133.5–4.0		1.444		25	122
$C_3H_3BrF_3I$	CF_3CH_2CHBrI	204		139–40		1.487		20	115
$C_3H_3BrF_4$	CF_3CH_2CHFBr	110		59.2–9.5		1.3441	1.7391 (25)	24	322
$C_3H_3Br_2ClF_2$	$CF_2ClCHBrCH_2Br$	201		151–2		1.474		21	122
$C_3H_3Br_2F_3$	$CF_3CHBrCH_2Br$	107	50	116		1.426		25	122
		201	25–86	115.8–6.0		1.4286	2.121(28)	25	115,150,161
	$CF_3CH_2CHBr_2$	203		111		1.4242	2.086	25	204,210
		204	26	110–12		1.426		25	115
	CF_2BrCH_2CHFBr	205	34	115–16		1.4256	2.0875	25	322
$C_3H_3ClF_3I$	CF_3CH_2CHClI	204	43	119		1.450		20	115
		205	97	120		1.453		20	132

TABLE 1 (*continued*)

Empirical Formula	Structural Formula	Method	Yield %	B.p. °C/mm.	F.p. or M.p. °C	n_D^t	d_4^t	t °C	Ref.
$C_3H_3ClF_4$	$CF_2ClCF_2CH_3$	104	86	19.90	−74.42	1.3012	1.3509	5	148
$C_3H_3Cl_2F_3$	$CF_3CCl_2CH_3$	203	72	48.8	13.8	1.3478	1.3842	20	178,211
$C_3H_3Cl_2F_3$	$CF_3CHClCH_2Cl$	107	47	76–7					122
		203	28–83	76.6–7.2		1.367		20	115,132,211
	$CF_3CH_2CHCl_2$	203		72.4	−93.2	1.3631	1.4408	20	178,204,211
		204	80	72.8–3.4/766		1.363		20	132
	$CH_3CF_2CFCl_2$	107	50	60–0.3		1.35377	1.4215	20	170,213
	$CH_3CFClCF_2Cl$		35	55.6	−30.48	1.3503	1.3956	20	176
$C_3H_3Cl_3F_2$	$CH_3CF_2CCl_3$	203	61.7	101–2	52.8–3.3				213
		203		102	47–49				170
	$CF_2ClCHClCH_2Cl$	201		113		1.415		20	122
		203		114.3		1.4116	1.499	28	211
	$CF_2ClCH_2CHCl_2$	203		107.8		1.4079	1.465	28	211
	$CFCl_2CFClCH_3$	104		97.7	27.6	1.4000	1.4572	30	148,176
	$CF_2ClCCl_2CH_3$	203		90.2	37.8				211
$C_3H_3Cl_4F$	$CH_3CFClCCl_3$	203		139.6	104–4.5				150,176
	$CH_2ClCFClCHCl_2$	203		50–1/14		1.4696	1.5782	20	150
$C_3H_3F_4I$	CF_3CH_2CHFI	205	84	86.2/757		1.4024		20	132
$C_3H_4BrClF_2$	$CF_2Cl(CH_2)_2Br$	107	11	100–0.5					122
		203		100–101		1.4140	1.726	24–26	204,210
	$CF_2ClCHBrCH_3$	104	9.6	90		1.4045	1.662	28	210,211
		203	3	90		1.4045	1.662	25	210
$C_3H_4BrF_3$	$CF_3(CH_2)_2Br$	107	51–56.6	62–64		1.3606		20–22	122,278
		202	40	60.5–2.5		1.3602	1.654	20	156,162
		203		62–2.5		1.3572	1.653	25	204,210
		204	13–90	63		1.358		25	115,132
	$CF_3CHBrCH_3$	104,	203						210
		203		48.4–9.0					204
		208		49			1.633	15	312
$C_3H_4Br_2F_2$	$CF_2Br(CH_2)_2Br$	205	23	62/86		1.4450	2.0353	25	320
	$CH_2BrCF_2CH_2Br$	107	45.3	136		1.4586	2.132	28	211

$C_3H_4ClF_3$	$CF_3(CH_2)_2Cl$	107	61	45–6		1.324		25	122
		202		45–6		1.3379		20	156
		203	16–90	45.1	−106.5	1.3350	1.3253	20	115,132,178, 204
	$CF_3CHClCH_3$	104	80	30		1.3150		20	178,211
		203							204,211
$C_3H_4Cl_2F_2$	$CF_2ClCHClCH_3$	203	13	69.3		1.3708	1.304	28	211
		201	90	70–0.5					122
	$CH_3CF_2CHCl_2$	203	10.4	78.5–9.5		1.38327	1.3666	20	170,213
	$CH_2ClCF_2CH_2Cl$	104	80	96.69	−30.04	1.3959	1.4156	20	148
	$CF_2ClCH_2CH_2Cl$	107	10	81–1.5		1.325		20	122
		203	28	80–8		1.3775	1.339	28	211
$C_3H_4Cl_3F$	$CH_3CHClCCl_2F$	104		113.5		1.4435	1.381	28	211
	$CH_2ClCFClCH_2Cl$	104		130.8	−67.8	1.4466	1.4579	20	148
	$CH_3CFClCHCl_2$	203		116.7		1.4360	1.4238	20	150
$C_3H_4F_3I$	$CF_3(CH_2)_2I$	205		90		1.423		17	110
$C_3H_4F_4$	$CF_3(CH_2)_2F$	104	41	29					132
		211	79	28.5–30		1.2765	1.2584	25	132,322
C_3H_5BrClF	$CH_3CHBrCHClF$	104	12.9	112.5		1.4460	1.626	28	211
	$CH_3CFClCH_2Br$			110–12		1.45503	1.6475	20	170
$C_3H_5BrF_2$	$C_2H_5CF_2Br$	202	53	46–6.5					124
	$CH_3CHBrCHF_2$	202	93	72–3					124
		104	10	72.6		1.3890	1.601	28	211
	$CH_3CF_2CH_2Br$			76.2–6.3		1.38860	1.6102	20	170
$C_3H_5Br_2F$	$CH_2FCHBrCH_2Br$	201		162.5		1.5092	2.089(25)	23	183,224
$C_3H_5ClF_2$	$C_2H_5CF_2Cl$	107	10	25.8		1.3330	1.3111	8	178
		109	60						176
		110	67.5						110
		202	68	25					124
	$CH_3CF_2CH_2Cl$	104		51					148
		109	4	55–5.2	−56.2	1.3520	1.2001	20	150,165
		203		55.1		1.3506	1.2023	20	170
	$CH_3CHClCHF_2$	104	13.6	52		1.3495	1.183	28	211
	$CH_3CHFCHFCl$	104	5.5	52.9		1.3487	1.191	28	211
$C_3H_5Cl_2F$	$C_2H_5CFCl_2$	110	12.7	66.6					211

TABLE 1 (*continued*)

Empirical Formula	Structural Formula	Method	Yield %	B.p. °C/mm.	F.p. or M.p. °C	n_D^t	d_4^t	t °C	Ref.
		202	12						126
$C_3H_5Cl_2F$	$CH_3CFClCH_2Cl$	202	30–74	88.5	−92.5	1.4121	1.2618	20	2,150,165, 176
	$CH_3CHClCHClF$	104		93		1.4055	1.251	28	211
	$CH_2ClCHClCH_2F$	201		118–9			1.327	18	224
$C_3H_5F_3$	$CF_3C_2H_5$	104	90						176
		107	63–85	−13	−148				124,178
		110	88.5						211
		205	33						110
		211	41–51	−12					132,322
		212							116
C_3H_6BrF	$F(CH_2)_3Br$	101		101.4		1.4295	1.542(25)	23	183,184
		216	70.6						184
C_3H_6ClF	$F(CH_2)_3Cl$	216	81.3	82.1		1.3855	1.0992 (25)	27.5	184
	$CH_3CFClCH_3$		35.2			1.35856	1.0072	20	170
$C_3H_6F_2$	$CF_2HC_2H_5$	104	80	7–8					172
	$F(CH_2)_3F$	101		41.6		1.3190	1.0057 (25)	26	183,184
	$CH_3CF_2CH_3$	107	85	−0.6 to −0.2			0.92	0	146,148
		202		−0.1	−104.8				4,95
C_3H_7F	$H(CH_2)_3F$	208	63.3	−2.3/768					78
		110	80	−3.2	−159	1.3226		−20	94
				−3					224
				−2.5	−159	1.3225	0.7818	−2.5	96
	$(CH_3)_2CHF$			−9.4	−133.4	1.3282	0.9692	−9.4	96
		202	62	−10.1	−133.4	1.3240		−20	94
		207	75–82						245,246
		208	50.7	−10					78
C_4BrF_9	$F(CF_2)_4Br$	203		43–4					125
		207	95	44					117

$C_4Br_2Cl_2F_6$	$CF_2BrCFBrCF_2CFCl_2$	201	91	65/5		1.427		20	127
$C_4Br_2Cl_4F_4$	$CFClBrCFBrCFClCFCl_2$	201		149–50/52		1.4949	2.2459	25	273
		201		138–40/35		1.493		20	131
$C_4Br_2Cl_2F_6$	$(CF_2BrCFCl—)_2$	209		75/20		1.427		20	118
$C_4Br_2F_8$	$Br(CF_2)_4Br$	207		97/740		1.3495	2.0979	25	40
	$C_2F_5CBrFCBrF_2$	201	58	95/740		1.3511	2.1279	25	40
	$(CF_3)_2CBrCBrF_2$	201		96/740					40
	$CF_3CBrFCBrFCF_3$	201		96/740		1.3538	2.2673	25	40
$C_4Br_4F_6$	$(CF_2BrCFBr—)_2$	201		130/70		1.464		25	118
C_4ClF_9	$F(CF_2)_4Cl$	203		29–30			1.610	25	29,125
		207	89	30					117
$C_4Cl_2F_8$	$CF_3(CF_2)_2CFCl_2$	107	77	62.8		1.3067	1.633(25)	20	209
	$(CF_3)_2CClCF_2Cl$	203	88	63		1.306		20	136
	$C_2F_5CCl_2CF_3$	203	90	64		1.316		20	120
	$CF_3(CFCl)_2CF_3$	106		62.9		1.3100	1.6801	20	163
		108		58–9.5		1.3156		8	92
		112							236
$C_4Cl_3F_6I$	$CF_2ClCFClCF_2CFClI$	205	26	74/24		1.4405	2.182	22	201
		205	75	80/25					110
$C_4Cl_3F_7$	$CF_3(CF_2)_2CCl_3$	203	55–60	96.2–6.5		1.3441	1.688	25	209,326
		217	30						327
	$CF_3CFClCCl_2CF_3$	107	53	97.5		1.3530	1.7484	20	163
	$CF_2ClCFClCF_2CF_2Cl$	204	83	96–7					126
		205	84	99–100					127
		207	66						126
$C_4Cl_4F_6$	$(CF_3CCl_2—)_2$	201		131	83–4				154
		203		136	83.4				26
		215							235
	$(CF_2ClCFCl—)_2$	112	6.5–44						236
		201	91	131–33					126,131
		203	93	134					131
		205	7	78/100					127
$C_4Cl_4F_6$		207	55–69	132–4					127,128
		209	51–82	134–4.5		1.3832		14	118,167
		210		132–3		1.3852		20	231
	$CF_2ClCF_2CCl_2CF_2Cl$	107		134.2		1.3856	1.7625	20	163

TABLE 1 (*continued*)

Empirical Formula	Structural Formula	Method	Yield %	B.p. °C/mm.	F.p. or M.p. °C	n_D^t	d_4^t	t °C	Ref.
$C_4Cl_4F_6$	$CF_2ClCFClCF_2CFCl_2$	201							127
		204	96	133–134					127
$C_4Cl_5F_5$	$CF_3CCl_2CF_2CCl_3$	203		170.5	−79.5	1.4227	1.8128	20	154
	$CF_2ClCCl_2CF_2CFCl_2$	107		171.3		1.4221	1.8047	20	163
$C_4Cl_6F_4$	$(CCl_3CF_2—)_2$	203		209	9.9	1.4502	1.8087	20	154
	$(CF_2ClCCl_2—)_2$	107		125–6/76		1.457		28	231
	$(CFCl_2CFCl—)_2$	112	2.1–4.4	84–6/8.5					231,236
		201	97	207–8		1.457			131
	$CCl_3CF_2CCl_2CF_2Cl$	107		209		1.4551	1.8392	20	163
$C_4Cl_7F_3$	$CF_3(CCl_2)_2CCl_3$	203			167–9				162
	$CF_2Cl(CCl_2)_2CFCl_2$	104		160–5/100					231
$C_4Cl_8F_2$	$CCl_3CF_2C_2Cl_5$	203		98/2	−8.2	1.5198	1.8990	20	152,172
	$CCl_3(CCl_2)_2CF_2Cl$	201		161/25	41.9–2.4		1.8047	25	173
$C_4F_8I_2$	$I(CF_2)_4I$	207		150	−9	1.4273	1.4739	27	107,249
C_4F_9I	$C_2F_5CFICF_3$	205	94	65.5		1.340		20	123
	$CF_3(CF_2)_3I$	113		67					286
		203	89	67					117
C_4F_{10}	$CF_3(CF_2)_2CF_3$			−1.7 ± 0.2					84
		101	87	1					123
		105	78–84	1					123
		108	45–58	−2					43,58
		112		4	−84.5				283,284
		205	85	1					129
$C_4HBrCl_2F_6$	$CF_2BrCFClCF_2CFClH$	202	4	130		1.386		20	118
C_4HBrF_8	$Br(CF_2)_4H$	202	12	66		1.309		20	135
$C_4HBr_2ClF_6$	$CF_2BrCFClCHFCF_2Br$	205	16.2	61.5/40		1.4330	2.013	20	201,378
$C_4HBr_3F_6$	$CF_3CBr_2CHBrCF_3$	201		79/45					116
C_4HClF_8	$Cl(CF_2)_4H$	214		50		1.30	1.607	20	13,25,75,77
$C_4HCl_2F_6I$	$CF_2ClCFClCHFCF_2I$	205	79	56/23		1.4224	2.110	28	318
$C_4HCl_2F_7$	$CF_3(CF_2)_2CHCl_2$	203	24.9	76.5		1.3212	1.612(20)	25	209
$C_4HCl_3F_6$	$CF_3CHClCCl_2CF_3$	201	92	104		1.3636	1.6968	25	116,154
		203		106		1.3660		20	26

$C_4HCl_3F_6$	$(CF_3)_2CHCCl_3$	203		106.5–7.5		1.3690	1.7095		175
$C_4HCl_7F_2$	$CF_2Cl(CCl_2)_2CHCl_2$	201		158/48		1.5112	1.8476	25	173
C_4HF_8I	$(CF_3)_2CHCF_2I$	205	80	80		1.347		20	136
C_4HF_9	$CF_3(CF_2)_2CF_2H$	107		14–15					29
		207	84	14/740					196
		211		14					125
	$(CF_3)_3CH$	202		11–12					40
$C_4H_2BrF_7$	$CF_3(CF_2)_2CH_2Br$	208	26	69/732		1.3182		20	193
		208	70–91.2	69.1		1.3166	1.780	25	209,326
$C_4H_2Br_2ClF_5$	$CF_2BrCFClCH_2CF_2Br$	205	44	70.1/50		1.4230	2.063	27	201,318
$C_4H_2Br_2F_6$	$CF_3(CHBr)_2CF_3$	201	82	60/120					116
$C_4H_2ClF_7$	$CF_3(CF_2)_2CH_2Cl$	208	78–95.5	54		1.2906	1.523	25	209,326
$C_4H_2Cl_2F_6$	$C_2F_5CFClCH_2Cl$	201	73.2	72		1.3386	1.471(25)	20	209
	$CF_3(CHCl)_2CF_3$	201	79	78					116
$C_4H_2Cl_3F_4I$	$CF_2ClCFClCH_2CFClI$	205	45	70/10		1.4741	2.075	22	201,318
$C_4H_2Cl_3F_5$	$CF_3CH_2CF_2CCl_3$	203		121.5	−31.9	1.3762	1.6299	20	154
$C_4H_2Cl_5F_3$	$CF_3CH_2C_2Cl_5$	203		87/30	−22	1.4528	1.7153	25	154
$C_4H_2Cl_6F_2$	$CF_2ClCHClCCl_2CHCl_2$	104		99.3/11		1.4095	1.7750	25	173
$C_4H_2Cl_7F$	$CFCl_2CHClCCl_2CHCl_2$	104		123/11		1.523	1.7729	20	173
$C_4H_2F_7I$	$C_2F_5CH_2CF_2I$	205	91	88		1.354		20	136
	$CF_3(CF_2)_2CH_2I$	218	58	91–1.5/740		1.3603		20	193
		208	82.7–84	91/740		1.3603	2.019	25	209,326
$C_4H_2F_8$	$C_2F_5CH_2CF_3$	104	48	18					136
	$(CF_3)_2CHCHF_2$	211	63	17					136
$C_4H_3BrCl_3F_3$	$CF_3CHBrCH_2CCl_3$	205		76–7/36–7		1.4415		20	162
$C_4H_3BrF_6$	$CF_3CHBrCH_2CF_3$	204		70					116
	$(CF_3)_2CHCH_2Br$	202	93	78					124
$C_4H_3Br_2ClF_4$	$CF_2BrCFClCH_2CHFBr$	205	74	72/32		1.4405	2.075	25	201,318
$C_4H_3Br_2F_5$	$C_2F_5CHBrCH_2Br$	201	50	123		1.4060		20	214
$C_4H_3ClF_6$	$CF_3CHClCH_2CF_3$	204	76	51		1.298		25	116
	$(CF_3)_2CHCH_2Cl$	202	67	58					124
$C_4H_3Cl_2F_5$	$CF_3CCl(CH_3)CF_2Cl$			75.3		1.3440	1.5133	20	175
		201	100	75.6		1.345		23	124
$C_4H_3Cl_3F_3I$	$CF_3CHICH_2CCl_3$	205	57	120/53					119
$C_4H_3Cl_3F_4$	$CH_3(CF_2)_2CCl_3$	203		123	−90	1.3908	1.5682	20	154

TABLE 1 (*continued*)

Empirical Formula	Structural Formula	Method	Yield %	B.p. °C/mm.	F.p. or M.p. °C	n_D^t	d_4^t	t°C	Ref.
$C_4H_3Cl_4F_3$	$CF_3CCl(CH_3)CCl_3$			148–9	115.6–16.4				175
$C_4H_3F_6I$	$CF_3CHICH_2CF_3$	205		80–80.5		1.3617		20	162
		205	65–98	87.5–7.8		1.371		25	116
$C_4H_4BrCl_3F_2$	$CF_2BrCH(CH_3)CCl_3$	205	65	60–5/0.1					124
$C_4H_4BrF_5$	$CF_3CH(CH_3)CF_2Br$	202	45	78					124
$C_4H_4Br_2ClF_3$	$CF_2BrCFClCH_2CH_2Br$	205	58	67/20		1.4563	2.035	25	201,317
$C_4H_4ClF_5$	$CF_3CH(CH_3)CF_2Cl$	202	56	58–9					124
$C_4H_4Cl_2F_3I$	$CF_2ClCFCl(CH_2)_2I$	205	94	62.1/25		1.4720	1.990	20	256
$C_4H_4Cl_3F_3$	$CF_3(CH_2)_2CCl_3$	203							153
	$CF_3CCl(CH_3)CHCl_2$	201		123.7		1.4084	1.5201	20	175
$C_4H_4Cl_4F_2$	$CH_3CF_2CCl_2CHCl_2$	203		165–7/745		1.4500	1.556	32	212
$C_4H_4F_5I$	$CF_3CH(CH_3)CF_2I$	205		95, 57/200		1.394			124
$C_4H_4F_6$	$CF_3(CH_2)_2CF_3$	205		25					162
		212		24.6	−53.7	1.2732	1.3702(0)	3	116,147
	$(CF_3)_2CHCH_3$	107		21.5	−106.7	1.2717	1.3725(0)	2.9	175
	$CF_3CH(CH_3)CF_3$	107	70	20					124
	$CF_2H(CHF)_2CF_2H$	202	90–98	63–65		1.300		20	131
$C_4H_5BrClF_3$	$CF_3CH_2CHBrCH_2Cl$	107		135–35.5		1.4156	1.698	25	319
$C_4H_5BrCl_2F_2$	$CF_2ClCH_2CHBrCH_2Cl$	107	17	52.4/10		1.4151	1.731	25	319
$C_4H_5BrCl_3F$	$CFCl_2CH_2CHBrCH_2Cl$	107	6.2	77.4/10		1.4916	1.784	25	319
$C_4H_5Br_2F_3$	$CF_3CBr(CH_3)CH_2Br$	216		130.8/754	−53 to −55	1.4410	1.9825	14.5	311
	$CF_2BrCHFCHBrCH_3$	205	55	56/43		1.4403	1.9438	25	322
	$CF_2BrCH_2CFBrCH_3$	205	58	52/35		1.4346	1.9352	25	322
$C_4H_5ClF_3I$	$CF_3CH_2CHICH_2Cl$	205	89	88/69		1.476		20	130
$C_4H_5ClF_4$	$CF_2ClCH_2CF_2CH_3$	107		69/745		1.3340		26	212
$C_4H_5Cl_2F_3$	$CF_3CH_2CCl_2CH_3$	203		89.90	−48	1.335	1.374	20	153
	$CF_3(CH_2)_2CHCl_2$	203		110					153
$C_4H_5Cl_2F_3$	$CF_3CH_2CHClCH_2Cl$	203		115					153
	$CF_3CCl(CH_3)CH_2Cl$	201, 107		93.5		1.3782	1.3899	20	175
	$CF_2ClCH_2CHFCH_2Cl$	107	20	118.4–8.5		1.3881	1.428	27	319
	$CFCl_2CH_2CF_2CH_3$	107		102/745		1.3758	1.357	26	212
$C_4H_5Cl_3F_2$	$CF_2ClCCl(CH_3)CH_2Cl$			131–2		1.4326	1.441	20	175

$C_4H_5Cl_3F_2$	$CH_3CF_2CCl_2CH_2Cl$	203		140–1/745		1.4238	1.443	32	212
	$CH_3CF_2CH_2CCl_3$	203		139.15	−29.5	1.4245	1.4366	20	152
$C_4H_5F_5$	$CF_3CH_2CF_2CH_3$	203		40.14	−35.01	1.2824	1.2666	20	152
$C_4H_6BrClF_2$	$CF_2ClCH_2CHBrCH_3$	205		117.2, 43.5/50		1.4175	1.5737	25	66
		205		55–6/55		1.4194	1.5784	25	321
$C_4H_6BrF_3$	$CF_3CH_2CHBrCH_3$	110	50	84		1.3740		24	322
$C_4H_6Br_2F_2$	$CF_2BrCH_2CHBrCH_3$	205	66.8	60–1/50		1.4469	1.8586	25	320
	$CH_2BrCHBrCF_2CH_3$	201		155–7/745	−12	1.4594	1.933	27	212
$C_4H_6ClF_3$	$CF_3(CH_2)_2Cl$	203		80.60	−67.25	1.3505	1.2425	20	153
	$CF_3CH_2CHClCH_3$	203		65.63	−79.24	1.3433	1.2133	20	153
		204	93	65.4–6.6		1.3438		20	132
	$CF_3CHClC_2H_5$			58.3	<−100	1.3369	1.1967	20	153
	$CH_3CF_2CFClCH_3$	109		53/745	−19	1.3358		22	212
$C_4H_6Cl_2F_2$	$CH_3CF_2CHClCH_2Cl$	201, 203		123.1		1.404	1.328	20	152
	$CH_3CF_2CH_2CHCl_2$	203		119.26	−66.99	1.4017	1.3138	20	152
	$CH_3CF_2CCl_2CH_3$	203		89.84	43.66	1.3752	1.2393	50	152
	$CH_3CHClCF_2CH_2Cl$	203		115.67	−60.5	1.4025	1.3276	20	152
	$CH_2ClCF_2CH_2CH_2Cl$	203		142.28	−28.7	1.4153	1.3652	20	152
	$CF_2ClCHClC_2H_5$	201		96.98	<−100	1.3878	1.2715	20	153
	$CHCl_2CF_2C_2H_5$	203	40	111.22	−54.39	1.3978	1.3113	20	152
$C_4H_6Cl_3F$	$CH_3CHClCFClCH_2Cl$		53						152
	$C_2H_5CFClCHCl_2$		14						152
$C_4H_6F_3I$	$CF_3(CH_2)_3I$	216	70	126–7		1.4326	1.851(20)	23	322
	$CF_3CH_2CHICH_3$	205	98	103.5		1.4277		20	132
$C_4H_6F_4$	$CH_3(CF_2)_2CH_3$			16.9	−52.4	1.2915	1.1633	0	154
$C_4H_7BrF_2$	$C_2H_5CF_2CH_2Br$	110		103–4					71
$C_4H_7Br_2F$	$CH_3CBrFCHBrCH_3$	201		155–162					74
$C_4H_7ClF_2$	$CH_3CF_2CH_2CH_2Cl$	203		93.22	−76.08	1.3709	1.1552	20	152
	$CH_3CF_2CHClCH_3$	104, 107		72–3		1.363	1.128(25)	20	189
		203		72.32	−92.1	1.3631	1.1259	20	152
	$CF_2Cl(CH_2)_2CH_3$	109	15	56.03	−119.39	1.3462	1.0752	20	153,165
		211		55.5		1.3476		25	321
	$CH_2ClCF_2C_2H_5$	203		82.72	−78.96	1.3685	1.1553	20	152

TABLE 1 (*continued*)

Empirical Formula	Structural Formula	Method	Yield %	B.p. °C/mm.	F.p. or M.p. °C	n_D^t	d_4^t	t°C	Ref.
$C_4H_7Cl_2F$	$CFCl_2(CH_2)_2CH_3$	109	33	95.3	−111.4	1.4007	1.1578	20	153
	$CFCl_2CH(CH_3)_2$	202	35	105–9		1.4558		20	165
	$CH_3CFClCHClCH_3$	104, 107		106–9		1.417	1.197	25	189
		203		108/745		1.4163	1.198	26	212
	$CH_3CFClCH_2CH_2Cl$	203		123/745		1.4220	1.227	26	212
$C_4H_7F_3$	$CF_3(CH_2)_2CH_3$	109	96–99	16.74	−114.79	1.2921	1.0144(0)	10	153
		211		18					132
C_4H_8BrF	$F(CH_2)_4Br$	101	19.6	134.2		1.4443	1.4372	25	184
C_4H_8ClF	$F(CH_2)_4Cl$	101	36.6	114.7		1.4023	1.0627 (25)	23	183,184
	$CH_3CFClC_2H_5$	202		67.7	−110	1.3782	0.9982	20	165
		203		67.65	−110.06	1.3782	0.9982	20	152
	$(CH_3)_2CHCHClF$	202		82.5	−69.3	1.3891	1.0324	20	165
$C_4H_8F_2$	$F(CH_2)_4F$	101		77.8		1.3433	0.9767	25	123
	$CH_3CF_2C_2H_5$	107		30.8		1.3182	0.9164 (10)	20	172
		109	51.3	30.92	−117.53	1.3138	0.9159	20	152
		109, 110	67	31	−114	1.3189	0.9170	10	267,269
		202		30.92	−117.3	1.3192	0.9159	10	164
		202	46	30.4–0.6/747	−116.9	1.333	0.9016	20	95
$C_4H_8F_2$		212		30		1.321	0.911(10)	20	19
				32		1.318	0.89(10)	20	292
C_4H_9F	$CH_3(CH_2)_3F$	101		32.5/755					60
		104		31.95–1.98/745		1.3419	0.7761 (20)	15	70
	$(CH_3)_2CHCH_2F$	102							241
	$CH_3CHFC_2H_5$	104		25.25–5.27/765		1.3366	0.7700(5)	12	70
		207	61						245
		212							17

C_4H_9F				25.1	−121.4	1.3299	0.7559	25.1	96
	$(CH_3)_3CF$			12.1	−77	1.3241	0.7535	12.1	96
		101				1.3320		1.5	60
$C_5BrCl_5F_6$	$CFClBrCF_2CFClCF_2CCl_3$	205	24	93–94.5/6		1.4350	2.0096	20	166
C_5BrF_{11}	$CF_3(CF_2)_4Br$	203		74–5					125
		204		73.9		1.2920	1.8522 (27.8)	28.4	105
		207		73.9		1.3042	1.9324	0	249
		207	91	74.5					117
C_5ClF_{11}	$CF_3(CF_2)_4Cl$	204		59.5		1.2736	1.6540 (25.8)	25.4	105
		203		59–60			1.655	25	29,125
		207	85	60		1.280		10	117
		207		59.5		1.2845	1.7150	0	249
$C_5Cl_2F_9I$	$CF_3CF_2CFClCF_2CFClI$	205	9–50	68/32, 70/34		1.400		20	133
$C_5Cl_3F_9$	$C_2F_5CFClCF_2CFCl_2$	204	70	119		1.345		20	133
$C_5Cl_{10}F_2$	$C_2Cl_5CF_2C_2Cl_5$	201			89.6 ± .02				146
	$CCl_3(CCl_2)_2CF_2CCl_3$	203			10–15				172
$C_5F_{11}I$	$CF_3(CF_2)_4I$	207		94.4		1.3243	2.0349	27.8	105
		207		94.4		1.3389	2.1141(0)	0.5	249
		207	89	95		1.320		20	95
C_5F_{12}	$CF_3(CF_2)_3CF_3$	108	58	29.4–9.5					43
		112		30					284
				30.1	−96.5		1.664	20	44
	$(CF_3)_2CFC_2F_5$			29.3	−126.2		1.620	20	44
	$C(CF_3)_4$			28.5–9.5					75A
C_5HClF_{10}	$CF_2Cl(CF_2)_3CF_2H$	214		77		1.30	1.661	20	25,72,75,251
$C_5HCl_2F_8I$	$CF_2ClCCl(CF_3)CHFCF_2I$	205	63	67–69/45		1.4174	2.150	25	323
C_5HF_{11}	$CF_3(CF_2)_3CF_2H$	107		45			1.614	25	29
		207	80	46					196
		211		44					125
$C_5H_2Br_2F_8$	$CF_2Br(CHFCF_2)_2Br$	205	18	60–3/24.8		1.4237	1.9254	25	322
$C_5H_2ClF_8I$	$CF_3CH_2CI(CF_3)CF_2Cl$	205	69						125
$C_5H_2Cl_2F_7I$	$CF_2ClCCl(CF_3)CH_2CF_2I$	205	77	79/40		1.4308	2.098	25	323
$C_5H_2F_9I$	$(CF_3)_2CICH_2CF_3$	205	71	20–1/20					125

TABLE 1 (*continued*)

Empirical Formula	Structural Formula		Method	Yield %	B.p. °C/mm.	F.p. or M.p. °C	n_D^t	d_4^t	t °C	Ref.
$C_5H_2F_{10}$	$CF_3CF(CHF_2)CF_2CF_2H$	207		63–5					9	
$C_5H_3Br_2F_7$	$CF_3(CF_2)_2CHBrCH_2Br$	201	48	140–1		1.3874		20	260	
$C_5H_3Cl_2F_6I$	$CF_3CHICH_2CFClCF_2Cl$	205		61/18		1.4275	2.013	22	201,318	
$C_5H_4BrF_7$	$CF_3(CF_2)_2(CH_2)_2Br$	202	85	97.8/747		1.3378		20	260	
$C_5H_4Br_2F_6$	$CF_2BrCH_2CF_2CH_2CF_2Br$	205	23	54.2/14		1.4032	2.003	25	322	
$C_5H_4Cl_2F_5I$	$CF_2ClCFClCH(CH_3)CF_2I$	205	71–89	75.5/20		1.46567	1.994	25	201,318,323	
$C_5H_4F_7I$	$CF_3(CH_2CF_2)_2I$	205		125/634		1.3826	1.981	20	257	
$C_5H_5Br_2F_5$	$C_2F_5CBr(CH_3)CH_2Br$	201	43	135		1.4168	1.955	20	214	
$C_5H_5Br_2Cl_2F_3$	$CF_2BrCFClCH_2CHBrCH_2Cl$	205	45	90/6		1.1462	1.9963	27	317	
$C_5H_6Br_2ClF_3$	$CF_2BrCFClCH_2CHBrCH_3$	205	83	66/11		1.4560	1.890	27	317	
$C_5H_6Br_2F_4$	$CF_2BrCH_2CHFCH_2CHFBr$	205	10	71.5/38		1.4560	1.8259	25	322	
$C_5H_7Br_2F_3$	$CF_2BrCH(CH_3)CFBrCH_3$	205	75	65/29.5		1.4469	1.8414	25	322	
$C_5H_7Cl_2F_3$	$(CH_3)_2CHCFClCF_2Cl$	206		26–6.2/30		1.3870	1.3004	25	12	
$C_5H_7Cl_3F_2$	$(CH_3)_2CHCCl_2CF_2Cl$	206		66–8/30		1.4078			12	
	$CF_2ClCH_2CCl(CH_3)CH_2Cl$	203		48–8.5/10		1.4311	1.3843	25	316	
$C_5H_8BrClF_2$	$(CH_3)_2CBrCH_2CF_2Cl$	205	22	69/86		1.4281	1.4960	25	321	
	$CF_2ClCH(CH_3)CHBrCH_3$	205		140–1/736		1.4299	1.508	25	66	
		205		62/49		1.4321	1.5322	25	321	
$C_5H_8Br_2F_2$	$CF_2BrCH(CH_3)CHBrCH_3$	205		77–9/50		1.4588	1.786(24)	20	66	
		205	75	72/39		1.4621	1.7730	25	320	
	$CF_2BrCH_2CBr(CH_3)CH_3$	205	64	79/66		1.4632	1.750	25	320	
$C_5H_8ClF_3$	$CF_3(CH_2)_4Cl$	107		121		1.3691	1.217	27	149	
	$CF_3CH_2CCl(CH_3)_2$	109		81–1.2		1.3548	1.1518	25	273	
$C_5H_8Cl_2F_2$	$CF_2ClCH_2CH(CH_3)CH_2Cl$	203		73–6/90		1.4055	1.237	25	273	
	$C_2H_5CF_2CHClCH_2Cl$	203		146.7 ± 0.1		1.4140	1.2840	20	146	
	$(CH_3)_2CClCH_2CF_2Cl$	203		56–9/90		1.3993	1.316	25	316	
	$CH_2ClCH_2CF_2(CH_2)_2Cl$	203		176.3 ± 0.1	−24.9 ± 0.2	1.4261	1.3179	20	146	
	$CH_2ClCH_2CF_2CHClCH_3$	203		154.8		1.4179	1.2899	20	146	
$C_5H_8F_3I$	$CF_3(CH_2)_3CH_2I$	205		153		1.439			110	
	$CF_3(CH_2)_2CHICH_3$	216		137		1.4335		25	216	
	$CF_3CH(CH_3)CH_2CH_2I$	216	32	143		1.4362		30	332	
$C_5H_8F_4$	$(CH_2F)_4C$	101	57–60	110–10.2	92				97	

$C_5H_9ClF_2$	$CF_2ClCH(CH_3)C_2H_5$	211	30	74.5–5.0		1.3636	1.0487	25	321
	$CF_2ClCH_2CH(CH_3)_2$	211	65	74.5–5.5		1.3665	1.064	25	321
		109	60.3	77		1.3598	1.039	25	316
	$C_2H_5CF_2(CH_2)_2Cl$	203		117.9 ± 0.2		1.3859	1.1278	20	146
	$C_2H_5CF_2CHClCH_3$	203		99.4 ± 0.1		1.3788	1.1085	20	146
$C_5H_9Cl_2F$	$CFCl_2CH_2CH(CH_3)_2$	202		112–13		1.4158	1.101	25	316
$C_5H_9F_3$	$CF_3(CH_2)_3CH_3$	205	26	47					110
	$CF_3CH_2CH(CH_3)_2$	109	2.3	37–8		1.3226	0.9788	25	316
$C_5H_{10}BrF$	$CH_2F(CH_2)_3CH_2Br$	101	31.4	162		1.4405	1.3604	25	184
$C_5H_{10}ClF$	$CH_2F(CH_2)_3CH_2Cl$	101	38.5	143.2		1.4120	1.0325	25	183,184
$C_5H_{10}F_2$	$CH_2F(CH_2)_3CH_2F$	101		105.5		1.3618	0.9572	25	183
	$CH_3CF_2(CH_2)_2CH_3$	107		59.8		1.3357	0.8958	20	172
		109, 110	64	60.1	−98.1	1.3360	0.8987	20	267
		202	84	59.7	−93	1.3350	0.8932	20	164,181
	$C_2H_5CF_2C_2H_5$	109, 110	54	60.8	−94	1.3390	0.9106	20	267,269
		202		60.2	−94	1.3370	0.9023		164
$C_5H_{11}F$	$CH_3(CH_2)_3CH_2F$	101		64.2		1.3590		20	60
		101		64.4		1.3569	0.7852	25	184
		104		62.8	<−80		0.7880	20	309
	$CH_3CHFCH_2C_2H_5$			48–50/756					31
		101		56.2/756		1.3578		20	60
	$(CH_3)_2CHCH_2CH_2F$	102					0.69415	19.6	329
		102		53.5					309
		101		56.2/756		1.3547		20	60
	$(CH_3)_3CCH_2F$	101		44.8	−121.1	1.3481		20	60,96
C_6BrF_{13}	$CF_3(CF_2)_4CF_2Br$	203		100–1					125
		207	90	100					117
		207		90–2/735		1.3205			39
C_6ClF_{13}	$CF_3(CF_2)_4CF_2Cl$	107, 203					1.705	25	29
		203		85–6					125
		207		86		1.287		15	117
$C_6Cl_2F_{12}$	$(C_2F_5CFCl—)_2$	209	11–68	110–12		1.324		20	133
		205		50/200					133

TABLE 1 (*continued*)

Empirical Formula	Structural Formula	Method	Yield %	B.p. °C/mm.	F.p. or M.p. °C	n_D^t	d_4^t	t °C	Ref.
$C_6Cl_2F_{12}$	$(CF_3)_2CClCCl(CF_3)_2$	109	60						236
	$(CF_3CClFCF_2—)_2$	215							235
	$CF_2Cl(CF_2)_4CF_2Cl$			114–15					29
$C_6Cl_3F_{11}$	$CF_3(CF_2)_4CCl_3$	217	51–63	143		1.3383		25	327
$C_6Cl_4F_9I$	$CF_2ClCFClCF_2CFClCF_2$-$CFClI$	205	14	140–42/30					127
$C_6Cl_6F_8$	$(CF_2ClCFClCFCl—)_2$	107		119.5–20.5/26		1.4240		25	275
$C_6Cl_8F_6$	$(CCl_3CF_2CFCl—)_2$	205, 209	81.5		40				158
	$(CFCl_2CFClCFCl—)_2$	201		132–4.5/5		1.4738	1.1918	25	275
$C_6F_{13}I$	$CF_3(CF_2)_4CF_2I$	207		109–12/736		1.3540			39
		207	90	117		1.322		20	117
C_6F_{14}	$(CF_3CF_2CF_2—)_2$	107		58	<−74		1.68	25	29
		112		60	−4				284
		207	81–84.5	56		1.2514		22	104,129,192
		209	15–77	57					137,145
$C_6HBrCl_3F_9$	$CF_2BrCFClCF_2CFClCF_2$-$CFClH$	202	0.5	140/100		1.405		20	135
C_6HBrF_{12}	$CF_2Br(CF_2)_4CF_2H$	202	0.5						135
C_6HClF_{12}	$CF_2Cl(CF_2)_4CF_2H$	206	58	209–11/22		1.5072		25	3
		214		100–1		1.3012	1.719(20)	5	25,72,79,213
C_6HF_{13}	$CF_3(CF_2)_4CF_2H$	107		71–2			1.684	25	29
		211		69–70					125
$C_6H_2Br_2ClF_9$	$CF_2BrCFCl(CHFCF_2)_2Br$	205		79.5/15		1.3943	2.007	25	318
$C_6H_2ClF_{11}$	$CF_3(CF_2)_4CH_2Cl$	208	78	103.6		1.2293	1.651	25	326
$C_6H_2F_{11}I$	$CF_3(CF_2)_4CH_2I$	208	87	133		1.3500	2.018	25	326
$C_6H_4Br_2ClF_7$	$CF_2BrCFCl(CH_2CF_2)_2Br$	205	23.4	90–1/20		1.4112	2.014	27	318
$C_6H_5Br_2F_7$	$CF_3CF_2CF_2(CHBr)_2CH_3$	201	47.3	97.2/64		1.4009		20	261
$C_6H_5Cl_2F_6I$	$CF_2ClCFClCH_2CI(CF_3)CH_3$	205	87	65.5/12		1.4418		22	318
$C_6H_6Br_2ClF_5$	$CF_2BrCFCl(CH_2CHF)_2Br$	205	6.4	104.5/15		1.4428	1.946	27	318
$C_6H_6ClF_6I$	$CF_2ClCF(CF_3)CH_2CHICH_3$	205		54/15		1.4242	1.846	25	323

$C_6H_8Br_2ClF_3$	$CF_2BrCFClCH(CH_3)$-$CHBrCH_3$	205	35	49/2.5		1.4592	1.8180	24	317
	$CF_2BrCFClCH_2CBr(CH_3)_2$	205	43	43–5/2		1.4590	1.8003	25	317
$C_6H_9Cl_2F_3$	$(CH_3)_3CCFClCF_2Cl$	206	5–10	55–7/50		1.4020		25	12
$C_6H_9Cl_3F_2$	$(CH_3)_3CCCl_2CF_2Cl$	206		77–80/25		1.4405		25	12
$C_6H_{10}F_4$	$CF_2HCF_2(CH_2)_3CH_3$	205		83–4.5		1.3354	1.1110	25	16
	$(CH_3)_3CCF_2CF_2H$	206		82.7–85					16
$C_6H_{12}F_2$	$CFH_2(CH_2)_4CFH_2$	101		129.9		1.3739	0.9407	25	183
	$C_2H_5(CHF)_2C_2H_5$	202	76	86/742		1.3546	0.9020	20	95
	$CH_3CF_2(CH_2)_3CH_3$	202		87.4	−82.5	1.3526	0.8922	20	164
		202	85	86–6.2/750		1.3535	0.8923	20	95,181
				116		1.373	0.89	20	292
	$CH_3CF_2CH_2CH(CH_3)_2$	109, 110	70.5	78.2	−112.7	1.3515	0.8823	20	267,269
$C_6H_{13}F$	$CH_3(CH_2)_4CH_2F$	101	20	92.5–3.0					98
		104	50	91.15/755		1.3740	0.8002	20	70
	$CH_3CHF(CH_2)_3CH_3$	102, 104		82–6					259
				69–72/759					31
	$CH_2FCH_2C(CH_3)_3$	206		75–7		1.3732	0.782	20	175,282
C_7BrF_{15}	$CF_3(CF_2)_5CF_2Br$	207	31	118–18.5		1.3010			198
		207	86	123–4					117
		203		109–10					125
		203		112–13			1.746	25	29
		207	80	109		1.2592		15	117
$C_7Cl_3F_{12}I$	$C_2F_5(CFClCF_2)_2CFClI$	205	15	72/17					133
$C_7F_{15}I$	$CF_3(CF_2)_5CF_2I$	205	85	137–8		1.323		30	117
	$CF_3(CF_2)_4CFICF_3$	205	51	135–9					123
C_7F_{16}	$CF_3(CF_2)_5CF_3$	107	83–4						29
		108	68	81–82	−80	1.267	1.741	25	83,112,124
		112	62	82		1.272	1.69(20)	26	48,242
				82.51 ± 0.05	−51.29				251
				82.47		1.2617	1.7333	20	84
				82		1.265	1.69(20)	21	292
C_7HClF_{14}	$CF_2Cl(CF_2)_5CF_2H$	213		123		1.3070	1.738	20	25,72
		214		123		1.3070	1.730(20)	5	75

TABLE 1 (*continued*)

Empirical Formula	Structural Formula	Method	Yield %	B.p. °C/mm.	F.p. or M.p. °C	n_D^t	d_4^t	t °C	Ref.
				122.5		1.3070	1.738(20)	5	254
C_7HF_{15}	$CF_3(CF_2)_5CF_2H$	107		96.7			1.725	25	29
		207	60	94		1.2690		25	196
		211		96					125
$C_7H_6F_9I$	$CF_3(CH_2CF_2)_3I$	205		180/634		1.3869	1.931	20	257
	$CF_3CHICH_2CH(CF_3)$-CH_2CF_3	205	5–11	76–8/25					116
$C_7H_7Br_2F_7$	$CF_3(CF_2)_2CHBrCBr(CH_3)_2$	201	33	84/27		1.4019	1.974	20	218
	$CF_3(CF_2)_2CHBrCHBrC_2H_5$	201	59	85/30		1.4052	1.875	20	218
$C_7H_{14}F_2$	$CH_3CF_2(CH_2)_4CH_3$	202		112.7	−62.2	1.3653	0.8855	20	95,164
	$CH_3(CH_2)_5CF_2H$	107	80	119.7	−82	1.37098	0.8959	20	169,172
$C_7H_{15}F$	$CH_3(CH_2)_5CFH_2$	104		119/755	−73	1.3855	0.8079 (20)	21.5	309
		206		109–11		1.3810	0.791	20	202
		208	24.7–55.1	119.2/750		1.3860		20	78
C_8ClF_{17}	$CF_2Cl(CF_2)_6CF_3$	203		132–53			1.778	25	29
$C_8Cl_5F_{12}I$	$CF_2ClCFCl(CF_2CFCl)_3I$	205	17	135–40/0.1		1.425			127
$C_8Cl_6F_{12}$	$CF_2Cl(CFClCF_2)_3CFCl_2$	205	9	145–47/20		1.408		22	127
	$(CF_2ClCFClCF_2CFCl—)_2$	209	81	142–44/20		1.408		22	128
C_8F_{18}	$CF_3(CF_2)_6CF_3$	107		107					29
		112		104		1.282	1.73	20	242,292
C_8HClF_{16}	$CF_2Cl(CF_2)_6CF_2H$	214		143		1.3088	1.778(20)	5	25,72,75,254
C_8HF_{17}	$CF_3(CF_2)_6CF_2H$	211		69–70/149					125
$C_8H_2Cl_4F_{12}$	$(CF_3)_2CHCCl_2CCl_2CH$-$(CF_3)_2$	203		118					175
$C_8H_{10}F_8$	$CH_3(CH_2)_3(CF_2)_4H$	205		128–31		1.3300	1.3271	25	16
	$(CH_3)_3C(CF_2)_4H$	206		120–33					16
$C_8H_{16}F_2$	$CH_3CF_2(CH_2)_5CH_3$	109, 110	58.9	136.3–6.6	−50.0	1.3766	0.8867	20	267,269
	$CH_3(CH_2)_2CF_2(CH_2)_3CH_3$	202		137.2	−45.9	1.3780	0.8919	20	164
$C_8H_{17}F$	$CH_3(CH_2)_6CH_2F$	102		130–4			0.798	0	259
		104		142.5/750			0.8036	21	209

$C_8H_{17}F$		211		69–70/149					125
	$CH_3CHF(CH_2)_5CH_3$	104		139.3					209
C_9ClF_{19}	$CF_3(CF_2)_7CF_2Cl$	203		150–1			1.805	25	29
$C_9Cl_4F_{15}I$	$CF_3(CF_2CFCl)_4I$	205	26	110/10					133
$C_9F_{19}I$	$CF_3(CF_2)_7CF_2I$	205		83–7/45					125
C_9F_{20}	$CF_3(CF_2)_7CF_3$	107		127			1.78	25	29
		108		125.3	−16	1.276	1.799	25	112
		112		122.5–3.5		1.283	1.80	20	242,292
C_9HClF_{18}	$CF_2H(CF_2)_7CF_2Cl$	214		162–3			1.81	25	75,254
C_9HF_{19}	$CF_2H(CF_2)_7CF_3$	107		138–9			1.795	25	29
$C_9H_{10}Br_4F_6$	$CH_2BrCBr(CH_3)(CF_2)_3$- $CBr(CH_3)CH_2Br$	201	56	131/1	32				218
$C_9H_{10}Cl_4F_6$	$CH_2ClCCl(CH_3)(CF_2)_3$- $CCl(CH_3)CH_2Cl$	201	56	104/1		1.4403	1.575	20	218
$C_9H_{16}Br_2F_2$	$CF_2BrCH_2CHBr(CH_2)_5CH_3$	205	55	76/1		1.4591	1.4715	25	320
$C_9H_{16}F_4$	$CH_3CF_2(CH_2)_5CF_2CH_3$	202		82/20	−2.3	1.3712	1.0507	20	164
$C_9H_{17}ClF_2$	$CH_2Cl(CH_2)_2CF_2(CH_2)_4CH_3$	202		87–92/11		1.4732		20	248
	$CH_2Cl(CH_2)_3CF_2(CH_2)_3CH_3$	202		92–97/11		1.4235		20	248
$C_{10}ClF_{21}$	$CF_2Cl(CF_2)_8CF_3$	203		169–71					29
$C_{10}Cl_6F_{15}I$	$CF_2ClCFCl(CF_2CFCl)_4I$	205		185–90/0.1		1.432		20	127
$C_{10}Cl_6F_{16}$	$(CF_2ClCF_2CFClCF_2$- $CFCl—)_2$	107	50.0	125–30/6		1.3914	1.9248	20	166
$C_{10}Cl_7F_{15}$	$CF_2Cl(CF_2CFCl)_4CFCl_2$	205	8	135–39/0.1		1.413		22	127
$C_{10}Cl_8F_{14}$	$(CFCl_2CF_2CFClCF_2$- $CFCl—)_2$	107	76.2	168–74/6		1.4239	1.9361	20	166
$C_{10}Cl_{10}F_{12}$	$(CCl_3CF_2CFClCF_2$- $CFCl—)_2$	209	80		94.5–95				166
$C_{10}F_{21}I$	$CF_3(CF_2)_8CF_2I$	205		102–6/45					125
$C_{10}F_{22}$	$CF_3(CF_2)_8CF_3$	107		150					29
		108		144.2	36	1.271	1.770	45	112
$C_{10}HClF_{20}$	$CF_2Cl(CF_2)_8CF_2H$	205		177–8	46				75,254
$C_{10}HF_{21}$	$CF_2H(CF_2)_8CF_3$	107		159–60	31–2				29
$C_{10}H_9F_{12}I$	$CF_3CHICH_2CH(CF_3)$- $CH_2CH(CF_3)CH_2CF_3$	205	4	90/5					116
$C_{10}H_{10}Br_4F_8$	$CH_2BrCBr(CH_3)(CF_2)_4CBr$- $(CH_3)CH_2Br$	201			70				218

TABLE 1 (*continued*)

Empirical Formula	Structural Formula	Method	Yield %	B.p. °C/mm.	F.p. or M.p. °C	n_D^t	d_4^t	t °C	Ref.
$C_{10}H_{10}Cl_4F_8$	$CH_2ClCCl(CH_3)(CF_2)_4CCl$-$(CH_3)CH_2Cl$	201	63	125/1	30				218
$C_{10}H_{10}F_{12}$	$CH_3(CH_2)_3(CF_2)_5CF_2H$	205		167–80		1.3291	1.4864	25	16
$C_{10}H_{16}Br_2$-ClF_3	$CF_2BrCFClCH_2CHBr$-$(CH_2)_5CH_3$	205	34	84/0.3		1.4612	1.5580	24	217
$C_{10}H_{21}F$	$CH_3(CH_2)_8CH_2F$	104		183.5			0.792	10.5	309
$C_{11}F_{24}$	$CF_3(CF_2)_9CF_3$			160.8	57.8	1.268	1.745	70	112
$C_{11}HClF_{22}$	$CF_2H(CF_2)_9CF_2Cl$	214		191	52				75,254
$C_{11}H_{23}F$	$CH_3(CH_2)_9CH_2F$	205		115–20/43					125
		101	18	89–91/12					98
$C_{12}ClF_{25}$	$CF_2Cl(CF_2)_{10}CF_3$	203							29
$C_{12}Cl_7F_{18}I$	$CF_2Cl(CFClCF_2)_5CFClI$	205		200–08/0.01		1.428		20	127
$C_{12}Cl_8F_{18}$	$CF_2Cl(CFClCF_2)_5CFCl_2$	205	12	190–5/0.1					127
$C_{12}Cl_8F_{18}$	$[CF_2ClCFCl$-$(CF_2CFCl)_2—]_2$	209	74	195–200/0.1					128
$C_{12}F_{25}I$	$CF_3(CF_2)_{10}CF_2I$			108–10/18					125
$C_{12}HClF_{24}$	$CF_2Cl(CF_2)_{10}CF_2H$	205		202–3	78–9				75
				202					254
		214		226					25,72
$C_{12}H_{10}F_{16}$	$CH_3(CH_2)_3(CF_2)_8H$	205		78–82/8		1.3288	1.5715	25	16
$C_{13}F_{27}I$	$CF_3(CF_2)_{11}CF_2I$	205		102–4/10					125
$C_{13}F_{28}$	$CF_3(CF_2)_{11}CF_3$	107		193–6	70.1				29
$C_{13}HClF_{26}$	$CF_2Cl(CF_2)_{11}CF_2H$	214		213–14	86–7				75,254
$C_{13}HF_{27}$	$CF_3(CF_2)_{11}CF_2H$	107		202–4	72–3				29
$C_{14}Cl_8F_{21}I$	$CF_2Cl(CFClCF_2)_6CFClI$	205	12	230–40/.001					127
$C_{14}Cl_9F_{21}$	$CF_2Cl(CFClCF_2)_6CFCl_2$	205	14	235–40/0.1–0.01					127

$C_{14}F_{29}I$	$CF_3(CF_2)_{12}CF_2I$	205		93–7/5					125
$C_{14}HClF_{28}$	$CF_2Cl(CF_2)_{12}CF_2H$	205		226–8	94.5				75,254
$C_{14}H_{10}F_{20}$	$CH_3(CH_2)_3(CF_2)_{10}H$	205		100.5/116		1.3292	1.6366	25	16
$C_{15}F_{31}I$	$CF_3(CF_2)_{12}CF_2I$	205		99–105/3					125
$C_{16}Cl_{10}F_{24}$	$Cl(CF_2CFCl)_8Cl$		10						110
$C_{16}F_{33}I$	$CF_3(CF_2)_{14}CF_2I$	205		87–94/0.5					125
$C_{16}H_{33}F$	$CH_3(CH_2)_{14}CH_2F$	104		287.5, 181/24			0.809	17.5	209
$C_{16}F_{34}$	$CF_3(CF_2)_{14}CF_3$	108		238–40					43

TABLE 2 CYCLIC ALKANES

Empirical Formula	Structural Formula	Method	Yield %	B.p. °C/mm.	F.p. or M.p. °C	n_D^t	d_4^t	t °C	Ref.
C_3F_6	$CF_2CF_2CF_2$	209							100
		210		−31					100
		214		−28					214
$C_4Br_2F_6$	$CFBrCFBrCF_2CF_2$	201	52	96–7		1.389	2.191	20	45, 100
C_4ClF_7	$CF_2CF_2CF_2CFCl$	210	34						13
$C_4Cl_2F_6$	$CF_2CFClCF_2CFCl$	210	20–59	59.5–6.0		1.336		14	45
		210		56	−17				281
		210		58–9		1.339	1.6462	20	100
		210		58–9					101
		210	80	58.97	−24	1.3340	1.6441	20	173
$C_4Cl_3F_5$	$CF_2CF_2CClFCCl_2$	210		94–5	31.5–3.5				194
$C_4Cl_4F_4$	$CF_2CF_2CCl_2CCl_2$	210	92	131.6/762	84.8				173
		210	90	131	82				281
	$CF_2CCl_2CF_2CCl_2$	210		128–9	81				100
	$CFClCFClCFClCFCl$	201	95	129	45–6				131
C_4F_7I	$CF_2CF_2CF_2CFI$	201		63					286

C_4F_8	$CF_2CF_2CF_2CF_2$	112		18.4	−83		1.72	0	247
		210		−5	−48				100
		210		−5.5	−40				1
		214		−5					19,72,75
		214	17						30
C_4HBrF_6	$CHFCF_2CF_2CFBr$	202		55.94/632.3		1.3402	1.8504	25	258
$C_4HBr_2F_5$	$CF_2CF_2CHBrCFBr$	201		107–9					47
$C_4HCl_3F_4$	$CF_2CF_2CCl_2CHCl$	210	18	109–10.5		1.3995	1.5720	25	62
$C_4H_2Cl_2F_4$	$CF_2CF_2CH_2CCl_2$	210		84–5					14
		210	46	84–4.7		1.3702	1.5298	25	62
$C_4H_2F_6$	$CF_2CF_2CHFCHF$	211		26.6–7.0					47
$C_4H_3ClF_4$	$CF_2CF_2CHClCH_2$	210	23	73–4		1.3462	1.4251	25	14,62
$C_4H_4F_4$	$CF_2CF_2CH_2CH_2$	210	40	50–0.7		1.3046	1.2752	25	14,62,74
		214	50						74
$C_5Cl_4F_6$	$CCl_2CCl_2CF_2CF_2CF_2$	201			151–3 (Sub.)				180
C_5F_{10}	$CF_2CF_2CF_2CF_2CF_2$	108	28–29	23.5–3.7					43,83
$C_5H_5ClF_4$	$CF_2CF_2CH_2CHCH_2Cl$	210	42	115–16		1.3745	1.3971	25	62

TABLE 2 (*continued*)

Empirical Formula	Structural Formula	Method	Yield %	B.p. °C/mm.	F.p. or M.p. °C	n_D^t	d_4^t	t °C	Ref.
$C_5H_6F_4$	$CF_2CF_2CH_2CHCH_3$	210	72	68.5–8.8		1.3191	1.1961	25	14,62
$C_5H_8F_2$	$CF_2C(CH_3)_2CH_2$	209	27	41.5–2.1		1.3455	0.891	25	332
	$CF_2CH(CH_3)CH(CH_3)$	211	39	55–6		1.3521	0.926	25	332
C_5H_9F	$CH_2(CH_2)_3CHF$	207	39	51–2/300		1.3919		25	246
C_6BrF_{11}	$CF_2(CF_2)_4CFBr$	207		90–0.8					198
$C_6Br_2F_{10}$	$CFBrCFBr(CF_2)_3CF_2$	203	31	139–40.5	31–2.5	1.367		45	324
$C_6Br_4F_8$	$CF_2(CFBr)_2CF_2CFBrCFBr$	201		99/20	40–2				82
	$CF_2(CFBr)_4CF_2$	201		105/20	42–3				82
C_6ClF_{11}	$CFCl(CF_2)_4CF_2$	108	13		30–1	1.301		40	324
$C_6Cl_2F_{10}$	$CFCl(CF_2)_4CFCl$	108	16						324
$C_6Cl_2F_{10}$		201	56	108	34				272,324
$C_6Cl_4F_8$	$CF_2(CFCl)_4CF_2$	201		49–50/20	59–60				82

$C_6F_{11}I$	$CFI(CF_2)_4CF_2$	201		112					286
C_6F_{12}	$CF_2(CF_2)_4CF_2$	108		52		1.2685	1.684(20)	30	292,324
		112		50	48–9				87
	$CF_3CF_2(CF_2)_3CF_2$	108	77	76.33		1.2816	1.7996	20	43,83,84
$C_6HBr_2F_9$	$CHBr(CF_2)_4CFBr$	201		147/150		1.394		6	272
C_6HF_{11}	$CFH(CF_2)_4CF_2$	211		63–3.5/757	46–8	1.275		50	324
		112		62	41–3				87
$C_6H_2F_{10}$	$CFH(CF_2)_4CFH$	211		91–2/753	−16	1.291		50	272
	$CFHCF_2CFH(CF_2)_2CF_2$	108		78–9	34–6	1.286		46	272
$C_6H_7ClF_4$	$CH_3C(CH_2Cl)CH_2CF_2CF_2$	210	45	122–4		1.3846	1.3161	25	14,62
$C_6H_7F_5$	$CF_2CF_2CH_2CFC_2H_5$	210		89–90		1.3295	1.2570	25	62
$C_6H_8F_4$	$CF_2CF_2CH_2CHC_2H_5$	212		90–1		1.3370	1.1506	25	14,15, 17,62
	$CF_2CF_2CH_2C(CH_3)_2$	210	30	82–3		1.3395	1.1446	25	14,62
	$CF_2CF_2CH(CH_3)CHCH_3$	210	5	87–7.5					14,62

TABLE 2 (*continued*)

Empirical Formula	Structural Formula	Method	Yield %	B.p. °C/mm.	F.p. or M.p. °C	n_D^t	d_4^t	t °C	Ref.
$C_6H_{11}F$	$\overline{CH_2(CH_2)_4CHF}$	202	70	60–3/200	12–13	1.4130		25	221
		202	80	71.2/300	13	1.4147		20	94
		202		43.2/100		1.4149		20	60
		207	36–58	73–4/300		1.4145		25	245,246
		104	30	100.2		1.4146	0.9296	20	315
C_7BrF_{13}	$\overline{CFBr(CF_2)_4CF}CF_3$	204		115.2–16.1					9
$C_7Br_2F_{12}$	$\overline{CFBrCFBr(CF_2)_3CF}CF_3$	201		156–9					9
C_7ClF_{13}	$\overline{CFCl(CF_2)_4CF}_2CF_3$	108		101.7–3.1		1.314		18	9
		204		100.7–1.7		1.315		14	9
$C_7Cl_2F_{12}$	$\overline{CFClCFCl(CF_2)_3CF}CF_3$	201		129–31					9
C_7F_{12}	CF_2—CF—CF_2 | | | | CF_2 | | | | CF_2—CF—CF_2	102		70/746		1.283(20)	1.767	30	180
C_7F_{14}	$\overline{CF_2(CF_2)_4CF}CF_3$	108	38	71.5–1.8		1.2765	1.7760	20	43
		108		75.5–5.8		1.285		17	9
		112		76.2	−38	1.276	1.784	25	139,289
	$\overline{CF_2(CF_2)_3CF}C_2F_5$			75.05		1.2772	1.7707	20	84

		108		72.5–4.0		1.276	1.7555	20	293
	$CF_2(CF_2)_3C(CF_3)_2$			71.67		1.2705	1.7660	20	84
C_7HF_{13}	$CFH(CF_2)_4CFCF_3$	211		86.6–8.0					9
		214		85.1–6.3					9
$C_7H_4F_8$	$CF_2CF_2CH_2CCH_2CF_2CF_2$	210		107–9		1.3325	1.5137	25	62
$C_7H_4F_{10}$	$CH_2(CF_2)_2CH_2CF_2CFCF_3$	112		64.5/162		1.3225		25	88
$C_7H_6Br_2F_6$	$CF_3CFCF_2CH_2(CHBr)_2CH_2$	201	91	89/10		1.4343		20	215
$C_7H_9Br_2F_3$	$CF_3CHCH_2(CHBr)_2CH_2CH_2$	201	97	91/10		1.4871		20	215
$C_7H_7F_7$	$CF_3CFCHFCH_2(CHF)_2CH_2$	112		55/162		1.3399		25	88
$C_7H_{10}F_4$	$(C_2H_5)(CH_3)CCH_2CF_2CF_2$	212		107.8		1.3529	1.1285	25	62
$C_7H_{10}F_4$	$CH_3(CH_2)_2CHCH_2CF_2CF_2$	212		113		1.3516	1.1190	25	62
$C_7H_{11}F_3$	$CF_3CH(CH_2)_4CH_2$			105.8		1.3739	1.0766	25	270
		212		107.05/761	<−78	1.37945	1.0870	15	308
C_8F_{16}	$C_2F_5CF(CF_2)_4CF_2$	102		99–9.8/748					217
		112		101.5	−60	1.283	1.826	25	139

TABLE 2 (*continued*)

Empirical Formula	Structural Formula	Method	Yield %	B.p. °C/mm.	F.p. or M.p. °C	n_D^t	d_4^t	t °C	Ref.
	$CF_3CFCF(CF_3)(CF_2)_3CF_2$	108 112	42	102.1–2.4 101.5	 −56	1.2923 1.283	1.8672 1.829	20 25	43 139
	$CF_3CFCF_2CF(CF_3)(CF_2)_2CF_2$	108	50	101.7–1.9		1.2908	1.8560	20	43
	$CF_3CF(CF_2)_2CF(CF_3)CF_2CF_2$	108 112	42	100.5–0.6 101		1.2897	1.8503	20	43 88
	$CF_2(CF_2)_6CF_2$	112		101.5	−5 to −6	1.283	1.829	25	138,247
$C_8H_5F_{11}$	$CF_3CF(CHF)_2CF(CF_3)CHFCH_2$	112		72/70.5		1.3309		25	88
$C_8H_6Br_2F_6$	CHBr—CH—CF—CF_3 CH_2 CHBr—CH—CF_2	201	89	92–3/10		1.4580		20	215
$C_8H_6F_8$	$CF_2CF_2CH_2CH$—$CHCH_2CF_2CF_2$	210	11	150–8	49–50				62
$C_8H_8F_8$	$CF_3CHCF_2CH_2CH(CF_3)CH_2CH_2$	112		128		1.3485		25	88
$C_8H_9Br_2F_3$	CHBr—CH—CF—CF_3 CH_2 CHBr—CH—CH_2	201	85	119/10		1.5013		20	215

$C_8H_9Br_2F_5$	$C_2F_5CH(CH_2)_2(CHBr)_2CH_2$	201	84	91/10		1.4606		20	215
$C_8H_{11}Br_2F$	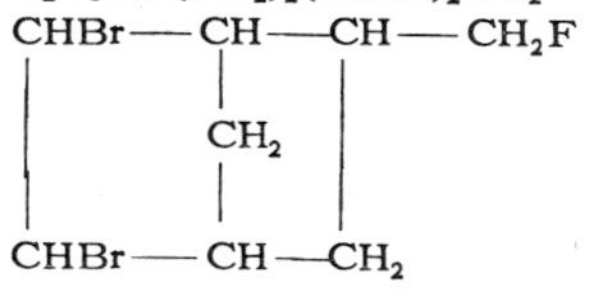	201	52	121–3/3		1.5524		20	215
$C_8H_{11}Br_2F_3$	$(CF_3)(CH_3)C(CH_2)_2(CHBr)_2CH_2$	201	73	110/10		1.4896		20	215
$C_8H_{12}F_4$	$CH_2(CH_2)_4CHCF_2CF_2H$	205		75–7/21		1.3625		25	16
		205		141.5–2.0		1.3841		25	18
C_9F_{16}	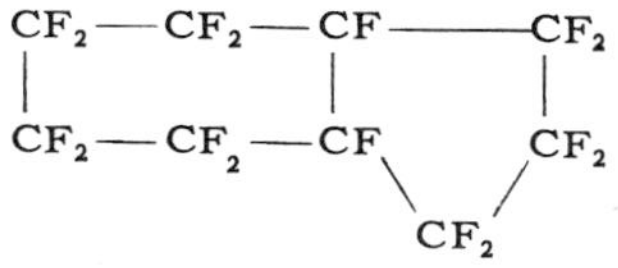	102		116–17/747	−15	1.303	1.884	20	208
C_9F_{18}	$CF_3(CF_2)_2CF(CF_2)_4CF_2$	108		123–6		1.293	1.888	25	112
	$(CF_3)_2CFCF(CF_2)_4CF_2$	102		123/751					217
	$CF_3CFCF(CF_3)CF_2CF(CF_3)CF_2CF_2$	112		124–6		1.296	1.881	25	139
	$CF_3CFCF_2CF(CF_3)CF_2CF(CF_3)CF_2$	112		124–5.5					82
		108		124.7–5.1	27	1.2995	1.9025	20	43
C_9HF_{17}	$CF_3CFCF_2CF(CF_3)CF_2CF(CF_3)CHF$	112		130		1.3040		25	88

TABLE 2 (*continued*)

Empirical Formula	Structural Formula	Method	Yield %	B.p. °C/mm.	F.p. or M.p. °C	n_D^t	d_4^t	t °C	Ref.
$C_9H_2F_{16}$	$CF_3CFCF_2CF(CF_3)CHFCF(CF_3)CHF$ (ring)	112		74.6/106		1.3113		25	88
$C_9H_9Br_2F_5$	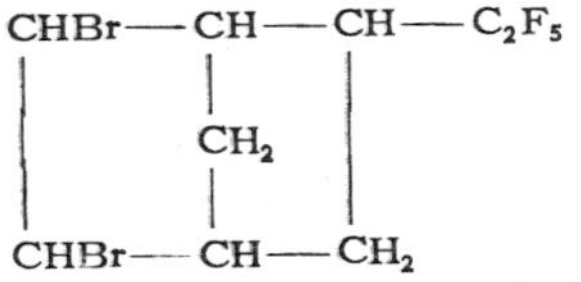	201	85	121–2/10		1.4711		20	215
$C_9H_{11}Br_2F_3$	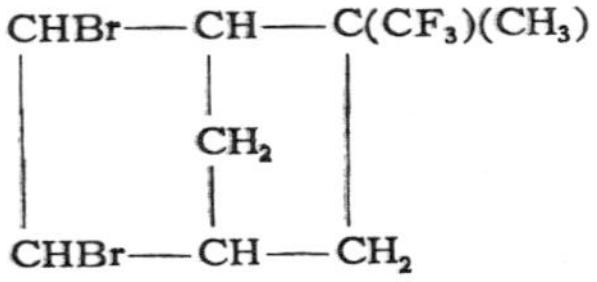	201	53	126–28/10		1.5037		20	215
$C_{10}H_{12}F_8$	$H(CF_2)_4CH(CH_2)_4CH_2$ (ring)	205		74–7/21		1.3626		25	18
$C_{10}H_{12}F_8$		205		98–106/21		1.3570		25	16
$C_{10}F_{18}$	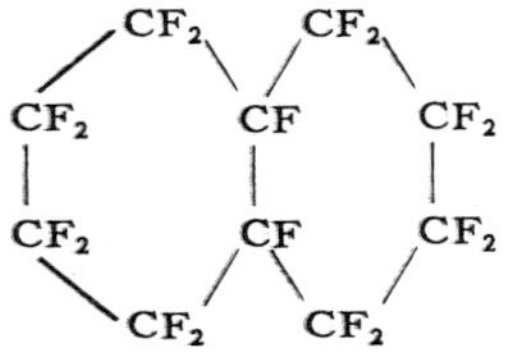	112		142	−15	1.309	1.919	25	138
				138		1.314	1.92	20	292
		102		140/750	−10	1.312	1.946	20	208

	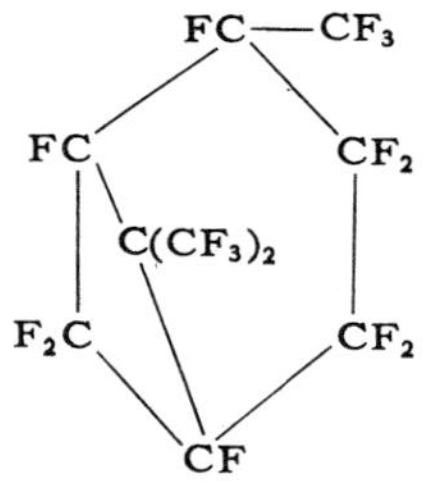	102		139/746		1.304	1.897	20	207
$C_{10}F_{20}$	$CF_3CF(CF_2)_4CFCF(CF_3)_2$	102	80	143–4/743					217
		108		144–6		1.3006		16	9
		108		146.5	−45	1.2965	1.902	25	112
$C_{11}F_{20}$	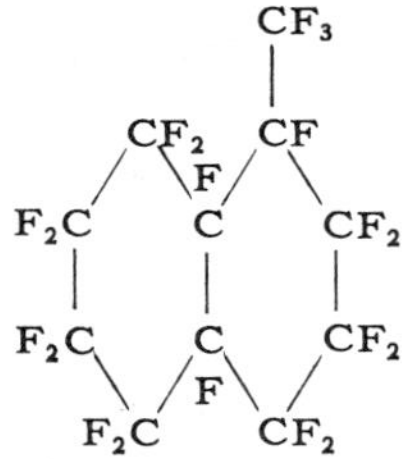	102		161/757		1.317	1.960	20	208
	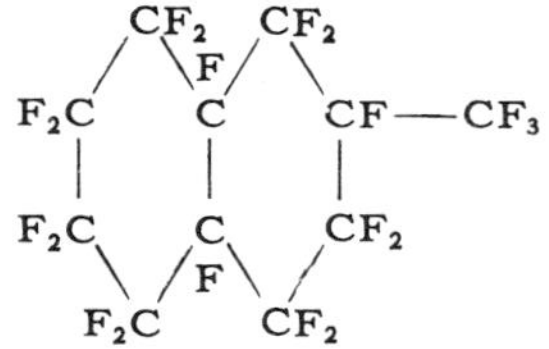	102		160–1/744		1.316	1.963	20	208
$C_{11}F_{22}$	$CF_3(CF_2)_4CF(CF_2)_4CF_2$	108		145–7		1.298	1.899	25	112

TABLE 2 (*continued*)

Empirical Formula	Structural Formula	Method	Yield %	B.p. °C/mm.	F.p. or M.p. °C	n_D^t	d_4^t	t °C	Ref.
$C_{12}F_{20}$	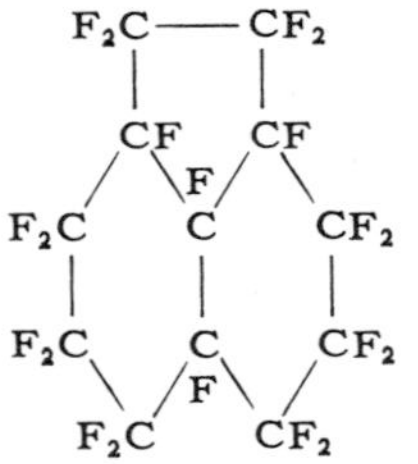	102		172.5–3.5/750		1.329	1.988	20	206
$C_{12}F_{22}$	$CF_2(CF_2)_4CF—CF(CF_2)_4CF_2$	108	52	179	74–5				8, 10
$C_{12}H_{12}F_{12}$	$H(CF_2)_6CH(CH_2)_4CH_2$	112		90/90	19–21				87
		205		67–77/1.5					16
$C_{13}F_{22}$	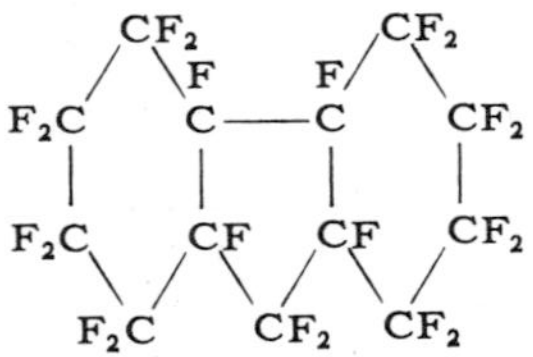	102		190		1.326	1.982	20	206
$C_{13}F_{24}$	$CF_2(CF_2)_4CFCF_2CF(CF_2)_4CF_2$	108	45	190.5	41–2				8

$C_{14}F_{24}$	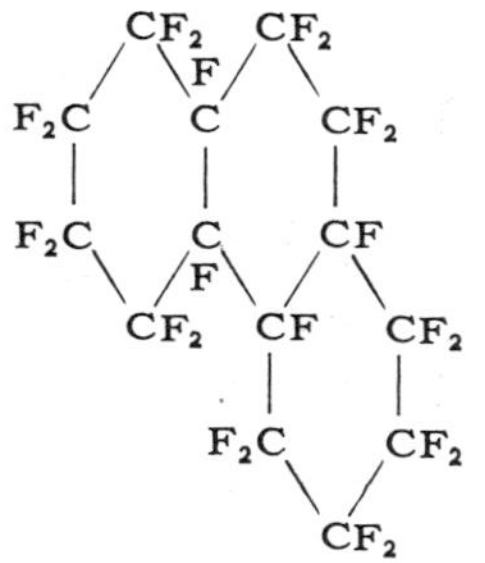	102		205–6		1.331	2.020	20	206
$C_{14}F_{26}$	$CF_2(CF_2)_4CF(CF_2)_2CF(CF_2)_4CF_2$	108	66		71–72				8
$C_{15}F_{28}$	$CF_2(CF_2)_4CF(CF_2)_3CF(CF_2)_4CF_2$	108	33	225–6		1.3220	1.9829	25	8
$C_{16}F_{26}$	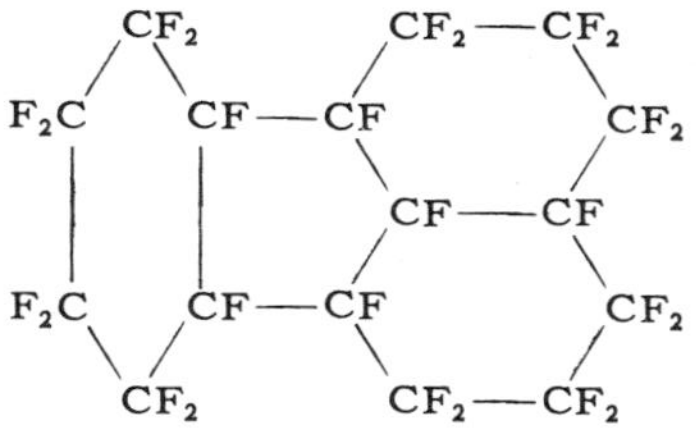	102		235–9		1.346	2.060	20	206
$C_{16}F_{30}$	$CF_2(CF_2)_4CF(CF_2)_4CF(CF_2)_4CF_2$	108	28	236–8	75–6				8
$C_{17}F_{32}$	$CF_2(CF_2)_4CF(CF_2)_5CF(CF_2)_4CF_2$	108	24	256–7	48				8
$C_{18}F_{34}$	$CF_2(CF_2)_4CF(CF_2)_6CF(CF_2)_4CF_2$	108	8	275–7	91				8

BIBLIOGRAPHY

1. Atkinson, B., and Trenwith, A. B., *J. Chem. Soc.*, **1953,** 2083.
2. Arnold, R. C., U. S. Patent 2,558,703 (1951).
3. Austin, P. R., U. S. Patent 2,449,360 (1948).
4. Austin, P. R., and Coffman, D. D., *J. Am. Chem. Soc.*, **75,** 4834 (1953).
5. Aynsley, E. E., and Watson, R. H., *J. Chem. Soc.*, **1955,** 576.
6. Baker, B. L., and Whaley, A. M., *J. Am. Chem. Soc.*, **73,** 4010(1951).
7. Banks, A. A., Emeleus, H. J., *et al.*, *J. Chem. Soc.*, **1948,** 2188.
8. Barbour, A. K., Barlow, G. B., and Tatlow, J. C., *J. Applied Chem.* **2,** 127(1952).
9. Barlow, G. B., Stacey, M., and Tatlow, J. C., *J. Chem. Soc.*, **1955,** 1741.
10. Barlow, G. B., and Tatlow, J. C., *J. Chem. Soc.*, **1952,** 4695.
11. Barnhart, W. S., British Patent 713,522(1954).
12. Barr, J. T., Gibson, J. D., and Lafferty, R. H., *J. Am. Chem. Soc.*, **73,** 1352(1951).
13. Barrick, P. L., U. S. Patent 2,427,116(1947).
14. Barrick, P. L., U. S. Patent 2,462,345(1949).
15. Barrick, P. L., U. S. Patent 2,462,347(1949).
16. Barrick, P. L., U. S. Patent 2,540,088(1951).
17. Barrick, P. L., U. S. Patent 2,550,953(1951).
18. Barrick, P. L., and Christ, R. E., U. S. Patent 2,436,135(1948).
19. Bayer, British Patent 684,117(1952).
20. Benning, A. F., U. S. Patent 2,230,925(1940).
21. Benning, A. F., U. S. Patent 2,426,172(1947).
22. Benning, A. F., Downing, F. B., and Park, J. D., U. S. Patent 2,394,381(1946).
23. Benning, A. F., Downing, F. B., and Plunkett, R. J., U. S. Patent 2,365,516(1944).
24. Benning, A. F., Downing, F. B., and Plunkett, R. J., U. S. Patent 2,393,304(1946).
25. Benning, A. F., and Park, J. D., U. S. Patent 2,384,499(1945).
26. Benning, A. F., and Park, J. D., U. S. Patent 2,407,246(1946).
27. Benning, A. F., and Park, J. D., U. S. Patent 2,420,222(1947).
28. Benning, A. F., and Park, J. D., U. S. Patent 2,437,993(1948).
29. Benning, A. F., and Park, J. D., U. S. Patent 2,490,764(1949).
30. Benning, A. F., and Young, U. S. Patent 2,615,926(1952).
31. Bergmann, E., Polyani, M., and Szabo, A. L., *Trans. Faraday Soc.*, **32,** 843(1936).
32. Berry, K. L., and Sturtevant, J. M., *J. Am. Chem. Soc.*, **64,** 1599(1942).
33. Bigelow, L. A., and Pearson, J. H., *J. Am. Chem. Soc.*, **56,** 2773(1934).
34. Booth, H. S., Mong, W. L., and Burchfield, P. E., *Ind. Eng. Chem.*, **24,** *328(1932).*
35. Bordner, C. A., U. S. Patent 2,615,925(1952).
36. Brandt, G. R. A., Emeleus, H. J., and Haszeldine, R. N., *J. Chem. Soc.*, **1952,** 2252.
37. Brice, T. J., Pearlson, W. H., and Simons, J. H., *J. Am. Chem. Soc.*, **68,** 968(1946).
38. Brice, T. J., Pearlson, W. H., and Simons, J. H., *J. Am. Chem. Soc.*, **71,** 2499(1949).
39. Brice, T. J., and Simons, J. H., *J. Am. Chem. Soc.*, **73,** 4016(1951).

40. Brice, T. J., LaZerte, J. D., and Pearlson, W. H., *J. Am. Chem. Soc.*, **75**, 2698(1953).
41. Brown, J. H., and Whalley, W. B., British Patent 576,190(1946).
42. Brown, J. H., and Whalley, W. B., *J. Soc. Chem. Ind.*, **67**, 331(1948).
43. Burford, W. B., Fowler, R. D., *et al.*, *Ind. Eng. Chem.*, **39**, 319(1947)
44. Burger, L. L., and Cady, G. H., *J. Am. Chem. Soc.*, **73**, 4243(1951).
45. Buxton, M. W., Ingram, D. W., *et al.*, *J. Chem. Soc.*, **1952**, 3830.
46. Buxton, M. W., Stacey, M., and Tatlow, J. E., *J. Chem. Soc.*, **1954**, 366.
47. Buxton, M. W., and Tatlow, J. C., J. *Chem. Soc.*, **1954**, 177.
48. Cady, G. H., Grosse, A. V., *et al.*, *Ind. Eng. Chem.*, **39**, 291(1947).
49. Calfee, J. D., and Bigelow, L. A., *J. Am. Chem. Soc.*, **59**, 2072(1937).
50. Calfee, J. D., and Bratton, F. H., U. S. Patent 462,359(1949).
51. Calfee, J. D., and Florio, P. A., U. S. Patent 2,469,290(1949).
52. Calfee, J. D., and Florio, P. A., U. S. Patent 2,499,129(1950).
53. Calfee, J. D., and Jewett, U. S. Patent 2,606,937(1952).
54. Calfee, J. D., and Miller, C. B., U. S. Patent 2,674,630(1954).
55. Calfee, J. D., and Smith, L. B., U. S. Patent 2,417,059(1947).
56. Calfee, J. D., Fukuhara, N., *et al.*, *J. Am. Chem. Soc.*, **62**, 267(1940).
57. Calfee, J. D., and Smith, L. B., U. S. Patent 2,566,163(1951).
58. Chabrie, C., *Compt. rend*, **110**, 280(1890).
59. Chabrie, C., *Compt. rend*, **111**, 747(1890).
60. Chapman, N. B., and Levy, J. L., J. *Chem. Soc.*,**1952**, 1673.
61. Coffman, D. D., Cramer, R., and Rigby, G. W., *J. Am. Chem. Soc.*, **71**, 749(1949).
62. Coffman, D. D., Barrick, P. L., *et al.*, *J. Am. Chem. Soc.*, **71**, 490(1949).
63. Coffman, D. D., Raasch, M. S., *et al.*, *J. Org. Chem.*, **14**, 747(1949).
64. Collie, N., *J. Chem. Soc.*, **55**, 111(1889).
65. Conly, J. C., U. S. Patent 2,678,953(1954).
66. Crane, G., and Barnhart, W. S., U. S. Patent 2,686,207(1954).
67. Crawford, G. H., and Simons, J. H., *J. Am. Chem. Soc.*, **77**, 2605(1955).
68. Cucolo, J. A., and Bigelow, L. A., *J. Am. Chem. Soc.*, **74**, 710(1952).
69. Davis, H. W., and Whaley, A. M., *J. Am. Chem. Soc.*, **72**, 4637(1950).
70. Desreux, V., *Bull. sci. acad. roy. Belg.*, **20**, 457(1934).
71. Dickey, J. B., U. S. Patent 2,624,746(1953).
72. Downing, F. B., Benning, A. F., and McHarness, R. C., U. S. Patent 2,384,821(1945).
73. Downing, F. B., Benning, A. F., and McHarness, R. C., U. S. Patent 2,413,696(1947).
74. Downing, F. B., Benning, A. F., and McHarness, R. C., U. S. Patent 2,480,560(1949).
75. Downing, F. B., Benning, A. F., and McHarness, R. C., U. S. Patent 2,551,573(1951).
75A. Dresdner, R. D., *J. Am. Chem. Soc.*, **78**, 876(1956).
76. Dumas, and Peligot, *Ann.*, **15**, 59.
77. duPont de Nemours, British Patent 583,874(1947).
78. Edgell, W. F., and Parts, L., *J. Am. Chem. Soc.*, **77**, 4899(1955).
79. Edgell, W. F., and Parts, L., *J. Am. Chem. Soc.*, **77**, 5515(1955).
80. Ellis, J. F., and Musgrave, W. K. R., *J. Chem. Soc.*, **1953**, 1063.
81. Emeleus, H. J., and Haszeldine, R. N., *J. Chem. Soc.*, **1949**, 2948.
82. Evans, D. E. M., and Tatlow, J. C., *J. Chem. Soc.*, **1954**, 3779.

83. Fowler, R. D., Burford, W. B., *et al.*, *Ind. Eng. Chem.*, **39**, 293(1947).
84. Fowler, R. D., Hamilton, J. M., *et al.*, *Ind. Eng. Chem.*, **39**, 375(1947).
85. Fremy, Ann., **92**, 247.
86. Fukuhara, N., and Bigelow, L. A., *J. Am. Chem. Soc.*, **63**, 788(1941).
87. Fukuhara, N., and Bigelow, L. A., *J. Am. Chem. Soc.*, **63**, 2793(1941).
88. Gilbert, A. R., and Bigelow, L. A., *J. Am. Chem. Soc.*, **72**, 2411(1950).
89. Gilman, H., and Jones, R. G., *J. Am. Chem. Soc.*, **65**, 1458(1943).
90. Gilman, H., and Jones, R. G., *J. Am. Chem. Soc.*, **65**, 2037(1943).
91. Gleave, W. W., British Patent 463,930(1937).
92. Gochenour, C. I., U. S . Patent 2,555,857(1951).
93. Gottleib, H. B., and Park, J. D., U. S. Patent 2,670,387(1954).
94. Grosse, A. V., and Linn, C. B., *J. Org. Chem.*, **3**, 26(1938).
95. Grosse, A. V., and Linn, C. B., *J. Am. Chem. Soc.*, **64**, 2289(1942).
96. Grosse, A. V., Wackher, R. C., and Linn, C. B., *J. Phys. Chem.*, **44**, 275(1942).
97. Gryszkiewicz-Trochimowski, E., and Gryszkiewicz-Trochimowski, O., *Bull. soc. chim. France*, **1953**, 123.
98. Gryszkiewicz-Trochimowski, E., Sporzynski, A., and Wnuk, J., *Rec. trav. chim.*, **66**, 413(1947).
99. Harmon, J., U. S. Patent 2,399,024(1946).
100. Harmon, J., U. S. Patent 2,404,374(1946).
101. Harmon, J., U. S. Patent 2,436,142(1948).
102. Hauptschein, M., *J. Am. Chem. Soc.*, **73**, 1428(1951).
103. Hauptschein, M., and Bigelow, L. A., *J. Am. Chem. Soc.*, **73**, 5591(1951).
104. Hauptschein, M., and Grosse, A. V., *J. Am. Chem. Soc.*, **74**, 4454(1952).
105. Hauptschein, M., Kinsman, R. L., and Grosse, A. V., *J. Am. Chem. Soc.*, **74**, 849(1952).
106. Hauptschein, M., Nodiff, E. A., and Grosse, A. V., *J. Am. Chem. Soc.*, **74**, 1347(1952).
107. Hauptschein, M., Stokes, C. S., and Grosse, A. V., *J. Am. Chem. Soc.*, **74**, 848(1952).
108. Hauptschein, M., Stokes, C. S., and Grosse, A. V., *J. Am. Chem. Soc.*, **74**, 1974(1952).
109. Hauptschein, M., and Grosse, A. V., *J. Am. Chem. Soc.*, **73**, 2461(1951).
110. Haszeldine, R. N., *J. Chem. Soc.*, **1949**, 2856.
111. Haszeldine, R. N., *Nature*, **165**, 152(1950).
112. Haszeldine, R. N., *J. Chem. Soc.*, **1950**, 3617.
113. Haszeldine, R. N., *J. Chem. Soc.*, **1951**, 584.
114. Haszeldine, R. N., *J. Chem. Soc.*, **1951**, 588.
115. Haszeldine, R. N., *J. Chem. Soc.*, **1951**, 2485.
116. Haszeldine, R. N., *J. Chem. Soc.*, **1952**, 2504.
117. Haszeldine, R. N., *J. Chem. Soc.*, **1952**, 4259.
118. Haszeldine, R. N., *J. Chem. Soc.*, **1952**, 4423.
119. Haszeldine, R. N., *J. Chem. Soc.*, **1953**, 922.
120. Haszeldine, R. N., *J. Chem. Soc.*, **1953**, 1749.
121. Haszeldine, R. N., *J. Chem. Soc.*, **1953**, 2075.
122. Haszeldine, R. N., *J. Chem. Soc.*, **1953**, 3371.
123. Haszeldine, R. N., *J. Chem. Soc.*, **1953**, 3559.
124. Haszeldine, R. N., *J. Chem. Soc.*, **1953**, 3565.
125. Haszeldine, R. N., *J. Chem. Soc.*, **1953**, 3761.
126. Haszeldine, R. N., *J. Chem. Soc.*, **1954**, 4026.

127. Haszeldine, R. N., *J. Chem. Soc.*, **1955**, 4291.
128. Haszeldine, R. N., *J. Chem. Soc.*, **1955**, 4302.
129. Haszeldine, R. N., and Leedham, K., *J. Chem. Soc.*, **1953**, 1548.
130. Haszeldine, R. N., Leedham, K., and Steele, B. R., *J. Chem. Soc.*, **1954**, 2040.
131. Haszeldine, R. N., and Osborne, J. E., *J. Chem. Soc.*, **1955**, 3880.
132. Haszeldine, R. N., and Steele, B. R., *J. Chem. Soc.*, **1953**, 1199.
133. Haszeldine, R. N., and Steele, B. R., *J. Chem. Soc.*, **1953**, 1592.
134. Haszeldine, R. N., and Steele, B. R., *J. Chem. Soc.*, **1954**, 923.
135. Haszeldine, R. N., and Steele, B. R., *J. Chem. Soc.*, **1954**, 3747.
136. Haszeldine, R. N., and Steele, B. R., *J. Chem. Soc.*, **1955**, 3005.
137. Haszeldine, R. N., and Walaschewski, E. G., *J. Chem. Soc.*, **1953**, 3607.
138. Haszeldine, R. N., and Walaschewski, E. G., *J. Chem. Soc.*, **1950**, 2787.
139. Haszeldine, R. N., and Walaschewski, E. G., *J. Chem. Soc.*, **1950**, 2689.
140. Henne, A. L., and Arnold, R. C., *J. Am. Chem. Soc.*, **70**, 1968(1948).
141. Henne, A. L., U. S. Patent 1,990,692(1935).
142. Henne, A. L., U. S. Patent 2,007,198(1935).
143. Henne, A. L., *J. Am. Chem. Soc.*, **59**, 1200(1937).
144. Henne, A. L., *J. Am. Chem. Soc.*, **60**, 1569(1938).
145. Henne, A. L., *J. Am. Chem. Soc.*, **75**, 5750(1953).
146. Henne, A. L., and DeWitt, E. G., *J. Am. Chem. Soc.*, **70**, 1548(1948).
147. Henne, A. L., and Finnegan, W. G., *J. Am. Chem. Soc.*, **71**, 298(1949).
148. Henne, A. L., and Flanagan, J. V., *J. Am. Chem. Soc.*, **65**, 2362(1949).
149. Henne, A. L., and Fox, C. J., *J. Am. Chem. Soc.*, **75**, 5750(1953).
150. Henne, A. L., and Haeckl, F. W., J. *Am. Chem. Soc.*, **63**, 2692(1941).
151. Henne, A. L., and Haeckl, F. W., *J. Am. Chem. Soc.*, **63**, 3476(1941).
152. Henne, A. L., and Hinkamp, J. B., *J. Am. Chem. Soc.*, **67**, 1194(1945).
153. Henne, A. L., and Hinkamp, J. B., *J. Am. Chem. Soc.*, **67**, 1197(1945).
154. Henne, A. L., Hinkamp, J. B., and Zimmerscheid, W. J., *J. Am. Chem. Soc.*, **67**, 1906(1945).
155. Henne, A. L., and Hubbard, D. M., *J. Am. Chem. Soc.*, **58**, 404(1936).
156. Henne, A. L., and Kaye, S., *J. Am. Chem. Soc.*, **72**, 3369(1950).
157. Henne, A. L., and Kraus, D. W., *J. Am. Chem. Soc.*, **73**, 5303(1951).
158. Henne, A. L., and Kraus, D. W., *J. Am. Chem. Soc.*, **76**, 1175(1954).
159. Henne, A. L., and Ladd, E. C., *J. Am. Chem. Soc.*, **58**, 402(1936).
160. Henne, A. L., and Ladd, E. C., *J. Am. Chem. Soc.*, **60**, 2491(1938).
161. Henne, A. L., and Nager, M., *J. Am. Chem. Soc.*, **73**, 1042(1951).
162. Henne, A. L., and Nager, M., *J. Am. Chem. Soc.*, **73**, 5527(1951).
163. Henne, A. L., and Newby, T. H., *J. Am. Chem. Soc.*, **70**, 130(1948).
164. Henne, A. L., and Plueddeman, E. P., *J. Am. Chem. Soc.*, **65**, 587(1943).
165. Henne, A. L., and Plueddeman, E. P., *J. Am. Chem. Soc.*, **65**, 1271(1943).
166. Henne, A. K., and Postelnek, W., Unpublished Observations, 1954.
167. Henne, A. L., and Postelnek, W., *J. Am. Chem. Soc.*, **77**, 2334(1955).
168. Henne, A. L., and Renoll, M. W., *J. Am. Chem. Soc.*, **58**, 887(1936).
169. Henne, A. L., and Renoll, M. W., *J. Am. Chem. Soc.*, **58**, 889(1936).
170. Henne, A. L., and Renoll, M. W., *J. Am. Chem. Soc.*, **59**, 2434(1937).
171. Henne, A. L., and Renoll, M. W., *J. Am. Chem. Soc.*, **61**, 2849(1939).
172. Henne, A. L., Renoll, M. W., and Leicester, H. M., *J. Am. Chem. Soc.*, **61**, 938(1939).
173. Henne, A. L., and Ruh, R. P., *J. Am. Chem. Soc.*, **69**, 279(1947).
174. Henne, A. L., and Ruh, R. P., *J. Am. Chem. Soc.*, **70**, 1025(1948).

175. Henne, A. L., Sheppard, W., and Young, E. J., *J. Am. Chem. Soc.*, **72,** 3577(1950).
176. Henne, A. L., and Waalkes, T. P., *J. Am. Chem. Soc*, **68,** 496(1946).
177. Henne, A. L., and Whaley, A. M., *J. Am. Chem. Soc.*, **64,** 1157(1942).
178. Henne, A. L., Whaley, A. M., and Stevenson, J. K., *J. Am. Chem. Soc.*, **63,** 3478(1941).
179. Henne, A. L., and West, E. G., *J. Am. Chem. Soc.*, **62,** 2051(1940).
179A. Henne, A. L., and Zimmer, W. F., *J. Am. Chem. Soc.*, **73,** 1362(1951).
180. Henne, A. L., and Zimmerscheid, W. J., *J. Am. Chem. Soc.*, **67,** 1235(1945).
181. Hillyea, J. C., and Wilson, J. F., U. S. Patent 2,471,525(1949).
182. Hoffmann, F. W., *J. Am. Chem. Soc.*, **70,** 2596(1948).
183. Hoffmann, F. W., *J. Org. Chem.*, **14,** 105(1949).
184. Hoffmann, F. W., *J. Org. Chem.*, **15,** 425(1950).
185. Hovey, R. S., and Carnell, P. H., U. S. Patent 2,439,299(1948).
186. Husted, D. R., and Ahlbrecht, A. H., *J. Am. Chem. Soc.*, **74,** 5422(1952).
187. Husted, D. R., and Kohlhase, W. L., *J. Am. Chem. Soc.*, **76,** 5141(1954).
188. James, W. R., Pearlson, W. H., and Simons, J. H., *J. Am. Chem. Soc.*, **72,** 1761(1950).
189. Johnson, F. W., U. S. Patent 2,398,181(1946).
190. Joyce, R. M., U. S. Patent 2,462,402(1949).
191. Kinetic Chemicals Inc., British Patent 612,992(1948).
192. Kirshenbaum, A. D., Streng, A. G., and Hauptschein, M., *J. Am. Chem. Soc.*, **75,** 3141(1953).
193. Krogh, L. C., Reid, T. C., and Brown, H. A., *J. Org. Chem.*, **19,** 1124(1954).
194. Kropa, E. L., and Padbury, J. J., U. S. Patent 2,590,001(1952).
195, Kwasnik, W., U. S. Patent 2,658,927(1953).
196. LaZerte, J. D., Hals, L. J., *et al.*, *J. Am. Chem. Soc.*, **75,** 4525(1953).
197. LaZerte, J. D., and Koshar, R. J., *J. Am. Chem. Soc.*, **77,** 910(1955).
198. LaZerte, J. D., Pearlson, W. H., and Kauck, E. A., U. S. Patent 2,647,933(1953).
199. LaZerte, J. D., Pearlson, W. H., and Kauck, E. A., U. S. Patent 2,704,776(1955).
200. Lebeau, P., and Damiens, A., *Compt. rend.*, **191,** 939(1930).
201. Lilyquist, M. R., Ph. D. Dissertation, University of Florida (1955).
202. Linn, C. B., and Schmerling, L., U. S. Patent 2,539,668(1951).
203. Locke, E. G., Brode, W. R., and Henne, A. L., *J. Am. Chem. Soc.*, **56,** 1936(1934).
204. McBee, E. T., U. S. Patent 2,644,845(1953).
205. McBee, E. T., U. S. Patent 2,637,747(1953).
206. McBee, E. T., and Bechtol, L. D., U. S. Patent 2,459,780(1949).
207. McBee, E. T., and Bechtol, L. D., U. S. Patent 2,459,781(1949).
208. McBee, E. T., and Bechtol, L. D., U. S. Patent 2,459,782(1949).
209. McBee, E. T., Campbell, D. H., and Roberts, C. W., *J. Am. Chem. Soc.*, **77,** 3149(1955).
210. McBee, E. T., Hass, H. B., *et al.*, *Ind. Eng. Chem.*, **39,** 409(1947).
211. McBee, E. T., Hass, H. B., *et al.*, *J. Am. Chem. Soc.*, **69,** 944(1947).
212. McBee, E. T., and Hausch, W. R., *Ind. Eng. Chem.*, **39,** 418(1947).
213. McBee, E. T., Henne, A. L., *et al.*, *J. Am. Chem. Soc.*, **63,** 3340(1940).
214. McBee, E. T., Higgins, J. F., and Pierce, O. R., *J. Am. Chem. Soc.*, **74,** 1387(1952).
215. McBee, E. T., Hsu, C. G., *et al.*, *J. Am. Chem. Soc.*, **77,** 915(1955).

216. McBee, E. T., Kelly, A. E., and Rapkin, E. J., *J. Am. Chem. Soc.*, **72**, 5071(1950).
217. McBee, E. T., and Ligett, W. B., U. S. Patent 2,606,212(1952).
218. McBee, E. T., Pierce, O. R., and Chen, M. C., *J. Am. Chem. Soc.*, **75**, 2324(1953).
219. McBee, E. T., Truchan, A., and Bolt, R. O., *J. Am. Chem. Soc.*, **70**, 2023(1948).
220. McCombie, H., and Saunders, B. C., *Nature*, **158**, 382(1946).
221. McElvain, S. M., and Langston, J. W., *J. Am. Chem. Soc.*, **66**, 1759(1944).
222. McGrew, F. C., and Price, E. H., U. S. Patent 2,687,440(1954).
223. Meslans, M., *Ann. de chim. et phys.*, (7) **1**, 94(1894).
224. Meslans, M., *Ann. de chim. et phys.*, (7) **1**, 363(1894).
225. Meslans, M., *Compt. rend.*, **110**, 717(1890).
226. Midgley, T., and Henne, A. L., U. S. Patent 2,013,062(1935).
227. Midgley, T., Henne, A. L., and McNary, R. R., U. S. Patent 2,007,208(1935).
228. Miller, W. T., *J. Am. Chem. Soc.*, **62**, 341(1940).
229. Miller, E. T., *J. Am. Chem. Soc.*, **62**, 993(1940).
230. Miller, W. T., *J. Am. Chem. Soc.*, **72**, 705(1950).
231. Miller, W. T., U. S. Patent 2,668,182(1954).
232. Miller, W. T., and Howald, J. M., Private Communication (1955).
233. Miller, W. T., and Calfee, J. D., U. S. Patent 2,676,996(1954).
234. Miller, W. T., Calfee, J. D., and Bigelow, L. A., *J. Am. Chem. Soc.*, **59**, 198(1937).
235. Miller, W. T., and Fager, C. W., U. S. Patent 2,598,411(1952).
236. Miller, W. T., Ehrenfeld, R. L., *et al.*, *Ind. Eng. Chem.*, **39**, 401(1947).
237. Miller, C. B., and Bratton, F. H., U. S. Patent 2,478,932(1949).
238. Miller, C. B., and Smith, L. B., U. S. Patent 2,669,590(1954).
239. Moissan, H., *Compt. rend.*, **110**, 952(1890).
240. Moissan, H., *Ann. de chim. et phys.*, (6) **19**, 272(1891).
241. Moissan, H., and Meslans, M., *J. Fort. Chem.*, **1888**, 931.
242. Musgrave, W. K. R., and Smith, F., *J. Chem. Soc.*, **1949**, 3021.
243. Murray, W. S., U. S. Patent 2,426,637(1947).
244. Murray, W. S., U. S. Patent 2,426,638(1947).
245. Nakanski, S., Myers, T. G., and Jensen, E. V., *J. Am. Chem. Soc.*, **77**, 3099(1955).
246. Nakanski, S., Myers, T. C., and Jensen, E. V., *J. Am. Chem. Soc.*, **77**, 5033(1955).
247. Neudorffer, J., *Compt. rend*, **244**, 1983(1952).
248. Newman, M. S., Renoll, M. W., and Averbach, I., *J. Am. Chem. Soc.*, **70**, 1023(1948).
249. Nodiff, E. A., Grosse, A. V., and Hauptschein, M., *J. Org. Chem.*, **18**, 235(1953).
250. Olah, Gy., and Pavlath, A., *Acta. Chim. Acad. Sci. Hung.*, **3**, 191(1953).
251. Oliver, G. D., Blumkin, S., and Cunningham, C. W., *J. Am. Chem. Soc.*, **73**, 5722(1951).
252. Otto, M., Theobald, H., and Melon, J., German Patent 859,887(1952).
253. Pailthorp, J. R., U. S. Patent 2,694,739(1954).
254. Park, J. D., Benning, A. F., *et al.*, *Ind. Eng. Chem.*, **39**, 354(1947).
255. Park, J. D., Lycan, W. R., and Lacher, J. R., *J. Am. Chem. Soc.*, **73**, 711(1951).
256. Park, J. D., Rausch, D. A., and Lacher, J. R., Private Communication (1955).

257. Park, J. D., Seffl, R., and Lacher, J. R., *J. Am. Chem. Soc.*, **78**, 59(1956).
258. Park, J. D., Sharrah, M. L., and Lacher, J. R., *J. Am. Chem. Soc.*, **71**, 2339(1949).
259. Paterno, E., and Spallino, R., *Atti. Acad. Lincei*, **16**,(2) 160, 1900.
260. Pierce, O. R., McBee, E. T., and Cline, R. E., *J. Am. Chem. Soc.*, **75**, 5618(1953).
261. Pierce, O. R., McBee, E. T., and Judd, G. F., *J. Am. Chem. Soc.*, **76**, 474(1954).
261A. Postelnek, W., Rausch, D. A., and Lovelace, A. M., 130th Meeting Am. Chem. Soc., Atlantic City, New Jersey, September 1956.
262. Price, E. H., and Johnson W. S., U. S. Patent 2,687,441(1954).
263. Prober, M., *J. Am. Chem. Soc.*, **73**, 4495(1951).
264. Prober, M., *J. Am. Chem. Soc.*, **76**, 4189(1954).
265. Raasch, M. W., U. S. Patent 2,424,677(1947).
266. Razumonskii, V. V., and Fridenberg, A. E., *Zhur. Obschei Khim.*, **19**, 92(1949).
267. Renoll, M. W., *J. Am. Chem. Soc.*, **64**, 1115(1942).
268. Renoll, M. W., U. S. Patent 2,344,061(1944).
269. Renoll, M. W., U. S. Patent 2,364,818(1944).
270. Roberts, J. D., Webb, R. L. and McElhill, E. A., *J. Am. Chem. Soc.*, **72**, 408(1950).
271. Rogers, G. C., and Cady, G. H., *J. Am. Chem. Soc.*, **73**, 3523(1951).
272. Roylance, J., Tatlow, J. C., Worthington, R. E., *J. Chem. Soc.*, **1954**, 4426.
273. Ruh, R. P., U. S. Patent 2,676,193(1954).
274. Ruh, R. P., and Davis, R. A., U. S. Patent 2,639,301(1953).
275. Ruh, R. P., Davis, R. A., and Allswede, K. A., U. S. Patent 2,705,229(1953).
276. Ruh, R. P., and Gordon, A. F., U. S. Patent 2,681,940(1954).
277. Ruff, O., and Brettschneider, O., *Z. Anorg. Allgem. Chem.*, **210**, 173(1933).
278. Ruff, O., *Ber.*, **69B**, 229(1936).
279. Saunders, B. C., Stacey, G. T., and Wilding, I. G. E., *J. Chem. Soc.*, **1949**, 773.
280. Scherer, O., U. S. Patent 2,146,354(1939).
281. Scherer, O., German Patent 856,145(1952).
282. Schmerling, L., U. S. Patent 2,533,052(1950).
283. Simons, J. H., and Block, L. P., *J. Am. Chem. Soc.*, **59**, 1407(1937).
284. Simons, J. H., and Block, L. P., *J. Am. Chem. Soc.*, **61**, 2962(1939).
285. Simons, J. H., Bond, R. I., and McArthur, R. E., *J. Am. Chem. Soc.*, **62**, 3477(1940).
286. Simons, J. H., and Brice, T. J., U. S. Patent 2,614,131(1952).
287. Simons, J. H., Brice , T. J., and Pearlson, W. H., U. S. Patent 2,658,928(1953).
288. Simons, J. H., Pearlson, W. H., and Jones, W. K., U. S. Patent 2,494,064(1950).
289. Smith, F., Stacey, M., *et al.*, *J. Apl. Chem.*, **2**, 97(1952).
290. Smorgonski, L. M., *J. Gen. Chem. (USSR)*, **17**, 416(1947).
291. Soll, J., German Patent 641,878(1937).
292. Stacey, M., *Royal Inst. Chem. Gt. Brit. and Ireland*, **1948**, 1.
293. Stilmar, F. B., Struve, W. S., and Lulek, N., U. S. Patent 2,503,077(1950).
294. Stover, W. A., U. S. Patent 2,622,106(1952).
295. Stover, W. A., U. S. Patent 2,622,106(1952).
296. Swarts, F., *Bull. acad. roy. Belg.*, (3), **24**, 474(1891).

297. Swarts, F., *Bull. acad. roy. Belg.*, (3), **26**, 102(1893).
298. Swarts, F., *Rec. trav. chim.*, **17**, 231(1898).
299. Swarts, F., *Bull. acad. roy. Belg.*, (3), **34**, 307(1897).
300. Swarts, F., *Bull. acad. roy. Belg.*, **1901**, 383.
301. Swarts, F., *Bull, acad. roy. Belg.*, **1903**, 438.
302. Swarts, F., *Rec. trav. chim.*, **27**, 128(1908).
303. Swarts, F., *Rec. trav. chim.*, **28**, 166(1909).
304. Swarts, F., *Bull, acad. roy. Belg.*, **1909**, 728.
305. Swarts, F., *Bull. sci. acad. roy. Belg.*, **1910**, 113.
306. Swarts, F., *Bull. sci. acad. roy. Belg.*, **1911**, 563.
307. Swarts, F., *Bull. sci. acad. roy. Belg.*, **1914**, 7.
308. Swarts, F., *Bull. acad. roy. Belg.*, **1920**, 399.
309. Swarts, F., *Bull. soc. chim. Belg.*, **30**, 302 (1921).
310. Swarts, F., *Bull, acad roy. Belg.*, ext. *Bull. Classe Sci.*, **Jun 1922**, 331.
311. Swarts, F., *Bull. soc. chim. Belg.*, **36**, 192(1927).
312. Swarts, F., *Bull. soc. chim. Belg.*, **38**, 99(1929).
313. Swarts, F., *Bull. soc. chim. Belg.*, **42**, 102(1933).
314. Swarts, F., *Compt. rend.*, **197**, 1261(1933).
315. Swarts, F., *Bull. sci. acad. roy. Belg.*, **22**, 105(1936).
316. Tarrant, P., Attaway, J., and Lovelace, A. M., *J. Am. Chem. Soc.*, **76**, 2343(1954).
317. Tarrant, P., and Gillman, E., J. *Am. Chem. Soc.*, **76**, 5423(1954).
318. Tarrant, P., and Lilyquist, M. R., *J. Am. Chem. Soc.*, **76**, 3640(1954).
319. Tarrant, P., Lilyquist, M. R., and Attaway, J., *J. Am. Chem. Soc.*, **76**, 944(1954).
320. Tarrant, P., and Lovelace, A. M., *J. Am. Chem. Soc.*, **76**, 3466(1954).
321. Tarrant, P., and Lovelace, A. M., *J. Am. Chem. Soc.*, **77**, 768(1955).
322. Tarrant, P., Lovelace, A. M., and Lilyquist, M. R., *J. Am. Chem. Soc.*, **77**, 2783(1955).
323. Tarrant, P., and Lutz, R., Private Communication (1955).
324. Tatlow, J. C., and Worthington, R. E., *J. Chem. Soc.*, **1952**, 1251.
325. Thornton, N. V., Burg, A. B., and Schlesinger, H. I., *J. Am. Chem. Soc.*, **55**, 3177(1933).
326. Tiers, G. V. D., *J. Am. Chem. Soc.*, **75**, 5978(1953).
327. Tiers, G. V. D., *J. Am. Chem. Soc.*, **77**, 6703(1955).
327A. Tiers, G. V. D., 128th Meeting American Chemical Society, Minneapolis, Minnesota (1955).
328. Towne, F. B., and Dickey, J. B., U. S. Patent 2,500,218(1950).
329. Tronov, B. V., and Krieger, E. A., *J. Russ. Phys. Chem. Soc.*, **56**, 167(1937).
330. Van Arkel, E. A., and Janetsky, E. F. *J., Rec. trav. chim.*, **56**, 167(1937).
331. Waalkes, T. P., U. S. Patent 2,466,189(1949).
332. Walborsky, H. M., Baum, M., and Loncrini, D. F., *J. Am. Chem. Soc.*, **77**, 3737(1955).
332A. Wethington., J. A. Jr., Private Communication, Univ. of Florida (1956).
333. Whalley, W. B., British Patent 580,140(1946).
334. Whalley, W. B., British Patent 589,167(1947).
335. Whalley, W. B., *J. Chem. Soc. Ind.*, **66**, 427(1947).
336. Young, D. S., Fukuhara, N., and Bigelow, L. A., *J. Am. Chem. Soc.*, **62**, 1171(1940).

CHAPTER III

Alkenes and Alkynes

TABLE OF CONTENTS

		PAGE
Introduction		100
Method Number		
301	Dehydrohalogenation	101
302	Dehalogenation	104
303	Dehydration of Alcohols	106
304	Addition of Hydrogen Halides to Alkynes	106
305	Pyrolysis of Esters	106
306	Decarboxylation of Salts of of Fluorocarboxylic Acids	107
307	Free Radical Addition	107
308	Disproportionation	108
309	Pyrolytic Reactions	108
310	Reaction of Organometallic Compounds with Olefins	109
311	Dimerization of Olefins	110
Table 3	Alkenes	113
Table 4	Dienes and Trienes	122
Table 5	Alkynes and Allenes	125
Table 6	Cyclic Alkenes	126
Bibliography		132

INTRODUCTION

Fluorine-containing olefins are generally prepared in the same manner employed in the preparation of non-fluorinated olefins. However several reactions which are not generally applicable in organic chemistry are very important for the preparation of this class of compounds. These are: a) decarboxylation of carboxylic acid salts, b) free radical addition, c) disproportionation, and d) reaction of organometallic compounds with olefins.

Fluorine-containing olefins are important intermediates in the preparation of alkanes, acids, amides, acyl halides, ethers, nitriles and a variety of other fluorinated compounds.

The widest commercial use of fluoroolefins has been in the production of plastics, elastomers, oils and greases. Polytetrafluoroethylene, sold in the United States under the trade name "Teflon" and in Britain as "Fluon," is inert to all reagents except fluorine and molten alkali metals. In addition to its outstanding chemical properties "Teflon" has excellent electrical properties. The thermal degradation of "Teflon" begins at about 450° with the evolution of volatile products, some of which are very toxic. Polychlorotrifluoroethylene, marketed under the trade name of "Kel-F" and "Fluorothene," also possesses excellent chemical and electrical properties. Lower molecular-weight polymers of chlorotrifluoroethylene find application as lubricating oils and greases. Many fluorine-containing elastomers have also been prepared which have outstanding chemical and thermal resistance. "Kel-F" elastomer (M. W. Kellogg Company), a copolymer of $CF_2{=}CFCl$ and $CF_2{=}CH_2$, has outstanding acid resistance and is used as a surface coating material. This elastomer can also be cured to give a chemically inert rubber. "Viton-A," a copolymer of $CF_3CF{=}CF_2$ and $CF{=}CH_2$, has recently been announced by E. I. du Pont de Nemours Company. This elastomer promises to have outstanding chemical and thermal stability.

METHOD 301 Dehydrohalogenation

The widely used dehydrohalogenation reaction for olefin preparation can be carried out by the following means: base catalyzed elimination, high temperature catalysis, and pyrolysis.

The base catalyzed elimination of hydrogen halide is perhaps the most common laboratory procedure and may be accomplished using a variety of metal hydroxides or alkoxides. The elimination appears to proceed by the following generally accepted mechanism:

$$\text{I} \quad B{:}^{\ominus} + H{:}C{-}C{-}X \rightleftarrows BH + {}^{\ominus}{:}C{-}CX$$

$$\text{II} \quad {}^{\ominus}{:}C{-}C{-}X \rightarrow C{=}C + {:}X^{\ominus}$$

$$(X = F,\ Cl,\ Br,\ I;\ B{:}^{-} = {:}OH^{-},\ {:}OR^{-})$$

As indicated, the reaction is initiated by the attack of base on a hydrogen atom which is beta to the halogen atom to be eliminated; thus a transitory carbanion is formed (Step I). Displacement of the halogen ion (X) by the free electron pair results in the formation of a carbon-carbon double bond (Step II).

In compounds of the type $CF_2ClCHBrCH_2Cl$ where two olefinic structures are possible, the relative electropositive character of the carbon atoms is of considerable importance in determining which hydrogen atom will be attacked. Examination of a number of base catalyzed dehydrohalogenations indicates that the carbon atom adjacent to a fluorine-containing carbon atom is the most electropositive in character and the hydrogen atom attached to this carbon atom, being more acidic, is most readily attacked by base. This is illustrated by the following examples of base catalyzed dehydrohalogenation: $CF_3CH_2CHBrCH_3 \rightarrow CF_3CH{=}CHCH_3$,[194] $CF_2ClCHClCH_2Cl \rightarrow CF_2ClCCl{=}CH_2$.[64] This effect is also illustrated by the dehydrohalogenation of $CF_3CH_2CCl{=}CH_2$ with alcoholic potassium hydroxide[73] to produce a 44 percent yield of $CF_3CH{=}C{=}CH_2$ and a 22 percent yield of $CF_3CH_2C{\equiv}CH$.

In general the ease of displacement of the halogen ion (X) (Step II) decreases in the following order: I > Br > Cl > F; for example, hydrogen iodide is preferentially eliminated from $CF_2ICHFCFClCF_2Cl$ instead of hydrogen chloride.[131] Halogen atoms on the carbon atom adjacent to $-CF_2-$ or $-CF_3$ groups are stabilized towards elimination in dehydrohalogen reactions. Henne and Hinkamp[93] found that dehydrohalogenation of $CF_3CHClCH_2CH_3$ with alcoholic potassium hydroxide does not take place but dehydrochlorination of $CF_3CH_2CHClCH_3$ proceeds very readily.

The elimination of hydrogen halide does not readily occur when either the hydrogen atom or the halogen atom is attached to a carbon atom containing fluorine. For example, the dehydrohalogenation of $CHCl_2CCl_2CHF_2$[29] and $CCl_3CH_2CF_2Cl$[168] yield $CCl_2{=}CClCHF_2$ and $CCl_2{=}CHCF_2Cl$, respectively, instead of $CHCl_2CCl{=}CF_2$ and $CCl_3CH{=}CF_2$.

Although alcohols are the most commonly used solvents for base catalyzed dehydrohalogenations, the elimination reaction may be complicated by ether formation in the case of highly fluorinated alkanes (cf. Methods 501 and 502). Water may be used as a solvent for this reaction and in this case the product, as it is formed, may be rapidly steam distilled from the aqueous alkali. Dehydrohalogenations may also be accomplished by using anhydrous potassium hydroxide and this method appears to be the most desirable for the preparation of fluorine-containing alkynes. For example, Haszeldine[59] obtained a good yield of

$CF_3C{\equiv}CH$ from $CF_3CBr{=}CH_2$. Park and co-workers[158] dehydrohalogenated $CF_2ClCFHI$ and $CF_2BrCHFBr$ using anhydrous potassium hydroxide pellets in mineral oil. During the reaction it was necessary to employ very vigorous stirring in order to remove the potassium halide from the surface of the potassium hydroxide pellets. This latter procedure was successfully applied by Jacobs and Bauer[119A] to the preparation of tetrafluoroallene from $CF_2BrCH{=}CF_2$. These workers were unsuccessful in an attempt to prepare tetrafluoroallene by the dehalogenation of $CF_2ICCl{=}CF_2$ which had been previously reported.[150]

In addition to sodium and potassium hydroxide, sodium ethoxide can be used as a basic reagent for the elimination of hydrogen halide from alkanes. Henne and Fox[90] used sodium ethoxide in ethanol to prepare $CCl_2{=}CFCF_2Cl$ in a 55 percent yield from $CHCl_2CFClCF_2Cl$ and in a 70 percent yield from $CHCl_2CF_2CF_2Cl$. However, the removal of hydrogen fluoride from $CHCl_2CF_2CF_2Cl$ by the use of alcoholic potassium hydroxide gave only a 56 percent yield of the same olefin. Among other reagents that have proved effective in certain cases for the removal of hydrogen halide are calcium hydroxide,[178] calcium carbonate,[183] and a mixture of potassium acetate and potassium carbonate.[185]

Tarrant and co-workers[188,192,194] have shown that tertiary amines at elevated temperatures (180° to 200°) are effective dehydrohalogenating agents for fluorinated alkanes. The reaction appears to proceed through the formation and subsequent decomposition of a quaternary salt to yield the fluoroolefin. The amines which are most effective in this reaction are tri-*n*-butylamine and dimethylaniline. However if the temperature of the reaction exceeds 200°, a considerable amount of 1-butene is formed from tri-*n*-butylamine and methyl halide is formed when dimethylaniline is employed. The use of tertiary amines is most effective in the removal of two moles of hydrogen halide to produce conjugated dienes whereas alkali may yield only a monoolefin:

$$CF_2BrCH(CH_3)CHBrCH_3 \xrightarrow[180^\circ]{(n\text{-}C_4H_9)_3N} CF_2{=}C(CH_3)CH{=}CH_2 \quad (23\%)^{192}$$

$$CF_2BrCH(CH_3)CHBrCH_3 \xrightarrow[25^\circ]{NaOH} CF_2BrC(CH_3){=}CHCH_3 \quad (47\%)^{27}$$

The reaction of 1,3-dichloro-1,1-difluoro-3-methylbutane and tri-*n*-butylamine at 180° yields $CF_2{=}CHC(CH_3){=}CH_2$, whereas at lower temperatures $CF_2ClCH{=}C(CH_3)CH_3$ is formed. Under either condition, 1,4-dichloro-1,1-difluoro-3-methylbutane failed to yield any unsaturated product.[188] This would indicate that the elimination of two moles of hydrogen halide from a butane to yield a 1,3-butadiene proceeds through the formation of an intermediate 2-butene, followed by 1,4-elimination and rearrangement.

Crane and Barnhart[27] report that simultaneous dehydrohalogenation and rearrangement of the double bond occurs when olefins of the type $CF_2XC(R){=}CHCH_3$ (R=H or CH_3; X=Cl or Br) are treated with ferric chloride or zinc chloride, to yield $CF_2{=}CRCH{=}CH_2$. By use of this technique, $CF_2ClCH{=}CHCH_3$ when added slowly to ferric chloride is converted in a 45 percent yield to $CF_2{=}CHCH{=}CH_2$.

High temperature catalytic means may be employed for the elimination of hydrogen halide from alkanes. For example, vinyl fluoride is formed in a 37 percent yield by passing CH_3CHF_2 over aluminum sulfate at 400°.[174] Hydrogen chloride is eliminated from CH_3CF_2Cl at 250° to 400° using aluminum oxide or aluminum fluoride as a catalyst.[145]

Dehydrohalogenation can also be accomplished by thermal cracking. The pyrolysis of $C_2H_5CF_3$ at 830° to 850° yields $CH_3CH{=}CF_2$, $CH_2{=}CF_2$, and $CH_2{=}CHF$.[32] By passing CH_3CF_2Cl through a tube at 870° either hydrogen chloride or hydrogen fluoride is removed, resulting in a 67 percent yield of $CH_2{=}CF_2$ and a 31.5 percent yield of $CH_2{=}CFCl$.[40] In the commercial preparation of tetrafluoroethylene, chlorodifluoromethane undergoes intermolecular elimination of hydrogen chloride at temperatures above 650° to give excellent yields of the product[31,120,156] (cf. Method 214).

METHOD 302 Dehalogenation

The most convenient method of dehalogenating fluorine-containing alkanes is by the use of zinc and a polar solvent such as alcohol. Zinc will effect elimination of chlorine, bromine, and iodine, but not fluorine. Compound halogens such as iodine-chlorine, bromine-chlorine and in some cases iodine-fluorine or chlorine-fluorine can also be eliminated by this procedure.

In choosing an alcohol to be used as a solvent, consideration should be given to the relative boiling points of the solvent and the desired product in order to facilitate separation. The reactions are usually carried out at the reflux temperature of the solvent; however, Benning, *et al.*[9] report that in order to effect dehalogenation of CF_2ClCF_2Cl in methanol, 110° at 200 psi for 5 hours is required. Zinc halide is often added to the zinc-solvent mixture in small amounts to shorten the induction period. The yield of olefin is usually good but in some cases the reaction may be accompanied by the reductive elimination of a halogen atom. Henne[89] obtained mainly $CF_3CCl{=}CHCF_3$ from the attempted dehalogenation of $CF_3CCl{=}CClCF_3$; some of the acetylenic derivative was also obtained.

Two moles of halogen may be removed simultaneously by this procedure as illustrated by the preparation of 1,3-perfluorobutadiene in a 98 percent yield from the 1,2,3,4-tetrachloro derivative.[62]

The role of the solvent in the zinc dehalogenation is that of a Lewis base which ties up the ZnX_2 formed and removes it from the surface of the zinc in the form of a complex. Although alcohols are the most commonly used solvents, dioxane, acetic anhydride, acetic acid, ethyl acetate, dimethyl formamide and acetone can be used. For example, the reaction of $CF_2ClCFClCFClCF_2Cl$ with zinc in dioxane yields 40 percent of $CF_2ClCF{=}CFCF_2Cl$ and only 15 percent of the diene, while a 98 percent yield of the diene was obtained using zinc and alcohol.[62] Park, *et al.*[157] were unable to prepare pure $CF_2{=}CFCONH_2$ from $CF_2BrCFBrCONH_2$ using zinc and alcohol, probably due to the addition of the alcohol to the resulting acrylamide. However, when acetone was employed as the solvent good yields of the acrylamide were obtained. Haszeldine[64] obtained $CF_2ClCH{=}CH_2$ in a 41 percent yield and $CF_2{=}CHCH_3$ in a 52 percent yield by treatment of $CF_2ClCHBrCH_2Cl$ with zinc in glacial acetic acid. The latter compound was formed by a simultaneous reduction and dehalogenation.

In several cases chlorine-fluorine and iodine-fluorine have been removed from alkanes by this procedure. McBee and co-workers[133] prepared $C_2F_5CF{=}CH_2$ in a 93 percent yield by treating $C_2F_5CF_2CH_2I$ with zinc in glacial acetic acid, while Haszeldine[76] obtained a 53 percent yield of $CF_3CF{=}CHF$ from CF_3CF_2CHClF using zinc in refluxing alcohol. Perfluoropropene has been obtained in poor yields by treating C_3F_7I with zinc in dioxane at 70° and in a 58 per cent yield by heating C_3F_7ZnI in a sealed tube[80] (cf. Method 1203). Gilman and Jones[42] prepared vinylidene fluoride in a 90 percent yield by the reaction of CF_3CH_2I with magnesium. Treatment of $CH_3CClFCH_2F$ with magnesium and iodine in refluxing ether for 18 hours results in the formation of 2-fluoropropene.[2]

Chlorotrifluoroethylene was prepared in a 92 to 98 percent yield by the addition of sodium to $CF_2ClCFCl_2$ in methanol.[39] The simultaneous reduction and dehalogenation of $CF_3CHBrCHBrCO_2C_2H_5$ to $CF_3CH{=}CHCH_2OH$ has been accomplished using lithium aluminum hydride (cf. Method 403). The dechlorination of $CF_2ClCFCl_2$, CF_2ClCF_2Cl and CF_2ClCCl_3 was effected by passing a mixture of the alkane and hydrogen over nickel at 200° to 700°.[13,23] Ehrenfeld[36] has prepared $CF_2{=}CHF$ by the electrolysis of $CF_2ClCFCl_2$ in a solution of zinc chloride in aqueous ethanol.

METHOD 303 Dehydration of Alcohols

Dehydration of fluorine-containing alcohols is accomplished in good yields by heating with phosphoric anhydride or concentrated sulfuric acid.[108,137,139] McBee, *et al.*[139] prepared $C_3F_7CH{=}CHC_2H_5$ in an 85 percent yield by heating $C_3F_7CH(OH)C_3H_7$ with phosphoric anhydride at 150° to 200°. Dehydration of the diol, $[n\text{-}C_3H_7CH(OH)CF_2CF_2{-}]_2$ with phosphoric anhydride yields only 10 percent of $(C_2H_5CH{=}CHCF_2CF_2{-})_2$ and 11 percent of $n\text{-}C_3H_7CH(OH)(CF_2)_4CH{=}CHC_2H_5$. However, by heating $CF_2[CF_2C(CH_3)_2OH]_2$ with concentrated sulfuric acid at 160°, $CF_2[CF_2C(CH_3){=}CH_2]_2$ was obtained in an 85 percent yield. The dehydration of some fluoroalcohols is very difficult due to the strengthening of the C—O bond resulting from the inductive effect of the fluorine atoms. For example, no dehydration occurs when $n\text{-}C_6H_{13}CH(OH)CF_3$ is heated with concentrated sulfuric acid, 85 percent phosphoric acid, or phosphoric anhydride. However, this alcohol may be converted to the olefin by pyrolysis of its ester[20] (cf. Method 305).

METHOD 304 Addition of Hydrogen Halides to Alkynes

Hydrogen fluoride readily adds to acetylene at elevated temperatures in the presence of AlF_3, Al_2O_3 or mercuric salts catalysts to yield a mixture of $CH_2{=}CHF$ and CH_3CHF_2[116,117,153] (cf. Methods 109 and 202). Hydrogen fluoride may also be added to vinyl acetylene using mercuric salts as catalyst to yield the mono- and di-addition products, $CH_2{=}CHCF{=}CH_2$ and $CH_2{=}CHCF_2CH_3$.[6,26,152,172] The addition of HF, HCl, HBr, or HI to $CF_3C{\equiv}CH$ gives good yields of compounds of the type $CF_3CH{=}CHX$.[60] Haszeldine[72] added hydrogen chloride to $CF_3C{\equiv}CCH_3$ using aluminum chloride catalyst and obtained $CF_3CH{=}CClCH_3$.

METHOD 305 Pyrolysis of Esters

Vapor phase pyrolysis of esters of fluorine-containing alcohols is of value for the preparation of olefins in cases where direct dehydration of the alcohol is unsuccessful. For example, Campbell, *et al.*[20] observed that $n\text{-}C_6H_{13}CH(OH)CF_3$ could not be dehydrated when heated with either concentrated sulfuric acid or phosphoric anhydride. However, the carbinol was converted to the olefin in a 59 percent yield by pyrolysis of its acetate over glass wool at 500°. Higher temperatures caused considerable carbonization; the ester was recovered unchanged at a reaction temperature of 450°.

Henne and Hinkamp[95] pyrolyzed the diacetate of $CF_3CH(OH)$-$CH_2CH(OH)CH_3$, and obtained a 75 percent yield of $CF_3CH{=}CHCH{=}CH_2$;

the pyrolysis of the bis(trifluoroacetate) of the same diol resulted in only a 40 percent yield of the diene.

METHOD 306 Decarboxylation of Salts of Fluorocarboxylic Acids

The decarboxylation of acid salts to produce olefins appears to be a reaction unique to the fluorine-containing acids; under certain conditions perfluoroalkyl halides and hydrides are produced (cf. Method 207). Terminally unsaturated olefins up to perfluoro-1-nonene can be prepared by pyrolysis of the sodium salts of the acids $CF_3(CF_2)_nCO_2Na$ (where n = 1–8) at 200° to 350°. However, decarboxylation of sodium trifluoroacetate gives only trifluoroacetyl fluoride (cf. Method 808), but when decarboxylation is carried out in the presence of sodium hydroxide, tetrafluoroethylene is obtained as the main product.[123] Brice[15] has shown that the pyrolysis of the sodium salt of perfluoropentanoic acid at 290° to 300° yields only perfluoro-1-butene while pyrolysis of the potassium salt at 165° to 200° yields 80 percent of perfluoro-2-butene and 20 percent of perfluoro-1-butene. Disodium perfluoroadipate has been pyrolyzed to perfluorobutadiene in a 30 percent yield.[67] The pyrolysis of $C_3F_7CHFCF_2CO_2Na$ at 200° yields $C_3F_7CH{=}CF_2$.[125]

In the pyrolysis of the sodium salts of carboxylic acids which contain fluorine and chlorine in the β-position, sodium chloride is preferentially eliminated. The pyrolysis of $CFCl_2CF_2CO_2Na$ yields 83 percent of $CFCl{=}CF_2$.[68] In no case has a ketone synthesis been reported by the pyrolysis of alkaline earth salts of perfluorocarboxylic acid which might be expected to occur by anology to hydrocarbon chemistry. For example, pyrolysis of barium perfluorobutyrate only yields perfluoro-1-propene.

METHOD 307 Free Radical Addition

Olefins can also be prepared by the free radical addition of perfluoroalkyl iodides to alkynes. The addition is accomplished by heating the reactants at 220° to 250° for 15 to 25 hours or by exposing the reactants to ultraviolet light for 3 to 5 days. Although the one-to-one adduct is produced as the main product, small amounts of telomers are also obtained. For example, by heating C_2F_5I with acetylene at 220° to 260° for 15 to 20 hours, $C_2F_5CH{=}CHI$ and $C_2F_5(CH{=}CH)_2I$ are obtained in 72 and 0.5 percent yields, respectively.[70]

The addition of trifluoromethyl iodide to propyne gives an 89 percent yield of $CF_3CH{=}CICH_3$ and traces of $CF_3CH{=}C(CH_3)CH{=}CICH_3$. However, the addition of trifluoromethyl iodide to trifluoropropyne results in a 38 percent yield of $CF_3CH{=}CICF_3$ and 9 percent yield of $CF_3CH{=}C(CF_3)CH{=}CICF_3$.[126] The reaction of trifluoromethyl iodide and allene in the presence of ultraviolet light for 48 hours results in a 96 percent yield of $CF_3CH_2CI{=}CH_2$.[73]

Park and co-workers[158] demonstrated that trifluorovinyl iodide undergoes addition to ethylene and fluoroethylenes to yield 1-butenes when irradiated with ultraviolet light. For example, $CF_2{=}CFI$ adds to ethylene to give $CF_2{=}CFCH_2CH_2I$ in good yields. The addition was also accomplished with $CHF{=}CH_2$, $CH_2{=}CF_2$ and other substituted ethylenes. The mode of addition is the same as described in Method 205.

METHOD 308 Disproportionation

The interchange of halogen atoms between two different compounds or the intramolecular rearrangement of the halogen atoms on a carbon skeleton can be effected with $AlCl_3$ (cf. Method 215). Disproportionation occurs when a mixture of hexachloropropene and chlorodifluoromethane is heated in the presence of aluminum chloride at 100° for ten hours; a mixture of $CCl_2FCCl{=}CCl_2$, $CClF_2CCl{=}CCl_2$ and $CF_3CCl{=}CCl_2$ is obtained.[34,52] Intramolecular disproportionation of $CF_2ClCCl{=}CCl_2$ in the presence of a metal halide yields $CCl_2FCCl{=}CCl_2$ and $CF_3CCl{=}CCl_2$.[162]

METHOD 309 Pyrolytic Reactions

The thermal cracking of many fluorine-containing materials may lead to olefins as well as alkanes (cf. Method 214). Pyrolytic reactions are best carried out by passing the material through a heated tube constructed of an inert material such as platinum or carbon. Very high pyrolysis temperatures may be obtained by the use of an electric arc or heated filament. It is very difficult to predict the course of this type of reaction for the products obtained may depend upon the temperature, contact time and pressure.

Upon heating "Teflon" at 500° to 700° in an inert chamber, $CF_2{=}CF_2$, $CF_3CF{=}CF_2$, $(CF_3)_2C{=}CF_2$ and other fluorocarbons are obtained in varying proportions depending upon the pressure.[8A,32,35] At 5 mm. pressure, $CF_2{=}CF_2$ is obtained in a 97 percent yield; at 41 mm. pressure, the yield of $CF_2{=}CF_2$ is 85.7 percent and $CF_3CF{=}CF_2$, 14.3 percent while at atmospheric pressure a mixture of fluorocarbons is produced which contains only a small amount of tetrafluoroethylene.

Hexafluoropropene and isomeric octafluorobutenes are obtained upon pyrolysis of tetrafluoroethylene at 600° to 700° at one atmosphere pressure. Similar results are observed when the olefin is passed over a platinum filament at 1000° to 1450° at 50 to 500 mm. pressure.[1,8A,179]

As previously stated, conditions play an important role in determining the products obtained from pyrolytic reactions. For example, the pyrolysis of perfluorocyclobutane at 400° to 600° produces a mixture of $CF_3CF{=}CF_2$ and $C_2F_5CF{=}CF_2$,[149] while pyrolysis of the same material at 700° to 725° yields a mixture of $(CF_3)_2C{=}CF_2$ and $CF_3CF{=}CFCF_3$.[15,159] Miller[149] reports that a mixture of $CF_2{=}CFCl$ and $CF_2{=}CFCClFCClF_2$ is obtained upon passing $\overline{CF_2CF_2CFClCFCl}$ (cyclic) through a tube at 560°, while pyrolysis of the same material in the presence of hydrogen yields only $CF_2{=}CFCl$.[10]

Haszeldine[74] has shown that the pyrolysis of perfluorocyclobutene at 600° gives only a 10 percent yield of perfluorobutadiene, while pyrolysis of perfluorobutadiene at 600° produces an 82 percent yield of perfluorocyclobutene. In similar manner 1,4-dichlorotetrafluorobutadiene is converted into 2,3-dichlorotetrafluorocyclobutene in 56 percent yield at a temperature of 250°. This would indicate that the cyclic olefins are the more thermodynamically stable structures.

METHOD 310 Reaction of Organometallic Compounds with Olefins

Dixon[30A] reports that fluoroolefins of the type, $FCY{=}CX_1X_2$ (where Y is F or fluoroalkyl and X_1X_2 are halogens) react in ether with organolithium compounds to give new olefins, $RCY{=}CX_1X_2$ and lithium fluoride. For example, the reaction of methyllithium with tetrafluoroethylene or chlorotrifluoroethylene at −80° produces $CH_3CF{=}CF_2$ and $CH_3CCl{=}CF_2$, respectively. No reaction occurred when vinylidene fluoride or 1,2-dichloro-1,2-difluoroethylene were treated with methyllithium. Although the reaction of alkyllithium compounds with tetrafluoroethylene gave only monoalkylated products, the reaction of alkyllithium compounds with cyclic fluoroolefins gave both monoalkyl and dialkyl perfluorocyclobutenes. For example, the reaction of methyllithium with perfluorocyclobutene yielded both $\overline{CF_2CFCF{=}CCH_3}$ (cyclic) and $\overline{CF_2CF_2C(CH_3){=}CCH_3}$ (cyclic). In the case of the reaction between phenyllithium and tetrafluoroethylene at low temperatures α,β,β-trifluorostyrene and α,β,-difluorostilbene are obtained. All fluorine atoms in $CF_2{=}CF_2$ may be replaced, to yield tetraphenylethylene when the reaction is carried out at 25°.

A similar reaction has been described by Tarrant and Warner[196] using alkyl Grignard reagents instead of alkyllithium compounds but poorer yields of olefins are obtained. For example, the reaction of ethylmagnesium bromide with $CF_2{=}CCl_2$ results in 10 percent conversion to

C_2H_5CF=CCl_2. It is interesting to note, however, that the reaction of methylmagnesium bromide with CF_2=$CFCF_2I$ results in a 24 percent conversion to CH_3CF_2CF=CF_2 and no CH_3CF=$CFCF_2I$ is obtained.

METHOD 311 Dimerization of Olefins

The dimerization of highly fluorinated olefins to cyclic butanes has been discussed previously (cf. Method 210). Generally, the dimerization of fluoroolefins containing not more than one fluorine atom per carbon atom leads to a linear product.[173] Upon heating CFCl=CFCl at 275° for 11 hours, a mixture of CFCl=CFCFClCFCl₂ (68%) and CFCl=CF(CFCl)₃CFCl (20%) is obtained.[74,170]

The codimerization or cycloalkylation of fluoroolefins with hydrocarbon dienes has been studied by a number of workers.[7,8,24] The codimerization appears to occur more easily than simple dimerization of fluoroolefins. Coffman and Barrick[8] studied the cycloalkylation reactions of tetrafluoroethylene and dienes and found that when a mixture of tetrafluoroethylene, butadiene and an inhibitor is heated at 125° for 8 hours

$\overline{CF_2CF_2CH_2CHCH}$=$CH_2$ is obtained in a 90 percent yield. These workers observed that no tetrafluorocyclohexane was formed as would be expected in a Diels-Alder condensation. When excess tetrafluoroethylene is employed a second cycloalkylation takes place to produce

$$
\begin{array}{cccc}
CF_2\!\!-\!\!CF_2 & CF_2\!\!-\!\!CF_2 \\
| \quad\quad | & | \quad\quad | \\
CH_2\!\!-\!\!CH\!\!-\!\!CH\!\!-\!\!CH_2
\end{array}
$$

The same reaction was carried out with other dienes with the following results:

$$CF_2\!=\!CF_2 + CH_2\!=\!CHC\!\equiv\!CH \xrightarrow[16.5\ \text{hrs.}]{100°}$$

$$
\begin{array}{c}
CF_2\!\!-\!\!CF_2 \\
|\quad\quad| \\
CH_2\!\!-\!\!CH\!\!-\!\!C\!\equiv\!CH\ (45\%)\ +
\end{array}
$$

$$
\begin{array}{c}
CF_2\!\!-\!\!CF_2 \\
|\quad\quad| \\
CH\!=\!C\!\!-\!\!CH\!=\!CH_2\ (45\%)\ +
\end{array}
$$

$$
\begin{array}{c}
CF_2\!\!-\!\!CF_2 \quad CF_2\!\!-\!\!CF_2 \\
|\quad\quad| \quad\ |\quad\quad| \\
CH_2\!\!-\!\!CH\!\!-\!\!C\!=\!CH\ (5\%)\ +
\end{array}
$$

$$
\begin{array}{c}
CH \\
\diagup\!\!\diagup \\
CH \quad\ CH \quad CF_2\!\!-\!\!CF_2 \\
|\quad\ \ \| \quad\ \ |\quad\quad| \\
CH \quad\ C\!\!-\!\!CH\!\!-\!\!CH_2 \\
\diagdown\!\!\diagup \\
CH
\end{array}
$$

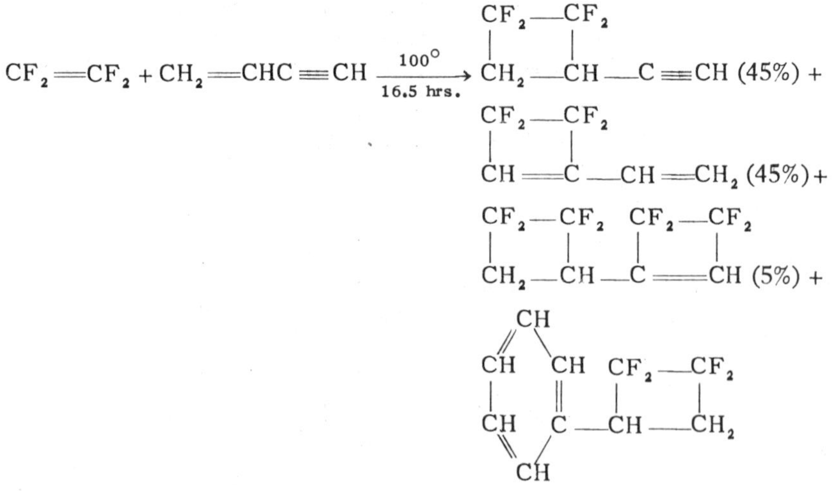

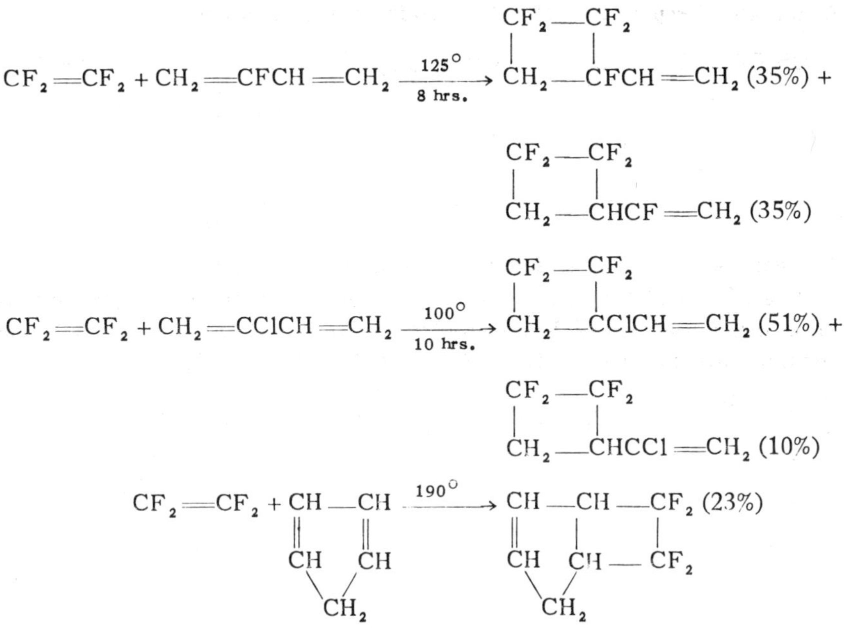

In all the cases studied only 1,2-addition occurred and no condensation products were obtained that could be explained by a Diels-Alder condensation.

More recently McBee, Pierce and Roberts[138] have reported the successful Diels-Alder reaction of several fluoroolefins with cyclopentadiene, butadiene, and anthracene. The reactions were carried out in sealed tubes in the presence of hydroquinone; benzene was used as a solvent in the case of anthracene. The fluoroolefins studied as dienophiles were found to have the following order of reactivity: $CF_3CF{=}CF_2 > C_2F_5CH{=}CH_2 > CF_3CH{=}CH_2 > CH_2FCH{=}CH_2 > CF_3C(CH_3){=}CH_2$. All these olefins reacted with cyclopentadiene at temperatures of 135° and 190° to give adducts in 60 to 70 percent yield. Allyl fluoride and 2-methyl-3,3,3-trifluoropropene were considerably less reactive. The following reactions are indicative of the results obtained from this work:

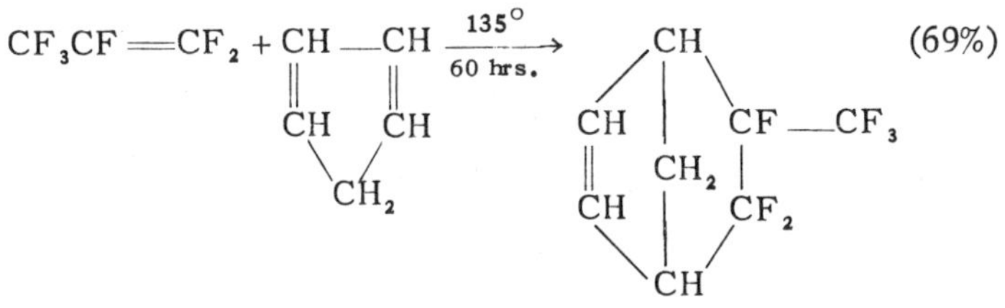

At a higher temperature (190°) bis-adducts were isolated,

$$CF_3CF = CF_2 + CH_2 = CHCH = CH_2 \xrightarrow[\text{24 hrs.}]{180°}$$

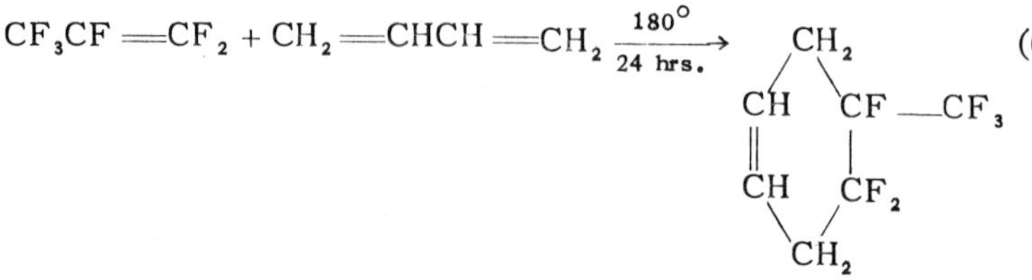

(64%)

The anthracene adducts were proven to be 9, 10-adducts.

Pruett[163] found that treatment of perfluorocyclobutene with pyridine at room temperature for 18 hours yielded as the main product a trimer of the possible structure

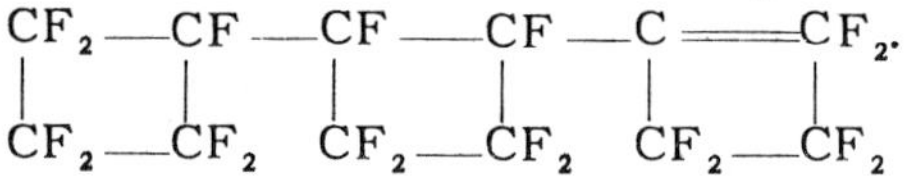

TABLE 3

ALKENES

Empirical Formula	Structural Formula	Method	Yield %	B.p. °C/mm.	F.p. or M.p. °C	n_D^t	d_4^t	t °C	Ref.
C_2BrF_3	$CF_2{=}CFBr$	301		−6.5/628					158, 181
$C_2Br_2F_2$	$CFBr{=}CFBr$	301		70.5/771		1.45345	2.3121		180
	$CF_2{=}CBr_2$	301							185
C_2Br_3F	$CFBr{=}CBr_2$	301		147.2			2.6699		180
C_2ClF_3	$CF_2{=}CFCl$	301	33	−26.8					30, 155, 175, 203
		302	77–92						12, 13, 23, 39, 107, 132
		306	83						68
		309	57						10
$C_2Cl_2F_2$	$CFCl{=}CFCl$ (cis)	302		21.1	−130.5	1.3777	1.4950	0	12, 132
	(trans)			22	−110.3	1.3798	1.4936	0	
		306	84						74
	$CF_2{=}CCl_2$	301	70	18.9–19	−116 to −115				135, 155
		302	90						13, 113
		309	71						18, 147
C_2Cl_3F	$CFCl{=}CCl_2$	301		71–72					178
		302		71.0	−108.9	1.4379	1.5460	20	12, 107, 132
		110	50						146
C_2F_3I	$CF_2{=}CFI$	301	76	28/627		1.4143	2.284	0	158
C_2F_4	$CF_2{=}CF_2$	301	76–87	−76					31, 120, 156
		302							9, 13
		306	80–90						49, 50, 71, 123, 124
		309	to 90						4, 10, 32, 35, 127, 160
C_2HBrF_2	$CFBr{=}CHF$	302		19.6/770		1.3846	1.8434	0	180
	$CF_2{=}CHBr$	301		6.1	−115.4		1.8175	0.5	107, 185
C_2HBr_2F	$CFBr{=}CHBr$	301		88.8			2.289	17.5	185
	$CHF{=}CBr_2$	301		90.3/748		1.4954	2.2908	17.5	180
C_2HClF_2	$CHCl{=}CF_2$			−17.7	−138.5				97, 107

TABLE 3 (*continued*)

Empirical Formula	Structural Formula	Method	Yield %	B.p. °C/mm.	F.p. or M.p. °C	n_D^t	d_4^t	t °C	Ref.
C_2HCl_2F	$CHCl=CClF$	301		35.1		1.4032	1.372	16.5	14,97,178
	$CHF=CCl_2$			37.3	−108.8	1.4036	1.3833	20	97
C_2HF_3	$CF_2=CHF$	302	85	−51					22,36,78,181
		306	35			1.3011		−72	47
C_2H_2BrF	$CH_2=CFBr$	301		12.5					183,184
		302		6.8					185
	$CHBr=CHF$	301		36					184
		302							180
C_2H_2ClF	$CH_2=CFCl$	301		−24.0	−169				14,40,107,145
		302							164,177
	$CHF=CHCl$	302		10					182
$C_2H_2F_2$	$CF_2=CH_2$	301	to 90	−82					32,33,40,42, 107,144,183
C_2H_3F	$CHF=CH_2$	301	70	−72					25,32,119,154, 174,198
		302							85,183,184
		304	82						21,116,117, 153,176,201
C_3BrF_5	$CF_2=CFCF_2Br$	301	59	28		1.3324		25	194
C_3ClF_5	$CF_2=CFCF_2Cl$	302	86	7.6		1.3050	1.5116	20	101
	$CF_2=CClCF_3$	302		6.8	−130				110
		107	47						112
	$CFCl=CFCF_3$	107	82	7.7–7.9	−156.8				101
$C_3Cl_2F_4$	$CCl_2=CFCF_3$	107	37	46.4	−139.6	1.3504	1.5389	20	92,110,112
	$CFCl=CClCF_3$	302		47.3	−137	1.3511	1.5468	20	110
	$CFCl=CFCF_2Cl$	302		43.5			1.555	10	105
$C_3Cl_3F_3$	$CF_2=CFCCl_3$	306	50	89–91		1.4027		25	199
	$CCl_2=CFCF_2Cl$	301	50–70	86.2/745		1.3950	1.576	25	90,169
		107	27						92
	$CCl_2=CClCF_3$	308		88.1	−114.6	1.4096	1.617	20	34,52,162
		107	43–77						15,28,112
		110							16,17
$C_3Cl_4F_2$	$CCl_2=CClCF_2Cl$	308		128.3	−102.2	1.4575	1.659	20	34,52,162

$C_3Cl_4F_2$		107	28						112
		110							16,331
C_3Cl_5F	$CCl_2{=}CClCFCl_2$	308		170		1.5052	1.702	20	34,162
		107	13						112
		110							16,331
	$CCl_2{=}CFCCl_3$	301		171.1	−77	1.506	1.7064	20	110
C_3F_5I	$CF_2{=}CFCF_2I$	204		53.4		1.389	2.109	20	151
C_3F_6	$CF_2{=}CFCF_3$	302	90	−29.4	−156.2				80,83,110,161
		306	97						49,50,61,124
		309							1,8A,32,149, 179
		107							149
		112							148
C_3HBrF_4	$CF_2{=}CHCF_2Br$	301	72	35		1.3463	1.747		194
$C_3HBr_2F_3$	$CHBr{=}CBrCF_3$	301	90	96		1.4322		20	58,98
C_3HClF_4	$CHCl{=}CFCF_3$	107		15	−115.8				110
$C_3HCl_2F_3$	$CCl_2{=}CHCF_3$	107		54.5		1.3688		20	111,112
	$CHCl{=}CFCF_2Cl$	302		58/748		1.3701	1.4643	25	167
				isomers					
				67/748		1.3825	1.4955	25	167
	$CHCl{=}CClCF_3$	107	92	53.7	−109.2	1.3670	1.4653	20	111,112,200
$C_3HCl_3F_2$	$CCl_2{=}CClCHF_2$	301		114.4		1.4452		20	29
		302							84
		107	24						200
	$CCl_2{=}CHCF_2Cl$	301		94.8/748		1.4190	1.5043	25	168
	$CHCl{=}CClCF_2Cl$	107	21	97		1.4253		20	200
C_3HCl_4F	$CHCl{=}CFCCl_3$	301		147.8		1.4870	1.5877	20	110
C_3HF_5	$CF_2{=}CHCF_3$	301	60–80	−21	−153				77,110,194
		302							141
	$CHF{=}CFCF_3$	302	53	−18.5					76
$C_3H_2BrClF_2$	$CH_2{=}CBrCF_2Cl$	301	89	78.5		1.415		20	64
$C_3H_2BrCl_2F$	$CCl_2{=}CFCH_2Br$	203		52/20		1.5130	1.8069	25	82
$C_3H_2BrF_3$	$CH_2{=}CBrCF_3$	301	90	33.0–33.5		1.3503		25	58,98
		107	85						64
	$CHBr{=}CHCF_3$	301	12	39–39.5		1.3580		23	58
		304	100						60,100

TABLE 3 (*continued*)

Empirical Formula	Structural Formula	Method	Yield %	B.p. °C/mm.	F.p. or M.p. °C	n_D^t	d_4^t	t °C	Ref.
$C_3H_2BrF_3$	$CHF{=}CHCF_2Br$	301	41	41–42		1.3666	1.667	25	194
$C_3H_2ClF_3$	$CH_2{=}CClCF_3$	301	50	14–15					58
		107	81						64
	$CHCl{=}CHCF_3$	301	82	20.8					58,75,111
		304	100						60
	$CH_2{=}CFCF_2Cl$	301		11.9	−143.7				110
$C_3H_2Cl_2F_2$	$CHCl{=}CClCHF_2$	107	82	89		1.4150		20	86,200
	$CH_2{=}CClCF_2Cl$	301	91	57–58		1.378		22	64
	$CH_2{=}CFCFCl_2$	301	40	54.4	−115.9	1.3851	1.3523	20	110
$C_3H_2F_3I$	$CF_3CH{=}CHI$	304	65	70–71					60
		307	80						54,56
$C_3H_2F_4$	$CH_2{=}CFCF_3$	107		−28.3	−152.24				110
	$CHF{=}CHCF_3$	301	80	−16					75
		304							60
	$CHF{=}CFCHF_2$	302		15–23					83
C_3H_3BrClF	$CHCl{=}CFCH_2Br$	203	45	39–40/40		1.4917		20	81
				isomers					
				61–62/40		1.5040		20	81
$C_3H_3BrF_2$	$CH_2{=}CHCF_2Br$	301	64	42		1.3773	1.543	25	194
$C_3H_3ClF_2$	$CH_2{=}CHCF_2Cl$	301	84	17.5					64
		302	72						64
$C_3H_3Cl_2F$	$CHCl{=}CFCH_2Cl$	216	38	41.7/100		1.4411	1.3510	20	81
				isomers					
				46/44		1.4571	1.3769	20	81
	$CCl_2{=}CFCH_3$		51	76.5–78		1.4196	1.3026	25	82
$C_3H_3F_3$	$CH_2{=}CHCF_3$	301	75	−18 to −16					58,75,134,194
		302							110
		107	51						64,98
	$CF_2{=}CFCH_3$	310	20	−18					30A
		302							110
C_3H_4ClF	$CHCl{=}CFCH_3$			29/747		1.3770	1.0812	20	81
				isomers					
				59/747		1.3920	1.1139	20	81

$C_3H_4F_2$	$CF_2{=}CHCH_3$	301		−29 to −27					32
		302	52						64
C_3H_5F	$CH_2{=}CFCH_3$	301	90	−24/757					3
		302							2
	$CH_2{=}CHCH_2F$	102							143
$C_4Br_2F_6$	$CF_3CBr{=}CBrCF_3$	301	78	106		1.396		25	59
C_4ClF_7	$CF_3CF{=}CClCF_3$	302		32.2		1.2946	1.5482	20	101
		107							46
$C_4Cl_2F_5I$	$CF_2{=}CFCF_2CCl_2I$	307	5	160/624		1.4635	2.232	20	158
$C_4Cl_2F_6$	$CF_3CCl{=}CClCF_3$	301	87	67.8	−67.3	1.3459	1.6233	20	59,94
		106							101
		107	95						46,109
	$CF_2ClCF{=}CFCF_2Cl$	302	40	65		1.339		25	62
	$CF_2{=}CFCF_2CFCl_2$	302	78	70–71					68
		306	63						68
	$CF_2{=}CFCFClCF_2Cl$	301	72	65.5–67		1.3440	1.615	22	131
		302							150
		309							149
		311							150
	$(CF_3)_2C{=}CCl_2$	301	83	74.5	−98.2	1.3517	1.6429	20	108
$C_4Cl_3F_5$	$CF_2{=}CClCF_2CFCl_2$	302		104.1		1.3840	1.6671	20	101
	$CCl_2{=}CClCF_2CF_3$	107		140.7		1.4040	1.7421	20	101
$C_4Cl_4F_4$	$CFCl{=}CFCFClCFCl_2$	309	57	140.5		1.429		20	74
		311	85						74,170,173
	$CF_2{=}CClCF_2CCl_3$	302		142.4		1.4254	1.7084	20	101
$C_4Cl_6F_2$	$CCl_2{=}CClCF_2CCl_3$	302	31	85–6/10		1.5052	1.7842	20	87,101
	$CCl_2{=}CClCCl_2CClF_2$	301		125.8/47	−50.7	1.5073	1.8047	25	106
$C_4F_6I_2$	$CF_2{=}CFCF_2CFI_2$	307		146/622		1.4794	2.522	20	158
C_4F_7I	$CF_2{=}CFCF_2CF_2I$	207	72	70/760					67
C_4F_8	$CF_2{=}CFCF_2CF_3$	306	91	1/740			1.5443	0	15,49,50,61, 124
		309							1,149
	$CF_3CF{=}CFCF_3$	302	52	0/740			1.5297	0	101,148
		306	80						15
		309							1
		107	80						62

TABLE 3 (*continued*)

Empirical Formula	Structural Formula	Method	Yield %	B.p. °C/mm.	F.p. or M.p. °C	n_D^t	d_4^t	t °C	Ref.
C_4F_8	$CF_2=C(CF_3)_2$	302	88	7.0			1.5922	0	79
		309	70						15,159,179
$C_4HBrClF_5$	$CF_2=CHCFClCF_2Br$	301	49	91		1.3837	1.838	24	131,190
C_4HBrF_6	$CF_3CH=CBrCF_3$	301	58	55					59
		304	68						60
C_4HClF_5I	$CF_2=CFCHClCF_2I$	307	4	127/627		1.4391	2.177	20	158
C_4HClF_6	$CF_2=CFCF_2CFClH$	302	75	56					78
	$CF_3CH=CClCF_3$	301	80	34.5-35.5	−106.1	1.2996	1.4909	20	59
		302							89
		304	65						60
		107							94
$C_4HCl_3F_3I$	$CF_3CI=CHCCl_3$	307	74	108/27					63
$C_4HCl_3F_4$	$CFCl=CHCFClCF_2Cl$	301	39	102.5		1.3993	1.586	24	131,190
$C_4HCl_4F_3$	$CF_3CH=CClCCl_3$	301		143.2		1.4360	1.6236	25	94
$C_4HCl_5F_2$	$CHCl_2CCl=CClCF_2Cl$	301		140.9/23	−51	1.4838	1.683	20	106
C_4HF_6I	$CF_3CH=CICF_3$	307	38	75.5		1.3758		16	126
	$CF_2=CFCFHCF_2I$	307	39	83/631		1.4006	2.103	20	158
$C_4H_2BrClF_4$	$CHF=CHCFClCF_2Br$	301	48	97/97.3		1.3961	1.781	25	131,190
$C_4H_2ClF_5$	$CH_2=C(CF_2Cl)CF_3$	301	28	52-55					66
$C_4H_2Cl_3F_3$	$CF_3CH=CHCCl_3$	301		128-130					63
		211	63						63
$C_4H_2F_5I$	$CF_2=CFCH_2CF_2I$	307	24	92/633		1.4118	2.060	20	158
	$CF_3CF_2CH=CHI$	307	72	84.4		1.392		25	70
$C_4H_2F_6$	$CF_3CF_2CF=CH_2$	302	93	3-7					133
	$CF_3CH=CHCF_3$	301	95	8.5					59,99
		212	91						59,89
$C_4H_2F_6$	(trans)	211	70	9.1					126
		212		33.2	−90.5	1.2825	1.4128(0)	2.2	89
	$(CF_3)_2C=CH_2$	107	93	11-13					66
$C_4H_3BrClF_3$	$CF_2BrCFClCH=CH_2$	301	68	99.5		1.4092	1.678	25	131,190
$C_4H_3Br_2F_3$	$CF_3CBr=CBrCH_3$	301	76	133-134		1.4568		19	72
$C_4H_3Cl_2F_3$	$CF_3C(CH_3)=CCl_2$	301		88.4		1.9947	1.4248	20	108
		107	42						66

$C_4H_3Cl_2F_3$	$CF_2ClCFClCH=CH_2$	301	91	71.8/631	Glass	1.3769	1.348	20	157
$C_4H_3F_4I$	$CF_2=CFCH_2CHFI$	307	50	107/633		1.4370	2.052	20	158
$C_4H_3F_5$	$CF_2=CFCF_2CH_3$	310	24	24–26		1.3571	1.57	11	196
	$CH_2=CHCF_2CF_3$	303							137
	$CF_3C(CH_3)=CF_2$	301	69	12.8–13.5/745					66,108
$C_4H_4BrF_3$	$CF_2=CFCH_2CH_2Br$	302		95		1.4022	1.660	22	131
$C_4H_4BrF_3$	$CF_3CH=CBrCH_3$	301	16	79–82		1.403		20	72
$C_4H_4ClF_3$	$CF_3CH=CClCH_3$	301	76	58–60					76
		304	56						76
	$CF_3C(CH_3)=CHCl$	301		46.4	−120.3	1.3489	1.2395	20	108
		107	70						108
	$CF_3C(CH_2Cl)=CH_2$	107		64.1		1.3520	1.2824	20	108
$C_4H_4Cl_2F_2$	$CF_2ClC(CH_3)=CHCl$	107		86–7		1.4023	1.3406	20	108
$C_4H_4F_3I$	$CF_2=CFCH_2CH_2I$	307	67	112/623		1.4554	1.957	20	158
	$CF_3CH_2CI=CH_2$	307	96	58–59/160		1.4312		20	73
	$CF_3CH=CICH_3$	307	91	94.5		1.4352		20	72,126
$C_4H_5BrF_2$	$CF_2BrCH=CHCH_3$	205		76.5/760		1.3872	1.3847	25	192
$C_4H_5ClF_2$	$CH_3CF_2CH=CHCl$	301		72/745		1.3720	1.157	27	136
	$CF_2ClCH_2CH=CH_2$	302	79	49.2/760		1.3550	1.103	25	191
	$CF_2ClCH=CHCH_3$	301	46	59.5–60		1.3656	1.1100	25	27,193
$C_4H_5Cl_2F$	$CFCl_2CH_2CH=CH_2$	302		88/760		1.4104	1.188	27	191
	$CH_3CH_2CF=CCl_2$	310	10	96.5–98		1.4219	1.217	25	196
$C_4H_5F_3$	$CF_3CH_2CH=CH_2$	302	80	10.5					73
		211	82						73
	$CH_3CH_2CF=CF_2$	310	20	13					30A
		302							131
$C_4H_5F_3$	$CF_3CH=CHCH_3$	301	80	17.7					75,194
		211	83	16.5					126
	$CF_3C(CH_3)=CH_2$	303	97	6.7					108,187
C_4H_6ClF	$CFCl=CHCH_2CH_3$	301	90	54.4	−144.9	1.3851	1.0216	20	93
$C_4H_6F_2$	$CF_2=CHCH_2CH_3$	301	83	3.71	−164.9	1.3253	0.9284	0	93
	$CH_3CF_2CH=CH_2$	304		24.0–24.5		1.327	0.937	10	26,152
	$CH_2=C(CH_2F)_2$	101		61.4–61.6		1.3621	1.0217	21.2	48
C_4H_7F	$CH_2=CFCH_2CH_3$	301		23.5/745		1.3492	0.824	15	136
	$CH_3CF=CHCH_3$	301		26/745		1.3302		10	32
		107							136
$C_5Cl_2F_8$	$CF_3CF_2CClFCF=CClF$	302	50	67		1.306		20	76

TABLE 3 (*continued*)

Empirical Formula	Structural Formula	Method	Yield %	B.p. °C/mm.	F.p. or M.p. °C	n_D^t	d_4^t	t °C	Ref.
$C_5Cl_2F_8$	$CF_2ClCCl(CF_3)CF=CF_2$	301	40	89/760		1.339	1.727	25	195
C_5F_{10}	$CF_2=CF(CF_2)_2CF_3$	306	90	29–30		1.2571		25	49,50,124
$C_5HCl_2F_7$	$CF_2ClCCl(CF_3)CH=CF_2$	301		92/760		1.3478	1.665	25	195
C_5HF_8I	$CF_3CH=CICF_2CF_3$	307	29	84–86		1.3623		16	126
C_5HF_9	$CF_3(CF_2)_2CH=CF_2$			30/740					125
	$(CF_3)_2C=CHCF_3$	301	81	33					66
		107	45						66
$C_5H_2Cl_2F_6$	$CF_2ClCFClCH=CHCF_3$	301	63	87.5		1.3472	1.519	23	131,190
$C_5H_2F_7I$	$CF_3(CF_2)_2CH=CHI$	307		101.5/772					55
$C_5H_2F_8$	$CF_3CH_2C(CF_3)=CF_2$	302	91						66
$C_5H_3Cl_2F_5$	$CF_2ClCCl(CF_3)CH=CH_2$	301	44	96/760		1.3627	1.510	25	195
$C_5H_3Cl_2F_5$	$CF_2ClCFClC(CH_3)=CF_2$	301	57	100.5		1.3746	1.515	22	131,190
$C_5H_3F_7$	$CF_3(CF_2)_2CH=CH_2$	303	95	31					160
$C_5H_5BrClF_3$	$CF_2BrCFClCH=CHCH_3$	301	45	74–75/93		1.4100	1.5684	26	189
$C_5H_5F_5$	$CF_3CF_2C(CH_3)=CH_2$	303	65	30			1.184	3	137
$C_5H_7BrF_2$	$CF_2BrC(CH_3)=CHCH_3$	301		103–105		1.425	1.423	20	27
	$CF_2BrCH=C(CH_3)_2$			96/760		1.4095	1.3476	25	192
$C_5H_7ClF_2$	$CH_2ClCH(CH_3)CH=CF_2$	301	11	93.9		1.3881	1.1255	25	188
	$CF_2ClC(CH_3)=CHCH_3$	301	44	86–87.5		1.3924	1.105	25	27
	$CH_2=C(CH_3)CH_2CF_2Cl$	302	56	75.1–75.6		1.3736	1.0831	25	188
	$CF_2ClCH=C(CH_3)_2$	301	78	87		1.3960	1.083	25	188,193
$C_5H_7F_3$	$CF_3CH=CHCH_2CH_3$	305	95	48.2–49.2/750		1.3254	0.9971	20	20
	$CF_3CH=C(CH_3)_2$	301	79	49.5–50		1.3296	1.0114	25	188
$C_5H_8F_2$	$CH_2=CHCF_2CH_2CH_3$	301		51					88
	$CF_2=CHCH(CH_3)_2$	301	59	27.8		1.33	0.8711	25	188
C_5H_9F	$CH_2F(CH_2)_2CH=CH_2$	101		61.9–62.1					118
$C_6Cl_3F_9$	$CF_2=CFCF_2CFClCF_2CFCl_2$	302	59	80–82/105					68
$C_6Cl_6F_6$	$CCl_3CF_2CF=CFCF_2CCl_3$	302	52			1.4501	1.8126	28	96
	$CFCl=CF(CFCl)_3CFCl_2$	311	20	224.4/760	−28.8	1.4441	1.764	25	170
C_6F_{12}	$CF_2=CF(CF_2)_3CF_3$	306	65	57					61
	$CF_3CF_2CF=CFCF_2CF_3$	302	58	49					76
	$CF_2=C(CF_3)CF_2CF_2CF_3$	302	53	60					79
	$(CF_3)_2C=C(CF_3)_2$	302	92						148

$C_6HF_{10}I$	$CF_3(CF_2)_2CH{=}CICF_3$	307	38	110				126
$C_6H_2F_9I$	$CF_3CF_2CF(CF_3)CH{=}CHI$	307	83	74–76/148				65
$C_6H_4Cl_2F_6$	$CF_2ClCFClCH{=}C(CH_3)CF_3$	301	40	109.5	1.3675	1.485	20	131,190
$C_6H_5ClF_6$	$CF_2ClCF(CF_3)CH{=}CHCH_3$	301		90/760	1.3405	1.367	25	195
$C_6H_5F_7$	$CF_3(CF_2)_2C(CH_3){=}CH_2$	303	71	55	1.2983	1.303	20	91,139
	$CF_3(CF_2)_2CH{=}CHCH_3$	303	70	62/743	1.3018		20	161
$C_6H_7BrClF_3$	$CF_2BrCFClCH{=}C(CH_3)_2$	301	50	42/39	1.4423	1.5274	24	189
$C_6H_8BrF_3$	$CF_2{=}CFCH(CH_3)CHBrCH_3$	302		79/65	1.4160	1.442	22	189
$C_6H_9ClF_2$	$CH_3(CH_2)_3CF{=}CFCl$	310	60	109				30A
$C_6H_9F_3$	$CH_3(CH_2)_3CF{=}CF_2$	310	80	70				30A
$C_6H_{11}F$	$CH_2F(CH_2)_3CH{=}CH_2$	101		91–92	1.3869		26	118
C_7F_{14}	$CF_3(CF_2)_4CF{=}CF_2$	306	86	81	1.2782		15	61,124
$C_7H_4F_{10}$	$CF_3(CF_2)_2CFHCF_2CH{=}CH_2$	303		91–92/740	1.3005		25	125
$C_7H_7F_7$	$CF_3(CF_2)_2CH{=}CHCH_2CH_3$	303	85	86	1.3178	1.253	20	139
	$CF_3(CF_2)_2CH{=}C(CH_3)_2$	303	68	82	1.3254	1.288	20	139
C_8F_{16}	$CF_3(CF_2)_5CF{=}CF_2$	306	47	105				61
$C_8H_6F_{10}$	$CF_3(CF_2)_2CHFCF_2C$- $(CH_3){=}CH_2$	303		113–114/740	1.3143		25	125
$C_8H_{13}F_3$	$CF_3CH{=}CH(CH_2)_4CH_3$	305	59	123.4/749	1.3682	0.962	20	20
C_9F_{18}	$CF_3(CF_2)_6CF{=}CF_2$	306	65	123	1.2868		20	49,50,124
$C_9H_{10}Cl_2F_6$	$CH_2{=}C(CH_3)CF_2CF_2CF_2C$- $(CH_3)ClCH_2Cl$	201	42	62/2	1.4403	1.508	25	139
$C_{10}Cl_4F_{16}$	$(CF_2ClCF_2CFClCF_2CF{=})_2$	302	30	86–90/6	1.3675	1.8349	20	104
$C_{10}H_{15}BrClF_3$	$CF_2BrCFClCH{=}CH(CH_2)_5CH_3$	301	70	62/0.5	1.4410	1.329	24	189
$C_{14}H_{25}F_3$	n-$C_{12}H_{25}CF{=}CF_2$	310	51	71/1				30A

TABLE 4

DIENES AND TRIENES

Empirical Formula	Structural Formula	Method	Yield %	B.p. °C/mm.	F.p. or M.p. °C	n_D^t	d_4^t	t °C	Ref.
C_4ClF_5	$CF_2{=}CClCF{=}CF_2$			37					150
$C_4Cl_2F_4$	$CFCl{=}CFCF{=}CFCl$	302	78	82.7–83.2/740		1.4053	1.561	20	74,150
		309	14						74
	$CF_2{=}CClCCl{=}CF_2$	302		67.2					150
	$CFCl{=}CClCF{=}CF_2$	302		72					150
$C_4Cl_3F_3$	$CFCl{=}CClCCl{=}CF_2$	302		104.5/740					150
C_4F_6	$CF_2{=}CFCF{=}CF_2$	302	67–98	7.4–7.6					62,69,74,103, 131,150
		306	30–70						67,69
		309	3–12						74
C_4HClF_4	$CF_2{=}CFCH{=}CFCl$	302	64	53		1.3804	1.431	24	131,190
C_4HF_5	$CF_2{=}CFCH{=}CF_2$	302	80	15.5					131,190
$C_4H_2F_4$	$CF_2{=}CFCH{=}CHF$	302	80	16.5		1.3427	1.342	0	131,190
$C_4H_3F_3$	$CF_2{=}CFCH{=}CH_2$	302	65–88	7.8–8.0					131,157,190
		301	20	8.5					194
	$CF_2{=}CHCF{=}CH_2$	304	42	16.9		1.3462	1.113	4	194
C_4H_4ClF	$CH_2{=}CFCCl{=}CH_2$	301							11
	$CFCl{=}CHCH{=}CH_2$	301		53.4/760		1.4267	1.066	25	191
$C_4H_4F_2$	$CF_2{=}CHCH{=}CH_2$	301	50	3.5–4.0/760		1.338	1.0	2	27,191,192
	$CH_2{=}CFCF{=}CH_2$	302		5–8	−92	1.373	1.001	0	202
C_4H_5F	$CH_2{=}CFCH{=}CH_2$	304	23–68	11.5–12		1.400	0.843	4	6,26,152,172
$C_5Cl_6F_2$	$CF_2(CCl{=}CCl_2)_2$	302	91	101/13	−40.8	1.5170	1.7480	20	88
C_5F_8	$CF_2{=}C(CF_3)CF{=}CF_2$	302		30–31/760		1.3000	1.527	0	195
				or 39					150
C_5HF_7	$CF_2{=}C(CF_3)CH{=}CF_2$	302	78	32.8/760		1.3087	1.494	0	195

$C_5H_2F_6$	$CF_2{=}CFCH{=}CHCF_3$	302	72	50.5		1.3322	1.389	22	131,190
$C_5H_3F_5$	$CF_2{=}CFC(CH_3){=}CF_2$	302	74	37		1.3250	1.289	20	131,190
	$CF_2{=}C(CF_3)CH{=}CH_2$	302	78	32.5/760		1.3372	1.310	0	195
$C_5H_5F_3$	$CF_2{=}CFCH_2CH{=}CH_2$	302	65	38/760		1.3435	1.0324	27	189
	$CF_2{=}CFCH{=}CHCH_3$	302	60	44–45/760		1.3689	0.9974	24	189
	$CF_3CH{=}CHCH{=}CH_2$	305	75	45.2–45.9		1.3571	1.027	20	95
	$CF_2{=}C(CH_3)CF{=}CH_2$	301	60	50		1.3631	1.095	25	194
	$CH_2{=}C(CF_3)CH{=}CH_2$	301	20	34–35		1.3485	1.064	20	95
		303		40–1/745					115
$C_5H_6F_2$	$CH_2{=}CHCF_2CH{=}CH_2$	301	63	46.8	−135.3	1.3552	0.9368	20	88
	$CF_2{=}C(CH_3)CH{=}CH_2$	301	23	39		1.3760	0.9582	25	192
		301		38		1.342	0.90	21	27
	$CF_2{=}CHC(CH_3){=}CH_2$	301	61	35.5		1.3705	0.946	25	188,192
C_5H_7F	$CH_2{=}C(CH_3)CF{=}CH_2$	304		47.3–7.5		1.397	0.847	25	26
$C_6Cl_2F_6$	$CFCl{=}CFCF{=}CFCF{=}CFCl$	302	46	132–4		1.4324	1.6116	25	171
C_6F_8	$CF_2{=}CFCF{=}CFCF{=}CF_2$	302	56	65–66/748		1.537	1.537	25	170
$C_6H_4F_5I$	$CF_3CF_2CH{=}CHCH{=}CHI$	307	0.5	104/46					70
$C_6H_4F_6$	$CF_2{=}CFCH{=}C(CH_3)CF_3$	302	72	71.5		1.3531	1.350	22	131,190
$C_6H_7F_3$	$(CH_3)_2C{=}CHCF{=}CF_2$	302	42	52–54/760		1.3606	0.8538	24	189
	$CF_3CH{=}CHC(CH_3){=}CH_2$	305	58	74–75		1.3780	1.052	20	95
$C_7H_2F_9I$	$CF_3CI{=}CHC(CF_3){=}CHCF_3$	307	9						126
$C_7H_8F_3I$	$CF_3CH{=}C(CH_3)CH{=}CICH_3$	307		54–55/7					126
$C_8Cl_2F_{12}$	$(CFClCF_2CF{=}CF_2)_2$	302	51	58/20					69
	$[CCl{=}C(CF_3)_2]_2$	301		123		1.3462	1.6838	20	108
C_8F_{12}	$CF_2{=}CFCF_2CF{=}CFCF_2CF{=}CF_2$	302	78	99–100					69

TABLE 4 (*continued*)

Empirical Formula	Structural Formula	Method	Yield %	B.p. °C/mm.	F.p. or M.p. °C	n_D^t	d_4^t	t °C	Ref.
$C_9H_2F_{13}I$	$CF_3CH{=}C(C_2F_5)CI{=}CHCF_2CF_3$	307	4	86–88/100					126
	$CF_3CI{=}CHC(CF_3){=}CH(CF_2)_2CF_3$	307		83/56					126
$C_9H_{10}F_6$	$CF_2[CF_2C(CH_3){=}CH_2]_2$	303	85	31/4		1.3620	1.228	20	139
$C_9H_{14}F_2$	$CH_2{=}CF(CH_2)_5CF{=}CH_2$	304		87/4	1.19	1.4036	0.9978	20	102
$C_{10}H_{10}F_8$	$[CF_2CF_2C(CH_3){=}CH_2]_2$	303	74	140		1.3682	1.110	20	139
$C_{10}H_{15}F_3$	$CF_2{=}CFCH{=}CH(CH_2)_5CH_3$	302	72	25/35		1.3810	0.838	24	189
$C_{11}H_{14}F_6$	$CF_2(CF_2CH{=}CHC_2H_5)_2$	303	12	86/19		1.3884	1.214	20	139
$C_{12}Cl_2F_{18}$	$(CF_2{=}CFCF_2CFClCF_2CF{=})_2$	302		115–120/20					69
$C_{12}H_{14}F_8$	$(CF_2CF_2CH{=}CHCH_2CH_3)_2$	303	10	92/14		1.3800	1.250	20	139

TABLE 5
ALKYNES AND ALLENES

Empirical Formula	Structural Formula	Method	Yield %	B.p. °C/mm.	F.p. or M.p. °C	n_D^t	d_4^t	t °C	Ref.
C_3F_4	$CF_2=C=CF_2$	301		− 38					119A
C_3HF_3	$CF_3C\equiv CH$	301	68–75	− 48					54, 57
C_4F_6	$CF_3C\equiv CCF_3$	301	68	− 24					59
		302	90						43, 59, 89
C_4HF_5	$CF_3CF_2C\equiv CH$	301	64	− 12					70
$C_4H_3F_3$	$CF_3C\equiv CCH_3$	302	39	18–18.5					72
	$CF_3CH=C=CH_2$	301	44	16					73

TABLE 6 CYCLIC ALKENES

Empirical Formula	Structural Formula	Method	Yield %	B.p. °C/mm.	F.p. or M.p. °C	n_D^t	d_4^t	t °C	Ref.
C_4ClF_5	$CF_2CF_2CCl{=}CF$	302	80	33–33.4		1.3208		25	121
$C_4Cl_2F_4$	$CF_2CF_2CCl{=}CCl$	302		67.1	−43.4	1.3699	1.534	25	106,173
	$CFClCFClCF{=}CF$	302	83	65.5		1.375			74
		309	74						74
C_4F_6	$CF_2CF_2CF{=}CF$	302	to 94	5–6	−60				18,51,53, 106,173
		309	82						74
C_4HF_5	$CF_2CF_2CF{=}CH$	301	64	25–26					19
$C_5Cl_2F_6$	$CF_2CF_2CF_2CCl{=}CCl$	107	72	90.7	−105.8	1.3676	1.6546	20	114,122,142
$C_5Cl_3F_5$	$CF_2CFClCF_2CCl{=}CCl$	107		122.98	glass	1.4069	1.6852	20	114
$C_5Cl_4F_2$	$CF_2CCl{=}CClCCl{=}CCl$	302	63	45/4		1.5008			140
$C_5Cl_4F_4$	$CF_2CCl_2CF_2CCl{=}CCl$	107		155.19	glass	1.4429	1.7165	20	114
$C_5Cl_5F_3$	$CF_2CCl_2CFClCCl{=}CCl$	107		185–190		1.48			114

$C_5Cl_6F_2$	$CFClCCl_2CFClCCl{=}CCl$ (cyclic)	107		90–93/10		1.513			114
	$CF_2CCl_2CCl_2CCl{=}CCl$ (cyclic)	107	58	93/10		1.5161		20	140
	or								
	$CCl_2CF_2CCl_2CCl{=}CCl$ (cyclic)								
C_5Cl_7F	$CFClCCl_2CCl_2CCl{=}CCl$ (cyclic)	107		116–118/10		1.546		20	114
$C_5H_3F_5$	$CF_2CF_2CF{=}CCH_3$ (cyclic)	310	30	50					30A
$C_5H_4F_4$	$CF_2CF_2CH_2C{=}CH_2$ (cyclic)	311		64–6		1.3318	1.2288	25	8,24
$C_6Br_2F_8$	$CF_2CFBrCFBrCF_2CF{=}CF$ (cyclic)	201		40/13					37
$C_6Cl_2F_8$	$CF_2(CF_2)_3CCl{=}CCl$ (cyclic)	107	44	111–113					142
		113		113/750	−70	1.375	1.719	20	130
C_6F_8	$CF_2CF_2CF{=}CFCF{=}CF$ (cyclic)	302		56–57/743	6	1.3149	1.601	20	128
		301		63–64		1.329		18	37,38
	$CF_2CF{=}CFCF_2CF{=}CF$ (cyclic)	301		57–58		1.318		18	37
C_6F_{10}	$CF_2(CF_2)_3CF{=}CF$ (cyclic)	301	82	52–53/750		1.296		15	197

TABLE 6 (*continued*)

Empirical Formula	Structural Formula	Method	Yield %	B.p. °C/mm.	F.p. or M.p. °C	n_D^t	d_4^t	t °C	Ref.
C_6HF_9	$CF_2CHFCF_2CF_2CF{=}CF$ (cyclic)	301		70–71		1.311		18	38
	$CHF(CF_2)_3CF{=}CF$ (cyclic)	301		69		1.311		18	38
	$CF_2(CF_2)_3CF{=}CH$ (cyclic)	301		64–65/750		1.310		12	165
$C_6H_4F_4$	$CF_2CF_2CH{=}CCH{=}CH_2$ (cyclic)	311 301	45	98–99 98–100		1.3742	1.2588	25	7,8,24 53
	$CF_2CF_2CH_2CHC{\equiv}CH$ (cyclic)	311	45	82–84		1.3553	1.2498	25	7,8,24
$C_6H_5ClF_4$	$CF_2CF_2CH_2CClCH{=}CH_2$ (cyclic)	311	51	108		1.3833	1.3483	25	8,24
	$CF_2CF_2CH_2CHCCl{=}CH_2$ (cyclic)	311	10	122–124		1.3868	1.3654	25	8,24
$C_6H_5F_5$	$CF_2CF_2CH_2CHCF{=}CH_2$ (cyclic)	311	35	95		1.3458	1.3193	25	8,24
	$CF_2CF_2CH_2CFCH{=}CH_2$ (cyclic)	311	35	85		1.3405	1.2941	25	8,24
$C_6H_6F_4$	$CF_2CF_2CH_2CHCH{=}CH_2$ (cyclic)	311	90	83–85		1.3489	1.1866	25	7,24

$C_3Cl_4F_2$	$CF_2CF_2C(CH_3)=CCH_3$	310	35	104					30A
C_7F_{12}	$CF_2CF_2CF(CF_3)CF_2CF=CF$	301		75.4–75.9		1.293		20	5
$C_7H_6F_4$	$CF_2CF_2CHCHCH=CHCH_2$	311	23	120–123		1.3865		25	24
$C_7H_6F_6$	$CH_2CF(CF_3)CF_2CH_2CH=CH$	311	64	97		1.3430		20	138
$C_7H_8F_4$	$CF_2CF_2CH_2CHCH=CHCH_3$	311	68	111		1.3698	1.1607	25	24
$C_7H_8F_4$	$CF_2CF_2CH_2C(CH_3)CH=CH_2$	311	83	103		1.3649	1.1655	25	24
$C_7H_9F_3$	$CH_2CH(CF_3)CH_2CH_2CH=CH$	303							186
		311	35	104		1.3856		20	138
$C_8H_2F_{10}$	$CF_2C(CF_3)=CHCF_2C(CF_3)=CH$	112		111.5	−16	1.3310		25	41
$C_8H_2F_{12}$	$CF_2CF(CF_3)CHFCF_2C(CF_3)=CH$	112		69.3/70.5		1.3250		25	41
$C_8H_4F_8$	$CF_2CF_2CH_2CHC=CHCF_2CF_2$	311	5	49–50/13		1.3596	1.5147	25	7,24
$C_8H_6F_6$	$CH=CHCHCH_2CHCF_2CFCF_3$	311	69	141		1.3741		20	138

TABLE 6 (*continued*)

Empirical Formula	Structural Formula	Method	Yield %	B.p. °C/mm.	F.p. or M.p. °C	n_D^t	d_4^t	t °C	Ref.
$C_8H_8F_4$	$CH{=}CHCH_2CH_2CHCHCF_2CF_2$	311	50	147–149		1.4019		25	24
$C_8H_9F_3$	$CH{=}CHCHCH_2CHCH_2CHCF_3$	311	65	119		1.4051		20	138
$C_8H_9F_5$	$CF_2CF_2CF{=}C(CH_2)_3CH_3$	310	20	112					30A
	$CH_2CH(C_2F_5)CH_2CH_2CH{=}CH$	311	38	119		1.3725		20	138
$C_8H_{11}F$	$CH{=}CHCHCH_2CHCH_2CHCH_2F$	311	27	66/55		1.4548		20	138
$C_8H_{11}F_3$	$CH_2CH_2CH{=}CHCH_2C(CH_3)CF_3$	311	15	122		1.3989		20	138
$C_9H_2F_{14}$	$CF(CF_3)CF_2CF(CF_3)CHFC(CF_3){=}CH$	112		67.5/106		1.3172		25	41
$C_9H_3F_{13}$	$CF(CF_3)CHFCF(CF_3)CHFC(CF_3){=}CH$	112		64.5/106		1.3238		25	41
$C_9H_9F_5$	$CH{=}CHCHCH_2CHCH_2CHC_2F_5$	311	66	130		1.3853		20	138

$C_9H_{11}F_3$	$CH{=}CHCHCH_2CHCH_2C(CH_3)CF_3$ (cyclic)	311	22	136		1.4168	20	138
$C_{12}F_{18}$	$CF_2-CF-CF-CF-C{=}CF$ $CF_2-CF_2 \quad CF_2-CF_2 \quad CF_2-CF_2$	311		51–52/17		1.3246	25	163
$C_{12}H_{18}F_4$	$CF_2CF_2C(C_4H_9){=}CC_4H_9$ (cyclic)	310	40	110/20				30A

BIBLIOGRAPHY

1. Atkinson, B., and Trenwith, A. B., *J. Chem. Soc.*, **1953,** 2083.
2. Austin, P. R., U. S. Patent 2,585,529(1952).
3. Austin, P. R., Coffman, D. D., *et al.*, *J. Am. Chem. Soc.*, **75,** 4834(1953).
4. Aynsley, E. E., and Watson, R. H., *J. Chem. Soc.*, **1955,** 576.
5. Barlow, G. B., Stacey, M. S., and Tatlow, J. C., *J. Chem. Soc.*, **1955,** 1749.
6. Barney, A. L., U. S. Patent 2,437,148(1948).
7. Barrick, P. L., U. S. Patent 2,462,345(1949).
8. Barrick, P. L., U. S. Patent 2,462,347(1949).

8A. Benning, A. F., Downing, F. B., and Park, J. D., U. S. Patent 2,394,581(1946).

9. Benning, A. F., Downing, F. B., and Plunkett, R. J., U. S. Patent 2,401,897(1946).
10. Benning, A. F., and Young, E. G., U. S. Patent 2,615,926(1952).
11. Bock, W. German Patent 737,276(1943).
12. Booth, H. S., Burchfield, P. E., *et al.*, *J. Am. Chem. Soc.*, **55,** 2231(1933).
13. Bordner, C. A., U. S. Patent 2,615,925(1952).
14. Bratton, F. H., and Weimann, G. M., U. S. Patent 2,478,933(1949).
15. Brice, T. J., LaZerte, J. D., and Pearlson, W. H., *J. Am. Chem. Soc.*, **75,** 2698 (1953).
16. Brown, J. H., and Whalley, W. B., British Patent 576,190(1946).
17. Brown, J. H., and Whalley, W. B., *J. Soc. Chem. Ind.*, **67,** 331(1948).
18. Buxton, M. W., Ingram, D. W., *et al.*, *J. Chem. Soc.*, **1952,** 3830.
19. Buxton, M. W., and Tatlow, J. C., *J. Chem. Soc.*, **1954,** 1177.
20. Campbell, K. N., Knoblock, J. A., and Campbell, B. K., *J. Am. Chem. Soc.*, **72,** 4380(1950).
21. Clark, J. W., U. S. Patent 2,626,963(1953).
22. Clark, J. W., British Patent 698,386(1953).
23. Clark, J. W., U. S. Patent 2,685,606(1954).
24. Coffman, D. D., Barrick, P. L., *et al.*, *J. Am. Chem. Soc.*, **71,** 490(1949).
25. Coffman, D. D., and Cramer, R. D., U. S. Patent 2,461,523(1949).
26. Coffman, D. D., and Salisbury, L. F., U. S. Patent 2,451,612(1948).
27. Crane, G., and Barnhart, W. S., U. S. Patent 2,686,207(1954).
28. Crawford, J. W. C., Walisgrove, E. R., and Imperial Chemical Industries Ltd., British Patent 623,227(1949).
29. Davis, H. W., and Whaley, A. M., *J. Am. Chem. Soc.*, **72,** 4637(1950).
30. Dittman, A. L., and Wrightson, J. M., U. S. Patent 2,690,459(1954).

30A. Dixon, S., *J. Org. Chem.*, **21,** 400(1956).

31. Downing, F. B., Benning, A. F., and McHarness, R. C., U. S. Patent 2,384,821(1945).
32. Downing, F. B., Benning, A. F., and McHarness, R. C., U. S. Patent 2,480,560(1949).
33. Downing, F. B., Benning, A. F., and McHarness, R. C., U. S. Patent 2,551,573(1951).
34. duPont, British Patent 581,662(1946).
35. duPont, British Patent 593,997(1947).
36. Ehrenfeld, R., U. S. Patent Appl. 762,873, *Official Gaz.*, **646,** 1377(1951).
37. Evans, D. E. M., and Tatlow, J. C., *J. Chem. Soc.*, **1954,** 3779.
38. Evans, D. E. M., and Tatlow, J. C., *J. Chem. Soc.*, **1955,** 1184.
39. Farbenfabriken Bayer, British Patent 681,067(1952).

40. Feasly, C. F., and Stover, W. A., U. S. Patent 2,627,529(1953).
41. Gilbert, A. R., and Bigelow, L. A., *J. Am. Chem. Soc.*, **72,** 2411(1950).
42. Gilman, H., and Jones, R. G., *J. Am. Chem. Soc.*, **65,** 2037(1943).
43. Gochenour, C. I., U. S. Patent 2,546,997(1951).
44. Gochenour, C. I., U. S. Patent 2,554,857(1951).
45. Gochenour, C. I., U. S. Patent 2,558,703(1951).
46. Gochenour, C. I., and Kyker, G. D., U. S. Patent 2,436,357(1948).
47. Grosse, A. V., and Linn, C. B., *J. Am. Chem. Soc.*, **64,** 2289(1942),
48. Gryszkiewicz-Trochimowski, E., and Gryzkiewicz-Trochimowski, O., *Bull. soc. chim. France*, **1953,** 123.
49. Hals, L. J., *J. Am. Chem. Soc.*, **73,** 4054(1951).
50. Hals, L. J., Reid, T. S., and Smith, G. H., U. S. Patent 2,668,864(1954).
51. Harmon, J., U. S. Patent 2,404,374(1946).
52. Harmon, J., U. S. Patent 2,404,706(1946).
53. Harmon, J., U. S. Patent 2,436,142(1948).
54. Haszeldine, R. N., *Nature*, **165,** 152(1950).
55. Haszeldine, R. N., *J. Chem. Soc.*, **1950,** 2789.
56. Haszeldine, R. N., *J. Chem. Soc.*, **1950,** 3037.
57. Haszeldine, R. N., *J. Chem. Soc.*, **1951,** 588.
58. Haszeldine, R. N., *J. Chem. Soc.*, **1951,** 2485.
59. Haszeldine, R. N., *J. Chem. Soc.*, **1952,** 2504.
60. Haszeldine, R. N., *J. Chem. Soc.*, **1952,** 3490.
61. Haszeldine, R. N., *J. Chem. Soc.*, **1952,** 4259.
62. Haszeldine, R. N., *J. Chem. Soc.*, **1952,** 4423.
63. Haszeldine, R. N., *J. Chem. Soc.*, **1953,** 922.
64. Haszeldine, R. N., *J. Chem. Soc.*, **1953,** 3371.
65. Haszeldine, R. N., *J. Chem. Soc.*, **1953,** 3559.
66. Haszeldine, R. N., *J. Chem. Soc.*, **1953,** 3565.
67. Haszeldine, R. N., *J. Chem. Soc.*, **1954,** 4026.
68. Haszeldine, R. N., *J. Chem. Soc.*, **1955,** 4291.
69. Haszeldine, R. N., *J. Chem. Soc.*, **1955,** 4302.
70. Haszeldine, R. N., and Leehdam, K., *J. Chem. Soc.*, **1952,** 3483.
71. Haszeldine, R. N., and Leedham, K., *J. Chem. Soc.*, **1953,** 1548.
72. Haszeldine, R. N., and Leedham, K., *J. Chem. Soc.*, **1954,** 1261.
73. Haszeldine, R. N., Leedham, K., and Steele, B. R., *J. Chem. Soc.*, **1954,** 2040.
74. Haszeldine, R. N., and Osborne, J. E., *J. Chem. Soc.*, **1955,** 3880.
75. Haszeldine, R. N., and Steele, B. R., *J. Chem. Soc.*, **1953,** 1199.
76. Haszeldine, R. N., and Steele, B. R., *J. Chem. Soc.*, **1953,** 1592.
77. Haszeldine, R. N., and Steele, B. R., *J. Chem. Soc.*, **1954,** 923.
78. Haszeldine, R. N., and Steele, B. R., *J. Chem. Soc.*, **1954,** 3747.
69. Haszeldine, R. N., and Steele, B. R., *J. Chem. Soc.*, **1955,** 3005.
80. Haszeldine, R. N., and Walaschewski, E. G., *J. Chem. Soc.*, **1953,** 3607.
81. Hatch, L. F., and McDonald, D. W., *J. Am. Chem. Soc.*, **74,** 2911(1952).
82. Hatch, L. F., and McDonald, D. W., *J. Am. Chem. Soc.*, **74,** 3328(1952).
83. Hauptschein, M., and Bigelow, L. A., *J. Am. Chem. Soc.*, **73,** 1428(1951).
84. Hauptschein, M., and Bigelow, L. A., *J. Am. Chem. Soc.*, **73,** 5591(1951).
85. Henne, A. L., *J. Am. Chem. Soc.*, **60,** 2275(1938).
86. Henne, A. L., U. S. Patent 2,371,751(1945).
87. Henne, A. L., *J. Am. Chem. Soc.*, **75,** 5750(1953).
88. Henne, A. L., and DeWitt, E. G., *J. Am. Chem. Soc.*, **70,** 1548(1948).

89. Henne, A. L., and Finnegan, W. G., *J. Am. Chem. Soc.*, **71**, 298(1949).
90. Henne, A. L., and Fox, C. J., *J. Am. Chem. Soc.*, **76**, 479(1954).
91. Henne, A. L., and Francis, W. C., *J. Am. Chem. Soc.*, **75**, 992(1953).
92. Henne, A. L., and Haechl, F. W., *J. Am. Chem. Soc.*, **63**, 3476(1941).
93. Henne, A. L., and Hinkamp, J. B., *J. Am. Chem. Soc.*, **67**, 1197(1945).
94. Henne, A. L., Hinkamp, J. B., and Zimmerschied, W. J., *J. Am. Chem. Soc.*, **67**, 1906(1945).
95. Henne, A. L., and Hinkamp, P. E., *J. Am. Chem. Soc.*, **76**, 5147(1954).
96. Henne, A. L., and Kraus, D. W., *J. Am. Chem. Soc.*, **76**, 1175(1954).
97. Henne, A. L., and Ladd, E. C., *J. Am. Chem. Soc.*, **58**, 402(1936).
98. Henne, A. L., and Nager, M., *J. Am. Chem. Soc.*, **73**, 1042(1951).
99. Henne, A. L., and Nager, M., *J. Am. Chem. Soc.*, **73**, 5527(1951).
100. Henne, A. L., and Nager, M., *J. Am. Chem. Soc.*, **74**, 650(1952).
101. Henne, A. L., and Newby, T. H., *J. Am. Chem. Soc.*, **70**, 130(1948).
102. Henne, A. L., and Plueddeman, E. P., *J. Am. Chem. Soc.*, **65**, 587(1943).
103. Henne, A. L., and Postelnek, W., *J. Am. Chem. Soc.*, **77**, 2334(1955).
104. Henne, A. L., and Postelnek, W., Private Communication.
105. Henne, A. L., and Renoll, M. W., *J. Am. Chem. Soc.*, **61**, 2489(1939).
106. Henne, A. L., and Ruh, R. P., *J. Am. Chem. Soc.*, **69**, 279(1947).
107. Henne, A. L., and Ruh, R. P., *J. Am. Chem. Soc.*, **70**, 1025(1948).
108. Henne, A. L., Shepard, J. W., and Young, E. J., *J. Am. Chem. Soc.*, **72**, 3577(1950).
109. Henne, A. L., and Trott, P. J., *J. Am. Chem. Soc.*, **69**, 1820(1947).
110. Henne, A. L., and Waalkes, T. P., *J. Am. Chem. Soc.*, **68**, 496(1946).
111. Henne, A. L., and Whaley, A. M., *J. Am. Chem. Soc.*, **64**, 1157(1942).
112. Henne, A. L., Whaley, A. M., and Stevenson, J. K., *J. Am. Chem. Soc.*, **63**, 3478(1941).
113. Henne, A. L., and Wiest, E. G., *J. Am. Chem. Soc.*, **62**, 2051(1940).
114. Henne, A. L., and Zimmerschied, W. J., *J. Am. Chem. Soc.*, **67**, 1235(1945).
115. Hill, H. M., and Toune, E. B., U. S. Patent 2,490,758(1949).
116. Hillyea, J. C., and Wilson, J. F., U. S. Patent 2,471,525(1949).
117. Hillyea, J. C., and Wilson, J. F., U. S. Patent 2,634,300(1953).
118. Hoffmann, F. W., *J. Org. Chem.*, **14**, 105(1949).
119. Imperial Chemical Industries Ltd., British Patent 619,394(1949).
119A. Jacobs, T. L., and Bauer, R. S., *J. Am. Chem. Soc.*, **78**, 4815(1956).
120. Kinetic Chemicals Inc., British Patent 581,045(1946).
121. Kropa, E. L., and Padbury, J. J., U. S. Patent 2,590,019(1952).
122. Latif, A., *J. Indian Chem. Soc.*, **30**, 524(1953).
123. LaZerte, J. D., U. S. Patent 2,601,536(1952).
124. LaZerte, J. D., Hals, L. J., *et al.*, *J. Am. Chem. Soc.*, **75**, 4525(1953).
125. LaZerte, J. D., and Koshar, R. J., *J. Am. Chem. Soc.*, **77**, 910(1955).
126. Leedham, K., and Haszeldine, R. N., *J. Chem. Soc.*, **1954**, 1634.
127. Lewis, E. E., and Naylor, M. A., *J. Am. Chem. Soc.*, **69**, 1968(1947).
128. Ligett, W. B., McBee, E. T., and Lindgren, V. V., U. S. Patent 2,432,997(1947).
129. Ligett, W. B., McBee, E. T., and Lindgren, V. V., U. S. Patent 2,498,891(1950).
130. Ligett, W. B., McBee, E. T., and Lindgren, V. V., U. S. Patent 2,509,156(1950).
131. Lilyquist, M. R., Ph. D. Thesis, Univ. of Florida (1955).
132. Locke, E. G., Brode, W. R., and Henne, A. L., *J. Am. Chem. Soc.*, **56**, 1926(1934).

133. McBee, E. T., Campbell, D. H., and Roberts, C. W., *J. Am. Chem. Soc.*, **77**, 3149(1955).
134. McBee, E. T., and Hass, H. B., *J. Am. Chem. Soc.*, **69**, 944(1947).
135. McBee, E. T., Hass, H. B., *et al.*, *Ind. Eng. Chem.*, **39**, 409(1947).
136. McBee, E. T., and Hausch, W. R., *Ind. Eng. Chem.*, **39**, 418(1947).
137. McBee, E. T., Higgins, J. F., and Pierce, O. R., *J. Am. Chem. Soc.*, **74**, 1387(1952).
138. McBee, E. T., Hsu, C. G., *et al.*, *J. Am. Chem. Soc.*, **77**, 915(1955).
139. McBee, E. T., Pierce, O. R., and Chen, M. C., *J. Am. Chem. Soc.*, **75**, 2324(1953).
140. McBee, E. T., Smith, D. K., and Ungnade, H. E., *J. Am. Chem. Soc.*, **77**, 387(1955).
141. McBee, E. T., Truchan, A., and Bolt, R. O., *J. Am. Chem. Soc.*, **70**, 2023(1948).
142. McBee, E. T., Wiseman, P. A., and Bachman, G. B., *Ind. Eng. Chem.*, **39**, 415(1947).
143. Meslans, M., *Comp. rend.*, **111**, 882(1890).
144. Miller, C. B., U. S. Patent 2,628,989(1953).
145. Miller, C. B., and Bratton, F. H., U. S. Patent 2,478,932(1949).
146. Miller, C. B., and Calfee, J. D., U. S. Patent 2,670,388(1954).
147. Miller, C. B., and Calfee, J. D., U. S. Patent 2,674,631(1954).
148. Miller, W. T., Ehrenfeld, R. L., *et al.*, *Ind. Eng. Chem.*, **39**, 401(1947).
149. Miller, W. T., U. S. Patent 2,664,449(1953).
150. Miller, W. T., U. S. Patent 2,668,182(1954).
151. Miller, W. T., U. S. Patent 2,671,799(1954).
152. Mochel, W. E., Salisbury, L. F., *et al.*, *Ind. Eng. Chem.*, **40**, 2285(1948).
153. Newkirk, A. E., *J. Am. Chem. Soc.*, **68**, 2467(1946).
154. Otto, M., Theabald, H., and Melon, R., German Patent 859,887(1952).
155. Padbury, J. J., and Tarrant, P., U. S. Patent 2,566,807(1951).
156. Park, J. D., Benning, A. F., *et al.*, *Ind. Eng. Chem.*, **39**, 354(1947).
157. Park, J. D., Rausch, D. A., and Lacher, J. R., Private Communication.
158. Park, J. D., Seffl, R., and Lacher, J. R., *J. Am. Chem. Soc.*, **78**, 59(1956).
159. Pearlson, W. H., and Hals, L. J., U. S. Patent 2,617,836(1952).
160. Pierce, O. R., McBee, E. T., and Cline, R. E., *J. Am. Chem. Soc.*, **75**, 5618(1953).
161. Pierce, O. R., McBee, E. T., and Judd, G. F., *J. Am. Chem. Soc.*, **76**, 474(1954).
162. Prober, M., *J. Am. Chem. Soc.*, **76**, 4189(1954).
163. Pruett, R. L., Bahnes, C. T., and Smith, H. A., *J. Am. Chem. Soc.*, **74**, 1638(1952).
164. Renoll, M. W., U. S. Patent 2,344,061(1944).
165. Roylance, J., Tatlow, J. C., and Worthington, R. E., *J. Chem. Soc.*, **1954**, 4426.
166. Ruff, O., and Bretschneider, O., *Z. anorg. allgem. Chem.*, **210**, 173(1933).
167. Ruh, R. P., U. S. Patent 2,628,987(1953).
168. Ruh, R. P., U. S. Patent 2,628,988(1953).
169. Ruh, R. P., U. S. Patent 2,673,173(1954).
170. Ruh, R. P., Davis, R. A., and Allswede, K. A., U. S. Patent 2,705,229(1955).
171. Ruh, R. P., and Davis, R. A., U. S. Patent 2,705,247(1955).
172. Salisbury, L. F., U. S. Patent 2,519,199(1950).
173. Scherer, O., German Patent 856,145(1952).

174. Skiles, B. F., U. S. Patent 2,674,632(1954).
175. Smith, L. B., and Miller, C. B., U. S. Patent 2,635,121(1953).
176. Soll, J., German Patent 641,878(1937).
177. Soll, J., German Patent 816,992(1951).
178. Soll, J., German Patent 816,698(1951).
179. Steunenberg, R. K., and Cady, G. H., *J. Am. Chem. Soc.*, **74**, 4165(1952).
180. Swarts, F., *Bull. acad. roy. Belg.*, (3), **34**, 307(1897).
181. Swarts, F., *Bull. acad. roy. Belg.*, (3), **37**, 357(1899).
182. Swarts, F., *Mem. couronnes acad. roy. Belg.*, **61**, 94(1901).
183. Swarts, F., *Bull. acad. roy Belg.*, **1901**, 383.
184. Swarts, F., *Bull. acad. roy. Belg.*, **1909**, 728.
185. Swarts, F., *Bull. acad roy. Belg.* , **1911**, 563.
186. Swarts, F., *Bull. soc. chim. Belg.*, **32**, 367(1923).
187. Swarts, F., *Bull. soc. chim. Belg.*, **36**, 191(1927).
188. Tarrant, P., Attaway, J., and Lovelace, A. M., *J. Am. Chem. Soc.*, **76**, 2343(1954).
189. Tarrant, P., and Gillman, E. G., *J. Am. Chem. Soc.*, **76**, 5423(1954).
190. Tarrant, P., and Lilyquist, M. R., *J. Am. Chem. Soc.*, **77**, 3640(1955).
191. Tarrant, P., Lilyquist, M. R., and Attaway, J., *J. Am. Chem. Soc.*, **76**, 944(1954).
192. Tarrant, P., and Lovelace, A. M., *J. Am. Chem. Soc.*, **76**, 3466(1954).
193. Tarrant, P., and Lovelace, A. M., *J. Am. Chem. Soc.*, **76**, 768(1955).
194. Tarrant, P., Lovelace, A. M., and Lilyquist, M. R., *J. Am. Chem. Soc.*, **77**, 2783(1955).
195. Tarrant, P., and Lutz, R., Private Communication.
196. Tarrant, P., and Warner, D. A., *J. Am. Chem. Soc.*, **76**, 1624(1954).
197. Tatlow, J. C., and Worthington, R. E., *J. Chem. Soc.*, **1952**, 1251.
198. Thomas, C. L., U. S. Patent 2,673,884(1954).
199. Tiers, G. V. D., *J. Am. Chem. Soc.*, **77**, 6704(1955).
200. Whaley, A. M., and Davis, H. W., *J. Am. Chem. Soc.*, **70**, 1026(1948).
201. Whitman, G. M., U. S. Patent 2,401,850(1946).
202. Wiseman, P. A., British Patent 675,372(1952).
203. Wrightson, J. M., and Dittman, A. L., U. S. Patent 2,667,518(1954).

CHAPTER IV

Alcohols

TABLE OF CONTENTS

		PAGE
Introduction		137
Method Number		
401	Reaction of Organometallic Compounds with Esters	138
402	Reaction of Organometallic Compounds with Aldehydes, Ketones, Epoxides, and Acyl Chlorides	140
403	Chemical Reduction of Acids, Esters, Acyl Chlorides, Aldehydes, and Ketones	141
404	Catalytic Reduction of Esters, Anhydrides, Ketones, and Amides	142
405	Free Radical Addition of Alcohols to Olefins	143
406	Reaction of Epoxides and Hydrogen Fluoride	143
407	Hydrolysis of Haloalkanes	143
408	Hydrolysis of Epoxides	144
409	Hydrolysis of Esters	144
410	Oxidation of Grignard Reagents	144
TABLE 7	Alcohols	145
TABLE 8	Diols	151
TABLE 9	Unsaturated Alcohols	152
Bibliography		153

INTRODUCTION

The properties of fluorine-containing alcohols are dependent on the position of fluorine in the molecule with respect to the hydroxyl group. The preparation of monofluoromethanol has been reported but all efforts to prepare di- or trifluoromethanol have been unsuccessful and these compounds are considered to be inherently unstable. The 1,1-dihydroperfluoroalcohols are quite stable and are readily prepared. Fluorine-containing alcohols are acidic in nature and the acidity increases markedly from CH_2FCH_2OH to CF_3CH_2OH. Monofluoroethanol is weakly acidic whereas the acidity of difluoroethanol compares to that of phenol and reacts with potassium carbonate, but not bicarbonate, to form the alcoholate. Trifluoroethanol is still more acidic and forms the alcoholate upon treatment with both carbonates and bicarbonates. The acidity of the *t*-perfluoroalcohols approaches still more closely the ionization constant of phenol (1×10^{-9}). The following table of ionization constants shows the increase in acidity observed in going from a primary to a tertiary alcohol.

Alcohol	K_i	Reference	Alcohol	K_i	Reference
CF_3CH_2OH	4.0×10^{-12}	22	$C_3F_7CH_2OH$	4.3×10^{-12}	18
CF_3 CHOH CH_3	6.0×10^{-12}	22	C_3F_7 CHOH C_3H_7	4.3×10^{-12}	18
CF_3 CH_3—COH CH_3	2.5×10^{-12}	22	C_3F_7 CHOH C_3F_7	2.2×10^{-11}	18
CF_3 CF_3—COH CF_3	3.0×10^{-10}	14A	C_3F_7 C_3F_7—COH C_3F_7	1.0×10^{-10}	14A

The effect of fluorine on the hydroxyl group in fluorinated alcohols readily diminishes as it is further removed from the hydroxyl group. In alcohols of the type $R_f(CH_2)_nOH$, the effect of the fluorine is diminished as n increases. This effect is very pronounced when n is changed from one to two.

METHOD 401 Reaction of Organometallic Compounds with Esters

Organometallic compounds react with esters of perfluorocarboxylic acids to yield either secondary or tertiary alcohols, or in many cases a mixture of the two. When a methylmagnesium halide reacts with an ester of a perfluorocarboxylic acid, good yields of tertiary alcohol are formed as the sole product. For example, methylmagnesium halide reacts with $CF_3CO_2C_2H_5$ and n-$C_3F_7CO_2C_2H_5$ to yield 80 percent of $CF_3C(CH_3)_2OH$ [9] and 76 percent of $C_3F_7C(CH_3)_2OH$,[39] respectively. McBee and co-workers [39] report the preparation of $[CF_2CF_2C(CH_3)_2OH]_2$ in a 98 percent yield from the reaction of the corresponding diethyl ester and methylmagnesium halide.

Ethylmagnesium halide reacts with a perfluorocarboxylic acid ester to yield a mixture of secondary and tertiary alcohols. McBee, *et al.*[40] show that the ratio of tertiary to secondary alcohol is greatly reduced as the chain length of the acid is increased:

$$C_2H_5MgBr + CF_3CO_2CH_3 \longrightarrow CF_3C(C_2H_5)_2OH\ (56\%) + CF_3CH(OH)C_2H_5\ (35\%)$$

$$C_2H_5MgBr + C_3F_7CO_2C_2H_5 \longrightarrow C_3F_7C(C_2H_5)_2OH\ (12\%) + C_3F_7CH(OH)C_2H_5\ (68\%)$$

By reacting ethylmagnesium halide with diethyl perfluoroadipate, 5 percent of $CF_2[CF_2C(C_2H_5)_2OH]_2$ and 23 percent of $CF_2[CF_2CH(C_2H_5)OH]_2$ are obtained.[39]

Pierce, *et al.*[54] report that a secondary alcohol may be obtained as the sole product when a perfluorocarboxylic acid ester is treated with a mixture of either methyl- or ethylmagnesium bromide and isopropylmagnesium bromide. This is illustrated as follows:

$$CF_3CO_2CH_3 + CH_3MgBr/i\text{-}C_3H_7MgBr \longrightarrow CF_3CH(OH)CH_3\ (54\%) + CF_3CH(OH)CH(CH_3)_2\ (14\%)$$

$$C_2F_7CO_2CH_3 + CH_3MgBr/i\text{-}C_3H_7MgBr \longrightarrow C_3F_7CH(OH)CH_3\ (68\%) + C_3F_7CH(OH)CH(CH_3)_2\ (11\%)$$

Similar results are obtained when a mixture of the ethyl- and isopropyl-Grignard reagents are employed. It is interesting to note that when the ethyl ester is employed in the above reaction, only secondary alcohols but no isopropyl derivatives are obtained. For example, when ethyl heptafluorobutyrate is treated with a mixture of methyl- and isopropylmagnesium bromide a 63 percent yield of $C_3F_7CH(OH)CH_3$ is obtained as the sole product.

Isopropyl-, *n*-propyl- or hexylmagnesium halides when reacted with perfluorocarboxylic acid esters produce only secondary alcohols. For example, the esters of trifluoroacetic, heptafluorobutyric, and hexafluoroglutaric acids when treated with *n*-propylmagnesium bromide yield respectively $CF_3CH(OH)C_3H_7$,[3] $C_3F_7CH(OH)C_3H_7$[39] and $CF_2[CF_2CH(OH)C_3H_7]_2$.[39] Similarly:

$$C_2F_5CO_2C_2H_5 + i\text{-}C_3H_7MgBr \longrightarrow C_2H_5CH(OH)CH(CH_3)_2$$ [36]

$$CF_3CO_2C_2H_5 + n\text{-}C_6H_{13}MgBr \longrightarrow CF_3CH(OH)C_6H_{13}$$ [3]

McBee, *et al.*[44] reported that *t*-butylmagnesium chloride reacts with methyl perfluorobutyrate to yield a mixture of $C_3F_7CH_2OH$ and $C_3F_7CH(OH)C(CH_3)_3$.

Fluorinated secondary and tertiary alcohols may also be obtained by reacting perfluoropropylmagnesium iodide with carboxylic acid esters at low temperatures. Haszeldine[13] reports that the reaction of perfluoropropylmagnesium iodide with ethyl acetate, -propionate and -butyrate or with esters of perfluorocarboxylic acids gives relatively low yields of the corresponding tertiary and secondary alcohols. Other investigators report that fluorinated alcohols can be obtained by the reaction of perfluoropropyllithium with ethyl perfluorobutyrate.[46,52] Fluorine-containing ketones are also obtained by these type reactions (cf. Method 602).

METHOD 402 Reaction of Organometallic Compounds with Aldehydes, Ketones, Epoxides, and Acyl Chlorides

Perfluoroaldehydes react with Grignard reagents to produce either secondary alcohols by addition, primary alcohols by reduction, or a mixture of both.

When methylmagnesium bromide reacts with perfluoroaldehydes, only the addition products are obtained, as illustrated by the preparation of $CF_3CH(OH)CH_3$ and $C_2F_5CH(OH)CH_3$ from fluoral and perfluoropropionaldehyde, respectively.[40] However, when a Grignard reagent other than CH_3MgX is employed both reduction and addition products are obtained. The amount of addition product formed is greatly decreased in going from fluoral to perfluoropropionaldehyde, and only slightly decreased in going from perfluoropropionaldehyde to perfluorobutyraldehyde. This is illustrated in the following examples:

$$C_2H_5MgBr + CF_3CHO \longrightarrow CF_3CH(OH)C_2H_5\ (60\%) + CF_3CH_2OH\ (20\%)$$
$$C_2H_5MgBr + C_2F_5CHO \longrightarrow C_2F_5CH(OH)C_2H_5\ (34\%) + C_2F_5CH_2OH\ (56\%)$$
$$C_2H_5MgBr + C_2F_7CHO \longrightarrow C_3F_7CH(OH)C_2H_5\ (19\%) + C_3F_7CH_2OH\ (61\%)$$

The ratio of reduction to addition products is also greatly affected by the reducing strength of the Grignard reagent employed. For example, if fluoral is treated with ethylmagnesium bromide a 60 percent yield of $CF_3CH(OH)C_2H_5$ and 20 percent of CF_3CH_2OH is obtained whereas upon treatment of fluoral with isopropylmagnesium bromide only CF_3CH_2OH is formed in an 87 percent yield.[40] The influence of reaction temperature, solvent, and other variables on the nature of the products is discussed by McBee.[43]

Perfluoropropylmagnesium iodide reacts with aldehydes to yield only addition products. This is exemplified by the following reactions:[12,13]

$$C_3F_7MgI + H_2CO \longrightarrow C_3F_7CH_2OH\ (42\%)$$
$$C_3F_7MgI + C_3H_7CHO \longrightarrow C_3F_7CH(OH)C_3H_7\ (40\%)$$
$$C_3F_7MgI + CF_3CHO \longrightarrow C_3F_7CH(OH)CF_3\ (29\%)$$

Pierce, *et al.*[51] report the preparation of $C_3F_7CH(OH)C_2H_5$ in good yield by the reaction of C_3F_7Li and C_2H_5CHO at −42 °. Park and co-workers[50] have prepared $CF_2{=}CClCH_2OH$ in a 54 percent yield by the reaction of $CF_2{=}CClMgI$ with formaldehyde.

Either secondary or tertiary alcohols or a mixture of both are obtained by reacting organometallic compounds with ketones. Methylmagnesium iodide reacts with $C_3F_7COCH_3$ to yield only $C_3F_7C(CH_3)_2OH$ as would be expected.[13] However, the nature of the Grignard reagent and the length of the perfluoroalkyl group in the ketone greatly influence the ratio of addition to reduction product as illustrated in the following examples:[40]

$$C_2H_5MgX + CF_3COCH_3 \longrightarrow CF_3CH(OH)CH_3\ (13\%) + CF_3C(CH_3)(C_2H_5)OH\ (79\%)$$
$$C_2H_5MgX + C_3F_7COCH_3 \longrightarrow C_3F_7CH(OH)CH_3\ (62\%) + C_3F_7C(CH_3)(C_2H_5)OH\ (18\%)$$
$$i\text{-}C_3H_7MgX + C_2F_5COCH_3 \longrightarrow C_2F_5CH(OH)CH_3\ (54\%)$$

Perfluoroorganometallic reagents react with ketones to produce only tertiary alcohols as illustrated by the preparation of $C_3F_7C(CH_3)_2OH$.[12,19,51,53]

Haszeldine[14] reports that $CF_3CH_2CH_2OH$ can be prepared by reacting CF_3MgI with ethylene oxide. Trifluoroacetyl chloride reacts with di(*n*-hexyl)cadmium to produce a mixture of $CF_3C(C_6H_{13})_2OH$ and $C_6H_{13}COCF_3$[3] (cf. Method 603).

METHOD 403 Chemical Reduction of Acids, Esters, Acyl Chlorides, Aldehydes, and Ketones

Lithium aluminum hydride is the most widely used reagent for the reduction of fluorine-containing acids, esters, acyl chlorides, aldehydes, and ketones to the corresponding alcohols. The reduction of a perfluorocarboxylic acid with $LiAlH_4$ in ether produces a mixture of the 1,1-dihydroperfluoroalcohol and the aldehyde hydrate (cf. Method 619). However, the reduction of acids which contain fluorine which is removed from the carboxyl group yields only the alcohol:

$$C_3F_7CO_2H + LiAlH_4 \longrightarrow C_3F_7CH_2OH + C_3F_7CH(OH)_2$$ [26,28]
$$CF_3CH(CH_3)CH_2CO_2H + LiAlH_4 \longrightarrow CF_3CH(CH_2)CH_2CH_2OH$$ [67]

The reduction of esters of fluorine-containing carboxylic acids with $LiAlH_4$ results in very good yields (75–90%) of the corresponding alcohols and under certain conditions, aldehydes may be obtained as the principal product (cf. Method 619). Campbell[3] prepared trifluoroethanol in a 76 percent yield from butyl trifluoroacetate. Reduction of the diesters of perfluorodicarboxylic acids produces the glycols in 88 to 93 percent yields.[38,56] McBee and co-workers[38,45] prepared diols in excellent yields by the $LiAlH_4$ reduction of fluorinated hydroxy esters. It has been reported that fluoromethanol can be prepared by the $LiAlH_4$ reduction of ethyl fluorocarbonate.[49] The reaction of $CF_3CHBrCHBrCO_2C_2H_5$ with $LiAlH_4$ resulted in simultaneous reduction and debromination to yield $CF_3CH{=}CHCH_2OH$.[45]

Perfluorinated acyl chlorides can also be reduced to the primary alcohols with lithium aluminum hydride as illustrated by the synthesis of n-$C_7F_{15}CH_2OH$ from n-$C_7F_{15}COCl$.[7] McBee[37] reduced $CF_3(CH_2)_2CHO$ with $LiAlH_4$ to $CF_3(CH_2)_2CH_2OH$.

Ketones are also readily reduced to the corresponding secondary alcohols in good yields using $LiAlH_4$. Haszeldine[13] prepared $C_3F_7CH(OH)CH_3$ in a 67 percent yield and $C_3F_7CH(OH)CF_3$ in a 61 percent yield from the respective ketones. Fluorine-containing α-bromoketones have been reduced to the α-bromoalcohols with $LiAlH_4$, without reduction of the bromine occurring.[35,55]

Sodium borohydride,[35] sodium trimethoxyborohydride[45] and aluminum isopropoxide[20,35] have also been used to a limited extent for the reduction of fluorine-containing carbonyl compounds. Fluorine-containing carbonyl compounds are also readily reduced with some Grignard reagents (cf. Methods 401 and 402).

METHOD 404 Catalytic Reduction of Esters, Anhydrides, Ketones, and Amides

Secondary fluoroalcohols are readily obtained by the catalytic reduction of ketones while primary alcohols are produced from fluorinated esters, amides and acid anhydrides. Platinum oxide, Raney nickel, and copper-chromium oxide have been employed as catalysts for the reduction of ketones to alcohols.[34,64,68] For example, Gilman and Jones[8] reduced CF_3COCH_3 to the alcohol in a 90 percent yield using platinum oxide catalyst while Henne and Hinkamp[20] obtained the diol in an 85 percent yield from $CF_3COCH_2COCH_3$ using Raney nickel as the catalyst.

Trifluoroacetamide[8] and acetic anhydride[65] are readily reduced to trifluoroethanol by the use of platinum oxide catalyst. However, the reduction of the anhydride tends to proceed beyond the alcohol stage to yield some CF_3CH_3.

Husted and Ahlbrecht[28] report that the reduction of the esters of perfluorocarboxylic acids to the corresponding alcohols proceeds when copper-chromium oxide catalyst is used at 210° and 3,500 psi pressure.

METHOD 405 Free Radical Addition of Alcohols to Olefins

Fluorine-containing primary, secondary and tertiary alcohols having the general formula R_fCHFCF_2CXYOH (where X and Y may be H or alkyl groups) can be prepared by the organic peroxide induced addition of alcohols to perfluoroolefins. LaZerte and Koshar[34] show that the reaction proceeds in the following manner:

$$CF_3CF{=}CF_2 + CH_3OH \xrightarrow{\text{Peroxide}} CF_3CHFCF_2CH_2OH\ (90\%)$$

$$CF_3(CF_2)_2CF{=}CF_2 + CH_3OH \longrightarrow CF_3(CF_2)_2CHFCF_2CH_2OH\ (87\%)$$

$$CF_3(CF_2)_2CF{=}CF_2 + C_2H_5OH \longrightarrow CF_3(CF_2)_2CHFCF_2CH(CH_3)OH\ (70\%)$$

$$CF_3(CF_2)_2CF{=}CF_2 + n\text{-}C_3H_7OH \longrightarrow CF_3(CF_2)_2CHFCF_2CH(C_2H_5)OH\ (20\%)$$

$$CF_3(CF_2)_2CF{=}CF_2 + i\text{-}C_3H_7OH \longrightarrow CF_3(CF_2)_2CHFCF_2C(CH_3)_2OH\ (40\%)$$

$$CF_3CF{=}CFCF_3 + CH_3OH \longrightarrow CF_3CHFCF(CH_2OH)CF_3\ (72\%)$$

In the above examples only the one to one addition products were obtained. However, Joyce[29] found that methanol reacts with tetrafluoroethylene to yield a series of alcohol telomers of the type $H(CF_2CF_2)_nCH_2OH$ (where n = 1–12); other alcohols react similarly.

METHOD 406 Reaction of Epoxides and Hydrogen Fluoride

Beta fluoro alcohols are obtained upon heating hydrogen fluoride with epoxides at 100° for six hours.[31,33] For example, hydrogen fluoride reacts with ethylene oxide to yield CH_2FCH_2OH; some $CH_2FCH_2OCH_2CH_2OH$ is also obtained. With unsymmetrical epoxides cleavage occurs in such a manner as to produce either secondary or tertiary alcohols to the exclusion of primary alcohols. For example, hydrogen fluoride reacts with propylene oxide and isobutylene oxide to yield $CH_2FCH(OH)CH_3$ and $(CH_3)_2C(OH)CH_2F$, respectively.

METHOD 407 Hydrolysis of Haloalkanes

Fluorine-containing alcohols can be obtained in good yields by the hydrolysis of fluoroalkyl or fluoroalkenyl bromides or chlorides.

Swarts[58,59] effected the hydrolysis of CHF_2CH_2Br to CF_2HCH_2OH in a 93 percent yield by treating the bromide with lead oxide or mercuric oxide and water in a sealed tube at 160°. The ease of hydrolysis of the allylic bromine in $CCl_2{=}CFCH_2Br$ is illustrated by its conversion to the alcohol upon treatment with 10 percent aqueous sodium carbonate at 70°.[11]

METHOD 408 Hydrolysis of Epoxides

Several fluorine-containing 1,2-diols were prepared by the hydrolysis of epoxides with dilute sulfuric acid. McBee and Burton[35] hydrolyzed CF_3CHCH_2O to $CF_3CH(OH)CH_2OH$ by refluxing with 1 percent sulfuric acid for twelve hours. However, Rausch, Lovelace, and Coleman[55] found that the hydrolysis of $C_3F_7CHCHC_2H_5$ required heating with 20 percent sulfuric acid at 105° for sixty hours.

METHOD 409 Hydrolysis of Esters

One technique for the preparation of fluorine-containing alcohols involves the fluorination of the ester of the haloalcohol rather than the fluorination of the alcohol itself. The fluoroalcohols are then obtained by hydrolysis of the ester. For example, the fluorination of chloroethanol using potassium fluoride is not readily accomplished. However, the fluorination of its ester proceeds readily. Using this technique, a number of monofluoroalcohols have been prepared[9,60] (cf. Method 101).

METHOD 410 Oxidation of Grignard Reagents

Several fluorine-containing alcohols have been prepared by the oxidation of a Grignard reagent. This procedure is illustrated by the preparation of $CF_3CH_2CH_2OH$ in a 39 percent yield from $CF_3CH_2CH_2MgCl$.[47]

TABLE 7

ALCOHOLS

Empirical Formula	Structural Formula	Method	Yield %	B.p. °C/mm.	F.p. or M.p. °C	n_D^t	d_4^t	t°C	Ref.
CF_4O	CF_3OF	112		-95					30
CH_3FO	CH_2FOH	403		51					49
$C_2H_3F_3O$	CF_3CH_2OH	402	77						13, 40
		403	76	73.9–74.1/750			1.3842	20	3, 16, 26
		404		74.05	-43.5	1.2907	1.3739	22	65, 8
$C_2H_4F_2O$	CHF_2CH_2OH	407	93.2	95.5–96			1.3084	17	58, 59
C_2H_5FO	CH_2FCH_2OH	101	42.8	103.3		1.3633	1.1002	25	24, 25, 32, 48
		101	42	103.5	-43		1.1150	10	57
		406	40	102–4		1.364	1.102	20	33, 31
		409	90	103.3/757	-27	1.3647	1.1112	18.3	9, 60
$C_3H_3BrF_4O$	$CF_3CH(OH)CHBrF$	403	85	124					41
$C_3H_3F_5O$	$CF_3CF_2CH_2OH$	402	58	81–83					40, 43
		403	38–50	80–81/740		1.295		15	15, 26, 27, 36
$C_3H_4BrF_3O$	$CF_3CH(OH)CH_2Br$	403	74.8	124.5/743.3	-3.0	1.4009	1.8608	20	35
$C_3H_5F_3O$	$CF_3CH_2CH_2OH$	402		100–101					14
		410	40	100		1.3200	1.2937	28	47
	$CF_3CH(OH)CH_3$	401	60	76–7					54
		402	31–70	76–8					13, 20, 43, 40
		403	84	77					22
		404	97	77.7/754	-52	1.3172	1.2799	15	8, 62, 64, 68
C_3H_6ClFO	$CH_2ClCH(OH)CH_2F$	406		153–6		1.4360	1.300	20	31
$C_3H_6F_2O$	$CH_2FCH(OH)CH_2F$	406		59/40		1.3800	1.244	20	31,32,33
C_3H_7FO	$CH_2FCH_2CH_2OH$	101	50	126–8		1.3771	1.0390	25	9, 25
	$CH_2FCH(OH)CH_3$	406	56	107–8		1.3822	1.0214	20	33
		409		106–8					9
$C_4H_3F_7O$	$CF_3(CF_2)_2CH_2OH$	401		95					44
		402	42–72	96.5		1.299		20	12, 13, 40

TABLE 7 (*Continued*)

Empirical Formula	Structural Formula	Method	Yield %	B.p. °C/mm.	F.p. or M.p. °C	n_D^t	d_4^t	t°C	Ref.
$C_4H_3F_7O$		403	40	96/740		1.294	1.600	20	26, 88
$C_4H_4F_6O$	$CF_3CFHCF_2CH_2OH$	405	90	114		1.3115		25	34
$C_4H_5F_5O$	$CF_3CF_2CH(OH)CH_3$	401	55	86–7.5					54
		402	85	85		1.3126	1.406	20	36, 40
$C_4H_6BrF_3O$	$CF_3CH(OH)CHBrCH_3$	403	79	65.5/63		1.4080	1.697	20	55
$C_4H_6F_4O$	$CHF_2CF_2C_2H_4OH$	405		110					29
$C_4H_7Cl_2FO$	$CCl_2FC(CH_3)_2OH$	401		41.0–41.5/13					9
$C_4H_7F_3O$	$CF_3(CH_2)_2CH_2OH$	403	75–86	122		1.3743		25	37
		403	75	124–5		1.3410		25	67
	$CH_3CH(CF_3)CH_2OH$	403		108.5–109.5		1.3399		20	2
	$CF_3CH(OH)CH_2CH_3$	401	31	90.8–1.8/752		1.3403	1.166	20	3, 54
		402	60						40
	$CF_3C(CH_3)_2OH$	401	80–97	81.6–81.7/761	20.75	1.3324	1.1903	22.6	9, 23, 63
C_4H_9FO	$CH_2F(CH_2)_2CH_2OH$	409		52–3/11					9
	$CH_2FC(CH_3)_2OH$	406		58/82		1.3913	0.9610	20	31, 33
$C_5F_2F_{10}O$	$CF_3(CF_2)_2CH(OH)CF_3$	401	8						13
		402	29						13
		403	61	51–52/209					13
$C_5H_3F_9O$	$CF_3(CF_2)_3CH_2OH$	403		111					28
$C_5H_4F_8O$	$CHF_2(CF_2)_3CH_2OH$	405		140					6, 29
	$CF_3CF_2CHFCF_2CH_2OH$	405	76	124		1.3083		25	34
	$CF_3CHFCF(CH_2OH)CF_3$	405	70	118		1.3118		25	34
$C_5H_5F_7O$	$CF_3(CF_2)_2CH(OH)CH_3$	401	68	101–2					13, 54
		402	37–41	101					12, 13, 40
		403	67						13
$C_5H_6F_4O$	$CF_2CF_2CH_2CHCH_2OH$ (ring: CF_2–CH bonded)	210	45	155–7		1.3670	1.3998	25	4

$C_5H_7F_5O$	$CF_3CF_2CH(OH)CH_2CH_3$	401	48	99–100					54
		402	28–57	97–98		1.3280	1.329	20	36, 40, 43
	$CF_3CF_2C(CH_3)_2OH$	401	76			1.3292	1.240	20	36
$C_5H_8BrF_3O$	$CF_3CH(OH)CHBrCH_2CH_3$	403	34	94.0–94.5/116		1.4148	1.602	20	55
	$CF_3CH(OH)CBr(CH_3)_2$	403	42	67.5/47		1.4159	1.591	20	55
$C_5H_8F_4O$	$HCF_2CF_2C_3H_6OH$	405		120					29
$C_5H_9F_3O$	$CF_3(CH_2)_3CH_2OH$	410		80–5/69					17
	$CF_3CH(CH_3)CH_2CH_2OH$	403	61	60–3/28					67
	$CF_3(CH_2)_2CH(OH)CH_3$	402	63	126		1.3330		25	37
	$CF_3CH(OH)(CH_2)_2CH_3$	401	75	109.2–11.5		1.3533	1.136	20	3
		402	5	110–12					13
		606	23	107–8/735					5
	$CF_3CH(OH)CH(CH_3)_2$	401	14	99–100					54
		606	9.7	97–100/739					5
	$CF_3C(OH)(CH_3)C_2H_5$	402	78	98.3		1.3540	1.161	20	40
		402	51	96–97					20
$C_6H_2F_{12}O$	$CF_3(CF_2)_2CH(OH)CF_2CF_3$	401	4–6						13
		402	30						13
		403	69	61/150					13
$C_6H_3F_{11}O$	$CF_3(CF_2)_4CH_2OH$	403		128					28
$C_6H_4F_{10}O$	$CF_3(CF_2)_2CFHCF_2CH_2OH$	405	85	138		1.3093		25	34
$C_6H_6BrF_7O$	$CF_3(CF_2)_2CH(OH)CHBrCH_3$	403	56	85/81		1.3709	1.748	20	55
$C_6H_6ClF_7O$	$CF_3(CF_2)_2CH(OH)CH_2CH_2Cl$	203		156/745	11–12	1.3560	1.558	20	42
	$CF_3(CF_2)_2CH(OH)CHClCH_3$	203		136–40/745 Decomp.					42
	$CF_3(CF_2)_2C(OH)(CH_3)CH_2Cl$	203		129/745	−2	1.3553	1.559	20	42
$C_6H_6F_8O$	$CHF_2(CF_2)_3C_2H_4OH$	405		140					29
	$CF_3CF_2CHFCF_2CH(OH)CH_3$	405	66	130		1.3202		25	34
		404		128–30		1.3190		25	34
$C_6H_7F_7O$	$CF_3(CF_2)_2CH(OH)C_2H_5$	401	56	113.5/745	−14	1.3255	1.439	20	7, 42, 54
		401	7–9						13

TABLE 7 (*Continued*)

Empirical Formula	Structural Formula	Method	Yield %	B.p.°C/mm.	F.p. or M.p. °C	n_D^t	d_4^t	t°C	Ref.
$C_6H_7F_7O$		402	45–68	112–14		1.3250		20	13, 40, 43, 51
		403	71						13
	$CF_3(CF_2)_2C(CH_3)_2OH$	401	76	108		1.3252	1.439	20	13, 39
		402	71						13
		402	29–32	107/743		1.3260		20	12, 51, 53
		402	10	100–110		1.3355		20	19
$C_6H_9F_5O$	$CF_3CF_2CH(OH)(CH_2)_2CH_3$	606	19	115–16/746					5
	$CF_3CF_2CH(OH)CH(CH_3)_2$	401	35	109		1.3428	1.289	20	36
		401	10	108–9					54
		606	7.5	107–9/737					5
	$CF_3CF_2C(OH)(CH_3)C_2H_5$	402	41.6			1.3460	1.251	20	36, 40
$C_6H_{11}F_3$9	$CF_3CH(OH)(CH_2)_3CH_3$	606	22	129–30/746					5
	$CF_3CH(OH)C(CH_3)_3$	401		110.5		1.3670	1.118	20	40
		606	6.4	109–12/740					5
	$CF_3(CH_2)_2C(CH_3)_2OH$	402		129		1.3645		20	21
	$CF_3C(CH_2CH_3)_2OH$	401	39	117.1–17.2		1.3723	1.145	20	3
$C_7H_2F_{14}O$	$(CF_3CF_2CF_2)_2CHOH$	401	42	114.3–117.5		1.293	1.668	20	46
		402	27	70/103					13
		403	83	58/78		1.2911	1.6735	20	13, 19
$C_7H_3F_{13}O$	$CF_3(CF_2)_5CH_2OH$	403		144					28
$C_7H_4F_{12}O$	$CHF_2(CH_2)_5CH_2OH$	405		169–70					29
$C_7H_6F_{10}O$	$CF_3(CF_2)_2CHFCF_2CH(OH)CH_3$	405	60	145		1.3183		25	34
$C_7H_8BrF_7O$	$CF_3(CF_2)_2CH(OH)CHBrCH_2CH_3$	403	65	75.0–75.8/32		1.3770	1.674	20	55
	$CF_3(CF_2)_2CH(OH)CBr(CH_3)_2$	403	54	83.9/62		1.3798	1.664	20	55
$C_7H_8F_8O$	$CHF_2(CF_2)_3C_3H_6OH$	405		150					29
$C_7H_9F_7O$	$CF_3(CF_2)_2CH(OH)(CH_2)_2CH_3$	401	88	131		1.3374	1.322	20	39
		401	10						13
		402	16	53.5/45		1.3391		20	19
		402	40	128–130					13

$C_7H_9F_7O$		606	8.9	130–31/741					5
	$CF_3(CF_2)_2CH(OH)CH(CH_3)_2$	401	87	123		1.3375	1.375	20	39
		401	11	124–5					54
		606	7.7	122–24/739					5
	$CF_3(CF_2)_2C(CH_3)(CH_2CH_3)OH$	402	18	125		1.3395	1.396	20	13, 40
$C_7H_{11}F_3O$	$CF_3CHCH_2CH(OH)(CH_2)_2CH_2$	212		182.7/765			1.2611	17	61
$C_7H_{11}F_5O$	$CF_3CF_2CHOH(CH_2)_3CH_3$	606	21.5	135/746					5
	$CF_3CF_2CH(OH)C(CH_3)_3$	401		120		1.3578	1.105	20	40
	$CF_3CF_2C(CH_2CH_3)_2OH$	401		127		1.3590	1.259	20	40
$C_8HF_{17}O$	$(CF_3CF_2CF_2)_2C(OH)(CF_3)$	401	5–8						13
$C_8H_3F_{15}O$	$CF_3(CF_2)_6CH_2OH$	403	56.8	142–3/739	36.5–7.0				7
		403		160					28
$C_8H_4F_{14}O$	$CF_3(CF_2)_4CHFCF_2CH_2OH$	405	90	170	38–39				34
	$(CF_3CF_2CF_2)_2C(OH)CH_3$	401	20–32	132–33		1.3031	1.763	25	13, 46
$C_8H_8F_{10}O$	$CF_3(CF_2)_2CHFCF_2C(CH_3)_2OH$	405	55	152		1.3291		25	34
$C_8H_{11}F_7O$	$CF_3(CF_2)_2CH(OH)(CH_2)_3CH_3$	606	22.6	69–70/27					5
	$CF_3(CF_2)_2CH(OH)C(CH_3)_3$	401		135		1.3485	1.310	20	44
	$CF_3(CF_2)_2C(CH_2CH_3)_2OH$	401	10–16	142/745	− 12	1.3526	1.295	20	7, 13, 42
$C_8H_{15}F_3O$	$CF_3CHOH(CH_2)_5CH_3$	401	77.8	165.7–6.2/751		1.3834	1.056	20	3
		606	27	167–8/740					5
$C_9HF_{19}O$	$(CF_3CF_2CF_2)_2C(CF_2CF_3)OH$	401	3–10						13
$C_9H_4F_{16}O$	$CHF_2(CF_2)_7CH_2OH$	405		157–158/200	65–7				29
$C_9H_6F_{14}O$	$(CF_3CF_2CF_2)_2C(CH_2CH_3)OH$	401	28						13
$C_9H_8F_{12}O$	$CHF_2(CF_2)_5C_3H_6OH$	405		183					29
$C_{10}HF_{21}O$	$(CF_3CF_2CF_2)_3COH$	401		115/743	10	1.2890		20	52
$C_{10}H_3F_{19}O$	$CF_3(CF_2)_8CH_2OH$	404		192	87.5				28
$C_{10}H_4F_{18}O$	$CF_3(CF_2)_6CHFCF_2CH_2OH$	405	90	201	80–81				34
$C_{10}H_8F_{14}O$	$(CF_3CF_2CF_2)_2C(OH)CH_2CH_2CH_3$	401	28						13
$C_{11}H_3F_{21}O$	$CF_3(CF_2)_9CH_2OH$	403		208					28
$C_{11}H_4F_{20}O$	$CHF_2(CF_2)_9CH_2OH$	405		180–181/200	95–7				29
$C_{12}H_3F_{23}O$	$CF_3(CF_2)_{10}CH_2OH$	403		224					28

TABLE 7 (*Continued*)

Empirical Formula	Structural Formula	Method	Yield %	B.p. °C/mm.	F.p. or M.p. °C	n_D^t	d_4^t	t°C	Ref.
$C_{13}H_3F_{25}O$	$CF_3(CF_2)_{11}CH_2OH$	403		240					28
$C_{13}H_4F_{24}O$	$CHF_2(CF_2)_{11}CH_2OH$	405			129–30				29
$C_{14}H_{27}F_3O$	$CF_3COH[(CH_2)_5CH_3]_2$	402		97.5–100/1.3		1.4180	0.9891	20	3
$C_{15}H_4F_{28}O$	$CHF_2(CF_2)_{13}CH_2OH$	405			156–60				29
$C_{17}H_4F_{32}O$	$CHF_2(CF_2)_{15}CH_2OH$	405			185–90				29
$C_{25}H_4F_{48}O$	$CHF_2(CF_2)_{23}CH_2OH$	405			280				29

TABLE 8

DIOLS

Empirical Formula	Structural Formula	Method	Yield %	B.p. °C/mm.	F.p. or M.p. °C	n_D^t	d_4^t	t °C	Ref.
$C_3H_5F_3O_2$	$CF_3CH(OH)CH_2OH$	408	26	69.5–70.1/10	25.3	1.3617	1.5051	20	35
$C_3H_6F_2O_2$	$HOCH_2CF_2CH_2OH$	103	85		52.5				38
$C_3H_7FO_2$	$CH_2FCH(OH)CH_2OH$	101	52	119–22/28					49A
		409		102.5–3.0/13					9
$C_4H_6F_4O_2$	$HOCH_2(CF_2)_2CH_2OH$	403	90		85				38
$C_4H_7F_3O_2$	$CF_3CH(OH)CH_2CH_2OH$	403	83	104–5/20					45
$C_5H_6F_6O_2$	$HOCH_2(CF_2)_3CH_2OH$	403	93		77.5				38
$C_5H_9F_3O_2$	$CF_3CH(OH)CH_2CH(OH)CH_3$	404	85	78/3		1.3798	1.294	20	20
$C_6H_6F_8O_2$	$HOCH_2(CF_2)_4CH_2OH$	403	88		68				38, 56
$C_6H_7F_7O_2$	$CF_3(CF_2)_2CH(OH)CH_2CH_2OH$	407			90–1				42
$C_7H_9F_7O_2$	$CF_3(CF_2)_2CH(OH)CH(OH)CH_2CH_3$	408			88				55
$C_9H_{14}F_6O_2$	$CF_2(CF_2CHOHCH_2CH_3)_2$	401	23		94–5				39
$C_9H_{14}F_6O_2$	$CF_2[CF_2C(CH_3)_2OH]_2$	401	82		78–9				39
$C_{10}H_{14}F_8O_2$	$[CF_2CF_2C(CH_3)_2OH]_2$	401	98		81–2				39
$C_{11}H_{18}F_6O_2$	$CF_2[CF_2CH(OH)CH_2CH_2CH_3]_2$	401	77		80–1				39
$C_{13}H_{22}F_3O_2$	$CF_2[CF_2C(CH_2CH_3)_2OH]_2$	401	5		68–9				39

TABLE 9

UNSATURATED ALCOHOLS

Empirical Formula	Structural Formula	Method	Yield %	B.p. °C/mm.	F.p. or M.p. °C	n_D^t	d_4^t	t °C	Ref.
$C_3H_3ClF_2O$	$CF_2{=}CClCH_2OH$	402	54	42–43/20		1.4028	1.427	20	50
$C_3H_3Cl_2FO$	$CCl_2{=}CFCH_2OH$	407	74	61/10		1.4670	1.5032	25	11
C_3H_4ClFO	$CHCl{=}CFCH_2OH$	407	71	48–9/15		1.4399	1.3472	20	10
			Isomers						
				65–6/15		1.4480	1.3519	20	
$C_4H_5F_3O$	$CF_3CH{=}CHCH_2OH$	403	50	128–128.5		1.3578	1.256	25	45
	$CH{\equiv}C(CF_3)(CH_3)OH$	402		97–8		1.3251	1.160	25	66
$C_6H_7F_3O$	$CF_3C{\equiv}CC(CH_3)_2OH$	402		110–11		1.3629		20	21
$C_6H_9F_3O$	$CF_3CH(OH)CH{=}C(CH_3)_2$	403	60	139–40		1.3823		20	20
$C_8H_{10}F_4O$	$CF_2CF_2CH{=}CCH(OH)CH(CH_3)_2$ (ring: first CF_2 bonded to the doubly bonded C)	210		87–95/28					1
$C_{12}H_{16}F_8O$	$CH_3(CH_2)_2CH(OH)(CF_2)_4CH{=}CHCH_2CH_3$	3	11	106–18		1.3954	1.247	20	39

BIBLIOGRAPHY

1. Barrick, P. L., U. S. Patent 2,462,345(1949).
2. Buxton, M. W., Stacey, M., and Tatlow, J. C., *J. Chem. Soc.*, **1954**, 366.
3. Campbell, K. N., Knoblock, J. O., and Campbell, K. B., *J. Am. Chem. Soc.*, **72**, 4380(1950).
4. Coffman, D. D., Barrick, P. L., *et al.*, *J. Am. Chem. Soc.*, **71**, 490(1949).
5. Dishart, K. T., and Levine, R., *J. Am. Chem. Soc.*, **78**, 2268(1956).
6. duPont, British Patent 583,874(1947).
7. Filler, R., Fenner, J. V., *et al.*, *J. Am. Chem. Soc.*, **75**, 2693(1953).
8. Gilman, H., and Jones, R. G., *J. Am. Chem. Soc.*, **70**, 1281(1948).
9. Gryszkiewicz-Trochimowski, E., Sporzynski, A., and Wnuk, J., *Rec. trav. chim.*, **66**, 427(1947).
10. Hatch, L. F., and McDonald, D. W., *J. Am. Chem. Soc.*, **74**, 2911(1952).
11. Hatch, L. F., and McDonald, D. W., *J. Am. Chem. Soc.*, **74**, 3328(1952).
12. Haszeldine, R. N., *J. Chem. Soc.*, **1952**, 3423.
13. Haszeldine, R. N., *J. Chem. Soc.*, **1953**, 1748.
14. Haszeldine, R. N., *J. Chem. Soc.*, **1954**, 1273.

14A. Haszeldine, R. N., 122nd Meeting American Chemical Society, Atlantic City, New Jersey, September 1952.

15. Haszeldine, R. N., and Leedham, K., *J. Chem. Soc.*, **1953**, 1548.
16. Henne, A. L., Alm, R. M., and Smook, M., *J. Am. Chem. Soc.*, **70**, 1968(1948).
17. Henne, A. L., and Fox, C. J., *J. Am. Chem. Soc.*, **75**, 5750(1953).
18. Henne, A. L., and Francis, W. C., *J. Am. Chem. Soc.*, **75**, 991(1953).
19. Henne, A. L., and Francis, W. C., *J. Am. Chem. Soc.*, **75**, 992(1953).
20. Henne, A. L., and Hinkamp, P. E., *J. Am. Chem. Soc.*, **76**, 5147(1954).
21. Henne, A. L., and Nagar, M., J. Am. Chem. *Soc.*, **74**, 650(1952).
22. Henne, A. L., and Pelley, R. L., *J. Am. Chem. Soc.*, **74**, 1426(1952).
23. Henne, A. L., Shepard, J. W., and Young, E. J., *J. Am. Chem. Soc.*, **72**, 3577(1950).
24. Hoffmann, F. W., *J. Am. Chem. Soc.*, **70**, 2596(1948).
25. Hoffmann, F. W., *J. Org. Chem.*, **15**, 425(1950).
26. Husted, D. R., and Ahlbrecht, A. H., *J. Am. Chem. Soc.*, **74**, 5422(1952).
27. Husted, D. R., and Ahlbrecht, A. H., *J. Am. Chem. Soc.*, **75**, 1605(1953).
28. Husted, D. R., and Ahlbrecht, A. H., U. S. Patent 2,666,797(1954).
29. Joyce, R. M., U. S. Patent 2,559,628(1951).
30. Kellogg, K. B., and Cady, G. H., *J. Am. Chem. Soc.*, **70**, 3986 (1948).
31. Knunyants, I. L., *Compt. rend. acad. sci. U.R.S.S.*, **55**, 223(1947).
32. Knunyants, I. L., Kil'disheva, O. V., and Bykhovskaya, E., *Zhur. Obshchei. Khim.*, **19**, 101(1949).
33. Knunyants, I. L., Kil'disheva, O. V., and Petrov, I. P., *Zhur. Obshchei. Khim.*, **19**, 95(1949).
34. LaZerte, J. D., and Koshar, R. J., *J. Am. Chem. Soc.*, **77**, 910(1955).
35. McBee, E. T., and Burton, T. M., *J. Am. Chem. Soc.*, **74**, 3022(1952).
36. McBee, E. T., Higgins, J. F., and Pierce, O. R., *J. Am. Chem. Soc.*, **74**, 1387(1952).
37. McBee, E. T., Kelley, A. E., and Rapkin, E., *J. Am. Chem. Soc.*, **72**, 5071(1950).
38. McBee, E. T., Marzluff, W. F., and Pierce, O. R., *J. Am. Chem. Soc.*, **74**, 444(1952).

39. McBee, E. T., Pierce, O. R., and Chen, M. C., *J. Am. Chem. Soc.*, **75**, 2324(1953).
40. McBee, E. T., Pierce, O. R., and Higgins, J. F., *J. Am. Chem. Soc.*, **74**, 1736(1952).
41. McBee, E. T., Pierce, O. R., and Kilbourne, H. W., *J. Am. Chem. Soc.*, **75**, 4091(1953).
42. McBee, E. T., Pierce, O. R., and Marzluff, W. F., *J. Am. Chem. Soc.*, **75**, 1609(1953).
43. McBee, E. T., Pierce, O. R., and Meyer, D. D., *J. Am. Chem. Soc.*, **77**, 83(1955).
44. McBee, E. T., Pierce, O. R., and Meyer, D. D., *J. Am. Chem. Soc.*, **77**, 917(1955).
45. McBee, E. T., Pierce, O. R., and Smith, D. D., *J. Am. Chem. Soc.*, **76**, 3725(1954).
46. McBee, E. T., Roberts, C. W., and Curtis, S. G., *J. Am. Chem. Soc.*, **77**, 6387(1955).
47. McBee, E. T., and Truchan, A., *J. Am. Chem. Soc.*, **70**, 2910(1948).
48. Olah, Gy., and Pavlath, A., *Acta Chim. Acad. Sci. Hung.*, **3**, 199(1953).
49. Olah, Gy., and Pavlath, A., *Acta Chim. Acad. Sci. Hung.*, **3**, 203(1953).
49A. Olah, Gy., and Pavlath, A., *Acad. Sci. Hung.*, **3**, 425(1953).
50. Park, J. D., Abramo, J., *et al.*, 128th Meeting American Chemical Society (1955).
51. Pierce, O. R., McBee, E. T., and Judd, G. F., *J. Am. Chem. Soc.*, **76**, 474(1954).
52. Pierce, O. R., McBee, E. T., and Judd, G. F., *J. Am. Chem. Soc.*, **76**, 479(1954).
53. Pierce, O. R., Meiners, A. F., and McBee, E. T., *J. Am. Chem. Soc.*, **75**, 2516(1953).
54. Pierce, O. R., Siegle, J. C., and McBee, E. T., *J. Am. Chem. Soc.*, **75**, 6324(1953).
55. Rausch, D. A., Lovelace, A. M., and Coleman, L. E. Jr., *J. Org. Chem.*, **21**, 1328(1956).
56. Roylance, J., Tatlow, J. C., and Worthington, R. E., *J. Chem. Soc.*, **1954**, 4426.
57. Saunders, B. C., Stacey, G. J., and Wilding, I. G. E., *J. Chem. Soc.*, **1949**, 773.
58. Swarts, F., *Bull. acad. roy. Belg.*, **1902**, 731.
59. Swarts, F., *Bull. acad. roy. Belg.*, **1908**, II, 272.
60. Swarts, F., *Bull. acad. roy. Belg.*, **1914**, 7.
61. Swarts, F., *Bull. soc. chim. Belg.*, **32**, 367(1923).
62. Swarts, F., *Bull. acad. roy. Belg.*, **13**, 175(1927).
63. Swarts, F., *Bull. soc. chim. Belg.*, **36**, 191(1927).
64. Swarts, F., *Bull. soc. chim. Belg.*, **38**, 99(1929).
65. Swarts, F., *Comp. rend.*, **197**, 1261(1933).
65A. Swarts, F., *Bull. soc. chim. Belg.*, **43**, 471(1934).
66. Tarrant, P., Warner, D. A., and Taylor, R. E., *J. Am. Chem Soc.*, **75**, 4360(1953).
67. Walborsky, H. M., Baum, M., and Loncrini, D. F., *J. Am. Chem. Soc.*, **77**, 3637(1955).
68. Wallsgrove, E. R., and Imperial Chemical Industries Ltd., British Patent 621,654(1949).

CHAPTER V

Ethers

TABLE OF CONTENTS

		PAGE
Introduction		155
Method Number		
501	Reaction of Alcohols and Olefins	156
502	Reaction of Alcohols and Alkyl Halides	158
503	Chlorination of Ethers	159
504	Codimerization of Olefins and Olefinic Ethers	160
505	Epoxidation	160
506	Halogen Interchange	161
507	Dehydration of Glycols	161
508	Reaction of Alcohols and Paraformaldehyde	162
509	Action of Diazomethane on Alcohols	162
510	Cyclic Trimerization of Ketones	162
511	Reaction of Alcohols and Epoxides	162
512	Reaction of Alkyl Sulfates or Sulfonates with Alcohols	163
513	Addition of Hydrogen Fluoride to Epoxides	163
TABLE 10	Aliphatic and Alicyclic Ethers	164
TABLE 11	Olefinic Ethers	169
TABLE 12	Cyclic Ethers	172
TABLE 13	Hydroxy Ethers	176
Bibliography		178

INTRODUCTION

This chapter deals with the preparation and, in part, the reactions of fluorine-containing ethers. As a class, the fluoroethers have received considerable attention both from the standpoint of their reactions as well as their potential use as polymerizable monomers.

The completely fluorinated ethers which have been prepared by either electrolytic fluorination or direct fluorination exhibit a high degree of thermal stability and undergo few chemical reactions. The perfluoroethers exhibit rather vividly the decrease in boiling point normally associated with the substitution of fluorine for the hydrogen of a hydrocarbon.

	b.p. °C Fluorocarbon	b.p. °C Hydrocarbon Analog
CF_3OCF_3	−59	−24.9
$C_2F_5OC_2F_5$	1	34.5
$C_3F_7OC_3F_7$	56	89
$C_5F_{11}OC_5F_{11}$	139	190
CF_3CFCF_2O (ring)	−42	35

Because of the extreme ease with which alcohols add to both fluoro- and chlorofluoroolefins, the preparation of numerous unsymetrical fluorinated ethers has resulted. Unlike the perfluoroethers they undergo various reactions. The particular grouping represented by —CF_2OCH_2— undergoes hydrolysis or alcoholysis rather readily to yield esters and ortho-esters.

Considerable emphasis has been placed on the polymers derived from the unsaturated fluoroethers and fluoroepoxides. The unsaturated fluoroethers exhibit a high degree of reactivity toward both homo- and copolymerization. However, at this time, no polymers of commercial utility have been announced. Attempted polymerization of fluoroepoxides by conventional means has resulted in only low molecular weight polyfluoroethers.

METHOD 501 Reactions of Alcohols and Olefins

The addition of alcohols to fluoroolefins to give good yields of ethers was first reported by Hanford and Rigby[18] with the addition of various alcohols to $CF_2{=}CF_2$, $CF_2{=}CFCl$ and $CF_2{=}CHCl$ using sodium as a catalyst. The procedure was adapted to both monohydric and dihydric alcohols. For example, with ethylene glycol and tetrafluoroethylene both $CHF_2CF_2OCH_2CH_2OH$ and $CHF_2CF_2OCH_2CH_2OCF_2CF_2H$ were obtained.

Miller and co-workers[44] have offered a mechanism to explain the ease of addition of alcoholates to fluorine-containing olefins. The reaction of methanol and base with $CF_2{=}CF_2$ proceeds in an exothermic manner from 0° to room temperature; $CFCl{=}CCl_2$ reacted with some loss of HX; while $CCl_2{=}CCl_2$ did not react at 0°. The following mechanism was proposed:

I 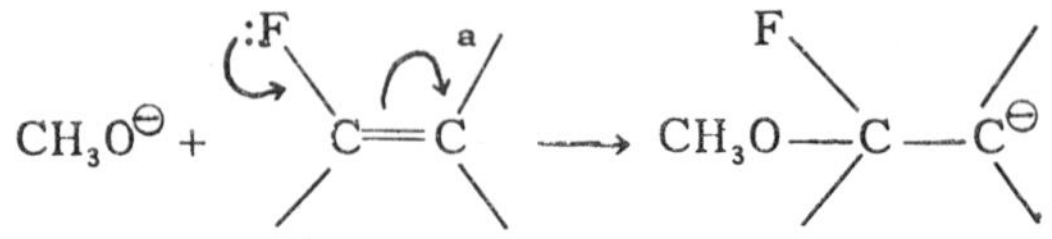

$$\text{II} \quad CH_3O-\underset{\diagup}{\overset{F}{\diagdown}}C-\overset{\diagup}{\underset{\diagdown}{C}}{}^{\ominus} + CH_3OH \longrightarrow CH_3O-\underset{\diagup}{\overset{F}{\diagdown}}C-\overset{\diagup}{\underset{\diagdown}{C}}-H + CH_3O^{\ominus}$$

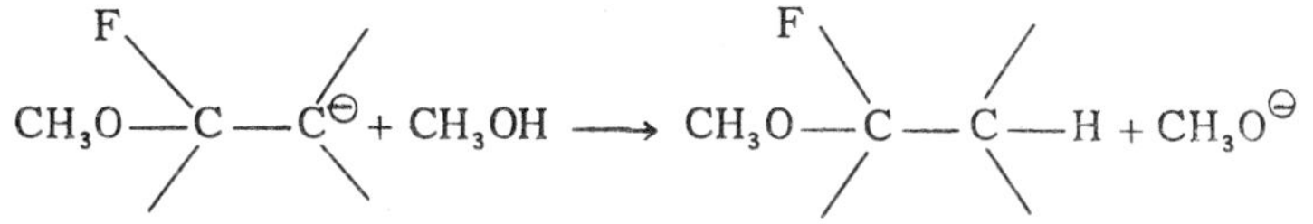

Step I is believed to be the rate controlling step while step II is fast. There is considerable reason to believe that fluorine is capable of greater electron release than chlorine as an activation mechanism. The role of fluorine relative to chlorine in its ability to promote addition of nucleophilic reagents as well as directing the orientation of addition is believed to be due to the greater tendency of fluorine to enter into resonance with the double bond, with the resultant polarization shown by arrow "a" in Step I above. The inductive effect of halogens on a double bond favors acceptor reactivity as contrasted with the strictly nuclephilic activity of simple ethylenic compounds.

The procedure has since been extended to include a considerable number of alcohols and olefins. Park and co-workers[50] have added methanol and ethanol to $CF_2{=}CFBr$ and $CF_2{=}CFI$ to give, respectively, CH_3OCF_2CFHBr and $C_2H_5OCF_2CFHI$. The addition of methanol, ethanol, n- and i-propanol and n-butanol to $CF_2{=}CFCF_3$ was reported[34] to yield ethers of the type $ROCF_2CFHCF_3$ when potassium hydroxide was used as a catalyst. Brice[6] has reported the uncatalyzed addition of ethanol to $CF_2{=}C(CF_3)_2$ to give $C_2H_5OCF_2CH(CF_3)_2$. The additions have been carried out both at atmospheric pressure and under autogenous pressure.

Tarrant and Brown[69] have studied the addition of methyl, ethyl, i-propyl and t-butyl alcohols to $CF_2{=}CFCl$, $CF_2{=}CCl_2$ and $CF_2{=}CHCl$ in the presence of base. The addition of t-butyl alcohol was found to proceed less readily than the other alcohols studied; $CF_2{=}CFCl$ was less reactive than $CF_2{=}CCl_2$ and $CF_2{=}CHCl$ when addition was attempted with t-butyl alcohol at atmospheric pressure. These workers also considered the thermal stability of alkyl fluoroethers. Ethers of the type $ROCF_2CClFH$ where R is a straight chain, are relatively stable, while those of the type $ROCF_2CCl_2H$ and $ROCF_2CH_2Cl$ have a tendency to split out hydrogen fluoride. The stability of this type of ether was found to be greatly influenced by the number of methyl groups substituted in the α position of the alkyl group. The reaction product of isopropyl alcohol and $CF_2{=}CHCl$ was a mixture of the saturated and unsaturated ethers. The reaction products of t-butyl alcohol with $CF_2{=}CFCl$ and $CF_2{=}CCl_2$ were the unsaturated ethers; $(CH_3)_3COCF{=}CFCl$ and $(CH_3)_3COCF{=}CCl_2$ respectively.

The addition of alcohols to fluoroalkynes has been reported by Chaney,[8]

Haszeldine[19] and Henne.[24] The addition of ROH to $CF_3C{\equiv}CH$ and $CF_3C{\equiv}CCF_3$ gives $CF_3CH{=}CHOR$ and $CF_3CH{=}C(CF_3)OR$, respectively. Addition of a second mole of ROH to $CF_3CH{=}C(CF_3)OR$ yields $CF_3CH_2C(OR)_2CF_3$.

Henne[26] has also reported the addition of fluoroalcohols to $CF_2{=}CF_2$. The reaction of CF_3CH_2OH and $CF_3CH_2CH_2OH$ with $CF_2{=}CF_2$ in the presence of sodium gave $CF_3CH_2OCF_2CF_2H$ and $CF_3CH_2CH_2OCF_2CF_2H$. Park, Sharrah and Lacher,[52] in studying the base catalyzed addition of alcohols to $CF_2CF_2CF{=}CF$, found that substitution predominated to the exclusion of the addition products that would be predicted on the basis of the reactions of $CF_2{=}CF_2$. They obtained $CF_2CF_2C(OR){=}COR$ rather than $CF_2CF_2CF(OR)CHF$ and point out that the vapor phase heat of chlorination of $CF_2{=}CF_2$ and $CF_2{=}CFCl$ are respectively 13.7 and 5.2 KCal greater than ethylene, while for $CF_2CF_2CF{=}CF$ it is 6.2 KCal less, ruling out the possibility of addition, but not substitution. However, Barr[1] using a quaternary ammonium base isolated the monosubstitution product with the structure $CF_2CF_2C(OR){=}CF$. Various mechanisms involving addition and elimination or substitution of allylic fluorine followed by rearrangement have been proposed to explain this reaction. Park and co-workers[48,54] have studied the reaction of alcohols with $CF_2CF_2CCl{=}CCl$ and $CF_3CCl{=}CCl_2$ in an attempt to explain the formation of products of the type $CF_2CF_2CCl{=}COR$ and $CF_3CCl{=}CClOR$. In the reaction with $CF_2CF_2CCl{=}CCl$ a triether of unknown structure was obtained. Similar results have been reported by Henne[23] on working with $CF_3CCl{=}CClCF_3$.

METHOD 502 Reaction of Alcohols and Alkyl Halides

The action of alcoholates on fluorocarbon halides to yield ethers was first reported by Swarts.[66] The reaction has since been adapted to numerous syntheses. At first it would appear to be a common Williamson synthesis for preparing ethers. For instance, it has been reported[73] that treatment of CHF_2CF_2Cl with ethanolic potassium hydroxide yields 66 to

70 percent of $CHF_2CF_2OC_2H_5$. Swarts[63,64] has reported that the action of the appropriate alcoholate on CF_2BrCH_2Br and CF_2BrCH_2F yielded $C_2H_5OCF_2CH_2Br$ and $CH_3OCF_2CH_2F$, respectively. Tarrant and Young[70] have since pointed out that a simple Williamson synthesis does not adequately explain in the products formed in some cases, nor the fact that the alkyoxy radical attaches itself to the carbon which contains the most fluorine. For example, these workers found that the treatment of $CHClFCHF_2$ with sodium ethylate at 120° gave a 53 percent yield of $CH_2ClCF_2OC_2H_5$. Other cases were also cited which can not be explained by a simple displacement reaction. It is proposed that intermediate fluoroolefins are formed, which in turn react with the alcoholate to form ethers as described in Method 501. Numerous examples may be found which appear to support this hypothesis. Gowland[14] reacted various alcoholates with CHF_2CCl_3 and obtained products with the structure $ROCF_2CHCl_2$.

The reaction of fluorine-containing alcoholates with alkyl halides can also be accomplished. McBee[42] reports that the reaction of CF_3CH_2ONa and C_2H_5Br yields $CF_3CH_2OC_2H_5$. The action of $CF_3CH_2CH_2ONa$ on CH_3Br and C_2H_5Br has been reported to yield 43 percent and 30 percent of $CF_3CH_2CH_2OCH_3$ and $CF_3CH_2CH_2OC_2H_5$, respectively.[26]

METHOD 503 Chlorination of Ethers

The photochemical chlorination of fluoroethers has been extensively studied. Park and co-workers[47,55] readily chlorinated CH_3OCF_2CFClH stepwise in the liquid phase to CCl_3OCF_2CFClH in yields of 90 to 95 percent using incandescent illumination. Some difficulty was experienced in replacing the hydrogen of the fluoroalkyl portion of the ether. However, complete chlorination was effected more slowly to yield $CCl_3OCF_2CFCl_2$. Stepwise chlorination of $C_2H_5OCF_2CFClH$ gave initially the α- and β-monochloroethers which on continued chlorination yielded $CH_2ClCHClOCF_2CFClH$ and $CHCl_2CHClOCF_2CFClH$. When the reaction was allowed to proceed to completion, $CCl_3CCl_2OCF_2CFCl_2$ was obtained. It was definitely established from this work that chlorination proceeds with an initial attack on the non-fluorinated portion of the ether and the hydrogen of the fluoroalkyl portion is only substituted with difficulty.

In general, in the substitution of chlorine for hydrogen in fluoroethers, the chlorine is directed away from the methyl and methylene groups adjacent to CF_3- and $-CF_2$-groups. This is not in general agreement with the directive effect of these groups in the chlorination of alkanes as discussed in Method 203. It is thought that the inductive effect of fluorine adjacent to hydrogen increases its protonic character with an accompaning decrease in ease of substitution. Park, Griffin and

Lacher[47] have also called attention to the fact that in ethers of the type RCH_2OCF_2R, radicals formed by the removal of hydrogen from the α-position of the hydrocarbon moiety may gain greater resonance stability than the radicals formed by removal of hydrogen from the β-position of the fluoroalkyl moiety. These factors appear to explain both the directive nature of such chlorinations as well as the difficulty of substitution for hydrogen adjacent to or isolated from the ether oxygen by carbons which contain fluorine.

Henne and Richter[25] chlorinated cyclic ethers of the type $\overline{CF_2CF_2CH_2OCH_2}$ and $\overline{CF_2CF_2CF_2CH_2OCH_2}$ to obtain $\overline{CF_2CF_2CCl_2OCCl_2}$ and $\overline{CF_2CF_2CF_2CCl_2OCCl_2}$ in 78 and 89 percent yields, respectively. The procedure which required two days employed a sun-lamp for illumination while chlorine was bubbled into the liquid.

METHOD 504 Codimerization of Olefins and Unsaturated Ethers

The codimerization of fluoroolefins is discussed in Method 210 and 311. Coffman[9] and Barrick[2,3] have reported the codimerization of fluoroolefins with a number of unsaturated compounds containing functional groups including the ethers. For example, the reaction of $CF_2 = CF_2$ and

$$CH_2 = CHCH \underset{O}{\overset{CH-CH}{\diagdown \diagup}} CH$$

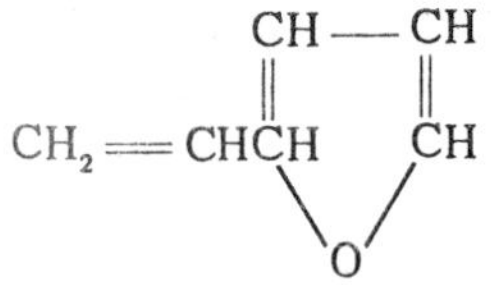

is reported[9] to give a 77 percent yield of

$$\begin{array}{c} CF_2-CF_2 \quad CH-CH \\ | \qquad | \qquad \| \quad \| \\ CH_2-CH-CH \underset{O}{\overset{}{\diagdown \diagup}} CH. \end{array}$$

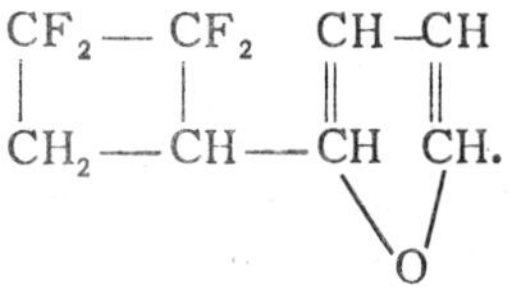

The yields of codimers from other olefinic ethers are reported to be considerably lower and range from 10 to 20 percent. The reaction is effected by heating a mixture of the fluoroolefin and the unsaturated ether with or without a peroxide catalyst. Representative temperatures which have been employed range from $100°$ to $150°$. The use of a polymerization inhibitor in this reaction is sometimes desirable depending upon the reactants employed.

METHOD 505 Epoxidation

The first reported epoxidation of fluoroalcohols utilized powdered potassium hydroxide in ether. Employing this procedure, Knunyants[31,33] reports good yields using both fluoro- and fluorochloroalcohols as shown:

$$\left.\begin{array}{l} CH_2ClCH(OH)CH_2F \\ CH_2FCH(OH)CH_2F \end{array}\right\rangle \xrightarrow{KOH} CH_2FCH{-}CH_2O \ (75\%)$$

McBee and co-workers[37, 39, 40] obtained high yields of epoxides from β-bromoalcohols using a 50 weight percent aqueous sodium hydroxide solution. For example, an 87 percent yield of CF_3CHCH_2O was obtained from $CF_3CH(OH)CH_2Br$. Other types of epoxides which were prepared by this procedure are:

$$CF_3CH{-}CHCH_3 \text{ (epoxide, O bridging)} \text{ and } C_3F_7CH{-}C{-}(CH_3)_2 \text{ (epoxide, O bridging)}.$$[59]

METHOD 506 Halogen Interchange

In a study of the reactivity of perfluoroethers, Tiers[71] discovered the first known chemical reaction of this type of compound. The treatment of perfluoro(α-alkyl)cyclic ethers with aluminum chloride resulted in replacement of the three α fluorine atoms with chlorine. For example, the treatment of $n{-}C_6F_{13}CFCF_2CF_2CF_2O$ with aluminum chloride gave a 60 percent yield of $n{-}C_6F_{13}CClCF_2CF_2CCl_2O$. In a continuation of this work which is discussed in Methods 217 and 805, Tiers showed that similar treatment of perfluoro-di-(n-alkyl) ethers and perfluorocyclic ethers which do not contain α-alkyl groups results in cleavage at the ether linkage as shown in the following examples:

$$R_fCF_2OCF_2R_f \xrightarrow{AlCl_3} [R_fCCl_2OCCl_2R_f] \longrightarrow R_fCOCl + R_fCCl_3$$

$$CF_2(CF_2)_nCF_2O \longrightarrow CCl_2(CF_2)_nCCl_2O \longrightarrow CCl_3(CF_2)_nCOCl$$

Park and co-workers[55] report the cleavage of fluorochloroethers with aluminum chloride to yield alkyl- and acyl halides.

METHOD 507 Dehydration of Glycols

$$HOCH_2(CF_2)_nCH_2OH + H_2SO_4 \longrightarrow CH_2(CF_2)_nCH_2O$$

A procedure for the preparation of cyclic fluoroethers was described by Henne and Richter[25] which involves the dehydration of a fluorine-containing glycol with sulfuric acid.

METHOD 508 Reaction of Alcohols and Paraformaldehyde

$$CH_2FCH_2OH + (CH_2O)_x + HCl\ (dry) \xrightarrow{0^\circ} CH_2FCH_2OCH_2Cl\ (60\%)$$

The reaction of fluoroalcohols with paraformaldehyde and dry hydrogen chloride is described by Knunyants[32] and Olah[46].

METHOD 509 Action of Diazomethane on Alcohols

Henne and Smook[26] reported that the action of diazomethane on trifluoroethanol results in the formation of the methyl ether.

$$CF_3CH_2OH + CH_2N_2 \xrightarrow{-10^\circ} CF_3CH_2OCH_3\ (27\%)$$

METHOD 510 Cyclic Trimerization of Ketones

The reaction of trifluoroacetone with sodium was reported by Henne and Hinkamp[22] to yield a condensation product:

$$CF_3COCH_3 + Na \longrightarrow$$

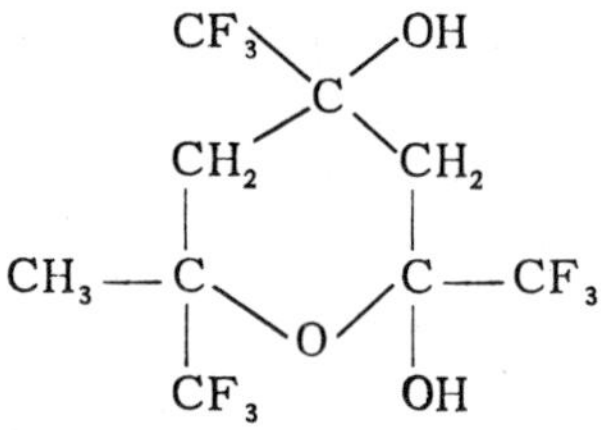

(81%)

METHOD 511 Reaction of Alcohols and Epoxides

$$\overset{O}{\overbrace{CH_2CH_2}} + CH_2FCH_2OH + Na_2SO_4 \xrightarrow{130^\circ} CH_2FCH_2OCH_2CH_2OH$$

This preparation of fluoroether alcohols was described by Buckle and co-workers[7].

Brey and Tarrant[5A] were successful in effecting the addition of more highly fluorinated alcohols to ethylene oxide. The reaction was carried out in an autoclave for 4 hours at 70° using a mixture of fluoroalcohol, ethylene oxide and potassium hydroxide. The yields ranged from 30 to 60 percent of the hydroxy ethers which had the general structure $RCH_2OCH_2CH_2OH$ (where R— is CF_3—, C_2F_5—, C_3F_7—, $CF_3C(CH_3)_2$—). These same workers studied the reaction of fluoroalcohols with epichlorohydrin. They observed that addition occurred in fair yields when a basic catalyst was used; only slight reaction was observed when acid catalysts were used. Trifluoroethanol reacted with epichlorohydrin in the presence of an excess of sodium hydroxide to give the glycidyl ether directly:

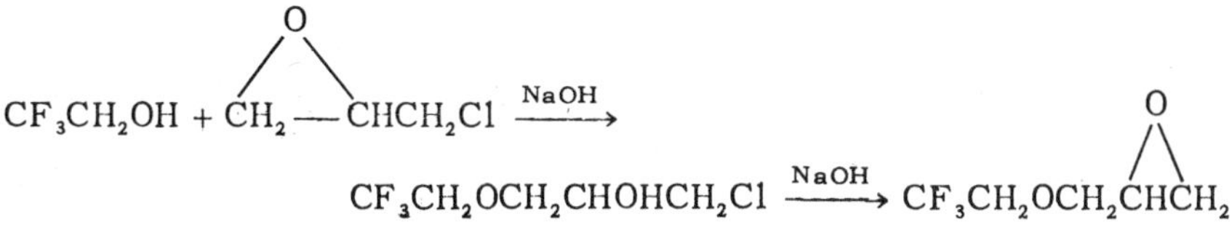

The reaction was complicated by the further reaction of the fluoroalcohol with the glycidyl ether:

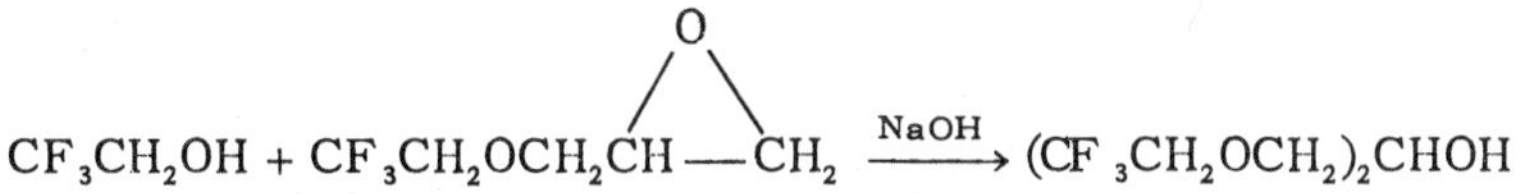

This procedure gives yields of 19 to 31 percent of the glycidyl ether and 19 to 24 percent of the diether. The three primary fluoroalcohols, CF_3CH_2OH, $C_2F_5CH_2OH$, and $C_3F_7CH_2OH$ undergo reaction to give the glycidyl ethers, however $CF_3C(CH_3)_2OH$ does not react appreciably. When pyridine is used as a catalyst, a 50 percent yield of the glycidyl ether is obtained from CF_3CH_2OH. The reactions where sodium hydroxide is used, are carried out in an aqueous medium at room temperature; the pyridine reaction can be run at 80° to 90° for 12 hours.

METHOD 512 Reaction of Alkyl Sulfates or Sulfonates with Alcohols

The treatment of fluorine-containing glycols with alkyl sulfates in the presence of sodium hydroxide and water to produce ethers was first reported by McBee and co-workers.[38] This procedure yielded ether alcohols as indicated by the following example:

$$HOCH_2(CF_2)_4CH_2OH + (CH_3O)_2SO_2 + NaOH + H_2O \xrightarrow{100^\circ} HOCH_2(CF_2)_4CH_2OCH_3$$

Faurote *et al.*[12A] reported the preparation of ethers from the decomposition of the tosylates of alcohols or glycols as illustrated below:

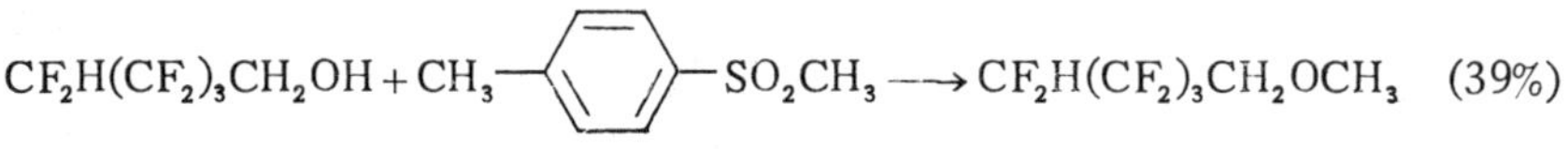

METHOD 513 Addition of Hydrogen Fluoride to Epoxides

This reaction as reported by Knunyants[31,33] was carried out using ethylene oxide, hydrogen fluoride and ether which contained 1 to 2 percent water and gave a 5 percent yield of the fluoroether shown below (cf. Method 406).

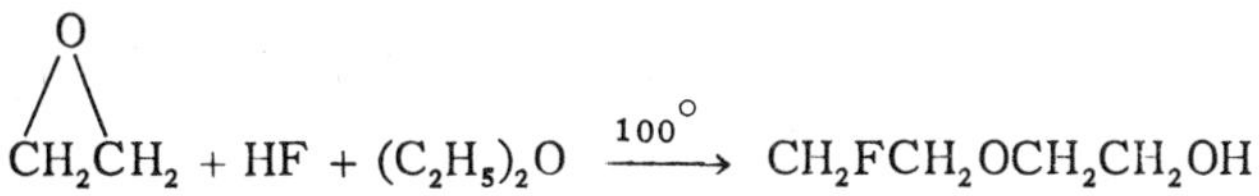

TABLE 10

ALIPHATIC AND ALICYCLIC ETHERS

Empirical Formula	Structural Formula	Method	Yield %	B.p. °C/mm.	F.p. or M.p. °C	n_D^t	d_4^t	t°C	Ref.
C_2F_6O	CF_3OCF_3	111		−59					61
$C_2H_3ClF_2O$	CF_2ClOCH_3	107		55.3	−105.1				5
$C_2H_3F_3O$	CF_3OCH_3 or CHF_2OCH_2F	107		30.1	−96.2				5
$C_3Cl_5F_3O$	$CFCl_2CF_2OCCl_3$	503		142/626		1.4187	1.7141	20	55
$C_3HCl_4F_3O$	$CFHClCF_2OCCl_3$	503		131/629		1.4090	1.6631	20	55
$C_3H_2Cl_3F_3O$	$CFHClCF_2OCHCl_2$	503		112.5/626		1.3883	1.5620	20	55
$C_3H_3ClF_4O$	$CF_2HCF_2OCH_2Cl$	503		72/628	−78	1.3311	1.4869	20	47
$C_3H_3Cl_2F_3O$	$CFHClCF_2OCH_2Cl$	503		112/745		1.3745	1.530	25	58
				104.5/624	Glass	1.3768	1.5269	20	47,55
$C_3H_3Cl_3F_2O$	$CHCl_2CF_2OCH_2Cl$	503		137/627	−31	1.4205	1.5679	20	47
$C_3H_4BrF_3O$	$CFHBrCF_2OCH_3$	501		82.5/631		1.3645	1.703	25	50
$C_3H_4ClF_3O$	$CFH_2CF_2OCH_2Cl$	503		85/625	−51	1.3514	1.4174	20	47
	$CFHClCF_2OCH_3$	501		64.4/630		1.3338	1.3632	20	56
		501		70.6	−92	1.3340	1.3636	20	44
		501	68	68.7/725		1.3315		25	1
$C_3H_4Cl_2F_2O$	$CH_2ClCF_2OCH_2Cl$	503		116/626	−44	1.3974	1.4594	20	47
	$CHCl_2CF_2OCH_3$	502		103–104.5					14
		501		104		1.3864	1.4226(20)	25	53
		501		105	−35	1.3861	1.4262	20	44
$C_3H_4F_4O$	$CF_2HCF_2OCH_3$	501		36.5	−107	< 1.3	1.2939	20	51,44
$C_3H_5ClF_2O$	$CH_2ClCF_2OCH_3$	501		27.5–28/130		1.3560	1.2592	25	69
$C_3H_5F_3O$	$CF_3CH_2OCH_3$	509	27	31.2/746		1.2942	1.1661	3	26
	$CFH_2CF_2OCH_3$	502		45					64
		501		45.2		1.2997	1.182(27.4)	25	49
C_3H_6ClFO	$CFH_2CH_2OCH_2Cl$	508	60	42–43/60		1.4120	1.190	20	32
$C_4Cl_3F_7O$	$CF_3CCl_2OCF_2CF_2Cl$	503		89.6		1.3303	1.6486	20	26
$C_4Cl_7F_3O$	$CFCl_2CF_2OCCl_2CCl_3$	503		94/10		1.4575	1.7819	20	55

$C_4F_{10}O$	$C_2F_5OC_2F_5$	111		1					61
	$CF_3OCF_2CF_2OCF_3$	111		13					61
$C_4H_3Cl_4F_3O$	$CFHClCF_2OCCl_2CH_2Cl$	503		85/23		1.4284	1.6633	25	58
	$CFHClCF_2OCHClCHCl_2$	503		85/23		1.4291	1.6438	20	55
$C_4H_3F_7O$	$CF_2HCF_2OCH_2CF_3$	501	78.5	56.7		1.2728	1.4874	20	26
$C_4H_4Cl_3F_3O$	$CFHClCF_2OCCl_2CH_3$	503		59/100	Glass	1.3776	1.4021	20	47
	$CFHClCF_2OCHClCH_2Cl$	503		97/100		1.4080	1.5426	20	55
$C_4H_4F_6O$	$CF_3CHFCF_2OCH_3$	501	83	54–55		1.2850	1.429	10	34
$C_4H_5ClF_3IO$	$CFHClCF_2OCH_2CH_2I$	216		93–103/36–38					35
$C_4H_5Cl_2F_3O$	$CFHClCF_2OCH_2CH_2Cl$	503		80/100	Glass	1.3935	1.4620	20	47
		503		84/100		1.3935	1.4620	20	55
		216	27	85/100		1.3882	1.4471	25	5A
	$CFHClCF_2OCHClCH_3$	503		63/100		1.3755	1.4020	20	55
		503		142–143/740		1.3920	1.4637	25	58
$C_4H_5Cl_3F_2O$	$CHCl_2CF_2OCH_2CH_2Cl$	216	27	86–87/33		1.4270	1.4833	25	5A
$C_4H_6BrF_3O$	$CF_2BrCFHOC_2H_5$	502		105–107		1.37938	1.6121	10.5	66
$C_4H_6Br_2F_2O$	$CHBr_2CF_2OC_2H_5$	502		67.2/25			1.9158	17.5	63
$C_4H_6ClF_3O$	$CFHClCF_2OC_2H_5$	501	88–92	82/630		1.3479	1.2726	20	56,12
		501		87–88.2		1.3451	1.2729	25	18
		501	47	87.2/725		1.3425		25	1
	$CF_3CH_2OCH_2CH_2Cl$	216	53	114–115		1.3590	1.3034	27	5A
$C_4H_6Cl_2F_2O$	$CHCl_2CF_2OC_2H_5$	501		63/100		1.3922	1.3145	25	69
		501		120		1.3895	1.3461(20)	25	53
		502		120.5					14
$C_4H_6F_3IO$	$CFHICF_2OC_2H_5$	501		122/630		1.4189	1.839	20	50
$C_4H_6F_4O$	$CF_2HCF_2OC_2H_5$	501		57.5		1.294	1.1978	25	10,11,18
		501		55.1/740		1.294	1.1978	25	26
		501		50.7/621.7	Glass	1.2961	1.1951	25	51
		502	66–70	57–58					73
$C_4H_7BrF_2O$	$CH_2BrCF_2OC_2H_5$	502		114.6		1.397	1.513	25	63,70
$C_4H_7ClF_2O$	$CH_2ClCF_2OC_2H_5$	502	53	89–93		1.368	1.168	25	70
		501		91–93					5,18

TABLE 10 (*continued*)

Empirical Formula	Structural Formula	Method	Yield %	B.p. °C/mm.	F.p. or M.p. °C	n_D^t	d_4^t	t °C	Ref.
$C_4H_7Cl_2FO$	$CHCl_2CFHOC_2H_5$	502		121			1.214	25	68
$C_4H_7F_3O$	$CF_3CH_2OC_2H_5$	502	60	49.9		1.3042	1.0910	20	5,26
		502		50.3		1.3065	1.065(25)	20	42
	$CF_3CH_2CH_2OCH_3$	502	43	54.9/753		1.3114	1.1129	20	26
C_4H_8ClFO	$CFH_2CH_2OCH_2CH_2Cl$	216	24	142–147		1.4170	1.137	20	32
$C_4H_8F_2O$	$CF_2HCH_2OC_2H_5$	502		66.3–66.7			1.039	15	67
C_4H_9FO	$CFH_2CH_2OC_2H_5$	101	40	74.5–75.5					15
$C_5F_{12}O$	$CF_3(CF_2)_3OCF_3$	111		35.4/742.8		1.240	1.581	27	61
$C_5H_4Br_2F_6O$	$CF_3CHBrCBr(OCH_3)CF_3$	201	100	58–59/25		1.408			20
$C_5H_5ClF_6O$	$CF_3CHFCF_2OCH_2CH_2Cl$	216	27	46/37		1.3349	1.4749	25	5A
$C_5H_5F_7O$	$CF_3CH_2CH_2OCF_2CF_2H$	501		88.2/744		1.3000	1.4087	20	26
$C_5H_6Br_2$-ClF_3O	$CFHClCF_2OCH_2CHBrCH_2Br$	201		110–111/19		1.4675	1.956	25	58
$C_5H_6ClF_5O$	$CF_3CF_2CH_2OCH_2CH_2Cl$	216	49	120–121		1.3448	1.3792	26	5A
$C_5H_6F_4O$	$CF_2CF_2CH_2CHOCH_3$	504		89–92					3
		504	13	88–91.8		1.3380	1.2612	25	9
$C_5H_6F_6O$	$CF_3CHFCF_2OC_2H_5$	501	79	64–65		1.2960	1.299	20	34
$C_5H_7F_5O$	$CF_3CH_2CF_2OC_2H_5$	502	25	77		1.326		20	20
$C_5H_8ClF_3O$	$CFHClCF_2OCH_2CH_2CH_3$	501		102.3/630		1.3575	1.2173	20	56
	$CFHClCF_2OCH(CH_3)_2$	501		94/630		1.3521	1.2010	20	56
$C_5H_8Cl_2F_2O$	$CHCl_2CF_2OCH_2CH_2CH_3$	501		136.5		1.3968	1.2636(20)	25	53
	$CHCl_2CF_2OCH(CH_3)_2$	501		28–30.2/9.0		1.3897	1.2331	25	69
$C_5H_8F_4O$	$CF_2HCF_2OCH_2CH_2CH_3$	501		71.7/626.7	Glass	1.3141	1.1549	25	51
$C_5H_9Br_2FO$	$CH_2BrCFBrCH_2OC_2H_5$	201		188					62
$C_5H_9ClF_2O$	$CH_2ClCF_2OCH(CH_3)_2$	501		53/121		1.3720	1.1627	25	69
$C_5H_9F_3O$	$CF_3CH_2CH_2OC_2H_5$	502	30	72.3/746		1.3258	1.0593	20	26
	$CF_3CH(CH_3)OC_2H_5$	502		63–64		1.3219	1.062	20	27

$C_5H_{10}BrFO$	$CH_2BrCFHCH_2OC_2H_5$	102	18.5	156.4–157.3					62
$C_5H_{10}F_2O$	$CF_2HCH_2OCH_2CH_2CH_3$	502		89					65
	$CFH_2CFHCH_2OC_2H_5$	102		114.5					62
$C_6F_{14}O$	$CF_3(CF_2)_2O(CF_2)_2CF_3$	111		56					61
$C_6H_4F_8O_2$	$CHF_2CF_2OCH_2CH_2OCF_2CF_2H$	501		86/100		1.3202	1.4726	25	11
$C_6H_6Br_2F_6O$	$CF_3CHBrCBr(OC_2H_5)CF_3$	201		72–73/32		1.409		20	19
$C_6H_6ClF_7O$	$CF_3(CF_2)_2CH_2OCH_2CH_2Cl$	216	67	75/80		1.3381	1.4673	25	5A
$C_6H_6Cl_4F_4O_2$	$CHCl_2CF_2OCH_2CH_2OCF_2CHCl_2$	501	18	90/2.2		1.5786	1.4194	25	5A
$C_6H_6F_8O$	$(CF_3)_2CHCF_2OC_2H_5$	501		83/743		1.2908	1.3946	25	6
	$CF_2HCF_2OCH_2CH_2CF_2CF_2H$	501		86/100		1.3202	1.4726	25	5,18
$C_6H_7ClF_6O_2$	$CF_3CHClC(OCH_3)_2CF_3$	501		141–142/747		1.3560	1.4854	20	23
$C_6H_8F_6O$	$CF_3CFHCF_2OCH_2CH_2CH_3$	501		92–93		1.3110	1.260	20	34
	$CF_3CFHCF_2OCH(CH_3)_2$	501		76		1.3220	1.280	22	34
$C_6H_8F_6O_2$	$CF_3CH_2C(OCH_3)_2CF_3$	501	53	50/100					19
$C_6H_{10}ClF_3O$	$CFHClCF_2O(CH_2)_3CH_3$	501		124.5/630		1.3680	1.1779	20	56
	$CFHClCF_2OC(CH_3)_3$	501	93	19–20/50		1.3653	1.1516	25	1
	$CF_3C(CH_3)_2OCH_2CH_2Cl$	216	45	135		1.3784	1.2102	25	5A
$C_6H_{10}Cl_2F_2O$	$CHCl_2CF_2O(CH_2)_3CH_3$	501		153		1.4029	1.2184	20	53
	$CHCl_2CF_2OCH(CH_3)C_2H_5$	502		154					14
$C_6H_{10}F_4O$	$CF_2HCF_2O(CH_2)_3CH_3$	501		22/23.5	Glass	1.3296	1.1163	25	51
$C_7H_{10}F_6O$	$CF_3CFHCF_2O(CH_2)_3CH_3$	501	34	108		1.3390	1.270	27	34
$C_7H_{12}Cl_2F_2O$	$CHCl_2CF_2O(CH_2)_4CH_3$	501		172.5		1.4157	1.1817(20)	25	53
$C_7H_{12}F_4O$	$CF_2HCF_2O(CH_2)_4CH_3$	501		31/20.3		1.3480	1.0726	25	51
$C_8F_{18}O$	$CF_3(CF_2)_3O(CF_2)_3CF_3$	111		100.7/741		1.2619	1.689	25	26,61
$C_8F_{18}O_3$	$C_2F_5OCF_2CF_2OCF_2CF_2OC_2F_5$	111		96.6/737		1.250	1.617	30	61
$C_8H_6F_{12}O$	$CH_3OCH_2(CF_2)_5CF_2H$	512	44	118.5/203		1.3164	1.6294	20	12A
$C_8H_9ClF_6O_3$	$CF_2(CF_2)_2CCl(OCH_3)C(OCH_3)_2$ (cyclic)	501		100–101.5/16		1.4220	1.4291	20	23
$C_8H_{11}F_6O_2$	$CF_3CHC(OC_2H_5)_2CF_3$	501	59	135		1.342		20	19
$C_8H_{12}F_4O$	$CF_2HCF_2OCH(CH_2)_4CH_2$ (cyclic)	501		86/100		1.3848	1.1526	25	10,18

TABLE 10 (*continued*)

Empirical Formula	Structural Formula	Method	Yield %	B.p. °C/mm.	F.p. or M.p. °C	n_D^t	d_4^t	t °C	Ref.
$C_8H_{12}F_6O_2$	$CF_3C(OC_2H_5)_2CH_2CF_3$	501		132–135		1.3394		25	8
$C_9H_{18}F_2O$	$CH_3CF_2(CH_2)_3O(CH_2)_3CH_3$	502		171.5		1.3889	0.9336	20	28
$C_9H_{18}F_2O_4$	$(CFH_2CH_2OCH_2CH_2O)_2CH_2$	508		120/3					46
$C_{10}F_{22}O$	$CF_3(CF_2)_4O(CF_2)_4CF_3$	111		138.4/755.6		1.268	1.758	25	61
$C_{12}F_{26}O$	$CF_3(CF_2)_5O(CF_2)_5CF_3$	111		179		1.278	1.803	25	61
$C_{14}H_{17}F_{11}O_5$	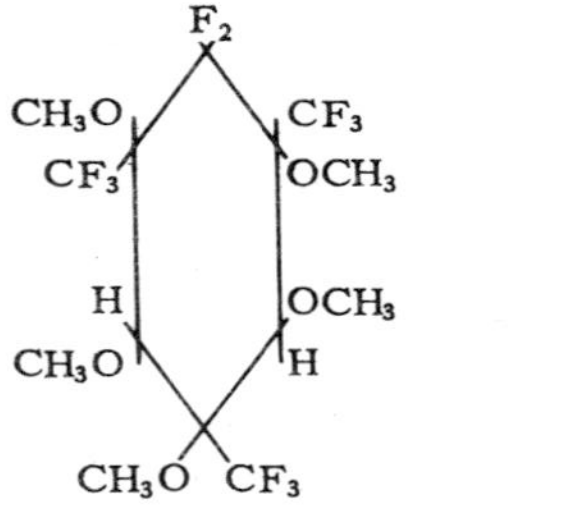	502		103/9	69.5–70.2				13
$C_{14}H_{26}F_4O$	$CHF_2CF_2OC_{12}H_{25}$	501	99	105/4		1.3968	0.9831	25	10,18
$C_{20}H_{18}F_{24}O_2$	$[(CH_2)_3OCH_2(CF_2)_5CF_2H]_2$	512	39	144/0.5	−50	1.3467	1.5776	20	12A
$C_{20}H_{38}F_4O$	$CF_2HCF_2OC_{18}H_{37}$	501	80	170/6	20–23	1.4144	0.9530	25	10

TABLE 11

OLEFINIC ETHERS

Empirical Formula	Structural Formula	Method	Yield %	B.p. °C/mm.	F.p. or M.p. °C	n_D^t	d_4^t	t°C	Ref.
$C_4Cl_5F_3O$	$CCl_2{=}CClOCF_2CFCl_2$	302		89/40		1.4440	1.7054	20	55
$C_4H_3Cl_2F_3O$	$CF_3CCl{=}CClOCH_3$	501	50	107–108/630		1.3917	1.4716(20)	18.5	48
$C_4H_3F_5O$	$CF_2{=}CFCF_2OCH_3$	502	70	38.5		1.296	1.358	20	43
$C_4H_4ClF_3O$	$CH_2{=}CHOCF_2CFClH$	301		71.4					35
		301	52	71–73		1.3531	1.2408	25	5A
$C_4H_5F_3O$	$CF_3CH{=}CHOCH_3$	501	92	83–84					19
	$CF_3CH_2OCH{=}CH_2$	301	32	42–48		1.3180	1.118	27	5A
$C_5H_3ClF_4O$	$CF_2CF_2CCl{=}COCH_3$ (cyclic)	501	75	117		1.3799	1.4614	20	54
		501		116.1/748		1.3752	1.4484	25	60
$C_5H_3ClF_6O$	$CF_3CCl{=}C(CF_3)OCH_3$	501		84–85/745		1.3370	1.4703(31)	20	23
$C_5H_3F_5O$	$CF_2CF_2CF{=}COCH_3$ (cyclic)	501	52	35–39/112 87/747	−42	1.3300	1.426(23)	25	1
$C_5H_4F_6O$	$CF_3CH{=}C(CF_3)OCH_3$	501	61	55–57					19
$C_5H_5Cl_2F_3O$	$CF_3CCl{=}CClOC_2H_5$	501		126/630		1.3980	1.3774(16)	18.5	48
$C_5H_5F_5O$	$CF_3CF_2CH_2OCH{=}CH_2$	301	21	54–60		1.3131	1.227	27	5A
$C_5H_6ClF_3O$	$CH_2{=}CHCH_2OCF_2CFClH$	501	45	109.2/750		1.3694	1.250	25	1
$C_5H_7F_3O$	$CF_3CH{=}CHOC_2H_5$	501	91	103		1.3494		21	19,24
C_5H_9FO	$CH_2{=}CFCH_2OC_2H_5$	301		77.5		1.3790	0.91659	15.1	62
$C_6H_3ClF_6O$	$CF_2CF_2CF_2C(OCH_3){=}CCl$ (cyclic)	501		130/742		1.3750	1.5645 (27.4)	20	23
$C_6H_3Cl_3F_2O$	$CF_2CCl{=}CClC(OCH_3){=}CCl$ (cyclic)	501	77	59–62/115		1.4755		20	41

TABLE 11 (*continued*)

Empirical Formula	Structural Formula	Method	Yield %	B.p. °C/mm.	F.p. or M.p. °C	n_D^t	d_4^t	t°C	Ref.
$C_6H_5ClF_4O$	$CF_2CF_2CCl{=}COC_2H_5$	501		129.5		1.3843	1.3642	20	54
$C_6H_5F_5O$	$CF_2CF_2CF{=}COC_2H_5$	501	33	29.5/36		1.3400	1.3233(20)	25	1
$C_6H_5F_7O$	$CF_3(CF_2)_2CH_2OCH{=}CH_2$	301	18	78–82		1.3111	1.343	26	5A
$C_6H_6F_4O_2$	$CF_2CF_2C(OCH_3){=}COCH_3$	501	12	47.4/15	−0.5 to 0	1.3714	1.330(23)	25	1
				36.8/11.3	−5.3	1.3690	1.3409	25	52
$C_6H_6F_6O$	$CF_3CH{=}C(CF_3)OC_2H_5$	501	57	72–5		1.409		20	8,19
$C_6H_7Cl_2F_3O$	$CF_3CCl{=}CClOCH_2CH_2CH_3$	501		147/630		1.4098		18.5	48
$C_6H_9ClF_2O$	$CFCl{=}CFOC(CH_3)_3$	501		18/0.8		1.3989	1.0940	25	69
				143/760					
$C_6H_9Cl_2FO$	$CCl_2{=}CFOC(CH_3)_3$	501		38/2.9		1.4315	1.1368	25	69
$C_7H_5ClF_4O$	$CF_2CF_2CCl{=}COCH_2CH{=}CH_2$	501		113.2		1.3861	1.337	25	60
$C_7H_7ClF_4O$	$CF_2CF_2CCl{=}COCH_2CH_2CH_3$	501		141		1.3900	1.2777	20	54
$C_7H_8F_6O_2$	$CF_3CH{=}C(CF_3)OCH_2CH_2CH_2OH$	501		83–4/30					8
$C_7H_9ClF_4O_3$	$CF_3CCl{=}C(OCH_3)CF(OCH_3)_2$	501		72/6		1.3985	1.3965(30)	20	23
$C_7H_9Cl_2F_3O$	$CF_3CCl{=}CClO(CH_2)_3CH_3$	501		166/630		1.4140	1.2473(22)	18.5	48

$C_8H_{10}F_4O_2$	$CF_2CF_2C(OC_2H_5){=}COC_2H_5$	501	5	61.6/11.5		1.3796		25	1
				52.8/10.3	−50.9	1.3790	1.2123	25	52
$C_{10}H_{14}F_4O$	$CF_2CF_2CH_2C(CH_3)CH_2OCH_2C(CH_3){=}CH_2$	504	20	70–2/19		1.3918		25	2,3,9
$C_{10}F_{14}F_4O_2$	$CF_2CF_2C(OCH_2CH_2CH_3){=}COCH_2CH_2CH_3$	501		82/17		1.3915	1.1501	25	52
$C_{12}H_{18}F_4O_2$	$CF_2CF_2C[O(CH_2)_3CH_3]{=}CO(CH_2)_3CH_3$	501		132–3/37.6	−49.2	1.4019	1.0965	25	52
$C_{18}H_{15}O_3$	CF_2—CF—CF—CF—$C(OC_2H_5)COC_2H_5$ CF_2—CF_2 CF_2—CF_2 CF_2—COC_2H_5	501	67		51.5–52.5				57

TABLE 12

CYCLIC ETHERS

Empirical Formula	Structural Formula	Method	Yield %	B.p. °C/mm.	F.p. or M.p. °C	n_D^t	d_4^t	t°C	Ref.
C_3F_6O	CF_3CFCF_2O	111		−42					30
	$CF_2CF_2CF_2O$	111		−38					29
$C_3H_2F_4O$	$CF_3CHCHFO$	505		37					39
$C_3H_3F_3O$	CF_3CHCH_2O	505	87.5	39.1–39.3/748.3		1.2997	1.3068	20	37
C_3H_5FO	CFH_2CHCH_2O	505	75	85–86.4		1.3730	1.090	20	31,33,45
		101	45	85.5–86					15
$C_4Cl_4F_4O$	$CF_2CF_2CCl_2OCCl_2$	503		131–2/742		1.4120	1.7382	20	25
C_4F_8O	$CF_2(CF_2)_3O$	111		1					29
$C_4H_4F_4O$	$CF_2CF_2CH_2OCH_2$	507		68/743		1.3244	1.4305	20	25
$C_4H_5F_3O$	$CF_3CHCHO(CH_3)$	505	90	58.5–59/747		1.3167	1.207	20	59
$C_5Cl_3F_7O$	$CF_3CClCF_2CF_2CCl_2O$	506	40	114		1.3620		25	71

$C_5Cl_4F_6O$	$CF_2CF_2CF_2CCl_2OCCl_2$	503		159/737	1.4008	1.7662	20	25
$C_5F_{10}O$	$CF_2(CF_2)_4O$	111 107		31–33 26/742	1.260	1.68(15)	29	29 25
$C_5H_4F_6O$	$CF_2CF_2CF_2CH_2OCH_2$	507		98–100/742	1.3250	1.5588	20	25
$C_5H_7F_3O$	$CF_3CHCHO(C_2H_5)$	505	83	78.8–79/745	1.3340	1.146	20	59
	$CF_3CHCO(CH_3)_2$	505	84	71.3–71.9/747	1.3292	1.125	20	59
$C_5H_7F_3O_2$	$CF_3CH_2OCH_2CHCH_2O$	511	31	132–135	1.3560	1.2666	25	5A
$C_5H_8F_2O$	$CH_2OCH_2C(CH_2F)_2$	101		141–142	1.3980	1.200	25	16
$C_6Cl_3F_9O$	$C_2F_5CClCF_2CF_2CCl_2O$	506	45	136	1.3566		25	71
$C_6H_5ClF_6O_2$	$CF_3CHClC(CF_3)OCH_2CH_2O$	501		85/48	1.3630	1.5920 (29)	20	23
$C_6H_5F_7O$	$CF_3CF_2CF_2CHCHO(CH_3)$	505	76	93.5/748	1.3091	1.424	20	59
$C_6H_5F_7O$	$CF_3CF_2CF_2C(CH_3)CH_2O$	505	93	93/745	1.3107	1.391	20	40
$C_6H_6F_4O$	$CF_2CF_2CH_2CHCHCH_2O$	504	9	74–76/67	1.3730		25	9

TABLE 12 (*continued*)

Empirical Formula	Structural Formula	Method	Yield %	B.p. °C/mm.	F.p. or M.p. °C	n_D^t	d_4^t	t °C	Ref.
$C_6H_6F_6O_2$	$CF_3CH_2CO(CF_3)CH_2CH_2O$	501		44–46/50		1.3318		25	8
$C_6H_7F_5O_2$	$CF_3CF_2CH_2OCH_2CHCH_2O$	511	19	81/86		1.3419	1.3534	25	5A
$C_6H_8F_4O_2$	$CF_2HCF_2CHCH_2OCH_2CH_2O$	501		153–157		1.3677		25	17
$C_7H_4ClF_5O_2$	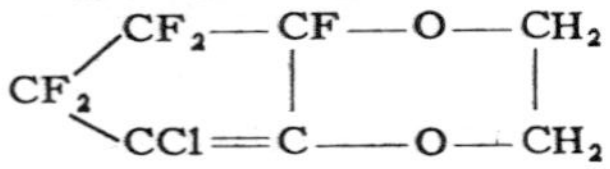	501		98/53		1.3993	1.5760 (29.5)	20	23
$C_7H_7F_7O$	$CF_3CF_2CF_2CHCO(CH_3)_2$	505	85	102.5–103/747		1.3187	1.351	20	59
	$CF_3CF_2CF_2CHCHO(C_2H_5)$	505	83	110.5–111/749		1.3218	1.358	20	59
$C_7H_7F_7O_2$	$CF_3(CF_2)_2CH_2OCH_2CHCH_2O$	511	23	79/49		1.3350	1.4429	25	5A
$C_8Cl_3F_{13}O$	$CF_3(CF_2)_3CClCF_2CF_2CCl_2O$	506	54	171		1.3494	1.813	25	71

$C_8H_6F_4O$	$CF_2CF_2CH_2CHC{=}CHCH{=}CHO$	504	77	86.5/80		1.4073	1.3341	25	9
$C_8H_8F_8O_2$	$CF_2H(CF_2)_3CHCH_2OCH_2CH_2O$	501		83–90/5		1.3484		25	17
$C_9H_5F_9O$	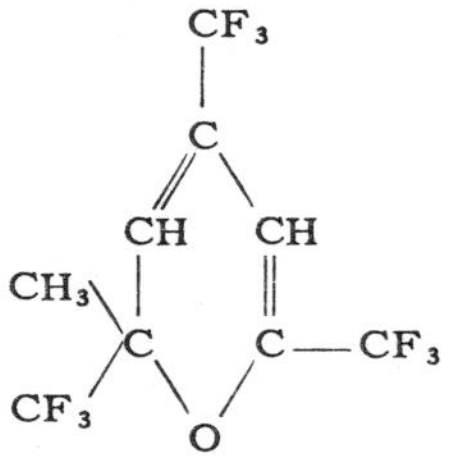	303		119–120	−27.3 to −26.3	1.3410	1.468	20	22
$C_{10}Cl_3F_{17}O$	$CF_3(CF_2)_5CClCF_2CF_2CCl_2O$	506	60	207		1.3455		25	71

TABLE 13

HYDROXY ETHERS

Empirical Formula	Structural Formula	Method	Yield %	B.p. °C/mm.	F.p. or M.p. °C	n_D^t	d_4^t	t°C	Ref.
$C_4H_6ClF_3O_2$	$CFClHCF_2OCH_2CH_2OH$	501		80.5–97		1.3808	1.456	25	35
		501	54	114–118/100		1.3795		21	5A
$C_4H_6Cl_2F_2O_2$	$CHCl_2CF_2OCH_2CH_2OH$	501	30	62–63/2		1.4245	1.4905	25	5A
$C_4H_6F_4O_2$	$CF_2HCF_2OCH_2CH_2OH$	501	15	94/100		1.3418	1.4159	25	10,11,18
$C_4H_7F_3O_2$	$CF_3CH_2OCH_2CH_2OH$	511	50	84/80		1.3502	1.2902	25	5A
$C_4H_9FO_2$	$CFH_2CH_2OCH_2CH_2OH$	513	5	172–174		1.4130	1.1150	20	31,33
		502		30/2.3					46
		511	70	81/22					7
$C_5H_6F_6O_2$	$CF_3CHFCF_2OCH_2CH_2OH$	501	25	72–74/40		1.3192	1.5227	25	5A
$C_5H_7F_5O_2$	$CF_3CF_2CH_2OCH_2CH_2OH$	511	32	87/84		1.3370	1.3806	25	5A
$C_5H_8ClF_3O_2$	$CF_3CH_2OCH_2CH(OH)CH_2Cl$	511	50	85–86/19		1.3951	1.3716	25	5A
$C_6H_6F_6O_2$	$CF_3CH{=}C(CF_3)OCH_2CH_2OH$	501		57/20		1.3450		25	8
$C_6H_7F_7O_2$	$CF_3(CF_2)_2CH_2OCH_2CH_2OH$	511	62	91–92/54		1.3300	1.4695	28	5A
$C_6H_{11}F_3O_2$	$CF_3C(CH_3)_2OCH_2CH_2OH$	511	35	92/77		1.3749	1.1931	22	5A
$C_6H_{13}FO_3$	$CFH_2CH_2OCH_2CH_2OCH_2CH_2OH$	511	15	132–133/30					7
$C_7H_8F_8O_2$	$CH_3OCH_2(CF_2)_4CH_2OH$	512		194–195		1.3	1.54	20	38
$C_7H_{10}F_6O_2$	$C_2H_5OCH_2(CF_2)_3CH_2OH$	512	48	190–191		1.3630	1.43(20)	24	38
$C_7H_{10}F_6O_3$	$(CF_3CH_2OCH_2)_2CHOH$	511	28	81/16		1.3528	1.3890	21	5A

$C_9H_9ClF_4O_4$	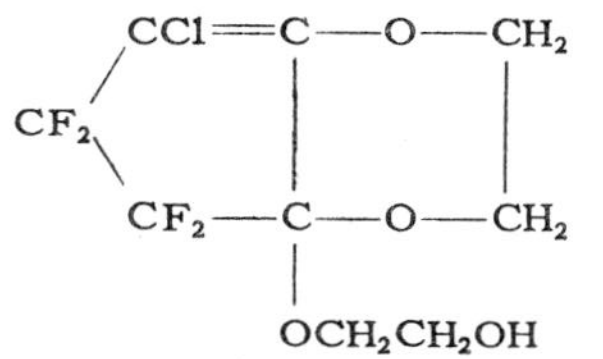	501		136–142/2–3		1.4508	1.5460(29)	20	23
$C_9H_9F_9O$	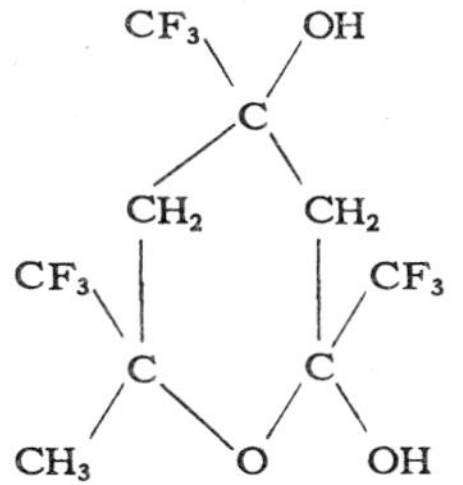	510	81	200–210	107.5–108.5				22
$C_{11}H_{10}F_{14}O_3$	$[CF_3(CF_2)_2CH_2OCH_2]_2CHOH$	511	26	112–115/15		1.3338	1.5569	25	5A

BIBLIOGRAPHY

1. Barr, J. T., Rapp, K. E., *et al.*, *J. Am. Chem. Soc.*, **72**, 4480(1950).
2. Barrick, P. L., U. S. Patent 2,462,347(1949).
3. Barrick, P. L., U. S. Patent 2,462,345(1949).
4. Benning, A. F., and Park, J. D., U. S. Patent 2,336,921(1943).
5. Booth, H. S., and Burchfield, P. E., *J. Am. Chem. Soc.*, **57**, 2070(1935).

5A. Brey, M. L., and Tarrant, P., Private Communication, 1956.

6. Brice, T. J., LaZerte, J. D., *et al.*, *J. Am. Chem. Soc.*, **75**, 2698(1953).
7. Buckle, F. J., and Saunders, B. C., *J. Chem. Soc.*, **1949**, 2774.
8. Chaney, D. W., U. S. Patent 2,522,566(1950).
9. Coffman, D. D., Barrick, P. L., *et al.*, *J. Am. Chem. Soc.*, **71**, 490(1949).
10. Coffman, D. D., Raasch, M. S., *et al.*, *J. Org. Chem.*, **14**, 747(1949).
11. duPont, British Patent 583,874(1947).
12. Englund, B., *Org. Synthesis*, **34**, 16(1954).

12A. Faurote, P. D., Murphy, C. M., and O'Rear, J. G., 127th Meeting American Chemical Society, Cincinnati, Ohio, April, 1955.

13. Gilbert, A. R., and Bigelow, L. A., *J. Am. Chem. Soc.*, **72**, 2411(1950).
14. Gowland, T. B., British Patent 523,449(1940).
15. Gryszkiewicz-Trochimowski, E., Sporzynski, A., and Wnuk, J., *Rec. Trav. Chim.*, **66**, 413(1947).
16. Gryszkiewicz-Trochimowski, E., and Gryszkiewicz-Trochimowski, O., *Bull. soc. chim. France*, **1953**, 123.
17. Hanford, W. E., U. S. Patent 2,433,844(1948).
18. Hanford, W. E., and Rigby, G. W., U. S. Patent 2,409,274(1946).
19. Haszeldine, R. N., *J. Chem. Soc.*, **1952**, 3490.
20. Haszeldine, R. N., and Steele, B. R., *J. Chem. Soc.*, **1954**, 923.
21. Henne, A. L., and Fox, C. J., *J. Am. Chem. Soc.*, **76**, 479(1954).
22. Henne, A. L., and Hinkamp, P. E., *J. Am. Chem. Soc.*, **76**. 5147(1954).
23. Henne, A. L., and Latif, K. A., *J. Indian Chem. Soc.*, **30**, 809(1953).
24. Henne, A. L., and Nager, M., *J. Am. Chem. Soc.*, **74**, 650(1952).
25. Henne, A. L., and Richter, S. B., J. *Am. Chem. Soc.*, **74**, 5420(1952).
26. Henne, A. L., and Smook, M. A., *J. Am. Chem. Soc.*, **72**, 4378(1950).
27. Henne, A. L., Smook, M. A., and Pelley, R. L., *J. Am. Chem. Soc.*, **72**, 4756(1950).
28. Henne, A. L., and Zimmerscheid, W. J., *J. Am. Chem. Soc.*, **69**, 281(1947).
29. Kauck, E. A., and Simons, J. H., U. S. Patent 2,594,272(1952).
30. Kauck, E. A., and Simons, J. H., British Patent 672,720(1952).
31. Knunyants, I. L., *Compt. rend. acad. sci. URSS*, **55**, 223(1947).
32. Knunyants, I. L., Kil'disheva, O. V., and Bykhovskaya, E., *Zhur. Obshchei Khim*, **19**, 101(1949).
33. Knunyants, I. L., Kil'disheva, O. V., and Petrov, I. P., *Zhur. Obshchei Khim*, **19**, 95(1949).
34. Knunyants, I. L., and Shchekotikhim, A. I., and Fokin, A. V., *Iyvest. akad. Nauk. S. S. S. R., Otdel. Khim. Nauk.*, **1953**, 282.
35. Lawson, J. K. Jr., U. S. Patent 2,631,975(1953).
36. McBee, E. T., U. S. Patent 2,574,649(1951).
37. McBee, E. T., and Burton, T. M., *J. Am. Chem. Soc.*, **74**, 3902(1952).
38. McBee, E. T., Marzluff, W. F., and Pierce, O. R., *J. Am. Chem. Soc.*, **74**, 444(1952).

39. McBee, E. T., Pierce, O. R., and Kilbourne, H. W., *J. Am. Chem. Soc.*, **75**, 4091(1953).
40. McBee, E. T., Pierce, O. R., and Marzluff, W. F., *J. Am. Chem. Soc.*, **75**, 1609(1953).
41. McBee, E. T., Smith, D. K., and Ungnade, H. E., *J. Am. Chem. Soc.*, **77**, 387(1955).
42. McBee, E. T., and Weesner, Wm. E., U. S. Patent 2,452,944(1948).
43. Miller, W. T., U. S. Patent 2,671,799(1954).
44. Miller, W. T., Fager, E. W., and Griswold, P. H., *J. Am. Chem. Soc.*, **70**, 431(1948).
45. Olah, Gy., and Pavlath, A., *Acta. Chim. Acad. Sci. Hung.*, **3**, 425(1953).
46. Olah, Gy., and Pavlath, A., *Acta. Chim. Acad. Sci. Hung.*, **4**, 89(1954).
47. Park, J. D., Griffin, D. M., and Lacher, J. R., *J. Am. Chem. Soc.*, **74**, 2292(1952).
48. Park, J. D., Halpern, E., and Lacher, J. R., *J. Am. Chem. Soc.*, **74**, 4104(1952).
49. Park, J. D., Lycan, W. R., and Lacher, J. R., *J. Am. Chem. Soc.*, **73**, 711(1951).
50. Park, J. D., Seffl, R., and Lacher, J. R., Private Communication.
51. Park, J. D., Sharrah, M. L., *et al.*, *J. Am. Chem. Soc.*, **73**, 1329(1951).
52. Park, J. D., Sharrah, M. L., and Lacher, J. R., *J. Am. Chem. Soc.*, **71**, 2337(1949).
53. Park, J. D., Snow, C. M., and Lacher, J. D., *J. Am. Chem. Soc.*, **73**, 861(1951).
54. Park, J. D., Snow, C. M., and Lacher, J. R., *J. Am. Chem. Soc.*, **73**, 2342(1951).
55. Park, J. D., Stricklin, B., and Lacher, J. R., *J. Am. Chem. Soc.*, **76**, 1387(1954).
56. Park, J. D., Vail, D. K., *et al.*, *J. Am. Chem. Soc.*, **70**, 1550(1948).
57. Pruett, R. L., Bahner, C. T., and Smith, H. A., *J. Am. Chem. Soc.*, **74**, 1638(1952).
58. Rapp, K. E., Barr, J. T., *et al.*, *J. Am. Chem. Soc.*, **74**, 749(1952).
59. Rausch, D. A., Lovelace, A. M., and Coleman, L. E. Jr., *J. Org. Chem.*, **21**, 1328(1956).
60. Ruh, R. P., U. S. Patent 2,613;228(1952).
61. Simons, J. H., U. S. Patent 2,500,388(1950).
62. Swarts, F., *Bull. Soc. Chim.*, **25**, 103(1919).
63. Swarts, F., *Bull. sci. acad. roy. Belg.*, **1911**, 563.
64. Swarts, F., *Bull. sci. acad. roy. Belg.*, **1911**, 563.
65. Swarts, F., *Bull. sci. acad. roy. Belg.*, **1901**, 401.
66. Swarts, F., *Bull. acad. roy. Belg.*, (3), **37**, 357(1899).
67. Swarts, F., *Bull. acad. roy. Belg.*, **1901**, 383.
68. Swarts, F., *Bull. soc. chim. France*, **1903**, 597.
69. Tarrant, P., and Brown, H. A., *J. Am . Chem. Soc.*, **73**, 1781(1951).
70. Tarrant, P., and Young, J. A., *J. Am. Chem. Soc.*, **75**, 932(1953).
71. Tiers, G. V. D., *J. Am. Chem. Soc.*, **77**, 4837(1955).
72. Whaley, A. M., U. S. Patent 2,451,185(1948).
73. Young, J. A., and Tarrant, P., *J. Am. Chem. Soc.*, **72**, 1860(1950).

CHAPTER VI

Ketones, Aldehydes and Acetals

TABLE OF CONTENTS

		PAGE
Introduction		181
Method Number		

KETONES

601	Base Catalyzed Condensation	182
602	Reaction of Esters with Organometallic Compounds	183
603	Reaction of Acyl Halides with Organometallic Compounds	183
604	Reaction of Nitriles with Grignard Reagents	183
605	Reaction of Acids or Acid Salts with Organometallic Compounds	184
606	Halogenation of Ketones	184
607	Oxidation of Secondary Alcohols	185
608	Oxidation of Olefins	185
609	Addition of Aldehydes to Olefins	186
610	Reaction of Esters with Sodium	186
611	Codimerization of Olefins with Vinyl Ketones	186
612	Decarboxylation of Sodium Salts of Keto Acids	186
613	Reduction of β-Diketones	186
614	Reduction of Olefinic Ethers	187
615	Hydrolysis of Olefinic Esters and Ketones	187
616	Dehydration of β-Hydroxy Ketones	187
617	Hydrolysis of Ketals	187
618	Hydrolysis of Chloroalkenes	187

ALDEHYDES AND ACETALS

619	Reduction of Acids, Acyl Halides, Esters and Nitriles	187
620	Oxidation of Alcohols and Alkanes	188
621	Reaction of Aldehydes with Alcohols	188
622	Codimerization of Olefins and Unsaturated Aldehydes	188
623	Action of Grignard Reagents on Orthoformates	189
624	Reduction of Carboxolamides	189
625	Reduction of Olefinic Ethers	189
TABLE 14	Ketones	190
TABLE 15	Diketones and Hydroxy Ketones	194
TABLE 16	Copper Chelates of β-Diketones	195
TABLE 17	Aldehydes	196
TABLE 18	Acetals and Hemiacetals	197
TABLE 19	Hydrates of Ketones and Aldehydes	197
Bibliography		198

INTRODUCTION

The large amount of effort directed toward the preparation of fluorine-containing ketones is indicative of the current interest in this particular class of compounds. In general the classical syntheses have been adapted for the preparation of fluorine-containing ketones with excellent results. However, such reactions as the decomposition of the double salts of perfluorocarboxylic acids have proved unfruitful for the preparation of fluoroketones. To date, no practical synthesis of perfluoroketones is available. More recently, several novel syntheses of alkyl perfluoroalkyl ketones have been described and research on these types of compounds should be stimulated by the greater accessibility of these compounds. The reactions of ketones of the type, R_fCOR, reflect the strong electron-withdrawing effect which the perfluoroalkyl group exerts on the carbonyl group. These ketones can readily be brominated or chlorinated in acid. No successful bimolecular reductions or base catalyzed condensations of these compounds have been reported.

In general, the fluorine-containing ketones are characterized by a high percentage of enol content and they easily form stable hydrates. In addition, the β-diketones easily form metal chelate complexes; a phenomenon which has been utilized to separate and purify various β-diketones, and conversely to separate various metals.

The aldehydes, due in part to their difficulty of preparation and purification, have not received as much attention. In the main, only aldehydes of the type R_fCHO have been prepared in any number, since they are generally synthesized by the reduction of a perfluorocarboxylic acid or its derivatives.

Fluorine-containing aldehydes readily polymerize to viscous oils or solids and also form stable hydrates and acetals.

KETONES

METHOD 601 Base Catalyzed Condensation

The base catalyzed condensation of various esters, ketones and keto-esters and subsequent hydrolysis of the condensation products has been used extensively for the preparation of fluorine-containing ketones and β-diketones (cf. Method 908). Trifluoroacetone is readily prepared by hydrolysis of ethyl trifluoroacetoacetate, which can be prepared by condensation of ethyl trifluoroacetate and ethyl acetate with various bases such as sodium ethylate and sodium hydride. Treatment of the acetoacetate with 10 to 40 percent sulfuric acid results in 75 to 100 percent yields of trifluoroacetone.[7,26,65]

McBee[42] prepared the following ketones in the yields indicated by refluxing the appropriate β-keto ester with 40 percent sulfuric acid; CH_2FCOCH_2F (74%), CF_3COCHF_2 (35%), CHF_2COCHF_2 (62%), CF_3COCH_2F (67%), CHF_2COCH_2F (65%). It is interesting to note that when either $CF_3COCF_2CO_2C_2H_5$ or $CHF_2COCF_2CO_2C_2H_5$ were hydrolyzed with 10 percent sulfuric acid only β-keto acids were obtained and not the expected ketones.

Henne and co-workers[26] first employed the condensation of perfluorocarboxylic acid esters and ketones for the preparation of β-diketones. A number of other workers have used this procedure to obtain yields of 35 to 85 percent of β-diketones.[1,6,52] Reid and Calvin[59] prepared a series of β-diketones in 45 to 87 percent yields by the hydrolysis of the condensation products of ethyl trifluoroacetoacetate and various ketones. A new procedure for working up the reaction mixture was also described.

The ease with which fluorine-containing β-diketones from chelates has been used as the basis for the isolation of this class of materials where a high state of purity is desired. The copper chelates have been prepared of a number of β-diketones; the β-diketone may be regenerated by decomposition of the chelate with hydrogen sulfide.

Treatment of the fluorine-containing acetoacetates with chlorine or bromine followed by decomposition of the ester can be employed to prepare mixed halogen-containing ketones (cf. Method 606).

METHOD 602 Reaction of Esters with Organometallic Compounds

The reaction of an ester with an alkyllithium or Grignard reagent has not been used extensively for the preparation of fluorine-containing ketones, because alcohols are generally obtained by this reaction (cf Method 401). However, several workers[15,23,40,46,54] have, reported successful preparation of ketones using this technique.

Henne and Francis[23] reported that a 20 percent yield of $C_3F_7COC_3F_7$ was obtained upon treatment of ethyl perfluorobutyrate with C_3F_7I and magnesium at −50°. McBee and co-workers[46] prepared the same compound in a 62 percent yield by treatment of ethyl perfluorobutyrate with phenylmagnesium bromide and C_3F_7I at −70°. The reaction of C_3F_7MgI at −40° with esters of both fluorinated acids and non-fluorinated acids produced the corresponding ketones in yields of 37 to 53 percent.[15]

Pierce, McBee and Judd[54] have described the preparation of $C_3F_7COC_3F_7$ in a 2 percent yield by the transmetalation of C_3F_7I with CH_3Li in the presence of ethyl heptafluorobutyrate at −45°. A 37 percent yield of $(C_3F_7)_3COH$ was obtained during the course of this reaction (cf. Method 401).

METHOD 603 Reaction of Acyl Halides with Organometallic Compounds

The reaction of perfluoroalkyl Grignard reagents with acyl chlorides have been studied extensively by Haszeldine.[15,17] The reaction of CF_3MgI with fluorinated or non-fluorinated acyl chlorides at low temperatures gave yields of 15 to 60 percent of the expected ketones. Similar reactions with C_3F_7MgI resulted in 15 to 40 percent yields of the fluorine-containing ketones.

Treatment of acetyl chloride with C_3F_7ZnI at 130° results in an 18 percent yield of $C_3F_7COCH_3$.[21]

Campbell[9] reports that the reaction of CF_3COCl and $(n\text{-}C_6H_{13})_2Cd$ yields $CF_3COC_6H_{13}$.

METHOD 604 Reaction of Nitriles with Grignard Reagents

The reaction of Grignard reagents with perfluoronitriles was studied by McBee and co-workers.[44] The interaction of ethylmagnesium iodide with C_3F_7CN gave a 79 percent yield of $C_3F_7COC_2H_5$ when the normal addition procedure was used. However, by the same procedure, $(CH_3)_3CMgCl$

yielded only 8 percent of $(CH_3)_3CCOC_3F_7$ and 33 percent of $(CH_3)_3CCN$. The reverse addition technique in the reaction of $(CH_3)_2CHMgBr$ and C_3F_7CN gave a 44 percent yield of $(CH_3)_2CHCOC_3F_7$ whereas normal addition yielded 35 percent of C_3F_7CHO (cf. Method 619).

Haszeldine[17] reports that the reaction of CH_3CN and CF_3MgI in a sealed tube yields 17 percent of CF_3COCH_3. A similar reaction between CF_3CN and CF_3MgI gives a 33 percent yield of CF_3COCF_3.

METHOD 605 Reaction of Acids or Acid Salts with Organometallic Compounds

Sykes, Tatlow and Thomas[66] reported that the reaction of perfluorocarboxylic acids with Grignard reagents gave ketones. The addition of a perfluorocarboxylic acid to an approximately three-fold excess of Grignard reagent yielded 25 to 63 percent of the desired ketone.

Dishart and Levine[11] concurrently studied this reaction with a number of Grignard reagents and reported that mixtures of ketones and carbinols were obtained with the ketones predominating. The yields of ketone ranged from 15 percent of $CF_3COC(CH_3)_3$ to 69 percent of n-$C_6H_{13}COCF_3$ while the yields of the secondary alcohols ranged from 6 percent to 27 percent.

A modification of this procedure which involves the addition of a slight excess (1.1 moles) of Grignard reagent to one mole of lithium salt of the perfluorocarboxylic acid has been reported.[56] This modification offers some advantage in that a large excess of Grignard reagent is not necessary and the yields of ketone are kept high at the expense of the formation of secondary alcohol.

The treatment of a perfluorocarboxylic acid lithium salt with an alkyllithium gives good yields of the perfluoroalkyl ketone.[3] Treatment of CF_3CO_2Li with n-C_4H_9Li gives a 61 percent yield of n-$C_4H_9COCF_3$.

METHOD 606 Halogenation of Ketones

The acid bromination or chlorination of fluorine-containing ketones can be carried out effectively in either concentrated sulfuric acid or in a mixture of acetic acid and sodium acetate at slightly elevated temperatures. McBee and co-workers[38] brominated CF_3COCH_3 in the presence of sulfuric acid to obtain an 80 percent yield of CF_3COCH_2Br. Bromination in the presence of sodium acetate and acetic acid gave only 19 percent of the β-bromoketone with small amounts of the dibromo-derivative. By the use of a larger excess of bromine in sulfuric acid, CF_3COCH_3 may be converted to $CF_3COCHBr_2$ in an 87 percent yield. Treatment of $CF_3COCHBr_2$ with bromine in the presence of sodium acetate and acetic acid gave an

81 percent yield of CF_3COCBr_3. Chlorination of fluorine-containing ketones proceeds with equal facility in concentrated sulfuric acid.

Rausch and Lovelace[56] brominated a series of fluoroalkyl ketones in concentrated sulfuric acid to obtain only the α-bromoketones in yields of 60 to 83 percent. It was observed that the bromination of ketones containing branched alkyl groups proceeded more slowly than the normal analogs.

Another procedure discussed briefly under Method 601 for introducing bromine or chlorine α to the carbonyl function of a ketone, is the reaction of a halogen with a fluorine-containing acetoacetic esters. For example, $CF_3COCHBrF$ and CF_3COCBr_2F are obtained directly by treatment of $CF_3COCHFCO_2C_2H_5$ with bromine in 40 percent sulfuric acid at moderate temperatures.[41]

In contrast to acid catalyzed chlorination of $C_3F_7COCH_2CH_3$ where a 93 percent yield of $C_3F_7COCHClCH_3$ is obtained, ultraviolet catalyzed chlorination of the same compound yields predominately the β-chloroketone, $C_3F_7COCH_2CH_2Cl$. The free radical chlorination of trifluoroacetone proceeds with extreme difficulty.

METHOD 607 Oxidation of Secondary Alcohols

The oxidation of fluorine-containing secondary alcohols has been successfully employed for the preparation of ketones by a number of investigators.[9,15,36,37,39,44] Sodium dichromate in sulfuric acid is the reagent most commonly employed and in some instances acetic acid is also added to the mixture. For example, the treatment of $C_2F_5CH(OH)CH_3$ with the mixture described gives a 67 percent yield of $C_2F_5COCH_3$.[39]

A second procedure reported by McBee[43] involves the oxidative chlorination of secondary alcohols. In this manner, $C_3F_7CH(OH)C_2H_5$ irradiated in carbon tetrachloride in the presence of chlorine, yields $C_3F_7COC_2H_5$, $C_3F_7CH(OH)CH_2CH_2Cl$ and $C_3F_7CH(OH)CHClCH_3$.

METHOD 608 Oxidation of Olefins

Several reagents have been used for the oxidation of fluoroolefins to ketones. Acidic potassium permanganate has been employed to oxidize $(CF_3)_2C{=}CCl_2$[29] and $(CF_3)_2C{=}CH_2$[16] to CF_3COCF_3. Aqueous potassium permanganate was used by Brice and co-workers[6] to convert $(CF_3)_2C{=}CF_2$ to 67 percent of CF_3COCF_3. Attempts to oxidize $(CF_3)_2C{=}CF_2$ with basic permanganate gave neither the expected cleavage product, fluoroform, nor hexafluoroacetone; instead, $(CF_3)_3CH$ was formed. Haszeldine[16] employed bromine and potassium permanganate to convert $(CF_3)_2C{=}CH_2$ to CF_3COCF_3 in a 55 percent yield.

Chromic oxide and acetic acid were employed by Swarts[63] to prepare $CF_3CHCH_2CH_2CH_2COCH_2$ from the cyclic olefin.

METHOD 609 Addition of Aldehydes to Olefins

LaZerte and Koshar[37] reported the novel procedure for the preparation of fluoro-ketones which involves the free radical addition of an aldehyde to a fluoroolefin. The reaction of acetaldehyde and $CF_3CF_2CF{=}CF_2$ in the presence of benzoyl peroxide gives a 76 percent yield of $CF_3CF_2CFHCF_2COCH_3$. A similar reaction between C_3H_7CHO and $CF_3CF{=}CF_2$ yields 70 percent of $CF_3CFHCF_2COC_3H_7$.

METHOD 610 Reaction of Esters with Sodium

$$C_3F_7CO_2C_2H_5 + Na/(C_2H_5)_2O \xrightarrow[60\%]{} C_3F_7COC_3F_7$$

This reaction is reported by Hauptschein[22] and is the only example of this reaction to date.

METHOD 611 Codimerization of Olefins with Vinyl Ketones

$$CF_2{=}CF_2 + CH_2{=}CHCOCH_3 \rightarrow CF_2CF_2CH_2CH\overset{\overset{O}{\|}}{C}CH_3$$ [2]

The technique employed in this reaction is similar to that which is described in Method 311.

METHOD 612 Decarboxylation of Sodium Salts of Keto Acids

The reaction shown below is the final step in the preparation of trifluoroacetone from the β-keto ester (cf. Method 601).

$$CF_3COCH_2CO_2Na + H_2O \xrightarrow{25^\circ} CF_3COCH_3$$ [64]

METHOD 613 Reduction of β-Diketones

Henne and Hinkamp[24] observed that fluorine-containing β-diketones may be selectively reduced to the hydroxy ketone:

$$CF_3COCH_2COCH_3 + H_2/\text{Raney Ni} \longrightarrow CF_3COCH_2CH(OH)CH_3$$

METHOD 614 Reduction of Olefinic Ethers

Haszeldine[14] reports that the following unusual reduction occurs:

$$CF_3CH{=}C(OCH_3)CF_3 + H_2/\text{Raney Ni} \longrightarrow CF_3CH_2COCF_3$$

METHOD 615 Hydrolysis of Olefinic Esters and Ketones

$$CH_3CO_2C(CF_3){=}CHCF_3 + C_4H_9OH + H_2SO_4 \xrightarrow{95\%} CF_3CH_2COCF_3\ ^{28}$$

$$CF_3CH{=}CHCOC_2H_5 + HgSO_4 + H_2O \longrightarrow CF_3COCH_3\ ^{25}$$

METHOD 616 Dehydration of β-Hydroxy Ketones

$$CF_3COCH_2C(OH)(CH_3)_2 \xrightarrow{55\%} CF_3COCH{=}C(CH_3)_2\ ^{24}$$

METHOD 617 Hydrolysis of Ketals

$$CF_3CH_2C(OCH_3)_2CF_3 + H_2SO_4/H_2O \xrightarrow{48\%} CF_3CH_2COCF_3\ ^{14}$$

METHOD 618 Hydrolysis of Chloroalkenes

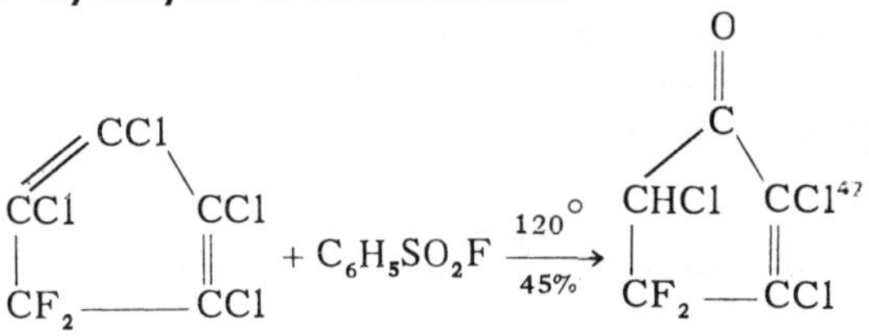

ALDEHYDES AND ACETALS

METHOD 619 Reduction of Acids, Acyl Halides, Esters and Nitriles

The reduction of perfluorocarboxylic acids to aldehydes was first reported by Husted and Ahlbrecht.[32,34] The procedure involved the addition of the acid to a cool slurry of $LiAlH_4$ followed by treatment with sulfuric acid. The yields of the aldehyde or aldehyde hydrate ranged from 20 to 40 percent and considerable amounts of the corresponding primary alcohols were formed (cf. Method 403). Baird and co-workers[4] reported much higher yields (60–78%) of the aldehyde with correspondingly lower conversions to the primary alcohol by use of a reverse addition technique. This involves the addition of the $LiAlH_4$ slurry to an ether solution of the acid at low temperatures.

Brown and Musgrave[8] carried out a Rosenmund reduction on CF_3COCl and obtained 64 percent of $CF_3CHO \cdot H_2O$.

Although the reduction of the esters of perfluorocarboxylic acids with $LiAlH_4$ usually results in the formation of alcohols, under certain conditions aldehydes can be preferentially produced. Pierce and Kane[53] using the reverse addition described above, set forth a general procedure for the reduction of fluorocarboxylic esters to give 70 to 80 percent yields of the aldehyde with little alcohol being formed.

Henne *et al.*[27] reacted CF_3CN with a $LiAlH_4$-ether slurry at Dry Ice temperatures and obtained 46 percent of CF_3CHO. McBee, Pierce and Meyer[44] using the normal addition procedure reacted $(CH_3)_2CHMgBr$ with C_3F_7CN at 0° and obtained 35 percent of C_3F_7CHO.

METHOD 620 Oxidation of Alcohols and Alkanes

Numerous oxidizing agents have been employed to convert fluorine-containing alcohols to aldehydes; the following are representative: $Na_2Cr_2O_2/H_2SO_4$ [27,67] HIO_4,[50] chlorine and ultraviolet light.[43] Yields of aldehydes as high as 60% have been reported.

Shechter and Conrad[62] effected the oxidation of $CF_3CH_2CH_3$ with nitric acid and oxygen and obtained 20 to 24 percent of CF_3CHO and 16 percent of $CF_3CH_2CH_2NO_2$.

METHOD 621 Reaction of Aldehydes with Alcohols

The preparation of acetals of fluorine-containing alcohols is accomplished in the usual fashion by reacting the alcohol and aldehyde in a stream of dry hydrogen chloride.[36,51]

Husted and Ahlbrecht[33] describe a procedure for the preparation of hemiacetals of fluoroaldehydes. The procedure consists of the reaction of an acyl halide of the type R_fCOCl with hydrogen in the presence of paladium on charcoal, quinoline and diethylether. The resulting intermediate, $R_fCHO \cdot HCl \cdot (C_2H_5)_2O$, is then treated with anhydrous alcohol to yield $R_fCH(OH)OR$; yields of the order of 75% of the hemiacetal are obtained.

METHOD 622 Codimerization of Olefins and Unsaturated Aldehydes

$$CF_2{=}CF_2 + CH_2{=}CHCHO \xrightarrow[12\%]{150^\circ} \overline{CF_2CF_2CH_2CH}CHO$$ [2,10]

METHOD 623 Action of Grignard Reagents on Orthoformates

$$CF_3CH_2CH_2MgBr + HC(OC_2H_5)_3 \xrightarrow[37\%]{} CF_3CH_2CH_2CHO \,[23,40]$$

METHOD 624 Reduction of Carboxolamides

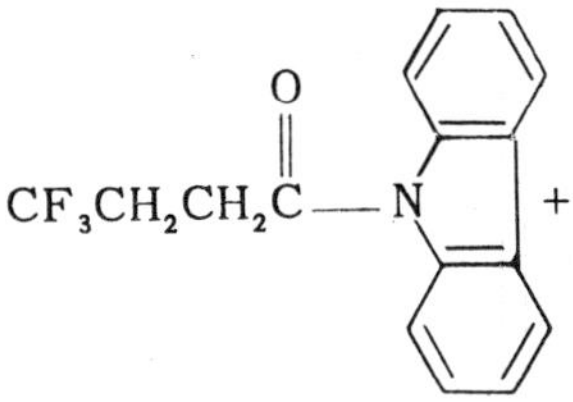

$$CF_3CH_2CH_2C-N \begin{array}{c} \end{array} + LiAlH_4 \xrightarrow[83\%]{} CF_3CH_2CH_2CHO \,[67]$$

METHOD 625 Reduction of Olefinic Ethers

$$CF_3CH=CHOC_2H_5 + H_2/Raney\ Ni \xrightarrow[79\%]{} CF_3CH_2CHO \,[14,25]$$

TABLE 14

KETONES

Empirical Formula	Structural Formula	Method	Yield %	B.p. °C/mm.	F.p. or M.p. °C	n_D^t	d_4^t	t °C	Ref.
$C_3Br_2F_4O$	CF_3COCBr_2F	606		81					41
$C_3Br_3F_3O$	CF_3COCBr_3	606	81.1	69.8–69.9/47	−39.5	1.4785	2.4751	20	38
C_3F_6O	CF_3COCF_3	112		−28	−129				12
		603	49						17
		604	33	−28					17
		608	16–55	−26 to −28					6,16,29, 55
C_3HBrF_4O	$CF_3COCHBrF$	601		65					41
$C_3HBr_2F_3O$	$CF_3COCHBr_2$	606	86.9	113.3–113.4/735.5	< −51	1.4311	2.1880	20	38
C_3HF_5O	CF_3COCHF_2	601	35	2–3					42
		603	59	4					42
$C_3H_2BrF_3O$	CF_3COCH_2Br	606	79.9	86.6/743	< −80	1.3750	1.8389	20	38
$C_3H_2ClF_3O$	CF_3COCH_2Cl	601		71–2		1.3440		20	30
$C_3H_2F_4O$	CF_3COCH_2F	601	67	44					42
		603	15	45–46					17
	CHF_2COCHF_2	601	62	58					42
$C_3H_3F_3O$	CF_3COCH_3	601	75–100	21–21.9					7,26,65
		603	59	21					17
		604	17	21					17
		605	56	21.5–22.5					66
		612							64
		615							25
	CHF_2COCH_2F	601	65	73					42
C_3H_4ClFO	CH_2FCOCH_2Cl	607		141.5–143.5		1.4235	1.296	20	36
$C_3H_4F_2O$	CH_2FCOCH_2F	601	74	101–102					42
	CHF_2COCH_3	601		46.5–46.7/757		1.3280	1.1644	20	10A
C_3H_5FO	CH_2FCOCH_3	105	66	72–72.5					57,58

C_3H_5FO		112		78					12
C_4F_8O	$CF_3COC_2F_5$	112		−0.5 to 0					31
$C_4H_2F_6O$	$CF_3CH_2COCF_3$	603	37	54–55					17
		608	65						16
		614							14
		615	95	54.2/747	−56	1.282	1.5589	20	28
		617	48						14
$C_4H_3F_5O$	$C_2F_5COCH_3$	605	28	40/740					11
		607	67	40			1.284	20	39
$C_4H_4BrF_3O$	$CF_3COCHBrCH_3$	606	82	93/748		1.3805	1.640	20	56
$C_4H_5F_3O$	$CF_3COC_2H_5$	601	8	44–45/738					1
		603	47	46					17
		605	52	45					66
	$CF_3CH_2COCH_3$	608		95–96					19
C_5F_8O	$CF_2CF_2CF_2CF_2CO$ (ring)	112		24					31
$C_5F_{10}O$	$CF_3CF_2CF_2COCF_3$	602	53						15
		603	36–43	29.5–30					15,17
		608	52	30					20
$C_5HCl_3F_2O$	$CF_2CCl{=}CClCOCHCl$ (ring)	618	45	64–66/4					47
$C_5H_3F_7O$	$CF_3CF_2CF_2COCH_3$	602	43						15
		603	15–18	58–60					15,21
		605	41	63–64					66
		607	71						15
$C_5H_4F_6O$	$CF_3COCH_2CH_2CF_3$	604	27	82		1.3020		25	40
$C_5H_5F_5O$	$C_2F_5COC_2H_5$	604	25	62		1.3015	1.259	20	44
		605	56.5	61–62/740					11
$C_5H_6BrF_3O$	$CF_3COCHBrC_2H_5$	606	83	61/124		1.3905	1.554	20	56
	$CF_3COCBr(CH_3)_2$	606	63	57.5/135		1.3920	1.547	20	56
$C_5H_7F_3O$	$CF_3COCH_2CH_2CH_3$	601	43	65–67/735					1
		603	51	68					17

TABLE 14 (*continued*)

Empirical Formula	Structural Formula	Method	Yield %	B.p. °C/mm.	F.p. or M.p. °C	n_D^t	d_4^t	t °C	Ref.
$C_5H_7F_3O$		604	53	67		1.3279	1.097	20	44
		605	51.2	65–67/731					11
	$CF_3COCH(CH_3)_2$	605	33.6–42	52–53/737					11,66
$C_6F_{12}O$	$CF_3CF_2CF_2COC_2F_5$	602	51						15
		603	41	52					15
$C_6H_4BrF_7O$	$CF_3CF_2CF_2COCHBrCH_3$	606	60	57/85		1.3491	1.686	20	56
$C_6H_4F_8O$	$C_2F_5CFHCF_2COCH_3$	607							37
		609	76	91–92/740		1.2988	1.693	25	37
$C_6H_5F_7O$	$CF_3CF_2CF_2COC_2H_5$	602	37						15
		603		78					15
		604	79	83		1.3028	1.370	20	44
		607	75						15
		607		70–74					43
$C_6H_6F_4O$	$CF_2CF_2CH_2CHCOCH_3$	611	18	134–135.5		1.3582	1.3114	25	2,10
$C_6H_7F_3O$	$CF_3COCH{=}C(CH_3)_2$	616	55	108		1.3802		20	24
$C_6H_7F_5O$	$C_2F_5COCH_2CH_2CH_3$	605	67	82/757					11
	$C_2F_5COCH(CH_3)_2$	605	42.5	73–74/737					11
$C_6H_9F_3O$	$CF_3CO(CH_2)_3CH_3$	605	52–63	90–92/741					11,66
		605	61	90/740		1.3410		20	3
	$CF_3COC(CH_3)_3$	605	15–25	70–73/740					11,66
$C_7F_{14}O$	$CF_3CF_2CF_2OCF_2CF_2CF_3$	602	20–62	75–76.5/740–743		1.26985	1.6250	20	23,46,54
		603	31	75					15
		610	60	75					22
$C_7H_6BrF_7O$	$CF_3CF_2CF_2COCHBrC_2H_5$	606	72	52/31		1.3594	1.627	20	56
	$CF_3CF_2CF_2COCBr(CH_3)_2$	606	66	62.1/61		1.3628	1.631	20	56
$C_7H_7F_7O$	$CF_3CF_2CF_2COCH_2C_2H_5$	601	51.5	99.5–101/741					1
		602	39						15

$C_7H_7F_7O$		603	21	100				15
		604	52	101.5	1.3181	1.334	20	44
		605	43.8	101–102/747				11
		607	68					15
	$CF_3CF_2CF_2COCH(CH_3)_2$	604	44	92.5	1.3100	1.308	20	44
		605	25	91–92/739				11
$C_7H_8F_6O$	$CF_3CFHCF_2COCH_2C_2H_5$	609	70	111–111.5/738	1.3268		25	37
	$CF_3CH_2CH_2COCH_2CH_2CF_3$	602	7	164	1.3435		25	40
$C_7H_9F_3O$	$CH_2CH_2CH_2CH(CF_3)CH_2CO$ (ring)	608		173–174/746		1.242	16	63
$C_7H_9F_5O$	$C_2F_5CO(CH_2)_3CH_3$	605	48.9	102–103/730				11
$C_7H_{11}F_3O$	$CF_3CO(CH_2)_4CH_3$	601	41.5	112–113.5/739				1
$C_8H_3F_3O$	$CF_3CO(CH_2)_5CH_3$	605	69	76/88				11
$C_8H_9F_7O$	$CF_3CF_2CF_2CO(CH_2)_3CH_3$	605	53.2	121–122/748				11
	$CF_3CF_2CF_2COC(CH_3)_3$	604	8	102	1.3268	1.254	20	44
		607		102	1.3268		20	44
$C_8H_{13}F_3O$	$CF_3CO(CH_2)_5CH_3$	603		70–72/187	1.3727	1.0498	20	9
		607	49					9
$C_9H_{13}F_3O$	$CF_3COCH_2CH(CH_2)_4CH_2$ (ring)			49–50/1				49
$C_{10}H_4F_{14}O$	$CH_3C(CF_2C_2H_5){=}CHCOCF_2C_2F_5$	604	46	53/4	1.3440	1.650	20	44

TABLE 15

DIKETONES AND HYDROXY KETONES

Empirical Formula	Structural Formula	Method	Yield %	B.p. °C/mm.	F.p. or M.p. °C	n_D^t	d_4^t	t °C	Ref.
$C_5H_2F_6O_2$	$CF_3COCH_2COCF_3$	601	72	63–65					26
$C_5H_5F_3O_2$	$CF_3COCH_2COCH_3$	601	62–80	107		1.3893		20	13,26, 52,59
$C_5H_7FO_2$	$CH_2FCOCH_2COCH_3$	601		25/15					13
$C_5H_7F_3O_2$	$CF_3COCH_2CHOHCH_3$	613		170–171/747		1.3719	1.3031	20	24
$C_6H_5F_5O_2$	$C_2F_5COCH_2COCH_3$	601	84.5	111–112/631		1.3729			52
$C_6H_7F_3O_2$	$CF_3COCH_2COC_2H_5$	601	84	124/755		1.3951	1.22	20.5	59
	$CF_3COCH(CH_3)COCH_3$	601	4.9	123/755		1.356	1.22	20	59
$C_6H_9F_3O_2$	$CF_3COCH_2COH(CH_3)_2$	402	26	30/2					24
$C_7H_5F_7O_2$	$CF_3CF_2CF_2COCH_2COCH_3$	601	78.5	55.5–56.8/38–39		1.3646		20	52
$C_7H_7F_3O_2$	$CF_3COCHCO(CH_2)_2CH_2$ (ring: CH and terminal CH_2 joined)	601	82.3	66/21–22		1.4312		20	52
$C_7H_9F_3O_2$	$CF_3COCH(CH_3)COC_2H_5$	601	66	148–151/735					1
		601	45	74/43		1.3921	1.22	20	59
$C_8H_5F_9O_2$	$CF_3(CF_2)_3COCH_2COCH_3$	601	80	68–68.5/33–34		1.3589		20	52
$C_8H_9F_3O_2$	$CF_3COCHCO(CH_2)_3CH_2$ (ring: CH and terminal CH_2 joined)	601		76–77/20–21		1.4522		20	52
$C_8H_{11}F_3O_2$	$CF_3COCH_2COCH_2CH(CH_3)CH_3$	601	87	78/64		1.4103	1.13	19	59
$C_9H_{13}F_3O_2$	$CF_3COCH(C_2H_5)COCH_2C_2H_5$	601	34	113–114/98					1
$C_{10}H_6F_{14}O_2$	$CF_3CF_2CF_2COH(CH_3)CH_2COCF_2CF_2CF_3$	603	6.24	68.5/29		1.3194		20	54
$C_{10}H_{15}F_3O_2$	$CF_3COCH_2CO(CH_2)_5CH_3$	601	55	65/6		1.4196	1.09	23	29

TABLE 16

COPPER CHELATES OF β-DIKETONES

Structural Formula Diketone	M.p. °C of Chelate	Ref.
$CF_3COCH_2COCF_3$	113-115	26
$CF_3COCH_2COCH_3$	189	52,59
$C_2F_5COCH_2COCH_3$	111.6-112	52
$CF_3COCH_2COC_2H_5$	154.5-155.3	59
$CF_3COCH(CH_3)COCH_3$	170.4-171.9	59
$CF_3CF_2CF_2COCH_2COCH_3$	55-55.2	52
$CF_3COCHCO(CH_2)_2CH_2$	175-176	52
$CF_3COCH(CH_3)COC_2H_5$	163-163.5	1
	164-165	59
$CF_3(CF_2)_3COCH_2COCH_3$	77.5-78	52
$CF_3COCHCO(CH_2)_3CH_2$	182-182.5	52
$CF_3COCH_2COCH_2CH(CH_3)CH_3$	124.5-125.3	59
$CF_3COCH_2CO(CH_2)_5CH_3$	71-72	59

TABLE 17

ALDEHYDES

Empirical Formula	Structural Formula	Method	Yield %	B.p. °C/mm.	F.p. or M.p. °C	n_D^t	d_4^t	t °C	Ref.
C_2HF_3O	CF_3CHO	619	26–78	−19.6 to −18/746					4,27,34,53
		620	20–24	−18.8 to −17.5					62
C_2H_3FO	CH_2FCHO	620	6	85–95					48,50,60
C_3HF_5O	C_2F_5CHO	619	20–75	1.5–2/746					4,34,53
$C_3H_3F_3O$	CF_3CH_2CHO	620	57	56–56.5/745		1.3168	1.365(20)	22	27
		625	28–79						14,28
C_4HF_7O	$CF_3CF_2CF_2CHO$	619	34–64	28–29/740		1.273	1.505(20)	4	4,32,34, 44,53
		620		29/745					43
$C_4H_3F_3O$	$CF_3CH{=}CHCHO$	620		70–76/70					45
$C_4H_5F_3O$	$CF_3CH_2CH_2CHO$	620	56	94–97					67
		623	37	96		1.3387		25	40
		624	83	93–97					67
C_5HF_9O	$CF_3(CF_2)_3CHO$	619		48/740					32
$C_5H_4F_4O$	$CF_2CF_2CH_2CHCHO$	622	12	117–117.5		1.3768	1.5089	25	2,10
$C_6H_6F_4O$	$CF_2CF_2CH_2C(CH_3)CHO$	622	50	120–122		1.3625	1.3113	25	2,10
$C_8HF_{15}O$	$CF_3(CF_2)_6CHO$	619	70	122		1.2913		20	53

TABLE 18

ACETALS AND HEMIACETALS

Empirical Formula	Structural Formula	Method	Yield %	B.p. °C/mm.	F.p. or M.p. °C	n_D^t	d_4^t	t°C	Ref.
$C_3H_5F_3O_2$	$CF_3CH(OH)OCH_3$	621		96–96.5/729		1.3259		25	33
$C_4H_7F_3O_2$	$CF_3CH(OH)OC_2H_5$	621	76.5	104–105/746		1.3408	1.241	25	33
$C_5H_5F_7O_2$	$CF_3CF_2CF_2CH(OH)OCH_3$	621		97–100/755		1.3140		25	33
$C_5H_7F_5O_2$	$C_2F_5CH(OH)OC_2H_5$	621		103		1.3302		20	33
$C_5H_{10}F_2O_2$	$CH_2(OCH_2CH_2F)_2$	621	50	162–164		1.3860	1.1302	20	36,51
$C_6H_7F_7O_2$	$CF_3CF_2CF_2CH(OH)OCH_2CH_3$	621		106–106.5/747		1.3245	1.411	20	33
$C_6H_{12}F_2O_2$	$CH_3CH(OCH_2CH_2F)_2$	621	20	80/30		1.3936	1.0914	20	36,51
$C_6H_{13}FO_2$	$CH_3CF(OC_2H_5)_2$	105							57

TABLE 19

HYDRATES OF KETONES AND ALDEHYDES

Empirical Formula	Structural Formula	Method	Yield %	B.p. °C/mm.	F.p. or M.p. °C	n_D^t	d_4^t	t°C	Ref.
$C_2H_3F_3O_2$	$CF_3CH(OH)_2$	619	64	50 (subl.)	68–70				8,32,34
$C_3H_3F_5O_2$	$C_2F_5CH(OH)_2$	619		92/732	52–53				32,34
$C_4H_3F_7O$	$CF_3CF_2CF_2CH(OH)_2$	619		95–96	61	1.3255		20	32,34
		623		92–98					23
$C_5H_6F_6O_4$	$CH_2[C(OH)_2CF_3]_2$				115 (subl.)				61
$C_6H_3F_9O_2$	$CF_3(CF_2)_4CH(OH)_2$	619		100/740					32
$C_9F_{19}CH(OH)_2$	$CF_3(CF_2)_8CH(OH)_2$	619		148/740	114				32

BIBLIOGRAPHY

1. Barkley, L. B., and Levine, R., *J. Am. Chem. Soc.*, **75**, 2059(1953).
2. Barrick, P. L., U. S. Patent 2,462,345(1949).
3. Bluhm, H. F., Donn, H. V., and Zook, H. D., *J. Am. Chem. Soc.*, **77**, 4406(1955).
4. Braid, M., Iserson, H., and Lawlor, F. E., *J. Am. Chem. Soc.*, **76**, 4027(1954).
5. Breslow, D. S., Walker, H. E., *et. al.*, *J. Am. Chem. Soc.*, **68**, 100(1946).
6. Brice, T. J., LaZerte, J. D., and Pearlson, W. H., *J. Am. Chem. Soc.* **75**, 2698(1953).
7. British Thomspon-Houston Company Ltd., British Patent 416,653(1934).
8. Brown, F., and Musgrave, W. K. R., *J. Chem. Soc.*, **1952**, 5039.
9. Campbell, K. N., Knoblock, J. O., and Campbell, B. K., *J. Am. Chem. Soc.*, **72**, 4380(1950).
10. Coffman, D. D., Barrick, P. L., *et.al.*, *J. Am. Chem. Soc.*, **71**, 490(1949).
10A. Desirant, Y., *Bull. sci. acad. roy. Belg.* (5), **19**, 325(1933).
11. Dishart, K. T., and Levine, R., *J. Am. Chem. Soc.*, **78**, 2268(1956).
12. Fukuhara, N., and Bigelow, L. A., *J. Am. Chem. Soc.*, **63**, 788(1941).
13. Haszeldine, R. N., *J. Chem. Soc.*, **1951**, 609.
14. Haszeldine, R. N., *J. Chem. Soc.*, **1952**, 3490.
15. Haszeldine, R. N., *J. Chem. Soc.*, **1953**, 1749.
16. Haszeldine, R. N., *J. Chem. Soc.*, **1953**, 3565.
17. Haszeldine, R. N., *J. Chem. Soc.*, **1954**, 1273.
18. Haszeldine, R. N., and Leedham, K., *J. Chem. Soc.*, **1953**, 1548.
19. Haszeldine, R. N., and Leedham, K., *J. Chem. Soc.*, **1954**, 1261.
20. Haszeldine, R. N., and Steele, B. R., *J. Chem. Soc.*, **1955**, 3005.
21. Haszeldine, R. N., and Walaschewski, E. G., *J. Chem. Soc.*, **1953**, 3607.
22. Hauptschein, M., and Braun, R. A., *J. Am. Chem. Soc.*, **77**, 4930(1955).
23. Henne, A. L., and Francis, W. C., *J. Am. Chem. Soc.*, **75**, 992(1953).
24. Henne, A. L., and Hinkamp, P. E., *J. Am. Chem. Soc.*, **76**, 5147(1954).
25. Henne, A. L., and Nagar, M., *J. Am. Chem. Soc.*, **74**, 650 (1952).
26. Henne, A. L., Newman, M. S., *et al.*, *J. Am. Chem. Soc.* **69**, 1819(1947).
27. Henne, A. L., Pelley, R. L., and Alm, R. M., *J. Am. Chem. Soc.*, **72**, 3370 (1950).
28. Henne, A. L., Schmitz, J. V., and Finnegan, W. G., *J. Am. Chem. Soc.*, **72**, 4195(1950).
29. Henne, A. L., Shepard, J. W., and Young, E. J., *J. Am. Chem. Soc.*, **72**, 3577(1950).
30. Hill, H. M., Towne, E. B., and Dickey, J. B., *J. Am. Chem. Soc.*, **72**, 3289(1950).
31. Holub, F. F., and Bigelow, L. A., *J. Am. Chem. Soc.*, **72**, 4879(1950).
32. Husted, D. R., and Ahlbrecht, A. H., U. S. Patent 2,568,500(1951).
33. Husted, D. R., and Ahlbrecht, A. H., U. S. Patent 2,681,370 (1954).
34. Husted, D. R., and Ahlbrecht, A. H., *J. Am. Chem. Soc.*, **74**, 5422(1952).

35. Knunyants, I. L., Kil'disheva, O. V., and Bykhovskaya, E., *Zhur. Obshchei Khim*, **19**, 101(1949).
36. Knunyants, I. L., Kil'disheva, O. V., and Petrov, I. P., *Zhur. Obshchei Khim*, **19**, 95(1949).
37. LaZerte, J. D., and Koshar, R. J., *J. Am. Chem. Soc.*, **77**, 910(1955).
38. McBee, E. T., and Burton, T. M., *J. Am. Chem. Soc.*, **74**, 3902(1952).
39. McBee, E. T., Higgins, J. F., and Pierce, O. R., *J. Am. Chem. Soc.*, **74**, 1387(1952).
40. McBee, E. T., Kelley, A. E., and Rapkin, E., *J. Am. Chem. Soc.*, **72**, 5071 (1950).
41. McBee, E. T., Pierce, O. R., and Kilbourne, H. W., *J. Am. Chem. Soc.*, **75**, 4091(1953).
42. McBee, E. T., Pierce, O. R., *et al.*, *J. Am. Chem. Soc.*, **75**, 3152(1953).
43. McBee, E. T., Pierce, O. R., and Marzluff, W. F., *J. Am. Chem. Soc.*, **75**, 1609(1953).
44. McBee, E. T., Pierce, O. R., and Meyer, D. D., *J. Am. Chem. Soc.*, **77**, 917(1955).
45. McBee, E. T., Pierce, O. R., and Smith, D. D., *J. Am. Chem. Soc.*, **76**, 3725(1954).
46. McBee, E. T., Roberts, C. W., and Curtis, S. G., *J. Am. Chem. Soc.*, **77**, 6387(1955).
47. McBee, E. T., Smith, D. K., and Ungnade, H. E., *J. Am. Chem. Soc.*, **77**, 387(1955).
48. McCombie, H., and Saunders, B. C., *Nature*, **158**, 382(1946).
49. Nes, W. R., and Burger, A., *J. Am. Chem. Soc.*, **72**, 5409(1950).
50. Olah, Gy., and Pavlath, A., *Acta. Chim. Acad. Sci. Hung.*, **3**, 425(1953).
51. Olah, Gy., and Pavlath, A., *Acta. Chim. Acad. Sci. Hung.*, **4**, 89(1954).
52. Park, J. D., Brown, H. A., and Lacher, J. R., *J. Am. Chem. Soc.*, **75**, 4753(1953).
52a. Park, J. D., Larsen, E. R., *et al.*, 130th Meeting American Chemical Society, Atlantic City, N. J., September, 1956
53. Pierce, O. R., and Kane, T. G., *J. Am. Chem. Soc.*, **76**, 300(1954).
54. Pierce, O. R., McBee, E. T., and Judd, G. F., *J. Am. Chem. Soc.*, **76**, 474(1954).
55. Pearlson, W. H., and Hals L. J., U. S. Patent 2,617,836(1952).
56. Rausch, D. A., Lovelace, A. M., and Coleman, L. E., Jr. *J. Org. Chem.*, **21**, 1328(1956).
57. Ray, P. C., Goswami, H. C., and Ray, A. C., *J. Ind. Chem. Soc.*, **12**, 93(1935).
58. Ray, P. C., Sarkar, P. B., and Ray, A. C., *Nature*, **132**, 749(1933).
59. Reid, J. C., and Calvin, M. *J. Am. Chem. Soc.*, **72**, 2948(1950).
60. Saunders, B. C., Stacey, G. J., and Wilding, I. G. E., *J. Chem. Soc.*, **1949**, 773.
61. Schultz, B. G., and Larsen, E. M., *J. Am. Chem. Soc.*, **71**, 3250(1949).
62. Shechter, H., and Conrad, F., *J. Am. Chem. Soc.*, **72**, 3371(1950).

63. Swarts, F., *Bull. soc. chim. Belg.*, **32**, 367(1923).
64. Swarts, F., *Bull. soc. acad. roy. Belg.*, **12**, 721(1926).
65. Swarts, F., *Bull. sci. acad. roy. Belg.*, **13**, 175(1927).
66. Sykes, A., Tatlow, J. C., and Thomas, C. L., *Chemistry and Industry*, **1955**, 630.
67. Walborsky, H. M., Baum, M., and Loncrini, D. F., *J. Am. Chem. Soc.*, **77**, 3637(1955).

CHAPTER VII

Carboxylic Acids

TABLE OF CONTENTS

		PAGE
Introduction		201
Method Number		
701	Hydrolysis of Amides, Nitriles, Esters and Acyl Halides	202
702	Oxidation of Fluoroolefins	203
703	Hydrolysis of Haloalkanes	204
704	Oxidation of Alcohols	205
705	Oxidation of Fluorocarbons	205
706	Electrolytic Fluorination	205
707	Carbonation of Organometallic Compounds	206
708	Addition of Formaldehyde to Olefins	206
709	Hydrolysis and Oxidation of Ethers	206
710	Hydrolysis of Triazines	207
711	Hydration of Olefins	207
712	Base Catalyzed Condensation	207
713	Diels-Alder Condensation	207
714	Decomposition of Diazo Compounds	207
715	Peroxide-Induced Coupling	208
716	Cleavage of Lactams	208
717	Synthesis of Amino Acids	208
TABLE 20	Monobasic Acids	210
TABLE 21	Dibasic Acids	215
Bibliography		216

INTRODUCTION

The fluorinated carboxylic acids are characterized by their highly acidic nature as compared to their hydrocarbon analogs. Increase in acidic character is noted with increasing fluorine content as shown in the table below:

Acid	$K \times 10^{-5}$	Acid	$K \times 10^{-5}$
CH_3CO_2H	1.8	$CF_3CF_2CF_2CO_2H$	68,000
CH_2FCO_2H	220	$CF_3CH_2CO_2H$	100
CHF_2CO_2H	5,700	$CF_3CH_2CH_2CO_2H$	7
CF_3CO_2H	59,000	$CF_3CH_2CH_2CH_2CO_2H$	3.2

The insulating effect of the — CH_2— groups can also be observed from these data. Henne and Fox[49] observed that unsaturated fluorinated acids are stronger than the corresponding saturated acids; $CF_3CH{=}CHCO_2H$, $K = 270 \times 10^{-5}$ as compared with $CF_3CH_2CH_2CO_2H$, $K = 3.2 \times 10^{-5}$.

The high acidity of the perfluorinated carboxylic acids accounts for the ease of solubility of most of their metal salts, including lead and silver salts, in water, alcohol and acetone.[70A] The alkali salts of the higher acids, due to their extremely low surface tension are effective wetting or dispersing agents in highly acidic media.

Peroxytrifluoroacetic acid, although it has not been isolated, has been used for the oxidation of nitrosoamines, anilines, olefins, for the ring enlargement of cyclic ketones and for the epoxidation of olefins. It is prepared *in situ* by the treatment of trifluoroacetic acid with hydrogen peroxide. The acid fluorides of peroxytrifluoroacetic acid and peroxypentafluoropropionic acid have been prepared by treatment of the respective fluorinated acids with fluorine and a trace of water. These acid fluorides are extremely explosive.

METHOD 701 Hydrolysis of Amides, Nitriles, Esters and Acyl Halides

Many of the fluorinated acids are prepared from intermediate fluorine-containing amides, nitriles, acyl halides and esters which can be more conveniently prepared than the acids themselves. For example, perfluorocarboxylic acyl halides result from the electrolytic fluorination of acids (cf. Method 706), and these halides, in turn, can be easily hydrolyzed in cold water. The preparation of fluorinated acids from the precursors mentioned above, with the exception of the nitriles, is in most cases straightforward and analogous to the usual preparation of the non-fluorinated carboxylic acids; the presence of a β — CF_2— group may cause anomalous results, and under certain conditions this group undergoes hydrolysis.

Nitriles can be converted to the corresponding carboxylic acids by treating with mineral acid or aqueous alkali. Coffman[19] and Barrick and

Cramer[6] treated $CF_2CF_2CH_2CHCN$ (cyclic) with 70 percent H_2SO_4 at 100° and obtained an 87 percent yield of the cyclic acid. However, the same nitrile, when treated with a 25 percent sodium hydroxide solution, yielded the dibasic acid, $HO_2CCF_2(CH_2)_2CO_2H$.[3] Similar results were obtained when Park, Rausch and Lacher[73] treated perfluoroacrylonitrile with concentrated sulfuric acid and obtained monofluoromalonic acid. However similar treatment of the dibromide, $CF_2BrCFBrCN$, resulted in the formation of $CF_2BrCFBrCO_2H$ as the sole product. Buckle and Saunders[13] hydrolyzed $CH_2FCH_2CH_2OCH_2CH_2CN$ to the corresponding acid upon treatment with concentrated hydrochloric acid at 100°. Treatment of $CH_2{=}C(CF_3)CN$ with dilute sulfuric acid, and treatment of $CH_2ClCH(CF_3)CN$ with concentrated sulfuric acid yielded, in each case, $CH_2OHCH(CF_3)CO_2H$.[15] Basic hydrolysis of CF_3CH_2CHICN, on the other hand, yielded $CF_3CH{=}CHCO_2H$.[31]

Esters can be readily hydrolyzed with either dilute mineral acid or base. Esters of the type $RCX_2CH_2CO_2R'$ where X is F, Cl or Br, when subjected to basic hydrolysis may yield unsaturated acids.

Amides can be hydrolyzed to the corresponding acid by the use of either acid or base. Buxton, Stacey and Tatlow[15] hydrolyzed $CH_3CH(CF_3)CONH_2$ to the acid in sulfuric acid at 120° for 5 hours. Jones[58] prepared $CF_3CH(OH)CH_2CO_2H$ by alkaline hydrolysis of the amide.

The acid can be isolated from the hydrolysis mixture by extraction with ether. However, highly fluorinated acids form constant boiling addition compounds with various ethers, ketones and other acids, and form hydrates as well. Hauptschein and Grosse[43] isolated and characterized addition compounds of $C_3F_7CO_2H$ and ethyl ether, butyl ether, ethyl cellosolve and diethyl carbitol. Lichtenberger, *et al.*[63] found addition compounds of CF_3CO_2H and ethyl acetate, dioxane and acetic acid. Henne and Fox[49] isolated mono- and hemi-hydrates of $CF_2HCF_2CO_2H$.

METHOD 702 Oxidation of Fluoroolefins

The method of oxidizing fluoroolefins to fluorinated carboxylic acids by alkaline permanganate in high yields was first reported by Henne, Alderson and Newman.[47] The position and number of fluorine atoms on the olefin plays a critical role in this reaction. For example, $CF_3CCl{=}CCl_2$ and $CHF_2CCl{=}CCl_2$ can be easily oxidized to the corresponding fluoroacetic acids in good yields because the resulting acids do not undergo the haloform reaction. However, $CH_2FCCl{=}CCl_2$

cannot be oxidized to monofluoroacetic acid.[47] Olefins with fluorine either on the α or γ carbon atoms are easily oxidized to the corresponding acids, but a β-fluoroolefin yields unsaturated acids due to dehydrofluorination in the alkaline medium; $CH_3CF_2CH_2CH{=}CH_2$ yields $CH_3CF{=}CHCO_2H$.[56] Symmetrical fluoroolefins such as $CF_3CCl{=}CClCF_3$ yield two moles of trifluoroacetic acid per mole of olefin; a more economical procedure than otherwise.[54]

The preparation of dibasic acids from the permanganate oxidation of cyclic fluoroolefins was first reported by Henne[45,46,55,56] who prepared hexafluoroglutaric acid from $\overline{CF_2(CF_2)_2CCl{=}CCl}$ and tetrafluorosuccinic acid from $\overline{CF_2CF_2CF{=}CF}$ and $\overline{CF_2CF_2CCl{=}CCl}$. Higher dibasic acids such as octafluoroadipic acid were prepared from 1,2-dichloroperfluorocyclohexene[65] or from the perfluorocyclohexene.[78,95] Henne and DeWitt[47A] prepared perfluoromalonic acid by permanganate oxidation of the dienes, $CH_2{=}CHCF_2CH{=}CH_2$ and $CCl_2{=}CClCF_2CCl{=}CCl_2$. Haszeldine[37] prepared this acid by the oxidation of the triene, $CF_2{=}CFCF_2CF{=}CFCF_2CF{=}CF_2$. Evans and Tatlow[24] prepared the same acid by the oxidation of 1,4-perfluorocyclohexadiene.

Either neutral or alkaline permanganate can be employed for this oxidation, although reaction times are necessarily longer in the former case. Reaction time can be considerably shortened by the addition of sodium hypochlorite to the alkaline permanganate. In the oxidation of $CF_3CCl{=}CCl_2$, the reaction was completed in 11.5 hours using this modification,[70] while the same oxidation employing neutral permanganate required 40 hours.[44]

Barrick[5] obtained the cyclic acid $\overline{CF_2CF_2CHCH}CO_2H$ upon oxidation of $\overline{CF_2CF_2CHCH}CH{=}CH_2$ with 50 percent nitric acid.

METHOD 703 Hydrolysis of Haloalkanes

The terminal $-CCl_3$ group of a fluoroalkane or a fluoroalkene can be hydrolyzed with concentrated sulfuric acid to the corresponding carboxylic acid. Benning and Park[7] treated CF_3CCl_3 with a mixture of mercurous and mercuric sulfate and oleum at 0° and obtained trifluoroacetic acid. Treatment of $CF_3CHBrCH_2CCl_3$ in 96 percent sulfuric acid at 125° by Henne and Fox[49] yielded γ,γ,γ-trifluorocrotonic acid. Haszeldine[33] hydrolyzed the unsaturated olefin $CF_3CH{=}CHCCl_3$ to trifluorocrotonic acid with concentrated sulfuric acid.

METHOD 704 Oxidation of Alcohols

Swarts[85,89] prepared monofluoroacetic acid by means of the permanganate or chromic acid oxidation of fluoroethanol. Difluoro-[85] and trifluoroacetic acids[93] were also made from the corresponding alcohols by chromic acid oxidation. Desirant[22] oxidized difluoroethanol to the corresponding acid using nitric acid as the oxidant. Longer chain fluorocarboxylic acids have also been prepared from the alcohols either by permanganate or chromic acid oxidation.[8,27,48,49,62] Joyce[59] prepared acids of the type $H(CF_2CFCl)_nCO_2H$ (where n = 1 to 3) by acidic permanganate oxidation of the alcohols resulting from the peroxide catalyzed addition of methanol to chlorotrifluoroethylene (cf. Method 405).

METHOD 705 Oxidation of Fluorocarbons

The first reported preparation of trifluoroacetic acid by Swarts[90] involved the chromic acid oxidation of *m*-trifluoromethylaniline. Swarts[91] also prepared trifluoromethyl adipic acid by oxidation of a trifluoromethylnitrocyclohexane with dilute nitric acid. The same worker also oxidized 1,1-difluoro-2-iodoethane to difluoroacetic acid by means of nitric acid.[84] Roylance, Tatlow and Worthington[78] prepared octafluoroadipic acid by the permanganate oxidation of 1,2-dihydroperfluorohexane.

Haszeldine[26,36] photochemically oxidized R_fCF_2H, R_fCCl_2I, R_fCF_2I, and $R_fCFClBr$ to the corresponding carboxylic acids, and obtained acyl fluorides as by-products. The oxidation of the hydrides, R_fCF_2H required from 10 to 45 days using either bromine or chlorine with oxygen. The halides of the type R_fCX_3 were oxidized in 0.5 to 10 hours under the same conditions as above. The iodides were more readily oxidized than the chlorides or bromides.

Oxidative bromination as described by Henne and Fox[49] provides for the oxidation of olefins containing a β-fluorine atom which ordinarily yield an unsaturated acid under alkaline oxidation conditions. Treatment of $CF_2ClCF{=}CCl_2$ with oxygen and bromine yields a mixture of $CF_2ClCFClCO_2H$ and $CF_2ClCFBrCO_2H$. The formation of an intermediate epoxide is postulated.

METHOD 706 Electrolytic Fluorination

The general method of the Simons process of electrolytic fluorination is discussed in Chapter I (cf. Method 111). This is perhaps the most practical commercial method available for the synthesis of various perfluorocarboxylic acids. The electrolytic cell has been exhaustively studied in the fluorination of hydrocarbon acids to the perfluorinated analogs.[57,70,23] Amides,[23] ethers[23] as well as anhydrides[60] also yield fluorinated acids. In a typical preparation, Kauck and Diesslin[60] used an electrolytic cell formed from a 5 inch iron pipe into which anhydrous HF was introduced. Nine nickel anodes and nine nickel cathodes were suspended from the top. Acetic anhydride was introduced and the cell was charged with a 50 amp. current at 5.2 volts and the temperature was kept at 20°. Trifluoroacetyl fluoride vaporized from the system as a gas.

In the electrolysis of higher molecular weight acids, acyl fluorides are recovered from the cell drainage, being more dense than and insoluble in liquid hydrogen fluoride. Some decarboxylation and fragmentation also occurs, yielding fluorocarbons and acids of shorter chain length than the starting material.

Method 111 describes an adaptation of this procedure whereby partially fluorinated carboxylic acids are produced electrolytically.

METHOD 707 Carbonation of Organometallic Compounds

This method is generally employed as a means of proving the formation of a fluorinated organometallic compound rather than as a general preparative method. The formation of organometallic compounds is discussed in Chapter XII. McBee and Truchan[69] carbonated $CF_3CH_2CH_2MgCl$ and obtained γ,γ,γ-trifluorobutyric acid. Henne and Francis[50] carbonated C_3F_7MgI at −80°, and obtained a 45 percent yield of perfluorobutyric acid. Haszeldine[30] obtained a 75 percent yield of the same compound by carbonating at −10°.

Haszeldine and Walschewski[42] prepared C_3F_7ZnI, but could not carbonate it to the corresponding acid. Pierce, McBee and Judd[75] prepared C_3F_7Li, but did not report its carbonation.

METHOD 708 Addition of Formaldehyde to Olefins

The addition of formaldehyde or paraformaldehyde to tetrafluoroethylene gives an 80 percent yield of the hydroxy acid, $HOCH_2CF_2CO_2H$.[18] The reaction is carried out in the presence of concentrated H_2SO_4 in a silver-lined autoclave at 80° for 15 hours.

$$CH_2O + CF_2{=\!=}CF_2 \longrightarrow HOCH_2CF_2CO_2H$$

METHOD 709 Hydrolysis and Oxidation of Ethers

It has been observed that α,α-difluoroethers can be readily hydrolyzed to a carboxylic acid. Swarts[88] treated $CH_2FCF_2OCH_3$ and $CHFBrCF_2OCH_3$ with nitric acid and obtained CH_2FCO_2H and $CHFBrCO_2H$, respectively. Haszeldine[31] hydrolyzed $CF_2HCF_2OC_2H_5$ with concentrated sulfuric acid to CHF_2CO_2H. When ethers of the type R_fCF_2OR are treated with concentrated sulfuric acid, esters of the type R_fCO_2R are obtained (cf. Method 906). Young and Tarrant[99] in studying this reaction found that $CH_2ClCF_2OC_2H_5$ hydrolyzes even in water to form ethyl chloroacetate.

The oxidation of fluorine-containing ethers has not been widely applied to the preparation of carboxylic acids. However, Swarts[84] reported the chromic acid oxidation of $CHF_2CH_2OC_2H_5$ yielded CHF_2CO_2H.

METHOD 710 Hydrolysis of Triazines

Fluorine-containing symmetrical triazines can be hydrolyzed with acid or base to yield carboxylic acids. Coffman[16,18] thus obtained CHF_2CO_2H from tris(difluoromethyl)-triazine in a yield of 22 percent. However, Henne and Pelley[51] obtained an 80 percent yield of this acid by hydrolysis of the same triazine with sodium hydroxide. Norton[71A] treated tris(trifluoromethyl)-triazine with various alcohols and obtained 90 percent yields of CF_3CO_2R (cf. Method 913).

METHOD 711 Hydration of Olefins

When water is added to tetrafluoroethylene in the presence of sodium sulfite and benzoyl peroxide at 120° and 325 to 350 psi, CF_2HCO_2H results.[4] Formic acid (100%) in the presence of *p*-toluenesulfonic acid hydrates $CF_3CH{=}CHCO_2Et$ to $CF_3CH(OH)CH_2CO_2H$.[97]

METHOD 712 Base Catalyzed Condensation

Trifluoroacetone and malonic acid react in pyridine with a catalytic amount of piperdine to yield the norleucine derivative, $CF_3C(OH)CH_3CH_2CO_2H$.[96] The decomposition of diethyl sodiofluoro-oxaloacetate with hydrochloric acid at 130°, yielded a small amount of fluoropyruvic acid, CH_2FCOCO_2H.[9]

METHOD 713 Diels-Alder Condensation

Maleic anhydride condenses with 2-fluorobutadiene to yield the dibasic acid, $\overline{CH_2CH(CO_2H)CH(CO_2H)CH_2CH{=}CF}$[17] (cf. Method 311).

METHOD 714 Decomposition of Diazo Compounds

The Wolff rearrangement of a diazo ketone (cf. Method 1121) to give γ,γ,γ-trifluoroproionic acid has been reported by Brown and Musgrave:[11]

$$CF_3COCHN_2 + Ag_2O \xrightarrow[Na_2S_2O_3]{\text{dioxane}} CF_3CH_2CO_2H$$

Park, *et al.*[72A] found that this rearrangement did not occur at all with the diazoketone prepared from $C_3F_7CO_2H$. The rearrangement occurred only slightly with $C_3F_7CH_2CO_2H$ and in good yield with $C_3F_7CH_2CH_2CO_2H$, to give $C_3F_7CH_2CH_2CH_2CO_2H$ (cf. Method 910).

METHOD 715 Peroxide-Induced Coupling

Kharasch [61] treated fluoroacetic acid with acetyl peroxide, and obtained $(CHFCO_2H)_2$. This compound reacts violently with water to yield hydrogen fluoride and maleic acid.

METHOD 716 Cleavage of Lactams

$$
\begin{array}{c}
\text{CH}_2 \\
\diagup \quad \diagdown \\
\text{CH}_2 \qquad \text{CH}_2 \\
| \qquad\qquad | \\
\quad\quad \text{CH}_2 \\
| \qquad\qquad | \\
\text{CH}_2 \qquad \text{C}=\text{O} \\
\diagdown \quad \diagup \\
\text{N} \\
\text{H}
\end{array}
\;+\;\text{HF (aqueous)}\;\xrightarrow[\text{NaNO}_2]{0^{\circ}}\; F(CH_2)_5CO_2H^{71}
$$

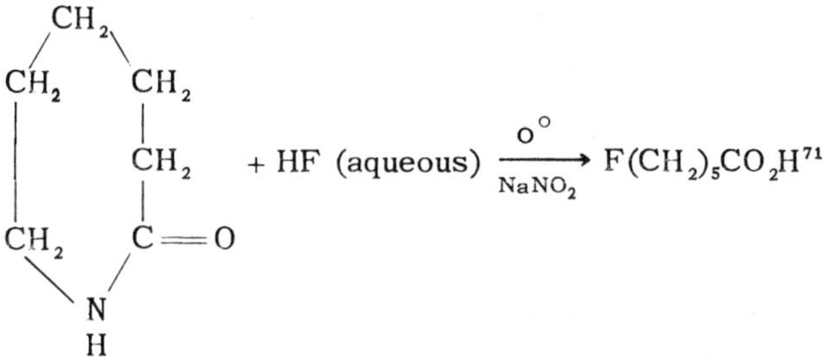

METHOD 717 Synthesis of Amino Acids

Fluorine-containing amino acids have been synthesized by Walborsky, *et al.*[92] One synthesis started with $CF_3CH_2CH_2CHO$, employing ammonium chloride and sodium cyanide, followed by hydrolysis with hydrobromic acid which resulted in a very poor yield of $CF_3CH_2CH_2CH(NH_2)CO_2H$. However, when the aldehyde was treated with ammonium carbonate and sodium cyanide (Strecker synthesis) and when the resulting hydantoin was hydrolyzed with barium hydroxide, a 30 percent yield of the amino acid was obtained. Another route as described by Walborsky is as follows:

$$
CF_3CH_2CH_2CH_2I +
\begin{array}{c}
CO_2C_2H_5 \\
| \\
HC-NHCHO \\
| \\
CO_2C_2H_5
\end{array}
\xrightarrow[59\%]{\text{NaH}}
$$

$$
\begin{array}{c}
CO_2C_2H_5 \\
| \\
CF_3CH_2CH_2CH_2C-NHCHO \\
| \\
CO_2C_2H_5
\end{array}
\xrightarrow[35\%]{10\%\ HCl}
CF_3CH_2CH_2CH_2CH(NH_2)CO_2H
$$

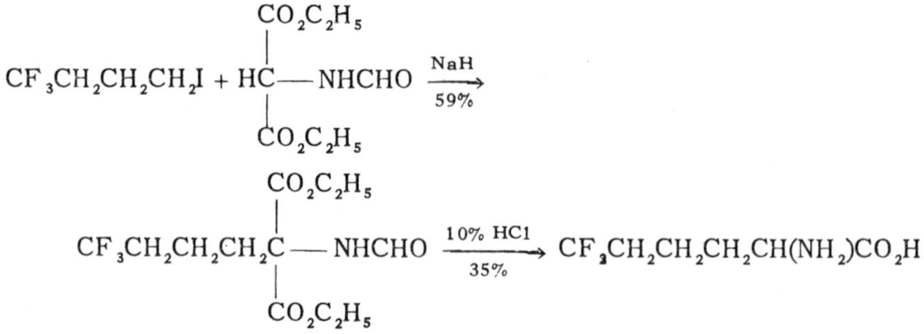

Lontz and Raasch[64] prepared $F(CH_2)_4CH(NH_2)CO_2H$ by the based cata-lyzed condensation of 1-fluoro-4-bromobutane with formamido-malonic ester and subsequent hydrolysis. These same workers employed the Strecker synthesis for the preparation of from trifluoro-

$$CF_3C \overset{\displaystyle CH_3}{\underset{\displaystyle NH_2}{|}} CO_2H$$

acetone.

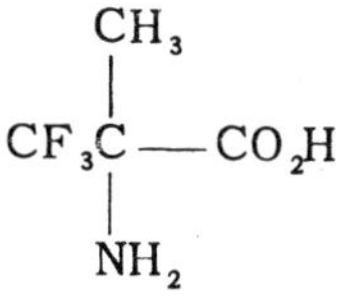

TABLE 20

MONOBASIC ACIDS

Empirical Formula	Structural Formula	Method	Yield %	B.p. °C/mm.	F.p. or M.p. °C	n_D^t	d_4^t	t°C	Ref.
$C_2HBrClFO_2$	$CBrClFCO_2H$	701		181	−5				82
$C_2HBrF_2O_2$	$CBrF_2CO_2H$	204		145–60	40				85
$C_2HBr_2FO_2$	CBr_2FCO_2H	701		198, 130/60	26.5				83
$C_2HClF_2O_2$	$CClF_2CO_2H$	203		121.5	22.9				86,87
		702	70						47
$C_2HCl_2FO_2$	CCl_2FCO_2H	701		162.5	−20				81
$C_2HF_3O_2$	CF_3CO_2H	702	87–90						47,54
		702	75						44
		703		72–3					7
		704							91,93
		705	6	72–72.5	−15.25				90
		706		72.4		1.2850	1.489	20	60,70A
		710	90						71A
$C_2H_2BrFO_2$	$CHBrFCO_2H$	701		183, 102/30	49				85
		709							88
$C_2H_2ClFO_2$	$CHClFCO_2H$	701	50	162		1.4085	1.532	25	98
$C_2H_2FIO_2$	$CHFICO_2H$	701			74				85
$C_2H_2F_2O_2$	CHF_2CO_2H	701		134					51
		702	86						44,47
		704		134.2/766, 67.70/20			1.539	10	85
		709	61						31,84
		705							84
		710	22	131					16,18
		711		132–3.5					4
$C_2H_3FO_2$	CH_2FCO_2H	104							1
		701	94.2	167–8.5	31–32				79

$C_2H_3FO_2$		701		165	33				82
		701	90						12
		704							89
				164–5	33–34				27
		709							88
$C_3HBrClF_3O_2$	$CF_2ClCFBrCO_2H$	705		85–86/15, 75/7	23.9	1.948		25	49
$C_3HBr_2F_3O_2$	$CF_2BrCFBrCO_2H$	701	32	72–3/2.5		1.4458	2.191	20	73
$C_3HCl_2F_3O_2$	$CFCl_2CF_2CO_2H$	702	62	83–85/20					36
	$CF_2ClCFClCO_2H$	705		83–85/30, 65/8		1.3868	1.591	25	49
$C_3HCl_3F_2O_2$	$CFCl_2CFClCO_2H$	702		115–18/25					39
$C_3HF_3O_2$	$CF_2{=}CFCO_2H$	302			35.5–6.5				49
$C_3HF_5O_2$	$CF_3CF_2CO_2H$	702	22	95.5–6.7		1.298		0	38
		705	51–73						26
		706		96/740			1.561	20	69
		706		95.5/738		1.2838	1.561(20)	25	57
$C_3H_2ClF_3O_2$	$CHF_2CFClCO_2H$	704		42/45					59
$C_3H_2F_2O_2$	$CF_2{=}CHCO_2H$	301							49
$C_3H_2F_4O_2$	$CF_2HCF_2CO_2H(+0.5\ H_2O)$	704		131.5–2.5					49
	$CF_2HCF_2CO_2H(+1\ H_2O$	704		136–7					49
$C_3H_3FO_2$	$CH_2{=}CFCO_2H$	302	55		51.5–2.0				49
$C_3H_3FO_3$	CH_2FCOCO_2H	712	9	98/5	50				9
$C_3H_3F_3O_2$	$CF_3CH_2CO_2H$	704		27–30/14–15	0				52
		714		144					11
$C_3H_4F_2O_2$	$CH_3CF_2CO_2H$	702	84.4	141	38–44				56
$C_3H_4F_2O_3$	$HOCH_2CF_2CO_2H$	701			49–53				18,76
		708	80						18
$C_3H_5FO_2$	CH_3CHFCO_2H	701		60–0.5/5–8					28
	$CH_2FCH_2CO_2H$	704	80	51.0–2.0/2					27
$C_4HCl_2F_5O_2$	$CF_2ClCFClCF_2CO_2H$	705	57	98–100/23					36
$C_4HCl_3F_4O_2$	$CCl_3CF_2CF_2CO_2H$	701	81	212		1.4132		26	95
$C_4HF_5O_3$	$CF_3COCF_2CO_2H$	701	56	56/3					68

TABLE 20 (*continued*)

Empirical Formula	Structural Formula	Method	Yield %	B.p. °C/mm.	F.p. or M.p. °C	n_D^t	d_4^t	t°C	Ref.
$C_4HF_7O_2$	$CF_3CF_2CF_2CO_2H$	706		120/735			1.651	20	60
		706		119/740	−17.5	1.293	1.651	20	23
		707	6–45						50
		707	75–80	120.5–1.1					30
$C_4H_2F_4O_3$	$CHF_2COCF_2CO_2H$	701	53	72/2					68
$C_4H_2F_6O_2$	$CF_3CHFCF_2CO_2H$	704		140/740		1.3100		25	62
$C_4H_3F_3O_2$	$CF_3CH{=}CHCO_2H$	701	72		51				31
		701	42.2–65	68–9/20	55–6				67
		703	48–68						33
		703			49.5–50.5				49
$C_4H_3F_3O_2$	$CH_2{=}C(CF_3)CO_2H$	303		146–8	50–2				15
$C_4H_3F_3O_3$	$CF_3COCH_2CO_2H$	701		79/8	72.8				92
$C_4H_3F_5O_2$	$CF_3CHFCHFCO_2H$	112		110–12/13					10
$C_4H_4BrF_3O_2$	$CF_3CHBrCH_2CO_2H$	216	93		39–41				97
		703		132–134					49
$C_4H_4ClF_3O_2$	$CH_2ClCH(CF_3)CO_2H$	202		169–70		1.3768		20	15
$C_4H_5FO_2$	$CH_3CF{=}CHCO_2H$	702		108–10/85	83				56
$C_4H_5F_3O_2$	$CF_3CH_2CH_2CO_2H$	701		70/12					40
		701	76	83–4.5/25	30–31				67
		707			33.2				69
	$CH_3CH(CF_3)CO_2H$	701	60	67/25			1.3444	20	15
$C_4H_5F_3O_3$	$CF_3CH(OH)CH_2CO_2H$	701	70	98/3	78–9				76
		701	97.2		69.5–70				58
		711	12		74–6				97
$C_4H_5F_3O_3$	$HOCH_2CH(CF_3)CO_2H$	701							15
	$CH_3C(CF_3)(OH)CO_2H$	701		189	88				21
$C_4H_6F_2O_2$	$CH_3CH_2CF_2CO_2H$	702		100–1/85	8.1	1.3618	1.2201	25	56
$C_4H_6F_3NO_2$	$CF_3C(CH_3)(NH_2)CO_2H$	717	58		250–300 (sub)				64

$C_4H_7FO_2$	$C_2H_5CHFCO_2H$	112		90/13					10
	$(CH_3)_2CFCO_2H$	112		80–2/13					10
	$CH_2F(CH_2)_2CO_2H$	704	75	60.0–2.0/2					27
$C_5HCl_3F_6O_2$	$CFCl_2CF_2CFClCF_2CO_2H$	702	57	135/18					36
$C_5HF_7O_2$	$CF_2{=}CFCF_2CF_2CO_2H$	306	21	75–6/59					35
$C_5HF_9O_2$	$CF_3(CF_2)_3CO_2H$	706		139/749			1.713	20	60
	$C_2F_5CF(CF_3)CO_2H$	702	51	135–6					34
$C_5H_2F_8O_2$	$C_2F_5CHFCH_2CO_2H$	704		152–3/740		1.3073		25	62
$C_5H_4F_4O_2$	$CF_2CF_2CH_2CHCO_2H$	701	87	100–0.5/24	61.5–63.0	1.3684	1.5103	25	6,19
		702		101/25					5
$C_5H_5F_3O_2$	$CF_3C(CH_3){=}CHCO_2H$	303	78	80–4					96
$C_5H_7F_3O_2$	$CF_3CH(CH_3)CH_2CO_2H$	212	89	90–91/25		1.3580		24	96
	$CF_3(CH_2)_3CO_2H$	704		94.8–95.0/15		1.3632	1.293	25	48
$C_5H_7F_3O_3$	$CF_3C(OH)(CH_3)CH_2CO_2H$	712	75	75–76/2	30				96
$C_5H_8F_3NO_2$	$CF_3(CH_2)_2CH(NH_2)CO_2H$	717	4.6–30		258(d)				96
$C_5H_9FO_3$	$CH_2FCH_2OCH_2CH_2CO_2H$	701	75	133–134/12					13
$C_5H_{10}FNO_2$	$F(CH_2)_3CH(NH_2)CO_2H$	701	27		190				64
$C_6HF_{11}O_2$	$CF_3(CF_2)_4CO_2H$	706		157/740		1.298	1.734(20)	29	23
		706		157/742			1.762	20	60
$C_6H_2F_{10}O_2$	$CF_3(CF_2)_2CHFCF_2CO_2H$	704		166–167/740		1.3120		25	62
$C_6H_3F_7O_2$	$CF_3(CF_2)_2CH{=}CHCO_2H$	701	86	80–81/10	48.5–49.0				67
$C_6H_5F_7O_2$	$CF_3(CF_2)_2(CH_2)_2CO_2H$	701	79	102.5–4.0/25	38–39				67
$C_6H_5F_7O_3$	$CF_3(CF_2)_2CH(OH)CH_2CO_2H$	701	90						67
$C_6H_6F_4O_2$	$CH_3CHCF_2CF_2CHCO_2H$	701			41–3	1.3744	1.4031	25	6
$C_6H_{10}F_2O_2$	$CH_3CF_2(CH_2)_3CO_2H$	702		85–86/15	34–35				56
$C_6H_{10}F_3NO_2$	$CF_3(CH_2)_3CH(NH_2)CO_2H$	717	56		272–274 (d)				96
$C_6H_{11}FO_2$	$F(CH_2)_5CO_2H$	716		67.8/0.6					71
		104	7.5	193/762					74

TABLE 20 (*continued*)

Empirical Formula	Structural Formula	Method	Yield %	B.p. °C/mm.	F.p. or M.p. °C	n_D^t	d_4^t	t°C	Ref.
$C_6H_{11}FO_3$	$F(CH_2)_2CH_2O(CH_2)_2CO_2H$	701	32	144–150/13					13
$C_6H_{12}FNO_2$	$F(CH_2)_4CH(NH_2)CO_2H$	717	55		144				64
$C_7HF_{11}O_2$	$\overline{CF_2(CF_2)_4CF}CO_2H$	706		168–170/740		1.325	1.798(20)	29	23
		706		170/742			1.780	20	60
$C_7HF_{13}O_2$	$CF_3(CF_2)_5CO_2H$	706		175/742			1.792	20	60
$C_7H_2Cl_3F_9O_2$	$H(CF_2CFCl)_3CO_2H$	704		100–130/3					59
$C_7H_2F_{12}O_2$	$H(CF_2CF_2)_3CO_2H$	704		190–193					8
$C_7H_6F_7NO_4$	$CF_3(CF_2)_2CH(CH_2NO_2)CH_2CO_2H$	701	48		46.5–48				20
$C_7H_{12}F_3NO_2$	$CF_3CH(CH_3)(CH_2)_2CH(NH_2)CO_2H$	717			254–256 (d)				96
$C_8HF_{13}O_2$	$\overline{CF_2(CF_2)_4CF}CF_2CO_2H$	706		184/735			1.813	20	60
$C_8HF_{15}O_2$	$CF_3(CF_2)_6CO_2H$	706		189/736					60
		706		190/740					23
$C_9HF_{19}O_2$	$CF_3(CF_2)_8CO_2H$	706		218/740					60
$C_9H_2F_{16}O_2$	$H(CF_2CF_2)_4CO_2H$	704		220–230	62–68				8
$C_9H_{17}FO_3$	$CH_3(CH_2)_3C(OH)(C_2H_5)CHFCO_2H$	701			92–93				66
	$CH_3(CH_2)_5CH(OH)CHFCO_2H$	701			69–70				66
$C_{10}HCl_5F_{14}O_2$	$Cl(CF_2CFCl)_4CF_2CO_2H$	705	57						36
$C_{10}HF_{19}$	$CF_3(CF_2)_8CO_2H$	706		130/30					23
$C_{10}H_4F_{16}O_3$	$CF_3(CF_2)_6CH(OH)CHFCO_2H$	701			156–158				66
$C_{10}H_5F_{15}O_3$	$CF_3(CF_2)_6CHOHCH_2CO_2H$	701			129–130				66
$C_{11}H_2F_{20}O_2$	$H(CF_2CF_2)_5CO_2H$	704			100–1				8
$C_{13}H_2F_{24}O_2$	$H(CF_2CF_2)_6CO_2H$	704			138				8
$C_{14}HF_{27}O_2$	$CF_3(CF_2)_{12}CO_2H$	706		270/740					56

TABLE 21

DIBASIC ACIDS

Empirical Formula	Structural Formula	Method	Yield %	B.p. °C/mm.	F.p. or M.p. °C	n_D^t	d_4^t	t°C	Ref.
$C_3H_2F_2O_4$	$CF_2(CO_2H)_2$	702	63		118				37
		702							47A
		702			117–118				24
$C_3H_3FO_4$	$CHF(CO_2H)_2$	701	45		135.8–136.5				73
$C_4H_2Cl_2F_2O_4$	$(\text{—}CFClCO_2H)_2$	702	62	100–105/0.1					39
$C_4H_2F_4O_4$	$(\text{—}CF_2CO_2H)_2$	702			120				80
		702	93		116–116.5				14
		702			115–116				24
		702	53		116				35
		702		150/15					46,53,56
$C_4H_4F_2O_4$	$(\text{—}CHFCO_2H)_2$	715							61
$C_5H_2F_6O_4$	$CF_2(CF_2CO_2H)_2$	702	86	134–138/3	78–88				45,55
		702							25
$C_5H_6F_2O_4$	$HO_2C(CH_2)_2CF_2CO_2H$	701	30	103–105					3
$C_6H_2Cl_2F_6O_4$	$(\text{—}CFClCF_2CO_2H)_2$	702	51						37
$C_6H_2F_8O_4$	$(\text{—}CF_2CF_2CO_2H)_2$	705			134				79
		702			134				79
		702	70		133–134				95
		702	83						65
$C_6H_3F_7O_4$	$HO_2CCF_2CFH(CF_2)_2CO_2H$	702			128–130				25
	$HO_2CCFH(CF_2)_3CO_2H$	702							25
$C_6H_7FO_7$	$HO_2CCHFC(OH)(CO_2H)CH_2CO_2H$	701							77
$C_7H_2F_{10}O_4$	$HO_2CCF_2CF(CF_3)(CF_2)_2CO_2H$	702			60–1				2
		705							91
$C_8H_9FO_4$	$CH_2CH(CO_2H)CH(CO_2H)CH_2CH{=}CF$ (ring: CH_2 bonded to CF)	713			163				17

BIBLIOGRAPHY

1. Alverez, S. B., *Rev. quin. farm.* **4,** 2(1947).
2. Barlow, G. B., Stacey, M., and Tatlow, J. C., *J. Chem. Soc.*, **1955,** 1749.
3. Barney, A. L., and Cairns, T. L., *J. Am. Chem. Soc.*, **72,** 3193(1950).
4. Barrick, P. L., U. S. Patent 2,403,207(1946).
5. Barrick, P. L., U. S. Patent 2,462,347(1949).
6. Barrick, P. L., and Cramer, R., U. S. Patent 2,441,128(1948).
7. Benning, A. F., and Park, J. D., U. S. Patent 2,396,076(1946).
8. Berry, K. L., U. S. Patent 2,559,629(1951).
9. Blank, I., Mager, J., and Bergmann, E. D., *J. Chem. Soc.*, **1955,** 2190.
10. Bockemuller, W., *Ann.*, **506,** 20(1933).
11. Brown, F., and Musgrave, W. K. R., *J. Chem. Soc.*, **1953,** 2087.
12. Buckle, F. J., and Saunders, B. C., *J. Chem. Soc.*, **1949,** 912.
13. Buckle, F. J., and Saunders, B. C., *J. Chem. Soc.*, **1949,** 2774.
14. Buxton, M. W., Ingram, D. W., *et al.*, *J. Chem. Soc.*, **1952,** 3830.
15. Buxton, M. W., Stacey, M., and Tatlow, J. C., *J. Chem. Soc.*, **1954,** 366.
16. Coffman, D. D., U. S. Patent 2,442,995(1948).
17. Coffman, D. D., and Salisbury, L. F., U. S. Patent 2,451,612(1948).
18. Coffman, D. D., Raasch, M. S., *et al.*, *J. Org. Chem.*, **14,** 747(1949).
19. Coffman, D. D., Barrick, P. L., *et al.*, *J. Am. Chem. Soc.*, **71,** 490(1949).
20. Cook, D. J., Pierce, O. R., and McBee, E. T., *J. Am. Chem. Soc.*, **76,** 83(1954).
21. Darrall, R. A., Smith, F., *et al.*, *J. Chem. Soc.*, **1951,** 2329.
22. Desirant, Y., *Bull. sci. acad. roy. Belg.*, **15,** 966(1929).
23. Diesslin, A. R., Kauck, E. A., and Simons, J. H., U. S. Patent 2,567,011(1951).
24. Evans, D. E. M., and Tatlow, J. C., *J. Chem. Soc.*, **1954,** 3779.
25. Evans, D. E. M., and Tatlow, J. C., *J. Chem. Soc.*, **1955,** 1184.
26. Francis, W. C., and Haszeldine, R. H., *J. Chem. Soc.*, **1955,** 2151.
27. Gryszkiewicz-Trochimowski, E., Sporzynski, A., and Wnuk, J., *Rec. trav. Chim.*, **66,** 419(1947).
28. Gryszkiewicz-Trochimowski, E., Sporzynski, A., and Wnuk, J., *Bull. Soc. Chim. France*, **1949,** 928.
29. Haszeldine, R. N., *J. Chem. Soc.*, **1952,** 2404.
30. Haszeldine, R. N., *J. Chem. Soc.*, **1952,** 3423.
31. Haszeldine, R. N., *J. Chem. Soc.*, **1952,** 3490.
32. Haszeldine, R. N., *J. Chem. Soc.*, **1952,** 4259.
33. Haszeldine, R. N., *J. Chem. Soc.*, **1953,** 922.
34. Haszeldine, R. N., *J. Chem. Soc.*, **1953,** 3559.
35. Haszeldine, R. N., *J. Chem. Soc.*, **1954,** 4026.

35A. Haszeldine, R. N., *Chem. Soc. Ann. Rep.*, **51,** 282(1954).

36. Haszeldine, R. N., *J. Chem. Soc.*, **1955,** 4291.
37. Haszeldine, R. N., *J. Chem. Soc.*, **1955,** 4302.
38. Haszeldine, R. N., and Leedham, K., *J. Chem. Soc.*, **1952,** 1548.
39. Haszeldine, R. N., and Osborne, J. E., *J. Chem. Soc.*, **1955,** 3880.
40. Haszeldine, R. N., and Steele, B. R., *J. Chem. Soc.*, **1953,** 1199.
41. Haszeldine, R. N., and Steele, B. R., *J. Chem. Soc.*, **1955,** 3005.
42. Haszeldine, R. N., and Walaschewski, E. G., *J. Chem. Soc.*, **1953,** 3607.
43. Hauptschein, M., and Grosse, A. V., *J. Am. Chem. Soc.*, **73,** 5139(1951).
44. Henne, A. L., U. S. Patent 2,371,751(1945).
45. Henne, A. L., U. S. Patent 2,438,484(1948).

46. Henne, A. L., U. S. Patent 2,438,485(1948).
47. Henne, A. L., Alderson, T., and Newman, M. S., *J. Am. Chem. Soc.*, **67,** 918(1945).
47A. Henne, A. L., and DeWitt, E. G., *J. Am. Chem. Soc.*, **70,** 1548(1948).
48. Henne, A. L., and Fox, C. J., *J. Am. Chem. Soc.*, **75,** 5750(1953).
49. Henne, A. L., and Fox, C. J., *J. Am. Chem. Soc.*, **76,** 479(1954).
50. Henne, A. L., and Francis, W. C., *J. Am. Chem. Soc.*, **73,** 3518(1951).
51. Henne, A. L., and Pelley, R. L., *J. Am. Chem. Soc.*, **74,** 1426(1952).
52. Henne, A. L., Pelley, R. L., and Alm, R. M., *J. Am. Chem. Soc.*, **72,** 3370(1950).
53. Henne, A. L., and Ruh, R. P., *J. Am. Chem.* Soc., **69,** 279(1947).
54. Henne, A. L., and Trott, P., *J. Am. Chem. Soc.*, **69,** 1820(1947).
55. Henne, A. L., and Zimmerscheid, W. J., *J. Am. Chem. Soc.*, **67,** 1235(1945).
56. Henne, A. L., and Zimmerscheid, W. J., *J. Am. Chem. Soc.*, **69,** 281(1947).
57. Husted, D. R., and Ahlbrecht, A. H., *J. Am. Chem. Soc.*, **75,** 1605(1953).
58. Jones, R. G., *J. Am. Chem. Soc.*, **70,** 143(1948).
59. Joyce, R. M., U. S. Patent 2,559,628(1951).
60. Kauck, E. A., and Diesslin, A. R., *Ind. Eng. Chem.*, **43,** 2332(1951).
61. Kharasch, M. S., U. S. Patent 2,426,244(1947).
62. LaZerte, J. D., and Koshar, R. J., *J. Am. Chem. Soc.*, **77,** 910(1955).
63. Lichtenberger, J., Baumann, and Breiss, *Bull. soc. Chim. France,* **1954,** 687.
64. Lontz, J. F., and Raasch, M. S., U. S. Patent 2,662,915(1953).
65. McBee, E. T., Park, J. D., *et al.*, *Ind. Eng. Chem.*, **39,** 415(1947).
66. McBee, E. T., Pierce, O. R., and Christman, D. L., *J. Am. Chem. Soc.*, **77,** 1581(1955).
67. McBee, E. T., Pierce, O. R., and Smith, D. D., *J. Am. Chem. Soc.*, **76,** 3722(1954).
68. McBee, E. T., Pierce, O. R., *et al.*, *J. Am. Chem. Soc.*, **75,** 3152(1953).
69. McBee, E. T., and Truchan, A., *J. Am. Chem. Soc.*, **70,** 2910(1949).
70. McGinty, L., British Patent 642,459(1950).
70A. Minnesota Mining and Manufacturing Company, "Trifluoroacetic Acid" and "Heptafluorobutyric Acid," St. Paul, Minnesota.
71. Nischk, and Muller, *Ann.*, **576,** 232(1952).
71A. Norton, T. R., *J. Am. Chem. Soc.*, **72,** 3527(1950).
72. Padbury, J. J., and Kropa, E. L., U. S. Patent 2,502,478(1950).
72A. Park, J. D., Larsen, E. R., *et al.*, 130th Meeting American Chemical Society, Atlantic City, New Jersey, September 1956.
73. Park, J. D., Rausch, D. A., and Lacher, J. R., Private Communication (1955).
74. Pattison, F. L. M., and Saunders, B. C., *J. Chem. Soc.*, **1948,** 2745.
75. Pierce, O. R., McBee, E. T., and Judd, G. F., *J. Am. Chem. Soc.*, **76,** 474(1954).
76. Pierce, O. R., and Smith, D. D., *J. Am. Chem. Soc.*, **76,** 3722(1954).
77. Rivett, D. E. A., *J. Chem. Soc.*, **1953,** 3710.
78. Roylance, J., Tatlow, J. C., and Worthington, R. E., *J. Chem. Soc.*, **1954,** 4426.
79. Saunders, B. C., and Stacey, G. J., *J. Chem. Soc.*, **1948,** 1773.
80. Scherer, O., German Patent 856,145(1952).
81. Swarts, F., *Bull. soc. chim. France* (3) **13,** 995(1895).
82. Sawrts, F., *Bull. acad. roy. Belg.*, (3) **35,** 849(1898).
83. Swarts, F., *Bull. soc. chim. France*, (3) **15,** 1134(1896).

84. Swarts, F., *Bull. soc. chim. France*, **1901,** 383.
85. Swarts, F., *Bull. soc. chim. France*, **1903,** 597.
86. Swarts, F., *Bull. soc. chim. France*, **1906,** 42.
87. Swarts, F., *Bull. soc. chim. France*, **1907,** 339.
88. Swarts, F., *Bull. soc. chim. France*, **1911,** 563.
89. Swarts, F., *Bull. soc. chim. France*, **1914,** 7.
90. Swarts, F., *Bull. sci. acad. roy. Belg.*, **8,** 343(1922).
91. Swarts, F., *Bull. sci. acad. roy. Belg.*, Ext. *Bull. Classe Sci.*, **Jun 1922,** 333.
92. Swarts, F., *Bull. acad. roy. Belg.*, **12,** 679(1926).
93. Swarts, F., *Compt. rend.*, **197,** 1261 (1933).
94. Tatlow, J. C., and Worthington, R. E., *J. Chem. Soc.*, **1952,** 1251.
95. Tiers, G. V. D., *J. Am. Chem. Soc.*, **77,** 6704(1955).
96. Walborsky, H. M., Baum, M., and Loncrini, D. F., *J. Am. Chem. Soc.*, **77,** 3637(1955).
97. Walborsky, H. M., and Schwarz, M., *J. Am. Chem. Soc.*, **75,** 3241(1953).
98. Young, J. A., and Tarrant, P., *J. Am. Chem. Soc.*, **71,** 2432(1949).
99. Young, J. A., and Tarrant, P., 120th Meeting American Chemical Society, New York, New York, September 1951.

CHAPTER VIII

Acyl Halides and Anhydrides

TABLE OF CONTENTS

		PAGE
Introduction		220
Method Number		
	ACYL HALIDES	
801	Action of Inorganic Acid Halides on Carboxylic Acids	220
802	Action of Phosphorus Halides on Carboxylic Acid Salts	221
803	Reaction of Carboxylic Acids with Benzoyl Halides.	221
804	Reaction of Acyl Halides with Hydrogen Halides or Inorganic Halides	221
805	Cleavage of Ethers with Aluminum Chloride	221
806	Oxidation of Alkenes and Alkanes	222
807	Reaction of Acid Anhydrides with Sodium Bromide.	222
808	Pyrolysis of Sodium Trifluoroacetate	222
809	Interaction of Carbon Tetrafluoride with Carbon Monoxide and Aluminum Chloride	222
	ANHYDRIDES	
810	Dehydration of Carboxylic Acids	223
811	Action of Acyl Halides on Carboxylic Acids or Their Salts	223
812	Pyrolysis of Silver Salts of Carboxylic Acids	223
813	Reaction of Anhydrides with Carboxylic Acids	223
TABLE 22	Acyl Halides	224
TABLE 23	Acid Anhydrides	226
Bibliography		227

INTRODUCTION

Generally, the preparation and reactions of fluorinated acyl halides are similar to those of their hydrocarbon analogs. They are useful intermediates in the preparation of esters and amides and also may be used in Freidel-Craft reactions with aromatic compounds to produce ketones. As discussed in Methods 112 and 706, the electrochemical fluorination of carboxylic acids and many of their derivatives leads to the production of perfluoroacyl fluorides.

Similarly, the preparation and properties of fluorine-containing acid anhydrides also resemble their hydrocarbon analogs. Trifluoroacetic anhydride has been rather extensively used as a promoter in esterification reactions.

ACYL HALIDES

METHOD 801 Action of Inorganic Acid Halides on Carboxylic Acids

Fluorine-containing carboxylic acids are readily converted to the acyl halides by the use of phosphorus halides or thionyl chloride. Attempts to prepare diacyl halides from fluorinated dicarboxylic acids and phosphorus pentachloride were unsuccessful due to decomposition upon distillation.

The action of phosphorus pentachloride on carboxylic acids at either room temperature or reflux temperature gives good yields of the acyl chlorides. For example, C_2F_5COCl can be obtained in a 90 percent yield using this procedure.[21] Although this is the most generally used procedure for the preparation of acyl chlorides, the separation from the by-product, phosphorus oxychloride is sometimes difficult. However, phosphorus trichloride may also be used successfully. For example, $C_3F_7CH_2O_2C(CF_2)_3COCl$ has been prepared in a 69 percent yield by treating the corresponding half-acid ester with phosphorus trichloride. In this case, phosphorous acid is the by-product.

Another procedure for the conversion of carboxylic acids to acyl chlorides is by the use of thionyl chloride at reflux temperatures. About one part pyridine per one hundred parts of the carboxylic acid is often employed as a catalyst. Although the yields of acyl chlorides produced using this procedure are slightly lower than when phosphorus pentachloride is used, the advantage lies in the fact that the only by-products are hydrogen chloride and sulfur dioxide.[5,8]

Acyl bromides are made from carboxylic acids by refluxing either with phosphorus tribromide[5,11] or with bromine and a small amount of red phosphorus.[30] The yields are about 50 percent.

The preparation of acyl iodides using the procedure has not been reported.

METHOD 802 Action of Phosphorous Halides on Carboxylic Acid Salts

Several examples are reported in which acyl chlorides are prepared by the action of phosphorus chlorides on the salts of carboxylic acids. When a mixture of phosphorus pentachloride and sodium fluoroacetate was allowed to react three weeks at room temperature an 83 percent yield of fluoroacetyl chloride resulted.[48] Knunyants[28] obtained the same product by heating sodium fluoroacetate with phosphorus trichloride at 140° to 150°. By refluxing barium trifluoroacetate with phosphorus trichloride for eighteen hours, a 53 percent yield of the acyl chloride was obtained.[36]

METHOD 803 Reaction of Carboxylic Acids with Benzoyl Halides

Fluorine-containing acyl halides are readily prepared by refluxing carboxylic acids with benzoyl halides. The desired acyl halide may be readily removed from the by-product, benzoic acid, by distillation. Using this procedure, Henne and co-workers[22] prepared trifluoroacetyl chloride in an 80 percent yield. The treatment of $C_8F_7CH{=}CHCO_2H$ with benzoyl chloride gave the corresponding acyl chloride in a 74 percent yield.[12]

Trifluoroacetyl and chlorodifluoroacetyl bromide have been prepared by heating the corresponding acids with benzoyl bromide.[47]

METHOD 804 Reaction of Acyl Halides with Hydrogen Halides or Inorganic Halides

Acyl chlorides are readily converted to acyl fluorides, bromides or iodides by the use of inorganic halides. Heptafluorobutyryl iodide has been prepared by treating the corresponding acyl chloride or bromide with calcium iodide.[11] Acyl chlorides also react with phosphorus tribromide to yield the acyl bromides.[16,36] It is also reported that CH_2FCOCl reacts with thallous fluoride to yield CH_2FCOF.[16]

Trifluoroacetyl iodide was prepared by treating trifluoroacetyl chloride with hydrogen iodide at 120° for eight hours.[17]

METHOD 805 Cleavage of Ethers with Aluminum Chloride

Although the preparation of acyl chlorides by the cleavage of highly fluorinated ethers is of little synthetic value at the present time, the method is of importance as a proof of structure for this type ether (cf. Method 503).

Tiers[46] has shown that n-$C_5F_{11}COCl$ is obtained when $(n\text{-}C_6F_{13})_2O$ is heated at 230° for 15 hours with aluminum chloride. Cyclic perfluoroethers may also be cleaved using this procedure. However, in this case, ω,ω,ω-trichloroperfluoroacyl chlorides are obtained. For example, by treating $\overline{O(CF_2)_3CF_2}$ with aluminum chloride at 170° for 13 hours, $CCl_3(CF_2)_2COCl$ was obtained in 55 percent yield. It is interesting to note that ethers of the general type, $R_f\overline{CF(CF_2)_nO}$, do not cleave under these conditions.

METHOD 806 Oxidation of Alkenes and Alkanes

Highly halogenated alkenes and alkanes can be converted to acyl halides by treatment with oxygen alone or oxygen in the presence of either chlorine or bromine.

Chaney[9] reports that a mixture of $CF_2ClCFClCOF$ and CF_2ClCCl_2COCl may be prepared from $CF_2ClCF{=}CCl_2$ by passing a mixture of oxygen and chlorine into the olefin under ultraviolet irradiation. The air oxidation of $CBr_2{=}CHF$ and $CFBr{=}CFBr$ yield $CHFBrCOBr$ and $CFBr_2COF$, respectively.[39] Chlorodifluoroacetyl fluoride has been prepared in a 43 percent yield by treating $CF_2{=}CFCl$ with oxygen at 25° to 50°.[26]

Francis and Haszeldine[14] reported that the photochemical vapor-phase oxidation of compounds of the type $CF_3CF_2CFX_2$ (X = H, F, Cl, Br, or I) to acyl halides may be readily accomplished. The photochemical oxidation of CF_3CF_2CFClI with a 4 to 1 molar ratio of oxygen to bromine yielded a mixture containing 69 percent C_2F_5COF and 21 percent CF_3COF. In the absence of chlorine or bromine as a sensitizer, carbon-carbon cleavage occurs readily and C_3F_7H, C_3F_7Cl, C_3F_7Br and C_3F_7I yield carbonyl fluoride (cf. Method 705).

METHOD 807 Reaction of Acid Anhydrides with Sodium Bromide

It is reported that the reaction between perfluorobutyric acid anhydride and sodium bromide results in a low yield of perfluorobutyryl bromide.[30]

$$(C_3F_7CO)_2O + NaBr \xrightarrow{\text{Reflux}} C_3F_7COBr$$

METHOD 808 Pyrolysis of Sodium Trifluoroacetate

$$CF_3CO_2Na \xrightarrow[205-340°]{} CF_3COF.^{44} \text{ (cf. Methods 207 and 306)}$$

METHOD 809 Interaction of Carbon Tetrafluoride with Carbon Monoxide and Aluminum Chloride

Carbon tetrachloride has been converted to trichloroacetyl chloride. Theobold[45] claims in a patent that trifluoroacetyl fluoride may be prepared by the same procedure from carbon tetrafluoride:

$$CF_4 + CO + AlCl_3 \xrightarrow[200^\circ\ 8\ \text{hrs.}]{900\ \text{atm.}} CF_3COF$$

ANHYDRIDES

METHOD 810 Dehydration of Carboxylic Acids

The simple anhydrides of fluorinated carboxylic acids are most readily obtained by refluxing the carboxylic acid with phosphorus pentoxide or phosphorus oxychloride. Using this procedure, Clark and Simons[10] prepared a series of anhydrides in good yields. The anhydride of perfluorosuccinic acid has been prepared in a similar manner.[24] By heating perfluorosuccinic acid[33] or perfluoroadipic acid[21] with phosphorus oxychloride, the cyclic anhydrides were prepared in good yields.

METHOD 811 Action of Acyl Halides on Carboxylic Acids or Their Salts

Fluoroacetic anhydride has been obtained in a 78 percent yield by reacting fluoroacetyl fluoride with fluoroacetic acid.[34] It has also been reported that perfluorobutyryl chloride reacts with sodium perfluorobutyrate to give perfluorobutyric anhydride.[11]

METHOD 812 Pyrolysis of Silver Salts of Carboxylic Acids

Haszeldine and Leedham[19] have reported that the pyrolysis of silver perfluorobutyrate at 500° yielded 11 percent of perfluorobutyric anhydride and 81 percent of perfluorohexane (cf. Method 207). However, in the presence of yellow phosphorus, the pyrolysis of silver trifluoroacetate gave a 61 percent yield of trifluoroacetic anhydride.[18]

METHOD 813 Reaction of Anhydrides with Carboxylic Acids

Mixed anhydrides have been prepared by reacting carboxylic acids with perfluorocarboxylic acid anhydrides or conversely. Thus, $CF_3\overset{\displaystyle O}{\overset{\|}{C}}O\overset{\displaystyle O}{\overset{\|}{C}}CH_3$ was prepared by treating acetic acid with trifluoroacetic anhydride at 20° or by distilling a mixture of trifluoroacetic acid and acetic anhydride through a column.[3]

TABLE 22

ACYL HALIDES

Empirical Formula	Structural Formula	Method	Yield %	B.p. °C/mm.	F.p. or M.p. °C	n_D^t	d_4^t	t°C	Ref.
C_2BrClF_2O	$CClF_2COBr$	803		93–4					47
	$CBrClFCOF$	107		51					38
C_2BrF_3O	CF_3COBr	804	59	−5	−130				36
		803		0					47
$C_2Br_2F_2O$	CBr_2FCOF	107		75.4/757					40
		807							39
C_2ClF_3O	CF_3COCl	803	79	−19 to −18					22,47
		801		−27					35
		802	53						36
	$CClF_2COF$	806	43	−18.5					26
$C_2Cl_2F_2O$	$CClF_2COCl$	803		49–50					47
	$CFCl_2COF$	107		25–40					37
C_2F_4O	CF_3COF	110		−59					15
		808							44
		809							45
		806							14
$C_2HBrClFO$	$CHBrFCOCl$	801		98/765			1.879	14.5	41
C_2HBr_2FO	$CHBrFCOBr$	806		112.5			2.331	10	39
C_2HClF_2O	CHF_2COCl	801		25					43
C_2HCl_2FO	$CHClFCOCl$	801	81	69.5		1.3992	1.468	25	49
C_2H_2BrFO	CH_2FCOBr	804		95–6					16
		801	47	87–88					2
C_2H_2ClFO	CH_2FCOCl	802	85	70–71/755		1.3835		27	48,28
		801	90	71.5–72.0/766					16,34
$C_2H_2F_2O$	CH_2FCOF	804		51.5–52					16
C_2F_3IO	CF_3COI	804	62	23					17
C_3ClF_5O	C_2F_5COCl	801	90	9.0					35,21

C_3ClF_5O		803	82	5/539.5, 9.4					27,19
$C_3Cl_2F_4O$	$CClF_2CClFCOF$	806							9
$C_3Cl_4F_2O$	$CClF_2CCl_2COCl$	806							9
C_3F_6O	CF_3CF_2COF	806							14
$C_3H_2ClF_3O$	CF_3CH_2COCl	801		70.3/745		1.3382	1.422	29.5	25
C_4BrF_7O	$CF_3(CF_2)_2COBr$	801		52–54/748		1.3261	1.735	20	11,30
		807		53/736					30
C_4ClF_7O	$CF_3(CF_2)_2COCl$	801		38–39		1.288	1.55	25	11,35
		805	30			1.2880		25	46
$C_4Cl_4F_4O$	$CCl_3CF_2CF_2COCl$	805	55	148		1.4105		25	46
C_4F_7IO	$CF_3(CF_2)_2COI$	804		77–78		1.353	2.00(20)	25	17,11
C_4HClF_6O	CF_3CFHCF_2COCl			54.4–55/735		1.3056		25	29
C_4HClF_6O	$CHF_2(CF_2)_2COCl$	801		39–41					5
$C_4H_2ClF_3O$	$CF_3CH{=}CHCOCl$	803	67	77–77.5		1.3703	1.362	20	31
$C_4H_4ClF_3O$	$CF_3(CH_2)_2COCl$	801		103/745		1.3610	1.361	24	25
$C_4H_4ClF_3O$	$CH_3CH(CF_3)COCl$	801		88–90					6
C_5ClF_9O	$CF_3(CF_2)_3COCl$	801		67.5–68/760					35
$C_5Cl_4F_6O$	$CCl_3(CF_2)_3COCl$	805	54	165		1.3966		25	46
C_5HBrF_8O	$CHF_2(CF_2)_3COBr$	801	70	97–101					15
C_5HClF_8O	$CHF_2(CF_2)_3COCl$	801	76	84.5/6.5					5,8
$C_5H_3ClF_4O$	$\overline{CH_2(CF_2)_2CH}COCl$ (ring)	801		70/124		1.3782	1.4915	25	1
$C_5H_8ClFO_2$	$CH_2FCH_2O(CH_2)_2COCl$		79	77–80/11					4
$C_6ClF_{11}O$	$CF_3(CF_2)_4COCl$	801		85.8–86/760		1.327	1.66	25	13,35
		805	43–51	87–93		1.2992		25	46
$C_6H_2ClF_7O$	$CF_3(CF_2)_2CH{=}CHCOCl$	803	73.7	65–73					12
$C_6H_{10}ClFO_2$	$CH_2F(CH_2)_2O(CH_2)_2COCl$			86–90/13					4
$C_8ClF_{15}O$	$CF_3(CF_2)_6COCl$	801	58	129–130/744		1.3025		25	20
$C_9HClF_{16}O$	$CHF_2(CF_2)_7COCl$	801		166.5					5
$C_9H_2ClF_{13}O_3$	$CF_3(CF_2)_2CH_2O_2C(CF_2)_3COCl$	801	69	95/42		1.3299		21	20
$C_{10}ClF_{19}O$	$CF_3(CF_2)_8COCl$	801		174–175/747	27–28				13

TABLE 23

ACID ANHYDRIDES

Empirical Formula	Structural Formula	Method	Yield %	B.p. °C/mm.	F.p. or M.p. °C	n_D^t	d_4^t	t °C	Ref.
$C_4F_4O_3$	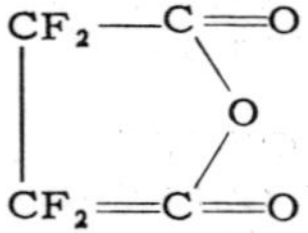	810		54–55		1.3240	1.6209	20	24,33
$C_4F_6O_3$	$(CF_3CO)_2O$	810		39.5–40.5	−65	1.269	1.490	25	10,44
		812	61						18
$C_4H_3F_3O_3$	$CF_3COOCOCH_3$	813		94–95		1.3253	1.38	25	3
$C_4H_4F_2O_3$	$(CH_2FCO)_2O$	811	77.7	88–89/12					34
$C_5F_6O_3$	$CF_2(CF_2CO)_2O$	810	76	72		1.3190	1.6541	25	21
$C_6F_{10}O_3$	$(CF_3CF_2CO)_2O$	810	57	69.8–70/735		1.273	1.571	25	10,19,27
		812	10						19
$C_6H_2F_8O_3$	$(CHF_2CF_2CO)_2O$	810		122.5–123.5/744					23
$C_8F_{14}O_3$	$(CF_3CF_2CF_2CO)_2O$	810		107–107.5		1.285	1.665	20	10
		811		106	−43	1.287	1.665	20	11
		812	11	107					19
$C_{10}F_{18}O_3$	$[CF_3(CF_2)_3CO]_2O$	810		137–137.5					10
$C_{12}F_{22}O_3$	$[CF_3(CF_2)_4CO]_2O$	810		175–176		1.295	1.769	25	10

BIBLIOGRAPHY

1. Barrick, P. L., and Cramer, R. D., U. S. Patent 2,441,128(1948).
2. Blank, I., Mayer, D., and Bergmann, E. D., *J. Chem. Soc.*, **1955**, 2190.
3. Bourne, E. J., *J. Chem. Soc.*, **1954**, 2006.
4. Buckle, F. J., and Saunders, B. C., *J. Chem. Soc.*, **1949**, 2774.
5. Bullitt, O. H. Jr., U. S. Patent 2,559,630(1951).
6. Buxton, M. W., Stacey, M., and Tatlow, J. C., *J. Chem. Soc.*, **1954**, 366.
7. Cady, G. H., and Kellogg, K. B., *J. Am. Chem. Soc.*, **75**, 2501 (1953).
8. Carnahan, J. E., and Sampson, H. J., U. S. Patent 2,646,449(1953).
9. Chaney, D. W., U. S. Patent 2,439,505(1948).
10. Clark, R. F., and Simons, J. H., *J. Am. Chem. Soc.*, **75**, 6305(1953).
11. Diesslin, A. R., Kauck, E. A., and Simons, J. H., U. S. Patent 2,567,011 (1951).
12. Filler, R., *J. Am. Chem. Soc.*, **76**, 1376 (1954).
13. Filler, R., O'Brien, J. F., *et al.*, *J. Am. Chem. Soc.*, **75**, 966 (1953).
14. Francis, W. C., and Haszeldine, R. N., *J. Chem. Soc.*, **1955**, 2151.
15. Fukuhara, N., and Bigelow, L. A., *J. Am. Chem. Soc.*, **63**, 788 (1941).
16. Gryskiewicz-Trochimowski, E., Sporzynski, A., and Wnuk, J., *Rec. trav. chim.*, **66**, 419(1947).
17. Haszeldine, R. N., *J. Chem. Soc.*, **1951**, 584.
18. Haszeldine, R. N., *J. Chem. Soc.*, **1952**, 4259.
19. Haszeldine, R. N., and Leedham, K., *J. Chem. Soc.*, **1953**, 1548.
20. Hauptschein, M.. O'Brien, J. F., *et al.*, *J. Am. Chem. Soc.*, **75**, 87(1953).
21. Hauptschein, M., Stokes, C. S., and Nodiff, E. A., *J. Am. Chem. Soc.*, **74**, 4005(1952).
22. Henne, A. L., Alm, R. M., and Smook, M., *J. Am. Chem. Soc.*, **70**, 1968(1948).
23. Henne, A. L., and Fox, C. J., *J. Am. Chem. Soc.*, **76**, 479(1954).
24. Henne, A. L., and Richter, S. B., *J. Am. Chem. Soc.*, **74**, 5420(1952).
25. Henne, A. L., and Stewart, J. J., *J. Am. Chem. Soc.*, **77**, 1901(1955).
26. Hurka, V. R., U. S. Patent 2,676,983(1954).
27. Husted, D. R., and Ahlbrecht, A. H., *J. Am. Chem. Soc.*, **75**, 1605(1953).
28. Knunyants, I. L., Kil'disheva, O. V., and Bykhovskaya, E., *Zhur. Obshchei Khim.*, **19**, 101(1949).
29. LaZerte, J. D., and Koshar, R. J., *J. Am. Chem. Soc.*, **77**, 910(1955).
30. LaZerte, J. D., Pearlson, W. H., and Kauck, E. A., U. S. Patent 2,704,776 (1955).
31. McBee, E. T., Pierce, O. R., and Smith, D. K., *J. Am. Chem. Soc.*, **76**, 3725 (1954).
32. Menefee, A., and Cady, G. H., *J. Am. Chem. Soc.*, **76**, 2020(1954).
33. Padbury, J. J., and Kropa, E. L., U. S. Patent 2,502,478(1950).
34. Saunders, B. C., and Stacey, G. J., *J. Chem. Soc.*, **1948**, 1773.
35. Simons, J. H., Black, W. T., and Clark, R. F., *J. Am. Chem. Soc.*, **75**, 5621 (1953).
36. Simons, J. H., and Rambler, E. O., *J. Am. Chem. Soc.*, **65**, 389(1943).
37. Swarts, F., *Bull. soc. chim. France*, (3), **13**, 992(1895).
38. Swarts, F., *Bull. soc. chim. France*, (3), **15**, 1135(1896).
39. Swarts, F., *Bull. acad. roy. Belg.*, (3), **35**, 532(1898).
40. Swarts, F., *Bull. acad. roy. Belg.*, (3), **35**, 849(1898).
41. Swarts, F., *Mem. couronnes acad. roy. Belg.*, **61**, 94(1901).

42. Swarts, F., *Bull. acad. roy. Belg.*, **1907**, 339.
43. Swarts, F., *Rec. trav. chim.*, **27**, 128(1908).
44. Swarts, F., *Bull. acad. roy. Belg.*, **8**, 343(1922).
45. Theobold, C. W., U. S. Patent 2,378,048(1945).
46. Tiers, G. V. D., *J. Am. Chem. Soc.*, **77**, 6703(1955).
47. Tinker, J. M., U. S. Patent 2,257,868(1941).
48. Truce, W. E., *J. Am. Chem. Soc.*, **70**, 2828(1948).
49. Young, J. A., and Tarrant, P., *J. Am. Chem. Soc.*, **71**, 2432(1949).

CHAPTER IX

Esters

TABLE OF CONTENTS

		PAGE
Introduction		230
Method Number		
901	Reaction of Acyl Halides with Alcohols	230
902	Reaction of Acids or Acid Salts with Alcohols	231
903	Reaction of Anhydrides with Alcohols	232
904	Addition of Acids to Alkenes and Alkynes	232
905	Interaction of Carboxylic Acid Salts and Haloalkanes	233
906	Hydrolysis of α,α-Difluoroethers	234
907	Malonic Ester Synthesis	234
908	Claisen Condensation	235
909	Reformatsky Synthesis	236
910	Reaction of Diazo Compounds with Acids and Alcohols	237
911	Transesterification	237
912	Codimerization of Olefins and Unsaturated Esters	238
913	Alcoholysis of Triazines	238
914	Reaction of Grignard Reagents with Alkyl Carbonates	238
915	Reaction of Aldehydes or Aldehyde Hydrates with Anhydrides	238
916	Reaction of Esters and Dimethylsulfone	238
TABLE 24	Monoesters	239
TABLE 25	Diesters and Triesters	246
TABLE 26	Unsaturated Monoesters	250
TABLE 27	Unsaturated Diesters	252

TABLE 28 Hydroxyesters 253
TABLE 29 Ketoesters 254
Bibliography 255

INTRODUCTION

Fluorine-containing esters may be readily prepared by a variety of reactions. The esterification of highly fluorinated alcohols presents a more difficult problem due to their acidic nature. This problem can be circumvented by employing several techniques described later in this Chapter.

The esters of both fluorine-containing acids and fluorine-containing alcohols have received some attention for possible application for specialty lubricating oils and hydraulic fluids. Acrylic esters of fluoroalcohols find use as monomers for the preparation of high temperature, solvent resistant elastomers (Minnesota Mining and Manufacturing Company). Polyesters derived from fluorinated glycols show promise as specialty rubbers which exhibit good thermal and oil resistance (Hooker Electrochemical Company).

METHOD 901 Reaction of Acyl Halides with Alcohols

The preparation of fluorine-containing esters by the reaction of an acyl halide with an alcohol can be treated by three possible cases; first the reaction of a fluoroacyl halide and a hydrocarbon alcohol, second, the esterification of a fluoroalcohol with a hydrocarbon acyl halide, and third, the case in which both reactants contain fluorine. The use of acyl halides has been widespread because early attempts at direct esterification resulted in low yields of ester when fluorinated alcohols were reacted with carboxylic acids. This was believed to be due to the highly acidic nature of the fluorinated alcohols. However, as indicated in Method 902, direct esterification of this combination can be accomplished in good yields. Not withstanding this development the acyl fluorides, chlorides and bromides have found considerable application for the preparation of esters. The following will serve only to demonstrate the types and yields of esters prepared by this reaction:

$$C_3F_7COCl + CH_3OH \xrightarrow[89\%]{} C_3F_7CO_2CH_3$$ [33,100]

$$C_3H_7COCl + CF_3CH_2OH \xrightarrow[71\%]{} C_3H_7CO_2CH_2CF_3$$ [41]

$$[(CH_2)_4COCl]_2 + C_3F_7CH_2OH \xrightarrow[75\%]{} [(CH_2)_4CO_2CH_2C_3F_7]_2$$ [41]

$$CH_2{=}CHCOCl + C_5F_{11}CH_2OH \xrightarrow[84\%]{} CH_2{=}CHCO_2CH_2C_5F_{11}$$ [3]

$$C_{17}F_{15}COCl + C_3F_7CH_2OH \xrightarrow[100\%]{} C_{17}F_{15}CO_2CH_2C_3F_7$$ [55]

$$C_3F_7COCl + CF_2(CF_2CH_2OH)_2 \xrightarrow[62\%]{} (C_3F_7CO_2CH_2CF_2)_2CF_2$$ [55]

The preparation of the esters of perfluorinated dibasic acids via the diacyl halide is not employed due to the difficulty of preparation and purification of the somewhat unstable diacyl halides.

METHOD 902 Reaction of Acids or Acid Salts with Alcohols

The direct esterification of an acid or its salt is the most useful and versatile procedure for the preparation of fluorine-containing esters. This procedure has now been shown to be generally applicable. Numerous catalysts have been employed among which are hydrogen chloride, concentrated sulfuric acid, fluorosulfonic acid and *p*-toluenesulfonic acid. It was formerly thought that the direct esterification of the α,α-dihydroperfluoroalcohols did not proceed very readily. More recently, however, Faurote and coworkers[35,36] have shown that concentrated sulfuric acid is an excellent catalyst for the direct esterification of highly fluorinated alcohols with hydrocarbon carboxylic acids.

Concentrated sulfuric acid proved superior to *p*-toluenesulfonic acid because of the higher rate of esterification and ease of purification of the desired ester. It is reported that the sulfonic acids form thermally and hydrolytically stable sulfonate esters which make purification of the products difficult.

Another catalyst found to be most useful in promoting esterification is trifluoroacetic anhydride. The use of trifluoroacetic anhydride in the preparation of esters of phenol is well known. Ahlbrecht, *et al.*[2] applied this technique to the esterification of 1,1-dihydroheptafluorobutanol with acrylic acid:

$$CH_2{=}CHCO_2H + C_3F_7CH_2OH + (CF_3CO)_2O \xrightarrow[85\text{-}90\%]{} CH_2{=}CHCO_2CH_2C_3F_7$$

Otherwise, acrylic anhydride or acrylyl chloride are needed to effect this esterification. As observed by other investigators, only a single ester was obtained and no trifluoroacetyl esters were isolated.

Direct esterification can also be effected if the water is removed as it is formed. In this procedure chloroform has been found useful to azeotrope the water from the reaction.[14] This was observed to work only when a fluorocarboxylic acid is esterified with a hydrocarbon alcohol; upon substitution of a fluorine-containing alcohol, no ester was obtained. Benzene and other solvents may also be used as azeotroping agents.[8,40]

The reaction of a carboxylic acid salt with an alcohol may also be considered to be direct esterification. The ethyl ester of trifluoroacetic acid is formed when the sodium or silver salt is treated with ethanol in sulfuric acid.[43,122,125] No esters of fluorocarboxylic acids have been prepared by the ammonium salt method described by Filachione,[37] although hydrocarbon esters can be readily prepared in this manner.

METHOD 903 Reaction of Anhydrides with Alcohols

The role of trifluoroacetic anhydride as a direct esterification promoter is mentioned in the previous method. It may also be used to esterify alcohols directly in the same fashion as acetic anhydride. For example:

$$(CF_3CO)_2O + HOCH_2CHClCO_2C_2H_5 \xrightarrow[91\%]{0^\circ} CF_3CO_2CH_2CHClCO_2C_2H_5 \quad {}^{32}$$

Acetic anhydride may also be used to acetylate fluoroalcohols in good yields:

$$(CH_3CO)_2O + C_2F_5CHOHCH_3 \xrightarrow[61\%]{} CH_3CO_2CH(CH_3)C_2F_5 \quad {}^{85}$$

The cyclic anhydrides of fluorine-containing dibasic acids have been used with limited success in making diesters. Hauptschein and coworkers[55] report the following reaction:

$$\overline{OC(CF_2)_3COO} + C_3F_7CH_2OH \longrightarrow C_3F_7CH_2O_2C(CF_2)_3CO_2H \ (26\%)$$
$$+$$
$$C_3F_7CH_2O_2C(CF_2)_3CO_2CH_2C_3F_7 \ (59\%)$$

METHOD 904 Addition of Acids to Alkenes and Alkynes

A most useful synthesis of vinyl esters is found in the addition of perfluoromonocarboxylic acids to acetylene. Howk, *et al.*[73] first described the synthesis of vinyl trifluoroacetate by the liquid phase addition of trifluoroacetic acid to acetylene in the presence of mercuric oxide, mercuric sulfate and hydroquinone. This same reaction is reported by Dickey[31] to occur when mercuric oxide and oleum are used. Coover, Stanin and Dickey[26A] prepared vinyl esters by the vapor-phase addition using either zinc or cadmium oxide as catalysts.

Reid[114] was successful in adding a number of perfluorocarboxylic acids to acetylene in the liquid phase using catalytic amounts of mercuric oxide and phosphorus pentoxide. The reaction is deleteriously affected by the presence of water. Although yields of esters in excess of 70 percent were obtained, the phosphorus pentoxide formed undesirable solid products. It was demonstrated that anhydrides of the perfluorocarboxylic acids could be employed as water scavengers, in this reaction, with excellent results. In the cases where the anhydride of the acid to be added was not available trifluoroacetic anhydride could be substituted:[115]

$$C_2F_5CO_2H + CH{\equiv}CH + HgO + (C_2F_5CO)_2O \xrightarrow[61\%]{} C_2F_5CO_2CH{=}CH_2$$

$$C_4F_9CO_2H + CH{\equiv}CH + HgO + (C_4F_9CO)_2O \xrightarrow[73\%]{} C_4F_9CO_2CH{=}CH_2$$

$$C_9F_{19}CO_2H + CH{\equiv}CH + HgO + (CF_3CO)_2O \xrightarrow[38\%]{} C_9F_{19}CO_2CH{=}CH_2$$

$$\overline{CF_2(CF_2)_4CF}CO_2H + CH{\equiv}CH + HgO + (CF_3CO)_2O \xrightarrow[56\%]{} \overline{CF_2(CF_2)_4CF}CO_2CH{=}CH_2$$

Joullie[80] reports that the addition of trifluoroacetic acid to isobutylene proceeds spontaneously at 50° with the evolution of heat to yield 75 percent of the *t*-butyl trifluoroacetate.

The addition of acetic acid to hexafluoro-2-butyne has been reported by Henne, *et al.*[65] to yield both mono- and diesters as well as other byproducts:

$$CF_3C{\equiv}CCF_3 + CH_3CO_2H + CH_3CO_2Na + (CH_3CO)_2O \longrightarrow CH_3CO_2\overset{\displaystyle CF_3}{\overset{|}{C}}{=}CHCF_3 + (CH_3CO_2)_2\overset{\displaystyle CF_3}{\overset{|}{C}}CH_2CF_3$$

METHOD 905 Interaction of Carboxylic Acid Salts and Haloalkanes

The interaction of a silver salt of a perfluorocarboxylic acid and an alkyl halide in a suitable solvent gives good yields of the ester. Filler, *et al.*[40] reacted silver perfluorobutyrate with a number of α,ω-polymethylene diiodides in Freon 113 and obtained the diesters in 80 percent yields. This procedure is also applicable to the preparation of *t*-butyl heptafluorobutyrate from the reaction of silver heptafluorobutyrate and *t*-butyl chloride.[100]

Pierce and co-workers[108] refluxed $C_3F_7CH_2CH_2Br$ with sodium acetate in glacial acetic acid and obtained 35 percent of the amylacetate.

It would appear that this would be a method for the synthesis of completely fluorinated esters which are not known to exist. However, Hauptschein and Grosse[54A] found that upon heating $C_3F_7CO_2Ag$ and C_3F_7I at 275° to 335° only n-C_6F_{14} was obtained (cf. Method 207).

METHOD 906 Hydrolysis of α,α-Difluoroethers

Swarts[123A] first reported that the acid hydrolysis of α,α-difluoroethers resulted in the formation of acids (cf. Method 709). A synthesis of fluorine-containing esters was described by Young and Tarrant[137] and also involves the hydrolysis of an α,α-difluoroether with concentrated sulfuric acid. Examples of this reaction are as follows:

$$CHClFCF_2OCH_3 + H_2SO_4 \xrightarrow[55\%]{} CHClFCO_2CH_3$$

$$CHClFCF_2OC_2H_5 + H_2SO_4 \xrightarrow[83\%]{} CHClFCO_2C_2H_5$$

$$CHClFCF_2OC_3H_7 + H_2SO_4 \xrightarrow[60\%]{} CHClFCO_2C_3H_7$$

$$CHF_2CF_2OC_2H_5 + H_2SO_4 \xrightarrow[60\%]{} CHF_2CO_2C_2H_5$$

The reaction is usually carried out at 0° to 15° and powdered glass may be added to facilitate the removal of the hydrogen fluoride formed.

Other α,α-difluoroethers have been shown to undergo this hydrolysis at slightly higher temperatures:

$$CF_3CHFCF_2OCH_3 + H_2SO_4 \xrightarrow[66\%]{60\text{–}65^\circ} CF_3CHFCO_2CH_3$$ [83]

$$CF_3CHFCF_2OC_2H_5 + H_2SO_4 \xrightarrow[60\%]{60\text{–}65^\circ} CF_3CHFCO_2C_2H_5$$ [83]

The basic alcoholysis of α,α-difluoroethers of the type CH_2ClCF_2OR, $CHCl_2CF_2OR$ and $CHClFCF_2OR$ has been shown by Tarrant and coworkers[132] to yield the orthoesters:

$$CHCl_2CF_2OC_2H_5 + C_2H_5OH + KOH \longrightarrow CHCl_2C(OC_2H_5)_3$$

$$CHClFCF_2OC_2H_5 + C_2H_5OH + KOH \longrightarrow CHClFC(OC_2H_5)_3$$

When this reaction was carried out at higher temperatures or when the products were allowed to stand in the presence of water, the acetates were formed, except in the case of $CHClFCF_2OC_2H_5$ where the resulting orthoester $CHClFC(OC_2H_5)_3$ was isolated. No ethyl chlorofluoroacetate was formed in the latter case. McBee and Filler[84] have also reported that the reaction of $CF_3CCl{=}CF_2$ with sodium ethylate in ethanol results in a 35 percent yield of $CF_3CHClCO_2C_2H_5$.

METHOD 907 Malonic Ester Synthesis

The malonic ester synthesis has been employed for the preparation of a number of ω-fluoroalkylmalonic esters. The reaction is carried out by treating the malonic ester with the desired chlorofluoro- or bromofluoroalkane in an alcoholic solution of sodium ethoxide. Bruce, *et al.*[16] condensed 1-bromo-3-fluoropropane and 1-chloro-5-fluoropentane with alkyl malonic esters and obtained yields of 24 to 46 percent. Attempts to condense CH_2FCH_2Cl, CH_2FCH_2Br, $CHClF_2$, C_3F_7I and $CH_3CF_2CH_2Cl$ under the same conditions gave either an intractable mixture or an incomplete reaction. Hoffmann[70] had earlier described the condensation of $F(CH_2)_3Br$ or $F(CH_2)_5Br$ with diethyl malonate to give 52 to 75 percent yields of the ω-fluoroalkylmalonates. In addition, $F(CH_2)_3Br$ was successfully condensed with ethyl acetoacetate. Henne and Latif[61] were successful in condensing $CF_3CCl{=}CClCF_3$ with the sodium derivative of diethyl malonate to obtain

$$CF_3CCl{=}\overset{\displaystyle CF_3}{\overset{|}{C}}CH(CO_2C_2H_5)_2.$$

METHOD 908 Claisen Condensation

The Claisen condensation of the esters of fluorine-containing carboxylic acids has found wide application in the preparation of β-ketoesters which are one of the important precursors to fluoroketones (cf. Method 601). The procedures employed for carrying out this reaction are generally those of a conventional base catalyzed condensation. Various reagents have been employed, namely sodium, sodium hydride and sodium alkoxides.

Swarts[127] first reported the preparation of ethyl γ,γ,γ-trifluoroacetoacetate by the condensation of ethyl acetate and ethyl trifluoroacetate in the presence of sodium ethoxide. Later this procedure was applied to the preparation of ethyl γ,γ-difluoroacetoacetate.[30,62]

The use of sodium ethoxide for the self-condensation of ethyl difluoroacetate, however, has not been found to be successful. McBee, *et al.*[89] in studying the Claisen condensation of fluorine-containing esters found sodium hydride to be effective for this condensation. Using sodium hydride, fluorine-containing acetoacetic esters were prepared in good yields. The effectiveness of sodium hydride is attributed to the irreversability of the first step of the reaction, namely, the conversion of the ester to a carbanion. The following example indicate the applicability and selectivity of this procedure:

$$CHF_2CO_2C_2H_5 + CH_2FCO_2C_2H_5 + NaH \xrightarrow[68\%]{30^\circ} CHF_2COCHFCO_2C_2H_5$$

$$CHF_2CO_2C_2H_5 + CHF_2CO_2C_2H_5 + NaH \xrightarrow[81\%]{70^\circ} CHF_2COCF_2CO_2C_2H_5$$

$$CF_3CO_2C_2H_5 + CH_3CO_2C_2H_5 + NaH \xrightarrow[84\%]{50^\circ} CF_3COCH_2CO_2C_2H_5$$

$$CF_3CO_2C_2H_5 + CH_2FCO_2C_2H_5 + NaH \xrightarrow[86\%]{50^\circ} CF_3COCHFCO_2C_2H_5$$

$$CF_3CO_2C_2H_5 + CHF_2CO_2C_2H_5 + NaH \xrightarrow[20\%]{75^\circ} CF_3COCF_2CO_2C_2H_5$$

In the first example, the selectivity of the reaction was attributed to the fact that the reaction was conducted at a temperature lower than that at which the ethyl difluoroacetate condenses with itself. In the case of the last example, an improved yield (65%) of the pentafluoroacetoacetic ester was obtained when the butyl esters were employed at a reaction temperature of 90°; the product was isolated as the hemi-ketal.

The condensation of ethyl fluoroacetate with diethyl oxalate has been effected using sodium ethoxide:[10,11,12,116]

$$(CO_2C_2H_5)_2 + CH_2FCO_2C_2H_5 + C_2H_5ONa \xrightarrow[55-67\%]{} C_2H_5O_2CCOCHFCO_2C_2H_5 \quad ^{12,116}$$

METHOD 909 Reformatsky Synthesis

The Reformatsky reaction has been extended by McBee and co-workers[91] to include the use of ethyl bromofluoroacetate for the preparation of α-fluoro-β-hydroxyesters. These workers report that although the reaction is more sluggish than when ethyl bromoacetate is employed, the yields of hydroxy esters are comparable and of the order of 40 to 80 percent. The reaction is carried out in xylene or toluene and does not require any special treatment of the zinc for activation and no other catalyst is required.

The reaction of both ethyl bromoacetate and ethyl bromofluoroacetate has successfully been carried out with a number of ketones and aldehydes:

$$CF_3CHO + CH_2BrCO_2C_2H_5 + Zn \xrightarrow[87\%]{} CF_3CHOHCH_2CO_2C_2H_5 \quad ^{93}$$

$$(C_3F_7)_2CO + CH_2BrCO_2C_2H_5 + Zn \xrightarrow[44\%]{} C_3F_7COH(C_3F_7)CH_2CO_2C_2H_5 \quad ^{91}$$

$$n\text{-}C_6H_{13}CHO + CHBrFCO_2C_2H_5 + Zn \xrightarrow[50\%]{} C_6H_{13}CHOHCHFCO_2C_2H_5 \quad ^{91}$$

$$n\text{-}C_7F_{15}CHO + CHBrFCO_2C_2H_5 + Zn \xrightarrow[61\%]{} C_7F_{15}CHOHCHFCO_2C_2H_5 \quad ^{91}$$

$$(CH_3)_3CCHO + CHBrFCO_2C_2H_5 + Zn \xrightarrow[39\%]{} (CH_3)_3CCHOHCHFCO_2C_2H_5 \quad ^{91}$$

$$C_2H_5O_2CCOCHFCO_2C_2H_5 + CH_2BrCO_2C_2H_5 + Zn \xrightarrow[12\%]{} C_2H_5O_2CCHFCOH(CO_2C_2H_5)CH_2CO_2C_2H_5 \quad ^{116}$$

Ethyl bromofluoroacetate gives poor results in condensations with perfluorinated ketones; fair yields of hydroxy esters are obtained when ethyl bromoacetate is used.

METHOD 910 Reaction of Diazo Compounds with Acids and Alcohols

Various diazo compounds have been used in the preparation of selected fluorine-containing esters. Brown and Musgrave[15] effected the Wolff rearrangement in the preparation of ethyl β,β,β-trifluoropropionate:

$$CF_3COCHN_2 + C_2H_5OH + Ag_2O \xrightarrow[40\%]{} CF_3CH_2CO_2C_2H_5$$

More recently Park[105] has studied the Arndt-Eistert reaction with $C_3F_7CO_2H$, $C_3F_7CH_2CO_2H$ and $C_3F_7CH_2CH_2CO_2H$. The diazoketone derived from $C_3F_7CO_2H$ failed to undergo the Wolff rearrangement. Small amounts of $C_3F_7CH_2CH_2CO_2CH_3$ were obtained from the rearrangement of the diazoketone prepared from $C_3F_7CH_2CO_2H$. However, the diazoketone derived from $C_3F_7CH_2CH_2CO_2H$ rearranged in a normal fashion. It was therefore concluded that perfluorinated acids of four carbon atoms or more fail to undergo the Arndt-Eistert reaction and two methylene groups must separate the perfluoroalkyl group from the carbonyl function before good yields are obtained. In all cases it was observed that the diazoketone apparently formed, but the Wolff rearrangement failed to take place in every case.

Buckle and Saunders[18] used diazoesters and diazomethylketones to prepare alkoxy esters:

$$N_2CHCO_2C_2H_5 + CH_2FCH_2OH + Ag_2O \longrightarrow CH_2FCH_2OCH_2CO_2C_2H_5 \; [18]$$

$$CH_2FCH_2O(CH_2)_2COCHN_2 + C_2H_5OH + Ag_2O \longrightarrow CH_2FCH_2O(CH_2)_3CO_2C_2H_5 \; [29]$$

The reaction of diazomethane with fluorine-containing carboxylic acids also yields the expected methyl esters:

$$CF_2(CO_2H)_2 + CH_2N_2 \xrightarrow[81\%]{} CF_2(CO_2CH_3)_2 \; [51,58]$$

$$CH_2FCOCO_2H + CH_2N_2 \xrightarrow[60\%]{} CH_2FCOCO_2CH_3 \; [12]$$

METHOD 911 Transesterification

$$R_fCO_2R + R'OH + p\text{-}CH_3\phi SO_2Cl \longrightarrow R_fCO_2R' + ROH$$

Transesterification has been applied to the preparation of fluorocarboxylic acid esters of higher alcohols. The procedure is generally the same as that employed in conventional acid catalyzed transesterifications. *Para*-toluenesulfonic acid or phosphoric acid may be used as a catalyst and the lower boiling alcohol is distilled from the reaction to drive it to completion.[4,28,57,72,137]

METHOD 912 Codimerization of Olefins and Unsaturated Esters

$$CF_2 = CF_2 + CH_2 = CHCO_2CH_3 \rightarrow \overline{CF_2CF_2CH_2CHCO_2CH_3}\ ^{7,24}$$

(cf. Method 210)

METHOD 913 Alcoholysis of Triazines

$$+ ROH + HCl/H_2O \rightarrow CF_3CO_2R$$

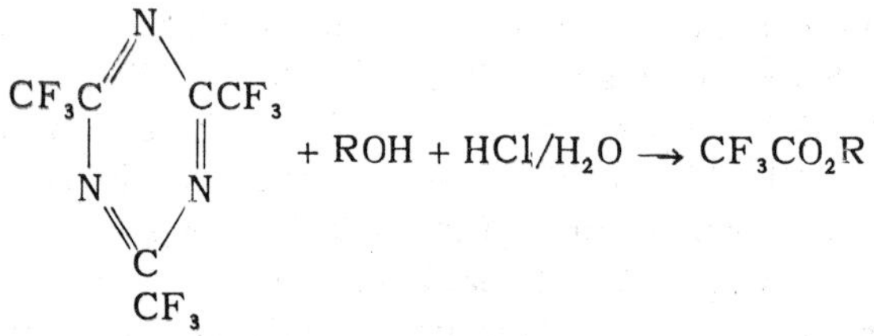

A unique method for the preparation of esters of trifluoroacetic acid is described by Norton.[102] It involves the hydrolysis of 2,4,6-tris(trifluoromethyl)-1,3,5-triazine with dilute mineral acid in the presence of an alcohol. Trifluoroacetic acid can also be prepared by this general method (cf. Method 710). The procedure is also adaptable to the preparation of difluoroacetic esters from the 2,4,6-tris(difluoromethyl)-1,3,5-triazine.[63]

METHOD 914 Reaction of Grignard Reagents with Alkyl Carbonates

$$CF_3CH_2CH_2MgX + (RO)_2CO \rightarrow CF_3CH_2CH_2CO_2R$$

Low yields of esters are obtained by the reaction of a fluorine-containing Grignard reagent with alkyl carbonates.[86] The reaction is further complicated by the formation of ketones and other by-products.

METHOD 915 Reaction of Aldehydes or Aldehyde Hydrates with Anhydrides

$$R_fCHO + (RCO)_2O \xrightarrow{H_2SO_4} R_fCH(O_2CR)_2$$

The diesters of fluorine-containing *gem* diols can be prepared by reaction of the fluoroaldehyde or its hydrate with an acid anhydride in the presence of a trace of sulfuric acid.[74] Pyridine has also been employed as a catalyst to promote this reaction.[75] No attempts have been reported in which a fluorine-containing acid anhydride was used.

METHOD 916 Reaction of Esters and Dimethylsulfone

$$R_fCO_2CH_3 + (CH_3)_2SO_2 \rightarrow R_fC(OCH_3)_3$$

This procedure is described by Holm[71] as a general procedure for the preparation of ortho esters of perfluorinated carboxylic acids.

TABLE 24

MONOESTERS

Empirical Formula	Structural Formula	Method	Yield %	B.p. °C/mm.	F.p. or M.p. °C	n_D^t	d_4^t	t°C	Ref.
$C_3H_3Cl_2FO_2$	$CFCl_2CO_2CH_3$	107		116–116.5					47
$C_3H_3F_3O_2$	$CF_3CO_2CH_3$			43–43.5					47
$C_3H_4ClFO_2$	$CHClFCO_2CH_3$	203	50	110–111					47
		906	55	116		1.3903	1.323	25	137
	$ClCO_2CH_2CH_2F$	901	81	129–131		1.4020	1.3620	20	82,104
$C_3H_4F_2O_2$	$CHF_2CO_2CH_3$	101	18	85–86					46
$C_3H_5FO_2$	$CH_2FCO_2CH_3$	101	43–90	104.5		1.3679	1.1744	20	46,103,118
		102		104.5			1.16126	15	131
		104		104					112
$C_4F_6O_2$	$OCF_2CF_2CF_2CO$	208	44–56	18	−59		1.6646	−32.4	56
$C_4H_2F_6O_2$	$CF_3CO_2CH_2CF_3$	404		55	−65.5	1.2812	1.4725	18	129
$C_4H_3F_5O_2$	$CF_3CF_2CO_2CH_3$	901		59.3–59.8/742		1.2869	1.390(20)	25	100
		902	70–85	61/739		1.2884	1.393	20	52,76
$C_4H_4F_4O_2$	$CHF_2CF_2CO_2CH_3$			93–94/754		1.3152		29	59
	$CF_3CHFCO_2CH_3$	906	65.5	96		1.3192	1.353	20	83
$C_4H_5Br_2FO_2$	$CFBr_2CO_2C_2H_5$	902		173			1.7709	30	120
	$CH_2BrCBrFCO_2CH_3$	104	24	76–78/9		1.4885	1.99	27	59
$C_4H_5BrClFO_2$	$CBrClFCO_2C_2H_5$	102		151					131
$C_4H_5ClF_2O$	$CF_2ClCO_2C_2H_5$	901, 902		97			1.252	22.8	112,123
$C_4H_5Cl_2FO_2$	$CFCl_2CO_2C_2H_5$			130					130
$C_4H_5F_3O_2$	$CF_3CO_2C_2H_5$	404	12	55–56/741		1.2772	1.464	20	75
		901		77.8		1.3219	1.3058	16	129
		902	73–90	60–62			1.1952	16.7	43,113,125
		913	92.5						102
				60.5		1.3093		15	62

TABLE 24 (*continued*)

Empirical Formula	Structural Formula	Method	Yield %	B.p. °C/mm.	F.p. or M.p. °C	n_D^t	d_4^t	t°C	Ref.
$C_4H_5F_3O_2$	$CH_3CO_2CH_2CF_3$	901		78		1.3202		20	63
$C_4H_6BrFO_2$	$CHBrFCO_2C_2H_5$	901		154		1.55866		17	121
	$CH_2FCO_2CH_2CH_2Br$	901		115–122/75					37
	$CH_2BrCO_2CH_2CH_2F$	901	50	87–90/12		1.4530	1.659	20	82
	$CH_2BrCHFCO_2CH_3$	104	56	92–94/80		1.4389	1.624	30	59
$C_4H_6ClFO_2$	$CHClFCO_2C_2H_5$	906	65–83	128		1.3927	1.225	25	34,137
	$CH_2FCO_2CH_2CH_2Cl$	901	77	178–179	−8.7		1.3230	20	119
	$CH_2ClCO_2CH_2CH_2F$	901	30–93	78–79/15		1.3900	1.4065	20	82,119
$C_4H_6F_2O_2$	$CHF_2CO_2C_2H_5$	902		70–70.5/28		1.4059	1.2418	20	30,99,121
		906	60						138
	$CH_3CO_2CH_2CHF_2$	901		106–106.5					63
	$CH_2FCO_2CH_2CH_2F$	104	25	78–80/35		1.3900	1.2862	20	82
		901	77	90.5–91/58	−25.4		1.2906	20	99,119
		902		146–147					47
$C_4H_6FIO_2$	$CHFICO_2C_2H_5$	204		180			1.6716	11	121
	$CH_2ICO_2CH_2CH_2F$	901	40	99–105/15		1.5080	1.991	20	82
$C_4H_7FO_2$	$CH_2FCO_2C_2H_5$	101	14–75	117–118					4,8,46, 103,118
		105		126					112
		901							99
	$CH_3CO_2CH_2CH_2F$	101	50	117–118					46
		102		119.3/753		1.37792	1.0982	20	124
		901	52	115–116		1.382	1.090	20	82,104
	$CH_2FCH_2CO_2CH_3$	902		117–118					48
	$CH_3CHFCO_2CH_3$	101	50	106.5–108.5					46,118
$C_5H_3F_7O_2$	$CF_3CF_2CF_2CO_2CH_3$	901	89	80	−86	1.293	1.483	20	33,100
$C_5H_5Br_2F_3O_2$	$CF_2BrCFBrCO_2C_2H_5$	902	45	178/622	Glass	1.4309	1.898	20	107
	$CF_3CBr(CH_2Br)CO_2CH_3$	202	71	89–90/32		1.4461		20	19

$C_5H_5Cl_2F_3O_2$	$CF_2ClCFClCO_2C_2H_5$	901		142	1.3830	1.405	23	21,22
		902		138–139/630	1.3827		20	107
$C_5H_5Cl_3F_2O_2$	$CF_2ClCCl_2CO_2C_2H_5$	901		172.5	1.4188	1.460	23	21,22
$C_5H_5F_5O_2$	$CF_3CF_2CO_2C_2H_5$	901		75–76/738	1.2990	1.294(20)	25	100
		902	60–80	75–75.6/738.5	1.2988	1.299(20)	25	52,76,85
$C_5H_6ClF_3O_2$	$CF_3CHClCO_2C_2H_5$	906	35	128–129	1.3635	1.322	20	84
	$CF_3CH(CH_2Cl)CO_2CH_3$	202		126–130	1.3690		13	19
$C_5H_6F_4O_2$	$CF_3CHFCO_2C_2H_5$	906	60	108–109	1.3260	1.289	20	83
$C_5H_6F_3IO_2$	$CF_3CH_2CHICO_2CH_3$	205		82/42	1.440		20	53
$C_5H_7F_3O_2$	$CF_3CO_2CH_2CH_2CH_3$	913	89	82.5	1.3233	1.1285 (25)	22.5	102
	$CF_3CO_2CH(CH_3)_2$	913	80	73.5	1.3165	1.077(25)	24	102
	$CF_3CH_2CO_2C_2H_5$	910	40	50/12	1.3912		24	15
	$CF_3CH_2CH_2CO_2CH_3$	914	27	113	1.3450		25	86
	$CF_3CH(CH_3)CO_2CH_3$	212, 902		100–102	1.3370		20	19
	$CH_3CO_2CH_2CH_2CF_3$	901		112.8–113	1.3410	1.219	20	63
	$CH_3CO_2CH(CH_3)CF_3$	901		85.6	1.3314	1.1823	15	63,128
		903		87				60
	$CH_2FCO_2CH(CH_2F)_2$	104	15	121/5	1.4295	1.414	20	82
$C_5H_7F_2IO_2$	$CH_2ICO_2CH(CH_2F)_2$	901	80	113–115/5	1.518	1.907	20	82
$C_5H_8ClFO_2$	$CHClFCO_2CH_2CH_2CH_3$	906	66	147	1.3994	1.170	25	137
$C_5H_8F_2O_2$	$CH_2FCO_2CH(CH_3)CH_2F$	104	40	166–168	1.398	1.202	20	82
$C_5H_8FIO_2$	$CH_2ICO_2CH(CH_3)CH_2F$	901	60	100–104/15	1.4918	1.7800	20	82
$C_5H_9FO_2$	$CH_2FCO_2CH_2CH_2CH_3$	101	69	135–137				118
	$CH_2FCO_2CH(CH_3)_2$	101	42	124				118
	$CH_3CHFCO_2C_2H_5$	101	50	122.5–123				45,46
	$CH_2FCH_2CH_2CO_2CH_3$	902		135–137				48
	$(CH_3)_2CFCO_2CH_3$	102		108–109				118
	$CH_3CO_2CH_2CHFCH_3$	101	30	123–125				46
	$CH_3CO_2CH_2CH_2CH_2F$	101	40	137–138				46

TABLE 24 (*continued*)

Empirical Formula	Structural Formula	Method	Yield %	B.p. °C/mm.	F.p. or M.p. °C	n_D^t	d_4^t	t°C	Ref.
$C_5H_9F_3O_3$	$CF_3C(OCH_3)_3$	916		106	−53 to −55	1.3380		25	71
$C_6H_2F_{10}O_2$	$CF_3(CF_2)_2CO_2CH_2CF_3$	901		92/737		1.278	1.565	25	55
$C_6H_3F_9O_2$	$CF_3CF_2CF(CF_3)CO_2CH_3$			101–102					50
$C_6H_5ClF_4O_2$	$CF_2CF_2CH_2CClCO_2CH_3$ (ring)	912	21	56.7/36		1.3850	1.4478	25	24
$C_6H_5F_7O_2$	$CF_3(CF_2)_2CO_2C_2H_5$	901	83	95/744		1.3032	1.394	20	100
	$CH_3CO_2CH_2(CF_2)_2CF_3$	903		105		1.3110	1.435	20	77
$C_6H_6F_4O_2$	$CH_3CO_2CHCH_2CF_2CF_2$ (ring)	912	27	138.5–139.5		1.3660	1.3310	25	7,24
$C_6H_7Br_2F_3O_2$	$CF_3CHBrCHBrCO_2C_2H_5$	202	85	90–92/15		1.4448	1.823(25)	20	94
$C_6H_7F_5O_2$	$C_2F_5CO_2CH(CH_3)_2$	902	45	86.5/741.5		1.3074	1.224	25	76
	$CH_3CO_2CH(CH_3)C_2F_5$	903	65	96		1.3220	1.229	20	85
$C_6H_8BrF_3O_2$	$CF_3CHBrCH_2CO_2C_2H_5$	202	80	98–99/100		1.3940		24.5	136
	$CF_3CH_2CHBrCO_2C_2H_5$	901	43	156–157		1.3962	1.524(20)	23	135
$C_6H_9F_3O_2$	$CF_3CO_2(CH_2)_3CH_3$	901		100.2		1.353	1.0268	22	1
	$CF_3CO_2C(CH_3)_3$	904	75	83		1.3300		25	80
	$CF_3CH_2CH_2CO_2C_2H_5$	212	86	126.5–127		1.3520		20	93
		914	31	127		1.3620		25	86
	$CH_3CO_2C(CH_3)_2CF_3$	901		94–95		1.3424	1.14	25	63
	$CH_3(CH_2)_2CO_2CH_2CF_3$	901	71.2	113/747		1.3452	1.137	25	41
$C_6H_9F_3O_3$	$CH_3OCH_2CH(CF_3)CO_2CH_3$			137–140					19
$C_6H_9F_5O_3$	$C_2F_5C(OCH_3)_3$	916		116		1.3289		25	71
$C_6H_{10}ClFO_2$	$CHClFCO_2(CH_2)_3CH_3$	911	70	165–166		1.4067	1.124	25	137
$C_6H_{10}F_2O_2$	$CHF_2CO_2(CH_2)_3CH_3$			136.5–137		1.3720		20	89
	$CH_3CH_2CF_2CO_2C_2H_5$	109	35	127–128		1.3665	1.082	20	68

$C_6H_{11}FO_2$	$CH_2FCO_2C(CH_3)_3$			129.5–131		1.386	0.9904	20	12
	$CH_3CH_2CHFCO_2C_2H_5$	102		138–141					13
$C_6H_{11}FO_2$	$CH_3CO_2(CH_2)_3CH_2F$	101	55	55.5–56/11					46
$C_6H_{11}FO_3$	$CH_2FCH_2OCH_2CO_2C_2H_5$	910		81/21					18
$C_7H_3F_{11}O_2$	$CF_3(CF_2)_4CO_2CH_3$	901		122		1.297	1.618	29	33
$C_7H_5F_9O_2$	$CF_3(CF_2)_3CO_2C_2H_5$			110/627		1.3060		20	106
$C_7H_7F_7O_2$	$CF_3(CF_2)_2CO_2CH(CH_3)_2$	901		106/739	−84 to −90	1.310	1.324	20	33,100
	$CH_3CO_2CH_2CH_2(CF_2)_2CF_3$	905	35	137–137.5		1.3276		20	108
$C_7H_8F_4O_2$	$CF_2CF_2CH_2C(CH_3)CO_2CH_3$	912	64	70/56		1.3656	1.28890	25	7,24
$C_7H_9F_7O_3$	$CF_3(CF_2)_2C(OCH_3)_3$	916		142		1.3207		25	71
$C_7H_{11}F_3O_2$	$CH_3CO_2CH(CF_3)CH_2CH_2CH_3$	901	85	119–124/744		1.3587		20	20
		903		112					60
$C_7H_{13}FO_2$	$CH_2F(CH_2)_3CO_2C_2H_5$	102		56–60/16					17
$C_7H_{13}FO_3$	$CH_2FCH_2OCH_2CH_2CO_2C_2H_5$	910	67	92/16					18
$C_8H_2F_{14}O_2$	$CF_3(CF_2)_2CO_2CH_2(CF_2)_2CF_3$	901		118–120		1.290	1.612	20	77
$C_8H_3F_{13}O_2$	$CF_3(CF_2)_5CO_2CH_3$	901		139		1.316		29	33
$C_8H_9F_7O_2$	$CF_3(CF_2)_2CH_2CH_2CO_2C_2H_5$	212	89	152–152.2		1.3360	1.342(25)	20	93
	$CF_3(CF_2)_2CO_2(CH_2)_3CH_3$	901		132/740		1.3249	1.296(20)	25	100
	$CF_3(CF_2)_2CO_2CH(CH_3)C_2H_5$	901		126/741		1.3212	1.284(20)	25	100
	$CF_3(CF_2)_2CO_2C(CH_3)_3$	901		116		1.318	1.280	20	33
		905		116/740	−92	1.318	1.278	20	100
$C_8H_{12}F_3NO_4$	$CH_3CO_2CH_2CH_2N(CH_2CF_3)O_2CCH_3$	903		79–80/1–2					27
$C_8H_{13}F_2NO_4$	$CH_3CO_2CH_2CH_2N(CH_2CHF_2)O_2CCH_3$	903		96–97/0.5					27
$C_8H_{13}F_3O_2$	$CF_3CO_2CH_2CH(CH_3)CH_2C_2H_5$	902		138–142					14
	$CH_3CH_2CH(CF_3)CH_2CO_2C_2H_5$		40	62–65/25		1.3750	1.110(25)	20	94
$C_8H_{14}BrFO_2$	$CH_2Br(CH_2)_4CO_2CH_2CH_2F$	902	53	142/13					17
$C_8H_{14}F_2O_2$	$CH_2F(CH_2)_4CO_2CH_2CH_2F$	102		103–105/14					17
$C_8H_{15}FO_2$	$CH_2F(CH_2)_4CO_2C_2H_5$	102	27	82–84/14					17

TABLE 24 (*continued*)

Empirical Formula	Structural Formula	Method	Yield %	B.p. °C/mm.	F.p. or M.p. °C	n_D^t	d_4^t	t°C	Ref.
$C_8H_{15}FO_3$	$CH_2FCO_2CH_2CH_2O(CH_2)_3CH_3$	911		95–100/5					57
	$CH_2FCH_2O(CH_2)_3CO_2C_2H_5$	910	28	99–100/12					18
$C_8H_{16}ClFO_3$	$CHClFC(OC_2H_5)_3$	906		67.5/10		1.4059	1.0815	25	132
$C_9H_3F_{13}O_3$	$CF_3(CF_2)_2CH_2O_2C(CF_2)_3CO_2H$	903	26	117/8		1.3285		22	55
$C_9H_3F_{15}O_2$	$CF_3(CF_2)_6CO_2CH_3$	901		158		1.304	1.684(20)	27	33
$C_9H_{10}F_7NO_4$	$CF_3(CF_2)_2CH(CH_2NO_2)CH_2CO_2C_2H_5$		64	96/5		1.3770		20	26
$C_9H_{11}F_7O_2$	$CF_3(CF_2)_2CO_2(CH_2)_4CH_3$	905	80	144/763		1.3334	1.2471	27	40
$C_9H_{13}F_3O_2$	$CH_3CO_2CH(CH_2)_3CH(CF_3)CH_2$ (ring: CH joined to CH_2)	902		192.5–194					126
$C_9H_{15}F_3O_2$	$CH_3CH(CH_3)CH(CF_3)CH_2CO_2C_2H_5$		40	98–99/65		1.3850	1.113(25)	20	94
$C_9H_{17}FO_3$	$CH_2F(CH_2)_2O(CH_2)_3CO_2C_2H_5$	910	10	110–111/14					18
$C_{10}H_{13}F_7O_2$	$CF_3(CF_2)_2CO_2(CH_2)_5CH_3$	903	76	74/20		1.3452	1.2315	20	35
$C_{10}H_{17}F_3O_2$	$CF_3CO_2CH(CH_3)(CH_2)_5CH_3$	901	71	78.5–79/20		1.3744	1.000	25	134
	$CH_3CO_2CH(CF_3)(CH_2)_5CH_3$	901	93	177.2–177.5		1.3800	1.041	20	20
$C_{10}H_{18}F_2O_2$	$CH_2F(CH_2)_6CO_2CH_2CH_2F$	102	21	128–130/13					17
$C_{10}H_{18}FIO_2$	$CH_2I(CH_2)_6CO_2CH_2CH_2F$	902	62.5	122–124/0.8					17
$C_{10}H_{19}FO_2$	$CH_2FCO_2CH_2CH(C_2H_5)(CH_2)_3CH_3$	911	80	65–68/2		1.4173		25	4,72
	$CH_2F(CH_2)_6CO_2C_2H_5$	102	70	191					17
$C_{11}H_3F_{19}O_2$	$CF_3(CF_2)_8CO_2CH_3$	901		193		1.308	1.760(20)	31	33
$C_{12}H_2F_{22}O_2$	$CF_3(CF_2)_6CO_2CH_2(CF_2)_2CF_3$	901	100	124		1.2875	1.6547	21.2	55
$C_{12}H_5F_{19}O_2$	$CH_3CO_2CH_2(CF_2)_8CF_3$			208		1.3189	1.709	20	77

$C_{12}H_9F_{15}O_2$	$CF_3(CF_2)_6CO_2(CH_2)_3CH_3$	902	93.2	96/20	−53	1.3246	1.5328	20	35
$C_{12}H_{17}F_7O_2$	$CF_3(CF_2)_2CO_2(CH_2)_7CH_3$	903		108/27		1.3582	1.185(20)	25	100
$C_{12}H_{22}BrFO_2$	$CH_2Br(CH_2)_8CO_2CH_2CH_2F$	902		184–188					17
$C_{12}H_{22}F_2O_2$	$CH_2F(CH_2)_8CO_2CH_2CH_2F$	102	17	145–149/12					17
$C_{12}H_{23}FO_2$	$CH_2F(CH_2)_8CO_2C_2H_5$	102	20	135–138/10					17
$C_{13}H_6F_{20}O_2$	$CH_3CO_2CH_2(CF_2)_9CF_2H$	903	81.6	134/20					35
$C_{13}H_{10}F_{16}O_2$	$CH_3(CH_2)_2CO_2CH_2(CF_2)_7CF_2H$	903	69.6	130/20		1.3368	1.5780	20	35
$C_{13}H_{25}FO_2$	$CH_2F(CH_2)_9CO_2C_2H_5$	102	81	140–141/11					17
$C_{14}H_{27}FO_2$	$CH_2FCO_2(CH_2)_{11}CH_3$	911		106–128/1		1.4317		25	4
	$CH_2F(CH_2)_{10}CO_2C_2H_5$	102	12	152–153/11					17
$C_{17}H_{18}F_{16}O_2$	$CH_3(CH_2)_4CH(C_2H_5)CO_2CH_2$-$(CF_2)_7CF_2H$	902	94	99/0.5	−18	1.3555	1.4384	20	35
$C_{17}H_{25}F_7O_2$	$CF_3(CF_2)_2CO_2(CH_2)_{11}CH_3$			158/23		1.3802	1.120(20)	25	100
$C_{20}H_{33}F_7O_2$	$CF_3(CF_2)_2CO_2(CH_2)_{15}CH_3$			208/31		1.3950	1.074(20)	25	100
$C_{22}H_{37}F_7O_2$	$CF_3(CF_2)_2CO_2(CH_2)_{17}CH_3$	902	93.1	144/0.5	12	1.4027	1.0560	20	35
				185/4		1.4020	1.0560	20	100

TABLE 25

DIESTERS AND TRIESTERS

Empirical Formula	Structural Formula	Method	Yield %	B.p. °C/mm.	F.p. or M.p. °C	n_D^t	d_4^t	t °C	Ref.
$C_5H_6F_2O_4$	$CF_2(CO_2CH_3)_2$	910		58–59/9	−35	1.3721	1.3059	20	58
		910	81	60–62/12					51
$C_5H_7FO_4$	$CHF(CO_2CH_3)_2$	101	40	80–82/12					46
$C_5H_8F_2O_3$	$(CH_2FCH_2O)_2CO$	901	45	95–98/16		1.3940	1.2552	20	82,104
$C_5H_9FO_3$	$CH_2FCH_2OCO_2C_2H_5$	902		56–57/14					18
$C_6H_6F_4O_4$	$(CF_2CO_2CH_3)_2$			173–176		1.3555		25	66
$C_6H_7F_3O_4$	$(CH_3CO_2)_2CHCF_3$	915		146–146.5/743.2		1.3530	1.291	20	74,75
$C_6H_8F_2O_4$	$(CHFCO_2CH_3)_2$	711	53	68–70/0.7					81
$C_7H_6F_6O_4$	$CF_2(CF_2CO_2CH_3)_2$	902	80	100–100.3/34	−31.8 to −33.6	1.3518	1.4856	20	67
$C_7H_7F_5O_4$	$(CH_3CO_2)_2CHC_2F_5$	915		157/743		1.346	1.361	20	74
$C_7H_8ClF_3O_4$	$CF_3CO_2CH_2CHClCO_2C_2H_5$	903	91	72–74/8–9					32
$C_7H_9F_3O_4$	$CH_3CO_2C(CH_3)(CF_3)O_2CCH_3$	902	91						19
$C_7H_{10}F_2O_4$	$CH_3O_2C(CH_2)_2CF_2CO_2CH_3$		70	65/12					6
$C_8H_6Cl_2F_6O_4$	$(CFClCF_2CO_2CH_3)_2$	910		155–158/2–4					51
$C_8H_7F_7O_4$	$(CH_3CO_2)_2CH(CF_2)_2CF_3$	915	75	165/743		1.3378	1.431	20	74,75
$C_8H_8F_6O_4$	$(CH_3CO_2)_2C(CF_3)CH_2CF_3$	904			97–97.8				65
$C_8H_{11}F_3O_4$	$CF_3C(O_2CCH_3)(CH_3)CO_2C_2H_5$	901	90	65–69/26		1.3669		20	19
$C_9H_7F_9O_4$	$CF_3CO_2CH(CF_3)CH_2CH(O_2CCF_3)CH_3$	903	75	158–160		1.3350		20	60
$C_9H_{10}F_6O_4$	$CF_2(CF_2CO_2C_2H_5)_2$	902	81–95	76–81/3–5		1.3585	1.3444(29)	20	64,66,88,97
	$(CF_3CO_2CH_2CH_2)_2CH_2$	902	81	75/4		1.3530	1.3286	25	40
$C_9H_{11}F_3O_6$	$CH_2FCO_2CH_2CH(O_2CCH_2F)CH_2O_2CCH_2F$	902		177–179/10					47
$C_9H_{13}F_3O_4$	$CH_3CO_2CH(CF_3)CH_2CH(O_2CCH_3)CH_3$	903	88	188–190		1.3809		20	60
$C_9H_{14}F_2O_4$	$C_2H_5O_2C(CH_2)_2CF_2CO_2C_2H_5$			127–128/28					6
$C_{10}H_{10}F_8O_4$	$(CF_2CF_2CO_2C_2H_5)_2$	902	72	215–219		1.4025	1.359(20)	29	96

$C_{10}H_{10}F_8O_4$				70–71/2–3		1.3541	1.4026(29)	20	88,97, 117, 133
$C_{10}H_{12}F_6O_4$	$(CH_2CH_2CO_2CH_2CF_3)_2$	901	68	70/0.6		1.3718	1.3316	25	41
$C_{10}H_{17}FO_4$	$CH_2F(CH_2)_2CH(CO_2C_2H_5)_2$	907	52	122/11		1.4176	1.0764	25	70
$C_{11}H_6F_{14}O_4$	$(CF_3CF_2CF_2CO_2CH_2)_2CH_2$	905	84	79/3.6		1.3225	1.5856	27.5	40
$C_{11}H_{10}F_{10}O_4$	$C_2H_5O_2CCF_2CF(CF_3)(CF_2)_2CO_2C_2H_5$	902			112–114	1.361		12	5
$C_{12}H_8F_{14}O_4$	$(CF_3CF_2CF_2CO_2CH_2CH_2)_2$	905	83	97/6.5		1.3288	1.5443	25	40
$C_{12}H_{14}F_8O_4$	$[CF_2CF_2CO_2CH(CH_3)_2]_2$	902		232–233/745					96
$C_{12}H_{15}F_7O_4$	$(CH_3CH_2CH_2CO_2)_2CH(CF_2)_2CF_3$	915		113/24		1.3626	1.269	20	74
$C_{12}H_{21}FO_4$	$CH_2F(CH_2)_4CH(CO_2C_2H_5)_2$	907	74	142/10		1.4237	1.0407	25	70
$C_{13}H_4F_{20}O_4$	$[CF_3(CF_2)_2CO_2CH_2CF_2]_2CF_2$	901	62	131/30		1.3140	1.7085	23	55
	$CF_2[CF_2CO_2CH_2(CF_2)_2CF_3]_2$	903	59	129/30		1.3142	1.7090	24	55
$C_{13}H_{10}F_{14}O_4$	$[CF_3(CF_2)_2CO_2(CH_2)_2]_2CH_2$	902	93	102/3.5		1.3350	1.5015	25	40
$C_{13}H_{18}F_6O_4$	$CF_2[CF_2CO_2(CH_2)_3CH_3]_2$	902		128/8		1.3741		25	40
$C_{14}H_4F_{22}O_4$	$[CF_3(CF_2)_2CH_2(CF_2)_2]_2$	901	72	85/1.5		1.360	1.734	25	55
$C_{14}H_7F_{19}O_4$	$(CH_3CO_2)_2CH(CF_2)_8CF_3$	915		222/750		1.333	1.673	20	74
$C_{14}H_{10}F_{16}O_4$	$[(CF_2)_4CO_2C_2H_5]_2$	902		156–159/27		1.341	1.592	25	49
$C_{14}H_{12}F_{14}O_4$	$[CF_3(CF_2)_2CO_2(CH_2)_3]_2$	902	95.6	133/10	−28	1.3413	1.4696	20	35
		905	82	110–111.5/4		1.3392	1.4670	27	40
	$[(CH_2)_2CO_2CH_2(CF_2)_2CF_3]_2$	901	71	100/1		1.3449	1.4893	25	41
	$CH_3CH[CH_2CO_2CH_2(CF_2)_2CF_3]_2$	902	82.8	85/0.5	−37	1.3448	1.4968	20	35
$C_{14}H_{18}F_8O_4$	$[(CF_2)_2CO_2(CH_2)_3CH_3]_2$	902	86	126/8.5		1.3725	1.2711	25	40
	$[(CF_2)_2CO_2CH(CH_3)C_2H_5]_2$	902	57	111/5		1.3680	1.2643	25	40
	$[(CF_2)_2CO_2CH_2CH(CH_3)_2]_2$	902		118/8		1.3697	1.2671	25	40
	$[(CF_2)_2CO_2C(CH_3)_3]_2$	902		100–110/8					40
	$[CH_3(CH_2)_2CO_2CH_2(CF_2)_2]_2$	901	77	112/1		1.3793	1.3181	25	41
$C_{14}H_{25}FO_4$	$CH_2F(CH_2)_5C(C_2H_5)(CO_2C_2H_5)_2$	907	29	135–138/4		1.4294		26	16
$C_{15}H_{12}F_{16}O_4$	$CH_2[CH_2CO_2CH_2(CF_2)_3CF_2H]_2$	902	92.1	134/0.5	−27	1.3560	1.5980	20	35
$C_{15}H_{14}F_{14}O_4$	$CH_2[CH_2CH_2CO_2CH_2(CF_2)_2CF_3]_2$	901	51	107/1		1.3506	1.4619	25	41
$C_{15}H_{27}FO_4$	$CH_2F(CH_2)_2C[(CH_2)_2CH(CH_3)_2](CO_2C_2H_5)_2$	907	26	120–123/6		1.4275	1.005	25	16
$C_{16}H_{14}F_{16}O_4$	$[(CH_2)_2CO_2CH_2(CF_2)_3CF_2H]_2$	902	96.0	139/0.5	−4	1.3605	1.5606	20	35

TABLE 25 (*continued*)

Empirical Formula	Structural Formula	Method	Yield %	B.p. °C/mm.	F.p. or M.p. °C	n_D^t	d_4^t	t°C	Ref.
$C_{16}H_{14}F_{16}O_4$	$CH_3CH[CH_2CO_2CH_2(CF_2)_3CF_2H]_2$	902	85.0	129/0.5	−60	1.3595	1.5570	20	35
	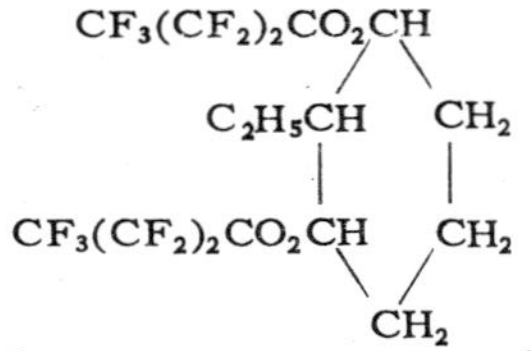			145/35		1.3488	1.413(20)	25	100
$C_{16}H_{16}F_{14}O_4$	$[(CH_2)_3CO_2CH_2(CF_2)_2CF_3]_2$	901	61	115/1		1.3542	1.4355	25	41
$C_{17}H_{10}F_{22}O_4$	$[CF_3(CF_2)_4CO_2CH_2CH_2]_2CH_2$	901	86	126–127/5		1.3305	1.6156	25	40
$C_{17}H_{18}F_{14}O_4$	$CH_2[(CH_2)_3CO_2CH_2(CF_2)_2CF_3]_2$	901	51	123/1		1.3578	1.4024	25	41
$C_{17}H_{26}F_6O_4$	$CF_2[CF_2CO_2(CH_2)_5CH_3]_2$	902	74	158–159/5		1.3938	1.1447	25	40
$C_{17}H_{31}FO_4$	$CH_2F(CH_2)_4C[(CH_2)_2CH(CH_3)_2](CO_2C_2H_5)_2$	907	24	133–137/2.5		1.4319	0.9844	26	16
$C_{18}H_{11}F_{21}O_6$	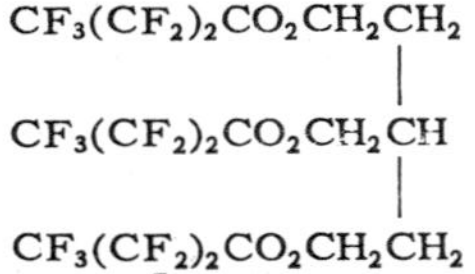	902	95.6	120/0.2	−60	1.3425	1.6135	20	35
$C_{18}H_{12}F_{22}O_4$	$CH_3CH[CH_2CO_2CH_2(CF_2)_4CF_3]_2$	902	84.2	115/0.5	−7	1.3386	1.6101	20	35
$C_{18}H_{20}F_{14}O_4$	$[CF_3(CF_2)_2CO_2(CH_2)_5]_2$	902	91.0	106/0.2	−38	1.3588	1.3594	20	35
		905	83	110.2/0.5		1.3568	1.3576	27	40
	$[(CH_2)_4CO_2CH_2(CF_2)_2CF_3]_2$	901	75	130/1		1.3615	1.3754	25	41
		902	78.4	133/0.5	2	1.3632	1.3837	20	35
	$[(CH_2)_2CO_2CH(C_2H_5)CF_2CF_2CF_3]_2$	901	73	108/0.9		1.3640	1.3782	25	41
$C_{18}H_{26}F_8O_4$	$[(CF_2)_2CO_2(CH_2)_5CH_3]_2$	902	58	155–156/3.5		1.3888	1.2038	25	40
$C_{20}H_{14}F_{24}O_4$	$[CF_2H(CF_2)_5CO_2(CH_2)_3]_2$	902	73	151/0.5	< −54	1.3474	1.6263	20	35
	$[(CH_2)_2CO_2CH_2(CF_2)_5CF_2H]_2$	902	89.4	157/0.5	10	1.3510	1.6516	20	35
	$CH_3CH[CH_2CO_2CH_2(CF_2)_5CF_2H]_2$	902	87.2	155/0.5	−50	1.3505	1.6484	20	35

$C_{20}H_{22}F_{16}O_4$	$[(CH_2)_4CO_2CH_2(CF_2)_3CF_2H]_2$	902	87.6	156/0.5	−9	1.3740	1.4385	20	35
$C_{21}H_{10}F_{30}O_4$	$[CF_3(CF_2)_6CO_2(CH_2)_2]_2CH_2$	901	59	159–160/7		1.3284	1.6846	25	40
$C_{21}H_{14}F_{24}O_6$	$CH_2CO_2CH_2(CF_2)_3CF_2H$ | $CHCO_2CH_2(CF_2)_3CF_2H$ | $CH_2CO_2CH_2(CF_2)_3CF_2H$	902	76	172/0.5	−40	1.3588	1.6800	20	35
$C_{22}H_{12}F_{30}O_4$	$[(CH_2)_2CO_2CH_2(CF_2)_6CF_3]_2$	901	56	173/3	39.5				41
		902	84.7	148/0.5	37–39				35
	$[CF_3(CF_2)_6CO_2(CH_2)_3]_2$	902	88.5	145/0.5	4	1.3341	1.6687	20	35
	$CH_3CH[CH_2CO_2CH_2(CF_2)_6CF_3]_2$	902	82.0	145/0.5	16	1.3363	1.6894	20	35
$C_{22}H_{34}F_8O_4$	$[(CF_2)_2CO_2CH_2CH(C_2H_5)(C_4H_9)]_2$	902		190–195/5		1.3990		25	40
$C_{23}H_{18}F_{24}O_4$	$CHCH_2CO_2CH_2(CF_2)_5CF_2H$ / \\ CH_2 $C(CH_3)_2$ \\ / $CHCO_2CH_2(CF_2)_5CF_2H$	902	67	165/0.5	−40	1.3646	1.6009	20	35
$C_{24}H_{14}F_{32}O_4$	$CH_3CH[CH_2CO_2CH_2(CF_2)_7CF_2H]_2$	902	91.1	175/0.5	25	1.3452	1.714	20	35
$C_{25}H_{10}F_{38}O_4$	$[CF_3(CF_2)_8CO_2(CH_2)_2]_2CH_2$	901	42	164/4		1.3286	1.735	25	40
$C_{28}H_{22}F_{32}O_4$	$(CH_3)_3CCHCH_2CO_2CH_2(CF_2)_7CF_2H$ | $CH_2CH_2CO_2CH_2(CF_2)_7CF_2H$	902	92.8	187/0.5	−7	1.3577	1.6238	20	35

TABLE 26

UNSATURATED MONOESTERS

Empirical Formula	Structural Formula	Method	Yield %	B.p. °C/mm.	F.p. or M.p. °C	n_D^t	d_4^t	t °C	Ref.
$C_4H_3F_3O_2$	$CF_3CO_2CH{=}CH_2$	904	16–43	39.5–40.5		1.3151	1.2031	25	31,73,115
$C_5H_2F_3NO_2$	$CF_3CO_2C(CN){=}CH_2$	903		140–142					31
$C_5H_3F_5O_2$	$CF_3CF_2CO_2CH{=}CH_2$	904	61–75	58/745		1.3095	1.319	20	52,115,100
$C_5H_5F_3O_2$	$CF_3CO_2C(CH_3){=}CH_2$	904		63–65					31
	$CF_2{=}CFCO_2C_2H_5$	302	70	93.6/629	−62	1.3652	1.244	20	107
	$CH_2{=}C(CF_3)CO_2CH_3$	305		103.8–105		1.3528		20	19
	$CH_2{=}CHCO_2CH_2CF_3$	901		45.9/125		1.3480	1.216	25	23
$C_5H_6F_2O_2$	$CH_2{=}CFCO_2CH_2CH_2F$	911		140–144		1.3981		20	28
$C_5H_7FO_2$	$CH_2FCO_2CH_2CH{=}CH_2$	901	46	136–137					119
$C_6H_3F_7O_2$	$CF_3CF_2CF_2CO_2CH{=}CH_2$	904	76	78–79/748		1.3086	1.418	20	100,108,114, 115
$C_6H_4F_6O_2$	$CH_3CO_2C(CF_3){=}CHCF_3$	904	40	94–94.2/748		1.3183	1.3840	25	65
$C_6H_5F_5O_2$	$CH_2{=}CHCO_2CH_2C_2F_5$	901		50.2/100		1.3363	1.32(Calc.)	20	23
$C_6H_7F_3O_2$	$CF_3CH{=}CHCO_2C_2H_5$	303	55–80	112.5–115		1.3600	1.125(25)	20	93,136
$C_7H_3F_9O_2$	$CF_3(CF_2)_3CO_2CH{=}CH_2$	904	73	97–99/732		1.3116	1.493	20	114,115
$C_7H_5F_7O_2$	$CH_2{=}CHCO_2CH_2CF_2CF_2CF_3$	901		43/40		1.3324	1.455	20	3,23,77
		902	85–90	51/50		1.3317	1.409	20	2

$C_8H_3F_{11}O_2$	$CF_3(CF_2)_4CO_2CH{=}CH_2$	904	44–50	65–66/100	1.3115	1.546	20	108,114,115
$C_8H_4F_{10}O_2$	$CF_3(CF_2)_2CH{=}CHCO_2CH_2CF_3$	901	37	132	1.3258		25	39
$C_8H_5F_9O_2$	$CH_2{=}CHCO_2CH_2(CF_2)_3CF_3$	901		57.5/30	1.3289	1.48(Calc.)	25	23
$C_8H_6F_8O_2$	$CH_2{=}CHCO_2CH_2(CF_2)_3CF_2H$	902		69–70/21	1.3421		25	9
$C_8H_7F_7O_2$	$CF_3(CF_2)_2CH{=}CHCO_2C_2H_5$	303	80	139.5–140	1.3444	1.352(25)	20	39,93
$C_8H_{11}F_3O_2$	$CH_3CO_2CH(CF_3){=}C(CH_3)_2$	903		122				60
$C_9H_3F_{11}O_2$	$\overline{CF_2(CF_2)_4CF}CO_2CH{=}CH_2$	904	56	59/45	1.3362	1.628	20	114,115
$C_9H_5F_{11}O_2$	$CH_2{=}CHCO_2CH_2(CF_2)_4CF_3$	901	84	62–63.5/20	1.3279	1.540(30)	20	3,23
$C_9H_8F_8O_2$	$CH_2{=}C(CH_3)CO_2CH_2(CF_2)_3CF_2H$	902		83–84/24	1.3553		25	9
$C_9H_{13}FO_2$	$(CH_3)_2C{=}CHCH{=}CFCO_2C_2H_5$	909		104–106/20	1.4532		20	91
$C_{11}H_5F_{15}O_2$	$CH_2{=}CHCO_2CH_2(CF_2)_6CF_3$	901	64	65/5	1.3279	1.631	20	3,23
$C_{12}H_3F_{19}O_2$	$CF_3(CF_2)_8CO_2CH{=}CH_2$	904	38	53/0.5	1.3176	1.707	20	114,115
$C_{13}H_5F_{19}O_2$	$CH_2{=}CHCO_2CH_2(CF_2)_8CF_3$	901	71.7	220/740	1.3279	1.689	20	3,23

TABLE 27

UNSATURATED DIESTERS

Empirical Formula	Structural Formula	Method	Yield %	B.p. °C/mm.	F.p. or M.p. °C	n_D^t	d_4^t	t°C	Ref.
$C_6H_5F_3O_4$	$CF_3CO_2CH{=}CHCO_2CH_3$	301		52–54/19–20					32
$C_6H_6F_2O_4$	$CHF_2CO_2CH{=}CHCO_2CH_3$	301		55–57/19–20					32
$C_7H_7F_3O_4$	$CF_3CO_2CH{=}CHCO_2C_2H_5$	301		43–45/8–9					32
$C_7H_8F_2O_4$	$CHF_2CO_2CH{=}CHCO_2C_2H_5$	301		46–48/8–9					32
$C_9H_{11}F_3O_4$	$CF_3CO_2CH{=}CHCO_2(CH_2)_3CH_3$	301		67–69/8–9					32
$C_9H_{12}F_2O_4$	$CHF_2CO_2CH{=}CHCO_2(CH_2)_3CH_3$	301		69–71/8–9					32
$C_{10}H_7F_7O_4$	$(CH_2{=}CHCO_2)_2CH(CF_2)_2CF_3$	915		89.5–90/15		1.3652	1.399	25	74,75
$C_{11}H_6Cl_4F_2O_4$	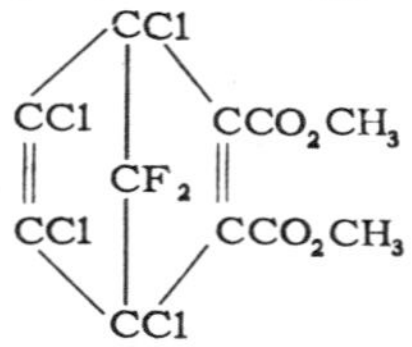	311	46	71–72					95
$C_{11}H_{11}ClF_6O_4$	$CF_3C[CH(CO_2C_2H_5)_2]{=}CClCF_3$	907		80–82/1		1.4018	1.3659(29)	20	61
$C_{12}H_{10}F_8O_4$	$(CF_2CF_2CO_2CH_2CH{=}CH_2)_2$	902		150–160/30					96
$C_{12}H_{15}F_3O_7$	$C_2H_5O_2CC(OC_2H_5){=}C(OCCF_3)CO_2C_2H_5$			141–142/14		1.4650	1.104	25	79
$C_{13}H_{21}FO_4$	$CH_2F(CH_2)_2C(CH_2CH{=}CH_2)(CO_2C_2H_5)_2$	907	56	121–126/7		1.4350	1.0414	24	16
$C_{15}H_{25}FO_4$	$CH_2F(CH_2)_4C(CH_2CH{=}CH_2)(CO_2C_2H_5)_2$	907	46	150–155/5		1.4376	1.012	25	16

TABLE 28

HYDROXYESTERS

Empirical Formula	Structural Formula	Method	Yield %	B.p. °C/mm.	F.p. or M.p. °C	n_D^t	d_4^t	t °C	Ref.
$C_5H_7F_3O_3$	$CH_2OHCH(CF_3)CO_2CH_3$	902		170–173					19
	$CH_3COH(CF_3)CO_2CH_3$			127–129/1		1.358		14	29
$C_5H_8F_2O_3$	$CH_2OHCF_2CO_2C_2H_5$	708		93–95/18					87
		902		181		1.3830		25	25,110
$C_6H_5F_7O_3$	$CF_3(CF_2)_2CO_2CH_2CH_2OH$			44/3.5		1.3325	1.542	20	100
$C_6H_9F_3O_3$	$CF_3CHOHCH_2CO_2C_2H_5$	404	90	180–180.2/748	26.9–27	1.3707	1.275	30	78,136
		909	87	81–83/15	25.5	1.3720	1.259	25	93
	$CF_3COH(CH_3)CO_2C_2H_5$	902	91	140–142		1.3577		20	19
$C_8H_9F_7O_3$	$CF_3(CF_2)_2CHOHCH_2CO_2C_2H_5$	909	94	90–92/15	17.3	1.3538	1.431(25)	20	93
	$CF_3(CF_2)_2CO_2(CH_2)_4OH$			141.6–142/742		1.3579		20	100
$C_8H_{13}FO_3$	$CH_3CH{=}CHCHOHCHFCO_2C_2H_5$	909	58	84–85/2		1.4410		20	91
$C_9H_{17}FO_3$	$(CH_3)_3CCHOHCHFCO_2C_2H_5$	909	39	115–116/16		1.4293		20	91
$C_{10}H_{12}F_8O_3$	$CH_3(CH_2)_2CO_2CH_2(CF_2)_4CH_2OH$	902	40	95/1.2		1.3714	1.4402	25	41
$C_{10}H_{13}F_7O_3$	$CF_3(CF_2)_2COH(C_2H_5)CH_2CO_2C_2H_5$	909	1.9	62–63/3		1.3688		20	91
$C_{10}H_{17}FO_3$	$\overline{CH_2(CH_2)_4C}(OH)CHFCO_2C_2H_5$ (ring)	909	38–44	126–127/11		1.4580		20	91
$C_{11}HF_{17}O_3$	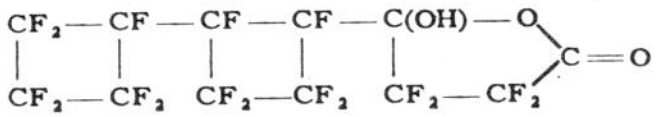	702	39	45.5–46.5/0.5–0.7		1.3332		22	109
$C_{11}H_8F_{14}O_3$	$CF_3(CF_2)_2COH[(CF_2)_2CF_3]CH_2CO_2C_2H_5$	909	44	65–66/3		1.3348		20	91
$C_{11}H_{21}FO_3$	$CH_3(CH_2)_5CHOHCHFCO_2C_2H_5$	909	50	128–130/4		1.4338		20	91
	$CH_3(CH_2)_3COH(C_2H_5)CHFCO_2C_2H_5$	909	56	110–111/5		1.4341		20	91
$C_{12}H_8F_{16}O_3$	$CF_3(CF_2)_6CHOHCHFCO_2C_2H_5$	909	61	113–114/4		1.3425		20	91
$C_{12}H_9F_{15}O_3$	$CF_3(CF_2)_6CHOHCH_2CO_2C_2H_5$	909	78	110–112/4		1.3429		20	91
$C_{12}H_{19}FO_7$	$C_2H_5O_2CCHFCOH(CO_2C_2H_5)CH_2CO_2C_2H_5$	909	12	120/0.1	41				116
$C_{12}H_{19}F_5O_4$	$CH_3(CH_2)_3OCOH(CF_3)CF_2CO_2(CH_2)_3CH_3$	908	65	79/15		1.3890		20	89

TABLE 29

KETOESTERS

Empirical Formula	Structural Formula	Method	Yield %	B.p. °C/mm.	F.p. or M.p. °C	n_D^t	n_4^t	t°C	Ref.
$C_4H_5FO_3$	$CH_2FCOCO_2CH_3$	910	60	85/14		1.423	1.510	20	12
$C_5H_6F_2O_3$	$CH_2FCOCHFCO_2CH_3$	908	35	97/14					118
$C_6H_5BrF_4O_3$	$CF_3COCBrFCO_2C_2H_5$	606		51–52/15					92
$C_6H_5Br_2F_3O_3$	$CF_3COCBr_2CO_2C_2H_5$	606		74–75/9		1.4420		26	101
$C_6H_5F_5O_3$	$CF_3COCF_2CO_2C_2H_5$	908	20	130–131					89
$C_6H_6ClF_3O_3$	$CF_3COCHClCO_2C_2H_5$	606		67–69/23		1.3890		19.5	69
$C_6H_6F_4O_3$	$CHF_2COCF_2CO_2C_2H_5$	908	81	143–144		1.3542		20	89
	$CF_3COCHFCO_2C_2H_5$	908	86	138–139					89
$C_6H_7F_3O_3$	$CF_3COCH_2CO_2C_2H_5$	908	54–84	131–132					62,89,90, 127
	$CHF_2COCHFCO_2C_2H_5$	908	68	159–160					89
$C_6H_8F_2O_3$	$CHF_2COCH_2CO_2C_2H_5$	908	35–83	162		1.4018		20	62,89
	$CH_2FCOCHFCO_2C_2H_5$	908	69	71–72/3					89
$C_8H_7F_7O_3$	$CF_3(CF_2)_2COCH_2CO_2C_2H_5$	908		150		1.355		24	54
$C_8H_{11}FO_5$	$C_2H_5O_2CCOCHFCO_2C_2H_5$	908	55–67	99/3		1.4203	1.261(20)	25	10,11,12, 116
$C_9H_{15}FO_3$	$CH_2F(CH_2)_2CH(OCCH_3)CO_2C_2H_5$	907	53.7	105.2/7		1.4237	1.064	25	70
$C_{12}H_{19}FO_5$	$(CH_3)_3CO_2CCOCHFCO_2C(CH_3)_3$	908			15				10,11,12

BIBLIOGRAPHY

1. Adams, R., "Organic Reactions," Vol. II, P. 89, John Wiley and Sons, Inc., New York (1944). (Chapter 2 by A. L. Henne.)
2. Ahlbrecht, A. H., and Codding, D. W., *J. Am. Chem. Soc.*, **75**, 984(1953).
3. Ahlbrecht, A. H., Reid, T. S., and Husted, D. R., U. S. Patent 2,642,416(1953).
4. Bacon, J. C., Bradley, C. W., *et al.*, *J. Am. Chem. Soc.*, **70**, 2653(1948).
5. Barlow, G. B., Stacey, M., and Tatlow, J. C., *J. Chem. Soc.*, **1955**, 1749.
6. Barney, A. L., and Cairns, T. L., J. *Am. Chem. Soc.*, **72**, 3193(1950).
7. Barrick, P. L., U. S. Patent 2,462,345(1949).
8. Bergmann, E. D., *J. Chem. Soc.*, **1953**, 3786.
9. Bittles, J. A., U. S. Patent 2,628,958(1953).
10. Blank, I., Mager, J., and Bergmann, E. D., *Bull Research Council Israel*, **3**, No. 1/2, 101(1953).
11. Blank, I., and Mager, J., *Experientia*, **10**, 77(1954).
12. Blank, I., Mager, J., and Bergmann, E. D., *J. Chem. Soc.*, **1955**, 2190.
13. Bockemuller, W., *Ann.*, **506**, 20(1933).
14. Burgoyne, E. E., and Condon, F. E., *J. Am. Chem. Soc.*, **72**, 3276(1950).
15. Brown, F., and Musgrave, W. K. R., *J. Chem. Soc.*, **1953**, 2087.
16. Bruce, W. F., and de V. Huber, R., *J. Am. Chem. Soc.*, **75**, 4668(1953).
17. Buckle, F. J., Pattison, F. L. M., and Saunders, B. C., *J. Chem. Soc.*, **1949**, 1471.
18. Buckle, F. J., and Saunders, B. C., *J. Chem. Soc.*, **1949**, 2774.
19. Buxton, M. W., Stacey, M., and Tatlow, J. E., *J. Chem. Soc.*, **1954**, 366.
20. Campbell, K. N., Knoblock, J. A., and Campbell, B. K., *J. Am. Chem. Soc.*, **72**, 4380(1950).
21. Chaney, D. W., U. S. Patent 2,456,768(1948).
22. Chaney, D. W., U. S. Patent 2,549,892(1951).
23. Codding, D. W., Reid, T. S., *et al.*, *J. Poly. Sci.*, **15**, 515(1955).
24. Coffmann, D. D., Barrick, P. L., *et al.*, *J. Am. Chem. Soc.*, **71**, 490(1949).
25. Coffmann, D. D., Raasch, M. S., *et al.*, *J. Org. Chem.*, **14**, 747(1949).
26. Cook, D. J., Pierce, O. R., and McBee, E. T., *J. Am. Chem. Soc.*, **76**, 83(1954).
26A. Coover, H. W., Stanin, T. E., and Dickey, J. B., U.S. Patent 2,525,526(1950).
27. Coover, H. W., and Dickey, J. B., U. S. Patent 2,585,230(1952).
28. Crawford, W. C., British Patent 616,849(1949).
29. Darrall, R. A., Smith, F., *et al.*, *J. Chem. Soc.*, **1951**, 2329.
30. Desirant, Y., *Bull. sci. acad. roy. Belg.*, **15**, 966(1929).
31. Dickey, J. B., and Stanin, T. E., U. S. Patent 2,525,530(1950).
32. Dickey, J. B., and Stanin, T. E., U. S. Patent 2,611,761(1952).
33. Diesslin, A. R., Kauck, E. A., and Simons, J. H., U. S. Patent 2,567,011(1951).
34. Englund, B., *Org. Syn.*, **34**, 49(1954).
35. Faurote, P. D., Murphy, C. M., and O'Rear, J. G., 127th Meeting American Chemical Society, Cincinnati, Ohio, April, 1955.
36. Faurote, P. D., and O'Rear, J. G., 130th Meeting American Chemical Society, Atlantic City, N. J., September 1956.
37. Filachione, E. M., Costello, E. J., and Fisher, C., H., *J. Am. Chem. Soc.*, **73**, 5265(1951).
38. Filler, R. J., *J. Am. Chem. Soc.*, **75**, 3016(1953).
39. Filler, R. J., *J. Am. Chem. Soc.*, **76**, 1376(1954).
40. Filler, R., O'Brien, J. F., *et al.*, *J. Am. Chem. Soc.*, **75**, 966(1953).

41. Filler, R., Fenner, J. V., *et al.*, *J. Am. Chem. Soc.*, **75,** 2693(1953).
42. Filler, R., O'Brien, J. F., *et al.*, *Ind. Eng. Chem.*, **46,** 544(1954).
43. Gilman, H., and Jones, R. G., *J. Am. Chem. Soc.*, **65,** 1458(1943).
44. Goswami, H. C., and Sarkar, P. B., *J. Indian Chem. Soc.*, **10,** 537(1933).
45. Gryszkiewicz-Trochimowski, E., and Gryszkiewicz-Trochimowski, O., *Bull. soc. chim. France*, **1949,** 928.
46. Gryszkiewicz-Trochimowski, E., Sporzynski, A., and Wnuk, J., *Rec. trav. chim.*, **66,** 413(1947).
47. Gryszkiewicz-Trochimowski, E., Sporzynski, A., and Wnuk, J., *Rec. trav. chim.*, **66,** 419(1947).
48. Gryszkiewicz-Trochimowski, E., Sporzynski, A., and Wnuk, J., *Rec. trav. chim.*, **66,** 430(1947).
49. Guenthner, R. A., U. S. Patent 2,606,206(1952).
50. Haszeldine, R. N., *J. Chem. Soc.*, **1953,** 3559.
51. Haszeldine, R. N., *J. Chem. Soc.*, **1955,** 4302.
52. Haszeldine, R. N., and Leedham, K., *J. Chem. Soc.*, **1953,** 1548.
53. Haszeldine, R. N., and Steele, B. R., *J. Chem. Soc.*, **1953,** 1199.
54. Hauptschein, M., and Braun, R. A., *J. Am. Chem. Soc.*, **77,** 4930(1955).
54A. Hauptschein, M., and Grosse, A. V., *J. Am. Chem. Soc.*, **74,** 4454(1952).
55. Hauptschein, M., O'Brien, J. F., *et al.*, *J. Am. Chem. Soc.*, **75,** 87(1953).
56. Hauptschein, M., Stokes, C. S., and Grosse, A. V., *J. Am. Chem. Soc.*, **74,** 1974(1952).
57. Hechenbleikner, I., U. S. Patent 2,456,586(1948).
58. Henne, A. L., and DeWitt, E. G., *J. Am. Chem. Soc.*, **70,** 1548(1948).
59. Henne, A. L., and Fox, C. J., *J. Am. Chem. Soc.*, **76,** 479(1954).
60. Henne, A. L., and Hinkamp, J. B., *J. Am. Chem. Soc.*, **76,** 5147(1954).
61. Henne, A. L., and Latif, K. A., *J. Indian Chem. Soc.*, **30,** 809(1953).
62. Henne, A. L., Newman, M. S., *et al.*, *J. Am. Chem. Soc.*, **69,** 1819(1947).
63. Henne, A. L., and Pelley, R. L., *J. Am. Chem. Soc.*, **74,** 1426(1952).
64. Henne, A. L., and Richter, S. B., *J. Am. Chem. Soc.*, **74,** 5420(1952).
65. Henne, A. L., Schmitz, J. W., and Finnegan, W. G., *J. Am. Chem. Soc.*, **72,** 4195(1950).
66. Henne, A. L., and Zimmer, W. F., *J. Am. Chem. Soc.*, **73,** 1103(1951).
67. Henne, A. L., and Zimmerscheid, W. J., *J. Am. Chem. Soc.*, **67,** 1235(1945).
68. Henne, A. L., and Zimmerscheid, W. J., *J. Am. Chem. Soc.*, **69,** 281(1947).
69. Hill, H. M., Towne, E. B., and Dickey, J. B., *J. Am. Chem. Soc.*, **72,** 3289(1950).
70. Hoffmann, F. W., *J. Org. Chem.*, **15,** 425(1950).
71. Holm, T., U. S. Patent 2,611,787(1952).
72. Horsefall, J. L., U. S. Patent 2,409,859(1946).
73. Howk, B. W., and Jacobson, R. A., U. S. Patent 2,436,144(1948).
74. Husted, D. R., and Ahlbrecht, A. H., U. S. Patent 2,568,501(1951).
75. Husted, D. R., and Ahlbrecht, A. H., *J. Am. Chem. Soc.*, **74,** 5422(1952).
76. Husted, D. R., and Ahlbrecht, A. H., *J. Am. Chem. Soc.*, **75,** 1605(1953).
77. Husted, D. R., and Ahlbrecht, A. H., U. S. Patent 2,666,797(1954).
78. Jones, R. G., *J. Am. Chem. Soc.*, **70,** 143(1948).
79. Jones, R. G., *J. Am. Chem. Soc.*, **73,** 5168(1951).
80. Joullie, M. M., *J. Am. Chem. Soc.*, **77,** 6662(1955).
81. Kharasch, M. S., Jensen, E. V., and Urry, W. H., *J. Org. Chem.*, **10,** 386(1945).

82. Knunyants, I. L., Kil'disheva, O. V., and Bykhovskaya, E., *Zhur. Obshchei Khim.*, **19**, 101(1949).
83. Knunyants, I. L., Shchekotikhim, A. I., and Fokin, A. V., *Iyvest. Akad. Nauk. S.S.S.R., Otdel. Khim. Nauk.*, **1953**, 282.
84. McBee, E. T., and Filler, R. J., *J. Org. Chem.*, **21**, 370(1956).
85. McBee, E. T., Higgins, J. F., and Pierce, O. R., *J. Am. Chem. Soc.*, **74**, 1387(1952) .
86. McBee, E. T., Kelly, A. E., and Rapkin, E. J., *J. Am. Chem. Soc.*, **72**, 5071(1950).
87. McBee, E. T., Marzluff, W. F., and Pierce, O. R., *J. Am. Chem. Soc.*, **74**, 444(1952).
88. McBee, E. T., Park, J. D., *et al.*, *Ind. Eng. Chem.*, **39**, 415(1947).
89. McBee, E. T., Pierce, O. R., *et al.*, *J. Am. Chem. Soc.*, **75**, 3152(1953).
90. McBee, E. T., Pierce, O. R., *et al.*, *J. Am. Chem. Soc.*, **75**, 4090(1953).
91. McBee, E. T., Pierce, O. R., and Christman, D. L., *J. Am. Chem. Soc.*, **77**, 1581(1955).
92. McBee, E. T., Pierce, O. R., and Kilbourne, H. W., *J. Am. Chem. Soc.*, **75**, 4091(1953).
93. McBee, E. T., Pierce, O. R., and Smith, D. D., *J. Am. Chem. Soc.*, **76**, 3722(1954).
94. McBee, E. T. Pierce, O. R., and Smith, D. D., *J. Am. Chem. Soc.*, **76**, 3725(1954).
95. McBee, E. T., Smith, D. K., and Ungnade, H. E., *J. Am. Chem. Soc.*, **77**, 387(1955).
96. McBee, E. T., and Wiseman, P. A., U. S. Patent 2,453,147(1948).
97. McBee, E. T., and Wiseman, P. A., U. S. Patent 2,515,246(1950).
98. McCombie, H., and Saunders, B. C., *Nature*, **158**, 382(1946).
99. Miller, W. T., and Prober, M., *J. Am. Chem. Soc.*, **70**, 2602(1948).
100. Minnesota Mining and Manufacturing Co., "Fluorochemicals-Heptafluorobutyric Acid," 1950.
101. Mosby, W. L., *J. Am. Chem. Soc.*, **74**, 844(1952).
102. Norton, T. R., *J. Am. Chem. Soc.*, **72**, 3527(1950).
103. Olah, Gy., and Pavlath, A., *Acta. Chim. Acad. Sci. Hung.*, **3**, 191(1953).
104. Olah, Gy., and Pavlath, A., *Acta. Chim. Acad. Sci. Hung.*, **4**, 89(1954).
105. Park, J. D., Larsen, E. R., *et al.*, 130th Meeting American Chemical Society, Atlantic City, N. J., September 1956.
106. Park, J. D., Lycan, W. R., and Lacher, J. R., *J. Am. Chem. Soc.*, **76**, 1388(1954).
107. Park, J. D., Rausch, D. A., and Lacher, J. R., Private Communication.
108. Pierce, O. R., McBee, E. T., and Cline, R. E., *J. Am. Chem. Soc.*, **75**, 5618(1953).
109. Pruett, R. L., Bahner, C. T., and Smith, H. A., *J. Am. Chem. Soc.*, **74**, 1638(1952).
110. Raasch, M. W., U. S. Patent 2,452,791(1948).
111. Ray, P. C., *Nature*, **132**, 173(1933).
112. Ray, P. C., and Ray, A. C., *J. Indian Chem. Soc.*, **13**, 427(1936).
113. Reid, J. C., *J. Am. Chem. Soc.*, **69**, 2069(1947).
114. Reid, T. S., U. S. Patent 2,592,069(1952).
115. Reid, T. S., Codding, D. W., and Bovey, F. A., *J. Poly. Sci.*, **18**, 417(1955).
116. Rivett, D. E. A., *J. Chem. Soc.*, **1953**, 3710.

117. Roylance, J., Tatlow, J. C., and Worthington, R. E., *J. Chem. Soc.*, **1954,** 4426.
118. Saunders, B. C., and Stacey, G. J., *J. Chem. Soc.*, **1948,** 1773.
119. Saunders, B. C., and Stacey, G. J., *J. Chem. Soc.*, **1949,** 916.
120. Swarts, F., *Bull. acad. roy. Belg.*, (3), **35,** 849(1898).
121. Swarts, F., *Bull. soc. chim. France*, **1903,** 597.
122. Swarts, F., *Rec. trav. chim.*, **25,** 250(1906).
123. Swarts, F., *Rec. trav. chim.*, **27,** 128(1908).
123A. Swarts, F., *Bull. soc. chim. France*, **1911,** 563.
124. Swarts, F., *Rec. trav. chim.*, **33,** 252(1914).
125. Swarts, F., *Bull. sci. acad. roy. Belg.*, **8,** 343(1922).
126. Swarts, F., *Bull. soc. chim. Belg.*, **32,** 367(1923).
127. Swarts, F., *Bull. sci. acad. roy. Belg.*, **12,** 692(1926).
128. Swarts, F., *Bull. soc. chim. Belg.*, **38,** 99(1929).
129. Swarts, F., *Compt. rend.*, **197,** 1261(1933).
130. Swarts, F., *Bull. soc. chim. France*, [3], **13,** 992(1895).
131. Swarts, F., *Bull. soc. chim. France*, [3], **15,** 1135(1896).
132. Tarrant, P., and Brown, H. A., *J. Am. Chem. Soc.*, **73,** 1781(1951).
133. Tatlow, J. C., and Worthington, R. E., *J. Chem. Soc.*, **1952,** 1251.
134. Traynham, J. G., *J. Am. Chem. Soc.*, **74,** 4277(1952).
135. Walborsky, H. M., Baum, M., and Loncrini, D. F., *J. Am. Chem. Soc.*, **77,** 3637(1955).
136. Walborsky, H. M., and Schwarz, M., *J. Am. Chem. Soc.*, **75,** 3241(1953).
137. Young, J. A., and Tarrant, P., *J. Am. Chem. Soc.*, **71,** 2432(1949).
138. Young, J. A., and Tarrant, P., *J. Am. Chem. Soc.*, **72,** 1860(1950).

CHAPTER X

Nitrogen Compounds—I

TABLE OF CONTENTS

PAGE

Introduction 261

Method Number

AMIDES

1001 Interaction of Ammonia or Amines with Esters 261
1002 Interaction of Ammonia or Amines with Acyl Halides. 261
1003 Interaction of Ammonia or Amines with Anhydrides . 262
1004 Addition of Amines to Fluoroolefins 262
1005 Hydrolysis of Nitriles 262
1006 Cleavage of Perfluoroalkyl Ketones with Ammonia 262
and Amines 263
1007 Addition of N-Bromoperfluoroamides to Olefins 263
1008 Ammonolysis and Rearrangement of Diazoketones ..

IMIDES

1009 Cyclization of Diamides 263

N-HALO AMIDES AND IMIDES

1010 Halogenation of Amides and Imides 263

AMIDINES

1011 Interaction of Ammonia with Perfluoronitriles...... 264

UREAS

1012 Hydrolysis of Isocyanates 264
1013 Synthesis of Barbituric Acid Derivatives.......... 264
1014 Synthesis of Substituted Hydantoins............. 264

CARBAMATES (URETHANES)

1015	Acylation of Ammonia or Amines with Chlorocarbonates	265
1016	Addition of Hydrogen Chloride to Isocyanates	265
1017	Acylation of Carbamates	265
1018	Interaction of Carbamates and Aldehydes	265

NITRILES

1019	Dehydration of Amides	265
1020	Addition of Ammonia to Fluoroolefins	265
1021	Addition of Hydrogen Cyanide to Aldehydes and Ketones	266
1022	Interaction of Allylic Halides and Sodium Cyanide	266
1023	Cyanoethylation	266

KETO NITRILES

1024	Interaction of Acyl Halides and Metallic Cyanides	266

ISOCYANATES

1025	Interaction of Phosgene with Amines	266
1026	Decomposition of Acyl Azides	267

THIOCYANATES

1027	Action of Potassium Thiocyanate on Alkyl Bromides	267

α-KETO THIOCYANATES

1028	Interaction of Acyl Halides and Silver Thiocyanate	267
TABLE 30	Amides	268
TABLE 31	Imides	272
TABLE 32	N-Bromo Amides	273
TABLE 33	Amidines	273
TABLE 34	Ureas	274
TABLE 35	Carbamates	275
TABLE 36	Nitriles	276
TABLE 37	Keto Nitriles	278
TABLE 38	Isocyanates	278
TABLE 39	Thiocyanates	279
TABLE 40	α-Keto Thiocyanates	279
Bibliography		280

INTRODUCTION

Because of their ease of preparation, the fluorine-containing amides have been used extensively as intermediates for the preparation of other organic fluorine compounds. Unlike their hydrocarbon analogs the perfluoroamides do not undergo the conventional Hofmann rearrangement to yield amines; instead perfluoroalkyl halides or hydrides are formed (cf. Method 213). More recently it has been observed that isocyanates are also formed in this reaction.

Perfluoroalkylamidines can be easily prepared from perfluoronitriles and anhydrous ammonia. The ease with which this reaction proceeds is in marked contrast to the preparation of the hydrocarbon analogs where an aluminum chloride catalyst is generally required. The perfluoroalkyldiamidines prepared from dinitriles polymerize to intractible resins when heated.

AMIDES

METHOD 1001 Interaction of Ammonia or Amines with Esters

This is the best general procedure for the preparation of amides. The reaction may be accomplished readily at 0° to room temperature with anhydrous ammonia or amines either in the presence or absence of solvents. Ether is the most generally used solvent. Concentrated ammonium hydroxide may also be employed but the subsequent drying of the product may be difficult.

The yields in this reaction are usually excellent, as illustrated by the preparation of CF_3CONH_2 in a 99 percent yield using anhydrous ammonia;[31] $CHClFCONH_2$ in a 98 percent yield using concentrated ammonium hydroxide,[89] and $CF_3(CF_2)_2CONHC_4H_9$ in an 80 percent yield from the corresponding amine.[49]

Although ammonia reacts with $CF_3CH{=}CHCO_2C_2H_5$ in ether to yield $CF_3CH{=}CHCO_2NH_2$, the same reaction when carried out in a sealed tube at 100° for 36 hours in the absence of a solvent yields 95 percent of $CF_3CH(NH_2)CH_2CONH_2$.[87]

The use of fluorine-containing amines to prepare substituted amides by this procedure has not been reported.

METHOD 1002 Interaction of Ammonia or Amines with Acyl Halides

This reaction may be carried out either by passing dry ammonia into a solution of the acyl halide in anhydrous ether or by the addition of cold concentrated aqueous ammonia.[20,27,41] The separation of the amide from the ammonium salt is usually accomplished by solvent extraction. When 28 percent aqueous ammonia is used, $H(CF_2)_4CONH_2$ is obtained from the corresponding acyl chloride in an 85 percent yield.[16] Coover and Dickey[23] prepared $CH_2{=}CHCONHCH_2CF_3$ from $CF_3CH_2NH_2$ and acrylyl chloride in a methylene chloride solution at a temperature below 5°, using triethylamine as an acid acceptor.

METHOD 1003 Interaction of Ammonia or Amines with Anhydrides

This method has been used chiefly for the acylation of amino acids with trifluoroacetic anhydride.[88] For example, the acylation of alanine with trifluoroacetic anhydride gave an 85 percent yield of $CH_3CH(NHCOCF_3)CO_2H$. Trifluoroacetic anhydride has been used to acetylate 3,3,3-trifluoropropylamine at 0°.[8]

METHOD 1004 Addition of Amines to Fluoroolefins

Under hydrolytic conditions, amides are prepared in a one step synthesis in good yields by the interaction of amines with fluoroolefins. For example, upon heating $CF_2{=}CF_2$ or $CF_2{=}CFCl$ with butylamine and borax at 100° for 8 hours, $CHF_2CONHC_4H_9$[28] and $CHClFCONHC_4H_9$[70] were obtained, respectively. The reaction of amines with $CF_2{=}CFCl$ yields only chlorofluoroacetamide.[69] Under similar conditions, $CF_3CHFCON(C_2H_5)_2$ was obtained from diethylamine and perfluoropropene.[50]

Using anhydrous conditions, Pruett, *et al.*[69] added diethylamine to $CF_2{=}CFCl$ and obtained $CHClFCF_2N(C_2H_5)_2$, which upon treatment with water, hydrolyzed quantitatively to $CHClFCON(C_2H_5)_2$ (cf. Method 1105).

METHOD 1005 Hydrolysis of Nitriles

Although fluorine-containing nitriles are usually prepared by the dehydration of the corresponding amide, the reverse of this reaction has been used in several cases for amide preparation.[14,25,67]

Buxton, *et al.*[14] obtained $CH_2{=}C(CF_3)CONH_2$ by treating the corresponding nitrile with concentrated sulfuric acid at 120° to 130° for 30 minutes. Upon the hydrolysis of $CF_2BrCFBrCN$ with 85 percent sulfuric acid at 150° for eight hours, $CF_2BrCFBrCO_2NH_2$ was obtained in a 90 percent yield.[67]

METHOD 1006 Cleavage of Perfluoroalkyl Ketones with Ammonia and Amines

Hauptschein and Braun[38] found that when $(C_3F_7)_2C{=}O$ was treated with certain primary and secondary amines such as ethanolamine, diisobutylamine, or dicyclohexylamine, cleavage of the perfluoroketone occurred with formation of the corresponding amides of perfluorobutyric acid. Ammonia reacted similarly, but the less basic aromatic amines such as aniline failed to undergo this reaction.

METHOD 1007 Addition of N-Bromoperfluoroamides to Olefins

In a study of the bromination of cyclohexene with N-bromoperfluoroamides, Park, *et al.*[66] found that allylic bromination as well as addition of bromine across the double bond occurred. However, some amides of the type $R_fCONH\overline{CH(CH_2)_4CH}Br$ were also isolated. The treatment of cyclohexene with $CF_3CF_2CONHBr$ resulted in an 11.5 percent yield of 3-bromocyclohexene, a 9.5 percent yield of 1,2-dibromocyclohexane, and a 16.9 percent yield of the adduct, $CF_3CF_2CONH\overline{CH(CH_2)_4CH}Br$.

METHOD 1008 Ammonolysis and Rearrangement of Diazoketones

Brown and Musgrave[10] report that the diazoketone, CF_3COCHN_2, derived from trifluoroacetic acid, undergoes the Wolff rearrangement in the presence of ammonia and silver oxide to yield $CF_3CH_2CONH_2$. However, Park, *et al.*[65A] found that the diazoketone derived from $C_3F_7CO_2H$ failed to undergo the Wolff rearrangement while the diazoketone from $C_3F_7(CH_2)_2CO_2H$ rearranged in a normal fashion and in good yield (cf. Methods 714 and 910).

IMIDES

METHOD 1009 Cyclization of Diamides

The cyclization of a diamide to an imide can be effected by heating with either 95 percent sulfuric acid or phosphoric anhydride. Perfluoroglutarimide was prepared in an 89 percent yield by heating the diamide with 95 percent sulfuric acid.[42] However, by heating the same diamide with phosphoric anhydride, a mixture of the imide and the dinitrile $NC(CF_2)_3CN$, was obtained.[54]

N-HALO AMIDES AND IMIDES

METHOD 1010 Halogenation of Amides and Imides

N-Bromoamides and-imides are readily prepared by treating the amide or imide with silver oxide to obtain the N-silver derivative. Bromination of the N-silver derivative in anhydrous trifluoroacetic acid gives good yields of the N-bromo product. A number of N-bromoamides and N-bromoimides have been prepared by this procedure.[42,65,66]

AMIDINES

METHOD 1011 Interaction of Ammonia with Perfluoronitriles

Husted[44] has shown that perfluoroalkylamidines can be prepared in high yields by the reaction of perfluoronitriles with anhydrous liquid ammonia. A series of perfluoroalkylamidines, $CF_3(CF_2)_nC(NH_2){=}NH$ (where n varies from 0 to 10) has been prepared under these conditions. Perfluoroalkylamidines are weakly basic and readily form salts with strong inorganic and organic acids. Hydrolysis of perfluoroalkylamidines yields the corresponding amides.

UREAS

METHOD 1012 Hydrolysis of Isocyanates

The hydrolysis of 1,1-dihydroperfluoroalkyl isocyanates yields symmetrical dialkyl ureas. For example, the hydrolysis of $CF_3CF_2CH_2NCO$ yields $(CF_3CF_2CH_2NH)_2C{=}O$.[60] However, hydrolysis of perfluoroalkyl isocyanates yield only perfluoroalkyl amides containing one less $-CF_2-$ group than the starting isocyanate.[1] Lindgren and Cassaday[52] prepared ureas directly from fluorine-containing amines without isolation of any intermediate isocyanate by treating the amine with phosgene in an aqueous solution of sodium hydroxide.

METHOD 1013 Synthesis of Barbituric Acid Derivatives

$$F(CH_2)_3C(C_2H_5)(CO_2C_2H_3) + Na + NaOEt + H_2NCONH_2 \longrightarrow$$

$$F(CH_2)_3\overline{C(C_2H_5)CONHCONHCO}$$ [11]

METHOD 1014 Synthesis of Substituted Hydantoins

$$CH_3COCF_3 + C_2H_5OH + H_2O + (NH_4)_2CO_3 + NaCN \xrightarrow[50-60°]{1.5\ hr.}$$

$$\overline{NHCONHCOC}(CH_3)CF_3$$ [53]

CARBAMATES (URETHANES)

METHOD 1015 Acylation of Ammonia or Amines with Chlorocarbonates

The most general procedure for the preparation of fluorine-containing carbamates is by the acylation of ammonia or amines with chlorocarbonates. In this manner, $CH_2FCH_2OCONH_2$ was obtained in a 95 percent yield from CH_2FCH_2OCOCl.[74]

METHOD 1016 Addition of Hydrogen Chloride to Isocyanates

Chlorocarbamates are prepared by the addition of hydrogen chloride to isocyanates. In this manner $CF_3(CF_2)_2CH_2NHCOCl$ was prepared from $CF_3(CF_2)_2CH_2NCO$.[60]

METHOD 1017 Acylation of Carbamates

$$CH_2FCH_2OCONH_2 + CH_3COCl \longrightarrow CH_2FCH_2OCONHCOCH_3$$ [63,74]

METHOD 1018 Interaction of Carbamates and Aldehydes

$$CH_2FCH_2OCONH_2 + CH_3CHO \xrightarrow{HCl} CH_3CH(NHCO_2CH_2CH_2F)_2$$ [74]

NITRILES

METHOD 1019 Dehydration of Amides

The most generally used method for the preparation of fluorine-containing nitriles is the dehydration of amides with phosphoric anhydride at 150° to 200°. By this procedure CF_3CN was obtained in a 74 percent yield by heating an intimate mixture of CF_3CONH_2 and phosphoric anhydride.[31]

METHOD 1020 Addition of Ammonia to Fluoroolefins

Anhydrous ammonia adds to fluoroolefins to produce nitriles, probably in the following manner:

$$R_fCF{=}CF_2 + NH_3 \longrightarrow [R_fCHFCF_2NH_2] \xrightarrow{2NH_3} R_fCHFCN + 2NH_4F$$

Ammonia reacts with perfluoropropene at dry ice temperatures to yield CF_3CHFCN.[51] Miller[59] has prepared both $CF_2{=}CFCN$ and $CF_2{=}CClCN$ by treating $CF_2ClCF{=}CF_2$ or $CF_2{=}CClCF_2Cl$ with anhydrous ammonia. The reaction was carried out in either benzene or dioxane at 0° to 100°.

METHOD 1021 Addition of Hydrogen Cyanide to Aldehydes and Ketones

The cyanohydrin of trifluoroacetone is prepared by treatment of the ketone with sodium cyanide and sulfuric acid.[25,26] Heptafluorobutyraldehyde in ethyl ether yields $C_3F_7CH(OH)CN$ when treated with hydrogen cyanide.[46]

METHOD 1022 Interaction of Allylic Halides and Sodium Cyanide

Miller[58] reports that $CF_2{=}CFCF_2Cl$ reacts with sodium cyanide in *t*-butanol to yield $CF_2{=}CFCF_2CN$.

METHOD 1023 Cyanoethylation

Cyanoethylation of fluoroethanol using a small amount of aqueous potassium hydroxide as catalyst at 60° gave a 64 percent yield of $CH_2FCH_2OCH_2CH_2CN$. Under similar conditions, a 76 percent yield of the cyanoethylated product of $CH_2FCH_2CH_2OH$ was obtained.[13]

Chaney[18] added ethanol to either $CF_2{=}CFCN$ or $CF_2{=}CClCN$ at room temperature in the absence of a catalyst, and obtained $C_2H_5OCF_2CHFCN$ and $C_2H_5OCF_2CHClCN$, respectively.

KETO NITRILES

METHOD 1024 Interaction of Acyl Halides and Metallic Cyanides

Keto nitriles can be prepared by the reaction of perfluoroacyl chlorides with silver cyanide at 80° to 95° for three days to three weeks. The longer reaction time is required for the higher members of the acyl chloride series. By this procedure, α-keto nitriles can be prepared from CF_3COCl, C_2F_5COCl, C_3F_7COCl and $C_5F_{11}COCl$.[68] The α-keto nitrile from monofluoroacetyl bromide is obtained by heating the acyl bromide with cuprous cyanide at 120° for 6 hours.[7]

Patton and Simons[68] have established by molecular weight determinations that the α-keto nitriles exist in the vapor phase as "dimers" of the general formula, $(R_fCOCN)_2$. The α-keto nitriles are readily hydrolyzed by water to yield perfluorocarboxylic acids.

ISOCYANATES

METHOD 1025 Interaction of Phosgene with Amines

Isocyanates of the general formula, $CF_3(CF_2)_nCH_2NCO$, have been prepared by treatment of the corresponding 1,1-dihydroperfluoroalkylamines in ethyl cellosolve with phosgene in the presence of calcium oxide.[60]

METHOD 1026 Decomposition of Acyl Azides

Ahlbrecht and Husted[1] have shown that perfluoroalkyl isocyanates can be prepared in good yields by reacting perfluoroacyl chlorides with sodium azide in toluene, followed by the *in situ* thermal decomposition of the intermediate perfluoroacyl azides. Isocyanates of the general formula $CF_3(CF_2)_nNCO$, (where n = 1 to 10) have been prepared by this method. Hydrolysis of these isocyanates yields perfluoroalkyl amides containing one —CF_2— group less than the starting isocyante.

THIOCYANATES

METHOD 1027 Action of Potassium Thiocyanate on Alkyl Bromides

Fluorine-containing thiocyanates can be prepared by treating fluoroalkyl bromides with potassium thiocyanate in refluxing ethanol. For example, CH_2FCH_2SCN was obtained in a 78 percent yield from CH_2FCH_2Br by this procedure.[56,73]

α-KETO THIOCYANATES

METHOD 1028 Interaction of Acyl Halides and Silver Thiocyanate

Fluorocarbon acyl chlorides react with silver thiocyanate at 60° to 80° to yield α-keto thiocyanates, $R_fCO(SCN)$.[68A] These thiocyanate derivatives are readily hydrolyzed by water to yield the perfluorocarboxylic acids and thiocyanic acid.

TABLE 30

AMIDES

Empirical Formula	Structural Formula	Method	Yield %	B.p. °C/mm.	F.p. or M.p. °C	n_D^t	d_4^t	t°C	Ref.
CF_3NO	$FCONF_2$				−152.5				71
$C_2H_2BrClFNO$	$CBrClFCONH_2$				131.5				76
$C_2H_2Br_2FNO$	CBr_2FCONH_2	1001			136				77
$C_2H_2ClF_2NO$	$CClF_2CONH_2$	1001		93/18	78.5				81
$C_2H_2Cl_2FNO$	CCl_2FCONH_2			215	126.5				75
$C_2H_2F_3NO$	CF_3CONH_2	1001	99	162.5	74.8				31,82
C_2H_3BrFNO	$CHBrFCONH_2$	1001			44				
C_2H_3ClFNO	$CHClFCONH_2$	1001	98	72/1		1.4535	1.510	25	89
C_2H_3FINO	$CHFICONH_2$	1001			92.5				79
$C_2H_3F_2NO$	CHF_2CONH_2	1001			51				65
C_2H_4FNO	CH_2FCONH_2	1001	80–100		108				2,9,12, 56,76
		107	65						85
$C_3H_2Br_2F_3NO$	$CF_2BrCFBrCONH_2$	1005	90		60.6–61.0				67
$C_3H_2Cl_2F_3NO$	$CF_2ClCFClCONH_2$	1001	68		90.6–91.1				67
		1002							20
$C_3H_2Cl_3F_2NO$	$CF_2ClCCl_2CONH_2$	1002		135–148/29	57–58.5				17,19, 20,21
$C_3H_2F_3NO$	$CF_2{=}CFCONH_2$	302	65		121.4–121.9				67
$C_3H_2F_5NO$	$CF_3CF_2CONH_2$	1001	94		95				37,45
$C_3H_3F_4NO$	$CF_2HCF_2CONH_2$	1001			58.4–59.4				40
$C_3H_4F_2N_2O_2$	$CF_2(CONH_2)_2$	1001			206–207				9,36,39
$C_3H_4F_3NO$	$CF_3CH_2CONH_2$	1002			108.8				41
		1008							10
C_3H_6FNO	$CH_3CHFCONH_2$				75–76				32
	$CH_2FCONHCH_3$	1001	75		64				12,56
$C_4H_2Cl_3F_4NO$	$CCl_3(CF_2)_2CONH_2$	1002			126.5–127				84
$C_4H_2F_7NO$	$CF_3(CF_2)_2CONH_2$	1002			105				27

$C_4H_4F_3NO$	$CF_3CH{=}CHCONH_2$	1001			146.5–147.5	87
	$CH_2{=}C(CF_3)CONH_2$	1005			104	14
$C_4H_4F_3NO_3$	$CF_3CONHCH_2CO_2H$	1003			120–121	88
$C_4H_4F_4N_2O_2$	$(CF_2CONH_2)_2$	1001	98		259.8–260.3	42,64
$C_4H_5ClF_3NO$	$CH_2ClCH(CF_3)CONH_2$	1005			118	14
$C_4H_6F_3NO$	$CF_3(CH_2)_2CONH_2$	1002			136.4	41
$C_4H_6F_3NO$	$CH_3CH(CF_3)CONH_2$	1002			139.5	14
		212				14
$C_4H_6F_3NO_2$	$CH_2(OH)CH(CF_3)CONH_2$				134	14
	$CH_3C(OH)(CF_3)CONH_2$	1005			142–144	14,25
	$CF_3CH(OH)CH_2CONH_2$	1001	90		124–125	48
C_4H_7ClFNO	$CH_2FCONHCH_2CH_2Cl$	216	87.1	77/0.3	65	12
		1001				56
$C_4H_7F_3N_2O$	$CF_3CH(NH_2)CH_2CONH_2$	1001	95		120.5–121	86,87
$C_4H_8FNO_2$	$CH_2FCONHCH_2CH_2OH$	1001	91	114/0.1	21	12,56
$C_5H_2Cl_3F_6NO$	$CCl_3(CF_2)_3CONH_2$	1002			138.3–138.4	84
$C_5H_2F_5N_2O_2$	$CO(CF_2)_3CONHNH$ (cyclic)	1001			186–187	54
$C_5H_2F_9NO$	$CF_3CF_2CF(CF_3)CONH_2$	1001			106–107	35
$C_5H_3F_8NO$	$CHF_2(CF_2)_3CONH_2$	1002	85		79–80	16
$C_5H_4F_6N_2O_2$	$(CF_2)_3(CONH_2)_2$	1001	96		208–209	30,42, 54,55
$C_5H_5F_6NO$	$CF_3CONHCH_2CH_2CF_3$	1003			51–52	8
$C_5H_6F_3NO$	$CH_2{=}CHCONHCH_2CF_3$	1002		73–74/2		23
$C_5H_6F_3NO_3$	$CH_3CH(NHCOCF_3)CO_2H$	1003	85		120.5	88
$C_5H_7F_2NO$	$CH_2{=}CHCONHCH_2CHF_2$	1002			86–90/3	23
$C_6H_2F_{11}NO$	$CF_3(CF_2)_4CONH_2$	1002			117	27
$C_6H_4F_8N_2O_2$	$(CF_2)_4(CONH_2)_2$	1001			237	54,55
$C_6H_5F_7N_2O_2$	$H_2NCOCF_2CFH(CF_2)_2CONH_2$	1001			205–206	30
$C_6H_6F_7NO_2$	$CF_3(CF_2)_2CONHCH_2CH_2OH$	1006			56.5–57.5	38

TABLE 30 (*continued*)

Empirical Formula	Structural Formula	Method	Yield %	B.p. °C/mm.	F.p. or M.p. °C	n_D^t	d_4^t	t°C	Ref.
$C_6H_8F_3NO_2$	$CF_3CONCH_2CH_2OCH_2CH_2$	1001	87	47/1		1.4177		25	49
$C_6H_8F_3NO_3$	$CF_3CONHCH_2CO_2CH_2CH_3$	1003			51.5				88
$C_6H_{10}Cl_2FNO$	$CH_2FCON(CH_2CH_2Cl)_2$		40	102/0.04					12
		1001							56
$C_6H_{10}FNO_3$	$CH_2FCONHCH_2CO_2C_2H_5$	1002			50–50.5				73A
$C_6H_{10}F_3NO$	$CF_3CON(CH_2CH_3)_2$	1001	60	30/2		1.3780		25	49
$C_6H_{10}F_3NO_2$	$CF_3CH(OH)CH_2CONHCH_2CH_2OH$	1001	95	186–188/2	59–61				48
$C_6H_{11}ClFNO$	$CHClFCONH(CH_2)_3CH_3$	1004		98.5–98.7/0.5		1.4431	1.1376	25	28,70
	$CHClFCON(CH_2CH_3)_2$	1004	100	47/0.7		1.4499	1.1635	25	69
$C_6H_{11}F_2NO$	$CHF_2CONH(CH_2)_3CH_3$	1004		113/30		1.4112	1.1029	25	28,70
$C_7H_2F_{11}NO$	$CF_2(CF_2)_4CFCONH_2$	1002			112				27
$C_7H_4F_{10}N_2O_2$	$H_2NCOCF_2CF(CF_3)CF_2CF_2CONH_2$	1001	70		168–169				3
$C_7H_8F_3NO_5$	$HO_2C(CH_2)_2CH(NHCOCF_3)CO_2H$	1003	76		192				88
$C_7H_8F_5NO_2$	$CF_3CF_2CONCH_2CH_2OCH_2CH_2$	1001	85	59/1					49
$C_7H_{10}ClF_2NO$	$CF_2ClCON(CH_2)_7CH_2$	1001	90	98/1		1.4520		25	49
$C_7H_{10}F_3NO$	$CF_3CON(CH_2)_4CH_2$	1001	84	44/1		1.4153		25	49
$C_7H_{10}F_5NO$	$CF_3CF_2CONH(CH_2)_3CH_3$	1001	80	48/1		1.3642		25	49
$C_7H_{11}F_2NO$	$CHF_2CON(CH_2)_4CH_2$	1001	85	66/3		1.4500		25	49
$C_7H_{11}F_4NO$	$CF_3CHFCON(CH_2CH_3)_2$	1004		98/22		1.3910	1.228	20	50

$C_8H_2F_{13}NO$	$CF_2(CF_2)_4CFCF_2CONH_2$	1002			119				27
$C_8H_2F_{15}NO$	$CF_3(CF_2)_6CONH_2$	1002			138				27
$C_8H_8F_7NO$	$CF_3(CF_2)_2CON(CH_2)_3CH_2$	1001	76	65/2		1.3755		25	49
$C_8H_8F_7NO_2$	$CF_3(CF_2)_2CON(CH_2)_2OCH_2CH_2$	1001	89	72/2		1.3850		25	49
$C_8H_{10}F_7NO$	$CF_3(CF_2)_2CONH(CH_2)_3CH_3$	1001	80	56/2		1.3568		25	49
$C_8H_{11}F_3N_2O_4$	$CF_3CONHCH_2CONHCH_2CO_2C_2H_5$	1003	60		145				88
$C_8H_{12}F_4N_2O_4$	$(CF_2CONHCH_2CH_2OH)_2$	1001			142–148				64
$C_8H_{14}FNO$	$CH_2FCONHCH(CH_2)_4CH_2$	1001	61		99–100				2
$C_9H_3F_{16}NO$	$CHF_2(CF_2)_7CONH_2$	1002	48		143–145				16
$C_9H_{10}F_7NO$	$CF_3(CF_2)_2CON(CH_2)_4CH_2$	1001	85	57/2		1.3846		25	49
$C_9H_{11}BrF_5NO$	$CF_3CF_2CONHCH(CH_2)_4CHBr$	1007			126				66
$C_{10}H_2F_{19}NO$	$CF_3(CF_2)_8CONH_2$	1002			150				27
$C_{10}H_4F_{16}N_2O_2$	$(CF_2)_8(CONH_2)_2$	1001			233				33
$C_{10}H_{10}F_8N_2O_2$	$(CF_2)_4(CH_2NHCOCH_3)_2$	1003			180–181				54
$C_{10}H_{11}BrF_7NO$	$CF_3(CF_2)_2CONHCH(CH_2)_4CHBr$	1007			139				66
$C_{10}H_{16}F_4N_2O_2$	$(CH_2)_6(NHCOCHF_2)_2$	1004							28
$C_{10}H_{16}F_4N_2O_2$	$[(CH_2)_3NHCOCHF_2]_2$	1004		115/5		1.43		25	70
$C_{10}H_{19}F_2NO$	$CHF_2CON(C_4H_9)_2$	1004		107/10		1.427	1.0158	25	70
$C_{10}H_{19}F_2NO$	$CHF_2CONHC_8H_{17}$	1004		115/5		1.4300		25	28
	$CHF_2CON(C_4H_9)_2$	1004		95/1.5		1.5036	1.2305	25	28
$C_{10}H_{19}F_8N_2O_2$	$(CF_2CF_2CH_2NHCOCH_3)_2$	1003							55

TABLE 30 (*continued*)

Empirical Formula	Structural Formula	Method	Yield %	B.p. °C/mm.	F.p. or M.p. °C	n_D^t	d_4^t	t°C	Ref.
$C_{11}H_{11}BrF_9NO$	$CF_3(CF_2)_2CONHCH(CH_2)_4CHBr$	1007			133				66
$C_{11}H_{18}FNO_5$	$CH_3CONHC(CO_2C_2H_5)_2CH_2CH_2F$				74–76				53
$C_{12}H_{18}F_7NO$	$CF_3(CF_2)_2CON(C_4H_9\text{-}t)_2$				155				38
$C_{12}H_{20}FNO_5$	$CH_2F(CH_2)_2C(NHCOCH_3)(CO_2C_2H_5)_2$		63		76–77				53
$C_{12}H_{20}F_4N_2O_2$	$[CF_2CONH(CH_2)_3CH_3]_2$	1001			130–132				64
$C_{14}H_{28}FNO$	$CH_2FCONH(CH_2)_{11}CH_3$	1001	74		63–66				2
$C_{16}H_{22}F_7NO$	$CF_3(CF_2)_2CON[CH(CH_2)_4CH_2]_2$	1006			179.5–180				38
$C_{16}H_{28}F_4N_2O_2$	$[CF_2CON(C_3H_7\text{-}i)_2]_2$	1001							64
$C_{20}H_{48}FNO$	$CH_2FCONH(CH_2)_{17}CH_3$	1001	39		73–75				2
$C_{40}H_{76}F_4N_2O_2$	$[CF_2CONH(CH_2)_{17}CH_3]_2$	1001			105–108				64

TABLE 31

IMIDES

Empirical Formula	Structural Formula	Method	Yield %	B.p. °C/mm.	F.p. or M.p. °C	n_D^t	d_4^t	t°C	Ref.
$C_4HF_4NO_2$	$COCF_2CF_2CONH$	1009	80	178	66.0–66.5				42
$C_5HF_6NO_2$	$CO(CF_2)_3CONH$	1009	89	159	27				42,54

TABLE 32

N-BROMO AMIDES

Empirical Formula	Structural Formula	Method	Yield %	B.p. °C/mm.	F.p. or M.p. °C	n_D^t	d_4^t	t°C	Ref.
C_2HBrF_3NO	$CF_3CONHBr$	1010	63		63				65
$C_2H_2BfF_2NO$	$CHF_2CONHBr$	1010	40		43				65
C_3HBrF_5NO	$CF_3CF_2CONHBr$	1010			69				66
$C_4BrF_4NO_2$	$CO(CF_2)_2CONBr$ (cyclic)	1010							42
C_4HBrF_7NO	$CF_3(CF_2)_2CONHBr$	1010			80				47,66
$C_5BrF_6NO_2$	$CO(CF_2)_3CONBr$ (cyclic)	1010							42
C_5HBrF_9NO	$CF_3(CF_2)_3CONHBr$	1010			87				66

TABLE 33

AMIDINES

Empirical Formula	Structural Formula	Method	Yield %	B.p. °C/mm.	F.p. or M.p. °C	n_D^t	d_4^t	t°C	Ref.
$C_2H_3F_3N_2$	$CF_3C(NH_2){=}NH$	1011		40–44/14					44
$C_3H_3F_5N_2$	$CF_3CF_2C(NH_2){=}NH$	1011	100		49.6–50				44
$C_4H_3F_7N_2$	$CF_3(CF_2)_2C(NH_2){=}NH$	1011	100		52				44
$C_6H_3F_{11}N_2$	$CF_3(CF_2)_4C(NH_2){=}NH$	1011			66				44
$C_8H_3F_{15}N_2$	$CF_3(CF_2)_6C(NH_2){=}NH$	1011			86–88				44
$C_{10}H_3F_{19}N_2$	$CF_3(CF_2)_8C(NH_2){=}NH$	1011			116–130				44

TABLE 34

UREAS

Empirical Formula	Structural Formula	Method	Yield %	B.p. °C/mm.	F.p. or M.p. °C	n_D^t	d_4^t	t°C	Ref.
$C_5H_5F_3N_2O_2$	NHCONHCOC(CH$_3$)CF$_3$	1014	23		137				53
$C_5H_6F_6N_2O$	(CF$_2$CH$_2$NH)$_2$CO	1012	84		158–159				15,52
$C_7H_6F_{10}N_2O$	(CF$_3$CF$_2$CH$_2$NH)$_2$CO	1012			166–167				60
$C_7H_7F_4N_2O_2$	NHCONHCOCHCH(CH$_3$)CF$_2$CF$_2$	1014			241–243				53
$C_9H_{13}FN_2O_3$	CH$_2$F(CH$_2$)$_2$C(CH$_2$CH$_3$)CONHCONHCO	1013	52		154–155				11
$C_{10}H_{13}FN_2O_3$	CH$_2$F(CH$_2$)$_2$C(CH$_2$CH=CH$_2$)CONHCONHCO	1013	36		145–146				11
$C_{11}H_{17}FN_2O_3$	CH$_2$F(CH$_2$)$_4$C(C$_2$H$_5$)CONHCONHCO	1013	38		120–122				11
$C_{12}H_{17}FN_2O_3$	CH$_2$F(CH$_2$)$_4$C(CH$_2$CH=CH$_2$)CONHCONHCO	1013	21		105–106				11
$C_{12}H_{19}FN_2O_3$	CH$_2$F(CH$_2$)$_2$C[CH$_2$CH$_2$CH(CH$_3$)$_2$]CONHCONHCO	1013	9.4		139–141				11
$C_{14}H_{23}FN_2O_3$	CH$_2$F(CH$_2$)$_4$C[CH$_2$CH$_2$CH(CH$_3$)$_2$]CONHCONHCO	1013	16		118–120				11
$C_{21}H_6F_{38}N_2O$	[CF$_3$(CF$_2$)$_8$CH$_2$NH]$_2$CO	1012			144–146				60

TABLE 35

CARBAMATES

Empirical Formula	Structural Formula	Method	Yield %	B.p. °C/mm.	F.p. or M.p. °C	n_D^t	d_4^t	t°C	Ref.
$C_3H_6FNO_2$	$CH_2FCH_2OCONH_2$	1015	96	128–130/40	23–24				62,74
$C_4H_8FNO_2$	$CH_2FCH_2OCONHCH_3$	1015		71–74/2					62
$C_5H_3ClF_7NO$	$CF_3(CF_2)_2CH_2NHCOCl$	1016			9				60
$C_5H_7ClFNO_3$	$CH_2FCONHCO_2CH_2CH_2Cl$	1017	24		59–61				63
$C_5H_8FNO_3$	$CH_3CONHCO_2CH_2CH_2F$	1017	35		79–80.5				74
$C_5H_8FNO_3$	$CH_2FCONHCO_2CH_2CH_3$	1017	16		72–74				63
$C_5H_9F_2NO_2$	$CHF_2CH_2NHCO_2CH_2CH_3$	1015		184–185.5	37.6				80
$C_5H_{10}FNO_2$	$CH_3CH_2NHCO_2CH_2CH_2F$	1015		116–117/30					74
	$(CH_3)_2NCO_2CH_2CH_2F$	1015		55–58/2					62
$C_7H_{12}FNO_3$	$CH_2CH_2OCH_2CH_2NCO_2CH_2CH_2F$ (ring)	1015		101–104/3					62
$C_7H_{12}F_2N_2O_9$	$CH_2(NHCO_2CH_2CH_2F)_2$	1018	60		152–153				74
$C_7H_{14}FNO_2$	$(CH_3CH_2)_2NCO_2CH_2CH_2F$	1015		46–49/2					62
$C_8H_{10}F_4N_2O_4$	$C_2H_5O_2CNCF_2CF_2NCO_2C_2H_5$ (ring)	210		66/3		1.3853			24
$C_8H_{13}ClF_2N_2O_4$	$CH_2ClCH(NHCO_2CH_2CH_2F)_2$	1018	84		156–157				74
$C_8H_{14}F_2N_2O_4$	$CH_3CH(NHCO_2CH_2CH_2F)_2$	1018	90		158.5–159.5				74
$C_9H_{16}F_2N_2O_4$	$CH_3CH_2CH(NHCO_2CH_2CH_2F)_2$	1018	90		153–154				74

TABLE 36

NITRILES

Empirical Formula	Structural Formula	Method	Yield %	B.p. °C/mm.	F.p. or M.p. °C	n_D^t	d_4^t	t°C	Ref.
C_2F_3N	CF_3CN	1019	74	−63.9/743					31,82
C_2HClFN	$CHClFCN$	1019	65	66		1.3627	1.267	25	89
C_2HF_2N	CHF_2CN	1019		22.8–23.4			1.1130	14.5	83
C_2H_2FN	CH_2FCN	1019	65	80			1.0730	16	12,56,83
		102							34
$C_3Br_2F_3N$	$CF_2BrCFBrCN$	201	94	93.7/689	−59	1.4122	2.106	20	67
C_3ClF_2N	$CF_2{=}CClCN$	302		63		1.3793	1.3560	24	17
		1020							59
$C_3Cl_2F_2N$	$CF_2ClCFClCN$	1019		51.5		1.3436	1.4360	23	17,19,20,21
$C_3Cl_3F_2N$	CF_2ClCCl_2CN	1019		95.5	−33	1.3991	1.5171	23	17,19,20,21
C_3F_3N	$CF_2{=}CFCN$	302		17.7–18			1.312	10	17
		1020							59
C_3F_5N	CF_3CF_2CN	1019		−35					37
C_3HF_4N	CF_3CHFCN	1020		42					51
C_3H_4FN	CH_3CHFCN			83–83.5					32
C_4F_5N	$CF_2{=}CFCF_2CN$	1022		43–48					58
C_4HF_6N	$(CF_3)_2CHCN$	1020	85	64–64.5		1.2750		25	51
$C_4H_2Br_2F_3N$	$CH_2BrCBr(CF_3)CN$	201		57–58/20		1.4372		20	14
$C_4H_2F_3N$	$CH_2{=}C(CF_3)CN$	305		75.9–76.2/759		1.3239		20	14,26
$C_4H_3ClF_3N$	$CH_2ClCH(CF_3)CN$	202		134–135		1.3649		13	14
$C_4H_4F_3NO$	$CF_3C(CN)(OH)CH_3$	1021	65	138–139		1.3385		20	25,26
$C_5F_6N_2$	$(CF_2)_3(CN)_2$	1019		38/745					54,55
$C_5H_2F_7NO$	$CF_3(CF_2)_2CH(OH)CN$	1021		62.5–64/3					46
$C_5H_3F_4N$	$\overline{CF_2CF_2CH_2CH}CN$ (ring)	210	64	148		1.3568	1.3909	25	4,6,22

$C_5H_6ClF_2NO$	$CH_3CH_2OCF_2CHClCN$	1023		93/100					17,18
$C_5H_6F_3NO$	$CH_3CH_2OCF_2CHFCN$	1023		120–122					18
C_5H_8FNO	$CH_2FCH_2OCH_2CH_2CN$	1023	64	103–104/15					13
$C_6F_6N_2$	$CF_2CF_2CF(CN)CFCN$	210	30	73.5/634		1.3300	1.462	20	67
$C_6F_8N_2$	$(CF_2)_4(CN)_2$	1019	64	63		1.2770	1.4304	20	54,55
$C_6H_5F_4N$	$CF_2CF_2CH_2CHCH_2CN$	210		193–195		1.3748	1.3459	25	4,6
$C_6H_6F_3NO_2$	$CH_3C(O_2CCH_3)(CF_3)CN$	901		143–144					26
		901		150–152		1.355		15	25
$C_6H_{10}FNO$	$CH_2FCH_2CH_2OCH_2CH_2CN$	1023	76	105–108					13
$C_7H_7F_2NO$	$CF_2CH_2C(CN){=}COC_2H_5$			83/31					5
$C_9H_{13}F_2NO_2$	$CF_2CH_2CH(CN)C(OC_2H_5)_2$			81.1/4					5

TABLE 37

KETO NITRILES

Empirical Formula	Structural Formula	Method	Yield %	B.p. °C/mm.	F.p. or M.p. °C	n_D^t	d_4^t	t°C	Ref.
C_3H_2FNO	CH_2FCOCN	1024	25	88–93/20					7
$C_6F_6N_2O_2$	$(CF_3COCN)_2$	1024		83–84		1.440		25	68
$C_8F_{10}N_2O_2$	$(CF_3CF_2COCN)_2$	1024		106–108		1.532		25	68
$C_{10}F_{14}N_2O_2$	$(CF_3CF_2CF_2COCN)_2$	1024		136–138		1.606		25	68
$C_{14}F_{22}N_2O_2$	$[CF_3(CF_2)_4COCN]_2$	1024		190–193		1.719		25	68

TABLE 38

ISOCYANATES

Empirical Formula	Structural Formula	Method	Yield %	B.p. °C/mm.	F.p. or M.p. °C	n_D^t	d_4^t	t°C	Ref.
C_2F_3NO	CF_3NCO	1026							43
C_3F_5NO	CF_3CF_2NCO	1026		−9/742					1
$C_3H_2F_3NO$	CF_3CH_2NCO	1025		55/740		1.3486	1.387	27	60
C_4F_7NO	$CF_3(CF_2)_2NCO$	1026	76	24–26/739					1
$C_4H_2F_5NO$	$CF_3CF_2CH_2NCO$	1025		72/757		1.3350	1.487	20	37,60
C_5F_9NO	$CF_3(CF_2)_3NCO$	1026		52–53/753		1.279			1
$C_5H_2F_7NO$	$CF_3(CF_2)_2CH_2NCO$	1025		90/737	−78	1.3152	1.512	20	60
$C_6F_{11}NO$	$CF_3(CF_2)_4NCO$	1026	50	75–78/735		1.290	1.696	25	1
$C_6H_2F_9NO$	$CF_3(CF_2)_3CH_2NCO$	1025		110					60
$C_7F_{13}NO$	$CF_3(CF_2)_5NCO$	1026		99					1
$C_7H_2F_{11}NO$	$CF_3(CF_2)_4CH_2NCO$	1025		127					60
$C_8F_{15}NO$	$CF_3(CF_2)_6NCO$	1026		119					1
$C_8H_2F_{13}NO$	$CF_3(CF_2)_5CH_2NCO$	1025		147					60

$C_9F_{17}NO$	$CF_3(CF_2)_7NCO$	1026		140					1
$C_9H_2F_{15}NO$	$CF_3(CF_2)_6CH_2NCO$	1025		167					60
$C_{10}F_{19}NO$	$CF_3(CF_2)_8NCO$	1026		160–161/743		1.302	1.787	20	1
$C_{10}H_2F_{17}NO$	$CF_3(CF_2)_7CH_2NCO$	1025		184					60
$C_{11}F_{21}NO$	$CF_3(CF_2)_9NCO$	1026		180					1
$C_{11}H_2F_{19}NO$	$CF_3(CF_2)_8CH_2NCO$	1025		93/14	46–47				60
$C_{12}F_{23}NO$	$CF_3(CF_2)_{10}NCO$	1026		200					1

TABLE 39

THIOCYANATES

Empirical Formula	Structural Formula	Method	Yield %	B.p. °C/mm.	F.p. or M.p. °C	n_D^t	d_4^t	t°C	Ref.
C_3H_4FNS	CH_2FCH_2SCN	1027	78	77.5–78.5/19					56,73
$C_6H_8F_3NS$	$CF_3(CH_2)_4SCN$	1027		82/3					72

TABLE 40

α-KETO THIOCYANATES

Empirical Formula	Structural Formula	Method	Yield %	B.p. °C/mm.	F.p. or M.p. °C	n_D^t	d_4^t	t°C	Ref.
C_3F_3NOS	$CF_3CO(SCN)$	1028		72–74		1.369		25	68
C_4F_5NOS	$CF_3CF_2CO(SCN)$	1028		87		1.503		25	68
C_5F_7NOS	$CF_3(CF_2)_2CO(SCN)$	1028		106		1.644		25	68

BIBLIOGRAPHY

1. Ahlbrecht, A. H., and Husted, D. R., U. S. Patent 2,617,817(1952).
2. Bacon, J. C., Bradley, C. W., *et al.*, *J. Am. Chem. Soc.*, **70**, 2653(1948).
3. Barlow, G. B., Stacey, M., and Tatlow, J. C., *J. Chem. Soc.*, **1955**, 749.
4. Barrick, P. L., and Cramer, R. D., U. S. Patent 2,441,128(1948).
5. Barrick, P. L., U. S. Patent 2,437,289(1948).
6. Barrick, P. L., U. S. Patent 2,462,345(1949).
7. Blank, I., Mager, J., and Bergmann, E. D., *J. Chem. Soc.*, **1955**, 2190.
8. Bourne, E. J., Henery, C. E. M., *et al.*, *J. Chem. Soc.*, **1952**, 4014.
9. Bradley, C. W., U. S. Patent 2,403,576(1946).
10. Brown, F., and Musgrave, W. K. R., *J. Chem. Soc.*, **1953**, 2087.
11. Bruce, W. F., and de V. Huber, R., *J. Am. Chem. Soc.*, **75**, 4668(1953).
12. Buckle, F. J., Heap, R., and Saunders, B. C., *J. Chem. Soc.*, **1949**, 912.
13. Buckle, F. J., and Saunders, B. C., *J. Chem. Soc.*, **1949**, 2774.
14. Buxton, M. W., Stacey, M., and Tatlow, J. C., *J. Chem. Soc.*, **1954**, 366.
15. Cassady, J. T., and Lindgren, V. V., British Patent 678,910(1952).
16. Carnahan, J. E., and Sampson, H. J., U. S. Patent 2,646,449(1953).
17. Chaney, D. W., U. S. Patent 2,439,505(1948).
18. Chaney, D. W., U. S. Patent 2,443,024(1948).
19. Chaney, D. W., U. S. Patent 2,456,768(1948).
20. Chaney, D. W., U. S. Patent 2,514,473(1950).
21. Chaney, D. W., U. S. Patent 2,549,892(1951).
22. Coffman, D. D., Barrick, P. L., *et al.*, *J. Am. Chem. Soc.*, **71**, 490(1949).
23. Coover, H. W., and Dickey, J. B., U. S. Patent 2,521,902(1950).
24. Cramer, R. D., U. S. Patent 2,456,176(1948).
25. Darrell, R. A., Smith, F., *et al.*, *J. Chem. Soc.*, **1951**, 2329.
26. Dickey, J. B., U. S. Patent 2,541,466(1951).
27. Diesslin, A. R., Kauck, E. A., and Simons, J. H., U. S. Patent 2,567,011(1951).
28. duPont, British Patent 583,264(1946).
29. Evans, D. E. M., and Tatlow, J. C., *J. Chem. Soc.*, **1954**, 3779.
30. Evans, D. E. M., and Tatlow, J. C., *J. Chem. Soc.*, **1955**, 1184.
31. Gilman, H., and Jones, R. G., *J. Am. Chem. Soc.*, **65**, 1458(1943).
32. Gryszkiewicz-Trochimowski, E., *Bull. soc. chim. France*, **1949**, 928.
33. Guenthner, R. A., U. S. Patent 2,606,206(1952).
34. Halbedel, H. S., Cardon, S. Z., and Schenk, W. J., U. S. Patent 2,442,290(1948).
35. Haszeldine, R. N., *J. Chem. Soc.*, **1953**, 3559.
36. Haszeldine, R. N., *J. Chem. Soc.*, **1955**, 4302.
37. Haszeldine, R. N., and Leedham, K. J., *J. Chem. Soc.*, **1953**, 1548.
38. Hauptschein, M., and Braun, R. A., *J. Am. Chem. Soc.*, **77**, 4930(1955).
39. Henne, A. L., and DeWitt, E. G., *J. Am. Chem. Soc.*, **70**, 1548(1948).
40. Henne, A. L., and Fox, C. J., *J. Am. Chem. Soc.*, **76**, 479(1954).
41. Henne, A. L., and Stewart, J. J., *J. Am. Chem. Soc.*, **77**, 1901(1955).
42. Henne, A. L., and Zimmer, W. F., *J. Am. Chem. Soc.*, **73**, 1103(1951).
43. Huckel, W., *Nachr. Akad. Wiss Gottingen, Math-physik Klasse*, 1946, No. 1, 55.
44. Husted, D. R., U. S. Patent 2,676,985(1954).
45. Husted, D. R., and Ahlbrecht, A. H., *J. Am. Chem. Soc.*, **75**, 1605(1953).
46. Husted, D. R., and Ahlbrecht, A. H., U. S. Patent 2,681,370(1954).
47. Husted, D. R., and Kohlhase, W. L., *J. Am. Chem. Soc.*, **76**, 5141(1954).
48. Jones, R. G., *J. Am. Chem. Soc.*, **70**, 143(1948).

49. Joullie, M. M., *J. Am. Chem. Soc.*, **77,** 6662(1955).
50. Knunyants, I. L., Shchekotikhim, A. I., and Fokin, A. V., *Izvest. Akad. Nauk S.S.S.R., Otdel. Khim. Nauk*, **1953,** 282.
51. LaZerte, J. D., U. S. Patent 2,704,769(1955).
52. Lindgren, V. V., and Cassaday, J. T., U. S. Patent 2,656,384(1953).
53. Lontz, J. F., and Raasch, M. S., U. S. Patent 2,662,915(1953).
54. McBee, E. T., and Wiseman, P. A., U. S. Patent 2,515,246(1950).
55. McBee, E. T., Wiseman, P. A., and Bachman, G. B., *Ind. Eng. Chem.*, **39,** 415(1947).
56. McCombie, H., and Saunders, B. C., *Nature*, **158,** 382(1946).
57. Milani, V., Skolnik, S., and Evans, R., *J. Am. Chem. Soc.*, **77,** 2903(1955).
58. Miller, W. T., U. S. Patent 2,671,799(1954).
59. Miller, W. T., U. S. Patent 2,691,036(1954).
60. Minnesota Mining and Manufacturing Company, British Patent 689,425(1953).
61. Newman, M. S., Renoll, M. W., and Averback, I., *J. Am. Chem. Soc.*, **70,** 1023(1948).
62. Olah, Gy., and Pavlath, A., *Acta Chem. Acad. Sci. Hung.* **4,** 89(1954).
63. Oliverio, V. T., and Sawicki, E. J., *J. Org. Chem.*, **20,** 1733(1955).
64. Padbury, J. J., and Kropa, E. L., U. S. Patent 2,502,478(1950).
65. Park, J. D., Gerjovich, H. J., *et al.*, *J. Am. Chem. Soc.*, **74,** 2189(1952).
65A. Park, J. D., Larsen, E. R., *et al.*, 130th Meeting, American Chemical Society, Atlantic City, N. J., September 1956.
66. Park, J. D., Lycan, W. R., and Lacher, J. R., *J. Am. Chem. Soc.*, **76,** 1388(1954).
67. Park, J. D., Rausch, D. A., and Lacher, J. R., Private Communication.
68. Patton, R. H., and Simons, J. H., *J. Am. Chem. Soc.*, **77,** 2016(1955).
68A. Patton, R. H., and Simons, J. H., *J. Am. Chem. Soc.*, **77,** 2017(1955).
69. Pruett, R. L., Barr, J. T., *et al.*, *J. Am. Chem. Soc.*, **72,** 3646(1950).
70. Rigby, G. W., and Schroeder, H. E., U. S. Patent 2,409,315(1946).
71. Ruff, O., and Giese, M., *Ber.*, **69,** 684(1936).
72. Salzberg, P. L., U. S. Patent 2,407,292(1946).
73. Saunders, B. C., Stacey, G. J., and Wilding, I. G. E., *J. Chem. Soc.*, **1949,** 773.
73A. Saunders, B. C., and Wilding, I. G. E., *J. Chem. Soc.*, **1949,** 1279.
74. Sawicki, E., and Ray, F. E., *J. Org. Chem.*, **18,** 1561(1953).
75. Swarts, F., *Bull. soc. chim. France* (3), **13,** 992(1895).
76. Swarts, F., *Bull. soc. chim. France* (3), **15,** 1134(1896).
77. Swarts, F., *Bull. acad. roy. Belg.* (3), **35,** 849(1898).
78. Swarts, F., *Mem. couronnes acad. roy. Belg.* **61,** 94(1901).
79. Swarts, F., *Bull. soc. chim. France*, **1903,** 597.
80. Swarts, F., *Chem. Zentr.* II, 944(1904).
81. Swarts, F., *Bull. acad. roy. Belg.*, **1907,** 339.
82. Swarts, F., *Bull. acad. roy. Belg.* (5), **8,** 343(1922).
83. Swarts, F., *Bull. soc. chim. Belg.*, **31,** 364(1922).
84. Tiers, G. V. D., *J. Am. Chem. Soc.*, **77,** 6704(1955).
85. Umeda, T., Japanese Patent 3874(1952).
86. Walborsky, H. M., Baum, M., and Loncrini, D. F., *J. Am. Chem. Soc.*, **77,** 3637(1955).
87. Walborsky, H. M., and Schwarz, M., *J. Am. Chem. Soc.*, **75,** 3241(1953).
88. Weygand, F., and Leising, E., *Chem. Ber.*, **87,** 248(1954).
89. Young, J. A., and Tarrant, P., *J. Am. Chem. Soc.*, **71,** 2432(1949).

CHAPTER XI

Nitrogen Compounds—II

TABLE OF CONTENTS

PAGE

Introduction 283

Method Number

AMINES

1101 Reduction of Amides 285
1102 Ammonolysis of Alkyl Halides 285
1103 Reduction of Nitriles 285
1104 Reduction of Nitro Compounds 286
1105 Addition of Amines to Alkenes and Alkynes 286
1106 Action of Hypohalites on Amides 287
1107 Decomposition of Azides 287
1108 Synthesis of Tertiary Amines 287
1109 Reduction of Oximes 287
1110 Addition of Hydrogen Fluoride to Azomethines . 288
1111 Hydrolysis of Substituted Amides 288
1112 Reaction of Amines with Ethylene Oxide 288
1113 Interaction of Amines and Alcohols 288

AZOMETHINES

1114 Pyrolysis of Tertiary Amines 288
1115 Pyrolysis of Fluorocarbon Carbamyl Fluorides 288
1116 Pyrolysis of Oxazetidines 289

QUATERNARY AMMONIUM SALTS

1117 Interaction of Tertiary Amines with Alkyl Halides .. 289

TRIAZINES

1118 Reaction of Ammonia with Alkenes 289
1119 Trimerization of Nitriles and Amidines............ 290

DIAZO COMPOUNDS

1120 Action of Nitrous Acid on Amines................ 290
1121 Interaction of Diazomethane with Acyl Halides 290

NITROSO COMPOUNDS

1122 Reaction of Nitric Oxide with Fluorocarbon Iodides. 290
1123 Action of Nitrosyl Chloride on Silver Perfluorocarboxylates 291
1124 Action of Nitrous Acid on Amines................ 291

NITRO COMPOUNDS AND NITRITES

1125 Nitration of Alkanes 291
1126 Oxidation of Nitrosoalkanes.................... 292
1127 Addition of Nitrosyl and Nitryl Halides to Olefins .. 292
1128 Addition of Dinitrogen Tetroxide to Olefins and Alkyl Iodides 293
1129 Condensation of Nitroalkanes with Aldehydes, Ketones, and Unsaturated Esters................ 293
1130 Addition Reactions of Nitroolefins 294
1131 Action of Nitrous Acid on Alcohols 294
TABLE 41 Amines.. 295
TABLE 42 Imines and Azomethines 299
TABLE 43 Quaternary Ammonium Salts 299
TABLE 44 Triazines....................................... 300
TABLE 45 Diazo Compounds............................... 302
TABLE 46 Nitroso Compounds 302
TABLE 47 Nitro Compounds and Nitrites 303
TABLE 48 Miscellaneous Nitrogen Compounds 304
Bibliography 305

INTRODUCTION

The strong electronegativity of fluorine is observed again in the effect on the chemical properties of fluorine-containing amines. As representative of this class of compounds, the 1,1-dihydroperfluoroalkylamines exhibit slight basic properties as contrasted with their hydrocarbon analogs. They form stable diazo compounds and in this respect are more analogous to aromatic amines.

Completely fluorinated primary or secondary amines are unknown with exception of $(CF_3)_2NH$ which was prepared by the addition of hydrogen fluoride to $CF_3N{=}CF_2$.[3] The perfluorinated analogs of amines can be prepared by various fluorination procedures as discussed in Chapter I (cf. Methods 108, 111, 112). Such fluorination procedures produce compounds of the types R_fNF_2, $(R_f)_2NF$, and $(R_f)_3N$. These compounds can be considered as derivatives of NF_3 and are referred to as nitrides. The fluorocarbon nitrides as a class do not chemically resemble amines. Although the nitrides of the type $(R_f)_3N$ are very chemically inert, they undergo pyrolysis at 500° to 800° to yield perfluoroazomethines.

As representative of the class of azomethines, perfluoro-2-azapropene, $CF_3N{=}CF_2$, has received considerable attention. This compound is completely decomposed by water or aqueous base. When this compound is treated with anhydrous methanol it decomposes to yield dimethyl ether, dimethyl carbonate and ammonium fluoride. Attempts to effect the addition of chlorine and iodine have not been successful. As previously indicated, the addition of hydrogen fluoride occurs with the formation of the secondary amine.

When Ruff and Giese[63] treated silver cyanide with fluorine they obtained a low yield of a blue gas which they believed to be perfluoronitrosomethane. Because it was contaminated with a colorless gas, it was believed that isomerization took place to form trifluoroformamide:

$$CF_3NO \rightarrow FCONF_2$$

Ruff and Willenberg[64] who also directly fluorinated silver cyanide, isolated hexafluoroazomethane, $CF_3N{=}NCF_3$. This compound has also been reported by Gervasi, *et al.*[21 A] as a result of the action of elemental fluorine on either ethyleneimine or ethylenediamine. Hexafluoroazomethane is not attacked by water or aqueous hydrochloric acid at 100°; does not undergo cracking at 500°; but it spark explodes to yield nitrogen and hexafluoroethane.

More recent work as described in Methods 1122 to 1124 indicates that the disappearance of the blue color was due to the reaction of the nitrosomethane with nitrogen tetroxide (which is formed as a by-product) to form the nitromethane. If nitrogen tetroxide is removed as it is formed, the pure nitrosoalkane can be isolated. Perfluoronitrosoalkanes are extremely reactive and form dimers.

Perfluoronitrosoalkanes can be oxidized to nitro compounds (cf. Method 1116). They react with fluorine-containing olefins to form oxazetidines, and under certain conditions form copolymers of the type $[-CF_2CF_2N(R_f)-O-]_n$ with these olefins.

Little information is available on the chemistry of perfluoronitroalkanes. They are chemically stable but undergo pyrolysis at high temperatures to yield fluorocarbon olefins and acyl fluorides, among other products. Partially fluorinated nitroalkanes such as CF_2ClNO_2 and CF_2BrNO_2 when treated with SbF_3Cl_2 undergo cleavage at the carbon-nitrogen bond to form CF_3Cl and CF_3Br as well as NO_2F.

AMINES

METHOD 1101 Reduction of Amides

The reduction of fluoroalkyl amides to 1,1-dihydrofluoroalkylamines can be accomplished using an ethereal solution of lithium aluminum hydride. A series of amines having the general structure $CF_3(CF_2)_nCH_2NH_2$ (where n = 0 to 11) have been prepared by this procedure.[54,55] The yield varied from 50 to 80 percent. Other workers also prepared amines by this method.[6,11,12,33,38,53] Extreme precautions are necessary when this procedure is used as many hazardous explosions have been reported.

METHOD 1102 Ammonolysis of Alkyl Halides

Anhydrous ammonia reacts with halogens other than fluorine in such fluoroalkyl compounds as CHF_2CH_2Br or CF_3CH_2Cl. The reaction can be carried out at 120° to 185° and primary amines are produced, although Swarts[68,69] reports that the reaction of CHF_2CH_2Br and ethanolic ammonia in a sealed tube yields $CHF_2CH_2NH_2$ some $(CHF_2CH_2)_2NH$ and $(CHF_2CH_2)_2NC_2H_5$. The formation of the tertiary amine can probably be attributed to the presence of ethanol in the reaction mixture. The action of aqueous ammonia on fluoroalkyl halides also produces primary amines.[5,18,19]

When alkylamines are reacted with fluoroalkyl halides in the presence of anhydrous ammonium carbonate, secondary and tertiary amines are the resultant products.[73] For example, *n*-butylamine reacts with 1-fluoro-2-bromoethane producing $n\text{-}C_4H_9N(CH_2CH_2F)_2$ and $n\text{-}C_4H_9NHCH_2CH_2F$.

METHOD 1103 Reduction of Nitriles

Fluorocarbon nitriles can be hydrogenated over platinum catalyst to yield 1,1-dihydroalkylamines. For example, CF_3CN was reduced in an

80 percent yield to $CF_3CH_2NH_2$ by this procedure.[22] Hydrogenation of $(CF_2CF_2CN)_2$ to $(CF_2CF_2CH_2NHCOCH_3)_2$ was accomplished by McBee and Wiseman[50] using platinum oxide in acetic anhydride. The resultant compound is readily hydrolyzed with 20 percent sulfuric acid to the diamine sulfate. The Raney nickel-catalyzed reduction of $CH_2FCH_2OCH_2CH_2CN$ to the corresponding amine was accomplished by Buckle and Saunders.[10]

METHOD 1104 Reduction of Nitro Compounds

Fluorocarbon nitro compounds can be reduced to primary amines with hydrogen and Raney nickel catalyst; a 95 percent yield of $C_3F_7CH(OH)CH_2NH_2$ is obtained from the corresponding nitro alcohol.[16] Lithium aluminum hydride can be employed to reduce $C_3F_7CH_2CH(C_2H_5)NO_2$ to the corresponding amine in a 50 percent yield.[16]

METHOD 1105 Addition of Amines to Alkenes and Alkynes

Secondary amines add to fluoroolefins under anhydrous conditions to give fluorinated tertiary amines in good yields. If an excess of the secondary amine is used, dehydrofluorination of the tertiary amine occurs. The addition product of secondary amines and $\overline{CF_2CF_2CF{=}CF}$ have a greater tendency to lose hydrogen fluoride than do the addition products obtained from $CF_2{=}CFCl$.[61] For example, the addition of diethylamine to $\overline{CF_2CF_2CF{=}CF}$ yields $(C_2H_5)_2N\overline{C{=}CFCF_2CF_2}$ while the addition to $CF_2{=}CFCl$ yields only $(C_2H_5)NCF_2CFClH$. The addition of secondary amines to fluoroolefins under hydrolytic conditions yields substituted amides.

Primary or secondary amines when added to fluorine-containing alkynes yield unsaturated secondary or tertiary fluoroalkylamines. The addition of diethylamine to 1,1,1-trifluoropropyne catalyzed by cuprous chloride resulted in $CF_3CH{=}CHN(C_2H_5)_2$.[29] When cyclohexylamine was added to hexafluorobutyne-2, the formation of *cyclo*-$C_6H_{11}NHC(CF_3){=}CHCF_3$ was observed.[60]

The addition of primary amines to fluoroolefins under anhydrous conditions yields imines.[61] Butylamine reacts with $CF_2{=}CFCl$ to give a mixture of $C_4H_9N{=}CFCFClH$ and $C_4H_9N{=}C(NHC_4H_9)CHClF$. Butylamine also reacts with $\overline{CF_2CF_2CF{=}CF}$ to produce $C_4H_9N{=}\overline{CC({=}NC_4H_9)CF_2CHF}$ (also cf. Method 1004).

METHOD 1106 Action of Hypohalites on Amides

The Hofmann degradation of perfluoroamides was demonstrate by Husted and Kohlhase to yield only perfluoroalkyl halides rather than the expected amines (cf. Method 213). However, Henne and Stewart[36] indicate that amines are formed from amides of the type $R_fCH_2CONH_2$ and $R_f(CH_2)_2CONH_2$. Reaction of trifluoroporpionamide with alkaline hypobromite produced only a 3 percent yield of $CF_3CH_2NH_2$. The low yield was attributed to a loss of HF in the alkaline medium to form the acylamide $CF_2{=}CHCONHBr$ which then reacted with the free bromine present to give $CF_2BrCHBrCONHBr$. However, the Hofmann degradation of $CF_3(CH_2)_2CONH_2$ produced a 35 percent yield of $CF_2(CH_2)_2NH_2$.

METHOD 1107 Decomposition of Azides

The Schmidt-Curtius rearrangement of fluorine-containing azides to the amines was reported by Henne and Stewart.[36] The azide prepared from CF_3CH_2COCl was rearranged in the presence of concentrated sulfuric acid and a 25 percent yield of $CF_3CH_2NH_2$ was reported. Rearrangement of $CF_3(CH_2)_2CON_3$ resulted in an 81 percent yield of $CF_3(CH_2)_2NH_2$. Similar treatment of $C_3F_7CON_3$ gave a 76 percent yield of the isocyanate C_3F_7NCO, and a 10 percent yield of $C_2F_5CONH_2$ which was presumed to be formed by instantaneous hydrolysis of the expected amine $C_3F_7NH_2$.

METHOD 1108 Synthesis of Tertiary Amines

A novel synthesis of fluorocarbon tertiary amines has been reported by Dresdner.[20] This preparation involves the thermal reaction between perfluoroalkyl sulfurpentafluorides and perfluoroazomethines such as perfluoro-2-azapropene:

$$CF_3SF_5 + CF_3N{=}CF_2 \xrightarrow{540^\circ} (CF_3)_3N$$

The reaction which is carried out in nickel tube packed with sodium fluoride pellets does not proceed until the decomposition temperature of the perfluoroalkyl sulfurpentafluoride is exceeded. When $C_2F_5SF_5$ is reacted with the perfluoroazomethine reasonable yields of $C_2F_5N(CF_3)_2$ are obtained. It is interesting to note that the reaction of $(CF_3)_2SF_4$ with $CF_3N{=}F_2$ does not yield any tertiary amine. It appears that this reaction involves two simultaneous disproportionations resulting in the formation of C_2F_6, SF_4, CF_3SF_3 and CF_4.

METHOD 1109 Reduction of Oximes

The reduction of oximes to primary amines is accomplished with hydrogen and Raney nickel catalyst. The preparation of $CF_3CH(NH_2)CH_3$ from the oxime of CF_3COCH_3 was effected in this manner.[18,19]

METHOD 1110 Addition of Hydrogen Fluoride to Azomethines

The addition of hydrogen fluoride to perfluoro-2-azopropene proceeds easily and almost quantitatively to yield bistrifluoromethylamine $(CF_3)_2NH$. This reaction was carried out in an autoclave at 150° for 15 hours.[3] A previous patent by Pearlson and Hals[59] refers to the preparation of $C_2F_5NHCF_3$ by the addition of hydrogen fluoride to $C_2F_5N{=}CF_2$.

METHOD 1111 Hydrolysis of Substituted Amides

$$(CF_2CF_2CH_2NHCOCH_3)_2 \xrightarrow[40\%]{H_2SO_4} (CF_2CF_2CH_2NH_2)_2 \quad ^{51}$$

METHOD 1112 Reaction of Amines with Ethylene Oxide

$$CHF_2CH_2NH_2 + \overline{CH_2CH_2O} \xrightarrow[100°]{4\ hrs} CHF_2CH_2NHCH_2CH_2OH \quad ^{15}$$

METHOD 1113 Interaction of Amines and Alcohols

$$(C_2H_5)_2NH + CH_2FCH_2OH \xrightarrow[100°]{3\ hrs} (C_2H_5)_2NCH_2CH_2F \quad ^{46}$$

AZOMETHINES

METHOD 1114 Pyrolysis of Tertiary Amines

The pyrolysis of tertiary perfluoroalkylamines in a graphite tube at 600° to 800° results in a mixture of fluorocarbons and perfluoroazomethines of the proposed structure $R_fN{=}CF_2$.[59] For example, the pyrolysis of $(C_2F_5)_3N$ at 745° gives $C_2F_5N{=}CF_2$. However, pyrolysis of the same amine at 500° to 550° in the presence of AlF_3—Al_2O_3 catalyst yields $C_2F_5N{=}CFCF_3$.

METHOD 1115 Pyrolysis of Fluorocarbon Carbamyl Fluorides

Pyrolysis of bis(trifluoromethyl)carbamyl fluoride at 500° to 600° results in the quantitative formation of perfluoro-2-azapropene and carbonyl fluoride. The pyrolysis which is described by Young, *et al.*[75] takes place in a nickel tube filled with nickel packing. The starting material is obtained by the electrolytic fluorination of $(CH_3)_2NCOCl$ or other nitrogen-containing compounds (cf. Method 111).

METHOD 1116 Pyrolysis of Oxazetidines

The pyrolysis of the oxazetidine, $CF_3\overline{NCF_2CF_2O}$, in the absence of air at 550° resulted in the formation of quantitative amounts of perfluoro-2-azapropene and carbonyl fluoride. The oxazetidine was prepared by Barr and Haszeldine[2] by the addition of trifluoromethylnitrosomethane to tetrafluoroethylene. In this addition, adjunctive polymers of the type $-[CF_2CF_2\underset{\displaystyle CF_2}{\underset{|}{N}}O]_n-$ are formed which also pyrolyzes to the azomethine at 400°.

QUATERNARY AMMONIUM SALTS

METHOD 1117 Interaction of Tertiary Amines with Alkyl Halides

Tertiary amines react readily with 1-bromo-2-fluoroethane to yield quaternary salts.[47,65] For example, the reaction of $(CH_3)_3N$ with CH_2FCH_2Br gives $[(CH_3)NCH_2CH_2F]^+Br^-$. As discussed previously (cf. Method 301), tertiary amines react with fluoroalkyl halides to yield olefins through the apparent formation and decomposition of quaternary salts at elevated temperatures. However, decomposition of tetramethylammoniumfluoride yields CH_3F (cf. Method 218).

TRIAZINES

METHOD 1118 Reaction of Ammonia with Alkenes

The preparation of 1,3,5-tris(fluoroalkyl)triazines may be accomplished by the reaction of anhydrous ammonia and fluoroolefins in the presence of copper acetate.[14,21,62] Some examples are as follows:

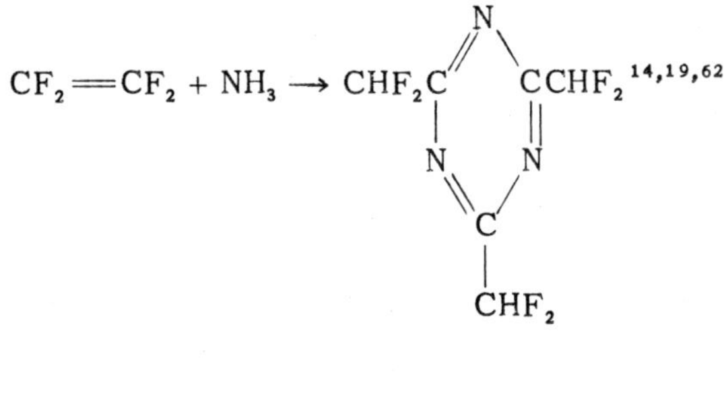

$$CF_2 = CFBr + NH_3 \rightarrow CHFBr - C \overset{\displaystyle N}{\underset{\displaystyle N}{\diagdown}} C - CHFBr$$

$$CHFBr$$

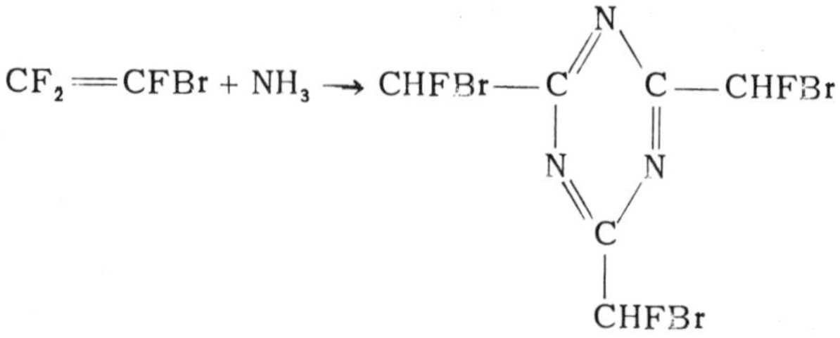

METHOD 1119 Trimerization of Nitriles and Amidines

Brown and Reilly[9] found that fluorocarbon nitriles R_fCN undergo trimerization to form 1,3,5-tris(fluoroalkyl)triazines. The trimerization occurs at $300°$ to $350°$ under autogenous pressure in the absence of catalysts.

An alternative synthesis used by these investigators involves heating a fluorocarbon amidine at atmospheric pressure. This results in the formation of a substituted triazine ring with the evolution of ammonia. Representative of the types of triazines prepared by these procedures are: 1,3,5-tris(trifluoromethyl)-, 1,3,5-tris(pentafluoroethyl)-, and 1,3,5-tris(heptafluoropropyl)triazine.

DIAZO COMPOUNDS

METHOD 1120 Action of Nitrous Acid on Amines

Diazo compounds can be prepared in good yields by the reaction of nitrous acid with 1,1-dihydroperfluoroalkylamines. For example, Gilman and Jones[22] prepared CF_3CHN_2 in a 68 percent yield from $CF_3CH_2NH_2$ (cf. Method 218).

METHOD 1121 Interaction of Diazomethane with Acyl Halides

Diazoketones can be prepared by the reaction of acyl halides with diazomethane. Brown and Musgrave[8] prepared CF_3COCHN_2 from CF_3COCl in a 63 percent yield using this procedure. Similarly, Park and co-workers[58] in a study of the Arndt-Eistert reaction prepared $C_3F_7COCHN_2$ and $C_3F_7(CH_2)_2COCHN_2$ (cf. Methods 714, 910).

NITROSO COMPOUNDS

METHOD 1122 Reaction of Nitric Oxide with Fluorocarbon Iodides

Nitric oxide reacts with perfluoroalkyl iodides to give deep blue gaseous nitrosoalkanes of the general formula $C_nF_{2n+1}NO$.[1,30] Other fluorine-containing nitroso compounds such as CF_2ClCF_2NO, CF_2BrCF_2NO, CF_2BrNO and CF_2ClNO are similarly obtained from the respective iodides.[30] The reactions involve the homolytic scission of R_fI to a fluorocarbon radical by means of ultraviolet light (in the presence of a small amount of mercury) and subsequent reaction with nitric oxide. The reaction as carried out by Banus[1] involves irradiation in the vapor-phase for several hours in a silica bulb at low temperatures without shaking, while Haszeldine[30] describes a method whereby the reactants are sealed in a silica tube and irradiated while shaking for several days. In either case, good yields are obtained.

It was discovered by Barr and Haszeldine[2] more recently, that removal of nitrogen tetroxide formed in this reaction offers a method for obtaining improved yields of perfluoroalkylnitroso compounds since dinitrogen tetroxide reacts with the nitroso compound to yield nitromethane upon irradiation.

When the reaction between trifluoromethyl iodide and nitric oxide is carried out in the presence of mercury at 100° for six days, trifluoronitromethane can be isolated.[41]

METHOD 1123 Action of Nitrosyl Chloride on Silver Perfluorocarboxylates

Perfluoroalkylnitroso compounds can also be prepared by the action of nitrosyl chloride on silver perfluorocarboxylates.[1,32] However, the yields are very low and separation from the numerous decomposition products is difficult. In addition to the nitroso compounds, small amounts of the nitro derivatives are also obtained.

METHOD 1124 Action of Nitrous Acid on Amines

N-Nitrosoamines can be prepared by treatment of a fluorocarbon amine with nitrous acid. The first such preparation of a fluorine-containing N-nitrosoamine by Swarts[68] involved the treatment of $(CHF_2CH_2)_2NH$ with nitrous acid to form $(CHF_2CH_2)_2NNO$. More recently, $(C_2F_5)_2NNO$ was prepared by Haszeldine and Mattinson[34] by this procedure.

NITRO COMPOUNDS AND NITRITES

METHOD 1125 Nitration of Alkanes

The preparation of fluorine-containing nitroalkanes by direct nitration is not readily accomplished. When 1,1,1-trifluoropropane is treated with concentrated nitric acid at 395° low yields of both $CF_3CH_2NO_2$ and

$CF_3CH_2CH_2NO_2$ are produced.[49] When the same nitration is carried out in the presence of oxygen at 440° to 460° a mixture of $CF_3CH_2CH_2NO_2$ and CF_3CHO results.[66]

METHOD 1126 Oxidation of Nitrosoalkanes

Perfluoroalkylnitroso compounds are readily oxidized to the nitro compounds by a variety of oxidizing agents. The highest yields of CF_3NO_2 are obtained when CF_3NO is treated with oxygen at 100° for 10 days. Jander and Haszeldine[39,41] report yields of 80 percent of perfluoronitromethane and observed that the completion of the reaction is indicated by the disappearance of the characteristic blue colored nitroso compound.

Another method for the oxidation of nitroso compounds employs hydrogen peroxide. Banus, prepared both CF_3NO_2 and $C_3F_7NO_2$ from the corresponding nitroso compounds in this manner.

Various metallic oxides such as Mn_2O_7, PbO_2, Pb_2O_3 and Cr_2O_3 have been shown by Haszeldine[30] to be useful in oxidizing fluorine-containing nitroso compounds:

$$CF_3NO + Mn_2O_7 \xrightarrow{49\%} CF_3NO_2$$

$$CF_3NO + Cr_2O_3 \xrightarrow{38\%} CF_3NO_2$$

$$CF_3NO + PbO_2 \xrightarrow{37\%} CF_3NO_2$$

$$C_2F_5NO + Mn_2O_7 \xrightarrow{33\%} C_2F_5NO_2$$

$$C_3F_7NO + Pb_2O_3 \xrightarrow{22\%} C_3F_7NO_2$$

When manganese heptoxide is used, explosions are likely to occur.

METHOD 1127 Addition of Nitrosyl and Nitryl Halides to Olefins

Nitrosyl halides can be added to fluoroolefins to give good yields of nitro compounds. The reaction probably proceeds through the nitroso compound which is oxidized to the nitro compound. It is believed that the addition occurs by the formation of the ionic intermediate NO^+X^- rather than by a free-radical mechanism. The halogen adds to the fluoroolefin to yield a dihalo-derivative as a by-product of the reaction.[30,74] From $CF_2{=}CFCl$ and NOCl, Haszeldine[30] obtained a 67 percent yield of $CF_2ClCFClNO_2$ and a 16 percent yield of $CFCl_2CF_2Cl$. Similarly, $CF_2{=}CF_2$ and NOBr yields a mixture of 37 percent of $CF_2BrCF_2NO_2$ and 10 percent of CF_2BrCF_2Br. In contrast, $CHF{=}CHCl$ reacts with NOCl and rearranges to yield 45 percent of the oxime $CHClFCCl{=}NOH$.[74]

Nitryl chloride, NO_2Cl, adds to $CF_2{=\!=}CF_2$ to give a 57 percent yield of $CF_2ClCF_2NO_2$.[30]

METHOD 1128 Addition of Dinitrogen Tetroxide to Olefins or Alkyl Iodides

When dinitrogen tetroxide was reacted with fluoroolefins, 1,2-dinitrofluoroalkanes were produced. This reaction as applied to fluoroolefins was first described by Hass and Whitaker[24] who obtained $NO_2CClFCF_2NO_2$ and $NO_2CF_2CF_2NO_2$ from chlorotrifluoroethylene and tetrafluoroethylene, respectively. Other olefins such as $CClF{=\!=}CClF$ were used by Haszeldine[30] and Coffman[14] to produce dinitrofluoroalkanes.

The reaction of heptafluoropropyl iodide with dinitrogen tetroxide is reported by Banus[1] to give low yields of perfluoronitropropane. This reaction is carried out by irradiation of the mixture in the presence of mercury as a sensitizer; and fluorocarbons such as C_3F_6 and C_6F_{14} were also isolated.

METHOD 1129 Condensation of Nitroalkanes with Aldehydes, Ketones, and Unsaturated Esters

Fluoroalkyl aldehyde hydrates condense with nitroalkanes producing the corresponding fluorine-containing nitroalcohols. The condensation of nitromethane, nitroethane and 1-nitropropane with various fluorine-containing aldehyde hydrates is summarized as follows:[16]

$$CF_3CHO \cdot H_2O + CH_3NO_2 + K_2CO_3 \xrightarrow{47\%} CF_3CHOHCH_2NO_2$$

$$C_3F_7CHO \cdot H_2O + CH_3CH_2NO_2 + K_2CO_3 \xrightarrow{70\%} C_3F_7CHOHCH(CH_3)NO_2$$

$$C_3F_7CHO \cdot H_2O + CH_3CH_2CH_2NO_2 + K_2CO_3 \xrightarrow{78\%} C_3F_7CHOHCH(C_2H_5)NO_2$$

The condensation of nitroalkanes with fluoroketones, however, yields only moderate amounts of nitroalcohol:

$$C_3F_7COCH_3 + CH_3NO_2 + K_2CO_3 \xrightarrow{28\%} C_3F_7C(CH_3)OHCH_2NO_2 \qquad (16)$$

The fluorine-containing nitroalcohols dehydrate readily to the corresponding nitroolefins.

A Michael type condensation of CH_3NO_2 with $CF_3CH{=\!=}CHCO_2R$ in the presence of triethylamine results in a 65 percent yield of $CF_3CH(CH_2NO_2)CH_2CO_2R$.[16]

METHOD 1130 Addition Reactions of Nitroolefins

The fluorine-containing nitroolefins show little reactivity toward acid catalyzed additions, however, base catalyzed additions proceed in the following manner:[16]

$$C_3F_7CH{=}CHNO_2 + CH_3NO_2 + NaOCH_3 \xrightarrow{68\%} C_3F_7CH(CH_2NO_2)_2$$

$$C_3F_7CH{=}CHNO_2 + C_2H_5OH \xrightarrow{35\%} C_3F_7CH(OC_2H_5)CH_2NO_2$$

$$C_3F_7CH{=}CHNO_2 + CH_2(CO_2C_2H_5)_2 + NaOC_2H_5 \xrightarrow{49\%} C_3F_7CH[CH(CO_2C_2H_5)_2]CH_2NO_2$$

$$C_3F_7CH{=}CHNO_2 + C_2H_5MgBr \longrightarrow C_3F_7CH(C_2H_5)CH_2NO_2$$

METHOD 1131 Action of Nitrous Acid on Alcohols

Fluoroalcohols can be esterified to yield the esters of nitrous acid by means of aqueous sodium nitrite and hydrochloric acid:

$$CH_2FCH_2OH + NaNO_2/HCl/N_2O \xrightarrow{40\%} CH_2FCH_2ONO$$ [46]

$$CF_3CH_2OH + NaNO_2/HCl/H_2O \xrightarrow{27\%} CF_3CH_2ONO$$ [34]

TABLE 41

AMINES

Empirical Formula	Structural Formula	Method	Yield %	B.p. °C/mm.	F.p. or M.p. °C	n_D^t	d_4^t	t °C	Ref.
CF_5N	CF_3NF_2	112			−122.1				13
C_2F_7N	$CF_3CF_2NF_2$	108		−34.3	glass				13,17
	$(CF_3)_2NF$	108	40–70	−37					71
C_2HF_6N	$(CF_3)_2NH$	1110	89	−6.7					3
$C_2H_2F_3N$	$CH_2{=}CFNF_2$	104							37,56
$C_2H_3F_4N$	$CH_3CF_2NF_2$	104							37,56
$C_2H_4F_3N$	$CF_3CH_2NH_2$	1101	80	37/740					6,53,54
		1102							5
		1103	80	37–37.3/743			1.2452	25	22
		1106	3	36/744		1.295	1.245	30	36
		1107	25						36
$C_2H_5F_2N$	$CHF_2CH_2NH_2$	1102		67.5–67.8/757		1.1757		11.9	68
		110							72
C_3F_9N	$(CF_3)_3N$	108		−6 to −7					25,28
		111		−11/735					44,45
		1108		−10.9(Calc.)	−114.7				20
C_3HF_8N	$C_2F_5NHCF_3$	1110							59
$C_3H_4F_5N$	$C_2F_5CH_2NH_2$	1101	80	49–49.5/739		1.297	1.400	20	33,38,54
$C_3H_6F_3N$	$CF_3(CH_2)_2NH_2$	1106	35	67.8/744		1.3332	1.162	30	36
		1107	81						36
$C_3H_6F_3N$	$CF_3CH(NH_2)CH_3$	1109		46–47		1.3210		20	18,19
$C_3H_6F_3NO \cdot HCl$	$CF_3CH(OH)CH_2NH_2 \cdot HCl$	1104	50		154–155				16
		1106			147–148				43
$C_3H_7F_2N$	$CH_3CF_2CH_2NH_2$	1102		75–77		1.3622		25	18,19
	$CHF_2(CH_2)_2NH_2$	1102		92–94		1.3650		20	18
	$CHF_2CH(NH_2)CH_3$	1109		80–82					19
$C_4F_{11}N$	$(CF_3)_2NC_2F_5$	108		20–22					25,28
		1108	46	20.5					20

TABLE 41 (*continued*)

Empirical Formula	Structural Formula	Method	Yield %	B.p. °C/mm.	F.p. or M.p. °C	n_D^t	d_4^t	t °C	Ref.
$C_4H_4F_7N$	$CF_3(CF_2)_2CH_2NH_2$	1101		68/740		1.298	1.493	20	54,55
$C_4H_7F_4N$	$(CHF_2CH_2)_2NH$	1102		124.4/757			1.3041	16.5	68
$C_4H_8FNO_2 \cdot HCl$	$CH_2FCH_2O_2CCH_2NH_2 \cdot HCl$		80		150				65
$C_4H_8F_3N$	$CH_3CH(CF_3)CH_2NH_2$	1101		50–110					11
$C_4H_9F_2N$	$C_2H_5CF_2CH_2NH_2$	1102		110–102					19
$C_4H_9F_2NO$	$CHF_2CH_2NHCH_2CH_2OH$	1112		63–65/2					15
$C_5F_{11}N$	$CF_2(CF_2)_4NF$ (cyclic)	111		48		1.281	1.744	20	67
$C_5H_{13}N$	$(C_2F_5)_2NCF_3$	108		45.5–46.5					25,28
		111		45/734					44,45
$C_5H_4F_9N$	$CF_3(CF_2)_3CH_2NH_2$	1101		87/740					55
$C_5H_5F_8N$	$H(CF_2)_4CH_2NH_2$	1101	51.7	123–124					12
$C_5H_6F_7O$	$C_3F_7CH(OH)CH_2NH_2$	1104	84	68–69					16
$C_5H_8F_6N_2$	$CF_2(CF_2CH_2NH_2)_2$	1103							50
$C_5H_{10}FNO$	$CH_2FCH_2O(CH_2)_3NH_2$	1103		160–164/760					10
C_6F_{13}									
$C_6F_{13}N$	$CF_2(CF_2)_4CFNF_2$ (cyclic)	108	0.2	75–76		1.286	1.787	25	27
		111		77		1.292		20	67
$C_6F_{15}N$	$(C_2F_5)_3N$	108		70.3		1.262	1.736	25	25,28
		111		68–69		1.258	1.708	25	44,45
$C_5H_4F_{11}N$	$CF_3(CF_2)_4CH_2NH_2$	1101		107/740					55
$C_6H_8F_7NO$	$C_3F_7CH(OH)CH(CH_3)NH_2$	1104	65		82–83				16
$C_6H_8F_8N_2$	$(CF_2CF_2CH_2NH_2)_2$	1103		65–66/5–6	44–45				50
		1110	40						51
$C_6H_{11}ClF_3N$	$(C_2H_5)_2NCF_2CFClH$	1105	87	32–33/5.5–6			1.19	25	61
$C_6H_{11}F_4N$	$(CHF_2CH_2CH_2)_2NH$	1102		91–94					18
	$(CHF_2CH_2)_2NC_2H_5$	1102		137/754					69
$C_6H_{14}FN$	$CH_2FCH_2N(C_2H_5)_2$	1112		107–113		1.400	0.8775	20	46

$C_6H_{14}FN \cdot HCl$	$CH_3(CH_2)_3NHCH_2CH_2F \cdot HCl$	1102			195–200				73
$C_7F_{15}N$	$CF(CF_3)(CF_2)_3CF(CF_3)NF$	108	5		94–95				26
$C_7F_{17}N$	$(C_2F_5)_2NC_3F_7$	111		93		1.270	1.764	25	44
$C_7H_4F_{13}N$	$CF_3(CF_2)_5CH_2NH_2$	1101		129/740		1.309	1.624	20	55
$C_7H_5F_{12}N$	$H(CF_2)_6CH_2NH_2$				118–119				12
$C_7H_9F_4NO_2$	$CH_2CF_2CF_2C(CH_3)CH(NH_2)CO_2H$	1110	68						48
$C_7H_{10}F_7N$	$C_3F_7CH(C_2H_5)CH_2NH_2$	1104	39	68/81		1.3443		20	16
	$C_3F_7CH_2CH(C_2H_5)NH_2$	1104	50	60/82		1.3388		20	16
$C_7H_{10}F_7NO \cdot HCl$	$C_3F_7CH(OH)CH(C_2H_5)NH_2 \cdot HCl$	1104	30		197–198				16
$C_7H_{12}F_3N$	$CF_3CH{=}CHN(C_2H_5)_2$	1105	28	40/105					29
$C_8F_{17}N$	$CF_2(CF_2)_4CFN(CF_3)_2$	111		110–111		1.286	1.835	20	44,45
$C_8F_{19}N$	$(C_2F_5)_2NC_4F_9$	111		113/743		1.275	1.792	26	44
	$[(CF_3)_2CF]_2NC_2F_5$	111		108/736		1.298		26	44,45
$C_8H_4F_{15}N$	$CF_3(CF_2)_6CH_2NH_2$	1101		146/740					55
$C_8H_{10}F_5N$	$(C_2H_5)_2NC{=}CFCF_2CF_2$	1105		76–77/52–54		1.3914	1.2271	25	61
$C_8H_{14}F_3NO$	$CF_3COCH_2CH_2N(C_2H_5)_2$		17	78–88/30					7
$C_8H_{16}FNO_2$	$CH_2FCO_2(CH_2)_2N(C_2H_5)_2$	902		96.5–97/16					23
$C_8H_{17}F_2N \cdot HCl$	$CH_3(CH_2)_3N(CH_2CH_2F)_2 \cdot HCl$	1102			66–68				73
$C_9F_{21}N$	$(C_3F_7)_3N$	108		129.9		1.279	1.822	25	25,28
		111		130		1.279	1.821	25	44
$C_9H_4F_{17}N$	$CF_3(CF_2)_7CH_2NH_2$	1101		165/740					55
$C_9H_5F_{16}N$	$H(CF_2)_8CH_2NH_2$	1101	60	86–89					12
$C_9H_{16}F_3N$	$CF_3CH(NH_2)CH_2CH(CH_2)_4CH_2$	1109	14	56–58/2					57

TABLE 41 (*continued*)

Empirical Formula	Structural Formula	Method	Yield %	B.p. °C/mm.	F.p. or M.p. °C	n_D^t	d_4^t	t°C	Ref.
$C_{10}F_{21}N$	$(C_2F_5)_2NCF(CF_2)_4CF_2$	111		145–149/738		1.300	1.854	21.5	44
$C_{10}F_{23}N$	$(C_3F_7)_2NCF_2CF(CF_3)_2$	108		146–148		1.283	1.84	25	25,28
$C_{10}F_{24}N_2$	$[CF_2N(C_2F_5)_2]_2$	111		185–187/736		1.291	1.858	27	44
$C_{10}H_4F_{19}N$	$CF_3(CF_2)_9CH_2NH_2$	1101		183/740	48				54,55
$C_{10}H_{13}F_6N$	$CH_2(CH_2)_4CHNHC(CF_3){=}CHCF_3$	1105		65–66/10		1.3874	1.2461	25	60
$C_{10}H_{14}F_5N$	$(C_3H_7)_2NC{=}CFCF_2CF_2$	1105	35	97–98/23		1.4016	1.160	25	61
$C_{11}F_{23}N$	$CF_2(CF_2)_4CFCF_2N(C_2F_5)_2$	111		163–165/742	69	1.304	1.892	26	44,45
$C_{11}H_4F_{21}N$	$CF_3(CF_2)_8CH_2NH_2$	1101		200/740					55
$C_{12}F_{27}N$	$(n\text{-}C_4F_9)_3N$	108		179.3		1.291	1.873	25	25,28
		111		177.2/755.3		1.290	1.856	25	44,45
$C_{12}H_4F_{23}N$	$CF_3(CF_2)_{10}CH_2NH_2$	1101		218/740					55
$C_{13}H_4F_{25}N$	$CF_3(CF_2)_{11}CH_2NH_2$	1101		235/740					55
$C_{15}F_{33}N$	$(C_5F_{11})_3N$(Isomeric Mixture)	111		215–216.5		1.301	1.923	25	44,45
	Cyclo-C_6F_9-1,3,5-$[CF_2N(CF_3)_2]_3$	111		221–45/740					44
$C_{18}F_{39}N$	$[CF_3(CF_2)_5]_3N$	111		258		1.305	1.923	25	44
$C_{18}F_{40}N_2$	$[CF_2N(C_4F_9)_2]_2$	111		242–248/751		1.308	1.902	25	44

TABLE 42

IMINES AND AZOMETHINES

Empirical Formula	Structural Formula	Method	Yield %	B.p. °C/mm.	F.p. or M.p. °C	n_D^t	d_4^t	t°C	Ref.
C_2F_5N	$CF_3N{=}CF_2$	1115	96	−33 to −31					75
		1116	Quant.	−33.7					2
C_2H_2FN	$CH_2{=}C{=}NF$	104							37,56
$C_2H_3F_2N$	$CH_3CF{=}NF$	104							37,56
C_3F_7N	$C_2F_5N{=}CF_2$	1114		13.2					59
C_4F_9N	$C_3F_7N{=}CF_2$	1114		12.3–12.5					59
	$C_2F_5N{=}CFCF_3$	1114		13–13.5					59
$C_5F_{11}N$	$CF_3(CF_2)_3N{=}CF_2$	1114		39					59
$C_6F_{13}N$	$C_3F_7N{=}CFC_2F_5$	1114		56.5–57.5					59
$C_6H_8F_3NO_2$	$CF_3C({=}NH)CH_2CO_2C_2H_5$			157/145	25.2				70
$C_6H_{10}ClF_2N$	$CH_3(CH_2)_3N{=}CFCHClF$	1105	33	51/26		1.4006	1.0936	25	61
$C_6H_{15}F_3N_2$	$C_3H_7N{=}CC({=}NC_3H_7)CF_2CHF$ (ring)	1105	56		88–89				61
$C_{10}H_{20}ClFN_2$	$CH_3(CH_2)_3N{=}C(NHC_4H_9)CHClF$	1105	12			1.4387			61
$C_{12}H_{19}F_3N_2$	$CH_3(CH_2)_3N{=}C{-}C({=}NC_4H_9)CF_2CHF$ (ring)	1105	72		65–66				61

TABLE 43

QUATERNARY AMMONIUM SALTS

Empirical Formula	Structural Formula	Method	Yield %	B.p. °C/mm.	F.p. or M.p. °C	n_D^t	d_4^t	t°C	Ref.
$C_5H_{13}BrFN$	$[(CH_3)_3(CH_2FCH_2)N]Br$	1117	14		274				47,65
$C_5H_{13}ClFN$	$[(CH_3)_3(CH_2FCH_2)N]Cl$	1117			244(dec.)				47
$C_5H_{13}FIN$	$[(CH_3)_3(CH_2FCH_2)N]I$	1117			250–251(dec.)				47
$C_7H_{15}ClFNO_2$	$[(CH_3)_3NCH_2CO_2CH_2CH_2F]Cl$	1117	80		122				65
$C_8H_{19}BrFN$	$[(C_2H_5)_3(CH_2FCH_2)N]Br$	1117			237				65

TABLE 44

TRIAZINES

Empirical Formula	Structural Formula	Method	Yield %	B.p. °C/mm.	F.p. or M.p. °C	n_D^t	d_4^t	t°C	Ref.
$C_6F_9N_3$	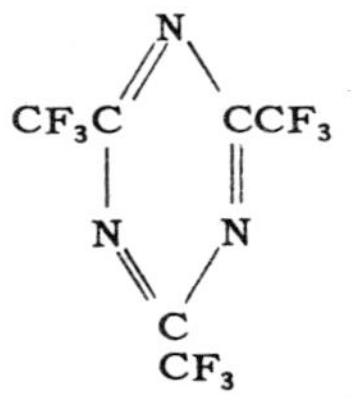	107		99	−24.8	1.3231	1.5857(26)	20	57A
		1119		95–96		1.3161	1.5930	25	9
$C_6H_3Br_3F_3N_3$	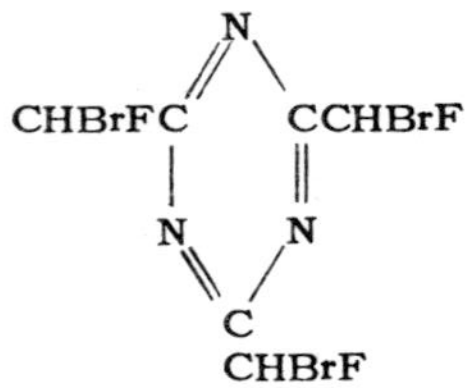	1118							62
$C_6H_3Cl_3F_3N_3$	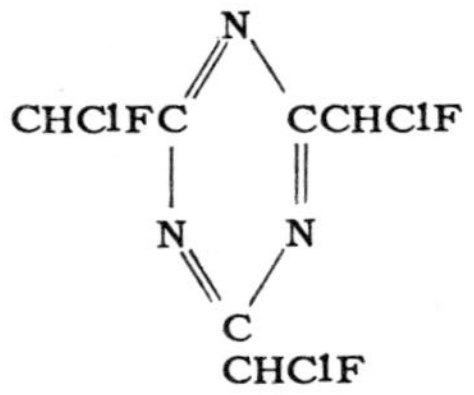	1118		95–96/3					21,62

$C_6H_3F_6N_3$	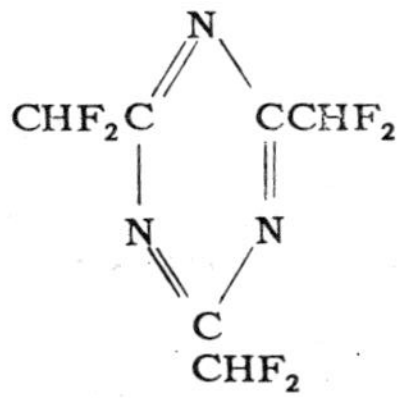	1118	72–73/9				14,19,62
$C_6H_6F_3N_3$	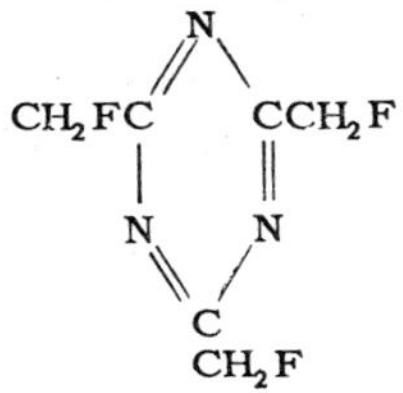	1118					62
$C_9F_{15}N_3$	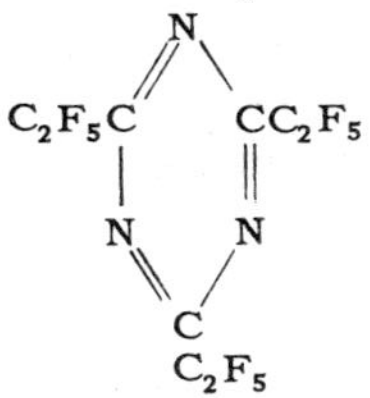	1119	121–122	1.3131	1.6506	25	9
$C_{12}F_{21}N_3$	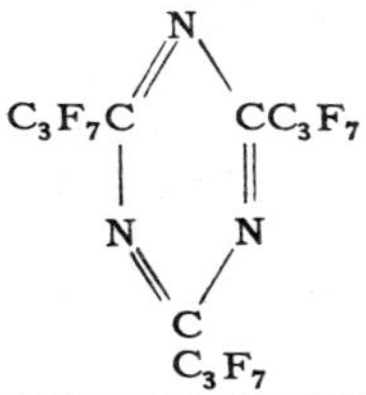	1119	165	1.3095	1.7158	25	9

TABLE 45

DIAZO COMPOUNDS

Empirical Formula	Structural Formula	Method	Yield %	B.p. °C/mm.	F.p. or M.p. °C	n_D^t	d_4^t	t°C	Ref.
$C_2F_6N_2$	$CF_3N{=}NCF_3$	112		−31.6/757	−133		2.19	−189	64
$C_3HF_2N_2O$	CF_3COCHN_2	1121	62.5	25/1					8
$C_2HF_3N_2$	CF_3CHN_2	1120	68	13–13.5/752					22
$C_6H_9FN_2O_2$	$CH_2FCH_2O(CH_2)_2COCHN_2$	1121							10

TABLE 46

NITROSO COMPOUNDS

Empirical Formula	Structural Formula	Method	Yield %	B.p. °C/mm.	F.p. or M.p. °C	n_D^t	d_4^t	t°C	Ref.
$CBrF_2NO$	$CBrF_2NO$	1122	50	−12					30
$CClF_2NO$	$CClF_2NO$	1122	50	−35					30
CF_3NO	CF_3NO	1122	75–90	−84					1,2,30, 39,41
		1123	16						1,32
		112		−94	−196.6				63
C_2BrF_4NO	CF_2BrCF_2NO	1122	52	18					30
C_2ClF_4NO	CF_2ClCF_2NO	1122	68	−2					30
C_2F_5NO	C_2F_5NO	1122	80	−42					30
C_3F_7NO	$CF_3(CF_2)_2NO$	1122	83	−12					1,30
C_4F_9NO	$C_2F_5CF(NO)CF_3$	1122	23	23–25					30,31
	$CF_3(CF_2)_3NO$	1122	81	16–17/730					30
$C_4H_4F_6N_2O$	$(CF_3CH_2)_2NNO$	1124	72	114–115		1.3374		18	34
$C_4H_6F_4N_2O$	$(CF_2HCH_2)_2NNO$	1124		178.6/755			1.4490	16.5	68
$C_5F_{11}NO$	$CF_3(CF_2)_4NO$	1122	71	19–20/730					30
$C_7F_{15}NO$	$CF_3(CF_2)_6NO$	1122	75	39–40/63					30

TABLE 47

NITRO COMPOUNDS AND NITRITES

Empirical Formula	Structural Formula	Method	Yield %	B.p. °C/mm.	F.p. or M.p. °C	n_D^t	d_4^t	t°C	Ref.
$CClF_2NO_2$	$CClF_2NO_2$	1126	15	24–25					30
CF_3NO_2	CF_3NO_2	1126	78	−31.1					1,30,39, 41
		1122	25						41
		1123	13						32
		113							37
$C_2BrF_4NO_2$	$CF_2BrCF_2NO_2$	1127	37	56–58					30
$C_2ClF_3N_2O_4$	$NO_2CClFCF_2NO_2$	1128	51	98–99/750		1.3748	1.674	25	24,30
$C_2ClF_4NO_2$	$CF_2ClCF_2NO_2$	1127	63	36–37		1.3145		22	30
$C_2Cl_2F_2N_2O_4$	$NO_2CFClCFClNO_2$	1128	47	81–82/103	12–18	1.4116	1.646	25	24,30
$C_2Cl_2F_3NO_2$	$CF_2ClCFClNO_2$	1127	67	77–78		1.3727	1.6202	20	30,74
$C_2F_4N_2O_4$	$NO_2CF_2CF_2NO_2$	1128	53	57–58/750	−41.5	1.348	1.595	25	14,24,30
$C_2F_5NO_2$	$CF_3CF_2NO_2$	1126	33	−1 to 0					30
$C_2HCl_3FNO_2$	$CHClFCCl_2NO_2$	1127	55	68–69/33		1.399	1.677	20	74
$C_2H_2F_3NO_2$	$CF_3CH_2NO_2$	1125		96		1.3394	1.3914	20	49
	CF_3CH_2ONO	1131	27	15.8					34
$C_2H_3ClFNO_2$	$CHClFCH_2NO_2$	1127	54	55.5/18					74
$C_2H_4FNO_2$	CH_2FCH_2ONO	1131	40	65–66		1.3572	1.1409	20	46
$C_3F_7NO_2$	$CF_3(CF_2)_2NO_2$	1126	41–68	23.2					1,30
$C_3H_4F_3NO_2$	$CF_3(CH_2)_2NO_2$	1125	16	134–134.8/748		1.3558	1.4220	20	66
		1125		135.5		1.3525	1.4259	20	49
$C_3H_4F_3NO_3$	$CF_3CH(OH)CH_2NO_2$	1129	47	84/17		1.3771		20	16
$C_5H_2F_7NO_2$	$C_3F_7CH{=}CHNO_2$	303	68	122		1.3403		20	16
$C_5H_4F_7NO_2$	$C_3F_7CH_2CH_2NO_2$	212	51	68/33		1.3335		20	16
$C_5H_4F_7NO_3$	$C_3F_7CH(OH)CH_2NO_2$	1129	75	56/2		1.3522		20	16
$C_6H_4F_7NO_2$	$C_3F_7CH{=}C(CH_3)NO_2$	303	63	136		1.3534		20	16
$C_6H_5F_7N_2O_4$	$C_3F_7CH(CH_2NO_2)_2$	1130	68		62–62.5				16

TABLE 47 (*continued*)

Empirical Formula	Structural Formula	Method	Yield %	B.p. °C/mm.	F.p. or M.p. °C	n_D^t	d_4^t	t°C	Ref.
$C_6H_6F_7NO_2$	$C_3F_7CH_2CH(CH_3)NO_2$	212	51	64/23		1.3412		20	16
	$C_3F_7CH(CH_3)CH_2NO_2$	1130	38	53/15		1.3447		20	16
$C_6H_6F_7NO_3$	$C_3F_7C(CH_3)OHCH_2NO_2$	1129	28	68/8		1.3624		20	16
	$C_3F_7CH(OH)CH(CH_3)NO_2$	1129	70	55/1		1.3589		20	16
$C_7H_6F_7NO_2$	$C_3F_7CH{=}C(C_2H_5)NO_2$	303	78	78/75		1.3574		20	16
$C_7H_8F_7NO_2$	$C_3F_7CH_2CH(C_2H_5)NO_2$	212	69	60/9		1.3493		20	16
	$C_3F_7CH(C_2H_5)CH_2NO_2$	1130	53	56/18		1.3543		20	16
$C_7H_8F_7NO_3$	$C_3F_7CHOHCH(C_2H_5)NO_2$	1129	78	73/5		1.3657		20	16
	$C_3F_7CH(OC_2H_5)CH_2NO_2$	1130	35	76/29		1.3488		20	16
$C_7H_{10}F_3NO_4$	$CF_3CH(CH_2NO_2)CH_2CO_2C_2H_5$	1129	68	105/9		1.4008		20	16
$C_{10}H_7F_{14}NO_2$	$C_3F_7CH(CH_2CH_2C_3F_7)CH_2NO_2$	1130	23	80/3		1.3361		20	16
$C_{12}H_{14}F_7NO_6$	$C_3F_7CH[CH(CO_2C_2H_5)_2]CH_2NO_2$	1130	49	145/9		1.3904		20	16

TABLE 48

MISCELLANEOUS NITROGEN COMPOUNDS

Empirical Formula	Structural Formula	Method	Yield %	B.p. °C/mm.	F.p. or M.p. °C	n_D^t	d_4^t	t°C	Ref.
$C_2F_6N_2O$	CF_3NONCF_3		47	6.9					39,42
$C_2F_6N_2O_2$	$CF_3ON(NO)CF_3$		~100	9.9					39,40
C_2HCl_2FNO	$CHClFCCl{=}NOH$	1127	45	76–78/60		1.4472	1.5749	20	74
$C_2H_4F_2N_2O_2$	$CHF_2CH_2NHNO_2$	1125		111–112/12	22.4				68
$C_3F_3N_3$	$(FCN)_3$	104		150					37
C_3F_7NO	$CF_3NCF_2CF_2O$ (ring: N–O bond closing the cycle)		62	−6.8					2
$C_3H_5FN_2O_2$	$CH_2FCON(NO)CH_3$								52

BIBLIOGRAPHY

1. Banus, J., *J. Chem. Soc.*, **1953,** 3755.
2. Barr, D. A., and Haszeldine, R. N., *J. Chem. Soc.*, **1955,** 1881.
3. Barr, D. A., and Haszeldine, R. N., *J. Chem. Soc.*, **1955,** 2532.
4. Barrick, P. L., U. S. Patent 2,437,289(1948).
5. Benning, A. F., and Park, J. D., U. S. Patent 2,348,321(1944).
6. Bourne, E. J., Henry, C. E. M., *et al.*, *J. Chem. Soc.*, **1952,** 4014.
7. Breslow, D. S., Walker, H. G., *et al.*, *J. Am. Chem. Soc.*, **68,** 100(1946).
8. Brown, F., and Musgrave, W. K. R., *J. Chem. Soc.*, **1953,** 2087.
9. Brown, H. C., and Reilly, W. L., 128th Meeting American Chemical Society, Minneapolis, Minnesota, September 1955.
10. Buckle, F. J., and Saunders, B. C., *J. Chem. Soc.*, **1949,** 2774.
11. Buxton, M. W., Stacey, M., and Tatlow, J. C., *J. Chem. Soc.*, **1954,** 366.
12. Carnahan, J. E., and Sampson, H. J., U. S. Patent 2,646,449(1953).
13. Coates, G. E., Harris, J., and Sutcliffe, T., *J. Chem. Soc.*, **1951,** 2762.
14. Coffman, D. D., Raasch, M. S., *et al.*, *J. Org. Chem.*, **14,** 747(1949).
15. Coover, H. W. Jr., and Dickey, J. B., U. S. Patent 2,585,230(1952).
16. Cook, D. J., Pierce, O. R., and McBee, E. T., *J. Am. Chem. Soc.*, **76,** 83(1954).
17. Cuculo, J. A., and Bigelow, L. A., *J. Am. Chem. Soc.*, **74,** 710(1952).
18. Dickey, J. B., U. S. Patent 2,537,976(1951).
19. Dickey, J. B., U. S. Patent 2,624,746(1953).
20. Dresdner, R., *J. Am. Chem. Soc.*, **79,** 69(1957).
21. duPont, and Rigby, G. W., British Patent 607,103(1948).
21A. Gervasi, J. A., Brown, M., and Bigelow, L. A., *J. Am. Chem. Soc.*, **78,** 1679(1956).
22. Gilman, H., and Jones, R. G., *J. Am. Chem. Soc.*, **65,** 1458(1943).
23. Gryszkiewicz-Trochimowski, E., Sporzynski, A., and Wnuk, J., *Rec. trav. chim.*, **66,** 427(1947).
24. Hass, H. B., and Whitaker, A. C., U. S. Patent 2,447,504(1948).
25. Haszeldine, R. N., *Research*, **3,** 430(1950).
26. Haszeldine, R. N., *J. Chem. Soc.*, **1950,** 1638.
27. Haszeldine, R. N., *J. Chem. Soc.*, **1950,** 1966.
28. Haszeldine, R. N., *J. Chem. Soc.*, **1951,** 102.
29. Haszeldine, R. N., *J. Chem. Soc.*, **1952,** 3490.
30. Haszeldine, R. N., *J. Chem. Soc.*, **1953,** 2075.
31. Haszeldine, R. N., *J. Chem. Soc.*, **1953,** 3559.
32. Haszeldine, R. N., and Jander, J., *J. Chem. Soc.*, **1953,** 4172.
33. Haszeldine, R. N., and Leedham, K. J., *J. Chem. Soc.*, **1953,** 1548.
34. Haszeldine, R. N., and Mattinson, B. J. H., *J. Chem. Soc.*, **1955,** 4172.
35. Hauptschein, M., and Braun, R. A., *J. Am. Chem. Soc.*, **77,** 4930(1955).
36. Henne, A. L., and Stewart, J. J., *J. Am. Chem. Soc.*, **77,** 1901(1951).
37. Huckel, W., *Nachr. Akad. Wiss. Gottinger, Math-physik Klasse*, **1946,** No. 1, 55.
38. Husted, D. R., and Ahlbrecht, A. H., *J. Am. Chem. Soc.*, **75,** 1605(1953).
39. Jander, J., and Haszeldine, R. N., *Naturwissenschaften*, **40,** 579(1953).
40. Jander, J., and Haszeldine, R. N., *J. Chem. Soc.*, **1954,** 696.
41. Jander, J., and Haszeldine, R. N., *J. Chem. Soc.*, **1954,** 912.
42. Jander, J., and Haszeldine, R. N., *J. Chem. Soc.*, **1954,** 919.

43. Jones, R. G., *J. Am. Chem. Soc.*, **70**, 143(1948).
44. Kauck, E. A., and Simons, J. H., U. S. Patent 2,616,927(1952).
45. Kauck, E. A., and Simons, J. H., British Patent 666,733(1952).
46. Knunyants, I. L., Kil'disheva, O. V., and Bykhovskaya, E., *Zhur. Obshchei Khim*, **19**, 101(1949).
47. Kubeczek, G., and Neugebauer, L., *Monatsh*, **80**, 395(1949).
48. Lontz, J. F., and Raasch, M. S., U. S. Patent 2,662,915(1953).
49. McBee, E. T., Hass, H. B., and Robinson, I. M., *J. Am. Chem. Soc.*, **72**, 3579(1950).
50. McBee, E. T., and Wiseman, P. A., U. S. Patent 2,515,246(1950).
51. McBee, E. T., Wiseman, P. A., and Bachman, G. B., *Ind. Eng. Chem.*, **39**, 415(1947).
52. McCombie, H., and Saunders, B. C., *Nature*, **158**, 382(1946).
53. McKay, A. F., and Vavasour, G. R., *Can. J. Chem.*, **32**, 639(1954).
54. Minnesota Mining and Manufacturing Company, British Patent 689,425(1953).
55. Minnesota Mining and Manufacturing Company, British Patent 717,232(1954).
56. Nerdel, F., *Naturwissenschaften*, **39**, 209(1952).
57. Nes, W. R., and Burger, A., *J. Am. Chem. Soc.*, **72**, 5409(1950).
57A. Norton, T. R., *J. Am. Chem. Soc.*, **72**, 3527(1950).
58. Park, J. D., Larsen, E. R., *et al.*, 130th Meeting, American Chemical Society, Atlantic City, N. J., September 1956.
59. Pearlson, W. H., and Hals, L. J., U. S. Patent 2,643,267(1953).
60. Pearson, F. G., U. S. Patent 2,558,875(1951).
61. Pruett, R. L., Barr, J. T., *et al.*, *J. Am. Chem. Soc.*, **72**, 3646(1950).
62. Rigby, G. W., U. S. Patent 2,484,528(1949).
63. Ruff, O., and Giese, M., *Ber.*, **69B**, 684(1936).
64. Ruff, O., and Willenberg, *Ber.*, **73B**, 724(1940).
65. Saunders, B. C., and Wilding, I. G. E., *J. Chem. Soc.*, **1949**, 1279.
66. Shechter, H., and Conrad, F., *J. Am. Chem. Soc.*, **72**, 3371(1950).
67. Simons, J. H., U. S. Patent 2,490,098(1949).
68. Swarts, F., *Bull. acad. roy. Belg.*, **1904**, 762.
69. Swarts, F., *Bull. acad. roy. Belg.*, **1904**, 955.
70. Swarts, F., *Bull. sci. acad. roy. Belg.*, **12**, 692(1926).
71. Thompson, J., and Emeleus, H., *J. Chem. Soc.*, **1949**, 3080.
72. Traube, W., and Peiser, E., *Ber.*, **53B**, 1501(1920).
73. Wilson, E., and Tishler, M., *J. Am. Chem. Soc.*, **73**, 3635(1951).
74. Yakubovich, A. Ya., Shpanskii, V. A., and Lemke, A. L., *Doklady Akad. Nauk. S.S.S.R.*, **96**, 773(1954).
75. Young, J. A., Simmons, T. C., and Hoffmann, F. W., *J. Am. Chem. Soc.*, **78**, 5637(1956).

CHAPTER XII

Organometallic and Organometalloid Compounds

TABLE OF CONTENTS

		PAGE
Introduction		309
Method Number		
	LITHIUM COMPOUNDS	
1201	Transmetallation	309
	MAGNESIUM COMPOUNDS	
1202	Reaction of Fluorocarbon Halides with Magnesium.	310
	ZINC COMPOUNDS	
1203	Reaction of Fluorocarbon Halides with Zinc	310
1204	Reaction of Fluorocarbon Halides with R_fZnI	311
	MERCURY COMPOUNDS	
1205	Reaction of Fluorocarbon Iodides with Mercury	311
1206	Reactions of Fluorocarbon Mercury Iodide Compounds	312
1207	Reaction of Fluorocarbon Mercury Iodides with Amalgams	312
1208	Reactions of Bis(Trifluoromethyl)Mercury	312
	CADMIUM COMPOUNDS	312
	SILICON COMPOUNDS	
1209	Reaction of Fluorocarbon Halides with Silicon	313

1210 Addition of Silanes to Fluoroolefins 313
1211 Addition of Fluorocarbon Halides to Vinyl Silanes 314
1212 Reaction of Organometallic Compounds with Silicon Halides or Alkoxides 314
1213 Codimerization of Fluoroolefins with Alkenyl Silanes 315

PHOSPHORUS COMPOUNDS ....

1214 Reaction of Fluorocarbon Iodides with Phosphorus 315
1215 Reaction of Silver Salts of Perfluorocarboxylic Acids with Phosphorus and Iodine 316
1216 Hydrolysis of Fluorocarbon Phosphines and Phosphine Iodides 316
1217 Reduction of Perfluoroalkyl Phosphine Iodides ... 316
1218 Halogenation of Fluorocarbon Phosphines........ 316
1219 Coupling of Fluorocarbon Phosphine Iodides 317
1220 Oxidation of Fluorocarbon Phosphines........... 317
1221 Reaction of Fluorocarbon Phosphine Iodides with Silver Cyanide 317
1222 Reaction of Phosphate Esters with Fluoroolefins . 317

ARSENIC COMPOUNDS ....

1223 Reaction of Fluorocarbon Iodides with Arsenic ... 317
1224 Hydrolysis of Fluorocarbon Arsines and Arsine Iodides.................................... 317
1225 Oxidation of Fluorocarbon Arsine Iodides 317
1226 Reduction of Fluorocarbon Arsine Iodides........ 318
1227 Halogenation of Fluorocarbon Arsines 318
1228 Coupling of Fluorocarbon Arsine Iodides......... 318
1229 Alkylation of Fluorocarbon Arsine Iodides 319
1230 Reaction of Fluorocarbon Arsine Iodides with Silver Salts 319

ANTIMONY COMPOUNDS 319

SELENIUM COMPOUNDS 319

TABLE 49 Lithium Compounds 320
TABLE 50 Magnesium Compounds 320
TABLE 51 Zinc Compounds............................. 320
TABLE 52 Mercury Compounds 321
TABLE 53 Cadmium Compounds 321

TABLE 54	Boron Esters	321
TABLE 55	Silicon Compounds	322
TABLE 56	Phosphorus Compounds	324
TABLE 57	Phosphorus Esters	325
TABLE 58	Arsenic Compounds	326
TABLE 59	Antimony Compounds	327
TABLE 60	Selenium Compounds	327
Bibliography		328

INTRODUCTION

In this chapter methods are described for preparation of compounds containing the R_f—M bond where R_f is a fluoroalkyl group and M is a metal or metalloid. Fluoroalkyl compounds of aluminum, boron, bismuth, tin, lead and gallium are unknown although an attempt to prepare the latter two was made by Emeleus and Haszeldine.[17] Trifluoromethyl acetylides of silver and copper were prepared by Haszeldine[24] but it is not clear whether or not these can be classified as true organometallic compounds. Fluorocarbon sulfur compounds are treated separately in Chapter XIII.

Fluoroalkyl esters of boric and phosphoric acids, although clearly not organometalloidal compounds are summarized in Tables 54 and 57.

LITHIUM COMPOUNDS

Unlike their hydrocarbon analogs, fluorocarbon lithium compounds are quite difficult to prepare. Unsuccessful attempts to prepare fluorocarbon lithium compounds by direct metallation of CF_3Cl were reported by Simons, Bond and McArthur[51] and by direct metallation of CF_3I by Emeleus and Haszeldine.[17]

METHOD 1201 Transmetallation

Preparation of C_3F_7Li was reported in high yields by Pierce, McBee and Judd[47] by reacting C_3F_7I with methyllithium in ether at $-74°$. Proof of its existence was established by reaction with aldehydes, ketones and other compounds. Upon heating C_3F_7Li, $CF_3CF{=}CF_2$ was obtained in a 95 percent conversion; hydrolysis with dilute sulfuric acid resulted in a quantitative conversion to C_3F_7H. Similar attempts to prepare CF_3Li[47] resulted in a vigorous reaction between CF_3I and CH_3Li, however, upon treatment of the reaction mixture with aldehydes, ketones or dilute acid, only tetrafluoroethylene was obtained. In the case of the reaction with aldehydes, aldol condensation products were also obtained.

MAGNESIUM COMPOUNDS

The fluorocarbon Grignard compounds are as versatile as other Grignard reagents and undergo many of their usual reactions. Thus far, it has been possible to prepare perfluoroalkyl Grignard compounds only from the iodides, with special precautions being necessary for the preparation of CF_3MgI. Hydrogen-containing fluoroalkyl chlorides, bromides as well as iodides have yielded Grignard compounds. It is interesting to note that while Grignard reagents of the type $C_nF_{2n+1}MgX$, and $C_nF_{2n+1}CH_2CH_2MgX$, have been prepared, compounds of the type $C_nF_{2n+1}CH_2MgX$ have not as yet been reported.

METHOD 1202 Reaction of Fluorocarbon Halides with Magnesium

The earliest attempt to react CF_3Cl with magnesium in the presence of dimethylamine resulted in a vigorous reaction, but no definite proof was established concerning the existence of CF_3MgCl.[51] Emeleus and Haszeldine[17] were unsuccessful in obtaining CF_3MgI and C_2F_5MgI by the usual Grignard procedure. However, subsequent work by Haszeldine[29] described the preparation of CF_3MgI by carefully purifying the magnesium and then reacting it with iodine at 150° prior to use. Reaction media used were either ethyl ether, butyl ether or tetrahydropyran. The reaction was carried out at temperatures from −60° to 60°; the highest yield of 45 percent was obtained at −15°. This Grignard compound yielded CHF_3 upon reaction with water, methanol or butylamine. Carbonation resulted in a 72 percent yield of CF_3CO_2H and reaction with CF_3CN yielded hexafluoroacetone. Brice, Pearlson and Simons[10] obtained C_3F_7H upon hydrolyzing the reaction mixture from C_3F_7Br and magnesium and ether, thus indicating the possible presence of the Grignard compound, although other reactions were not attempted. McBee, *et al.*[37,39] prepared $CF_3CH_2CH_2MgCl$ and reportedly carbonated it to the corresponding carboxylic acid. Henne and Francis[32] successfully prepared C_3F_7MgI at −80° in ether and carbonated it to the carboxylic acid in a 45 percent yield. Pierce and co-workers[45,46,48] prepared C_3F_7MgI and $C_3F_7CH_2CH_2MgBr$ and described their reactions with many compounds. Haszeldine[27,28,31] also prepared C_3F_7MgI in 65 to 80 percent yields. The preparation of $CF_2{=}CFMgI$ and $CF_2{=}CClMgI$ has been reported by Park.[41,42] The latter Grignard compound was reacted with formaldehyde to yield $CF_2{=}CClCH_2OH$.

ZINC COMPOUNDS

METHOD 1203 Reaction of Fluorocarbon Halides with Zinc

Miller, Fainberg and Bergman[39A,40] first reported the preparation of

C_3F_7ZnI by reacting C_3F_7I with zinc in the presence of dioxane or other ethers. This compound is reported to be stable at the boiling point of dioxane although it decomposes into perfluoropropene at higher temperatures.

Haszeldine and Walaschewski[31] also prepared C_3F_7ZnI in a 53 percent yield by reacting C_3F_7I with zinc in the presence of ether or tetrahydropyran at $-10°$. In the presence of dioxane, a solvated compound was isolated, the composition of which corresponded to one mole of C_3F_7ZnI and one mole of dioxane. Perfluoropropylzinciodide is not as reactive as the corresponding Grignard compound, viz., it does not carbonate to the acid nor react with carbonyl compounds, although it does react with acetyl chloride, yielding the ketone. Reaction with dilute acid, base or water results in quantitative yields of C_3F_7H.

METHOD 1204 Reaction of Fluorocarbon Halides with R_fZnI

Miller and Bergman[40] obtained $(C_3F_7)_2Zn \cdot CH_3OCH_2CH_2OCH_3$ and $(C_3F_7)_2Zn \cdot Et_2O$ by reacting C_3F_7ZnI with C_3F_7I in the appropriate ether, then separated the diperfluoroalkylzinc complex by distillation. Reaction of $(C_3F_7)_2Zn \cdot Et_2O$ with pyridine yielded $(C_3F_7)_2Zn \cdot 2Pyr$ and reaction of $(C_3F_7)_2Zn \cdot Et_2O$ with acyl chlorides gave ketones.

MERCURY COMPOUNDS

Fluorocarbon mercury compounds can be formed by heating a fluorocarbon iodide with mercury in the presence of ultraviolet light. The reaction of a Grignard compound on mercuric chloride, although used for the preparation of hydrocarbon mercury compounds, has not been employed for the preparation of fluorocarbon mercury compounds. Fluorocarbon mercury compounds have the unusual property of being solids and water soluble, unlike their hydrocarbon analogs.

METHOD 1205 Reaction of Fluorocarbon Iodides with Mercury

The first fluorocarbon mercury compounds were described by Banks, Emeleus, *et al.*[1] Trifluoromethyl iodide and mercury were heated in a sealed silica vessel and irradiated with ultraviolet light for 24 hours at 180° to 190° which resulted in quite low yields of CF_3HgI. Yields of 22 percent were realized by heating the reactants at 260° to 290° for 12 hours in a sealed tube.[17] Perfluoroethylmercuryiodide was prepared by Banks, Emeleus, *et al.*,[1] and by Emeleus and Haszeldine[17] in 50 to 55 percent yields by ultraviolet irradiation of C_2F_5I and mercury for 5 to 6 days at 120°. Both CF_3HgI and C_2F_5HgI are white crystalline solids readily subliming in vacuum and soluble in organic solvents as well as in water, although they slowly decompose in the latter solvent.[1,17]

METHOD 1206 Reactions of Fluorocarbon Mercury Iodide Compounds

The reactions of CF_3HgI are summarized below:[17]

$$CF_3HgI + I_2 \xrightarrow[120^\circ/2\text{ hrs. }(92\%)]{h\nu} CF_3I$$

$$CF_3HgI\text{ (aqueous)} + KI \xrightarrow[(72\%)]{3\text{-}10\text{ days}} CF_3H$$

$$CF_3HgI + Ag_2O \xrightarrow[(90\%)]{2\text{ hrs.}} CF_3HgOH$$

Trifluoromethylmercury hydroxide undergoes the following reactions.[17]

$$CF_3HgOH + \text{dil. }HCl \xrightarrow{(91\%)} CF_3HgCl$$

$$CF_3HgOH + \text{dil. }HBr \xrightarrow{(80\%)} CF_3HgBr$$

$$CF_3HgOH + \text{dil. }HNO_3 \longrightarrow CF_3HgNO_3$$

METHOD 1207 Reaction of Fluorocarbon Mercury Iodides with Amalgams

When CF_3HgI is treated with the amalgams of either silver, copper or cadmium at temperatures of 120° to 160° from 10 to 20 hours, bis(trifluoromethyl)mercury is obtained in high yields.[18] Barnes, *et al.*[2] prepared $(C_2F_5)_2Hg$ by this method. Bis(trifluoromethyl)mercury is a white solid, melting at 163° (sealed tube), is soluble in water and unstable to ultraviolet light.

METHOD 1208 Reactions of Bis(Trifluoromethyl)Mercury

This compound undergoes the following reactions:[18]

$$(CF_3)_2Hg + HgI \xrightarrow[(75\%)]{170^\circ} CF_3HgI$$

$$(CF_3)_2Hg + HgCl \xrightarrow[(62\%)]{170^\circ} CF_3HgCl$$

$$(CF_3)_2Hg + Zn\text{ or }Mg \xrightarrow[12\text{ hrs}]{140^\circ} \text{(hydrolysis)} \longrightarrow CHF_3$$

$$(CF_3)_2Hg + X_2 \xrightarrow{100^\circ} CF_3X \quad (X = Cl, Br\text{ or }I)$$

CADMIUM COMPOUNDS

It has been reported that cadmium fluorocarbon iodides can be prepared in solution by reaction of a fluorocarbon Grignard reagent with a cadmium salt.[15,26]

SILICON COMPOUNDS

Although Rochow[49] reported that the CF_3—Si linkage was cleaved by water, Pierce, McBee and Judd[47] found that the C_3F_7—Si linkage was stable in dilute acid at 100°, but cleaved in the presence of alcoholic potassium hydroxide. Fluoroalkyl groups such as $CF_3CH_2CH_2$— are not readily cleaved from silicon.

Fluoroalkyl silicone monomers can be easily hydrolyzed to the cyclic trimers or tetramers in a manner similar to dimethyldichlorosilane. However, Pierce, McBee and Cline[46] found that long-chain fluoroalkyl dichloro- or dialkoxysilanes yield only silanediols upon hydrolysis.

The preparation of a high molecular weight fluoroalkyl silicone elastomer has been recently announced by the Dow Corning Corporation (Silastic LS-53).

METHOD 1209 Reaction of Fluorocarbon Halides with Silicon

$$2RX + Si \longrightarrow R_2SiX_2$$

While this general method[49] is successfully used in the commercial preparation of dialkyldichlorosilanes, a true evaluation of its utility in the synthesis of the fluoroalkylsilanes must be deferred, due to the lack of specific information concerning physical and chemical properties of products claimed in patents. Izard and Kwolek[33] reacted CF_3Cl or C_2F_5Cl with silicon-copper alloy at 500° to 1,000°, and although an exothermic reaction was observed, SiX_4 was the only product. Patent claims were made for the preparation of CF_3SiBrF_2 and CF_3SiF_3 by reacting CF_3Br and silicon-copper alloy at 400°.[50] Another patent claims that mono-, bis- and tris-trifluoromethyl silicon halides are obtained by treating silicon-copper alloy with hydrogen at 900° to 1,200° for 3 hours prior to use, and then subsequent reaction with CF_3Cl, CF_3Br or CF_3I at 400° to 500°.[43]

METHOD 1210 Addition of Silanes to Fluoroolefins

$$R_fCY{=}CY_2 + HSi\!\!\mid\!\!— \longrightarrow R_fCYHCY_2Si\!\!\mid\!\!—, \quad (Y{=}H,\ F \text{ or } Cl)$$

This reaction has been reported to occur either by use of peroxide or platinum catalysts, or by purely thermal initiation. Peroxide catalyzed additions of this type are an adaptation of the method of Sommer, *et al.*,[53] who added trichlorosilane to octene-1. Using this technique, McBee, Roberts and Purckhauer[38] reported the preparation of $C_2F_5CH_2CH_2SiCl_3$ and $C_5F_{11}CHFCF_2SiCl_3$ by the addition of trichlorosilane to $C_2F_5CH{=}CH_2$

and $C_5F_{11}CF{=}CF_2$. The addition of trichlorosilane to $CCl_2{=}CClCF_3$ yielded a mixture of

$$\begin{array}{c} CF_3 \\ | \\ CCl_2{=}C{-}SiCl_3 \end{array} \text{ and } \begin{array}{c} CF_3 \\ | \\ CHCl_2CClSiCl_3 \end{array}$$

These reactions were carried out at 125° to 130° for a period of 60 hours.

Wagner[57] reported the use of a platinum on charcoal catalyst to effect the addition of trichlorosilane to $CF_2{=}CH_2$ at 100° to 300° and 30 to 1,000 psi to yield $CHF_2CH_2SiCl_3$. Tarrant and Butler[56] prepared $C_3F_7CH_2CH_2Si(CH_3)Cl_2$, $C_2F_5CH_2CH_2Si(CH_3)Cl_2$ and $CF_3CH_2CH_2Si(CH_3)Cl_2$ in good yields by this technique, using a reaction temperature of 225° to 250° for 16 hours. However, difficulty was encountered in the attempted additions of silanes to $CF_2{=}CFCl$ and perfluoroolefins using this procedure, and violent explosions resulted.

The thermal addition of trichlorosilane to tetrafluoroethylene has been reported by Haszeldine and Marklow[30] to proceed as follows:

$$nCF_2{=}CF_2 + HSiCl_3 \rightarrow H(CF_2CF_2)_nSiCl_3 \quad (n = 1 \text{ to } 10)$$

METHOD 1211 Addition of Fluorocarbon Halides to Vinyl Silanes

The addition of CF_3I to vinyltrichlorosilane to yield $CF_3CH_2CHISiCl_3$ was reported by Haszeldine and Marklow.[30] Tarrant[55] added CF_2Br_2 and $CF_2BrCFClBr$ to $CH_2{=}CHSi(CH_3)_3$ using benzoyl peroxide catalyst, and obtained $CF_2BrCH_2CHBrSi(CH_3)_3$ and $CF_2BrCFClCH_2CHBrSi(CH_3)_3$, respectively. These compounds, upon treatment with alkali, yield α,β-unsaturated products. The butenyl silane, $CF_2BrCFClCH{=}CHSi(CH_3)_3$ upon treatment with zinc, dehalogenates to yield both the butadienyl silane, $CF_2{=}CFCH{=}CHSi(CH_3)_3$ and the dimer,

$$\begin{array}{l} CF_2{-}CFCH{=}CHSi(CH_3)_3 \\ |\quad\;\;\; | \\ CF_2{-}CFCH{=}CHSi(CH_3)_3. \end{array}$$

METHOD 1212 Reaction of Organometallic Compounds with Silicon Halides or Alkoxides

Fluorocarbon Grignard reagents react with $SiCl_4$ or $Si(OR)_4$ to yield mixtures of partially and completely substituted fluoroalkyl silanes. Pierce, *et al.*[46] reported the reaction of $C_3F_7CH_2CH_2MgBr$ with tetrachloro- and tetraalkoxysilanes to give $(C_3F_7CH_2CH_2)_4Si$ together with intermediate compounds. McBee[37] obtained similar results upon reacting $CF_3CH_2CH_2MgCl$ with orthosilicates. Trifluoromethylmagnesiumiodide was added to silicon tetrachloride by Haszeldine and Marklow[30] who reported obtaining $(CF_3)_2SiCl_2$ and CF_3SiCl_3. Pierce, *et al.*[47] effectively utilized C_3F_7Li (cf. Method 1201) in the preparation of fluoroalkylsilanes. Simultaneous addition of diethyldichlorosilane and perfluoropropyl iodide to an ether solution of methyllithium at $-50°$ resulted in a low yield of $(C_2H_5)_2Si(C_3F_7)_2$.

METHOD 1213 Codimerization of Fluoroolefins with Alkenyl Silanes

When allylsilanes are reacted with tetrafluoroethylene in the presence of benzoyl peroxide, codimerization (cf. Method 210) is observed.[22] For example:

$$CH_2{=}CHCH_2Si(OEt)_2CH_3 + CF_2{=}CF_2 \xrightarrow[150°/16\ hrs]{Bz_2O_2} \begin{array}{l} CH_2-CH-CH_2Si(OEt)_2CH_3 \\ |\qquad\ \ | \\ CF_2-CF_2 \end{array}$$

PHOSPHORUS COMPOUNDS

The chemistry of fluorocarbon phosphorus compounds has been almost exclusively studied by the British group consisting of Emeleus, Bennett, Haszeldine, Brandt and Paul. Their approach has been to first prepare trifluoromethyl phosphine iodides or tris(trifluoromethyl)phosphine, then to obtain derivative compounds therefrom. It is interesting to note that while the preparation of the above mentioned compounds is accomplished directly from phosphorus and CF_3I, the non-fluorinated analogs have only been prepared by the reaction of alkyl Grignard reagents, zinc compounds or alkyl halides on phosphine or alkyl halides on phosphonium iodide, PH_4I.

Tris(trifluoromethyl)phosphine does not form addition compounds with sulfur, silver iodide or carbon disulfide as does its hydrocarbon analog.[15] No attempts have been made to prepare quarternary phosphonium compounds of the type, $[(CF_3)_4P]^+I^-$, similar to those obtained from the reaction of $(C_2H_5)_3P$ and C_2H_5I. It is also interesting to note that higher fluorocarbon phosphine homologs have not yet been reported.

METHOD 1214 Reaction of Fluorocarbon Iodides with Phosphorus

When CF_3I is heated with white or yellow phosphorus at 220° for 48 hours, a mixture of CF_3PI_2, $(CF_3)_2PI$ and $(CF_3)_3P$ results, with the latter compound predominating in an 84 percent yield.[3,4] These three compounds are liquids and are insoluble in water and are interconvertible through disproportionation.[15]

METHOD 1215 Reactions of Silver Salts of Perfluorocarboxylic Acids with Phosphorus and Iodine

Burg, *et al.*[11] describes a method whereby improved yields of CF_3PI_2 and $(CF_3)_2PI$ are obtained when CF_3CO_2Ag, red phosphorus and iodine are heated together. These compounds react with mercury to yield open-chain and ring compounds.

METHOD 1216 Hydrolysis of Fluorocarbon Phosphines and Phosphine Iodides

When CF_3PI_2, $(CF_3)_2PI$ or $(CF_3)_3P$ are treated with an excess of aqueous alkali, a quantitative yield of fluoroform results.[5] Controlled hydrolysis of $(CF_3)_3P$ with one equivalent of alkali yields trifluoromethyl*phosphonous* acid, $CF_3PHO(OH)$ which decomposes to fluoroform [through the unstable *phosphinous* acid $(CF_3)_2POH$] but which was isolated as a sodium salt.[5,6] Controlled hydrolysis of CF_3PI_2, $(CF_3)_2PI$ and CF_3PCl_2 with minimum amounts of water also gives high yields of the *phosphonous* acid,[5] which is also referred to as trifluoromethyl*phosphinic* acid.[16] In the controlled hydrolysis of CF_3PI_2 to $CF_3PHO(OH)$, subsequent evaporation by freeze drying also yielded CF_3PH_2.[6]

Oxidative hydrolysis of CF_3PI_2, $(CF_3)_2PI$, CF_3PCl_2 and $(CF_3)_2PCl$ with water and hydrogen peroxide (100 vol.) gives high yields of trifluoromethyl*phosphonic* acid, $CF_3PO(OH)_2$. Hydrolysis of $(CF_3)_2PCl_3$ with water yields $(CF_3)_2PO(OH)$, bis(trifluoromethyl)*phosphinic* acid, isolated as the silver salt.[20] Hydrolysis of $(CF_3)_3PCl_2$ in the presence of oxalic acid yields $(CF_3)_3PO$, tris(trifluoromethyl)*phosphine oxide*.[44]

The fluorocarbon acids of phosphorus are weaker than sulfuric and hydrochloric acids but stronger than perfluorocarboxylic and nitric acids.

METHOD 1217 Reduction of Perfluoroalkyl Phosphine Iodides

Bis(trifluoromethyl)phosphine can be prepared by reduction of $(CF_3)_2PI$ with Raney nickel and hydrogen and by photochemical reduction with hydrogen; however, $LiAlH_4$ is not effective in the reduction of this compound.[6] It can also be prepared by the hydrogenation of $(CF_3)_2PP(CF_3)_2$.[6]

Trifluoromethylphosphine CF_3PH_2, however, was prepared by the reduction of CF_3PI_2 with $LiAlH_4$, but this compound could not be reduced with hydrogen and Raney nickel.[6]

METHOD 1218 Halogenation of Fluorocarbon Phosphines

Chlorination of $(CF_3)_3P$ and $(CF_3)_2PCl$ at low temperatures resulted in the formation of the pentavalent compounds $(CF_3)_3PCl_2$ and $(CF_3)_2PCl_3$.[4,20]

However, the reaction of $(CF_3)_2PI$ and CF_3PI_2 with silver chloride at room temperature yielded $(CF_3)_2PCl$ and CF_3PCl_2.[4]

METHOD 1219 Coupling of Fluorocarbon Phosphine Iodides

$$(CF_3)_2PI + Hg \xrightarrow{\text{2 days}} (CF_3)_2PP(CF_3)_2.^{4}$$

METHOD 1220 Oxidation of Fluorocarbon Phosphines

$$CF_3PH_2 + HNO_3 \longrightarrow CF_3PO(OH)_2.$$

METHOD 1221 Reaction of Fluorocarbon Phosphine Iodides with Silver Cyanide

$$(CF_3)_2PI + AgCN \xrightarrow[\text{24 hours}]{20^\circ} (CF_3)_2PCN.^{4}$$

METHOD 1222 Reaction of Phosphate Esters with Fluoroolefins

$$(EtO)_2\overset{\overset{\displaystyle O}{\|}}{P}H + CF_2{=\!=}CF_2 \xrightarrow[90^\circ]{Bz_2O_2} \xrightarrow[100^\circ]{H_2SO_4} H(CF_2CF_2)_nPO(OH)_2.^{8}$$

ARSENIC COMPOUNDS

The same group of workers who studied the chemistry of fluorocarbon phosphorus compounds also contributed almost exclusively to the elucidation of perfluorocarbon arsenic chemistry. The preparation of trifluoromethylarsines is effected in a manner similar to the phosphorus analogs, *i.e.*, reaction of arsenic with CF_3I.

METHOD 1223 Reaction of Fluorocarbon Iodides with Arsenic

Trifluoromethyl iodide reacts with arsenic at 220° to form CF_3AsI_2, $(CF_3)_2AsI$ and $(CF_3)_3As$.[3,9,21,58]

METHOD 1224 Hydrolysis of Fluorocarbon Arsines and Arsine Iodides

The treatment of CF_3AsI_2, $(CF_3)_2AsI$ or $(CF_3)_3As$ with aqueous sodium hydroxide, yields fluoroform.[9] However, these compounds are stable to water.

METHOD 1225 Oxidation of Fluorocarbon Arsine Iodides

When $(CF_3)_2AsI$ and CF_3AsI_2 are treated with hydrogen peroxide (100 vol.) high yields of $(CF_3)_2AsO(OH)$ and $CF_3AsO(OH)_2$, are obtained in 15 minutes.[19,20] A longer reaction time yields fluoroform in the former case. Both acids readily form the silver salt upon treatment with moist silver oxide.[19] The anhydride of trifluoromethylarsonic acid CF_3AsO_2 was prepared by heating the acid under vacuum at 56°. This dehydration proceeds through the *pyro*-acid, $[CF_3AsO(OH)]_2O$ which can also be prepared by treating $CF_3AsO(OH)_2$ with P_2O_5. The trifluoromethylarsonic acids are stronger than nitric acid and perfluorocarboxylic acids but weaker than sulfuric, hydrochloric and trifluoromethylphosphonic acids.[16] Treatment of $(CF_3)_2AsI$ with mercuric oxide results in the formation of $[(CF_3)_2As]_2O$, a cacodyl oxide.[58]

METHOD 1226 Reduction of Fluorocarbon Arsine Iodides

Trifluoromethyl- and bis(trifluoromethyl)arsine were prepared from the iodides by reduction with $LiAlH_4$ in di-*n*-butyl ether in 49 percent and 16 percent yields respectively.[21] Yields of 98 percent and 43 percent were obtained by reduction with zinc-copper couple and dilute hydrochloric acid. By the latter method, 37 percent of $(CF_3)_2AsAs(CF_3)_2$ was also formed. Trifluoromethylarsine was also prepared by the photochemical reduction of CF_3AsI_2 in 85 percent yield.

METHOD 1227 Halogenation of Fluorocarbon Arsines

Liquid phase chlorination of $(CF_3)_3As$ at room temperature yields $(CF_3)_3AsCl_2$ and $(CF_3)_2AsCl_3$.[21] Heating $(CF_3)_3AsCl_2$ at 125° for 20 hours results in the formation of CF_3AsCl_2, $(CF_3)_2AsCl$ and $(CF_3)_3As$. The regeneration of tris(trifluoromethyl)arsine from $(CF_3)_3AsCl_2$ can also be effected in high yields by treatment with water or ethanol in a sealed tube.[19] Halogen exchange on fluorocarbon arsine halides has been accomplished by treating $(CF_3)_2AsI$ and CF_3AsI_2 with silver chloride, producing CF_3AsCl_2 and $(CF_3)_2AsCl$, respectively.[58] Bromination of $(CF_3)_3As$ does not oxidize arsenic to the pentavalent state, but results in the formation of $(CF_3)_2AsBr$ and CF_3AsBr_2.[21] Fluorination of $(CF_3)_3As$ with CoF_3 in a hot tube yields $(CF_3)_2AsF$. Replacement of iodine with fluorine in $(CF_3)_2AsI$ has been effected by the use of silver fluoride. Similarly, $(CF_3)_3AsCl_2$ has been fluorinated to the difluoride.

METHOD 1228 Coupling of Fluorocarbon Arsine Iodides

When $(CF_3)_2AsI$ is treated with mercury, the coupled diarsine, $(CF_3)_2AsAs(CF_3)_2$, is formed.[9] This same compound is also formed when $(CF_3)_2AsI$ is treated with zinc-copper couple (cf. Method 1226). Treatment of the diarsine with aqueous alkali yields fluoroform. When

$(CF_3)_3AsCl_2$ is reacted with mercury, a reduction occurs and $(CF_3)_3As$ is formed rather than a coupled product.[21]

METHOD 1229 Alkylation of Fluorocarbon Arsine Iodides

When $(CF_3)_2AsI$ or $(CF_3)AsI_2$ are reacted with methyl Grignard reagent, the mono- and dimethyl derivatives are formed, respectively.[19,20] Treatment of $(CF_3)_3As$ with methyl iodide in the presence of ultraviolet light also results in the formation of $(CF_3)_2AsCH_3$.[19,21]

METHOD 1230 Reaction of Fluorocarbon Arsine Iodides with Silver Salts

Bis(trifluoromethyl)iodoarsine reacts with silver cyanide and silver thiocyanate to form $(CF_3)_2AsCN$ and $(CF_3)_2AsSCN$, respectively. These compounds liberate fluoroform upon treatment with aqueous base.[21]

ANTIMONY COMPOUNDS

Preliminary reports on trifluoromethylstibines has been described in reviews by Emeleus.[15,16] Antimony and trifluoromethyl iodide, when reacted together at 170° to 175° form tris(trifluoromethyl)stibine and some $(CF_3)_2SbI$. The distibine $(CF_3)_2SbSb(CF_3)_2$ was prepared from $(CF_3)_2SbI$ and mercury, similar to the preparation of the phosphorus and arsenic analogs. Chlorination of $(CF_3)_3Sb$ yields $(CF_3)_3SbCl_2$ which gives a dihydrate upon treatment with water. Heating of the dihydrate with water gives a monobasic acid, $(CF_3)_2SbH_3O_3$, isolated as the silver salt.[16]

SELENIUM COMPOUNDS

These compounds have also been briefly described in reviews by Emeleus.[14,15,16] Reaction of CF_3I and selenium at 270° to 295° yields $(CF_3)_2Se$ and $(CF_3)_2SeSe(CF_3)_2$. Chlorination of the monoselenide in ultraviolet light yields CF_3SeCl_3 which hydrolyzes to the acid, $CF_3SeO(OH)$. Chlorination of the diselenide yields CF_3SeCl. An excess of chlorine converts the diselenide to CF_3SeCl_3. Treatment of CF_3SeCl with mercury results in the formation of $(CF_3Se)_2Hg$.

TABLE 49

LITHIUM COMPOUNDS

Empirical Formula	Structural Formula	Method	Yield %	B.p. °C/mm.	F.p. or M.p. °C	n_D^t	d_4^t	t °C	Ref.
C_3F_7Li	C_3F_7Li	1201	77						47

TABLE 50

MAGNESIUM COMPOUNDS

Empirical Formula	Structural Formula	Method	Yield %	B.p. °C/mm.	F.p. or M.p. °C	n_D^t	d_4^t	t °C	Ref.
CF_3IMg	CF_3MgI	1202	20–45						29
C_2ClF_2IMg	$CF_2{=}CClMgI$	1202							41
C_2F_3IMg	$CF_2{=}CFMgI$	1202							42
C_3F_7BrMg	C_3F_7MgBr	1202							10
C_3F_7IMg	C_3F_7MgI	1202	45						32
		1202	65						28,31
		1202	83						45,48
$C_3H_4ClF_3Mg$	$CF_3CH_2CH_2MgCl$	1202	82.8						37,39
$C_5H_4BrF_7Mg$	$C_3F_7CH_2CH_2MgBr$	1202							46

TABLE 51

ZINC COMPOUNDS

Empirical Formula	Structural Formula	Method	Yield %	B.p. °C/mm.	F.p. or M.p. °C	n_D^t	d_4^t	t °C	Ref.
C_3F_7IZn	C_3F_7ZnI	1203	14–53						31,39A,40

TABLE 52

MERCURY COMPOUNDS

Empirical Formula	Structural Formula	Method	Yield %	B.p. °C/mm.	F.p. or M.p. °C	n_D^t	d_4^t	t °C	Ref.
$CBrF_3Hg$	CF_3HgBr	1206	80						17
$CClF_3Hg$	CF_3HgCl	1206	91		76				17
CF_3IHg	CF_3HgI	1205	5–8		112.5 (sealed tube)				1
		1205	22		subl. 80				17
CF_3O_3NHg	CF_3HgNO_3	1206							17
CHF_3OHg	CF_3HgOH	1206	90						17
C_2F_5IHg	C_2F_5HgI	1205			87.5–88.5				1
		1205	60–65						17
C_2F_5OHg	C_2F_5HgO	1206			220–225				2
C_2F_6Hg	$(CF_3)_2Hg$	1207	80		163 (sealed tube)				18
$C_4F_{10}Hg$	$(C_2F_5)_2Hg$	1207	60		106–107 (sealed tube)				2
C_6F_6Hg	$(CF_3C{\equiv}C)_2Hg$				42–43				24

TABLE 53

CADMIUM COMPOUNDS

Empirical Formula	Structural Formula	Method	Yield %	B.p. °C/mm.	F.p. or M.p. °C	n_D^t	d_4^t	t °C	Ref.
CF_3ICd	CF_3CdI								26
C_3F_7ICd	C_3F_7CdI								26

TABLE 54

BORON ESTERS

Empirical Formula	Structural Formula	Method	Yield %	B.p. °C/mm.	F.p. or M.p. °C	n_D^t	d_4^t	t °C	Ref.
$C_6H_{12}F_3O_2B$	$(CH_2FCH_2O)_3B$			173					13

TABLE 55

SILICON COMPOUNDS

Empirical Formula	Structural Formula	Method	Yield %	B.p. °C/mm.	F.p. or M.p. °C	n_D^t	d_4^t	t°C	Ref.
$CBrF_5Si$	CF_3SiBrF_2	1209		12–13					50
		1212							30
CF_6Si	CF_3SiF_3	1209		−42					50
		1212							30
$C_2H_3Cl_3F_2Si$	$CHF_2CH_2SiCl_3$	1210		104–105.5					57
$C_3Cl_5F_3Si$	$CF_3(SiCl_3)C{=}CCl_2$	1210		165–166					38
$C_3HCl_6F_3Si$	$CF_3(SiCl_3)CClCHCl_2$	1210							38
$C_3H_3BrF_6Si$	$CF_3CH_2CHBrSiF_3$	1210	13	81		1.3434	1.7727 (26.4)	23	55
$C_4H_4Cl_3F_5Si$	$C_2F_5CH_2CH_2SiCl_3$	1210	88.5	127–127.8/75.8					38
$C_4H_7Cl_2F_3Si$	$CF_3CH_2CH_2Si(CH_3)Cl_2$	1210	73.5	76/85		1.3937	1.2323	27	56
$C_5H_7Cl_2F_5Si$	$C_2F_5CH_2CH_2Si(CH_3)Cl_2$	1210	62	52.5/40		1.3692	1.3240	25	56
$C_6H_7Cl_2F_7Si$	$C_3F_7CH_2CH_2Si(CH_3)Cl_2$	1210	58	146		1.3609	1.4024(30)	22	56
$C_6H_{11}BrF_2Si$	$CF_2BrCH{=}CHSi(CH_3)_3$	1211		57/40		1.4231	1.1789 (23.5)	23	55
$C_6H_{12}Br_2F_2Si$	$CF_2BrCH_2CHBrSi(CH_3)_3$	1211	61	74–76/9		1.4630	1.5521(16)	25	55
$C_6H_{13}F_3O_2Si$	$CF_3CH_2CH_2Si(CH_3)(OCH_3)_2$	1212	61.9	96.5/251		1.3576	1.0954	20	37
$C_6H_{13}F_3O_3Si$	$CF_3CH_2CH_2Si(OCH_3)_3$	1212	94	79.8–80.5/87		1.3547	1.137	20	37
$C_7HCl_3F_{14}Si$	$C_5F_{11}CHFCF_2SiCl_3$	1210	80						38
$C_7H_{10}ClF_7Si$	$(C_2H_5)_2SiCl(C_3F_7)$	1212	17.8	119/743		1.3538		20	47
$C_7H_{11}BrClF_2Si$	$CF_2BrCFClCH{=}CHSi(CH_3)_3$	1211	75	48/5		1.4323	1.3495(23)	24	55
$C_7H_{11}F_3Si$	$CF_2{=}CFCH{=}CHSi(CH_3)_3$	1211	78	36–37/40		1.4151	1.4159	24	55
$C_7H_{13}Br_2ClF_2Si$	$CF_2BrCHClCH_2CHBrSi(CH_3)_3$	1211	58.7–84.6	85–86/5		1.4647	1.6146(25)	22.5	55
$C_8H_{14}F_6O_2Si$	$(CF_3CH_2CH_2)_2Si(OCH_3)_2$	1212	82	100.5/57		1.3531	1.256	20	37

$C_9H_{16}Cl_2F_2OSi$	$CCl_2CF_2CH_2CHCH_2Si(OC_2H_5)(CH_3)_2$	1213		220			1.159	25	22
$C_9H_{16}F_4OSi$	$CF_2CF_2CH_2CHCH_2Si(OC_2H_5)(CH_3)_2$	1213		176			1.092	25	22
$C_{10}H_{10}F_{14}O_2Si$	$(C_3F_7CH_2CH_2)_2Si(OH)_2$	1212	65		64.5–65.0				46
$C_{10}H_{14}F_{14}Si$	$(C_2H_5)_2Si(C_3F_7)_2$	1212	10.2–32	79/12		1.3380		20	47
$C_{10}H_{17}F_7O_2Si$	$C_3F_7CH_2CH_2Si(OC_2H_5)_2(CH_3)$	1212	60–61	75.9/23, 92/42		1.3502		20	37
$C_{10}H_{18}F_4O_2Si$	$CF_2CF_2CH_2CHCH_2Si(OC_2H_5)_2(CH_3)$	1213		201			1.096	25	22
$C_{10}H_{19}F_5Si$	$C_2F_5CH_2CH_2Si(C_2H_5)_3$	1210	66.3	173.1/753		1.3800	1.110	20	38
$C_{11}H_{19}F_7O_3Si$	$C_3F_7CH_2CH_2Si(OC_2H_5)_3$	1212	20–71	92.5–93.0/25		1.211		20	37,46
$C_{12}H_{20}F_4O_2Si$	$CF_2CF_2CH_2CHCH_2Si(OC_2H_5)_2$-$(CH_2CH{=}CH_2)$	1213		103/10			1.096	25	22
$C_{12}H_{22}F_4Si_2$	$[(CH_3)_3SiCH{=}CHCF_2{-}]_2$	1211	23.6	60–62/6		1.4348	0.9009	22	55
$C_{14}H_{18}F_{14}O_2Si$	$(C_3F_7CH_2CH_2)_2Si(OC_2H_5)_2$	1212	25–77	117.5–118.0/25					37,46
$C_{14}H_{20}F_8O_2Si$	$(CF_2CF_2CH_2CHCH_2)_2Si(OC_2H_5)_2$	1213		117/3			1.259	25	22
$C_{14}H_{22}F_6Si$	$(CH_3)_3SiCH{=}CHCF{-}CF_2$ $(CH_3)_3SiCH{=}CHCF{-}CF_2$	1211	45	86/5		1.4168	1.0604(25)	26	55
$C_{15}H_{12}ClF_{21}Si$	$(C_3F_7CH_2CH_2)_3SiCl$	1212	47	133–134/15	34–35				46
$C_{15}H_{13}F_{21}OSi$	$(C_3F_7CH_2CH_2)_3SiOH$	1212	42	151–153/25		1.3378		20	46
$C_{15}H_{16}F_{28}Si$	$(C_3F_7CH_2CH_2)_4Si$	1212	2.9–10	71–72/25					37,46
$C_{30}H_{24}F_{42}OSi_2$	$[(C_3F_7CH_2CH_2)_3Si]_2O$	1212	33		66.5–67.0				46

TABLE 56

PHOSPHORUS COMPOUNDS

Empirical Formula	Structural Formula	Method	Yield %	B.p. °C/mm.	F.p. or M.p. °C	n_D^t	d_4^t	t°C	Ref.
CCl_2F_3P	CF_3PCl_2	1218	82	37					4
CF_3I_2P	CF_3PI_2	1214	1	69/29, 133/413					3,4
		1215	7						11
CH_2F_3P	CF_3PH_2	1217		−25.5					6
$CH_2F_3O_2P$	$CF_3PHO(OH)$	1216							5,6
$CH_2F_3O_3P$	$CF_3PO(OH)_2$	1216	80–88		81–82				5
		1220	96						6
C_2ClF_6P	$(CF_3)_2PCl$	1218	97	21					4
$C_2Cl_3F_6P$	$(CF_3)_2PCl_3$	1218	75	107					20
C_2F_6IP	$(CF_3)_2PI$	1214	15	73/755		1.403		15	3,4
		1215	30						11
C_2HF_6P	$(CF_3)_2PH$	1217	65	1					6
$C_2HF_6O_2P$	$(CF_3)_2PO(OH)$	1216	95	182					20
$C_3Cl_2F_9P$	$(CF_3)_3PCl_2$	1218	56	71/368	20.5				4
C_3F_6NP	$(CF_3)_2PCN$	1221	95	48		1.3248		20	4
C_3F_9P	$(CF_3)_3P$	1214	84	173					3,4
C_3F_9P		1215	35						11
C_3F_9PO	$(CF_3)_3PO$	1216	70	23.5					44
$C_4F_{12}P_2$	$(CF_3)_2PP(CF_3)_2$	1219	82	83–84					4

TABLE 57

PHOSPHORUS ESTERS

Empirical Formula	Structural Formula	Method	Yield %	B.p. °C/mm.	F.p. or M.p. °C	n_D^t	d_4^t	t °C	Ref.
$C_2H_4Cl_2O_2P$	$CH_2FCH_2OPOCl_2$		35.4	106–107/30		1.4400	1.5367	20	34
$C_3H_4Br_2FOP$	$CF_3CH(CH_3)OPBr_2$		48				1.988	15	53
$C_4H_7F_4O_3P$	$(CHF_2CH_2O)_2POH$			109–110/1.7					12
$C_6H_6F_9O_3P$	$(CF_3CH_2O)_3P$		78	130–131/743		1.3224	1.4866	25	35
$C_6H_6F_9O_4P$	$(CF_3CH_2O)_3PO$		68	74–75/9		1.3180		25	35
$C_6H_9F_6O_4P$	$(CHF_2CH_2O)_3PO$			233–235					53
$C_6H_{12}F_3O_3P$	$(CH_2FCH_2O)_3P$			114–116/8		1.417	1.285	20	34
$C_6H_{12}F_3O_4P$	$(CH_2FCH_2O)_3PO$		60	169/11		1.4043	1.365	20	34
$C_{10}H_7F_{16}O_4P$	$[H(CF_2)_4CH_2O]_2PO(OH)$			200/5					7
$C_{15}H_9F_{24}O_4P$	$[H(CF_2)_4CH_2O]_3PO$			161/7					7
$C_{16}H_6F_{21}O_3P$	$(C_3F_7CH_2O)_3P$		83	97.5–98.0/16			1.6618	20	35

TABLE 58

ARSENIC COMPOUNDS

Empirical Formula	Structural Formula	Method	Yield %	B.p. °C/mm.	F.p. or M.p. °C	n_D^t	d_4^t	t°C	Ref.
CBr_2F_3As	CF_3AsBr_2	1227	12	118/745		1.528		20	21
CCl_2F_3As	CF_3AsCl_2	1227		71/760		1.431		20	21,58
CF_3I_2As	CF_3AsI_2	1223	4–10	100/48, 183/760		1.688		20	9,21,58
CF_3O_2As	CF_3AsO_2								19
CH_2F_3As	CF_3AsH_2	1226	49–98	−12.5/753					21
$CH_2F_3O_3As$	$CF_3AsO(OH)_2$	1225	96						19
C_2BrF_6As	$(CF_3)_2AsBr$	1227	38	59.5/745		1.398		20	21
C_2ClF_6As	$(CF_3)_2AsCl$	1227		46		1.351		19	21,58
$C_2Cl_3F_6As$	$(CF_3)_2AsCl_3$	1227	30	92–95/722		1.423		20	21
C_2F_6IAs	$(CF_3)_2AsI$	1223	13–20	14/54		1.425		25	3,9,21, 58
C_2F_7As	$(CF_3)_2AsF$	1227		25/760					21,58
C_2HF_6As	$(CF_3)_2AsH$	1226	16–43						21
$C_2HF_6O_2As$	$(CF_3)_2AsO(OH)$	1225	86		$150/10^{-3}$ (sub.)				20
$C_2H_2F_6O_5As$	$[CF_3AsO(OH)]_2O$	1225							19
$C_3Cl_2F_9As$	$(CF_3)_3AsCl_2$	1227	34	98.5		1.386		19	19
C_3F_6NAs	$(CF_3)_2AsCN$	1230		89.5		1.359		20	21,58
C_3F_6NSAs	$(CF_3)_2AsSCN$	1230		117		1.445		20	21,58
C_3F_9As	$(CF_3)_3As$	1223	70–85	33.3					3,9,19, 21,58
$C_3F_{11}As$	$(CF_3)_3AsF_2$	1227							21
$C_3H_3F_6As$	$(CF_3)_2AsCH_3$	1229	50–63	52–53					19,21
$C_4F_{12}As_2$	$(CF_3)_2AsAs(CF_3)_2$	1228		106–7		1.372		19	9
$C_4F_{12}OAs_2$	$(CF_3)_2AsOAs(CF_3)_2$	1225		100		1.354		20	58

TABLE 59

ANTIMONY COMPOUNDS

Empirical Formula	Structural Formula	Method	Yield %	B.p. °C/mm.	F.p. or M.p. °C	n_D^t	d_4^t	t °C	Ref.
CCl_2F_3Sb	CF_3SbCl_2								16
C_3F_9Sb	$(CF_3)_3Sb$								15,16
$C_3H_3F_9O_3Sb$	$(CF_3)_3SbH_3O_3$								16
$C_4F_{12}Sb_2$	$(CF_3)_2SbSb(CF_3)_2$								16
C_6F_6ISb	$(CF_3)_2SbI$			72					16

TABLE 60

SELENIUM COMPOUNDS

Empirical Formula	Structural Formula	Method	Yield %	B.p. °C/mm.	F.p. or M.p. °C	n_D^t	d_4^t	t °C	Ref.
$CClF_3Se$	CF_3SeCl								14,16
CCl_3F_3Se	CF_3SeCl_3								14,15
$C_2F_6HgSe_2$	$(CF_3Se)_2Hg$								14,15
C_2F_6Se	CF_3SeCF_3			−1 to 0.5					16
$C_4F_{12}Se_2$	$(CF_3)_2SeSe(CF_3)_2$			72–73					14,15,16

BIBLIOGRAPHY

1. Banks, A. A., Emeleus, H. J., *et al.*, *J. Chem. Soc.*, **1948,** 2188.
2. Banus, J., Emeleus, H. J., and Haszeldine, R. N., *J. Chem. Soc.*, **1950,** 3041.
3. Bennett, F. W., Brandt, G. R. A., *et al.*, *Nature*, **166,** 225(1950).
4. Bennett, F. W., Emeleus, H. J., and Haszeldine, R. N., *J. Chem. Soc.*, **1953,** 1565.
5. Bennett, F. W., Emeleus, H. J., and Haszeldine, R. N., *J. Chem. Soc.*, **1954,** 3598.
6. Bennett, F. W., Emeleus, H. J., and Haszeldine, R. N., *J. Chem. Soc.*, **1954,** 3896.
7. Benning, A. F., U. S. Patent 2,559,749(1951).
8. Bittles, J. A., and Joyce, R. M., U. S. Patent 2,559,754(1951).
9. Brandt, G. R. A., Emeleus, H. J., and Haszeldine, R. N., *J. Chem. Soc.*, **1952,** 2252.
10. Brice, T. J., Pearlson, W. H., and Simons, J. H., *J. Am. Chem. Soc.*, **68,** 969(1946).
11. Burg, A. B., Slota, P. J., and Mahler, W., 129th Meeting American Chemical Society, Dallas, Texas, April, 1956.
12. Cook, H. G., Illet, J. D., *et al.*, *J. Chem. Soc.*, **1949,** 2921.
13. Cook, H. G., Illet, J. D., and Saunders, B. C., *J. Chem. Soc.*, **1950,** 3125.
14. Dale, J. W., Emeleus, H. J., and Haszeldine, R. N., 122nd Meeting American Chemical Society, Atlantic City, New Jersey, September, 1952.
15. Emeleus, H. J., in Simons "Fluorine Chemistry," Vol. II, New York, Academic Press, 1954.
16. Emeleus, H. J., *J. Chem. Soc.*, **1954,** 2979.
17. Emeleus, H. J., and Haszeldine, R. N., *J. Chem. Soc.*, **1949,** 2948.
18. Emeleus, H. J., and Haszeldine, R. N., *J. Chem. Soc.*, **1949,** 2953.
19. Emeleus, H. J., Haszeldine, R. N., and Paul, R. C., *J. Chem. Soc.*, **1954,** 881.
20. Emeleus, H. J., Haszeldine, R. N., and Paul, R. C., *J. Chem. Soc.*, **1955,** 563.
21. Emeleus, H. J., Haszeldine, R. N., and Walaschewski, E. G., *J. Chem. Soc.*, **1952,** 1552.
22. Frost, L. W., U. S. Patent 2,596,967(1952).
23. Haszeldine, R. N., *J. Chem. Soc.*, **1949,** 2856.
24. Haszeldine, R. N., *Nature*, **165,** 152(1950).
25. Haszeldine, R. N., *Nature*, **167,** 139(1951).
26. Haszeldine, R. N., *Nature*, **167,** 1028(1951).
27. Haszeldine, R. N., *J. Chem. Soc.*, **1952,** 3423.
28. Haszeldine, R. N., *J. Chem. Soc.*, **1953,** 1748.
29. Haszeldine, R. N., *J. Chem. Soc.*, **1954,** 1273.
30. Haszeldine, R. N., and Marklow, R. J., 128th Meeting American Chemical Society, Minneapolis, Minnesota, September, 1955.
31. Haszeldine, R. N., and Walaschewski, E. G., *J. Chem. Soc.*, **1953,** 3607.
32. Henne, A. L., and Francis, W. C., J. *Am. Chem. Soc.*, **73,** 3518(1951).
33. Izard, E. F., and Kwolek, S. L., *J. Am. Chem. Soc.*, **73,** 1156(1951).
34. Knunyants, I. L., Kil'disheva, O. V., and Bykhovshaya, E., *Zhur. Obschei. Khim.*, **19,** 101(1949).

35. Krogh, L. C., Reid, T. S., and Brown, H. A., *J. Org. Chem.*, **19**, 1124(1954).
36. McBee, E. T., Kelley, A. E., and Rapkin, E., *J. Am. Chem. Soc.*, **72**, 5071(1950).
37. McBee, E. T., Roberts, C. W., *et al.*, *J. Am. Chem. Soc.*, **77**, 1292(1955).
38. McBee, E. T., Roberts, C. W., and Puerckhauer, G. W. R., 130th Meeting American Chemical Society, Atlantic City, New Jersey, September, 1956.
39. McBee, E. T., and Truchan, A., *J. Am. Chem. Soc.*, **70**, 2910(1949).
39A. Miller, W. T., Fainberg, A. H., and Bergman, E., 122nd Meeting American Chemical Society, New York City, September, 1952.
40. Miller, W. T., and Bergman, E., 126th Meeting American Chemical Society, New York City, September, 1954.
41. Park, J. D., Abramo, J., *et al.*, 128th Meeting American Chemical Society, Minneapolis, Minnesota, September, 1955.
42. Park, J. D., Seffel, R. J., and Lacher, J. R., J. *Am. Chem. Soc.*, **78**, 59(1956).
43. Passino, H. J., and Rubin, L. C., U. S. Patent 2,686,194(1954).
44. Paul, R. C., *J. Chem. Soc.*, **1955**, 574.
45. Pierce, O. R., and Levine, M., *J. Am. Chem. Soc.*, **75**, 1254(1953).
46. Pierce, O. R., McBee, E. T., and Cline, R. E., *J. Am. Chem. Soc.*, **75**, 5618(1953).
47. Pierce, O. R., McBee, E. T., and Judd, G. F., *J. Am. Chem. Soc.*, **76**, 474(1954).
48. Pierce, O. R., Meiners, A. F., and McBee, E. T., *J. Am. Chem. Soc.*, **75**, 2516(1953).
49. Rochow, E. G., "An Introduction to the Chemistry of the Silicones," (2nd Ed.), New York, John Wiley and Sons, Inc. (1951).
50. Simons, J. H., and Dunlap, R. D., U. S. Patent 2,651,651(1953).
51. Simons, J. H., Bond, R. L., and McArthur, N. E., *J. Am. Chem. Soc.*, **62**, 3479(1940).
52. Sommer, L. H., Pietrusza, E. W., and Whitmore, F. C., *J. Am. Chem. Soc.*, **69**, 188(1947).
53. Swarts, F., *Rec. trav. chim.*, **28**, 166(1909).
54. Swarts, F., *Bull. soc. chim. Belg.*, **38**, 99(1929).
55. Tarrant, P., Dykes, G. W., *et al.*, 128th Meeting American Chemical Society, Minneapolis, Minnesota, September, 1955,
56. Tarrant, P., Butler, G. B., *et al.*, 130th Meeting American Chemical Society, Atlantic City, New Jersey, September, 1956.
57. Wagner, G. H., U. S. Patent 2,637,738(1953).
58. Walaschewski, E. G., *Chem. Ber.*, **86**, 272(1953).

CHAPTER XIII

Sulfur Compounds

TABLE OF CONTENTS

		PAGE
Introduction		332
Method Number		

SULFIDES

1301	Interaction of Fluorocarbon Iodides and Sulfur	332
1302	Reactions of Sulfides and Disulfides	333
1303	Addition of Mercaptans to Olefins	333
1304	Reaction of Alkyl Halides with Sodium Mercaptides	334
1305	Action of Iodine Pentafluoride on Carbon Disulfide	334
1306	Addition of Sulfur Monochloride or Alkanesulfenyl Chlorides to Olefins	334

FLUORINATION PRODUCTS OF SULFUR COMPOUNDS

1307	Fluorination of Carbon Disulfide	335
1308	Fluorination of Thiols, Sulfides and Thioacids	335

SULFOXIDES AND SULFONES

1309	Addition of Grignard Reagents to Alkanesulfonyl Fluorides	336
1310	Oxidation of Sulfides	337

THIOLS

1311	Reaction of Fluoroalkyl Halides and Sodium Hydrosulfide	337

1312 Hydrolysis of Thioesters 337
1313 Decomposition of Thiofluoroalkylmercurials 337

THIOESTERS

1314 Reaction of Mercaptans and Acyl Halides 338
1315 Reaction of Mercaptans and Acid Anhydrides ... 338
1316 Addition of Thioacids to Olefins 338
1317 Reaction of Thioacid Salts with Alkyl Halides ... 338
1318 Oxidation of Unsaturated Thioethers 338

ALKANESULFONIC ACIDS

1319 Addition of Sodium Sulfite or Bisulfite to Olefins 339
1320 Oxidation of Thiofluoroalkylmercurials 339

ALKANESULFONYL CHLORIDES

1321 Action of Phosphorus Pentachloride on Alkanesulfonic Acids 339
1322 Oxidation of Thiocyanates or Alkanesulfenyl Chlorides 339

ALKANESULFENYL CHLORIDES

1323 Preparation and Reaction of Fluoroalkanesulfenyl Chlorides 340

ESTERS OF ALKANESULFONIC ACIDS

1324 Reaction of Sulfonic Acids with Alcohols 340
1325 Reaction of Zinc Alkanesulfinates with Alkanesulfonic Chlorides 340
1326 Reaction of Silver Alkanesulfonates with Alkyl Iodides 341

AMIDES AND AMMONIUM SALTS OF ALKANESULFONIC ACIDS

1327 Reaction of Alkanesulfonyl Halides and Amines .. 341
1328 Reaction of Alkanesulfonic Acid Hydrates and Amines or Ammonia 341

ESTERS OF SULFURIC ACID

1329 Reaction of Alcohols with Sulfuryl Chloride...... 341
1330 Addition of Fluorosulfonic Acid to Olefins....... 341

MISCELLANEOUS SULFUR COMPOUNDS

1331	Thioformates and Thiocarbonates	342
1332	Esters of Sulfurous Acid	342
1333	Alkanesulfinic Acids	342
1334	Thioamides	343
TABLE 61	Sulfur Compounds	344
Bibliography		349

INTRODUCTION

This chapter refers to fluorine-containing sulfur compounds representing various oxidation states of sulfur. Fluorocarbon selenium compounds compounds are discussed in Chapter XII. Although most fluorocarbon analogs of alkyl sulfur compounds have been prepared, very slight emphasis has been placed on preparation of fluorocarbon thiols and no compounds representing the class of perfluorothiocarboxylic acids have been reported.

The addition of various sulfur-containing compounds to fluoroolefins appears to proceed with the ease exhibited by the nucleophilic addition of alcohols to fluoroolefins as discussed in Chapter V.

A number of fluoroalkyl sulfur compounds have been prepared using the electrolytic fluorination process (cf. Method 111). Representative of this class of materials is CF_3SF_5. These compounds exhibit a high degree of thermal stability.

Attempts to fluorinate thiophene directly to obtain cyclic sulfides have resulted only in the isolation of perfluorocyclobutane and perfluorocyclooctane.

Xanthate esters have been prepared by conventional techniques; however, difficulty has been experienced in attempting to pyrolyze the ester to an olefin.

SULFIDES

METHOD 1301 Interaction of Fluorocarbon Iodides and Sulfur

Fluorocarbon sulfides may be prepared by heating perfluoroalkyl iodides with sulfur either in a sealed tube or in an autoclave. This procedure generally results in a mixture of the mono-, di- and trisulfides as evidenced by the work of Hauptschein and Grosse[22] who obtained $C_3F_7SC_3F_7$, $C_3F_7SSC_3F_7$ and $C_3F_7SSSC_3F_7$ upon heating C_3F_7I and sulfur at 250° for fourteen hours. If this reaction is carried out at either higher temperatures or for longer periods of time higher sulfides are obtained to the exclusion of the monosulfide. Haszeldine and co-workers[3,16,19] observed these results while reacting CF_3I or C_3F_7I with sulfur employing the following times and temperatures; 265° for 24 hours, 310° for 36 hours or 410° for 14 hours. A free radical mechanism has been proposed to account for the formation of sulfides by this reaction.[3]

METHOD 1302 Reactions of Sulfides and Disulfides

Bistrifluoromethyltrisulfide or -disulfide yielded the monosulfide upon irradiation with ultraviolet light.[3,16] Photochemical decomposition of the trisulfide for seventeen days yielded both the disulfide and the monosulfide. Further irradiation of the disulfide for five days gave a 70 percent yield of the monosulfide.[16] When a mixture of bistrifluoromethylsulfide and mercury were irradiated for four days, a high yields of $(CF_3S)_2Hg$, bis(trifluoromethylthio)mercury was formed.[3,16] Treatment of the mercurial with chlorine gave a mixture of bistrifluoromethyldisulfide and trifluoromethylsulfenyl chloride, CF_3SCl (cf. Method 1322).

Treatment of the mercurial with thiocarbonylchloride results in a quantitative conversion to CF_3SHgCl. The disulfide and trisulfide decompose when heated for 12 hours at 60° with 15 percent aqueous base.[16] However, CF_3SCF_3 is stable to aqueous alkali.

Hydrogen-containing fluoroalkyl sulfides are slowly attacked by boiling alcoholic potassium hydroxide, but do not add bromine from a benzene solution or do not form sulfonium salts with methyl iodide as do ordinary alkyl sulfides.[33]

METHOD 1303 Addition of Mercaptans to Olefins

A versatile method for the preparation of unsymmetrical fluorine-containing sulfides is the addition of thiols to fluorine-containing olefins employing various catalysts. A British patent describes the preparation of sulfides by the addition of various thiols to fluorine-containing olefins in the presence of aluminum chloride or peroxide catalyst at 110°.[12]

A thorough study of the addition of thiols to fluoroolefins was made by Rapp, Pruett, *et al.*[34] by the use of either triethylamine or benzyltrimethylammonium chloride (Triton B) as catalysts. It was found that use of the latter catalyst resulted in higher yields of sulfide and the reaction can occur at temperatures as low as 25° to 46°. In the addition of alkyl sulfides to chlorotrifluoroethylene or 1,1-difluoro-2,2-dichloroethylene, the mode of addition was observed to yield sulfides of the type $RSCF_2CFClH$ and $RSCF_2CCl_2H$. The addition of $HOCH_2CH_2SH$ to $CF_2{=}CFCl$ indicated that the —SH group rather than the —OH group added preferentially to the olefin, resulting in the formation of $HOCH_2CH_2SCF_2CFClH$. In this reaction $NaSCH_2CH_2OH$ was employed as a catalyst. In the addition of *n*-butyl mercaptan to perfluorocyclobutene with Triton B as a catalyst, the resultant product was 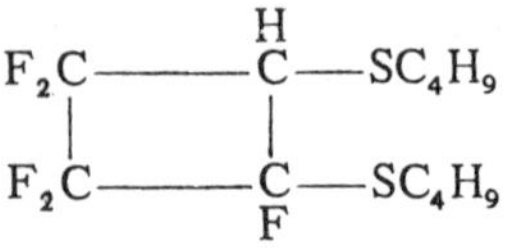 which indicated that dehydrofluorination of the intermediate compound, 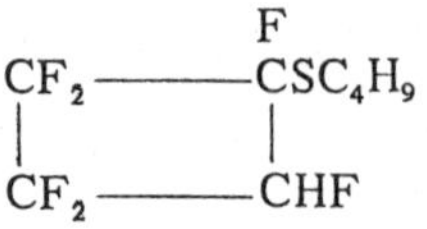 to 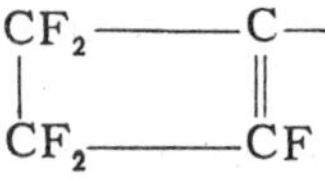 and the subsequent addition of another mole of C_4H_9SH occurred. When the addition was carried out in the presence of triethylamine catalyst, the unsaturated intermediate was isolated, as well as the unsaturated cyclic di-thio ether.[33]

Methyl, ethyl and isopropyl mercaptans were added to tetrafluoroethylene, chlorotrifluoroethylene and symmetrical dichlorodifluoroethylene at 115° to 125° for 6 hours in an autoclave using sodium hydroxide as a catalyst.[25] By the use of this technique, various mercaptans were added to perfluoropropene resulting in sulfides of the type, CF_3CHFCF_2SR.[27]

METHOD 1304 Reaction of Alkyl Halides with Sodium Mercaptides

Ethane 1,2-disulfides of the type $FCH_2CH_2SCH_2CH_2SCH_2CH_2F$ have been prepared by McCombie and Saunders[29] and Saunders and Stacey[36] as follows:

$$FCH_2CH_2Br + NaSH \longrightarrow FCH_2CH_2SH \xrightarrow{NaOH} FCH_2CH_2SNa$$

$$2FCH_2CH_2SNa + FCH_2CH_2Br \longrightarrow FCH_2CH_2SCH_2CH_2SCH_2CH_2F$$

METHOD 1305 Action of Iodine Pentafluoride on Carbon Disulfide

Haszeldine and Kidd[16] treated carbon disulfide with iodine pentafluoride for 12 hours at 195° in an autoclave and 76 percent of CF_3SSCF_3 and 7 percent of CF_3SSSCF_3 were formed (cf. Method 1307).

METHOD 1306 Addition of Sulfur Monochloride or Alkanesulfenyl Chlorides to Olefins

The formation of chlorofluoroalkyldisulfides have been reported by the addition of sulfur monochloride to fluoroolefins. Raasch[32] added a mixture of S_2Cl_2 and SCl_2 to tetrafluoroethylene in a silver-lined autoclave at 2,000 psi and at a temperature of 100° to 150°. A complex mixture of sulfides resulted from which $(CF_2ClCF_2)S_2$ was isolated.

Knunyants and Fokin[25A] obtained the same disulfide in this reaction employing a stainless steel autoclave at $100°$ to $120°$, but in addition, isolated $(CF_2ClCF_2)_2S$, $ClCF_2CF_2SCl$ and $ClCF_2CF_2SSCl$. The latter two compounds, a sulfenyl chloride (cf. Method 1222) and a thiosulfenyl chloride were added to hydrocarbon olefins and formed a sulfide and disulfide, respectively. Both ethylene and cyclohexene were added to CF_2ClCF_2SCl in a sealed tube and formed $CF_2ClCF_2SCH_2CH_2Cl$ and

$$
\begin{array}{c}
\text{CHCl} \\
\diagup \quad \diagdown \\
\text{CH}_2 \quad \text{CHSCF}_2\text{CF}_2\text{Cl}. \\
| \qquad | \\
\text{CH}_2 \quad \text{CH}_2 \\
\diagdown \quad \diagup \\
\text{CH}_2
\end{array}
$$

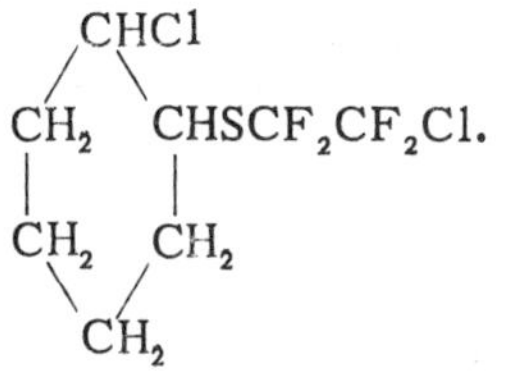

Reaction of CF_2ClCF_2SSCl with cyclohexene resulted in the formation of the disulfide,

$$
\begin{array}{c}
\text{CHCl} \\
\diagup \quad \diagdown \\
\text{CH}_2 \quad \text{CHSSCF}_2\text{CF}_2\text{Cl}. \\
| \qquad | \\
\text{CH}_2 \quad \text{CH}_2 \\
\diagdown \quad \diagup \\
\text{CH}_2
\end{array}
$$

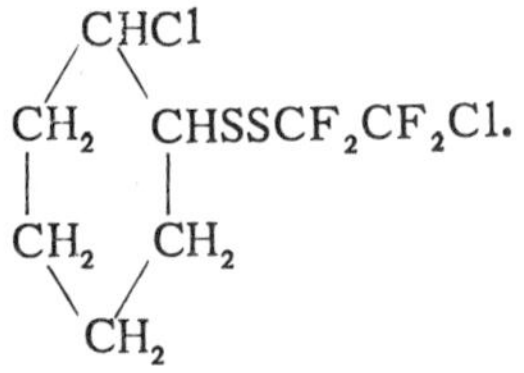

FLUORINATION PRODUCTS OF SULFUR COMPOUNDS

METHOD 1307 Fluorination of Carbon Disulfide

When carbon disulfide is treated with cobaltic fluoride, fluorinated in a Simons cell or directly reacted with fluorine, derivatives of sulfur hexafluoride are formed. In contrast, treatment with iodine pentafluoride forms sulfides (cf. Method 1305). Silvey and Cady[38] treated carbon disulfide with cobaltic fluoride at $250°$ and obtained trifluoromethylsulfur pentafluoride. The direct fluorination of carbon disulfide by Tyczkowski and Bigelow[40] also resulted in the formation of CF_3SF_5 (cf. Method 112).

Clifford, El-Shamy, et al.[6] treated carbon disulfide in the Simons cell for 45 hours and obtained a 90 percent yield of CF_3SF_5 and small amounts of $CF_2(SF_5)_2$ and $CF_2(SF_3)_2$; the latter compound is a derivative of sulfur tetrafluoride.

METHOD 1308 Fluorination of Thiols, Sulfides and Thioacids

Fluorination of thiols or sulfides result in the formation of derivatives of sulfur hexafluoride, but fluorination of thioacids result in the formation of sulfur tetrafluoride as well. Treatment of CH_3SH with cobaltic fluoride, by Silvey and Cady,[38] resulted in the formation of CF_3SF_5. Direct fluorination of the same thiol with fluorine resulted in the monohydro-derivative of CF_3SF_5 ($CSHF_7$).

Fluorination of dimethylsulfide in the Simons cell yielded 20 percent of CF_3SF_5 and small amounts of $(CF_3)_2SF_4$. Dresdner[11] similarly obtained a mixture of $C_2F_5SF_5$ and $(C_2F_5)_2SF_4$ from the electrolytic fluorination of diethyl sulfide. By the same method, mixtures of n-$C_4F_9SF_5$ and (n-$C_4F_9)_2SF_4$;[22A,37] $C_2F_5SF_5$ and $(C_2F_5)_2SF_4$; $C_3F_7SF_5$ and $(C_3F_7)_2SF_4$[22A] were obtained. In this reaction, fluorocarbons as well as SF_6 were also isolated. Similar treatment of the disulfide (n-$C_4H_9)_2S_2$ resulted in the formation of n-$C_4F_9SF_5$.[22A]

Fluorocarbon sulfurpentafluorides are remarkably thermally stable. When CF_3SF_5 was passed at 450° through a nickel tube packed with nickel filings, the starting material was recovered. However, at 500°, perfluoroethane and SF_4 were isolated.[10] Pyrolysis of $(C_4F_9)_2SF_4$ at 550° yielded a quantitative amount of C_8F_{18}.[37] In the presence of bromine under these conditions, a 58 percent yield of C_4F_9Br was recovered. The nature of the decomposition products suggest a free radical mechanism.[37]

Dresdner[11] reacted CF_3SF_5 with perfluoroazomethine, $CF_3N{=}CF_2$ at 519° and one atmosphere pressure in a nickel tube packed with sodium fluoride pellets and obtained $(CF_3)_3N$ (cf. Method 1108). The reaction of $C_2F_5SF_5$ and perfluoroazomethine carried out in an autoclave at 372° to 384° at 12 atmospheres yielded $(CF_3)_2NC_2F_5$. The addition of CF_3SF_5 to perfluoropropene at 425° to 518° resulted in a mixture of *neo-*, *iso-*, and *n*-perfluoropentanes as well as higher fluorocarbons.[10]

Haszeldine and Nyman[20] fluorinated thioglycollic acid in a Simons cell and obtained $SF_5CF_2CO_2H$ as well as $SF_3CF_2CO_2H$; the latter being a derivative of sulfur tetrafluoride. Pyrolysis of $SF_5CF_2CO_2Ag$ in the presence of chlorine yielded SF_5CF_2Cl (cf. Method 207). Similar treatment of $SF_3CF_2CO_2Ag$ resulted in the formation of thionyl fluoride, sulfuryl fluoride, and carbon dioxide.

SULFOXIDES AND SULFONES

METHOD 1309 Addition of Grignard Reagents to Alkanesulfonyl Fluorides

When alkyl Grignard reagents are reacted with fluorocarbon sulfonyl fluorides, sulfones are formed. By this method, Brown[4] prepared $CF_3SO_2CH_3$ and $C_8F_{15}SO_2CH_3$ by reacting methylmagnesium iodide with the respective fluorocarbon sulfonyl fluoride. In addition, β-disulfones of the type $R_fSO_2CH_2SO_2R_f$ are also formed.

METHOD 1310 Oxidation of Sulfides

The oxidation of fluorine-containing sulfides with nitric acid results in sulfoxide formation. Treatment of $(CH_2FCH_2)_2S$ with concentrated nitric acid yielded $(CH_2FCH_2)_2S \longrightarrow O$.[30] Oxidation of the same sulfide with chromic acid resulted in the formation of the sulfone, $(CH_2FCH_2)_2SO_2$. Truce, Birum and McBee[39] oxidized the unsymmetrical sulfides CH_3SCClF_2, CH_2ClSCF_3 and CH_3SCF_3 to the respective sulfones with chromic acid in glacial acetic acid. Potassium permanganate in glacial acetic acid was employed by Rapp, Pruett, *et al.*[34] in the oxidation to $C_2H_5SO_2CF_2CFClH$ n-$C_4H_9SO_2CF_2CFClH$ from the corresponding sulfides.

THIOLS

METHOD 1311 Reaction of Fluoroalkyl Halides and Sodium Hydrosulfide

The reaction of FCH_2CH_2Br and NaSH to yield FCH_2CH_2SH was reported by McCombie and Saunders.[29] The use of this method in the synthesis of more highly fluorinated thiols has not been reported.

METHOD 1312 Hydrolysis of Thioesters

Treatment of $FCH_2CH_2S\overset{\overset{\displaystyle O}{\|}}{C}CH_3$ with anhydrous hydrogen chloride in cyclohexanol at 60° for 24 hours has been reported by Ellingboe[13] to yield 74.4 percent of FCH_2CH_2SH.

METHOD 1313 Decomposition of Thiofluoroalkylmercurials

When bis(perfluoroalkylthio)mercury (cf. Method 1302) is treated with dry hydrogen chloride in a sealed tube for 24 to 48 hours, the fluorocarbon thiol is obtained. Haszeldine and Kidd[16,19] reported obtaining high yields of CF_3SH and C_3F_7SH from the respective mercurials. These are the only examples of fluorocarbon thiols yet reported. Trifluoromethanethiol, b.p. $-36.7°$, is decomposed by dilute aqueous sodium hydroxide and yields fluoride, carbonate, and sulfide ions. Aqueous hydrolysis gives thiocarbonyl fluoride, then carbonyl sulfide. Reaction with anhydrous ammonia gives carbonyl sulfide, silicon tetrafluoride, trifluoromethylfluorodithioformate (CF_3SCSF), and bistrifluoromethyltrithiocarbonate $(CF_3S)_2CS$.[19] These compounds are further discussed in Method 1334.

THIOESTERS

METHOD 1314　Reaction of Mercaptans and Acyl Halides

Saunders and Stacey[36] obtained a 63 percent yield of $CH_2FCOSCH_2CH_2Cl$ from the reaction of CH_2FCOCl and $HSCH_2CH_2Cl$ at 150°. In a similar manner, Hauptschein and co-workers[21] synthesized $CF_3COSC_2H_5$, $C_2F_5COSC_2H_5$ and other fluorinated esters derived from dithiols and perfluoroacyl chlorides.

METHOD 1315　Reaction of Mercaptans and Acid Anhydrides

When a perfluorodicarboxylic acid anhydride reacts with a thiol, the half-acid ester is formed. As expected $O{=}\overset{\displaystyle\lceil\!-\!-O\!-\!-\!\rceil}{C}CF_2CF_2CF_2\overset{}{C}{=}O$ and C_2H_5SH yielded $C_2H_5SOCCF_2CF_2CF_2CO_2H$.[21] Reaction of trifluoroacetic anhydride and 1,5-pentane dithiol resulted in the ester, $CH_2(CH_2CH_2SCOCF_3)_2$.[21]

METHOD 1316　Addition of Thioacids to Olefins

When thioacetic acid was added to vinyl fluoride in the presence of dibutyl disulfide and ultraviolet light, a 75 percent yield of the ester, $CH_3COSCH_2CH_2F$, resulted.[13]

METHOD 1317　Reaction of Thioacid Salts with Alkyl Halides

If the potassium salt of thioacetic acid reacts with 1-bromo-2-fluoroethane, the ester, $CH_3COSCH_2CH_2F$, is obtained.[14] In a similar manner, $CH_2FOSCH_2CH_2Cl$ is also formed.

METHOD 1318　Oxidation of Unsaturated Thioethers

Oxidation of the di-thioether of perfluorocyclobutene (cf. Method 1303) with potassium permanganate in glacial acetic acid yielded the dibutyl thioester of perfluorosucinnic acid.[34]

$$\begin{array}{cc}
CF_2{-}C{-}SC_4H_9 & \overset{O}{\underset{}{\|}} \\
\ \ |\ \ \ \|\ \ \ \ \ \ \ \ \ \xrightarrow{[o]}\ \ CF_2{-}C{-}SC_4H_9 \\
CF_2{-}C{-}SC_4H_9 & \ |\\
& CF_2{-}C{-}SC_4H_9 \\
& \underset{O}{\|}
\end{array}$$

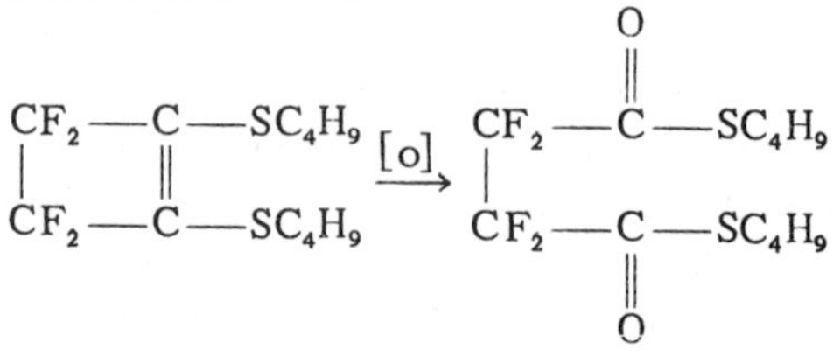

ALKANESULFONIC ACIDS

METHOD 1319 Addition of Sodium Sulfite or Bisulfite to Olefins

A convenient method for the preparation of fluoroalkanesulfonic acids is the addition of sodium sulfite to fluoroolefins using benzoyl peroxide as a catalyst. The reaction is carried out in an autoclave at autogenous pressure at 80° to 210°. The fluoroalkanesulfonic acid is generated from the sodium salt by sulfuric acid. Barrick[1,2] and Coffman[7] were thus able to prepare $CHF_2CF_2SO_3H$ in a 54 percent yield from tetrafluoroethylene. Koshar *et al.*[24] prepared $CF_3CFHCF_2SO_3H$, $C_3F_7CFHCF_2SO_3H$, and $C_5F_{11}CFHCF_2SO_3H$ in good yields from the fluoroolefins and sodium hydrogen sulfate and borax. Haszeldine,[15] using sodium sulfite and borax, prepared $CFCl_2CF_2CFHCF_2SO_3H$ and other chlorofluoroalkanesulfonic acids.

The fluoroalkanesulfonic acids are hydroscopic viscous liquids which liberate chloride ion from sodium chloride.[24] They form solid hydrates on exposure to atmospheric moisture. The acids can be regenerated from the hydrates by thionyl chloride.[7]

METHOD 1320 Oxidation of Thiofluoroalkylmercurials

Another method for the preparation of fluoroalkanesulfonic acids was reported by Haszeldine and Kidd,[17] who oxidized $(CF_3S)_2Hg$ with 35 percent hydrogen peroxide at 105°.

ALKANESULFONYL CHLORIDES

METHOD 1321 Action of Phosphorus Pentachloride on Alkanesulfonic Acids

Fluoroalkanesulfonyl chlorides can be made by the action of phosphorus pentachloride on a sulfonic acid at 100° for four hours. In this manner Haszeldine and Kidd[18] prepared CF_3SO_2Cl in a 63 percent yield. Barrick[2] and Coffman[7] likewise prepared $CHF_2CF_2SO_2Cl$.

METHOD 1322 Oxidation of Thiocyanates or Alkanesulfenyl Chlorides

Treatment of 2-fluoroethylthiocyanate with chlorine and water at 0° resulted in a 60 percent yield of $CH_2FCH_2SO_2Cl$.[35] Similar treatment of trifluoromethanesulfenyl chloride, CF_3SCl (cf. Method 1223), for 48 hours resulted in a 47 percent yield of trifluoromethanesulfonyl chloride.[18] When the reaction was allowed to proceed for 7 days, a 98 percent yield of the sulfonyl chloride was obtained. Oxidation of CF_3SCl with 35 percent H_2O_2 also results in the formation of CF_3SO_2Cl.[18]

ALKANESULFENYL CHLORIDES

METHOD 1323 Preparation and Reaction of Fluoroalkanesulfenyl Chlorides

Haszeldine and Kidd[16] found that when $(CF_3S)_2Hg$ (cf. Method 1302) was chlorinated in a sealed tube at $-22°$, a 72 percent yield of trifluoromethanesulfenyl chloride resulted. This compound, CF_3SCl is the acyl chloride of the hypothetical acid, trifluoromethanesulfenic acid, CF_3SOH. Attempts to hydrolyze the sulfenyl chloride failed to yield the acid.[18] Aqueous hydrolysis in a large excess of water, yielded 33 percent of trifluoromethanesulfinic acid, CF_3SO_2H (cf. Method 1333) and 66 percent yield of CF_3SSCF_3. Controlled aqueous hydrolysis yielded $CF_3SO_2SCF_3$ (cf. Method 1325). Basic hydrolysis of the sulfenyl chloride yielded fluoroform and sulfur.

The addition of sulfur monochloride to tetrafluoroethylene yielded, in addition to mono- and disulfides, some sulfenyl chlorides, CF_2ClCF_2SCl and CF_2ClCF_2SSCl (cf. Method 1306). When 2-chlorotetrafluoroethanesulfenyl chloride was reacted with diethylamine, the sulfenamide, $CF_2ClCF_2SN(C_2H_5)_2$ resulted.[25A] Treatment of CF_2ClCF_2SCl with an ethereal solution of potassium iodide liberated hydrogen iodide, and coupling to the disulfide was observed.

ESTERS OF ALKANESULFONIC ACIDS

METHOD 1324 Reaction of Sulfonic Acids with Alcohols

$$CHF_2CF_2SO_3H + C_2H_5OH \longrightarrow CHF_2SO_2C_2H_5$$ [2]

METHOD 1325 Reaction of Zinc Alkanesulfinates with Alkanesulfenyl Chlorides

When zinc trifluoromethanesulfinate (cf. Method 1333) was reacted with trifluoromethanesulfenyl chloride for a period of five days, trifluoromethylthiol trifluoromethanesulfonate, $CF_3SO_2SCF_3$ was produced in a 67 percent yield.[18] This ester could not be prepared by direct reaction of CF_3SO_2Cl and CF_3SH during a five day period in a sealed tube, nor could it be prepared by the reaction of $(CF_3S)_2Hg$ and CF_3SO_2Cl. It is interesting to note that controlled hydrolysis of CF_3SCl with small amounts of water also yielded 27 percent of the same ester.

Two ionic mechanisms for hydrolysis of CF_3SCl were proposed by Haszeldine and Kidd[18] to explain the reason for this ester formation.

METHOD 1326 Reaction of Silver Alkanesulfonates with Alkyl Iodides

Brown[4] reported that when silver trifluoromethanesulfonate is reacted with alkyl iodides, alkyl trifluoromethanesulfonates are obtained. These esters are strong alkylating agents and hydrolyze in water. In an attempt to prepare ethyl perfluorooctanesulfonate from C_2H_5I and $C_8H_{17}SO_3Ag$ in benzene, a 75 percent yield of ethylbenzene resulted, illustrating the powerful alkylating properties of these esters.

AMIDES AND AMMONIUM SALTS OF ALKANESULFONIC ACIDS

METHOD 1327 Reaction of Alkanesulfonyl Halides and Amines

The reaction of butylamine and dibutylamine with 2-hydrotetrafluoroethanesulfonyl chloride yielded sulfonamides in the normal fashion.[7] In this manner, $CHF_2CF_2SO_2NHC_4H_9$ and $CHF_2CF_2SO_2N(C_4H_9)_2$ were produced.

METHOD 1328 Reaction of Alkanesulfonic Acid Hydrates and Amines or Ammonia

When ammonia or alkylamines react with fluoroalkanesulfonic acid hydrates, ammonium salts or alkyl ammonium salts of the sulfonic acid are formed.[7] For example, the reaction of $CHF_2CF_2SO_3H \cdot H_2O$ with ammonia yielded $CHF_2CF_2SO_3NH_4$. The reaction of the same hydrate with methylamine yielded $CHF_2CF_2SO_3NH_3CH_3$, and with *n*-dodecylamine yielded $CHF_2CF_2SO_3NH_3C_{12}H_{25}$.

ESTERS OF SULFURIC ACID

METHOD 1329 Reaction of Alcohols with Sulfuryl Chloride

When fluorine-containing alcohols are reacted with sulfuryl chloride, fluoroalkylsulfates of the monosulfate, $(RO)_2SO_2$ are formed in the normal fashion. In addition, acyl chlorides of the monosulfate, $ROSO_2Cl$ are also formed. The esterification is best effected at temperatures of 60° to 70°. At this time, sulfuric acid esters of 2-fluoroethanol have been the only sulfates prepared by this method.[26,31,35]

METHOD 1330 Addition of Fluorosulfonic Acid to Olefins

Calfee and Florio[5] added fluorosulfonic acid to fluoroolefins at 30° and obtained the corresponding acid fluorides of the monosulfate. The addition of fluorosulfonic acid to vinylidene fluoride and chlorotrifluoroethylene yielded $CH_3CF_2OSO_2F$ and $CHClFCF_2OSO_2F$, respectively.

MISCELLANEOUS SULFUR COMPOUNDS

METHOD 1331 Thioformates and Thiocarbonates

Trifluoromethyl fluorodithioformate CF_3SCSF was prepared by Haszeldine and Kidd[19] in a 40 percent yield by the reaction of trifluoromethanethiol with anhydrous ammonia. The ammonia acts as an acceptor for hydrogen fluoride which is liberated:

$$CF_3SH \xrightarrow{NH_3} CSF_2 + HF$$

$$CF_3SH + CSF_2 \xrightarrow{NH_3} CF_3SCSF + HF\,.$$

Another product of the reaction between CF_3SH and ammonia is bistrifluoromethyl trithiocarbonate $(CF_3S)_2CS$ obtained in a 10 percent yield. It is believed to form in the following manner:[19]

$$CF_3SH + CSF_2 \longrightarrow CF_3SCSF + HF$$

$$CF_3SCSF + CF_3SH \longrightarrow (CF_3S)_2CS + HF\,.$$

Photochemical chlorination of the fluorodithioformate yielded chlorotrifluoromethane. Aqueous hydrolysis at room temperature to 75° yields hydrogen fluoride, carbonyl sulfide, carbon disulfide and a small amount of trifluoromethanethiol. Alternate means of preparing the trithiocarbonate are as follows:[19]

$$(CF_3S)_2Hg + CF_3SCSF \xrightarrow[24\ hrs.]{0^\circ} (CF_3S)_2CS\ (34\%)$$

$$(CF_3S)_2Hg + CSCl_2 \xrightarrow[24\ hrs.]{50^\circ} (CF_3S)_2CS\ (61\%)$$

METHOD 1332 Esters of Sulfurous Acid

Esterification of 2-fluoroethanol with thionyl chloride yielded bis(2-fluoroethyl)sulfite, $(CH_2FCH_2O)_2SO$.[31]

METHOD 1333 Alkanesulfinic Acids

Reduction of trifluoromethanesulfonyl chloride with zinc dust and water resulted in the formation of trifluoromethanesulfinic acid, isolated as the hydrated zinc salt.[18]

METHOD 1334 Thioamides

$$\underset{\overset{|}{CH_3}}{\overset{\overset{OH}{|}}{CF_3C}}\!-\!CN + EtOH + NH_3 \xrightarrow[\text{18 hrs.}]{H_2S} \underset{\overset{|}{CH_3}}{\overset{\overset{OH}{|}}{CF_3C}}\!-\!CSNH_2 \ ^{[8]}$$

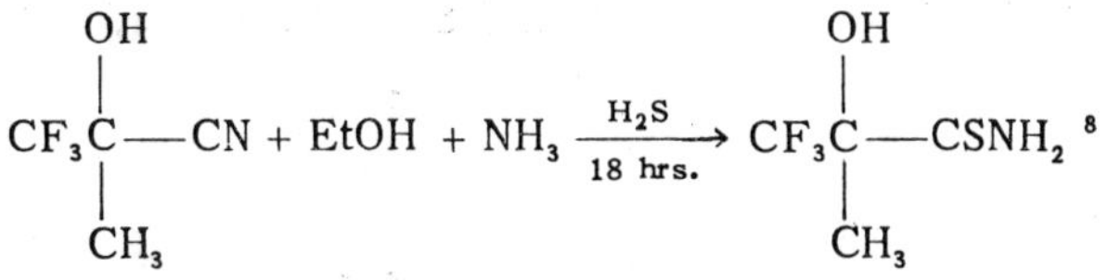

TABLE 61

SULFUR COMPOUNDS

Empirical Formula	Structural Formula	Method	Yield %	B.p. °C/mm.	F.p. or M.p. °C	n_D^t	d_4^t	t°C	Ref.
$CClF_3O_2S$	CF_3SO_2Cl	1321	63	31.6					18
		1322	40–98	31.6					18
$CClF_3S$	CF_3SCl	1323	72	−0.7					16
$CClF_3SHg$	CF_3SHgCl	1302	97		124–126				19
$CClF_7S$	CF_2ClSF_5	1308		16.5					20
CF_8S	CF_3SF_5	1307	90	−20 to −21	−86.9 ± 0.2				6,38,40
		1308	20	−20					6
CF_8S_2	$CF_2(SF_3)_2$	1307	0.5	35					6
$CF_{12}S_2$	$CF_2(SF_5)_2$	1307	0.5	60.5					6
CHF_3O_3S	CF_3SO_3H	1320	92	162, 42/1					17,18
CHF_3S	CF_3SH	1313	99	−36.7					16
CHF_7S		1308		5.1	−87				38
$CH_2F_3O_3SNa$	$CF_3SO_2Na \cdot H_2O$	1333	38						18
$C_2Cl_2F_4S$	CF_2ClCF_2SCl	1323		69.5		1.3890	1.605	20	25A
$C_2Cl_2F_4S_2$	CF_2ClCF_2SSCl	1323		126		1.4112	1.674	20	25A
$C_2F_4S_2$	CF_3SCSF	1331	40	42.9/762					19
$C_2F_6O_2S_2$	$CF_3SO_2SCF_3$	1325	67	69–70		1.3480		1	18
C_2F_6S	$(CF_3)_2S$	1302	62	−22.2					3,16
$C_2F_6S_2$	CF_3SSCF_3	1301	75						3,16
		1302	34–60						16
		1305	76	34					16
		1323	55–60						18
$C_2F_6S_2Hg$	$(CF_3S)_2Hg$	1302	90		37–38				3,16
$C_2F_6S_3$	CF_3SSSCF_3	1301	12	86.2		1.4023		20	16
		1305	7	86.4		1.4023		20	16
$C_2F_6S_4$	$CF_3SSSSCF_3$	1301	1	135		1.4608		20	16

$C_2F_{10}S$	$(CF_3)_2SF_4$	1308	2	20.5					7
	$C_2F_5SF_5$	1308	28	11.3					11
$C_2HClF_4O_2S$	$CHF_2CF_2SO_2Cl$	1321		90–92.5					2,7
$C_2HF_3O_5S$	$CF_3CO_2SO_3H$			40–42/30					9
$C_2HF_5O_2S$	$SF_3CF_2CO_2H$	1308		132.5					20
C_2HF_5S	CF_3SCHF_2	107	45	0.8–1.3					39
$C_2HF_7O_2S$	$SF_5CF_2CO_2H$	1308							20
$C_2H_2ClF_3O_2S$	$CH_2ClSO_2CF_3$	1310	46	139.9/751	−90	1.3859	1.6633	20	39
$C_2H_2ClF_3O_3S$	$CH_2ClCF_2OSO_2F$	1330		108					5
$C_2H_2ClF_3S$	CF_3SCH_2Cl	107	66	63.5/740		1.3818	1.4122	20	39
$C_2H_2Cl_2F_2S$	$CClF_2SCH_2Cl$	107	9	105.7/740		1.4408	1.510	20	39
$C_2H_2F_4O_3S$	$CHF_2CF_2SO_3H$	1319	100	59.5, 90–92/3–5					1,2,7
$C_2H_3ClF_2O_2S$	$CH_3SO_2CClF_2$	1310	62	165.1	21–21.6	1.4050	1.5685	20	39
$C_2H_3ClF_2S$	CH_3SCClF_2	107	32	56.3/755	−100.2	1.3926	1.298	20	39
$C_2H_3F_3O_2S$	$CH_3SO_2CF_3$	1309							4
		1310	40	128.9/737	14	1.3486	1.5141	20	39
$C_2H_3F_3O_3S$	$CF_3SO_3CH_3$	1326							4
	$CH_3CF_2OSO_2F$	1330		74–75					5
$C_2H_3F_3S$	CH_3SCF_3	107	38	11.5–11.7/750					39
$C_2H_4ClFO_2S$	$CH_2FCH_2SO_2Cl$	1322	60.6	84.5/13					35
$C_2H_4ClFO_3S$	$CH_2FCH_2OSO_2Cl$	1329	62	79–80/18		1.4198	1.4970	20	26,35
$C_2H_4F_4O_4S$	$CHF_2CF_2SO_3H \cdot H_2O$	1319		112–114.5/5	54				1,7
C_2H_5FS	CH_2FCH_2SH	1312	74.4	38.5/225		1.4288	1.082	25	13,29
$C_2H_5F_4NO_3S$	$CHF_2CF_2SO_3NH_4$				198				7
$C_3F_6S_3$	$(CF_3S)_2CS$	1331	10–61	110					19
C_3HF_7S	$CF_3CF_2CF_2SH$	1313		23.7/759					19
$C_3H_2F_6O_3S$	$CF_3CHFCF_2SO_3H$	1319		111–113/20					24
$C_3H_3ClF_2S$	$CH_3SCF{=}CFCl$	1303	57	88–89		1.4390	1.324	20	25
$C_3H_4ClF_3S$	CH_3SCF_2CFClH	1303		104		1.4083	1.389	20	25
$C_3H_4FOS_2Na$	$CH_2FCH_2OCS_2Na$		55	208–210					28
$C_3H_4F_4S$	$CH_3SCF_2CF_2H$	1303	77	63		1.3675	1.322	8	25
$C_3H_5Cl_2F_2S$	$CH_3SCClFCHClF$	1303	60	58.5/15		1.5900	1.355	20	25

TABLE 61 (*continued*)

Empirical Formula	Structural Formula	Method	Yield %	B.p. °C/mm.	F.p. or M.p. °C	n_D^t	d_4^t	t°C	Ref.
$C_3H_5F_3O_3S$	$CF_3SO_3C_2H_5$	1326							4
C_3H_6ClFOS	$CH_2FOSCH_2CH_2Cl$	1317		106–107/12					14
$C_3H_7F_4NO_3S$	$CH_2FCF_2SO_3NH_3CH_3$				119–120.5				7
$C_4Cl_2F_8S$	$CF_2ClCF_2SCF_2CF_2Cl$	1306		100–102		1.368	1.662	10	25A
$C_4Cl_2F_8S_2$	$CF_2ClCF_2SSCF_2CF_2Cl$	1306		139–140		1.3970	1.685	20	25A,32
$C_4Cl_2F_8S_3$	$CF_2ClCF_2SSSCF_2CF_2Cl$	1306		50–52/5		1.4340	1.707	20	25A
$C_4F_{14}S$	$(C_2F_5)_2SF_4$	1308	2.9	68		1.2753	1.875	25	11,22A
	$CF_3(CF_2)_3SF_5$	1308		70		1.2710	1.8451	25	22A,37
$C_4HF_7O_5S$	$CF_3CF_2CF_2CO_2SO_3H$			51–53/30					9
$C_4H_2Cl_2F_6O_3S$	$CFCl_2CF_2CHFCF_2SO_3H$	1319	69	118–120/3.5					15
C_4H_3FS	$SCH{=}CFCH{=}CH$ (ring)	107	14.5	82		1.4971		20	41
$C_4H_4ClF_3O_2S$	$CHClFCF_2SCH_2CO_2H$	1303	48	85/<0.01	19	1.4470	1.5847	25	34
$C_4H_4Cl_2F_4S$	$CF_2ClCF_2SCH_2CH_2Cl$	1306		85/100		1.4218	1.5828	20	25A
$C_4H_4F_6S$	$CF_3CHFCF_2SCH_3$	1303		87		1.3443	1.380	20	27
$C_4H_5ClF_2S$	$C_2H_5SCF{=}CFCl$	1303	90	106–107		1.4385	1.282	20	25
$C_4H_5F_3OS$	$CF_3COSC_2H_5$	1314	84	90.5		1.3755	1.2338	25	21
C_4H_6ClFOS	$CH_2FCOSCH_2CH_2Cl$	1314	63	104–105/33					36
$C_4H_6ClF_3OS$	$CHClFCF_2SCH_2CH_2OH$	1303	87	62.5/0.5		1.4426	1.4793	25	34
$C_4H_6ClF_3O_2S$	$C_2H_5SO_2CF_2CFClH$	1310	86	99/22	−18	1.4144	1.5009	25	34
$C_4H_6ClF_3S$	$C_2H_5SCF_2CFClH$	1303	95	69.1/100		1.4079	1.3212	25	34
$C_4H_6Cl_2F_2S$	$C_2H_5SCFClCHClF$	1303	62	138		1.4612	1.425	20	25
$C_4H_6F_3NOS$	$CH_3C(CF_3)(OH)CSNH_2$	1334		70–76/0.9	52				8
$C_4H_6F_4O_3S$	$CHF_2CF_2SO_3C_2H_5$	1324		96–100					1
$C_4H_6F_4S$	$C_2H_5SCF_2CF_2H$	1303	76	64/12		1.4740	1.3515	20	12,25
C_4H_6FOS	$CH_3COSCH_2CH_2F$	1316	75	87/100		1.4525	1.4041	25	13
		1317	65	41–42/12					14
C_4H_8ClFS	$CH_2ClCH_2SCH_2CH_2F$		22	91.5–92.5/30	−44	1.4852	1.228(20)	25	23

$C_4H_8F_2OS$	$(CH_2FCH_2)_2SO$	1310			102–103				30
$C_4H_8F_2O_2S$	$(CH_2FCH_2)_2SO_2$	1310			41–42				30
$C_4H_8F_2O_3S$	$(CH_2FCH_2O)_2SO$	1332		125/15					31
$C_4H_8F_2O_4S$	$(CH_2FCH_2O)_2SO_2$	1329		145/18					35
				80–81/2		1.4177	1.3678(25)	20	34A
				82–84/2		1.4080	1.3191	20	26,31
$C_4H_8F_2S$	$(CH_2FCH_2)_2S$	102		95–96/30					30
$C_5H_2F_{10}O_3S$	$CF_3(CF_2)_2CHFCF_2SO_3H$	1319	79	119–120/14					24
$C_5H_5F_5OS$	$C_2F_5COSC_2H_5$	1314	93	103		1.3592	1.3300	24	21
$C_5H_6F_6S$	$CF_3CHFCF_2SC_2H_5$	1303	34	100–101		1.3548	1.322	20	27
$C_5H_6F_7OS$	$CF_3CHFCF_2SCH_2CH_2OH$	1303	20.5	53–54/5		1.3835	1.546	20	27
$C_5H_7ClF_2S$	$(CH_3)_2CHSCF{=}CFCl$	1303	74	135		1.4178	1.278	20	25
$C_5H_8Cl_2F_2S$	$(CH_3)_2CHSCFClCHClF$	1303	52	159/738		1.4534	1.302	25	25
C_5H_9FOS	$CH_3SCOCH_2CH_2CH_2F$			54/6		1.4857	1.1135	20	34A
$C_6F_{14}S$	$(C_3F_7)_2S$								22
$C_6F_{14}S_2$	$(C_3F_7S)_2$	1301	36	122–122.2					19,22
$C_6F_{14}S_3$	$(C_3F_7S)_2S$	1301		152.5–153					22
$C_6F_{18}S$	$(C_3F_7)_2SF_4$	1308							22A
$C_6H_2Cl_3F_9O_3S$	$CFCl_2CF_2CFClCF_2CHFCF_2SO_3H$	1319	57	130–133/0.1					15
$C_6H_5F_7OS$	$C_3F_7COSC_2H_5$	1314	90	119		1.3544	1.4217	19	21
$C_6H_7F_5OS_2$	$C_2F_5CH(CH_3)OCS_2CH_3$		50	4/6		1.4157	1.387	20	28
$C_6H_{10}ClF_3O_2S$	$CH_3(CH_2)_3SO_2CF_2CHClF$	1310		70/0.01	−0.5 to 0.5	1.4517	1.3953	25	34
$C_6H_{10}ClF_3S$	$CH_3(CH_2)_3SCF_2CHClF$	1303	95	71.6/25		1.4196	1.224	25	34
$C_6H_{10}ClF_4NS$	$CF_2ClCF_2SN(C_2H_5)_2$	1323		66–67/60		1.4850	1.341	20	25A
$C_6H_{10}Cl_2F_2S$	$CH_3(CH_2)_3SCF_2CHCl_2$	1303	90	43/1		1.4545	1.2707	25	34
$C_6H_{11}F_4NO_2S$	$CHF_2CF_2SO_2NH(CH_2)_3CH_3$	1327	90	113/30		1.4112	1.1029	25	7
$C_6H_{12}F_2S_2$	$CH_2FCH_2S(CH_2)_2SCH_2CH_2F$	1304		139/17					29,36
$C_7H_2F_{14}O_3S$	$CF_3(CF_2)_4CFHCF_2SO_3H$	1319	73	119–120/3					24
$C_7H_5ClF_6O_2S$	$C_2H_5SCO(CF_2)_3COCl$		83	101/43		1.4016		25	21
$C_7H_6F_6O_3S$	$C_2H_5SCO(CF_2)_3CO_2H$	1315		131/8		1.4070		25	21
$C_8F_{22}S$	$[CF_3(CF_2)_3]_2SF_4$	1308							22A,37

TABLE 61 (*continued*)

Empirical Formula	Structural Formula	Method	Yield %	B.p. °C/mm.	F.p. or M.p. °C	n_D^t	d_4^t	t °C	Ref.
$C_8H_6F_4O_4S_2$	CF_2—$CSCH_2CO_2H$ CF_2—$CSCH_2CO_2H$	1303	23		116–117				34
$C_8H_9F_5S$	$CH_3(CH_2)_3SC{=}CFCF_2CF_2$	1303	23	61.7/18		1.4086	1.2555	25	34
$C_8H_{10}Cl_2F_4S$	$CF_2ClCF_2SCH(CH_2)_4CHCl$	1306		135–136/60		1.4595	1.388	20	25A
$C_8H_{10}Cl_2F_4S_2$	$CF_2ClCF_2SSCH(CH_2)_4CHCl$	1306		142/20		1.4915	1.456	20	25A
$C_9H_3F_{15}O_2S$	$CF_3(CF_2)_7SO_2CH_3$	1309							4
$C_9H_{10}F_6O_2S_2$	$(CF_3COSCH_2CH_2)_2CH_2$	1315	79	119/8		1.4269	1.3627	25	21
	$CF_2(CF_2COSC_2H_5)_2$	1314	90	122/8		1.4351	1.3858	25	21
$C_{10}H_{19}F_4NO_2S$	$CHF_2CF_2SO_2N[(CH_2)_3CH_3]_2$	1327	62	107/10		1.4270	1.0158	25	7
$C_{11}H_{10}F_{10}O_2S_2$	$(C_2F_5COSCH_2CH_2)_2CH_2$	1314	80	128/8		1.4006	1.4404	24	21
$C_{12}H_{18}F_4O_2S_2$	$(CF_2COSC_4H_9)_2$	1318				1.4719		25	33
$C_{12}H_{18}F_4S_2$	CF_2—CSC_4H_9 CF_2—CSC_4H_9	1303	33	45/<0.01	−41	1.4791	1.1645	25	34
$C_{12}H_{19}F_5S_2$	CF_2—$CFSC_4H_9$ CF_2—$CHSC_4H_9$	1303	30	50/<0.01	−31.5	1.4810	1.1588	25	34
$C_{12}H_{25}F_4NO_3S$	$CHF_2CF_2SO_3NH_3C_{10}H_{21}$	1328			225				7
$C_{13}H_{10}F_{14}O_2S_2$	$(C_3F_7COSCH_2CH_2)_2CH_2$	1314	80	142/8		1.3866	1.5220	25	21
$C_{14}H_{29}F_4NO_3S$	$CHF_2CF_2SO_3NH_3C_{12}H_{25}$	1328			155				7

BIBLIOGRAPHY

1. Barrick, P. L., U. S. Patent 2,403,207(1946).
2. Barrick, P. L., British Patent 579,897(1946).
3. Brandt, G. R. A., Emeleus, H. J., and Haszeldine, R. N., *J. Chem. Soc.*, **1952**, 2198.
4. Brown, H. A., 128th Meeting, American Chemical Society, Minneapolis, Minn., September 1955.
5. Calfee, J. D., and Florio, P. A., U. S. Patent 2,628,972(1953).
6. Clifford, A. F., El-Shamy, H. K., *et al.*, *J. Chem. Soc.*, **1953**, 2372.
7. Coffman, D. D., Raasch, M. S., *et al.*, *J. Org. Chem.*, **14**, 747(1949).
8. Darrall, R. A., Smith, F., *et al.*, *J. Chem. Soc.*, **1951**, 2329.
9. Dowdall, J. F., U. S. Patent 2,628,253(1953).
10. Dresdner, R., *J. Am. Chem. Soc.*, **77**, 6633(1955).
11. Dresdner, R., *J. Am. Chem. Soc.*, **79**, 69(1957).
12. duPont, British Patent 583,874(1947).
13. Ellingboe, E. K., U. S. Patent 2,439,203(1948).
14. Gryszkiewicz-Trochimowski, E., Sporzynski, A., and Wnuk, J., *Rec. Trav. Chim.*, **66**, 427(1947).
15. Haszeldine, R. N., *J. Chem. Soc.*, **1955**, 4291.
16. Haszeldine, R. N., and Kidd, J. M., *J. Chem. Soc.*, **1953**, 3219.
17. Haszeldine, R. N., and Kidd, J. M., *J. Chem. Soc.*, **1954**, 4228.
18. Haszeldine, R. N., and Kidd, J. M., *J. Chem. Soc.*, **1955**, 2901.
19. Haszeldine, R. N., and Kidd, J. M., *J. Chem. Soc.*, **1955**, 3871.
20. Haszeldine, R. N., and Nyman, F., 130th Meeting American Chemical Society, Atlantic City, N. J., September 1956.
21. Hauptschein, M., Stokes, C. S., and Nodiff, E. A., *J. Am. Chem. Soc.*, **74**, 4005(1952).
22. Hauptschein, M., and Grosse, A. V., *J. Am. Chem. Soc.*, **73**, 5461(1951).

22A. Hoffmann, F. W., and Simmons, T. C., *et al.*, 130th Meeting American Chemical Society, Atlantic City, N. J., September 1956.

23. Kharasch, M. S., Weinhouse, S., and Jensen, E. V., *J. Am. Chem. Soc.*, **77**, 3145(1955).
24. Koshar, R. J., Trott, P. W., and LaZerte, J. D., *J. Am. Chem. Soc.*, **75**, 4595(1953).
25. Knunyants, I. L., and Fokin, A. V., *Izvest. Akad. Nauk. S.S.S.R., Otdel, Khim. Nauk.*, **1952**, 261.

25A. Knunyants, I. L., and Fokin, A. V., *Izvest. Akad. Nauk. S.S.S.R., Otdel,* Khim. Nauk., **1955**, 705.

26. Knunyants, I. L., Kil'disheva, O. V., and Bykhovskaya, E., *Zhur. Obshchei Khim.*, **19**, 101(1949).
27. Knunyants, I. L., Shchekotikhin, A. I., and Fokin, A. V., *Izvest. Akad. Nauk. S.S.S.R., Otdel. Khim. Nauk.*, **1953**, 282.
28. McBee, E. T., Higgins, J. F., and Pierce, O. R., *J. Am. Chem. Soc.*, **74**, 1387(1952).
29. McCombie, H., and Saunders, B. C., *Nature*, **158**, 382(1946).
30. Malatesta, P., and D'Arti, B., *Ricerca Sci.*, **22**, 1589(1952).
31. Olah, Gy., and Pavlath, A., *Acta. Chim. Acad. Sci. Hung.*, **4**, 89(1954).
32. Raasch, M. S., U. S. Patent 2,451,411(1948).
33. Rapp, K. E., Barr, J. T., *et al.*, *J. Am. Chem. Soc.*, **74**, 749(1952).

34. Rapp, K. E., Pruett, R. L., *et al.*, *J. Am. Chem. Soc.*, **72,** 3642(1950).
34A. Redeman, C. E., Chaiken, S. W., *et al.*, *J. Am. Chem. Soc.*, **70,** 3604(1948).
35. Saunders, B. C., Stacey, G. J., and Wilding, I. G. E., *J. Chem. Soc.*, **1949,** 773.
36. Saunders, B. C., and Stacey, G. J., *J. Chem. Soc.*, **1949,** 916.
37. Severson, W. A., Bruce, T. J., and Coon, R. I., 128th Meeting, American Chemical Society, Minneapolis, Minn., September 1955.
38. Silvey, G. A., and Cady, G. H., *J. Am. Chem. Soc.*, **72,** 3624(1950).
39. Truce, W. E., Birum, G. H., and McBee, E. T., *J. Am. Chem. Soc.*, **74,** 3594(1952).
40. Tyczkowski, E. A., and Bigelow, L. A., *J. Am. Chem. Soc.*, **75,** 3523(1953).
41. Van Vleck, R. T., U. S. Patent 2,562,994(1951).

INDEX

Italicized page numbers refer to tabular material

Acetals, *197*
  preparation, 188
Acetoacetic esters, halogenation, 185
  hydrolysis of, 182–183, 185
Acetylenes (see Alkynes)
Acids (see Carboxylic acids)
Acyl azides, decomposition of, 267
Acyl bromides, preparation of, 220
Acyl chlorides, preparation from carboxylic acid salts, 221
  preparation using phosphorus halides, 220
  preparation using thionyl chloride, 220
Acyl fluorides, preparation by electrochemical process, 18, 205–206
  preparation by fluorocarbon oxidation, 205
  preparation using metallic fluorides, 6, 10
Acyl halides, *224–225*
  decarboxylation of, 42
  hydrolysis of, 202–203
  preparation from alkenes and alkanes, 222
  preparation from anhydrides, 222
  preparation from ethers, 221–222
  reaction with alcohols, 230–231
    with amines, 261–262
    with ammonia, 261–262
    with cadmium alkyls, 141
    with diazomethane, 290
    with hydrogen halides, 221
    with metallic cyanides, 266
    with silver thiocyanate, 267
    with sodium azide, 267
  reduction of, 141–142, 188
Alcohols, *145–150*
  acid nature of, 138
  addition to alkenes, 266
  cyanoethylation, 266
  dehydration of, 106
  olefinic, *152*
  oxidation of, 185, 188, 205
  preparation of, 138–144
  preparation by acid reduction, 141–142

Alcohols (Cont'd)
preparation by action of fluoroalkyl lithium reagents on aldehydes, 141
preparation by action of fluoroalkyl lithium reagents on esters, 140
preparation by action of Grignard reagents on aldehydes, 140–141
preparation by action of Grignard reagents on esters, 139–140
preparation by aldehyde reduction, 141–142
preparation by anhydride reduction, 142
preparation by amide reduction, 142
preparation by ester hydrolysis, 144
preparation by ester reduction, 141–143
preparation by free radical addition, 143
preparation by hydrolysis of haloalkanes, 143–144
preparation by ketone reduction, 141–142
preparation by oxidation of Grignard reagents, 144
preparation by reduction of acyl halides, 141–142
preparation from acyl halides, 141
preparation from epoxides, 143
preparation from ketones, 141
preparation using metallic fluorides, 3, 4
reaction with acyl halides, 230–231
with aldehydes, 188
with amines, 288
with anhydrides, 232
with carboxylic acids, 231–232
with carboxylic acid salts, 231–232
with diazo compounds, 237
with diazomethane, 162
with epoxides, 162
with nitroolefins, 294
with nitrous acid, 294
with thionyl chloride, 342
Alcoholates, reaction with alkyl halides, 158–159
with olefins, 156–158
Aldehyde hydrates, 182, 187–188, 194
Aldehydes, *196*
addition of hydrogen cyanide, 266
addition to olefins, 187
condensation with nitroalkanes, 293
olefinic, *196*
codimerization with olefins, 188
preparation by acyl halide reduction, 188
preparation by alcohol oxidation, 188
preparation by alkane oxidation, 188
preparation by carboxylic acid reduction, 187–188
preparation by carboxylic ester reduction, 188
preparation by nitrile reduction, 188
preparation from carboxalamides, 189
preparation from orthoformates and fluorocarbon Grignard reagents, 189
reaction with alcohols, 188

Aldehydes (Cont'd)
reaction with anhydrides, 238
with carbamates, 265
with fluoroalkyl lithium reagents, 141
with Grignard reagents, 140–141
Alkadienes (see Dienes)
Alkanes (see also Alkyl halides, Fluorocarbons and Haloalkanes)
acyclic, *49–79*
cyclic, *80–91*
preparation by olefin dimerization, 43
preparation by ring closure, 43
dehalogenation of, 104–105
dehydrohalogenation of, 101–104
nitration of, 291–292
oxidation of, 188, 222
preparation by disproportionation, 45–46
preparation by ether cleavage, 47
preparation by halide reduction, 44
preparation by Lewis acid catalyzed additions, 40
preparation by olefin reduction, 44–45
preparation by free radical addition, 37–40
preparation from acyl halides, 42
preparation from alcohols, 46
preparation from amides, 45
preparation from anhydrides, 42
preparation from carboxylic acids, 40
preparation from carboxylic acid salts, 41–42
preparation from ketones, 46
preparation from phosphorous acid esters, 43
preparation from quaternary salts, 47
preparation from tosylates, 42
reaction with dinitrogen tetroxide, 293
Alkenes (see also olefins), *113–121*
addition of alcohols, 266
addition of amines, 262, 286
addition of ammonia, 265
addition of carboxylic acids, 232
addition of N-Bromoperfluoroamides, 263
addition of silanes, 313–314
cyclic, *126–131*
dehydrohalogenation of, 101–104
disproportionation of, 108
dimerization with alkenyl silanes, 315
free radical addition to, 108
oxidation of, 222
preparation by addition of hydrogen halides to alkynes, 106
preparation by dehalogenation, 104–105
preparation by dehydrohalogenation, 101–104
preparation by pyrolysis, 106–109

Alkenes (Cont'd)
preparation from carboxylic acid salts, 107
reaction with ammonia, 289–290
with dinitrogen tetroxide, 293
with nitroso compounds, 289
with nitrosyl halides, 292–293
with nitryl halides, 292–293
with phosphate esters, 317
with sodium cyanide, 266
Alkyl carbonates, reaction with fluorocarbon Grignard Reagents, 238
Alkyl halides (see also Alkanes, Haloalkanes and Fluorocarbons)
reaction with mercaptides, 334
with sodium hydrosulfide, 337
Alkyl sulfates (see also Sulfuric acid esters), preparation of, 341–342
Alkynes, *125, 128*
addition of alcohols, 157–158
addition of carboxylic acids, 232–233
addition of hydrogen fluoride, 14–15
addition of hydrogen halides, 106
free radical addition to, 107–108
preparation by dehydrohalogenation, 102–103
preparation of, 102–103
Aluminum fluoride, use as fluorinating agent, 6, 14
Amides, *268–272*
cyclic, *270–272*
deamination of, 45
dehydration of, 265
electrochemical fluorination of, 206
hydrolysis of, 202–203, 288
olefinic, *268, 269*
preparation from acyl halides, 261–262
preparation from alkenes, 262, 263
preparation from amidines, 264
preparation from anhydrides, 262
preparation from diazoketones, 263
preparation from esters, 261
preparation from isocyanates, 264
preparation from ketones, 263
preparation from nitriles, 262
preparation using metallic fluorides, 3
reaction with hypohalites, 287
reduction of, 142, 285
Amidines, *273*
hydrolysis of, 264
preparation from nitriles, 264
trimerization of, 290
Amines, *295–298*
addition to alkenes, 286
addition to alkynes, 286

Amines (Cont'd)
addition to olefins, 262
cyclic, *296–298*
preparation from amides, 285, 287–288
preparation from azides, 287
preparation from haloalkanes, 285
preparation from azomethines, 287, 288
preparation from nitriles, 285, 286
preparation from nitro compounds, 286
preparation from oximes, 287–288
pyrolysis of, 288
reaction with alcohols, 288
with acyl halides, 261–262
with ammonia, 262
with chlorocarbonates, 265
with esters, 261
with ethylene oxide, 288
with ketones, 263
with nitrous acid, 290–291
with phosgene, 266–267
Amino acids, preparation of, 208–209
Ammonia, reaction with acyl halides, 261–262
with alkenes, 289–290
with anhydrides, 262
with chlorocarbonates, 265
with esters, 261
with haloalkanes, 288
with ketones, 263
with nitriles, 264
Anhydrides, *226*
decarboxylation of, 42
electrochemical fluorination of, 206
preparation by carboxylic acid dehydration, 223
preparation from acyl halides, 223
preparation by pyrolysis of carboxylic acid salts, 223
reaction with alcohols, 232
with aldehydes, 238
with amines, 262
with ammonia, 262
with carboxylic acids, 223
with sodium bromide, 222
reduction of, 142
Antimony fluorides, action on bromoalkanes, 8
action on chloroalkanes, 8
action on chloroalkenes, 9–10
use as fluorinating agents, 7–10
Antimony compounds, fluorocarbon (see also Stibines), 319, *327*
Arndt-Eistert reaction, 237, 290
Arsines, fluorocarbon, *326*
halides, *326*

Arsines (Cont'd)
halogenation of, 318
hydrolysis of, 317
iodides, alkylation of, 319
coupling of, 318–319
hydrolysis of, 317
oxidation of, 317–318
preparation using fluorocarbon iodides, 317
reaction with silver cyanide, 319
with silver thiocyanate, 319
reduction of, 318
preparation from fluorocarbon iodides, 318–319
preparation from fluorocarbon iodides, 317
preparation using metallic fluorides, 4
Arsonic acids, *326*
preparation of, 317–318
Azides, decomposition of, 287
Azomethines, *299*
addition of hydrogen fluoride, 288
preparation from *t*-amines, 288
preparation from fluorocarbon carbanyl fluorides, 288–289
preparation from oxazetidines, 289
reaction with trifluoromethyl sulfurpentafluoride, 336

Barbituric acid derivatives, 264
Boron esters, *321*
Boron trifluoride, use as fluorinating agent, 6, 14
Bromination, of fluorocarbons, 36
Bromination, oxidative, 205
Bromine, addition to olefins, 33–34
Bromine,monochloride, addition to olefins, 34
Bromine trifluoride, preparation of, 24
use as fluorinating agent, 24
N-Bromoamides, *273*
addition to olefins, 263

Cadmium compounds, fluorocarbon, *321*
iodides, preparation of, 312
reaction with acyl halides, 183
Calcium fluoride, use as fluorinating agent, 5
Carbamates (see also methanes), *275*
acylation of, 265
preparation from chlorocarbonates, 265
preparation from isocyanates, 265
reaction with aldehydes, 265
Carbamyl fluorides, pyrolysis of, 288–289
Carboxolamides, (see also amides) reduction of, 189
Carboxylic acids, addition to alkenes, 232
addition to alkynes, 232–233

Carboxylic acids (Cont'd)
decarboxylation of, 40
dehydration of, 223
dibasic, *215*
preparation by Diels-Alder condensation, 207
preparation by hydrolysis of nitriles, 203
direct fluorination of, 22
hydrates of, 203
ionization constants of, 202
molecular addition compounds of, 203
monobasic, *210–214*
preparation by carbonation of fluorocarbon Grignard reagents, 206, 310
preparation by cleavage of lactams, 208
preparation by electrochemical fluorination, 205–206
preparation by free radical coupling, 208
preparation by hydrolysis of acyl halides, 202–203
preparation by hydrolysis of amides, 202–203
preparation by hydrolysis of carboxylic esters, 202–203
perparation by hydrolysis of ethers, 206–207
preparation by hydrolysis of haloalkanes, 204
preparation by hydrolysis of nitriles, 202–203
preparation by hydrolysis of triazines, 207
preparation by olefin hydration, 207
preparation by oxidation of alcohols, 205
preparation by oxidation of ethers, 207
preparation by oxidation of fluorocarbons, 205
preparation by oxidation of olefins, 203
reaction with acyl halides, 223
with alcohols, 231–232
with anhydrides, 223
with benzoyl halides, 221
with diazo compounds, 237
with inorganic acid halides, 220
reduction of, 141–142
unsaturated, *211–215*
preparation by hydrolyic dehydrohalogenation, 203, 204
preparation by oxidation of dienes, 204
Wolff rearrangement of, 207–208
Carboxylic acid salts, decarboxylation of, 41–42, 107
pyrolysis of, 222, 223
reaction with acyl halides, 223
with alcohols, 231–232
with haloalkanes, 233
with organometallic compounds, 184
with phosphorus and iodine, 316
with phosphorus halides, 221
with nitrosyl chloride, 291
solubility of, 202
Carboxylic diesters, *246–249*

Carboxylic diesters (Cont'd)
unsaturated, *252*
Carboxylic esters, *239–245*
condensation with ketones, 182
hydrolysis of, 144, 202–203
preparation by the Claisen condensation, 235–236
preparation by the malonic ester synthesis, 234–235
preparation by the Reformatsky synthesis, 236
preparation from aldehydes, 238
preparation from alkyl carbonates, 238
preparation from anhydrides, 238
preparation from α,α-difluoroethers, 234
preparation from haloalkanes and carboxylic acid salts, 233
preparation from olefins and carboxylic acids, 232–233
preparation from triazines, 238
preparation using acyl halides, 230–231
preparation using anhydrides, 232
preparation using carboxylic acids and their salts, 231–232
preparation using metallic fluorides, 3, 4, 5, 6, 10
reaction with alkyllithium reagents, 183
with amines, 261
with ammonia, 261
with dimethylsulfone, 238
with fluoroalkyl lithium reagents, 140
with Grignard reagents, 139–141, 183
with nitroolefins, 294
reduction by sodium, 186
reduction of, 141–143. 187–188
transesterification of, 237
triesters, *246–249*
unsaturated, *250–251*
condensation with nitroalkanes, 293
dimerization of, 238
hydrolysis of, 187
Codimerization of olefins (see also Dimerization), 110–112
of fluorocarbon iodides and bromides, 43
Coupling, of fluorocarbon phosphine iodides, 317
free radical, of carboxylic acids, 208
Chlorine, addition to olefins, 33
Chlorination, of fluorocarbons, 35–36
oxidative, 185
Chlorine trifluoride, preparation, 23–24
use as fluorinating agent, 24
Chlorocarbonates, reaction with amines, 265
with ammonia, 265
Chromic fluoride, use as fluorinating agent, 12, 16
Claisen condensation, 235–236
Cobaltic fluoride, preparation of, 10
reaction with carbon disulfide, 335

Cobaltic fluoride (Cont'd)
  use as fluorinating agent, 10–11
Cobaltous fluoride, preparation of, 10
Codimerization, of olefins to vinyl ketones, 186
Copper fluoride, use as fluorinating agent, 3
Cyanoethylation, 266
Cyanohydrins, 266
  reaction with ammonia and hydrogen sulfide, 343
Cyanuric fluoride, *304*
Cycloalkylation (see also Dimerization, Codimerization), 110–112

Decarboxylation, of acyl halides, 42
  of anhydrides, 42
  of carboxylic acid salts, 41–42, 107
Dehalogenation, of haloalkanes, 104–105
Dehydration, of alcohols, 106
  of amides, 265
Dehydrohalogenation, of haloalkanes, 101–104
Diamides, cyclization of, 263
Diazo compounds, *302*
  preparation from acyl halides, 290
  preparation from amines, 290
Diazoketones, ammonolysis and rearrangement, 263
  rearrangement, 207–208
Diazomethane, reaction with alcohols, 162
Diels-Alder condensation, 110–112, 207
Dienes, *122–124*
  condensation with maleic anhydride, 207
  oxidation of, 204
  preparation by dehalogenation, 105
  preparation by dehydrohalogenation, 103–104
  preparation from dicarboxylic acid salts, 107
Diketones, *194*
β-Diketones, copper chelates of, 195
  metal chelates of, 181, 182
  preparation of, 182
  reduction of, 186
Dimerization of olefins (see also Codimerization), 43, 110–112
Diols (see also glycols), *151*
  preparation from epoxides, 144
  preparation of, 142
Disproportionation, 46, 108
Disulfides, preparation of, 332–333

Epoxidation, 160–161
Epoxides, hydrolysis of, 144
  preparation from halohydrins, 160–161
  reaction with alcohols, 162
  reaction with hydrogen fluoride, 143
Esters, carboxylic (see Carboxylic esters)

Ethers, alicyclic, *164–171*
chlorination of, 159
cleavage of, 47, 221–222
cyclic, *172–175*
cleavage of, 161
preparation from glycols, 161
preparation from ketones, 162
electrochemical fluorination of, 206
glycidyl, preparation of, 162–163
hydrolysis of, 156, 206–207, 234
hydroxy, *176*
preparation from epoxides, 163
olefinic, *169–171*
codimerization with olefins, 160
polymerization of, 156
preparation, 157
preparation by dehydration of β-hydroxyketones, 187
reduction of, 187
oxidation of, 207
preparation by electrochemical process, 18
preparation from alcohols and diazomethane, 162
preparation from alcohols and epoxides, 162
preparation from alcohols and paraformaldehyde, 162
preparation from alcoholates and alkyl halides, 158–159
preparation from glycols and alkyl sulfates,
preparation from olefins, 156–158
preparation using metallic fluorides, 3, 4, 5, 10
thermal stability of, 155–156
stability of, 157

Fluorination, direct, 20–23
electrochemical (see also Simons' process), 17–19, 205–206
jet process, 20–21
liquid phase, 21
use of hydrogen fluoride, 12–17, 23–24
use of metallic fluorides, 3–10
vapor phase, 20–21
Fluorine, action on aliphatic hydrocarbons, 20–21
action on aromatic hydrocarbons, 22
action on carbon, 21
action on nitrogen compounds, 22–23
action on oxygenated compounds, 22
action on sulfur compounds, 23
directive effect in chlorination, 159–160
isotopic exchange, 32
Fluorocarbonates, preparation of alkanes from, 42
Fluorocarbon halides, addition to vinyl silanes, 314
reaction with lithium alkyls, 309
with arsenic, 317
with magnesium, 310

Fluorocarbon halides (Cont'd)
  reaction with mercury, 311–312
    with phosphorus, 315
    with silicon, 313
    with sulfur, 332–333
    with zinc, 310
    with zinc alkyl compounds, 311
  hydrides, bromination of, 36
    preparation by olefin oxidation, 185
    preparation from amides, 45
    preparation from carboxylic acid salts, 42–43
Fluorocarbon nitriles (see also Nitriles),
  preparation by direct fluorination, 22–23
  preparation by electrochemical process, 18
  preparation using metallic fluorides, 6, 11
Fluorocarbon polymers, 101
Fluorocarbons (see also Alkanes, Alkyl halides and Haloalkanes)
  acyclic, *48–79*
  cyclic, *80–91*
    pyrolysis of, 45
  directive influence in halogenation of, 35–36
  halogenation of, 35
  oxidation of, 205
  preparation by direct fluorination, 20–22
  preparation by electrochemical process, 18–19
  preparation by olefin addition of hydrogen halides, 34–35
  preparation by pyrolysis, 45–46
  preparation by Swarts reaction, 7–9
  preparation using metallic fluorides, 3–12
  properties compared with hydrocarbons, 32
  pyrolysis of, 45–46
Free radical addition, catalysis of, 38
  mechanism of, 37–38
  of alcohols to olefins, 143
  of aldehydes to olefins, 186
  orientation in, 38–39

Gold hexafluorobromide, use as fluorinating agent, 5
Glycols, dehydration of, 161
  preparation of, 142
  reaction with alkyl sulfates, 163
Grignard reagents (see organomagnesium compounds)

N-Haloamides, preparation from amides, 263–264
Halogen fluorides, use as fluorinating agents, 23–24
Halogen interchange, 37
  in cyclic ethers, 161
Haloalkanes (see also Alkanes, Alkyl halides and Fluorocarbons)
  Ammonolysis of, 285

Haloalkanes (Cont'd)
hydrolysis of, 204
reaction with carboxylic acid salts, 233
reaction with nitric oxide, 290–291
Halogenation (see also chlorination and Bromination) of alcohols, 46
of amides, 263–264
of arsinis, 318
of fluorocarbon phosphine halides, 316–317
of imides, 263–264
of ketones, 46
of olefins, 33–34
N-Haloimides, preparation from imides, 263–264
Hemiacetals, *198*
preparation from aldehydes, 188
Hofmann degradation, 45, 287
Hydantoins, 208, 264
Hydrogen chloride, addition to isocyanates, 265
addition to olefins, 35
Hydrogen halides, action on acyl halides, 221
Hydrogen fluoride, addition to acetylene, 35
addition to alkynes, 14
addition to azomethines, 288
addition to olefins, 12–14, 34–35
cleavage of lactams, 208
reaction with cyclopropane, 13
with epoxides, 15, 143, 163
with haloalkanes, 12–17
use as fluorinating agent, 12–17
use in electrochemical fluorination, 17
Hydrolysis, of alkyllithiums, 309
of amides, 288
of amidines, 264
of α,α-difluoroethers, 234
of fluorocarbon arsine iodides, 317
of fluorocarbon arsines, 317
of fluorocarbon phosphine iodides, 316
of fluorocarbon phosphines, 316
of isocyanates, 264
of keto nitriles, 266
Hydroxy acids, 207
Hydroxy amines, *295–297*
preparation from ethylene oxide, 288
Hydroxy esters, *253*
Hydroxy ketones, *194*
dehydration of, 187
preparation by β-diketone reduction, 186
Hydroxylamines, *304*

Imides, *272*
preparation from diamides, 263

Imines, *299*
Iodine, additions to olefins, 34
Iodine monobromide, addition to olefins, 34
Iodine monochloride, addition to olefins, 34
Iodine pentafluoride, addition to olefins, 34
  preparation, 24
  reaction with carbon disulfide, 334
  use as fluorinating agent, 24
Isocyanates, *278–279*
  addition of hydrogen chloride, 265
  hydrolysis of, 264
  preparation from acyl azides,
  preparation from acyl halides, 267
  preparation from amines, 266–267

Ketals, hydrolysis of, 187
Keto acids, 207
  salts, 186
    decarboxylation of, 186
Keto esters, *254*
β-Keto esters, hydrolysis of, 182
Keto nitriles, *278*
  hydrolysis of, 266
  preparation from acyl halides, 266
α-Keto thiocyanates, *279*
  preparation from acyl halides, 267
Ketone hydrates, 181, *195*
Ketones, *190, 193*
  addition of hydrogen cyanide, 266
  cleavage with amines, 263
  cleavage with ammonia, 263
  condensation with malonic acid, 207
  condensation with nitroalkenes, 293
  cyclic, 186, 187, *191–194*
    preparation from cyclic chloroalkenes, 187
  direct fluorination of, 22
  halogenation of, 184–185
  olefinic, 186, *191, 192, 193*
    hydrolysis of, 187
  preparation by base catalyzed condensation, 182–183
  preparation by hydrolysis of β-ketoesters, 182
  preparation by ketal hydrolysis, 187
  preparation by olefin oxidation, 185–186
  preparation by oxidation of secondary alcohols, 185
  preparation by reaction of acyl halides with organometallic reagents, 183
  preparation by reaction of esters with organometallic reagents, 183
  preparation by reduction of carboxylic esters, 186
  preparation by reduction of olefinic ethers, 187
  preparation from acyl halides and organometallic reagents, 183
  preparation from carboxylic acid salts and organometallic compounds, 184

Ketones Cont'd)
preparation from keto acid salts, 186
preparation from nitriles and Grignard reagents, 183–184
reaction with fluorocarbon Grignard reagent, 141
reduction of, 141–142
trimerization of, 162

Lactams, cleavage, 207
Lead tetrafluoride, use as fluorinating agent
Lithium compounds, fluorocarbon (see Organolithium compounds)

Maleic anhydride, condensation with dienes, 207
Malonic acid condensation, 207
Malonic ester synthesis, 234–235
Manganese trifluoride, preparation of, 11
use as fluorinating agent, 11–12
Magnesium compounds, fluorocarbon (see Organomagnesium compounds)
Markownikoff's rule, 35
Metallic fluorides, reactivities of, 2
Mercaptans (also see thiols)
addition to olefins, 333–334
reaction with acyl halides, 338
with anhydrides, 338
Mercaptides, reaction with alkyl halides, 334
Mercuric fluoride, preparation of, 5
use as fluorinating agent, 5–6
Mercurous fluoride, preparation of, 5
use as fluorinating agent, 5
Mercury compounds, fluorocarbon (see Organomercury compounds)
Mercury fluorosilicate, use as fluorinating agent, 6
Monofluoroalkanes, instability of, 34

Nitrides (see also Fluorocarbon nitride), 284
Nitrides, *295–298*
Nitriles (see also fluorocarbon nitriles), *276–277*
cyclic, *276–277*
hydrolysis of, 202–203, 262
olefinic, *276–277*
preparation from alcohols, 266
preparation from aldehydes, 266
preparation from alkenes, 265, 266
preparation from amides, 265
preparation from ketones, 266
preparation using metallic fluorides, 4
reaction with ammonia, 264
with Grignard reagents, 183–184
reduction of, 188, 285–286
trimerization of, 290
Nitrites, 291–294

Nitrites (Cont'd)
preparation from alcohols, 294
Nitro alcohols, *303–304*
preparation of, 293
Nitro alkanes, *303–304*
condensation with aldehydes, 293
condensation with ketones, 293
condensation with unsaturated esters, 293
preparation from alkenes, 292–293
preparation from nitrosoalkenes, 292
reaction with nitroolefins, 294
Nitro alkenes, *303–304*
N-Nitroamides, *304*
Nitro compounds, 291–294
reduction of, 286
Nitro esters, *304*
Nitro olefins, *303–304*
addition reactions of, 294
preparation of, 293
Nitroso alkanes, *302*
oxidation of, 292
preparation from alkanes, 291–292
preparation from haloalkanes, 290–291
N-Nitroso amides, 304
preparation from amines, 291
N-Nitroso amines, *302*
preparation using carboxylic acid salts, 291
Nitroso compounds, 290–291
reaction with alkenes, 289

Olefins, *113–121*
addition of aldehydes to, 186
addition of halogens to, 33–34
addition of hydrogen fluoride to, 12–14
addition of hydrogen halides to, 35
addition of mercaptans to, 333–334
addition of sodium sulfite to, 339
addition of thioacids to, 338
codimerization with olefinic aldehydes, 188
codimerization with olefinic ethers, 160
cyclic, 187, *126–131*
dimerization of, 110–112
dimerization with unsaturated esters, 238
free radical addition of alcohols to, 143
free radical addition to, 37–40, 108
hydration of, 207
Lewis acid catalyzed additions to, 40
oxidation of, 185–186, 203
preparation by Swarts reaction, 9–10
pyrolysis of, 108–109

Olefins (Cont'd)
  reaction with alcoholates, mechanism, 156–157
  reaction with alkyl Grignard reagents, 109–110
  reaction with lithium alkyls, 109
Organoantimony compounds, fluorocarbon (see antimony compounds and stibines)
Organoarsenic compounds, fluorocarbon (see arsines)
Organocadmium compounds, fluorocarbon (see cadmium compounds)
Organolithium compounds, fluorocarbon, 206, *320*
  preparation by transmetallation, 309
  reaction with carboxylic acid salts, 184
    with carboxylic esters, 140, 183
    with olefins, 109
    with silicon halides, 324–315
Organomagnesium compounds, fluorocarbon, *320*
  carbonation of, 206
  oxidation of, 144
  preparation of, 310
  reactions of, 310
  reaction with acyl halides, 183
    with aldehydes, 140–141
    with cadmium salts, 312
    with carboxylic esters, 140, 183
    with ketones, 141
    with nitriles, 184
    with fluorocarbon arsine iodides, 319
    with silicon halides or alkoxides, 314
Organomagnesium compounds, reaction with carboxylic esters, 140
    with nitriles, 188
    with nitroolefins, 294
    with olefins, 109–110
Organomercury compounds, fluorocarbon, *321*
  iodides, reactions of, 312
    reaction with amalgams, 312
  preparation of, 132
  preparation using fluorocarbon halides, 311–312
  reactions of, 312
Organophosphorous compounds, fluorocarbon (see individual phosphorous compound)
Organoselenides, fluorocarbon (see selenides)
Organosilicon compounds, fluorocarbon (see silanes)
Organosulfur compounds, fluorocarbon (see individual sulfur compounds)
Organozinc compounds, fluorocarbon, 206, *320*
  preparation of, 311
  preparation using fluorocarbon halides, 310
  reactions of, 311
  reaction with acyl halides, 183
Ortho esters, preparation of, 234, 238
Orthoformates, reaction with fluorocarbon Grignard reagents, 189
Oxazetadines, *304*
  preparation of, 289

Oxazetadines (Cont'd)
pyrolysis of, 289
Oximes, reduction of, 287–288

Peroxycarboxylic acyl fluorides, 202
Peroxycarboxylic acids, 202
Phosphine halides, *324*
halogenation of, 316–317
preparation from phosphines, 316–317
Phosphine iodides, coupling of, 317
hydrolysis of, 316
reaction with silver cyanide, 317
preparation using carboxylic acid salts, 316
preparation using fluorocarbon iodides, 315
reduction of, 316
Phosphine oxides, 324
preparation of, 316
Phosphines, *324*
hydrolysis of, 316
oxidation of, 317
Fluorocarbon phosphines, preparation from phosphine iodides, 315–316
phosphinic acids, *324*
preparation of, 316
phosphonic acids, *324*
preparation of, 316, 317
phosphonous acids, *324*
preparation of, 316
Phosphorous acid esters, 43
Phosphorus esters, *325*
Polyethers, 156
Polymerization, of epoxides, 156
of olefinic ethers, 156
Polysulfides, *344*
Potassium fluoride, use as fluorinating agent, 3
Pyrolysis, of alkanes, 104
of carboxylic acid salts, 223
of carboxylic esters, 106–107
of fluorocarbons, 45–46
of lithium alkyl compounds, 309
of polymers, 45–46
of sodium trifluoroacetate, 222
of Teflon, 108

Quaternary ammonium fluorides, 47
Quaternary ammonium salts, 289, *299*
decomposition of, 289
preparation using *t*-amines, 289

Reduction, of acyl halides, 141–142
of aldehydes, 141–142

Reduction, of alkyl halides, 44
  of amides, 142
  of anhydrides, 142
  of carboxylic acids, 141–142
  of esters, 141–143
  of ketones, 141–142
  of olefins and dienes, 44–45
Reformatsky synthesis, 236
Ring formation, 43
Rosenmund reduction, 188

Schmidt-Curtiss rearrangement, 287
Selenides, *327*
  preparation of, 319
Silanes, *322–323*
  cyclic, *323*
  olefinic, *322–323*
  preparation from fluorocarbon halides, 313, 314
  preparation from olefins, 313, 314
  preparation from vinyl silanes, 314
  preparation using fluorocarbon Grignard reagents, 314
  preparation using fluorocarbon lithium compounds, 314–315
  preparation using silicon halides or alkoxides, 314–315
Silver difluoride, preparation of, 4
  use as fluorinating agent, 4
Silver fluoride, use as fluorinating agent, 3–4
Silver fluorosilicate, use as fluorinating agent, 6
Simons process, 17–19, 205–206, 335, 336
Sodium hydrosulfide, reaction with alkyl halides, 337
Stibine halides, *327*
Stibines (see also antimony compounds, fluorocarbon), *327*
  preparation of, 319
Strecker synthesis, 208–209
Sulfates (see also sulfuric acid esters), reaction with glycols, 163
Sulfenamides, preparation, 340
Sulfenyl chlorides, addition to olefins, 334–335
  hydrolysis of, 340–341
  oxidation of, 339–340
  preparation of, 340
  preparation from bis(perfluoroalkylthio)mercury, 333
  reactions of, 340
Sulfides, *344–348*
  cyclic, *346,348*
  fluorination of 335–336
  irradition of, 333
  oxidation of, 337
  preparation from alkyl halides and sodium mercaptides, 334
  preparation from carbon disulfide fluorination, 334
  preparation from fluorocarbon iodides and sulfur, 332–333
  preparation from mercaptans and olefins, 333–334

Sulfides (Cont'd)
preparation from sulfenyl chlorides and olefin, 334–335
preparation from sulfur monochloride and olefins, 334–335
reaction with bases, 333
with mercury, 333
unsaturated, *345, 346, 347, 348*
Sulfinic acids, preparation of, 340, 342
Sulfinates, zinc salts, reaction with sulfenyl halides, 340
Sulfites (see also sulfurous acid esters), 342
Sulfones, preparation by sulfide oxidation, 337
preparation from sulfonyl fluoride and Grignard reagents, 336
Sulfonamides, 341
Sulfonates, reaction with glycols, 163
Sulfonic acids, *334, 348*
addition to olefins, 341, 342
ammonium salts of, 341
hygroscopic nature of, 339
preparation of, 339
quaternery ammonium salts of, 341
reaction with alcohols,
silver salts of, 341
reaction with alkyl iodides, 341
with amines, 341
Sulfonic acid esters, preparation of, 341–342
properties of, 341
Sulfoxides, preparation by sulfide oxidation, 337
Sulfonyl chlorides, *344, 345*
preparation of, 339–340
Sulfonyl fluorides, reaction with Grignard reagents, 336
Sulfur compounds, preparation by electrochemical process, 18
preparation using halogen fluorides, 24
preparation using metallic fluorides, 10, 11
reaction with azomethines, 287
Sulfur hexafluoride, 336
fluorocarbon carboxylate derivatives of, 336
fluorocarbon derivatives of, 335, 336, *344, 347*
Sulfur monochloride, addition to olefins, 334–335
Sulfur tetrafluoride, fluorocarbon derivatives of, 335, 336, *344*
Sulfuric acid esters (see also sulfates), *345, 347, 348*
preparation of, 341–342
Sulfurous acid, esters of (see also sulfites), 342
Swarts reaction, 7–10

Teflon, pyrolysis of, 46, 108
Telomerization, 39–40, 107, 143
Thallous fluoride, use as fluorinating agent, 6
Thioacids, fluorination of, 335–336
reaction with alkyl halides, 338
Thioamides, *346–348*
preparation of, 343

Thiocarbonates, *344, 345*
preparation of, 342
Thiocyanates, *279*
oxidation of, 339–340
preparation from alkanes, 267
Thioesters, hydrolysis of, 337
preparation of, 338
Thioethers, unsaturated oxidation of, 338
Thioformates, *344*
preparation of, 342
reactions of, 342
Thioalkylmercurials, *334*
oxidation of, 339
reaction with hydrogen chloride, 337
Thiols, fluorination of, 335, 336
preparation of, 337
reaction with ammonia, 342
reactions of, 337
Tin tetrafluoride, use as fluorinating agent, 6–7
Titanium tetrafluoride, use as fluorinating agent, 12
Tosylates, preparation of alkanes from, 42
Transesterification, 237
Transmetallation, of alkanes, 309
Triazines, 289–290, *300–301*
alcoholysis of, 238
hydrolysis of, 207
preparation using alkenes, 289–290
preparation using amidines, 290
preparation using nitriles, 290
Trienes, *122–124*
Trifluoromethylsulfur pentafluoride, 335, 306
Trisulfides, preparation of, 332–333

Ureas, 264, *274*
preparation from amines, 266
preparation from isocyanates, 264
Urethanes (see also carbamates), 265

Williamson synthesis, 158
Wolff rearrangement, 207–208, 237, 263
Wurtz condensation 43

Xanthates, 332

Zinc compounds, fluorocarbon (see organozinc compounds)